Linux® Bible

2011 Edition

Linux® Bible

2011 Edition

Boot up to Ubuntu®, Fedora®, KNOPPIX, Debian®, openSUSE®, and 13 Other Distributions

Christopher Negus

WILEY

Wiley Publishing, Inc.

Linux® Bible 2011 Edition

Published by
Wiley Publishing, Inc.
10475 Crosspoint Boulevard
Indianapolis, IN 46256
www.wiley.com

Copyright © 2011 by Wiley Publishing, Inc., Indianapolis, Indiana

Published simultaneously in Canada

ISBN: 978-0-470-92998-8

ISBN: 978-1-118-02805-6 (ebk)

ISBN: 978-1-118-02975-6 (ebk)

ISBN: 978-1-118-02976-3 (ebk)

Manufactured in the United States of America

10 9 8 7 6 5 4 3 2 1

Library of Congress Control Number: 2010939960

As always, I dedicate this book to my wife, Sheree.

Credits

Acquisitions Editor
Mary James

Senior Project Editor
Ami Frank Sullivan

Technical Editor
David Duffey

Production Editor
Kathleen Wisor

Copy Editor
Nancy Rappoport

Editorial Director
Robyn B. Siesky

Editorial Manager
Mary Beth Wakefield

Freelancer Editorial Manager
Rosemarie Graham

Marketing Manager
Ashley Zurcher

Production Manager
Tim Tate

Vice President and Executive Group Publisher
Richard Swadley

Vice President and Executive Publisher
Barry Pruett

Associate Publisher
Jim Minatel

Project Coordinator, Cover
Katie Crocker

Compositor
Jeff Wilson, Happenstance Type-O-Rama

Proofreader
Louise Watson, Word One New York

Indexer
Robert Swanson

Cover Image
Joyce Haughey

Cover Designer
Michael Trent

About the Author

Chris Negus has written or co-written dozens of books on Linux and UNIX, including *Red Hat Linux Bible* (all editions), *CentOS Bible*, *Fedora and Red Hat Enterprise Linux Bible*, *Linux Troubleshooting Bible*, *Linux Toys*, and *Linux Toys II*. Recently, Chris co-authored several books for the new Toolbox series for power users: *Fedora Linux Toolbox*, *SUSE Linux Toolbox*, *Ubuntu Linux Toolbox*, *Mac OS X*, and *BSD UNIX Toolbox*.

For eight years Chris worked with the organization at AT&T that developed UNIX before moving to Utah to help contribute to Novell's UnixWare project in the early 1990s. When not writing about Linux, Chris enjoys playing soccer and just hanging out with his family.

Currently, Chris is employed by Red Hat, Inc. as a Linux instructor. He teaches classes and gives exams to those seeking Red Hat Certified Engineer (RHCE) and Red Hat Certified System Administrator (RHCSA) certifications.

About the Technical Editor

David Duffey is a Red Hat Certified Architect, Security Specialist, and Instructor and was the first Ubuntu Certified Instructor in the United States. He has worked with Dell as a Senior Business Development Manager for Red Hat and has worked with Canonical on their Ubuntu Server curriculum. David founded TreeO Technology in 2007, where he provides management consulting to companies using open standards.

David holds undergraduate degrees in Mathematics and Computer Science from Kansas State University and an Executive MBA from The University of Texas. He resides in Austin, Texas with his wife and daughter.

Acknowledgments

I consider anyone who has contributed to the free and open source software community to be a contributor to the book you are holding. The backbone of any Linux distribution is formed by the organizations that produce the distributions, the major projects included in Linux, and the thousands of people who give their time and code to support Linux. So, thanks to you all!

Special thanks to David Duffey for providing excellent feedback as technical editor of this edition. A smart TE makes it tough on the author, but the result is always a better book. Thanks to the folks at Wiley for helping me press through the project. As project editor, Ami Sullivan did an excellent job of gently prodding this busy author to meet his deadlines, as she managed the book between the various editors and production staff. Thanks to Margot Maley Hutchison and Maureen Maloney from Waterside Productions for contracting the book for me with Wiley.

And finally, special thanks to my wife, Sheree. There's no way I could do the work I do without the solid support I get on the home front. I love you, and thanks for taking such good care of Seth, Caleb, and me.

Contents at a Glance

Contents

Contents

Contents

Contents

Contents

Contents

Contents

Contents

Contents

Contents

Contents

Contents

Contents

Introduction

Insert the DVD that comes with this book into a PC. Within five minutes, you'll be able to try out Linux with a full range of desktop applications. Within an hour, you can have a full-blown Linux desktop or server system installed on your computer. If you are like most of us who have been bitten by the Linux bug, you won't ever look back.

Linux Bible 2011 Edition is here to open your eyes to what Linux is, where it came from, and where it's going. But, most of all, the book is here to hand you Linux and help you get started. Because Linux is the operating system of free speech and free choice, *Linux Bible* gives you choices in selecting the Linux that is right for you.

On the DVD that comes with this book are 18 different Linux distributions that you are free to install, try out, and keep. You learn how those distributions are alike or different, and the book leads you through the basics of installing and setting up your Linux system as:

- **A desktop computer user** — You have a full range of office, music, gaming, graphics, and other applications to use.
- **A Linux system administrator** — Learn how to install software, use shell commands, configure system services, and secure your computers and networks.
- **A Linux server administrator** — Using some of the world's best server software, you can set up your computer to be a Web server, file server, mail server, or print server.
- **A software developer** — You can draw on thousands of open source programming tools to develop your own software applications.

The Linux systems you have in your hand don't contain trialware or otherwise-hobbled software. On the contrary, they feature software created by world-class development projects, the same teams that build the software that powers many stock exchanges, space exploration, professional businesses, schools, home desktops, and Internet service providers. In other words, this truly first-rate software is from developers who have made a commitment to producing software that can be used in the ways that you choose to use it.

Most of the Linux distributions offered on the DVD that comes with this book are live CDs that let you try a Linux distribution without installing. Almost all of those live CDs include features that let you install the contents of those live CDs to your hard disk. For example, you can try out Fedora, Gentoo, Ubuntu, openSUSE, PCLinuxOS, and CentOS as live CDs, and then install those distributions permanently to your hard drive from icons on the desktops of those live CDs.

Unlike some other books on Linux, this book doesn't tie you to one Linux distribution. The book teaches you the essentials of Linux graphical desktop interfaces, shell commands, and basic system administration. Separate chapters break down many of the major Linux distributions available today. Then descriptions of the major software projects in most Linux distributions (KDE and GNOME desktops, Apache Web servers, Samba file and printer sharing, and so on) guide you in setting up and using those features, regardless of which Linux you choose.

Understanding the Linux Mystique

This book is designed to spark your imagination about what is possible with Linux, and then give you the software and instruction to jump right into Linux. From there, the approach is to help you learn by using it.

In the first chapter, you'll learn how to begin using the Linux of your choice by choosing from the Linux distributions included on the DVD that comes with this book. Then you'll learn how to configure the perfect Linux desktop to include everything you need to use Linux as your every-day desktop system.

If you are intrigued by what you learn here, I'll tell you how to find a staggering number of open source projects, forums, and mailing lists that are thriving today (and always looking for more people to get involved).

How This Book Is Organized

Learn the basics of what goes into Linux and you will be able to use all sorts of devices and computers in the future. The book is organized in a way that enables you to start off at the very beginning with Linux, but still grow to the point where you can get going with some powerful server and programming features, if you care to.

Part I includes two short chapters designed to get you started with Linux. Those two chapters describe

- What you need to get started with Linux and what advantages Linux gives you over other operating systems (Chapter 1)
- How you can create a desktop system with all the bells and whistles so you can use Linux to do everything you want to do with a desktop system (Chapter 2)

Part II provides in-depth details on how to use Linux desktops and associated applications. Chapters 3–5 describe

- The KDE, GNOME, and other desktop interfaces (Chapter 3)

- Applications for e-mail and Web browsing (Chapter 4)
- Tools for playing a range of multimedia content (music, video, and digital images) as well as applications for playing Linux games (Chapter 5)

In Part III, you learn how to administer Linux systems, including

- Basic graphical tools, commands, and configuration files for administering Linux systems (Chapter 6)
- Common installation tasks, such as disk partitioning and software package selection (Chapter 7)
- How to use commands to traverse the Linux file systems, manipulate files, and check the system (Chapter 8)
- Tools for adding users, working with removable media, and monitoring system performance (Chapter 9)
- Adding partitions, creating file systems, and mounting file systems (Chapter 10)
- Setting up wired and wireless connections to LANs and the Internet (Chapter 11)
- Using tools to communicate over networks and check network resources (Chapter 12)
- Techniques for securing Linux systems (Chapter 13)
- Creating shell scripts for administering systems (Chapter 14)

Linux creates powerful servers, and in Part IV you learn to

- Set up a Web server using Apache and related features in Linux (Chapter 15)
- Run a mail server (Chapter 16)
- Share printers with a CUPS print server (Chapter 17)
- Share files with a Samba or NFS file server (Chapter 18)

If you don't have Linux installed yet, this book helps you understand differences in Linux distributions, and then install the systems you want from the DVD that is included in this book. Part V (Chapters 19 through 24) describes each of those distributions and how to run them live or install them.

If you are coming to Linux for its programming environment, Part VI provides chapters that describe

- Programming environments and interfaces (Chapter 25)
- Programming tools and utilities (Chapter 26)

In addition, Appendix A tells you what's on the DVD, how to install from the DVD, and how to burn additional installation CDs from the software that you can get on the Internet.

New in Linux Bible 2011 Edition

Changes for this edition of the *Linux Bible* focus on areas such as improving your personal desktop system and extending your use of commands to work with Linux. There has also been less emphasis on comparing and contrasting Linux distributions.

Linux has reached the point where it is good enough to use as your everyday desktop system. However, some work may be needed to set up that desktop to do everything you want it to do. A new Chapter 2 was added to this edition to detail as many things as I could think of to help you transition from Windows to Linux as your everyday desktop.

The real power of Linux comes from the thousands of tools that support the operating system. Because finding some of those tools can be a challenge, I've enhanced descriptions for setting up disks (Chapter 10), working with network tools (Chapter 12), and other features to include more commands and options to use those tools effectively.

To make space for some of the new content, I've placed less emphasis on describing all the individual Linux distributions that are available. Although Ubuntu, Fedora, SUSE, and most of the other most popular Linux distributions are still described, descriptions of several less popular distributions were cut.

However, most Linux distributions rely on many of the same major software projects (GNOME, Apache, GNU Utilities, and so on). Therefore, most of the descriptions in this book can be helpful to you, regardless of which distributions you are using.

What You Will Get from This Book

By the time you finish this book, you'll have a good basic understanding of many of the major features in Linux and how you can use them. If you decide then that you want to go a bit deeper into any Red Hat–sponsored distribution, *Fedora Linux Bible* is a good next step, with content that includes how to set up many different types of Linux servers. You can find similar books for other distributions.

If you are more technically oriented, *Linux Troubleshooting Bible* (Wiley, 2004) can be a good way to learn more advanced skills for securing and troubleshooting Linux systems. Or a *Linux Toolbox* book for Fedora, Ubuntu, BSD, or SUSE (Wiley, 2007 and 2008) can provide you with more than 1,000 Linux command lines to help you become a Linux power user.

If you are looking for some fun, try out some projects with an old PC and free software from *Linux Toys II* (Wiley, 2005).

Conventions Used in This Book

Throughout the book, special typography indicates code and commands. Commands and code are shown in a monospaced font:

```
This is how code looks.
```

In the event that an example includes both input and output, the monospaced font is still used, but input is presented in bold type to distinguish the two. Here's an example:

```
$ ftp ftp.handsonhistory.com
Name (home:jake): jake
Password: ******
```

As for styles in the text:

- New terms and important words appear in *italics* when introduced.
- Keyboard strokes appear like this: Ctrl+A.
- Filenames, URLs, and code within the text appear like so: persistence.properties.

The following items call your attention to points that are particularly important.

Note
A Note provides extra information to which you need to pay special attention. ■

Tip
A Tip shows a special way of performing a particular task. ■

Caution
A Caution alerts you to take special care when executing a procedure, or damage to your computer hardware or software could result. ■

Cross-Reference
A Cross-Reference refers you to further information on a subject that you can find outside the current chapter. ■

Coming from Windows
A Coming from Windows icon provides tips to help you transfer your knowledge of Windows systems to the Linux world. ■

On the DVD
The On the DVD icons point out features related to the DVD that accompanies the book. ■

Part I

Getting Off the Ground with Linux

Starting with Linux

With Linux, you are free to erase your computer's entire hard disk and run nothing but free (as in freedom) software on it. As an alternative, you could run Linux from a live CD (ignoring your computer's contents without changing them) or install Linux to dual boot with your Windows or Mac OS X system as you choose. The bottom line is that with Linux you are free to do as *you* choose with your computer.

In only a few years, Linux has advanced from being considered a specialty operating system into the mainstream. Precompiled and preconfigured Linux systems can be installed with no technical expertise. Versions of Linux run on all kinds of devices, from mobile phones (see www.linuxdevices.com) to netbooks to supercomputers to Mars Rovers. In short, Linux has become a system that almost anyone can run almost anywhere.

On both desktop and server computers Linux has become a formidable operating system across a variety of business applications. Today, large enterprises can deploy thousands of systems using Linux distributions from companies such as Red Hat, Inc. and Canonical Ltd. Small businesses can put together the mixture of office and Internet services they need to keep their costs down.

The free and open source software (FOSS) development model that espoused sharing, freedom, and openness is now on a trajectory to surpass the quality of other operating systems outside of the traditional Linux servers and technical workstations. What were once weak components of Linux, such as less user-friendly desktops, missing multimedia codecs, and limited driver availability, have improved at a rapid pace. In areas of security, usability, connectivity, and network services, Linux has continued to improve and outshine the competition.

Computer industry heavy-hitters such as Microsoft and Oracle have taken notice of Linux. Microsoft has struck agreements with Linux companies including Novell and Xandros to form partnerships that primarily protect those companies against threatened Microsoft lawsuits. Oracle began producing its own enterprise-targeted Linux system to try to stem the flow of customers to Red Hat Enterprise Linux.

What does this all add up to? A growing swirl of excitement around the operating system that the big guys can't seem to get rid of. For people like yourself, who want the freedom to use your computer software as you like, it means great prospects for the future.

Let this book help you grab your first look at the distributions, applications, services, and community that make up the phenomenon that has become Linux.

Taking Your First Step

In your hands, you have more than a dozen Linux distributions (on DVD), thousands of applications, and instructions for getting it all running on your own computer. For you, right now, the worldwide Linux phenomenon is just a reboot away.

Linux Bible 2011 Edition brings you into the world of free and open source software that, through some strange twists and turns, has fallen most publicly under the "Linux" banner. Through descriptions and procedures, this book helps you

- Understand what people do with Linux and how you can use Linux for all your computing tasks.
- Sort through the various distributions of Linux to choose one (or more) that is right for you. You get several Linux systems on this book's DVD. (Linux is all about choice, too!)
- Try out Linux as a desktop computer, server computer, or programmer's workstation.
- Become connected to the open source software movement, as well as many separate high-quality software projects that are included with Linux.

What Comes in Linux Systems?

Whether you are using Linux for the first time or just want to try out a new Linux distribution, *Linux Bible 2011 Edition* is your guide to using Linux and the latest open source technology. Although different Linux distributions vary in the exact software they include, this book describes the most popular software available for Linux to

- Manage your desktop (menus, icons, windows, and so on)
- Listen to music, watch video, and store and arrange digital photos
- Browse the Web and send e-mail
- Play games
- Find thousands of other open source software packages you can get for free

Because most Linux distributions also include features that let them act as servers (in fact, that's one of the things Linux has always been best at), you'll also learn about software available for Linux that lets you do the following:

- Connect to the Internet or other network
- Use Linux as a firewall and router to protect and manage your private network
- Run a Web server (using Apache, MySQL, and PHP)
- Run a mail server (using Exim, Sendmail, or other mail transfer agent)
- Run a print server (using CUPS)
- Run a file server (using NFS, vsFTPd, or Samba)
- Use the exact same enterprise-quality software used by major corporations (such as Google and Amazon.com), universities, and businesses of all sizes

This book guides you through the basics of getting started with these Linux features, plus many more. After you've been through the book, you should be proficient enough in the basics to track down answers to your more advanced questions through the volumes of manual pages (usually referred to as man pages), FAQs, HOWTOs, and forums that cover different aspects of the Linux operating system.

To get started with Linux right now, all you need is a standard PC with a bootable DVD drive.

What Do You Need to Get Started?

Although Linux runs well on many low-end computers (even some old 486s and early Pentiums), if you are completely new to Linux, I recommend that you start with a PC that has a little more muscle. Here's why:

- Full-blown Linux operating systems with complete GNOME or KDE desktop environments (see Chapters 2 and 3) perform poorly on slow CPUs and less than the recommended amount of RAM. The bells and whistles come at the price of processing power. Lighter-weight options (such as the Xfce or LXDE desktop environments) often run well on computers that have limited resources, but they may offer fewer features.

- You can use streamlined graphical Linux installations that fit on small hard disks (as small as 100MB) and run fairly well on slow processors. Also, small live CD Linux distributions, such as Damn Small Linux (DSL), can be copied to hard disk and run from there (read about some of these small "bootables" in Chapter 24). The 50MB DSL desktop system can run fine on old Pentium machines with little RAM. But if you want to add some of the more demanding applications to these small systems, such as OpenOffice.org office applications, you will find you need more than minimal computer hardware.

If you are starting with a Pentium II, 400 MHz, your desktop will run slowly in default KDE or GNOME configurations with less than 128MB of RAM. A simpler desktop system, with just X and a window manager, will work, but won't give you the full flavor of a Linux desktop. (See Chapter 3 for information about different desktop choices and features.)

The good news is that cheap desktop PCs or netbooks that you can buy from big box retailers start at less than $200. Those systems will perform better than most PCs you have lying around that are more than a few years old, and some even come with Linux pre-installed. The bottom line is that the less you know about Linux, the more you should try to have computer hardware that is up to spec to have a pleasant experience.

Starting Right Now

If you are anxious to get started, insert the DVD accompanying this book into the DVD drive on your PC and reboot. When you see the boot screen you will be able to choose from a multitude of different Linux distributions. If you simply press Enter, or wait a few seconds for the timeout, the default distribution KNOPPIX will load. If you would like to try a different distribution more appropriate for you or your hardware, you can type in a boot label instead. I've highlighted two of the distributions available to you here:

- **KNOPPIX** — If you don't type anything, after a few seconds, a fully functional KNOPPIX desktop Linux system will boot directly from the DVD. From that Linux system, you can do everything you would expect to do from a modern desktop computing system: write documents, play music, communicate over the Internet, work with images, and so on. If you have a wired Ethernet connection that connects to the Internet when you started up Windows, most likely it will also connect automatically when KNOPPIX starts.
- **Damn Small Linux** — When the boot screen appears, you are prompted to type a name representing the Linux distribution you want to boot. Before the short time out, you can type the name of the Linux you want and press Enter. If you have a low-end or older computer, I suggest you type dsl to start Damn Small Linux.

By booting either KNOPPIX or Damn Small Linux, what you have in front of you is a functioning desktop system that you can install to your hard disk to use permanently, if you like. You can choose to add software from among thousands of software packages available for Linux. Depending on your Linux system, installing extra software might just take a few clicks.

The next sections step you through a few things you can do with KNOPPIX and Damn Small Linux.

Trying KNOPPIX

When KNOPPIX starts up, you bypass a login screen and go directly to a Lightweight X11 Desktop Environment (LXDE) that is loaded with free software for you to try. Figure 1-1 shows an example of the KNOPPIX LXDE desktop with desktop effects enabled. The image shows a window exploding as it is closed.

Note

If you have any trouble starting KNOPPIX, see Chapter 24 for descriptions of boot options to help you overcome certain problems (such as a garbled screen or hanging when certain hardware is encountered). That chapter also describes other KNOPPIX features. ∎

FIGURE 1-1

The KNOPPIX live Linux CD contains the LXDE desktop and many popular applications.

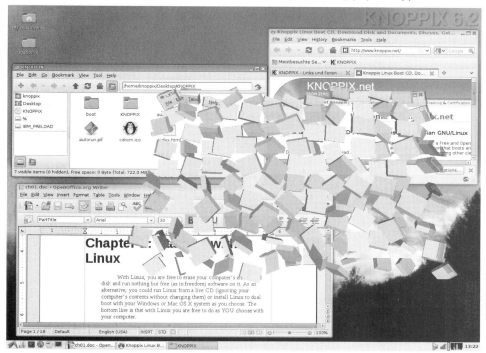

Here is a quick tour of the KNOPPIX desktop:

- **Browsing** — Select the Web Browser icon from the bottom panel to open the Iceweasel browser. The Iceweasel browser is a version of the Firefox Web browser that was rebranded by the Debian project (http://geticeweasel.org).

- **Managing files** — Select the My Documents icon from the desktop. A PCMan File Manager window opens to show your home folder (/home/knoppix). You will typically save files and folders to your home folder. Because you are running KNOPPIX as a live CD, any files you create will be lost when you reboot if you don't explicitly save them. Chapter 21 describes how to make a persistent desktop, so you can save the files you create in KNOPPIX permanently.

- **Accessing disks** — A live CD, such as KNOPPIX, is designed to run without touching the contents of your hard disk. However, if you have something on your hard disk you want to use with KNOPPIX (such as a music file or document), KNOPPIX makes doing it easy.

  Entries appear in the left column of the file manager, representing every partition on your hard disk as well as detected removable media (such as a USB flash drive). Select an icon to display the contents of the partition in that file manager window. To add content to that disk partition, simply drag and drop files from the desktop, or copy, move, or otherwise create files from the shell.

- **Special Knoppix features** — Because of the temporary nature of a live CD, you have to configure settings each time you boot, unless you take steps to save those settings. From the LXDE icon on the left side of the bottom panel, you can see a menu of selections to do special things to make KNOPPIX run from your hard disk. Select Preferences ⇨ KNOPPIX HD Install to install KNOPPIX so you can run it from your hard disk.

  Other KNOPPIX features are also available from that menu. You can select Install Components from the Preferences menu to add non-free software, such as Flash plug-ins or Windows fonts. Chapter 24 describes other KNOPPIX features.

- **Running applications** — Select the LXDE icon from the lower-left corner of the panel to see a menu of available applications. Choose Office to select from several OpenOffice.org office applications for writing documents, using spreadsheets, drawing pictures, and building presentations. Try out some communications applications, such as Icedove Mail/News reader and Pidgin Internet Messenger, from the Internet menu.

When you are done trying KNOPPIX, select Log Out from the LXDE menu and choose Shut Down. After KNOPPIX shuts down, it ejects the disc. After you remove the disc, you can use your computer again with whatever operating system you have installed there.

Trying Damn Small Linux

Because Damn Small Linux (DSL) is based on KNOPPIX, you may notice some similarities. DSL is smaller and faster, however, so you should get to the DSL desktop screen more quickly. Instead of LXDE, the DSL desktop features a simple window manager. Figure 1-2 shows an example of a Damn Small Linux desktop with several applications open.

Note
Many of the same boot options that come with KNOPPIX will work with DSL, so check Chapter 24 if you have trouble booting DSL. ■

Here are some things to try on your DSL desktop:

- **Web browsing** — With an active wired Internet connection, you should be able to connect to the Internet automatically when DSL boots up. The Dillo Web browser opens to a page of basic DSL information. Continue to browse the Web from Dillo, or open the Firefox icon from the desktop to browse with Firefox instead.

- **Install applications** — Open the MyDSL icon from the desktop and then, when prompted, download the applications database. After that, select categories from the left column to look through listings of hundreds of applications you can add to DSL. When you find one you like, choose Install Selected to download and install it.

- **Check out the desktop** — On the desktop itself, view information about your computer (CPU Usage, RAM, Swap, File Systems, and so on) in the upper-right corner. Select DSL in the lower-left corner of the bottom panel to see a menu of available applications. Then try a few applications. You can view the same menu by right-clicking on the desktop.

FIGURE 1-2

Damn Small Linux provides an efficient desktop Linux.

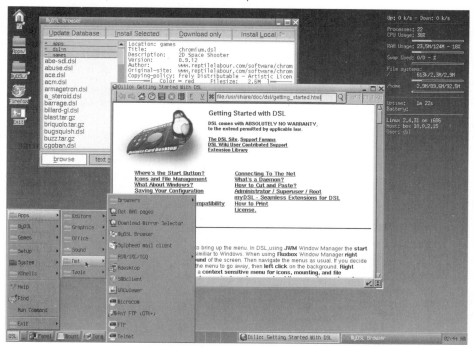

- **Change settings** — Select Setup from the main menu to adjust the date and time, change your desktop theme, configure your X display server, or set up a wireless or dial-up Internet connection.

- **Control the system** — Select System from the menu and choose Control Panel. From the control panel that appears, you can configure your printer, back up your files (remember that files disappear at reboot with live CDs if you don't save them to disk or removable media), or start login (SSH) or FTP services. Return to the main menu and select Apps ⇨ Tools to use some cool, specialized DSL features, such as install to hard disk or portable USB flash drive (pendrive). You can also remaster a MyDSL CD or make a boot floppy.

- **Trying applications** — Figure 1-2 shows a couple of applications open on the DSL desktop. Open the MyDSL folder to see application packages you can install (shown upper left). Select Apps ⇨ Net to see applications you could use to access the Internet (such as email clients, web browsers, and instant messaging clients).

Select the Exit icon from the desktop and choose Shutdown or Reboot to exit from DSL. Notice that the Backup box is selected. With that box selected, DSL gives you the option to save your files and settings (provided you set up a location to back up your files earlier from the Control Panel). With that information saved, the next time you boot DSL from that computer, you have those files and settings available.

Trying Other Linux Distributions

Of course you can try many other Linux distributions from the DVD that comes with this book besides KNOPPIX and Damn Small Linux. Ubuntu has a large, active following and can be run live from the DVD. Try Fedora or openSUSE if you want to try a Linux system that is being prepared for enterprise distros (Red Hat Enterprise Linux and SUSE Linux Enterprise, respectively).

Gentoo and Slackware often appeal to technically oriented users. On small machines, distros such as Puppy Linux or BackTrack may interest you. See Appendix A for information on these and other Linux systems included with this book.

Understanding Linux

People who don't know what Linux is sometimes ask me whether it's a program that runs on Microsoft Windows. When I tell them that Linux is, itself, an operating system like Windows and that they can remove (or never purchase) Windows, I sometimes get a surprised reaction, "A PC can run with nothing from Microsoft on it?" The answer is yes!

The next question about Linux is often, "How can Linux be free?" Although the full answer to that is a bit longer (and covered later), the short answer is, "Because the people who write the code license it to be freely distributed." Keep in mind, however, that the critical issue relating to the word "free" is "freedom," meaning that you are free to rebuild, reuse, reconfigure, and otherwise do what you like with the code. The only major responsibility related to most "free" software is that if you change the code, and want to redistribute your resulting applications, you pass your modified code forward so that others may benefit from your work as well.

Linux is a full-blown operating system that is a free clone of the powerful and stable UNIX operating system. Start your computer with Linux, and Linux takes care of the operation of your PC and manages the following aspects of your computer:

- **Processor** — Because Linux can run many processes from many different users at the same time (even with multiple CPUs on the same machine), Linux needs to be able to manage those processes. The Linux scheduler sets the priorities for running tasks and manages which processes run on which CPUs (if multiple processors are present). You can tune the scheduler differently for different types of Linux systems. If the scheduler is tuned properly, the most important processes get the quickest responses from the processor. For example, a Linux scheduler on a desktop system gives higher priority to things such as moving a window on the desktop than it does to a background file transfer.

- **Memory** — Linux tries to keep processes with the most immediate need in RAM, while managing how processes that exceed the available memory are moved to swap space. *Swap space* is a defined area on your hard disk that's used to handle the overflow of running processes and data. When RAM is full, processes are placed in swap space. When swap space is full (something that you don't want to happen), Linux will try to figure out which processes to keep and which to kill.

- **Devices** — Linux supports thousands of hardware devices, yet keeps the kernel a manageable size by including only a small set of drivers in the active kernel. Using loadable modules, the kernel can add support for other hardware as needed. Modules can be loaded and unloaded on demand, as you add and remove hardware. (The kernel, described in detail a bit later on, is the heart of a Linux operating system.)

- **File systems** — File systems provide the structure in which files are stored on hard disk, CD, DVD, floppy disks, or other media. Linux knows about different file system types (such as Linux ext3 and reiserfs file systems, or VFAT and NTFS from Windows systems) and how to manage them.

- **Security** — Like UNIX, Linux was built from the ground up to enable multiple users to access the system simultaneously. To protect each user's resources, every file, directory, and application is assigned sets of read, write, and execute permissions that define who can access them. In a standard Linux system, the root user has access to the entire system, some special logins have access to control particular services (such as Apache for Web services), and users can be assigned permission individually or in groups. Recent features such as Security Enhanced Linux and AppArmor enable more refined tuning and protection in highly secure computing environments.

What I have just described are components that are primarily managed by what is referred to as the Linux *kernel*. In fact, the Linux kernel (which is still maintained by Linus Torvalds, who created the Linux kernel as a graduate student in Finland) is what gives Linux its name. The kernel is the software that starts up when you boot your computer and interfaces with the programs you use so they can communicate effectively and simply with your computer hardware.

Components such as administrative commands and applications from other free and open source software projects work with the kernel to make Linux a complete operating system. The GNU project (www.gnu.org), in particular, contributed many implementations of standard UNIX components that are now in Linux. Apache, KDE, GNOME, and other major open source projects in Linux have also contributed to the success of Linux. Those other projects added such things as

- **Graphical user interfaces (GUIs)** — Consisting of a graphical framework (typically the X Window System), window managers, panels, icons, and menus, GUIs enable you to use Linux with a keyboard and mouse combination, instead of just typing commands (as was done in the old days).

- **Administrative utilities** — Including hundreds (perhaps thousands) of commands and graphical windows to do such things as add users, manage disks, monitor the network, install software, and generally secure and manage your computer.

- **Applications** — Although no Linux distribution includes all of them, literally thousands of games, office productivity tools, Web browsers, chat windows, multimedia players, and other applications are available for Linux.

- **Programming tools** — Including programming utilities for creating applications and libraries for implementing specialty interfaces.

- **Server features** — Enabling you to offer services from your Linux computer to another computer on the network. In other words, while Linux includes Web browsers to view Web pages, it can also be the computer that serves up Web pages to others. Popular server features include Web, mail, database, printer, file, DNS, and DHCP servers.

After Linus Torvalds and friends had a working Linux kernel, pulling together a complete open source operating system was possible because so much of the available "free" software was

- **Covered by the GNU Public License (GPL) or similar license** — That allowed the entire operating system to be freely distributed, provided guidelines were followed relating to how the source code for that software was made available going forward (see http://www.gnu.org/licenses/gpl.html).

- **Based on UNIX-like systems** — Clones of virtually all the other user-level components of a UNIX system had been created. Those and other utilities and applications were built to run on UNIX or other UNIX-like systems.

Linux has become one of the most popular results of the open source software movement. But the traditions of sharing code and building communities that made Linux possible started years before Linux was born. You could argue that it began in a comfortable think tank known as Bell Laboratories. Free software projects, such as the GNU Project, created free versions of UNIX utilities, and soon the ball was rolling.

Leveraging work done on UNIX and GNU projects helped to get Linux up and running quickly. The culture of sharing in the open source community and adoption of a wide array of tools for communicating on the Internet have helped Linux to move quickly through infancy and adolescence to become a mature operating system.

The simple commitment to share code is probably the single most powerful contributor to the growth of the open source software movement in general, and Linux in particular. That commitment has also encouraged involvement from the kind of people who are willing to contribute back to that community in all kinds of ways. The willingness of Linus Torvalds to incorporate code from others in the Linux kernel has also been critical to the success of Linux.

What's So Great About Linux?

If you have not used Linux before, you should expect a few things to be different from using other operating systems. Here is a brief list of some Linux features that you might find cool:

- **No constant rebooting** — Uptime is valued as a matter of pride (remember, Linux and other UNIX systems are most often used as servers, which are expected to, and do, stay up 24/7/365). After the original installation, you can install or remove most software without having to reboot your computer for almost any software besides the kernel itself.

- **Start/stop services without interrupting others** — You can start and stop individual services (such as Web, file, and e-mail services) without rebooting or even interrupting the work of any other users or features of the computer. In other words, you should not have to reboot your computer every time someone sneezes. (Installing a new kernel is just about the only reason you need to reboot.)

- **Portable software** — You can often change to another Linux, UNIX, or BSD system and still use the exact same software! Most open source software projects were created to run on any UNIX-like system and many also run on Windows systems, if you need them to. If it won't run where you want it to, chances are that you, or someone you hire, can port it to the computer you want. (*Porting* refers to modifying an application or driver so it works in a different computer architecture or operating system.)

- **Downloadable applications** — If the applications you want are not delivered with your version of Linux, you can often download and install them with a single command, using tools such as apt, urpmi, and yum.

- **No settings hidden in code or registries** — After you learn your way around Linux, you'll find that (given the right permissions on your computer) most configuration is done in plain-text files that are easy to find and change. In recent years, simplified graphical interfaces have been added to make working with configuration files even easier. Because Linux is based on openness, nothing is hidden from you. Even the source code, for GPL-covered software, is available for your review.

- **Mature desktop** — The X Window System (providing the framework for your Linux desktop) has been around longer than Microsoft Windows. The KDE and GNOME desktop environments provide graphical interfaces (windows, menus, icons, and so forth) that rival those on Microsoft systems. You have the freedom to choose lightweight window managers instead as well. Ease-of-use problems with Linux systems are rapidly evaporating.

- **Freedom** — Linux, in its most basic form, has no corporate agenda or bottom line to meet. You are free to choose the Linux distribution that suits you, look at the code that runs the system, add and remove any software you like, and make your computer do what you want it to do. Linux runs on everything from supercomputers to cell phones and everything in between. Many countries are rediscovering their freedom of choice and making the switch at government and educational levels. France, Germany, Korea, and India are just a few that have taken notice of Linux. The list continues to grow.

Some aspects of Linux make it hard for some new users to get started. One is that Linux is typically set up to be secure by default, so you must adjust to using an administrative login (root) to make most changes that affect the whole computer system. Although this can be a bit inconvenient, trust me, it makes your computer safer than just letting anyone do anything.

The Linux model was built around a true multiuser system. You can set up logins for everyone who uses your Linux computer, and you (and others) can customize your environment however you see fit without affecting anyone else's settings.

For the same reason, many services are off by default, so you need to turn them on and do at least minimal configuration to get them going. For someone who is used to Windows, Linux can be difficult just because it is different from Windows. But because you're reading this book, I assume you want to learn about those differences.

Summary

Getting started with Linux can be as easy as inserting the DVD accompanying this book into your PC and rebooting. Using that media, you can try out more than a dozen different Linux systems, either live or by installing them to hard disk.

You can use Linux as a desktop system (like Microsoft Windows); as a Web, file, or print server; or as a programmer's workstation. You have a lot of flexibility when it comes to how Linux is configured and what software you install and run on it.

Because you are free to use open source software as you please, many Linux enthusiasts have come up with interesting and innovative ways to use Linux and benefit from it. The rest of this book is devoted to helping you find the best ways to use Linux for whatever your computing needs are.

Creating the Perfect Desktop

2

IN THIS CHAPTER

Getting a computer for Linux

Installing a Linux desktop system

Configuring the desktop

Adding desktop applications

Transitioning from Windows

Before you abandon your Windows or Mac desktop for Linux as your primary desktop system, you want to make sure that your Linux setup can do everything you want it to do. That means being able to

- Run the applications you need to do your work, play your multimedia, and communicate over the Internet
- Transition the way you work and the stuff you work with (documents, music, spreadsheets, and so on) from your old desktop to your new Linux desktop

Getting the perfect Linux desktop system won't happen by itself. But using a basic Linux installation, a connection to the Internet, and the descriptions in this book, you should be able to match what you had on your Windows or Mac system in most ways and surpass it in many others.

In this chapter, I'm going to take you through the paces of setting up a Linux desktop system that will make the transition to Linux as easy as possible. To that end, I'll start you with a particular Linux distribution, describe what you want to add to it to make it a smoking desktop system, and suggest ways of tuning it to work best for you.

The software in this section draws on a variety of sources, including "The Perfect Desktop" how-to documents available from HowtoForge.com. Although this chapter focuses on Fedora, other documents at that site cover "Perfect Desktops" for Ubuntu, PCLinuxOS, and other Linux systems. Because some of the software described in this chapter and those documents contains "non-free" elements, you should read the "Beyond Free Software" sidebar relating to these non-free elements.

Beyond Free Software

Any time you add software to a computer, you should question yourself about the quality, safety, and legality of that software. Malicious software can give bad guys access to your computer. Poorly written code can hurt your system's performance. Software that includes non-free elements (proprietary code or patented ideas) can leave you open to legal problems.

Sticking to software from Linux distributions that have been carefully vetted for quality and legality (such as the software included in the Fedora Project) gives you the best chance at safe and healthy computing. Keep in mind that risks can arise when you stray outside those safe confines.

That said, I'm here to inform you, not lecture you. In the process of describing everything you might want on a Linux desktop, I'm going to tell you about software that some describe as "non-free." Non-free software can fall into a number of different categories, including the following:

- **Patent encumbered** — Some software has been totally rewritten as free software, but some person or company may claim to have patents on the ideas in that software. For example, there is open source software for playing MP3 audio that an organization claims royalties for because it holds a patent on the ideas that make MP3 codecs.

- **Cost-free, but not open** — The foundations of open source software include the ability to see, change, and freely redistribute the code. Some proprietary code, such as Flash and PDF players from Adobe, don't cost anything but are limited in those other ways.

- **Proprietary applications** — You may have legally purchased an application for Windows and feel you need that application for your desktop. If you can't find an equivalent Linux application, you often can run that application in Linux using the wine package (which provides a windows compatibility layer for running Windows applications) or by running an entire Windows system as a virtual guest in Linux. However, the ability to run that application in Linux may not be supported (or even legal) and you won't be able to change or redistribute that application.

As issues come up throughout the book, I'll try to point out the risks of using the various types of non-free software and what your other options are.

Starting with Your Linux Desktop

Let's face it: If you can't set up a Linux system to do what you expect from your Mac or Windows system, you probably won't want to use it as your everyday desktop. That's why this chapter is devoted to taking you step-by-step through the process of making a Linux system into a perfect desktop system.

Not every piece of software or every desktop setting will suit you perfectly right from the start. But by describing the choices you have for adding applications, tuning your system, and transitioning your stuff (documents, music, and so on) to Linux, I hope to make it so you don't even miss your old desktop.

Although this book is about freedom to choose your own Linux system and use it as you please, I'm going to choose a particular Linux distribution to start with and show you all the ways you can set it up. After that, you can use the rest of the book to apply what you have learned here to any Linux distribution you choose.

To do the desktop setup in this chapter, you will need to get a computer with an Internet connection, and then install and configure a Fedora Linux distribution from the DVD that comes with this book. If you prefer to start with a different Linux distribution, install one of those systems instead (see Appendix A). In many cases, you can use the information in this chapter to guide you to the same results.

Step 1: Getting a Computer

Linux distributions (many of which come with this book) are available to run on any computer, from a 486 processor to the latest enterprise-quality server. For a good desktop experience, however, I recommend you start with a PC that has some power.

Selecting Computer Hardware

Table 2-1 contains my recommendations for a computer to install the Fedora distribution that is on the DVD that comes with this book.

Depending on what you want to do with your Linux system, you may want to add other hardware. For example, you may want to add Webcams, scanners, speakers, printers, and external storage. One of the more challenging hardware components to get working, however, is a wireless card.

TABLE 2-1

Choosing a Computer for a Fedora Desktop

Requirement	Description
Processor	Choose a 400 MHz Pentium Pro or better. Although that's the minimum, you won't have a great desktop with less than a 1 GHz processor. We provide 32-bit versions of Linux, but those versions also work on 64-bit processors. (You can get 64-bit versions yourself if you choose, instead of using software that comes with the book.)
Memory	Have at least 512MB of RAM, although some larger applications will run poorly on computers with less than 1GB of RAM. Applications for things such as video editing and CAD/CAM can require much more RAM. (These days, a power-user desktop should start with 2GB to 4GB of RAM.)

continued

TABLE 2-1	*(continued)*
Requirement	**Description**
Disk space	I recommend at least 5GB of unassigned disk space (more is better). To get that space, your computer either needs to:
	• Have no operating system on it (or one that you are willing to delete); or
	• Have extra space on your hard disk that is not being used by another operating system (not free space on a Windows partition—it must be space that is not assigned to any partition); or
	• Have a USB port that you can use with a removable USB drive. For this option, you can buy something like an 8GB or 16GB USB flash drive. (With this type of install, you can later use that USB drive to boot Linux from almost any computer with a USB port. It will run slower than a system installed to hard disk, but faster than one running from a live CD.)
Other hardware	You need a DVD drive and network card. You must be able to boot from the DVD drive and connect your network card to the Internet. Also, although Linux can run without these things, the procedure here assumes you have a keyboard, screen, and mouse.

Choosing Networking Hardware

After you have acquired the computer you want to use, make sure that Internet access is available. Wired network interface cards will almost always work. However, not all wireless cards work out of the box.

Some wireless cards do work out of the box. For example, there are native Linux drivers that are already in Fedora or your other Linux distribution. Some wireless cards require that firmware be loaded, but otherwise use native Linux drivers. Intel's IPW wireless cards are examples of cards that require firmware from the manufacturer for them to work. Several releases ago, Fedora, Ubuntu, and several other Linux distributions relented and included firmware for Intel IPW wireless cards.

If the wireless card you have doesn't work, you might want to save yourself some trouble and get a card that is supported in Linux. Visit the Linux wireless LAN support page to fine one: http://linux-wless.passys.nl/query_alles.php.

To get an unsupported wireless card working, there are two projects that can help. Try the Linuxant DriverLoader site (http://linuxant.com/driverloader) for cards that don't include the required firmware or the NDISwrapper site (http://ndiswrapper.sourceforge.net) for information on how to load Windows drivers under Linux.

Step 2: Installing Your Linux Desktop

There are several desktop Linux distributions included on the DVD that comes with this book. Full-blown desktop systems include Fedora, Ubuntu, PCLinuxOS, and others. Lightweight Linux desktops include Damn Small Linux, Puppy Linux, and SLAX. For this procedure, I'm using Fedora as the example.

Note

There are several reasons for choosing Fedora for the demonstration system. Fedora software packages are carefully screened to only include software that is redistributable. So it's up to you what, if any, non-free software you use. Also, Fedora is developed as the basis for Red Hat Enterprise Linux, the world's most popular enterprise-quality Linux system. So the skills you learn using Fedora can transition easily into those that you use to become a professional software developer, systems analyst, or system administrator. ■

Starting with a Fedora Desktop

Here are the basic steps for installing Fedora to your computer's hard disk, as well as a few things you should do to prepare your desktop system to be able to add the software you need going forward:

1. **Get hardware.** Get the computer hardware in place, as described in Table 2-1.

2. **Start the install.** Insert the DVD into your computer's DVD drive, reboot your computer and, when you see the *Linux Bible 2011 Edition* boot screen, choose fedora.

3. **Run the install.** Follow the instructions in Chapter 20 for installing Fedora, including rebooting your computer when the install is done, running the Firstboot procedure, and logging in for the first time. (Be sure to remember passwords for the root user and the regular user you created.)

4. **Set up your Internet connection.** If you have a wired Internet connection, you may automatically be connected to the Internet. Open the Firefox browser and visit a Web site to check. To connect to a wireless network, click the NetworkManager icon in the top panel and select your network. If neither works, refer to Chapter 11 for information on configuring network interfaces.

5. **Get software updates.** From the desktop, select System ➪ Administration ➪ Software Update. (Note the amount of space needed to get the updates listed and make sure you have enough space.) Select Install Updates to begin downloading and installing them.

Preparing to Install Extra Software

The Fedora repository has been screened to contain only software that meets criteria that make it open and redistributable. In some instances, however, you may want to go beyond the Fedora repo. Before you do, however, you should understand that some third-party repositories

- Have less stringent requirements for redistribution and freedom from patent constraints than the Fedora repository has

- May introduce some software conflicts

- May include software that is not open source and, although it may be free for personal use, may not be redistributable

- May slow down the process of installing all of your packages (because metadata is downloaded for every repository you have enabled)

For those reasons, I recommend that you either don't enable any extra software repositories, or only enable the RPM Fusion repository at first. RPM Fusion represents a fusion of several popular third-party Fedora repositories (Freshrpms, Livna.org, and Dribble). See the repository's FAQ for details (http://rpmfusion.org/FAQ). To enable the free repository, do the following:

1. Open a Terminal window.

2. Type **su –** and enter the root password when prompted.

3. Type the following command (we had to break the line into two because it was too long, so be sure to type the entire address on one line with no space):

```
# rpm -Uvh http://download1.rpmfusion.org/free/fedora/
rpmfusion-free-release-stable.noarch.rpm
```

The RPM Fusion non-free repository contains such things as codecs needed to play many popular multimedia formats. To enable the non-free repository, type the following (again, type the following two lines on a single line, with no space between the two:

```
# rpm -Uhv http://download1.rpmfusion.org/nonfree/fedora/
rpmfusion-nonfree-release-stable.noarch.rpm
```

Most of the other third-party repositories that might interest you contain software that is not open source. I'll describe how to enable those repositories later in this chapter, when you learn how to add Skype and software from the Adobe repository.

Checking Available Software

Once your repositories are in place and accessible, you can list the available software packages and choose what you want to install. Select System ➪ Administration ➪ Add/Remove Software. The Add/Remove Software window should appear. From that window, select System ➪ Software Sources. Figure 2-1 shows an example of the Software Sources window.

You can see that the repositories containing the basic Fedora and Fedora Updates repositories are enabled. Likewise, the RPM Fusion (free and non-free) repositories (basic and updates repositories) are enabled here. The updates repositories include software packages that have been updated since Fedora was first released.

Now your Linux system should be ready for you to tune your Linux desktop and add the extra software you need from the Fedora repository. Before heading on to those sections, however, you can take a quick look at what software is now available for you to install. From the Add/Remove Software window, you can

- Type the name of a software package you are interested in and click the Find button.

- Select a category of applications that interest you to see applications you can install.

FIGURE 2-1

Check your Fedora software repository sources.

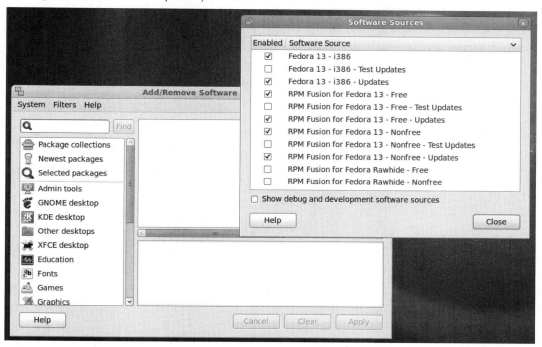

If you are looking for something to try, select Games ⇨ gnome-games-extra, to install a nice selection of simple desktop games. Once you have chosen packages to install, click the Apply button. You may be prompted to allow additional packages to be installed and to enter the root password. Packages are then downloaded and installed.

If you feel adventurous, you can type commands to find information about your installed packages. (See Chapter 8 if you are not familiar with how to use the shell in Linux.) Here are some examples of how to get information about available software packages from the shell:

1. **Open a Terminal window.** Select Applications ⇨ System Tools ⇨ Terminal.
2. **Become root user.** Type **su –** and enter the root password when prompted.
3. **Check Fedora Packages.** Look for packages you want first in the Fedora repository, to have the best chance of getting the best-of-breed, open source software. Type this command to see all packages available from all enabled repositories. Use the space bar to page through the packages. (I showed a few packages from the output that I thought might be of special interest.)

```
# yum --disablerepo="rpmfusion*" list available | more
Available Packages
...
audacity.i686                    Popular open source audio editor
blender.i686                     3D amimation, modeling and rendering software
chess.i686                       3D chess game
evolution.i686                   Email and groupware client
gimp.i686                        GNU image manipulation package
gnucash.i686                     Money management package
inkscape.i686                    Vector graphics editor
k3b.i686                         CD/DVD burner application
mediatomb.i686                   Multimedia management software
openoffice.org-calc.i686         Spreadsheet application
openoffice.org-draw.i686         Drawing application
openoffice.org-impress.i686      Presentation application
openoffice.org-math-core.i686    Mathematics application
openoffice.org-writer.i686       Word processing application
pidgin.i686                      Instant messaging application
samba.i686                       Windows file/print sharing application
sugar.noarch                     Sugar desktop environment


tvtime.i686                      TV viewer
wine.i686                        Software to run Windows applications in Linux
```

4. **Check rpmfusion packages.** Type the following command to see all packages available from the rpmfusion repositories. Use the space bar to page through more than 1800 packages. (I listed a few packages that I thought might be of special interest):

```
# yum -disablerepo="*" --enablerepo="rpmfusion*" list available | more
Available Packages...
DVDAuthorWizard.noarch       Create a DVD from MPEG-2 video files
SheepShaver.i586             Run-time environment to run old MacOS apps
VirtualBox-OSE.i686          General-purpose full virtualizer for the PC
broadcom-wl.noarch           Drivers for Broadcom wireless cards
bubbros.i686                 Game inspired by Bubble and Bobble Mac game
ffmpeg.i686                  Live audio/video encoder for many formats
gnome-mplayer.i686           Popular video player for GNOME desktop
gnome-video-arcade.i686      MAME arcade/console game player for GNOME
k3b-extras-freeworld.i686    Extra codecs for k3b CD/DVD burning
kino.i686                    Popular video editor for Linux
lame.i686                    Open source MP3 encoder
lastfm.i586                  Use http://last.fm to track what you listen to
lightspark.i686              Open source Flash implementation
motion.i686                  Motion detection software for video cameras
mpg123.i686                  Command-line MP3 audio player
mythtv.i686                  TV recorder/viewer and much more
ndiswrapper.i586             Lets Windows wireless drivers work in Linux
nvidia-*                     Packages for proprietary NVIdia video drivers
```

```
raine.i386            Emulator to run M68000, Z80, and M68705 games
unrar.i686            Utility to extract RAR archive files
xbill.i586            Game to kill an evil computer system thief
xbmc.i686             Popular multimedia center software
xorg-x11-drv-nvidia*  Proprietary Nvidia video driver packages
```

The next few steps describe how to add software packages to configure your desktop and run popular desktop applications.

Step 3: Configuring Your Desktop

There are many ways to configure the look, feel, and behavior of your GNOME desktop (which is the default desktop for Fedora and other Linux distributions). Before you start configuring your desktop, know that there are a few other choices for desktop environments in Fedora or other Linux systems that you can consider.

From the Add/Remove Software window, you can select any of the following desktop environments to install and use instead of GNOME (with multiple desktops installed, you'll be able to choose the one you want when you log in):

- **KDE desktop** (www.kde.org) — The other major desktop environment for Linux systems

- **XFCE desktop** (www.xfce.org) — A more efficient, streamlined desktop that is appropriate for netbooks or older computers

- **Other desktops** — Choose other lightweight desktop environments, such as the LXDE desktop or Sugar (the desktop used on the One Laptop Per Child project)

Choose the appropriate packages from the group noted in the preceding bulleted list if you want to use a desktop other than GNOME. Refer to Chapter 3 for descriptions of how to configure and use those desktops.

Note
There is an easy way to install a full desktop environment from the command line. Open a Terminal window and become the root user. Then type yum groupinstall *desktop* and replace *desktop* with one of the following: "KDE," "XFCE," or "Sugar Desktop Environment." ■

Details on configuring GNOME are contained in Chapter 3. Here are just a few things you can do to turn on some neat features and tailor the desktop to the way you like to use it.

- **Change desktop theme** — Select System ➪ Preferences ➪ Appearance to open the Appearance Preferences window. On the Themes tab, select the theme you like, and then choose Customize to select the controls, colors, border, icons, and pointer. If you want to choose from dozens of free themes, select Get More Themes Online. From the GNOME Art site (http:/art.gnome.org/themes), select to download the theme you want, and then choose to install it with the theme installer.

- **Change desktop background** — From the Appearance Preferences window, select the Background tab. Choose any image available from your desktop and drag-and-drop it onto the Background tab for that image to become your desktop background. The first image (upper-left corner) represents no desktop image and lets you select colors for your background instead.

- **Change desktop screensaver** — Select System ➪ Preferences ➪ Screensaver to see a list of available screen savers. Choose one and select Preview to see how it works. To get more choices, use the Add/Remove Software window to choose packages such as xscreensaver-extras and xscreensaver-extras-gss. The packages that are installed as a result also let you turn off the GNOME screen saver and use the X screen saver, which offers many alternative screen savers. Choose Picture Folder to use a slide show of one of your own picture folders as the screen saver.

- **Configure panel applications** — Right-click the top panel and select Add to Panel. Choose applications you might want to add to the panel so you can launch them with a single click. Choose the icon for any installed applications or special applets, such as Gnote note-taking software or System Monitor to watch the system load.

- **Desktop effects** — Although desktop effects don't work well in every environment, when they do work they provide some nice eye candy for your desktop. To enable Desktop Effects, select System ➪ Preferences ➪ Desktop Effects. Choose Compiz, then "Windows Wobble" and "Workspaces on a Cube" if you like. Then try a few effects, such as Alt+Tab (to step through your applications) or Ctrl+Alt+left mouse button (to rotate desktop workspaces on a cube). See Chapter 3 for other desktop effects.

Chapter 13 covers more features you can add to the desktop.

Step 4: Adding Applications

Adding applications to your desktop system is where you can go a little wild. In Fedora, there are more than 14,000 software packages available. Although you won't have all the same applications you would expect to find on a Windows or Mac OS X system, you will find alternatives to those applications in every category.

So, open your Add/Remove Software window and follow along with the descriptions of packages. Here are a few things to think about as you look to install packages:

- Make sure you have enough disk space to install the packages you choose. Select Applications ➪ System Tools ➪ Disk Usage Analyzer to open the Disk Usage Analyzer window. Select the Scan Filesystem button to see how much space is available.

- Once you have selected the software to install, and you have clicked Apply, you will be able to see how much disk space the install and its dependent packages will need. You can select Cancel at that point if you don't want to proceed.

Choosing Office Applications

When it comes to replacing Microsoft Office on their Linux desktops, most people start with the OpenOffice.org office productivity applications. From the Add/Remove Software window, search for openoffice.org to see what applications are available.

- **Word processing** — For a word processor, select OpenOffice.org Writer (see the openoffice.org-writer package). It supports a variety of word processing formats, including several versions of Microsoft Word (.doc) files.

- **Spreadsheets** — Choose OpenOffice.org Spreadsheet (openoffice.org-calc package) to provide an application for working with spreadsheets. In addition to supporting open source spreadsheet formats, this application also supports Microsoft Excel formats (.xls and .xlt).

- **Presentations** — The OpenOffice.org Presentation application (openoffice.org-impress package) lets you create presentations from scratch or transition your Microsoft Powerpoint applications to Linux. The OpenOffice.org Drawing application lets you create and save drawings.

The OpenOffice.org applications are among the largest applications that are commonly used in Linux. Expect to have to download several hundred megabytes of data to install a few OpenOffice.org applications. And expect it to take a while with a slow Internet connection. Figure 2-2 shows an example of a document open in Writer and a spreadsheet open in Calc.

FIGURE 2-2

Work with documents, spreadsheets, and other common office files using OpenOffice.org.

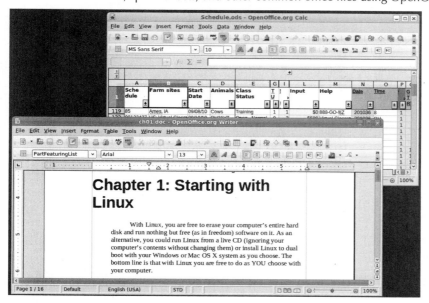

Other popular office applications include gnucash (for managing money) and scribus (for doing desktop publishing page layout).

Once your office applications are installed, select Applications ⇨ Office to select the applications you want to run.

Some non-free office software that some people like to add includes the Adobe PDF and Flash players. If you decide to add this software (and keep in mind that you don't need to because open source software exists to play this content), Adobe has a repository you can use to install this software. Here's how to enable the Adobe repository:

1. Open a Terminal window.

2. Type **su –** and enter the root password when prompted.

3. Type the following command (on one line, with no space in the Web address):

```
# rpm -Uvh http://linuxdownload.adobe.com/adobe-release/
adobe-release-i386-1.0-1.noarch.rpm
```

Here are some packages you might choose to install from that repository:

```
# yum install AdobeReader_enu        Installs Adobe PDF/PS Reader
# yum install flash-plugin           Installs the Adobe flash plug-in
```

Choosing Games

With an active games special interest group (SIG) associated with the Fedora Project, there are hundreds of open source games available to you for your Fedora desktop. These range from simple board games and card games to complex simulation and first-person shooter games. There are also many commercial computer games (such as Enemy Territory, Medal of Honor, and Eve Online) that have been released into the public domain and have been ported to Linux.

From the Add/Remove Software window, select Games in the left column. You can scroll through numerous games that are available to install on your Fedora system.

For a simple set of board games and card games, you can install the games that come with the GNOME and KDE desktops (gnome-games and kdegames packages, respectively). These games are engaging without being consuming and they don't take a lot of disk space.

On the other end of the spectrum are games that consume lots of disk space and lots of your time. You can try OpenArena (openarena package), or Doom (doom-shareware, prboom, and freedoom packages) to try out some legacy first-person shooter games.

See Chapter 5 for descriptions of other games.

Choosing Multimedia Applications

Multimedia is where you get into some of the non-free areas of software. While often available in open source software, some codecs for playing MP3 or other audio and video formats are patent-encumbered. In other words, there may be companies or individuals who expect royalties for using these codecs, even if they didn't write the code themselves.

I suggest you refer to Chapter 5 for descriptions of these formats and the various legal issues surrounding them before installing multimedia software in Linux. Here are some of the applications you might want to look into for playing your movies, music, and images.

- **Video players** — Consider totem, mplayer, and xine applications for playing video and audio content. See Chapter 5 for a description of the media plug-ins you need to add to make these video players useful. In particular, look into gstreamer plug-ins (good, bad, and ugly) to add to your Linux desktop. Some of these require access to the non-free RPM Fusion repositories. Also, see the "Choosing Office Applications" section for information on enabling the Adobe repository and adding the Flash plug-in to play Flash video through your browser.

- **Audio editors and players** — Rhythmbox comes installed on your Linux desktop and provides an excellent way of managing your music, podcasts, and streaming audio. Sound Juicer is already installed to rip and play music CDs. Amarok (amarok package) is another popular application for playing and managing music. To edit audio, consider installing Audacity (audacity package). To burn CDs and DVDs, Brasero Disc Burner is already installed. The k3b package offers an alternative application for burning and mastering CDs and DVDs.

- **Image editors and players** — GNU Image Manipulation Program (GIMP) is the most popular tool for manipulating digital images. Shotwell Photo Manager is already installed to manage images and do simple photo manipulations. F-Spot is an alternative photo manager.

Choosing Internet Applications

Once you are connected to the Internet, numerous applications are available to help you get around. Here are some examples:

- **Web browsers** — Firefox is included with Fedora and is by far the most popular Web browser available on Linux systems. Konqueror is a Web browser that comes with the KDE desktop, which can also be added to GNOME. Install SeaMonkey to get a Web browser (based on the Mozilla browser) and a full suite of Internet applications.

- **E-mail clients** — Evolution (evolution package) and Thunderbird (thunderbird package) are the most popular graphical e-mail clients available. For a text-based mail client, try the mutt command (mutt package).

- **File transfer applications** — Firefox can already be used to download files from Web sites and FTP sites. To share files using BitTorrent protocols, the Transmission

BitTorrent Client is also already installed. For a standalone FTP client, install the gftp package.

- **Instant messaging clients** — For instant messaging, install either the pidgin package or empathy package.

Besides the applications mentioned here, there are some non–open source applications you can add to Fedora. In particular, many people use Skype for video conferencing. While I recommend using open source software when possible, if you want to try Skype in Fedora, here is what you need to do:

1. Open a Terminal window.

2. Type **su –** and enter the root password when prompted.

3. Create a repo file for Skype using any text editor. For example, type **gedit /etc/yum. repos.d/skype.repo**. Then add the following text using that text editor:

```
[skype]
name=Skype Repository
baseurl=http://download.skype.com/linux/repos/fedora/updates/i586/
gpgkey=http://www.skype.com/products/skype/linux/rpm-public-key.asc
gpgcheck=0
```

4. Then, to install the Skype software, type the following:

```
# yum install skype
```

5. To start using Skype, select Applications ➪ Internet ➪ Skype.

Choosing Other Applications

This chapter has touched just the tip of the iceberg for applications you can install to enhance your Fedora desktop experience. Now that you know how to go about looking for software packages to install, here are a few other categories of applications you can look into:

- **Programming** — If you are a software developer, select the Programming heading in the left column to choose from hundreds of software development tools packages.

- **Admin tools** — Explore lots of tools for doing system administration of disks, networks, and other features.

- **Education** — Install applications for education, such as programs for doing flashcards, exploring outer space, and working with geometry. Install the childsplay package for a suite of educational games for small children.

Try searching for applications by keywords to find the ones you want. You could run out of disk space before you run out of interesting applications to install and try.

Step 5: Transitioning from Windows

Starting with a new Linux operating system means getting your content (documents, music, videos, images, and so on) from your Windows or Mac system and getting the applications you need to work with that content. Previous sections in this chapter should help you find new applications to meet most of your needs. Beyond that, this section will help you:

- Access or move your stuff from your old system to Linux
- Understand how to run an occasional Windows application in Linux (if you absolutely have to)

Getting Your Files from Windows to Linux

How you get your music, image, document, and other files from Windows to Linux depends on several things. Are you dual-booting Linux and Windows, so the content is on the local hard disk? Are you connected to a network and able to make your content available as a Windows share? Is the content on a totally disconnected computer?

Here are a few suggestions on ways to get your stuff from Windows to Linux.

Getting Windows Content from the Local Disk

If your Windows system is on another partition on your local hard disk, try mounting that partition in Linux and copying it over. Here's a way you could do that from your Fedora desktop:

Note

Traditionally, writing to NTFS partitions from Linux has risked some data corruption. Reading from those partitions, as described in this section, is believed to be quite stable. ■

1. Open a Terminal window.
2. Type **su –** and enter the root password when prompted.
3. Type the following command:

```
# fdisk -l | grep -i ntfs
/dev/sda1    *    1    2618    21029053+    HPFS/NTFS
```

4. If an NTFS partition appears, that's probably your Windows partition. Create a mount point and mount that partition on your Linux file system. With the example of /dev/sda1 shown in the preceding command output, you could type the following:

```
# mkdir /mnt/windows
# mount /dev/sda1 /mnt/windows
```

If no NTFS partition appears, repeat Steps 3 and 4, replacing ntfs with fat (to look for FAT and VFAT partitions). Then create another mount point and mount any other partitions you find.

To copy the content from the partition, right-click the Home icon on your desktop and select Browse Folder. Use the buttons to go to the root of the file system, then select the mnt and windows partitions (/mnt/windows). Look for the folders you want to copy from your Windows systems. Think about how big the folder is before starting the copy, then drag-and-drop it to your desktop.

Getting Windows Content over the Network

Linux has support for accessing Windows shares. If the content you want is available from a Windows share on your network, select Places ⇨ Connect to Server. From the Connect to Server window, select Windows Share and type in the name of the server, share, and user name. Then click Connect. You may be asked to enter a password.

As an alternative, you can just type the server name and choose from available shares. Then enter the name and password as needed.

If all goes well, a window representing the share should appear on your desktop. You can then drag-and-drop the files across that you want.

Putting Content on Removable Media

Massively large removable media is so cheap these days that you can move large amounts of data between systems that aren't even connected to a network. You can burn your content to a CD or DVD or just copy it onto a USB flash drive from Windows.

The Fedora desktop used in this chapter will be able to read content copied to USB flash drives that are formatted in NTFS or FAT formats. When you insert the drive with that content into your Fedora computer, a file manager window opens and you will be able to copy the files across to your local system.

Running Windows Applications in Linux

Despite having comparable Linux applications to replace most of the Windows applications you are used to, there may still be times that you want or need to run a particular Windows application. For those times, there are ways to run most Windows applications in Linux.

Here are a few ways you can go about it:

- **WINE** — Install the wine package (which stands for WINE is not an Emulator). Using wine, you can run installation programs for many Windows applications, and then run them from your Linux desktop.

- **Virtualization** — By installing virtualization tools, you can actually install and run an entire Windows system in Linux (providing you have hardware that will support it). In Fedora, try installing the virt-manager package and run the Virtual Machine Manager application to install and manage a virtual Windows system. VirtualBox is another application you can use to do virtualization in Linux.

Keep in mind that there are security risks inherent in running Windows applications in Linux. If at all possible, try using open source Linux applications instead.

Summary

Not everything you might want for a Linux desktop will be ready for you out of the box. By following the procedures in this chapter, however, you can find lots of ways to get the applications you need to move from your old desktop system to Linux without much trouble.

Although this chapter uses Fedora as an example of how to set up a Linux desktop system, most of the descriptions here will work with other desktop systems as well. When possible, I recommend that you look for open source alternatives to your Windows applications. However, if you must have a particular Windows application, you can install individual Windows applications using WINE or full Windows systems virtually from a Linux desktop.

Part II

Running a Linux Desktop

Getting into the Desktop

## 3

In the past few years, graphical user interfaces (GUIs) available for Linux have become as easy to use as those on the Apple Mac or Microsoft Windows systems. With these improvements, even a novice computer user can start using Linux without needing to have an expert standing by.

You don't need to understand the underlying framework of the X Window System, window managers, widgets, and whatnots to get going with a Linux desktop system. That's why I start by explaining how to use the two most popular desktop environments: KDE (K desktop environment) and GNOME. After that, if you want to dig deeper, I tell you how you can put together your own desktop by discussing how to choose your own X-based window manager to run in Linux.

Understanding Your Desktop

When you install Linux distributions such as Fedora, SUSE, or Ubuntu, you have the option to choose a desktop environment. Distributions such as Gentoo and Debian GNU/Linux, give you the option to go out and get whatever desktop environment you want (without an installer particularly prompting you for it). When you are given the opportunity to select a desktop during installation, your choices usually include one or more of the following:

- **K desktop environment** (www.kde.org) — In addition to all the features you would expect to find in a complete desktop environment (window managers, toolbars, panels, menus, key bindings, icons, and so on), KDE has many bells and whistles available. Applications for graphics, multimedia, office productivity, games, system administration, and many other uses have been integrated to work smoothly with KDE, which is the default desktop environment for SUSE and various other Linux distributions.

- **GNOME desktop environment** (www.gnome.org) — GNOME is a more streamlined desktop environment. It includes fewer customizations than KDE and is less complex, making it ideal for older systems. Some think of GNOME as a more business-oriented desktop. It's the default desktop for Red Hat–sponsored systems such as Fedora and RHEL, as well as Ubuntu, and others.

Note

The KDE 4 Desktop is based on the Qt graphical toolkit. GNOME is based on GTK+. Although graphical applications are usually written to either QT or GTK+, by installing both desktops you will have the libraries needed to run applications written for both toolkits from either environment. ■

- **Lightweight desktop environments** — Xfce (www.xfce.org) and LXDE (www.lxde.org) are examples of desktop environments that are built to run well with low-powered processors and less RAM. LXDE is currently the desktop environment used with KNOPPIX.

- **X and a window manager** (X.org) — You don't need a full-blown desktop environment to operate Linux from a GUI. The most basic, reasonable way of using Linux is to simply start the X Window System server and a window manager of your choice (you have dozens to choose from). Many advanced users go this route because it can offer more flexibility in how they set up their desktops. Window managers such as Xfce and fluxbox are particularly good on low-end, low-resource machines.

The truth is that most X applications run in any of the desktop environments just described (provided that proper libraries are included with your Linux distribution as noted earlier). So you can choose a Linux desktop based on the performance, customization tools, and controls that best suit you. Each of these three types of desktop environments is described in this chapter.

Starting the Desktop

Because the way that you start a desktop in Linux is completely configurable, different distributions offer different ways of starting up the desktop. After your Linux distribution is installed, it may just boot to the desktop, offer a graphical login, or offer a text-based login. Bootable Linux systems (which don't have to be installed at all) typically just boot to the desktop.

Boot to the Desktop

Some bootable Linux systems boot right to a desktop without requiring you to log in so you can immediately start working with Linux. KNOPPIX is an example of a distribution that boots straight to a Linux desktop from a CD. That desktop system usually runs as a particular username (such as knoppix, in the case of the KNOPPIX distribution). To perform system administration, you have to switch to the administrator's account temporarily (using the su or sudo command).

Caution

Using any computer operating system without password protection violates all basic security rules. Use a system without password protection only on a temporary basis on computers that have no access to critical data. To be more secure, you can assign a password to a live CD's primary user account, and certainly assign one if you install that live CD to hard disk. ■

Boot to Graphical Login

Most desktop Linux systems that are installed on your hard disk boot up to a graphical login screen. Although the X display manager (xdm) is the basic display manager that comes with the X Window System, KDE and GNOME each have their own graphical display managers that are used as login screens (kdm and gdm, respectively).

So chances are that you will see the login screen associated with KDE or GNOME (depending on which is the default on your Linux system). Display managers such as gdm offer you the opportunity to log in to different types of desktops, depending on what is installed on your system (GNOME, KDE, Xfce, or others).

Note

When Linux starts up, it enters into what is referred to as a run level or system state. For example, Fedora is set to start at run level 5. A Fedora system set to run level 3 boots to a text prompt. The Ubuntu GUI starts in run level 2. Some Linux distributions ignore the concept of run levels. In Fedora, the run level is set by the initdefault **line in the** /etc/inittab **file. Change the number on the** initdefault **line as you please between 3 and 5. Don't use any other number unless you know what you are doing. Never use 0 or 6. Those numbers are used to shut down and reboot the system, respectively. ■**

Because graphical login screens are designed to be configurable, you often find that the distribution has its own logo or other graphical elements on the login screen. With Fedora, the default login screen is based on the GNOME display manager (gdm). To begin a session, you can just enter your login (username) and password to start up your personal desktop environment.

Your selected desktop environment — KDE, GNOME, Xfce, or other — comes up ready for you to use. Although the system defines a desktop environment by default, you can typically change desktop environments on those Linux systems, such as Fedora, that offer multiple desktop environments.

Figure 3-1 shows a basic graphical login panel displayed by the gdm graphical display manager in Fedora.

To end a session, you can choose to log out. Figure 3-2 shows the graphical menu from a Fedora GNOME desktop for ending a session or changing the computer state (System ⇨ Shut Down).

FIGURE 3-1

A simple GNOME display manager (gdm) login screen

FIGURE 3-2

The Session menu in Fedora

X display managers can enable you to do a lot more than just get to your desktop. Although different graphical login screens offer different options, here are some you may encounter:

- **Session/Options** — Look for a Session or Options button on the login screen. From there, you can choose to start your login session with a GNOME, KDE, or other desktop environment.

- **Language** — Linux systems that are configured to start in multiple languages may give you the opportunity to choose a language (other than the default language) to boot into. For this to work, however, you must have installed support for the language you choose.

- **Accessibility** — Some display managers let you choose accessibility preferences. These selections let you hear text read aloud, magnify parts of the screen, use an onscreen keyboard, or do other things to overcome difficulty hearing, seeing, or using a keyboard.

If you don't like the way the graphical login screen looks, or just want to assert greater control over how it works, you can configure and secure X graphical login screens in many ways. Later, after you are logged in, you can use the following tools (as root user) to configure the login screen:

- **KDE login manager** — From the KDE Control Center, you can modify your KDE display manager using the Login Manager screen (from KDE Control Center, select System Administration ⇨ Login Manager). You can change logos, backgrounds, color schemes, and other features related to the look and feel of the login screen.

- **GNOME login manager** — The GNOME display manager (gdm) comes with a Login Window Preferences utility (from the desktop, run the `gdmsetup` command as root user). From the Login Window Preferences window, you can select the Local tab and choose a whole different theme for the login manager. On the Security tab, you may notice that all TCP connections to the X server are disallowed. Don't change this selection because no processes other than those handled directly by your display manager should be allowed to connect to the login screen. (The `gdmsetup` utility is not available in the current release of Fedora.)

After your login and password have been accepted, the desktop environment configured for your user account starts up. Users can modify their desktop environments to suit their tastes (even to the point of changing the entire desktop environment used).

Boot to a Text Prompt

Instead of a nice graphical screen with pictures and colors, you might see a login prompt that looks like this:

```
Welcome to XYZ Linux
yourcomputer login:
```

This is the way all UNIX and older Linux systems used to appear on the screen when they booted up. Now this is the login prompt that is typical for a system that is installed as a server or, for some reason, was configured not to start an X display manager for you to log in.

Just because you have a text prompt doesn't necessarily mean you can start a desktop environment. Many Linux experts boot to a text prompt because they want to bypass the graphical login screen or use the GUI only occasionally. Some Linux servers may not even have a desktop environment installed. However, if X and the other necessary desktop components are installed on your computer, you can typically start the desktop after you log in by typing the following command:

```
$ startx
```

The default desktop environment starts up, and you should be ready to go. What you do next depends on whether you have a KDE, GNOME, or some sort of homespun desktop environment.

Note

In most cases, the GUI configuration you set up during installation for your video card and monitor gets you to a working desktop environment. If, for some reason, the screen is unusable when you start the desktop, you need to do some additional configuration. The "Configuring Your Own Desktop" section later in this chapter describes some tools you can use to get your desktop working. ■

K Desktop Environment

KDE was created to bring a high-quality desktop environment to UNIX (and now Linux) workstations. Integrated within KDE are tools for managing files, windows, multiple desktops, and applications. If you can work a mouse, you can learn to navigate the KDE desktop.

The lack of an integrated, standardized desktop environment once held back Linux and other UNIX systems from acceptance on the desktop. While individual applications ran well, you mostly could not drag-and-drop files or other items between applications. Likewise, you couldn't open a file and expect the machine to launch the correct application to deal with it or save your windows from one login session to the next. With KDE, you can do all those things and much more. For example, you can

- Drag-and-drop a document from one folder window to another (to move it) or on an OpenOffice.org Writer icon (to open it for editing).
- Right-click an image file (JPEG, PNG, and so on), and the Open with menu lets you choose to open the file using an image viewer (KView), editor (The GIMP), slide show viewer (KuickShow), or other application.

To make more applications available to you in the future, KDE provides a platform for developers to create programs that easily share information and detect how to deal with different data types. The things you can do with KDE increase in number every day.

KDE is the default desktop environment for Mandriva and several other Linux systems. SUSE, openSUSE, and related distributions moved from KDE to GNOME as the default desktop, but still make KDE available. Red Hat Enterprise Linux and Fedora, which used to place less emphasis on KDE, now have much-improved support for KDE desktops, even offering a custom KDE desktop live CD/installer disk.

The past year has seen several point releases to improve the KDE 4 desktop. Despite many bold new features for managing the desktop, KDE 4 suffered from some instability. The latest version of KDE is much improved. The following section describes how to get started with KDE.

Using the KDE Desktop

The KDE 4 desktop, now available with Fedora, Ubuntu, and other major Linux distributions, offers the Plasma desktop and a relatively new framework for developing KDE applications. Some Linux distributions still use the more stable KDE 3.5, so you may have a choice of which KDE you use.

KDE 4 marked some major innovations for the KDE desktop. New libraries were added to support multimedia applications and improve handling of removable devices. There are new applications for viewing documents (such as Okular) and managing files (such as Dolphin). The most important new feature, however, is the Plasma desktop shell.

The Plasma desktop shell gives the KDE 4 desktop a whole new look and feel from the KDE 3.5 desktop. It features improved ways of finding and presenting information, such as KRunner and KickOff. The Plasma Panel incorporates lots of applets, as well as clocks, pagers, and other useful applications.

Elements in the Plasma desktop shell are referred to as *plasmoids*. What makes plasmoids different from components on many of today's desktop systems is that they can be combined in various ways to interact with each other and can be placed in different locations. For example, if a particular widget (such as a clock or a news ticker) is important to you, instead of having it represented by a tiny icon on the panel, you can put a big version of the applet on your desktop.

Figure 3-3 shows an example of a KDE desktop in openSUSE.

Some of the key elements of the KDE desktop include

- **Plasmoids** — Applets that you can add to the desktop as well as the panel are referred to as *plasmoids* in KDE 4. In Figure 3-3 you can see the clock, picture frame, and news ticker all added to the desktop. You can drag plasmoids around, group them together, and arrange them as you like on your desktop.

- **Konqueror** — The default web browser for KDE, which can also be used as a file manager

- **Dolphin** — A file manager for KDE

- **Panel** — The panel provides some quick tools for launching applications and managing the desktop. You can adapt the panel to your needs by resizing it, adding tools, and changing its location. By default, you start with an application launcher, taskbar, desktop pager, some mini applets, new device modifier, and a clock.

- **Application Launcher/Menu** — This panel button is the new KickOff Application menu, which helps you search for applications installed on your system and launch them. Choose between Favorites (applications you use often), Applications (application menus), Computer (places and storage devices), or Recently Used applications. If you prefer the classic KDE view, right-click the button and select Switch to Classic Menu Style. The desktop returns to a classic view of application categories and menus.

FIGURE 3-3

The KDE desktop includes a panel, desktop icons, and much more.

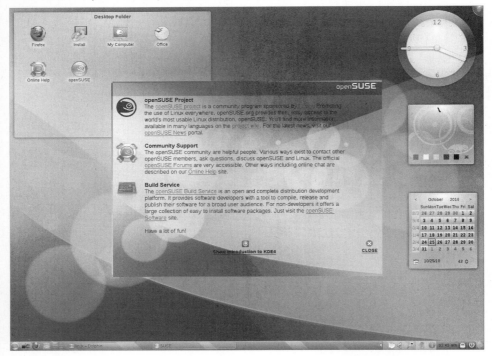

- **Taskbar** — This button shows the tasks that are currently running on the desktop. The button for the window that is currently active appears pressed in. Click a task to toggle between opening and minimizing the window.

- **Desktop Pager** — This box on the panel consists of your virtual desktops, and contain small views of each desktop. Four virtual desktops are available to you by default. These are labeled 1, 2, 3, and 4. You begin your KDE session on virtual desktop 1. If windows are on the desktop, small icons representing them may cover the desktop number. You can change to any of the four desktops by clicking it.

- **Mini applets** — Some applications, such as media players, clipboards, and battery power managers, will keep running after you have closed the related window. Some of those applications maintain a tiny applet in the panel. Clicking on these applets often restores the windows they represent. This feature is convenient for music players if you don't want to take up desktop space while you play music, but you want to be able to open the player quickly to change songs.

- **Clock** — The current time appears on the far-right side of the panel. Click it to see a calendar for the current month. Click the arrow keys on the calendar to move forward and back to other months.

To navigate the KDE desktop, you can use the mouse or key combinations. The responses from the desktop to your mouse depend on which button you click and where the mouse pointer is located.

Table 3-1 shows the results of clicking each mouse button with the mouse pointer placed in different locations. (You can change these and other behaviors from the KDE menu by selecting System Settings, and then choosing Keyboard & Mouse.)

TABLE 3-1

Single-Click Mouse Actions

Pointer Position	Mouse Button	Result
Window title bar or frame (current window active)	Left	Raises current window
Window title bar or frame (current window active)	Middle	Lowers current window
Window title bar or frame (current window active)	Right	Opens operations menu
Window title bar or frame (current window not active)	Left	Activates current window and raises it to the top
Window title bar or frame (current window not active)	Middle	Activates current window and lowers it
Window title bar or frame (current window not active)	Right	Opens operations menu without changing position
Inner window (current window not active)	Left	Activates current window, raises it to the top, and passes the click to the window
Inner window (current window not active)	Middle or Right	Activates current window and passes the click to the window
Any part of a window	Middle (plus hold Alt key)	Toggles between raising and lowering the window
Any part of a window	Right (plus hold Alt key)	Resizes the window
On the desktop area	Left (hold and drag)	Selects a group of icons
On the desktop area	Right	Opens system pop-up menu

Click a desktop icon to open it. Double-clicking a window title bar results in a window-shade action, where the window scrolls up and down into the title bar.

If you don't happen to have a mouse or you just like to keep your hands on the keyboard, you can use several keystroke sequences to navigate the desktop. Table 3-2 shows some examples.

TABLE 3-2

Keystrokes

Key Combination	Result	Directions
Alt+Tab	Step through windows	To step through each of the windows that are running on the current desktop, hold down the Alt key and press the Tab key until you see the one you want. Then release the Alt key to select it.
Alt+F2	Open Run Command box	To open a box on the desktop that lets you type in a command and run it, hold the Alt key and press F2. Next, type the command in the box and press Enter to run it. You can also type a URL into this box to view a web page.
Alt+F4	Close current window	To close the current window, press Alt+F4.
Ctrl+Alt+Esc	Close another window	To close an open window on the desktop, press Ctrl+Alt+Esc. When a skull and crossbones appear as the pointer, move the pointer over the window you want to close and click the left mouse button. (This technique is good for killing a window that has no borders or menu.)
Ctrl+F1, F2, F3, or F4 key	Switch virtual desktops	Go directly to a particular virtual desktop by pressing and holding the Ctrl key and pressing one of the following: F1, F2, F3, or F4. These actions take you directly to desktops one, two, three, and four, respectively. You could do this for up to eight desktops, if you have that many configured.
Alt+F3	Open window operation menu	To open the operations menu for the active window, press Alt+F3. When the menu appears, move the arrow keys to select an action (Move, Size, Minimize, Maximize, and so on), and then press Enter to select it. Press Esc to close the menu.

Managing Files with Dolphin and Konqueror

With KDE 4, the KDE desktop offers two file managers: the newer Dolphin File Manager and the existing Konqueror File Manager/Browser. Dolphin is a streamlined file manager that is now used by default when you open a folder in KDE. Konqueror can handle a wide range of content from local files and folders to remote web content. The two applications are described in the sections that follow.

Note

For further information on Dolphin, refer to the Dolphin File Manager home page (`http://dolphin .kde.org`). ■

Using the Dolphin File Manager

By adding Dolphin to KDE, the KDE project now offers an efficient way to manage your files and folders, without the overhead of a full-blown web browser (such as Konqueror). With Dolphin, you have a lot of flexibility and features for getting around your file system and working with the files and folders you encounter. Features in Dolphin include

- **Navigation** — The navigation bar lets you see the current folder in relation to your home directory or to the root of the file system. Select View ➪ Location Bar ➪ Editable Location to see (and change) the full path to your current folder. Select folders from the left column to go straight to that folder.

- **Listing Files and Folders** — Select icons in the toolbar to display files and folders as icons, with filename, size, and date, or with small icons in columns.

- **Properties** — Right-click on a file or folder and select Properties. Properties displayed include file type (such as folder or Ogg Vorbis audio), location (such as /home/joe), file/folder size, date/time modified, date/time accessed, and permissions. For folders, there are also some nice features that let you refresh the amount of disk space used by the folder or configure file sharing to share the folder with other computers on the network. Both Samba and NFS file sharing are supported.

- **Filter and Search** — Select Tools ➪ Show Filter Bar from the Dolphin toolbar. In the Filter box that appears, type a string of text to display any file or folder name containing that text string (for example, usi would match Music). Select Tools ➪ Find Files to open the kfind window to search for files (described later).

- **Preview** — Typically, files are represented by generic icons (text file, image file, and so on) in the Dolphin window. Click the Preview button on the toolbar and you can see small representations of the text or image contained in the file, instead of a generic icon.

To open the Dolphin File Manager, select File Manager from the main KDE menu. Figure 3-4 shows an example of the Dolphin File Manager.

FIGURE 3-4

Dolphin is an efficient file manager for KDE.

Working with Files

Because most of the ways of working with files in Dolphin are quite intuitive (by intention), Table 3-3 provides a quick rundown of how to do basic file manipulation.

TABLE 3-3

Working with Files in Dolphin

Task	Action
Open a file	Left-click the file. The contents of that file will open in the application window defined for that content. For example, images open in Gwenview and text files open in KWrite. You also can open directories, applications, and links by left-clicking them.
Open a file with a specific application	Right-click a data file, choose Open With from the pop-up menu, and then select one of the available applications to open the file. The applications listed are those that are set up to open the file. Select Other to choose a different application.
Delete a file	Right-click the file and select Move to Trash. You are asked whether you really want to move the file to trash. Click Yes to move the file to the trash.
Copy a file	Right-click the file and select Copy. This copies the file to your clipboard. After that, you can paste it to another folder. Click the Klipper (clipboard) icon in the panel to see a list of copied files. Klipper holds the seven most recently copied files, by default. Click the Klipper icon and select Configure Klipper to change the number of copied files Klipper will remember.
Paste a file	Right-click (an open area of a folder) and select Paste. A copy of the file you copied previously is pasted in the current folder.
Link a file	Drag-and-drop a file from one folder to another. When the menu appears, click Link Here. (A linked file lets you access a file from a new location without having to make a copy of the original file. When you open the link, a pointer to the original file causes it to open.)
Move a file Copy a file Create a link to a file	With the original folder and target folder both open on the desktop, click and hold the left mouse button on the file you want to move, drag the file to an open area of the new folder, and release the mouse button. From the menu that appears, click Move. (You also can use this menu to copy or create a link to the file.)

There are also several features for viewing information about the files and folders in your Dolphin windows:

- **View quick file information** — Positioning the mouse pointer over the file displays information such as its filename, size, and type in the window footer.

- **View hidden files** — Selecting View ➪ Show Hidden Files enables you to see files that begin with a dot (.). Dot files tend to be used for configuration and don't generally need to be viewed in your daily work.

- **View file details** — Selecting View ➪ View Mode ➪ Details provides a list of details regarding the contents of the current folder. You can click a folder in the details view to jump directly to that folder. Select View ➪ Additional Information to add more information about each file to the view, such as permissions, owner, group, and type. Columns and Icon views are also available.

To act on a group of files at the same time, you can take a couple of actions. Choose Edit ➪ Select All to highlight all files and folders in the current folder so they are ready for you to act on. Or, you can select a group of files by clicking in an open area of the folder and dragging the pointer across the files you want to select. All files within the box will be highlighted. When files are highlighted, you can move, copy, or delete the files as described earlier.

Searching for Files

If you are looking for a particular file or folder, use the Dolphin Find feature. To open a Find window to search for a file, open a local folder (such as /home/chris) and choose Tools ➪ Find File. The Find Files/Folders (kfind) window appears. You can also open this window by typing **kfind** from a Terminal window.

Figure 3-5 shows the Find Files/Folders window.

FIGURE 3-5

Search for files and folders from the kfind window.

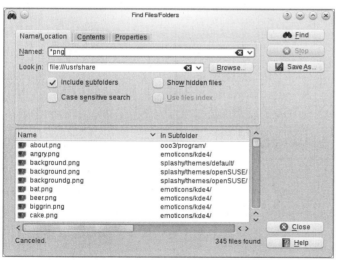

Simply type the name of the file you want to search for (in the Named text box) and the folder, including all subfolders, you want to search in (in the Look in text box). Then click the Find button. Use metacharacters, if you like, with your search. For example, search for `*.rpm` to find all files that end in `.rpm`, or `z*.doc` to find all files that begin with z and end with `.doc`. You can also select to have the search be case-sensitive or click the Help button to get more information on searching. The example in Figure 3-5 shows a search for PNG image files (ending in `.png`).

To further limit your search, you can click the Properties tab and then enter a date range (between), a number of months before today (during the previous *x* months), or the number of days before today (during the previous *x* days). You can also search for files that are of a certain size (File size is) in kilobytes, megabytes, or gigabytes. Select the Contents tab to choose to limit the search to files of a particular type (File Type) or files that include text that you enter (Containing Text).

Creating New Files and Folders

You can create a variety of file types when using the Dolphin window. Choose File ⇨ Create New, and select Folder (to create a new folder) or one of several different types under the File or Device submenu. Depending on which version of Dolphin you are using, you might be able to create some or all of the file types that follow:

- **Text File** — Opens a dialog box that lets you create a document in text format and place it in the Dolphin window. Type the name of the text document to create and click OK.

- **HTML File** — Opens a dialog box that lets you type the name of an HTML file to create.

- **Link to Location (URL)** — Selecting this menu item opens a dialog box that lets you create a link to a web address. Type a name to represent the address and type the name of the URL (web address) for the site. (Be sure to add the `http://`, `ftp://`, or other prefix.)

- **Link to Application** — Opens a window that lets you type the name of an application. Click the Permissions tab to set file permissions (Exec must be on if you want to run the file as an application). Click the Execute tab and type the name of the program to run (in the field Execute on click) and a title to appear in the title bar of the application (in the field Window Title). If it is a text-based command, select the Run in terminal check box. Select the check box to run as a different user and add the username. Click the Application tab to assign the application to handle files of particular MIME types. Click OK.

Under the Link to Device submenu, you can make the following selections:

- **CD-ROM Device** — Opens a dialog box that lets you type a new CD-ROM device name. Click the Device tab and type the device name (`/dev/cdrom`), the mount point (such as `/mnt/cdrom`), and the file system type (you can use iso9660 for the standard CD-ROM file system, ext2 for Linux, or msdos for DOS). When the icon appears, you can open it to mount the CD-ROM and display its contents.

- **CDWRITER Device** — From the window that opens, enter the device name of your CD writer.

- **Camera Device** — In the dialog box that opens, identify the device name for the camera device that provides access to your digital camera.

- **DVD-ROM Device** — Opens a dialog box that lets you type a new CD-ROM or DVD-ROM device name. Click the Device tab and type the device name (such as /dev/cdrom), the mount point (such as /mnt/cdrom), and the file system type (you can use iso9660 for the standard CD-ROM file system, ext2 for Linux, or msdos for DOS). When the icon appears, you can open it to mount the CD-ROM or DVD-ROM and display its contents.

- **Floppy Device** — Opens a dialog box in which you type a new floppy name. Click the Device tab and type the device name (/dev/fd0), the mount point (such as /mnt/floppy), and the file system type (you can use auto to autodetect the contents, ext2 for Linux, or msdos for DOS). When the icon appears, open it to mount the floppy and display its contents.

- **Hard Disk Device** — Opens a dialog box that lets you type the name of a new hard disk or hard-disk partition. Click the Device tab and type the device name (/dev/hda1), the mount point (such as /mnt/win), and the file system type (you can use auto to autodetect the contents, ext2 or ext3 for Linux, or vfat for a Windows file system). When the icon appears, you can open it to mount the file system and display its contents.

Creating MIME types and applications is described later in this chapter.

Using the Konqueror Web Browser/File Manager

Although Dolphin is now intended for pure file manager features, Konqueror is an excellent tool if you want to move between local and web content. Konqueror's greatest strengths over earlier file managers include the following:

- **Network desktop** — If your computer is connected to the Internet or a LAN, features built into Konqueror enable you to create links to files (using FTP) and web pages (using HTTP) on the network and open them in the Konqueror window. Those links can appear as file icons in a Konqueror window or on the desktop. Konqueror also supports WebDAV, which you can configure to allow local read and write access to remote folders (which is a great tool if you are maintaining a web server).

- **Web browser interface** — The Konqueror interface works like Firefox, Internet Explorer, or other web browsers in the way you select files, directories, and web content. Because Konqueror is based on a browser model, a single click opens a file, a link to a network resource, or an application program. You can also open content by typing web-style addresses in the Location box. The rendering engine used by Konqueror, called KHTML, is also used by Safari (the popular web browser for Apple Mac OS X systems) and supports advanced features, such as Cascading Style Sheets (CSS) 3.

Tip

Web pages that contain Java and JavaScript content run by default in Konqueror. To check that Java and JavaScript support is turned on, choose Settings ⇨ Configure Konqueror. From the Settings window, click Java & JavaScript and select the Java tab. To enable Java, click the Enable Java Globally box and click Apply. Repeat for the JavaScript tab. ∎

- **File types and MIME types** — If you want a particular type of file to always be launched by a particular application, you can configure that file yourself. KDE already has dozens of MIME types defined so that particular file and data types can be automatically detected and opened in the correct application. There are MIME types defined for audio, image, text, video, and a variety of other content.

Of course, you can also perform many standard file manager functions with Konqueror. For example, you can manipulate files by using features such as select, move, cut, paste, and delete; search directories for files; create new items (files, folders, and links, to name a few); view histories of the files and web sites you have opened; and create bookmarks. Most of these features work the same way as they do in Dolphin (as described earlier).

Using Bookmarking Features in Konqueror

Because Konqueror performs like a web browser as well as a file manager, it includes several browser features. For example, the bookmarks feature enables you to keep a bookmark list of web sites you have visited. Click Bookmarks, and a drop-down menu of the sites you have bookmarked appears. Select from that list to return to a site. There are several ways to add and change your bookmarks list:

- **Add Bookmark** — To add the address of the page currently being displayed to your bookmark list, choose Bookmarks ➪ Add Bookmark. The next time you click Bookmarks, you will see the bookmark you just added on the Bookmarks menu. In addition to web addresses, you can also bookmark any file or folder.

- **Edit Bookmarks** — Select Bookmarks ➪ Edit Bookmarks to open a tree view of your bookmarks. From the Bookmark Editor window that appears, you can change the URLs, the icon, or other features of the bookmark. Another nice feature lets you check the status of the bookmark (that is, the address available).

- **New Bookmark Folder** — You can add a new folder of bookmarks to your Konqueror bookmarks list. To create a bookmarks folder, choose Bookmarks ➪ New Bookmark Folder. Then type a name for the new Bookmarks folder, and click OK. The new bookmarks folder appears on your Bookmarks menu. You can add the current location to that folder by clicking on the folder name and selecting Add Bookmark.

Configuring Konqueror Options

You can change many of the visual attributes of the Konqueror window, including which menu bars and toolbars appear. You can have any of the following bars appear on the Konqueror window: Menubar, Toolbar, Extra Toolbar, Location Toolbar, and Bookmark Toolbar. Select Settings, and then click the bar you want to have appear (or not appear). The bar appears when a check mark is shown next to it.

You can modify a variety of options for Konqueror by choosing Settings ➪ Configure Konqueror. The Konqueror Settings window appears, offering the following options:

- **Performance** — Display configuration settings that can be used to improve Konqueror performance. You can preload an instance after KDE startup or minimize memory usage.

- **Bookmarks** — Configures the bookmarks home page.

- **File Management** — Submenus of this menu configure features such as navigation, services, general, file associations, and how trash is handled.

- **View Modes** — An icon in a Konqueror folder can be made to resemble the contents of the file it represents. For example, if the file is a JPEG image, the icon representing the file could be a small version of that image. Using the Previews features, you can limit the size of the file used (1MB is the default) because many massive files could take too long to refresh on the screen. You can also choose to have any thumbnail embedded in a file to be used as the icon or have the size of the icon reflect the shape of the image used.

- **Web Browsing** — Click the Browsing selection to open a window to configure the web browser features of Konqueror. Submenus of this menu include Proxy, Appearance, AdBlock Filters, web Shortcuts, Cache, History, Cookies, Browser Identification, Java & JavaScript, and Plug-ins. They are described here:

  - **Proxy** — Click Proxy to configure Konqueror to access the Internet through a proxy server (by default, Konqueror tries to connect there directly). You need to enter the address and port number of the computer providing HTTP and/or FTP proxy services. Alternatively, you can have Konqueror try to automatically detect the proxy configuration.

  - **Appearance** — Click here to modify the appearance of the Konqueror window.

  - **AdBlock Filters** — Click here to create a list of URLs that are filtered as you browse the web. Filtering is based on frame and image names. Filtered URLs can be either thrown away or replaced with an image. You can also import and export lists of filters here.

  - **Web Shortcuts** — Display a list of keyword shortcuts you can use to go to different Internet sites. For example, follow the word "ask" with a search string to search the Ask (www.ask.com) web site.

  - **Cache** — Indicate how much space on your hard disk can be used to store the sites you have visited (based on the value in the Disk Cache Size field).

  - **History** — Modify the behavior of the list of sites you have visited (the history). By default, the most recent 500 URLs are stored, and after 500 days (KNOPPIX) or 90 days (Fedora), a URL is dropped from the list. There's also a button to clear your history. (To view your history list in Konqueror, open the left panel, and then click the tiny scroll icon.)

  - **Cookies** — Choose whether cookies are enabled in Konqueror. By default, you are asked to confirm that it is okay each time a web site tries to create or modify a cookie. You can change that to either accept or reject all cookies. You can also set policies for acceptance or rejection of cookies based on host and domain names.

  - **Browser Identification** — Set how Konqueror identifies itself when it accesses a web site. By default, Konqueror tells the web site that it is the Mozilla web browser. You can select Konqueror to appear as different web browsers to specific sites. You must sometimes do this when a site denies you access because you do not have a specific type of browser (even though Konqueror may be fully capable of displaying the content).

- **Java and JavaScript** — Enable or disable Java and JavaScript content contained in web pages in your Konqueror window.

- **Plug-ins** — Display a list of directories that Konqueror will search to find plug-ins. Konqueror can also scan your computer to find plug-ins that are installed for other browsers in other locations.

Managing the KDE Desktop

If you have a lot of things open at the same time, organizing those items can make managing your desktop much easier. The KDE 4 Plasma desktop offers many of the traditional ways of managing desktop elements (windows, workspaces, panels, icons, menus, and so on). However, it also offers new ways of grouping and managing your desktop elements.

Managing Windows in the Taskbar

When you open a window, a button representing the window appears in the panel at the bottom of the screen. Here is how you can manage windows from the taskbar appearing on that panel:

- **Toggle windows** — Left-click any running task in the taskbar to toggle between opening the window and minimizing it.

- **Position windows** — You can choose to have the selected window be above or below other windows or displayed in full screen. Right-click the running task in the taskbar and select Advanced. Then choose Keep Above Others, Keep Below Others, or Fullscreen.

- **Move windows** — Move a window from the current desktop to any other virtual desktop. Right-click any task in the taskbar, select To Desktop, and then select any desktop number. The window moves to that desktop.

All the windows that are running, regardless of which virtual desktop you are on, appear in the taskbar.

Moving Windows

The easiest way to move a window from one location to another is to place the cursor on the window's title bar, hold down the mouse button and drag the window to a new location, and release the mouse button to drop the window. Another way to do it is to click the window menu button (top-left corner of the title bar), select Move, move the mouse to relocate the window, and then click again to place it.

Tip

If, somehow, the window gets stuck in a location where the title bar is off the screen, you can move it back to where you want it by holding down the Alt key and clicking the left mouse button in the inner window. Then move the window where you want it and release. ∎

Resizing Windows

To resize a window, grab anywhere on the outer edge of the window border, and then move the mouse until the window is the size you want. Grab a corner to resize vertically and horizontally at the same time. Grab a side to resize in only one direction.

You can also resize a window by clicking the window menu button (top-left corner of the title bar) and selecting Resize. Move the mouse until the window is resized and click to leave it there.

Pinning Windows on Top or Bottom

You can set a window to always stay on top of all other windows or always stay under them. Keeping a window on top can be useful for a small window that you want to always refer to (such as a clock or a small TV viewing window). To pin a window on top of the desktop, click the window menu button in the window title bar. From the menu that appears, select Advanced ⇨ Keep Above Others. Likewise, to keep the window on the bottom, select Advanced ⇨ Keep Below Others.

Using Virtual Desktops

To give you more space to run applications than will fit on your physical screen, KDE gives you access to several virtual desktops at the same time. Using the 1, 2, 3, and 4 buttons on the panel, you can easily move between the different desktops. Just click the one you want.

If you want to move an application from one desktop to another, you can do so from the window menu. Click the window menu button for the window you want to move, click To Desktop, and then select Desktop 1, 2, 3, or 4. The window will disappear from the current desktop and move to the one you selected.

Adding Widgets

You want to be able to quickly access the applications that you use most often. One of the best ways to make that possible is to add widgets to the panel or the desktop that can either run continuously (such as a clock or news ticker) or launch the applications you need with a single click.

To add a KDE widget to the panel:

1. Right-click anywhere on the panel.
2. Click Add Widgets.
3. Select the widget you want to add and click Add Widget.

An icon representing the widget should immediately appear on the panel. (If the panel seems a bit crowded, you might want to remove some widgets you don't use or add a widget directly to the desktop.) At this point, you can change any properties associated with the widget by right-clicking the widget in the panel and then selecting to change its settings.

If you decide later that you no longer want this widget to be available on the panel, right-click it and click Remove.

To add a widget to the desktop:

1. Right-click an open area of the desktop.
2. Select Add Widgets from the menu.
3. Select the widget you want from the list that appears and click Add Widget.

If you decide later that you no longer want this widget to be available on the desktop, hover the mouse over it and click the red X to delete it.

Configuring the Desktop

If you want to change the look, feel, or behavior of your KDE desktop, the best place to start is the Personal Settings window. The Personal Settings window lets you configure dozens of attributes associated with colors, fonts, and screen savers used by KDE. Selections from that window also let you do basic computer administration, such as changing date/time settings and modifying your display.

To open the Personal Settings window, select the KickOff menu button (represented by the open-SUSE logo icon in openSUSE) at the lower-left corner of the panel and choose Configure Desktop. The Personal Settings window appears, as shown in Figure 3-6.

FIGURE 3-6

Configure your system in KDE from the Personal Settings window.

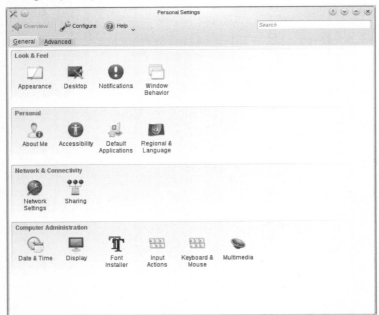

Click any item you want to configure, or type into the Search box to find a selection that matches what you type.

There are several ways you can change the look and feel of your desktop display from the Personal Settings window. Under the Look & Feel menu, you can select to change the appearance, desktop, notifications, or window behavior.

Here are a few of the individual desktop features you may want to change:

- **Change the screen saver** — Under the Look & Feel heading, select Desktop ⇨ Screen Saver. From the window that appears, only a few screen savers are available by default. However, by installing the kdeartwork-extras package, you can get a lot more screen savers to choose from. Under the Start Automatically box, select how many minutes of inactivity before the screen saver turns on. You can also click Require Password to require that a password be entered before you can access your display after the screen saver has come on.

Tip

If you are working in a place where you want your desktop to be secure, be sure to turn on the Require Password feature. This prevents others from gaining access to your computer when you forget to lock it or shut it off. If you have any virtual terminals open, switch to them and type vlock to lock each of them as well. (You need to install the vlock package if the vlock **command isn't available.)** ■

- **Change fonts** — You can assign different fonts to different places in which fonts appear on the desktop. Under the Look & Feel heading, select Appearance ⇨ Fonts. Select one of the categories of fonts (General, Fixed width, Small, Toolbar, Menu, Window title, Taskbar, and Desktop fonts). Then click the Choose box to select a font from the Select Font list box that you want to assign to that category. If the font is available, you will see an example of the text in the Sample text box.

- **Change colors** — Under the Look & Feel heading in the System Settings window, select Appearance ⇨ Colors. The window that appears lets you change the color of selected items on the desktop. Select a whole color scheme from the Color Scheme list box. Or select an item from the Colors tab to change a particular item. Items you can change include text, backgrounds, links, buttons, and title bars.

Tip

To use 100 dpi fonts, you must add an entry for 100 dpi fonts to the /etc/X11/xorg.conf **file. After you make that change, you must restart the X server for it to take effect.** ■

For most people, the panel is the place where they select which desktop is active and which applications are run. You can change panel behavior from the Configure Panel window. Right-click any empty space on your panel, and then select Panel Settings. You can change these features from the Settings window that appears:

- **Height/Width** — The Size selection lets you change the size of the panel from Normal to Tiny, Small, Large, or Custom. With Custom, select the exact point size (48 is the default).

- **Screen Edge** — Change the location of the panel from Bottom to Top, Right, or Left.

The GNOME Desktop

GNOME (pronounced *guh-nome*) the desktop environment that you get by default when you install Fedora, Ubuntu, and other Linux systems. This desktop environment provides the software that is between your X Window System framework and the look and feel provided by the window manager. GNOME is a stable and reliable desktop environment, with a few cool features.

As of this writing, GNOME 2.32 is the most recent version available, although the distribution you are using may or may not include this latest version. Recent GNOME releases include advancements in 3D effects (see "3D Effects with AIGLX" later in this chapter), improved usability features, and an application for using your webcam.

To use your GNOME desktop, you should become familiar with the following components:

- **Metacity (window manager)** — The default window manager for GNOME in Ubuntu, Fedora, RHEL, and others is Metacity. Metacity configuration options let you control such things as themes, window borders, and controls used on your desktop.

- **Compiz (window manager)** — You can enable this window manager in GNOME to provide 3D desktop effects.

- **Nautilus (file manager/graphical shell)** — When you open a folder (by double-clicking the Home icon on your desktop, for example), the Nautilus window opens and displays the contents of the selected folder. Nautilus can also display other types of content, such as shared folders from Windows computers on the network (using SMB).

- **GNOME panels (application/task launcher)** — These panels, which line the top and bottom of your screen, are designed to make it convenient for you to launch the applications you use, manage running applications, and work with multiple virtual desktops. By default, the top panel contains menu buttons (Applications, Places, and System), desktop application launchers (Evolution e-mail and Firefox web browser), a workspace switcher (for managing four virtual desktops), and a clock. Icons appear in the panel when you need software updates or SELinux detects a problem. The bottom panel has a Show Desktop button, window lists, a trashcan, and a workspace switcher.

- **Desktop area** — The windows and icons you use are arranged on the desktop area, which supports drag-and-drop between applications, a desktop menu (right-click to see it), and icons for launching applications. A computer icon consolidates CD drives, floppy drives, the file system, and shared network resources in one place.

GNOME also includes a set of preferences windows that enable you to configure different aspects of your desktop. You can change backgrounds, colors, fonts, keyboard shortcuts, and other features related to the look and behavior of the desktop. Figure 3-7 shows how the GNOME desktop environment appears the first time you log in, with a few windows added to the screen.

The desktop shown in Figure 3-7 is for Fedora. The following sections provide details on using the GNOME desktop.

FIGURE 3-7

The GNOME desktop environment

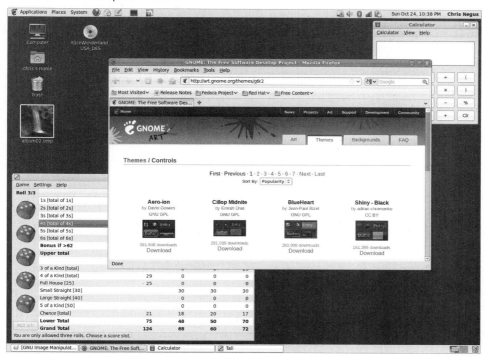

Using the Metacity Window Manager

The Metacity window manager seems to have been chosen as the default window manager for GNOME because of its simplicity. The creator of Metacity refers to it as a "boring window manager for the adult in you" — and then goes on to compare other window managers to colorful, sugary cereal, whereas Metacity is characterized as Cheerios.

Note
To use 3D effects, your best solution is to use the Compiz window manager, described later in this chapter. ■

There really isn't much you can do with Metacity (except get your work done efficiently). You assign new themes to Metacity and change colors and window decorations through the GNOME preferences (described later). A few Metacity themes exist, but expect the number to grow.

Basic Metacity functions that might interest you are keyboard shortcuts and the workspace switcher. Table 3-4 shows keyboard shortcuts to get around the Metacity window manager.

Another Metacity feature of interest is the workspace switcher. Four virtual workspaces appear in the Workspace Switcher on the GNOME panel. You can do the following with the Workspace Switcher:

- **Choose current workspace** — Four virtual workspaces appear in the Workspace Switcher. Click any of the four virtual workspaces to make it your current workspace.

- **Move windows to other workspaces** — Click any window, each represented by a tiny rectangle in a workspace, to drag-and-drop it to another workspace. Likewise, you can drag an application from the Window List to move that application to another workspace.

- **Add more workspaces** — Right-click the Workspace Switcher, and select Preferences. You can add workspaces (up to 32).

- **Name workspaces** — Right-click the Workspace Switcher and select Preferences. Click in the Workspaces pane to change names of workspaces to any names you choose.

You can view and change information about Metacity controls and settings using the gconf-editor window (type **gconf-editor** from a Terminal window). As the window says, it is not the recommended way of changing preferences, so when possible, you should change the desktop through GNOME preferences. However, gconf-editor is a good way to see descriptions of each Metacity feature.

From the gconf-editor window, select apps ➪ metacity, and then choose from general, global_keybindings, keybindings_commands, window_keybindings, and workspace_names. Click each key to see its value, along with short and long descriptions of the key.

TABLE 3-4

Metacity Keyboard Shortcuts

Actions		Keystrokes
Window focus	Cycle forward, with pop-up icons	Alt+Tab
	Cycle backward, with pop-up icons	Alt+Shift+Tab
	Cycle forward, without pop-up icons	Alt+Esc
	Cycle backward, without pop-up icons	Alt+Shift+Esc
Panel focus	Cycle forward among panels	Alt+Ctrl+Tab
	Cycle backward among panels	Alt+Ctrl+Shift+Tab
Workspace focus	Move to workspace to the right	Ctrl+Alt+right arrow
	Move to workspace to the left	Ctrl+Alt+left arrow
	Move to upper workspace	Ctrl+Alt+up arrow
	Move to lower workspace	Ctrl+Alt+down arrow

Actions	Keystrokes
Minimize/maximize all windows	Ctrl+Alt+D
Show window menu	Alt+Spacebar
Close menu	Esc

Using the GNOME Panels

The GNOME panels are placed on the top and bottom of the GNOME desktop. From those panels you can start applications (from buttons or menus), see what programs are active, and monitor how your system is running. There are also many ways to change the top and bottom panels — by adding applications or monitors or by changing the placement or behavior of the panel, for example.

Right-click any open space on either panel to see the Panel menu. Figure 3-8 shows the Panel menu on the top.

FIGURE 3-8

The GNOME Panel menu

From GNOME's Panel menu, you can choose from a variety of functions, including:

- **Use the menus** — The Applications menu displays most of the applications and system tools you will use from the desktop. The Places menu lets you select places to go, such as the Desktop folder, home folder, removable media, or network locations. The System menu lets you change preferences and system settings, as well as get other information about GNOME.

- **Add to Panel** — Add an applet, menu, launcher, drawer, or button.

- **Properties** — Change the panel's position, size, and background properties.

- **Delete This Panel** — Delete the current panel.

- **New Panel** — Add panels to your desktop in different styles and locations.

You can also work with items on a panel. For example, you can

- **Move items** — To move an item on a panel, right-click it, select move, and then drag-and-drop it to a new position.

- **Resize items** — You can resize some elements, such as the Window List, by clicking an edge and dragging it to the new size.

- **Use the Window List** — Tasks running on the desktop appear in the Window List area. Click a task to minimize or maximize it.

The following sections describe some things you can do with the GNOME panel.

Using the Applications and System Menus

Click Applications on the panel, and you see categories of applications and system tools that you can select. Click the application you want to launch. To add an item from a menu so that it can launch from the panel, drag-and-drop the item you want to the panel.

You can add items to your GNOME menus. To do that, right-click on any of the menu names, and then select Edit Menus. The window that appears lets you add or delete menus associated with the Applications and System menus. You can also add items to launch from those menus by selecting New Item and typing the name, command, and comment for the item.

Adding an Applet

You can run several small applications, called *applets*, directly on the GNOME panel. These applications can show information you may want to see on an ongoing basis or may just provide some amusement. To see what applets are available and to add applets that you want to your panel, perform the following steps:

1. Right-click an open space in the panel so that the Panel menu appears.

2. Select Add to Panel. An Add to Panel window appears.

3. Select from among several dozen applets, including a clock, dictionary lookup, stock ticker, and weather report. The applet you select appears on the panel, ready for you to use.

Figure 3-9 shows (from left to right) eyes, system monitor, weather report, Terminal, and Wanda the Fish.

FIGURE 3-9

Placing applets on the panel makes accessing them easy.

After an applet is installed, right-click it on the panel to see what options are available. For example, select Preferences for the stock ticker, and you can add or delete stocks whose prices you want to monitor. If you don't like the applet's location, right-click it, click Move, slide the mouse until the applet is where you want it (even to another panel), and click to set its location.

If you no longer want an applet to appear on the panel, right-click it, and then click Remove From Panel. The icon representing the applet disappears. If you find that you have run out of room on your panel, you can add a new panel to another part of the screen, as described in the next section.

Adding Another Panel

If you run out of space on the top or bottom panels, you can add more panels to your desktop. You can have several panels on your GNOME desktop. You can add panels that run along the entire bottom, top, or side of the screen. To add a panel, do the following:

1. Right-click an open space in the panel so that the Panel menu appears.
2. Select New Panel. A new panel appears on the side of the screen.
3. Right-click an open space in the new panel and select Properties.
4. From the Panel Properties, select where you want the panel from the Orientation box (Top, Bottom, Left, or Right).

After you've added a panel, you can add applets or application launchers to it as you did to the default panel. To remove a panel, right-click it and select Delete This Panel.

Adding an Application Launcher

Icons on your panel represent a web browser and several office productivity applications. You can add your own icons to launch applications from the panel as well. To add a new application launcher to the panel, do the following:

1. Right-click in an open space on the panel.
2. Select Add to Panel ⇨ Application Launcher from the menu. All application categories from your Applications and System menus appear.
3. Select the arrow next to the category of application you want, and then select Add. An icon representing the application appears on the panel.

To launch the application you just added, simply click the icon on the panel.

If the application you want to launch is not on one of your menus, you can build a launcher yourself as follows:

1. Right-click in an open space on the panel.

2. Select Add to Panel ⇨ Custom Application Launcher ⇨ Add. The Create Launcher window appears.

3. Provide the following information for the application that you want to add:

   - **Type** — Select Application (to launch a regular GUI application) or Application in Terminal. Use Application in Terminal if the application is a character-based or ncurses application. (Applications written using the ncurses library run in a Terminal window but offer screen-oriented mouse and keyboard controls.)

   - **Name** — A name to identify the application (this appears in the tooltip when your mouse is over the icon).

   - **Command** — The command line that is run when the application is launched. Use the full path name, plus any required options.

   - **Comment** — A comment describing the application. It also appears when you later move your mouse over the launcher.

4. Click the Icon box (it might say No Icon). Select one of the icons shown and click OK. Alternatively, you can browse your file system to choose an icon.

5. Click OK.

The application should now appear in the panel. Click it to start the application.

Note

Icons available to represent your application are contained in the `/usr/share/pixmaps` **directory. These icons are either in** `.png` **or** `.xpm` **formats. If there isn't an icon in the directory you want to use, create your own (in one of those two formats) and assign it to the application. ∎**

Adding a Drawer

A drawer is an icon that you can click to display other icons representing menus, applets, and launchers; it behaves just like a panel. Essentially, any item you can add to a panel you can add to a drawer. By adding a drawer to your GNOME panel, you can include several applets and launchers that together take up the space of only one icon. Click on the drawer to show the applets and launchers as if they were being pulled out of a drawer icon on the panel.

To add a drawer to your panel, right-click the panel and select Add to Panel ⇨ Drawer. A drawer appears on the panel. Right-click it, and add applets or launchers to it as you would to a panel. Click the icon again to retract the drawer.

Figure 3-10 shows a portion of the panel with an open drawer that includes an icon for launching a weather report, sticky notes, and stock monitor.

FIGURE 3-10

Add launchers or applets to a drawer on your GNOME panel.

Changing Panel Properties

Those panel properties you can change are limited to the orientation, size, hiding policy, and background. To open the Panel Properties window that applies to a specific panel, right-click on an open space on the panel and choose Properties. The Panel Properties window that appears includes the following values:

- **Orientation** — Move the panel to different locations on the screen by clicking on a new position.

- **Size** — Select the size of your panel by choosing its height in pixels (48 pixels by default).

- **Expand** — Select this check box to have the panel expand to fill the entire side, or clear the check box to make the panel only as wide as the applets it contains.

- **AutoHide** — Select whether a panel is automatically hidden (appearing only when the mouse pointer is in the area).

- **Show Hide buttons** — Choose whether the Hide/Unhide buttons (with pixmap arrows on them) appear on the edges of the panel.

- **Arrows on hide buttons** — If you select Show Hide Buttons, you can choose to have arrows on those buttons.

- **Background** — From the Background tab, you can assign a color to the background of the panel, assign a pixmap image, or just leave the default (which is based on the current system theme). Click the Background Image check box if you want to select an Image for the background, and then select an image, such as a tile from /usr/share/backgrounds/tiles or other directory.

Tip

I usually turn on the AutoHide feature and turn off the Hide buttons. Using AutoHide gives you more desktop space to work with. When you move your mouse to the edge where the panel is, the panel pops up — so you don't need Hide buttons. ■

Using the Nautilus File Manager

At one time, file managers did little more than let you run applications, create data files, and open folders. These days, as the information a user needs expands beyond the local system, file managers are expected to also display web pages, access FTP sites, and play multimedia content. The Nautilus file manager, which is the default GNOME file manager, is an example of just such a file manager.

When you open the Nautilus file manager window (for example, by opening the Home icon or other folder on your desktop), you see the name of the location you are viewing (such as the folder name) and what that location contains (files, folders, and applications). Double-click a folder to open that folder in a new window.

Select your folder name to see the file system hierarchy above the current folder. GNOME remembers whatever size, location, and other setting you had for the folder the last time you closed it and returns it to that state the next time you open it.

To see more controls, right-click a folder and select Browse Folder to open it. Icons on the toolbar of the Nautilus window let you move forward and back among the directories and web sites you visit. To move up the directory structure, click the up arrow. Figure 3-11 is an example of the file manager window displaying the home directory of a user named chris in browse mode.

FIGURE 3-11

The Nautilus file manager enables you to move around the file system, open directories, launch applications, and open Samba folders.

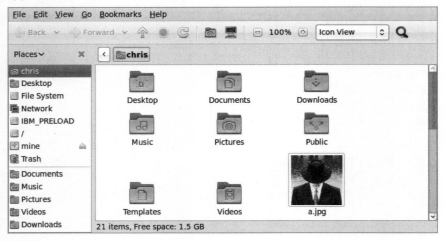

To refresh the view of the folder, click the Reload button. The Home button takes you to your home page, and the Computer button lets you see the same type of information you would see from a My Computer icon on a Windows system (CD drive, floppy drive, hard disk file systems, and network folders).

Icons in Nautilus often indicate the type of data that a particular file contains. The contents or file extension of each file can determine which application is used to work with the file, or you can right-click an icon to open the file it represents with a particular application or viewer.

Here are some of the more interesting features of Nautilus:

- **Sidebar** — From the Browse Folder view described previously, select View ➪ Side Pane to have a sidebar appear in the left column of the screen. From the sidebar, you can click a pull-down menu that represents different types of information you can select one at a time.

  The Tree tab, for example, shows a tree view of the directory structure, so you can easily traverse your directories. The Notes tab lets you add notes that become associated with the current Directory or web page, and the History tab displays a history of directories you have visited, enabling you to click those items to return to the sites they represent. There is also an Emblems tab that lets you drag-and-drop emblems on files or folders to indicate something about the file or folder (emblems include icons representing draft, urgent, bug, and multimedia).

- **Windows file and printer sharing** — If your computer is connected to a LAN on which Windows computers are sharing files and printers, you can view those resources from Nautilus. Type **smb:** in the Open Location box (select Go ➪ Location to get there) to see available workgroups. Click a workgroup to see computers from that workgroup that are sharing files and printers. Figure 3-12 shows an example of a local Nautilus window displaying icons representing folders shared from a Window computer named bluestreak that is accessible on the local LAN. The shared folder from that computer is named My Doc Blue.

FIGURE 3-12

Display shared Windows file and printer servers (SMB) in Nautilus.

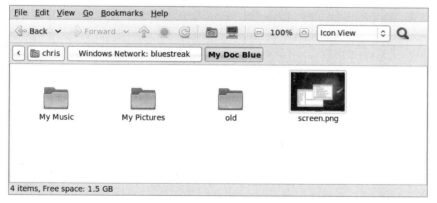

- **MIME types and file types** — To handle different types of content that may be encountered in the Nautilus window, you can set applications to respond based on MIME type and file type. With a folder displayed, right-click a file for which you want to assign an application. Click Open With Other Application. If no application or viewer has been assigned for the file type, click Associate Application to be able to select an application. From the Add File Types window, you can add an application based on the file extension and MIME type representing the file.

- **Drag-and-drop** — You can use drag-and-drop within the Nautilus window, between the Nautilus and the desktop, or among multiple Nautilus windows. As other GNOME-compliant applications become available, they are expected to also support the drag-and-drop feature.

If you would like more information on the Nautilus file manager, visit the GNOME web site (`http://live.gnome.org/Nautilus`).

3D Effects with AIGLX

Several different initiatives have made strides in recent years to bring 3D desktop effects to Linux. Ubuntu, openSUSE, and Fedora used AIGLX (`http://fedoraproject.org/wiki/RenderingProject/aiglx`).

The goal of the Accelerated Indirect GLX project (AIGLX) is to add 3D effects to everyday desktop systems. It does this by implementing OpenGL (`http://opengl.org`) accelerated effects using the Mesa (`www.mesa3d.org`) open source OpenGL implementation.

Currently, AIGLX supports a limited set of video cards and implements only a few 3D effects, but it does offer some insight into the eye candy that is in the works.

If your video card was properly detected and configured, you may be able to simply turn on the Desktop Effects feature to see the effects that have been implemented so far. To turn on Desktop Effects, select System ➪ Preferences ➪ Appearance Visual Effects. When the Desktop Effects window appears, select Enable Desktop Effects. Enabling this does the following:

- Stops the current window manager and starts the Compiz window manager.
- Enables the Windows Wobble When Moved effect. With this effect on, when you grab the title bar of the window to move it, the window will wobble as it moves. Menus and other items that open on the desktop also wobble.
- Enables the Workspaces on a Cube effect. Drag a window from the desktop to the right or the left and the desktop will rotate like a cube, with each of your desktop workspaces appearing as a side of that cube. Drop the window on the workspace where you want it to go. You can also click on the Workspace Switcher applet in the bottom panel to rotate the cube to display different workspaces.

Other nice desktop effects result from using the Alt+Tab keys to tab among different running windows. As you press Alt+Tab, a thumbnail of each window scrolls across the screen as the window it represents is highlighted.

Figure 3-13 shows an example of a Compiz desktop with AIGLX enabled. The figure illustrates a web browser window being moved from one workspace to another as those workspaces rotate on a cube.

FIGURE 3-13

Rotate workspaces on a cube with AIGLX desktop effects enabled.

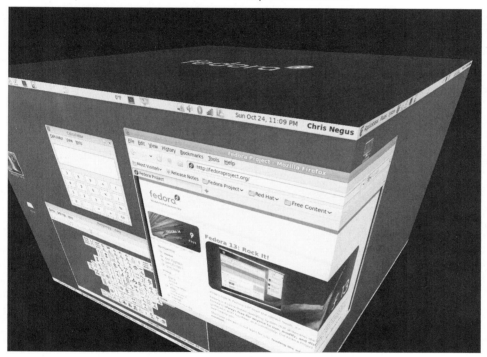

The following are some interesting effects you can get with your 3D AIGLX desktop:

- **Spin cube** — Hold Ctrl+Alt keys and press the right and left arrow keys. The desktop cube spins to each successive workspace (forward or back).

- **Slowly rotate cube** — Hold the Ctrl+Alt keys, press and hold the left mouse button, and move the mouse around on the screen. The cube will move slowly with the mouse among the workspaces.

- **Tab through windows** — Hold the Alt key and press the Tab key. You will see reduced versions of all your windows in a strip in the middle of your screen, with the current window highlighted in the middle. Still holding the Alt key, press Tab or Shift+Tab to move forward or backwards through the windows. Release the keys when the one you want is highlighted.

- **Scale and separate windows** — If your desktop is cluttered, hold Ctrl+Alt and press the up arrow key. Windows will shrink down and separate on the desktop. Still holding Ctrl+Alt, use your arrow keys to highlight the window you want and release the keys to have that window come to the surface.

- **Scale and separate workspaces** — Hold Ctrl+Alt and press the down arrow key to see reduced images of the workspace shown on a strip. Still holding Ctrl+Alt, use right and left arrow keys to move among the different workspaces. Release the keys when the workspace you want is highlighted.

- **Send current window to next workspace** — Hold Ctrl+Alt+Shift keys together and press the left and right arrow keys. The next workspace to the left or right, respectively, appears on the current desktop.

- **Slide windows around** — Press and hold the left mouse button, and then press the left, right, up, or down arrow keys to slide the current window around on the screen.

If you get tired of wobbling windows and spinning cubes, you can easily turn off the AIGLX 3D effects and return Metacity as the window manager. Select System ⇨ Preferences ⇨ Desktop Effects again and toggle off the Enable Desktop Effects button to turn off the feature.

If you have a supported video card, but find that you are not able to turn on the Desktop Effects, check that your X server started properly. In particular, make sure that your /etc/X11/xorg.conf file is properly configured. Make sure that dri and glx are loaded in the Module section. Also, add an extensions section anywhere in the file (typically at the end of the file) that appears as follows:

```
Section "extensions"
 Option "Composite"
EndSection
```

Another option is to add the following line to the /etc/X11/xorg.conf file in the Device section:

```
Option "XAANoOffscreenPixmaps"
```

The XAANoOffscreenPixmaps option will improve performance. Check your /var/log/Xorg.log file to make sure that DRI and AIGLX features were started correctly. The messages in that file can help you debug other problems as well.

Changing GNOME Preferences

There are many ways to change the behavior, look, and feel of your GNOME desktop. You can modify most GNOME preferences from submenus on the Preferences menu (select System ⇨ Preferences).

Unlike earlier versions of GNOME, boundaries between preferences related to the window manager (Metacity), file manager (Nautilus), and the GNOME desktop itself have been blurred. Preferences for all of these features are available from the Preferences menu.

The following items highlight some of the preferences you might want to change:

- **Accessibility** — If you have difficulty operating a mouse or keyboard or seeing the screen, the Assistive Technologies window lets you adapt mouse and keyboard settings to make operating your computer easier for you. It also lets you magnify selected applications. (Select System ➪ Preferences ➪ Assistive Technologies.)

- **Desktop Background** — You can choose a solid color or an image to use as wallpaper. Select System ➪ Preferences ➪ Appearance and then the Background tab. If you choose to use a solid color (by selecting No Desktop Background icon), click the Color box, select a color from the palette, and click OK.

  To use wallpaper for your background, open the folder containing the image you want to use, and then drag the image into the Desktop Wallpaper pane on the Desktop Preferences window. You can choose from a variety of images in the /usr/share/nautilus /patterns and /usr/share/backgrounds/tiles directories. Then choose to have the wallpaper image tiled (repeated pattern), centered, scaled (in proportion), or stretched (using any proportion to fill the screen).

- **Screensaver** — Choose from dozens of screen savers from the Screensaver window. Select System ➪ Preferences ➪ Screensaver. Choose Random to have your screen saver chosen randomly from available screen savers, or select one that you like from the list to use all the time. Next, choose how long your screen must be idle before the screen saver starts (default is 10 minutes). You can also choose to lock the screen when the screen saver is active, so a password is required to return to the desktop. If you only see a few screen savers, you might want to install the xscreensaver-extras and xscreensaver-gl-extras packages to get a bunch more.

- **Theme** — Choose an entire theme of elements to be used on your desktop, if you like. From the Appearance window, select the Theme tab. A desktop theme affects not only the background but also the way that many buttons and menu selections appear. Only a few themes are available for the window manager (Metacity) in the Fedora distribution, but you can get a bunch of other themes from themes.freshmeat.net (click Metacity).

  To modify a theme, select the Customize button and then click the Controls tab to choose the type of controls to use on your desktop. Click the Window Border tab to select from different themes that change the title bar and other borders of your windows. Click the Icons tab to choose different icons to represent items on your desktop. Themes change immediately as you click or when you drag a theme name on the desktop.

Exiting GNOME

When you are done with your work, you can either log out from your current session or shut down your computer completely. To exit from GNOME, do the following:

1. Click the System button from the panel.

2. Select Log Out from the menu. A pop-up window appears, asking whether you want to Log Out. Some versions will also ask whether you want to Shut Down or Restart the computer.

3. Select Log Out from the pop-up menu. This logs you out and returns you to either the graphical login screen or to your shell login prompt. (If you select Shut Down, the system shuts down, and if you select Restart, the system restarts.)

4. Select OK to finish exiting from GNOME.

If you are unable to get to the Log Out button (if, for example, your panel crashed), two other exit methods are available. Try one of these ways, depending on how you started the desktop:

- If you started the desktop from the graphical display manager or by typing **startx** from your login shell, select System ➪ Logout to end your GNOME session.

- If your screen is completely unresponsive (mouse and keyboard aren't working), you might just have to reboot your computer. If possible, log in to the computer over the network and type **reboot** (as root user) to reboot.

Although these ways are not the most graceful for exiting the desktop, they work. You should be able to log in again and restart the desktop.

Configuring Your Own Desktop

Today's modern desktop computer systems are made to spoon-feed you your operating system. In the name of ease of use, some desktop environments spend a lot of resources on fancy panels, complex control centers, and busy applets. In short, they can become bloated.

Many technically inclined people want a more streamlined desktop — or at least want to choose their own bells and whistles. They don't want to have to wait for windows to redraw or menus to come up. Linux enables those people to forget the complete desktop environments and configure the main elements:

- **X** — The X Window System provides the framework of choice for Linux and most UNIX systems. When you configure X yourself, you can choose the video driver, monitor settings, mouse configuration, and other basic features needed to get your display working properly.

- **Window manager** — Dozens of window managers are available to use with X on a Linux system. Window managers add borders and buttons to otherwise bare X windows. They add colors and graphics to backgrounds, menus, and windows. Window managers also define how you can use keyboard and mouse combinations to operate your desktop.

You need to configure X directly only if your desktop isn't working (the desktop may appear scrambled or may just plain crash). You may choose to configure X if you want to tune it to give you higher resolutions or more colors than you get by default.

Still to come in this chapter: examining tools for tuning X and, in particular, working with the `xorg.conf` file. You'll also explore a few popular window managers that you might want to try out. Slackware Linux is used to illustrate how to choose and configure a window manager because Slackware users tend to like simple, direct ways of working with the desktop (when they need a desktop at all).

Configuring X

Before 2004, most Linux distributions used the X server from the XFree86 project (`www.xfree86.org`). Because of licensing issues, many of the major Linux vendors (including Red Hat, SUSE, and Slackware) changed to the X server from X.Org (`www.X.org`). The descriptions of how to get X going on your machine assume you are using the X.Org X server.

If you are able to start a desktop successfully, and your mouse, keyboard, and screen all seem to be behaving, you may not have to do anything more to configure X. However, if you can't start the desktop or you want to adjust some basic features (such as screen resolution or number of colors supported), the following sections offer some ideas on how to go about doing those things.

Creating a Working X Configuration File

Most newer Linux distributions don't need an X configuration file at all to work. But, if your desktop crashes immediately or shows only garbled text, try to create a new X configuration file. With the X.Org X server, that file is `/etc/X11/xorg.conf`.

Note

In XFree86, the configuration file, which has basically the same format, is `/etc/X11/XF86Config`. ∎

In Fedora, before you try to reconfigure X, be sure that you are not in run level 5. That run level will continuously try to restart X. I recommend you change to run level 3 before reconfiguring X. (For Ubuntu, type **stop gdm** instead.) Press Ctrl+Alt+F1 and log in as root. Then type the following:

```
# init 3
```

Note

Some of the latest versions of X have split the xorg.conf file into a set of files contained in the `/etc/X11/xorg.conf.d` directory. So, instead of editing the information in the xorg.conf file, edit the files in that directory. ∎

Tip

One trick you might want to try before reconfiguring X is to simply remove the existing `xorg.conf` file. For example, type this as root: `mv /etc/X11/xorg.conf /etc/X11/old.xorg.conf`. Then restart X as described later. Often, simply starting X will cause a new, working `xorg.conf` file to be created. With the latest versions of X, move the files from the `xorg.conf.d` directory. ∎

To have X try to create a working `xorg.conf` file for you to use, do the following from a Terminal window as root user:

1. If Linux booted to a command prompt, go to the next step. However, if it tried to start X automatically, you might have an illegible screen. In that case, you need to stop X so that it doesn't just restart immediately. Open a Terminal window, log in as root, and type **init 3** (in Fedora) or **stop gdm** (in Ubuntu).

2. To have X probe your video hardware and create a new configuration file, type the following:

   ```
   # Xorg -configure
   ```

3. The file `x.org.conf.new` should appear in your home directory. To test whether this new configuration file works, type the following to start the X server:

   ```
   # X -xf86config /root/xorg.conf.new
   ```

   A gray background with an X in the middle should appear. Move the mouse to move the X pointer. If that succeeds, you have a working `xorg.conf` file to use.

4. Press Ctrl+Alt+F2 and Ctrl+c to exit the X server.

5. Copy the new configuration file to where it is picked up the next time X starts.

   ```
   # cp /root/xorg.conf.new /etc/X11/xorg.conf
   ```

Chances are that you have a very basic X configuration that you may want to tune further. In Fedora, after X is working you can return to run level 5 by typing the following as root user:

```
# init 5
```

For Ubuntu, type **start gdm** instead.

Getting New X Drivers

Working video drivers in Linux are available with most video cards you can purchase today. However, to get some advanced features from your video cards (such as 3D acceleration) you may need to get proprietary drivers directly from the video manufacturers. In particular, you may want to get drivers from NVidia and ATI.

For Ubuntu, Fedora, and many other major Linux distributions, NVidia and ATI drivers have been packaged for the particular kernel you are running. Because these drivers are not open source, however, you typically have to enable third-party or non-free software repositories to get them to work.

If your Linux system doesn't have such repositories available, to get new drivers for video cards or chipsets from NVidia, go to the NVidia site (`www.nvidia.com`) and select the Download Drivers button. Follow the link to Linux and FreeBSD drivers. Links from the page that appears will take you to a web page from which you can download the new driver and get instructions for installing it.

For ATI video cards and chipsets, go to www.ati.com and select Drivers & Software. Follow the links to Linux drivers and related installation instructions.

Tuning Up Your X Configuration File

The xorg.conf file might look a bit complicated when you first start working with it. However, chances are that you will need to change only a few key elements in it. As root user, open the /etc/X11/xorg.conf file in any text editor. Here are some things you can look for:

- **Mouse** — Look for an InputDevice section with a Mouse0 or Mouse1 identifier. That section for a simple two-button, PS2 mouse might look as follows:

```
Section "InputDevice"
    Identifier    "Mouse0"
    Driver        "mouse"
    Option        "Protocol" "PS/2"
    Option        "Device" "/dev/psaux"
EndSection
```

If you are unable to use some feature of the mouse, such as a middle wheel, you might be able to get it working with an entry that looks more like the following:

```
Section "InputDevice"
    Identifier    "Mouse0"
    Driver        "mouse"
    Option        "Protocol" "IMPS/2"
    Option        "Device" "/dev/psaux"
    Option        "ZAxisMapping" "4 5"
EndSection
```

Don't change the mouse identifier, but you can change the protocol and add the ZAxisMapping line to enable your wheel mouse. Try restarting X and trying your mouse wheel on something like a web page to see whether you can scroll up and down with it.

Your mouse might be connected in a different way (such as a bus or serial mouse) or may have different buttons to enable. Tools for configuring your mouse are distribution-specific. Try mouseconfig, mouseadmin, or system-config-mouse to reconfigure your mouse from the command line.

- **Monitor** — The monitor section defines attributes of your monitor. You can use some generic settings if you don't know the exact model of your monitor. Changing the Horizontal Sync and Vertical Refresh rates without checking your monitor's technical specifications is not recommended; you could damage the monitor. Here's an example of an entry that will work on many LCD panels:

```
Section "Monitor"
    Identifier    "Monitor0"
    VendorName    "Monitor Vendor"
    ModelName     "LCD Panel 1024x768"
    HorizSync     31.5 - 48.5
    VertRefresh   40.0 - 70.0
EndSection
```

Here's an entry for a generic CRT monitor that will work on many CRTs:

```
Section "Monitor"
    Identifier    "Monitor0"
    VendorName    "Monitor Vendor"
    ModelName     "Generic Monitor, 1280x1024 @ 74 Hz"
    HorizSync     31.5 - 79.0
    VertRefresh   50.0 - 90.0
EndSection
```

If a tool is available to select your monitor model directly, that would be the best way to go. For example, in Red Hat systems, you would run system-config-display to change monitor settings.

- **Video device** — The Device section is where you identify the driver to use with your video driver and any options to use with it. It is important to get this section right. The Xorg command described earlier usually does a good job detecting the driver. If you want to change to a different one, this is where to do so. Here's an example of the Device section after I added a video driver from NVIDIA to my system (the driver name is nv):

```
Section "Device"
    Identifier    "Card0"
    Driver        "nv"
    VendorName    "nVidia Corporation"
    BoardName     "Unknown Board"
    BusID         "PCI:1:0:0"
EndSection
```

- **Screen resolution** — The last major piece of information you may want to add is the screen resolution and color depth. There will be a screen resolution associated with each video card installed on your computer. The Screen section defines default color depths (such as 8, 16, or 24) and modes (such as 1024 × 768, 800 × 600, or 640 × 480). Set the DefaultDepth to the number of bits representing color depth for your system, and then add a Modes line to set the screen resolution.

To read more about how to set options in your `xorg.conf` file, type **man xorg.conf**.

Choosing a Window Manager

Fully integrated desktop environments have become somewhat unfriendly to changing out window managers. However, you can completely bypass KDE or GNOME, if you like, and start your desktop simply with X and a window manager of your choice.

Although I'm using Slackware as the reference distribution for describing how to change window managers, the concept is the same on other Linux systems. In general, if no desktop environment is running in Linux, you can start it by typing the following:

```
$ startx
```

This command starts up your desktop environment or window manager, depending on how your system is configured. Although a variety of configuration files are read and commands are run, essentially which desktop you get depends on the contents of two files:

- `/etc/X11/xinit/xinitrc` — If a user doesn't specifically request a particular desktop environment or window manager, the default desktop settings will come from the contents of this file. The `xinitrc` file is the system-wide X configuration file. Different Linux systems use different `xinitrc` files.

- `$HOME/.xinitrc` — The `.xinitrc` file is used to let individual users set up their own desktop startup information. Any user can add a `.xinitrc` file to his or her own home directory. The result is that the contents of that file will override any system-wide settings. If you do create your own `.xinitrc` file, it should have as its last line `exec` *windowmanager*, where *windowmanager* is the name of your window manager; for example:

  ```
  exec /usr/bin/blackbox
  ```

Slackware has at least seven different window managers from which you can choose, making it a good place to try out a few. It also includes a tool called `xwmconfig`, which lets you change the window manager system-wide (in the `/etc/X11/xinit/xinitrc` file). To use that tool, as the root user simply type **xwmconfig** from any shell on a Slackware system.

Select the window manager you want to try from that screen and select OK. That window manager will start the next time you run `startx` (provided you don't override it by creating your own `.xinitrc` file). Here are your choices:

- **LXDE** (`www.lxde.org`) — The Lightweight X11 Desktop Environment was created to perform quickly and elegantly, even in less powerful machines. These qualities make it particularly suitable for mobile devices, netbooks, and other hardware directed toward cloud computing. Figure 3-14 shows an example of an LXDE desktop.

FIGURE 3-14

Get special effects on low-powered machines with the Lightweight X11 Desktop Environment.

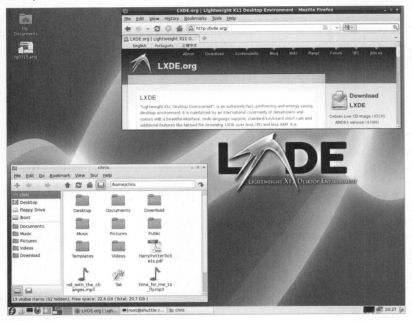

- **Xfce** (www.xfce.org) — The Xfce window manager is designed to be lightweight and fast. Xfce is very popular for running Linux on inexpensive PCs, such as the ASUS EeePC. Figure 3-15 shows an example of an Xfce desktop in Fedora.

- **Blackbox** (http://blackboxwm.sourceforge.net) — Another lightweight window manager that strives to require few library dependencies so it can run in many environments. Offers many features for setting colors and styles.

- **FluxBox** (http://fluxbox.sourceforge.net) — Based on Blackbox (0.61.1), FluxBox adds nice features such as window tabs (where you can join together multiple windows so they appear as multiple tabs on a single window). It also includes an icon bar and adds some useful mouse features (such as using your mouse wheel to change workspaces).

- **Window Maker** (www.windowmaker.info) — Window Maker is a clone of the NEXTSTEP graphical interface, a popular UNIX workstation of the 1980s and 1990s. It is a particularly attractive window manager, with support for themes, various window decorations, and features for changing backgrounds and animations, and adding applets (called *docapps*).

- **FVWM** (www.fvwm.org) — This window manager supports full internationalization, window manager hints, and improved font features. Interesting features include window shading in all directions (even diagonal) and side titles (including text displayed vertically).

FIGURE 3-15

Xfce offers many powerful features in an efficient desktop.

- **FVWM-95** (http://fvwm95.sourceforge.net) — A version of FVWM that was created to look and feel like Windows 95.

- **Twm (Tabbed Window Manager)** — Although no longer actively maintained, some people still use twm when they want a truly bare-bones desktop. Until you click the left mouse button in twm, there's nothing on the screen. Use the menu that pops up to open and close windows.

Many other window managers are available for Linux as well. To check out some more, visit the Xwinman web site (http://xwinman.org).

After the system default is set for your window manager, users can set their own window manager to override that decision. The following section describes how to do that.

Choosing Your Personal Window Manager

Simply adding an exec line with the name of the window manager you want to use to your own .xinitrc file in your home directory causes startx to start that window manager for you. Here is an example of the contents of a .xinitrc to start the Window Maker window manager:

```
exec /usr/bin/wmaker
```

Make sure that the file is executable (`chmod 755 $HOME/.xinitrc`). The Window Maker window manager should start the next time you start your desktop. Other window managers you can choose include Blackbox (`/usr/X11R6/bin/blackbox`), FluxBox (`/usr/X11R6/bin/fluxbox`), FVWM (`/usr/X11R6/bin/fluxbox`), FVWM-95 (`/usr/X11R6/bin/fvwm95`), and twm (`/usr/X11R6/bin/twm`).

Getting More Information

If you tried configuring X and you still have a server that crashes or has a garbled display, your video card may either be unsupported or may require special configuration. Here are a couple of locations you can check for further information:

- **X.Org** (`www.x.org`) — The latest information about the X servers that come with Fedora is available from the X.Org web site. X.Org is the freeware version of X used by most major Linux distributions.

- **X documentation** — README files specific to different types of video cards are delivered with the X.Org X server. Visit the X `doc` directory (`/usr/X11R6/lib/X11/doc`) for a README file specific to the type of video card (or more specifically, the video chipset) you are using. You can also find a lot of good information on the `xorg.conf` man page (type **man xorg.conf**).

Summary

Complete desktop environments that run in Linux can rival desktop systems from any operating system. KDE and GNOME are the most popular desktop environments available today for Linux. For people who want a sleeker, more lightweight desktop environment, Xfce and LXDE desktops and a variety of simple window managers (Blackbox, Xfce, FVWM, twm, FluxBox, and many others) are available to use in Linux as well.

The KDE desktop is well known for its large set of integrated applications (office productivity tools, games, multimedia, and other applications). The latest KDE offers a more efficient file manager called Dolphin and desktop applets called plasmoids.

GNOME has the reputation of being a more basic, business-oriented desktop. Most Linux distributions such as Slackware and Gentoo offer GNOME and KDE desktops that aren't changed much from how they are delivered from those desktop projects. Other Linux systems (such as Fedora) put their own look and feel on GNOME and KDE desktops.

Although the latest Windows systems won't run on many older Pentium machines, you can use an efficient Linux system such as Slackware, add a lightweight window manager, and get reasonably good performance with your desktop system on those machines.

E-mailing and Web Browsing

W eb browsers and e-mail clients available with Linux have seen incredible improvements over the past few years. Their features rival those you can get on the most popular Windows clients. Security issues with Outlook mail clients and Internet Explorer browsers have many people taking a fresh look at Linux and open source software for accessing the Internet.

This chapter describes some of the best Web, e-mail, chat, and related tools for accessing the Internet that you can get with the Linux distributions described with this book. If you have never worked with the Internet from Linux, or haven't for a few years, you might be blown away by what's available today.

Using E-mail

Any Linux desktop system worth the name *desktop system* will have at least one or two applications for sending, receiving, and working with your personal e-mail. Many users believe that superior tools for managing spam and generally better security mechanisms make Linux a great desktop platform for managing your e-mail.

Choosing an E-mail Client

Choices of e-mail clients range from those that look like clones of popular Windows e-mail programs to those that run in plain text from the shell. Interfaces vary widely with the e-mail clients that are available with Linux. Here are some different ways in which e-mail clients are integrated into Linux:

- **Standalone** — These days, most e-mail clients are standalone applications in their own right. The primary standalone e-mail application is Mozilla Thunderbird 2 (`www.mozilla.com/en-US/thunderbird/`), although you can find 50 or more choices on Linux such as Sylpheed (`sylpheed.sraoss.jp/en/`).

- **With a Web browser** — Many popular Web browsers include an integrated e-mail client. By configuring the e-mail client that comes with your browser, you are ready to launch a new e-mail message by clicking on a mailto link from a browser window. You can also easily open the e-mail client from your Web browser's toolbar.

  Feature-rich Mozilla SeaMonkey Mail (`www.seamonkey-project.org`) is part of a full suite of Internet client applications that includes a Web browser, an HTML composer, and other features. Most users, however, use the separated clients Thunderbird for e-mail and Firefox for Web browsing.

  The Opera Web browser (`www.opera.com`) also includes an integrated e-mail client. It is perhaps the most elegant of the e-mail clients that come with a Web browser. Opera is available for personal use without cost.

- **With groupware** — Some e-mail clients have been bundled with other personal productivity applications to form integrated groupware applications. The most popular of these in Linux is Evolution, which is bundled as the default e-mail client with several different Linux distributions. Besides e-mail, Evolution includes a calendar, task list, and contacts directory. Today, the GNOME project manages Evolution (`http://projects.gnome.org/evolution`).

- **From the shell** — Many old-school UNIX and Linux power users prefer to use an e-mail client that runs without a graphical desktop. Although not always intuitive to use, text-based e-mail readers run much faster than their graphical counterparts. The `mail` command dates back to the earliest UNIX systems (where there was no GUI). The Mutt e-mail client is popular among power users because of its capability to manage large mailboxes, message threads, and attachments efficiently.

If your web browser does not come with its own mail reader or you want to use a different mail client, you can configure the browser to launch your favorite mail client instead. If you use webmail to read your e-mail rather than a traditional e-mail client, you can install the "desktop-webmail" package in Ubuntu, which will launch a browser to your webmail whenever you click on a mailto link.

Features inside each e-mail client can help you distinguish between them. While most e-mail clients let you get, compose, send, and manage e-mail messages, here are a few extra features you might look for:

- **Filters and spam catchers** — Thunderbird, Evolution, and other mail clients offer message filters and junk mail detectors. You use filters to set up rules to sort incoming mail into different folders, delete certain messages, or otherwise respond to incoming mail. Some e-mail clients also have features that try to automatically detect when junk mail has arrived. If you get a lot of e-mail, these can be invaluable tools for managing your e-mail. (Select the Tools or Message menu from your e-mail client, and then look for a Filters or Junk Mail selection.)

- **Security features** — E-mail clients such as Thunderbird (`www.mozilla.com/en-US/thunderbird/`) enable you to use message encryption, digital signatures, and other security features to keep your e-mail private.

- **Sorting, searching, marking, and displaying** — Again, if you are managing lots of e-mail messages at once (some people manage thousands of messages), the capability to refer back to the one you want can be critical. Some clients let you sort by date, sender, priority, subject, and other items. You might be able to search message contents for text or choose how to display the messages (such as without showing attachments or with source code shown).

- **Mail composition tools** — Most recent mail composers let you include HTML in your messages, which enables you to add images, links, tables, colors, font changes, and other visual enhancements to your messages. One warning: Some mailing lists don't like you to send messages in HTML because some people still use plain-text readers that aren't HTML-aware.

- **Multiple accounts** — Many e-mail clients enable you to configure multiple e-mail accounts to be served by your e-mail reader. Early plain-text e-mail clients pointed to only one mailbox at a time.

- **Performance** — Some lightweight graphical e-mail clients give you much better performance than others. In particular, the Sylpheed e-mail client (which comes with Damn Small Linux) was created to use a minimal amount of memory and processing power, yet still provide a graphical interface. E-mail clients that run from the keyboard, in particular the mutt e-mail client, will run much faster than, say, most full-blown graphical e-mail clients such as Evolution.

Coming from Windows

For most home and small-business users, Evolution and the standalone Thunderbird are often available from a Linux desktop and will give you much the same experience you would expect from Microsoft Windows mail clients, such as Outlook Express. If you are using the KDE desktop, you can use the KDE groupware client Kontact, which includes KMail (the e-mail client), along with a contact manager, calendar, to-do list application, and more. ■

Even though the Linux distribution you are using may have only one or two of the e-mail clients described in this section, you can always add a client that interests you.

Transitioning Your E-mail from Windows

To understand how to transition your e-mail client from Windows to Linux, you need to know a bit about your current e-mail setup. Whether you are using Outlook, Outlook Express, or any other e-mail client running in Windows, here are some things you should know:

- **Server type** — Is your e-mail server a POP3 or IMAP server? If it is an IMAP server, all your messages are being stored on the server. Transitioning to a different e-mail server might simply mean pointing the new e-mail client at your server and continuing to use e-mail as you always have. If it is a POP3 server, your messages have probably been downloaded to your local client. To keep your old messages, you need to somehow bring your current mail folders over to your new client, which is a potentially tricky undertaking. When you sign up for your e-mail account or Internet service, the people providing the service should tell you whether the service is POP3 or IMAP. Some mail servers use secure versions of those protocols (IMAPS and POP3S).

- **Address book** — You need to export your current address book to a format that can be read by your new e-mail client, and import it to your new e-mail client. For example, from the Contacts section of the Evolution e-mail client, you can import address books and/or mailboxes in Berkeley mbox, Evolution, Outlook, Mozilla CVS or tab formats, vCard format, LDAP ldif format, or vCalendar (vcf) or iCalendar (ics) formats.

To transition to Linux, you may want to add a cross-platform e-mail client such as Thunderbird to your Windows system so that you can get at your resources (addresses, stored mail messages, and so on) during the transition to your new mail client. When you eventually move off Windows altogether, Thunderbird for Linux will work almost exactly as it does in Windows.

If your current e-mail server is a Microsoft Exchange server (2000, 2003, or 2007), you need to get the Evolution plug-in for Microsoft Exchange to allow Evolution to access information from that server. For Fedora, you need to install the evolution-exchange package and then identify your mail server as Microsoft Exchange when you create a new e-mail account.

Getting Started With E-mail

Most Linux systems include an e-mail client that you can select on a panel or by left-clicking on the desktop to bring up a menu. Look for an envelope icon on a panel or a submenu labeled something like "Internet". If you want a graphical e-mail reader, you can start by looking for one of these clients: Thunderbird, Evolution, Mozilla SeaMonkey Mail, or KMail.

After you have launched your chosen e-mail client, you need some information to use it. When you first start most graphical e-mail clients, a configuration screen of some sort asks you to set up an account. Here's how to begin setting up a mail account for the e-mail clients described in this chapter:

- **Thunderbird** — This is the next-generation mail client from the people who bring you Firefox and Mozilla (mozilla.org). Now at version 3.1, and with more advanced security features, you might consider Thunderbird. Not only is it faster than SeaMonkey Mail and Evolution, Thunderbird is an ideal complement to Mozilla Firefox Web browser. Firefox and Thunderbird run on a number of operating systems, including Linux, Solaris, Microsoft Windows, and Mac OS X.

- **Evolution** — The Evolution Setup Assistant starts the first time each user opens Evolution. After that, select Edit ⇨ Preferences from the main Evolution window. Then choose Mail Accounts and double-click the mail account you want to modify, or select Add to add a new account.

- **Mozilla SeaMonkey Mail** — An account wizard starts the first time you open SeaMonkey Mail. After that, you can set up or modify accounts from the SeaMonkey Mail window by clicking Edit ➪ Preferences ➪ Mail & Newsgroups.

- **Sylpheed** — The Sylpheed e-mail client (http://sylpheed.sraoss.jp/en/) is used on some mini-desktop distributions, such as Damn Small Linux. Sylpheed is particularly fast and efficient, but still has support for powerful features such as filtering, search, junk mail control, and digital signing and encryption (using GnuPG).

- **KMail** — From the KMail window, select Settings ➪ Configure KMail. From the Configure KMail window that appears, select the Network icon. From there, you can click Sending or Receiving tabs to configure your outgoing and incoming e-mail settings. KMail is developed by the KDE project (www.kde.org).

Initial configuration for text-based e-mail clients is described later in this chapter.

Information you will need to configure your e-mail accounts is much the same for the different graphical e-mail clients covered in this chapter:

- **Name** — Enter your name as you want it to appear on outgoing messages.

- **E-mail address** — Enter the e-mail address from which you are sending. You may also be offered the opportunity to supply a different reply-to address, if you want replies to go to an address other than the one you sent from.

- **Mail server type** — Most mail servers are POP3- or IMAP-type servers. (Configuring those types of servers is discussed in Chapter 16.)

- **Server names** — Enter the names of the servers you will use to send outgoing e-mail and receive incoming e-mail. The names can be fully qualified domain names (such as mail.linuxtoys.net) or IP addresses. In many cases, the incoming and outgoing mail servers are the same.

- **Username** — Enter the name by which the mail server knows you. For example, if your e-mail address is chris@linuxtoys.net, your username to the mail.linuxtoys.net server might simply be chris. However, your username on the mail server might be different, so you should find that out from the administrator of your mail server.

- **Account title** — Enter the name that you want to call this mail account so you can refer to it later in your list of mail and newsgroup accounts.

- **Authentication type** — Indicate the type of authentication to use when you get your mail (sometimes authentication is needed to send your mail as well). Password authentication is normal. Usually you can have your e-mail client remember your password if you want. Typically, you are prompted for the password the first time you connect to get your mail.

That is most of the basic information you need to start getting and sending e-mail. However, you may want to further tune how your e-mail client interacts when it gets and sends e-mail.

Tuning Up E-mail

With your basic settings done, you should be ready to start sending and receiving your e-mail. Before you do, however, you should consider some of the other settings that can affect how you use mail:

- **Automatically check messages** — You can set your e-mail client to automatically check and download your messages from the mail server every few minutes.

- **Leave messages on server** — If you turn this feature on for a POP3 server, your e-mail messages remain on the server after you have downloaded them to your e-mail client. People sometimes turn this feature on if they want to check their mail messages while they are on the road yet want to download their messages to their permanent desktop computer later.

- **Certificates** — Your e-mail client may provide a way of using certificates to sign your outgoing messages. For example, Evolution, Thunderbird, and SeaMonkey Mail all have Security tabs for your mail settings that let you enter information about your certificates and specify that your e-mail be signed. You can also choose to use the certificates for encryption.

Step through your mail account settings, because they are slightly different for each e-mail client.

Reading E-mail with Thunderbird

The Thunderbird e-mail client program is a full-featured mail and newsgroup reader that usually comes with most Linux desktop systems. The version of Thunderbird described in this section is 3.1.

Note
In the past, you may have run the integrated Mozilla suite of applications, now called Mozilla SeaMonkey. The more recent versions of Linux, however, have replaced SeaMonkey with separate e-mail and Web-browsing applications, Thunderbird and Firefox, respectively. If you are used to the older Mozilla suite, you should consider upgrading to Thunderbird. ■

Thunderbird includes features for:

- Sending, receiving, reading, and managing e-mail
- Managing multiple mail and newsgroup accounts
- Composing HTML e-mail messages
- Controlling junk e-mail
- Message encryption and signing

Coming from Windows
Thunderbird runs on Windows as well as Linux, so you can convert your organization to Thunderbird now, and then later migrate to Linux. ■

On most desktop Linux systems, either Thunderbird or Evolution (covered later in this chapter) will be the primary e-mail client for your Linux distribution. You can launch the e-mail application from the desktop from a menu such as Internet or Office.

For example, in Fedora and Ubuntu, you run an e-mail client from the Applications ➪ Office menu. Fedora defaults to Evolution as the primary e-mail client, so Evolution is listed as Evolution Mail and Calendaring on the Application ➪ Office menu. Thunderbird is listed as Thunderbird E-mail (if you install the Thunderbird package).

Setting Up an E-mail Account

When you launch Thunderbird for the first time, the application presents the Mail Account Setup wizard, which leads you through setting up an e-mail account (you can create more than one). Figure 4-1 shows this window. Follow these steps to create your e-mail account:

1. **Create e-mail account.** When the Mail Account Setup window appears, type in your name, e-mail address, and password, and then click continue.

   The Mail Account Setup wizard tries to guess the location of your incoming and outgoing mail servers. If it is able to do so, it presents the locations, as shown in Figure 4-2.

FIGURE 4-1

The Thunderbird Mail Account Setup wizard

FIGURE 4-2

Use or change settings found by the Mail Account Setup wizard.

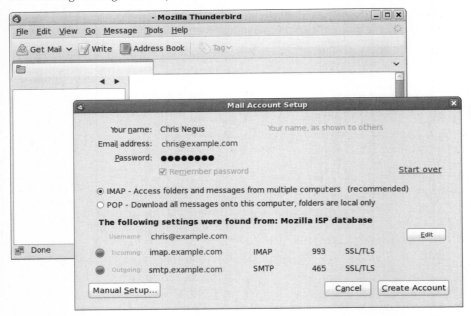

2. **Choose mail protocol.** The setup wizard may detect your incoming and outgoing mail servers, along with the types of mail retrieval protocols available from them.

   If both POP and IMAP are available, choose POP only if you want all your e-mail to be downloaded to your computer and stored there. Most people prefer to have their mail reside on the server, so they can access it on the Internet from any computer that has an e-mail client that supports IMAP.

3. **Choose server locations.** If the server locations detected by the wizard are correct, you can select Create Account to use those settings. Otherwise, select Edit to change the locations of your servers manually.

If your mail settings are correct, e-mail message headers will begin downloading to your Thunderbird e-mail client. Thunderbird is now ready to begin getting and sending mail messages. If you need to change any settings for the account you just set up (change defaults you have not had a chance to change or create another account), select Edit ➪ Account Settings from the Thunderbird window.

Tip

With the Junk Mail feature, Thunderbird automatically tags any message it believes to be junk mail with a blue recycle-bin icon. Using the Junk toolbar, you train the Junk Mail feature by telling it when a message is or isn't junk mail. After you have identified which messages are junk mail, you can automatically move incoming junk mail to the Junk folder. ■

Connecting to the Mail Server

After you have set up your mail accounts in Thunderbird, you can explicitly ask to download any available mail messages from the server (for POP3 accounts) or message headers (for IMAP). To do that, click the Get Mail button.

You may be prompted for the password for your account on the mail server. Using that password, Thunderbird downloads all your messages from the mail server. It downloads messages again every 10 minutes, or you can click the Get Mail button at any time.

If you want to change how often mail is downloaded, or other features of your account, choose Edit ⇨ Account Settings. Under the e-mail account you added are categories to change the setup and behavior of the account. (Click Server Settings to change how often, if at all, new messages are automatically downloaded from the mail server.)

Managing Incoming Mail

Select the Inbox title in the left column. It shows how many messages are in your Inbox that have not been read. Your incoming messages appear to the right, with the headers on top and the currently selected message text below it. Figure 4-3 shows Thunderbird displaying some e-mail headers and the current message.

Thunderbird offers various ways to store and manage these e-mail messages. Here's a quick rundown of how to manage incoming mail:

- **Mail folders** — Mail messages are stored in folders in the left column. There could be a separate heading for each mail account you have or you might have specified that Thunderbird use a global Inbox where messages from all accounts get placed in the same Inbox folder. For each mail account, incoming messages are stored (by default) in your Inbox folder. You can create additional folders to better keep track of your mail (right-click on Inbox, and select New Folder to add a folder). Other folders contain drafts of messages set aside for a time (Drafts), templates for creating messages (Templates), messages you have sent (Sent), and messages that you have discarded (Trash).

- **Sort messages** — Messages are sorted by date for the folder you select, in the upper-right corner of the display. Click the headings over the messages to sort by subject, sender, date, or priority. The icon on the far right of the Subject header lets you choose what information columns to display for the message headers (such as recipient, size, status, and so on). You can then sort on any of those columns.

FIGURE 4-3

Manage incoming mail from the Thunderbird window.

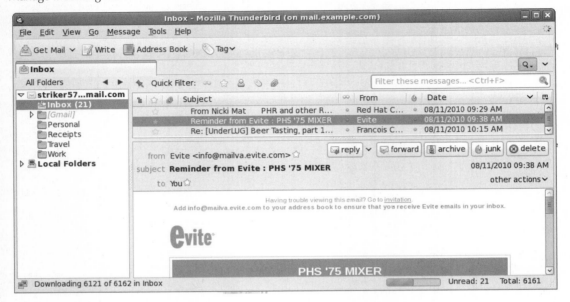

- **Read messages** — When you select a message, it appears in the lower-right corner of the display. Click the e-mail address from the sender and a menu enables you to add that address to your address book, compose mail to that address, copy mail to that address, or create a filter from that message.

- **Filter mail** — When Thunderbird grabs your e-mail from the mail server, it drops it into the global Inbox or one associated with your mail account, by default. Thunderbird provides some nice features for checking each message for information you choose, and then acting on that message to move it to another folder, label it, or change its priority. See the "Filtering mail and catching spam" section later in this chapter for details.

- **Search messages** — You can use the search feature to retrieve messages that are in one of your mail folders. With the folder you want to search being the current folder, type a word to search on into the Subject or Sender Contains box. Messages with sender names or subject lines that don't contain that string will disappear from the list of messages. To do more detailed searches, choose Edit ➪ Find ➪ Search Messages.

Composing and Sending Mail

To compose e-mail messages, you can either start from scratch or respond to an existing e-mail message. The following are some quick descriptions of how to create outgoing mail:

- **New messages** — To create a new message, choose Message ➪ New Message (or click Write on the toolbar).

- **Reply to messages** — To reply to a mail message, click the message on the right side of your screen and then choose Message ⇨ Reply (to reply only to the author of the message) or Message ⇨ Reply to All (to reply to everyone listed as a recipient of the message).

- **Forward messages** — To forward a mail message, click the message on the right side of your screen and then choose Message ⇨ Forward. You can also forward a message and have it appear in the text (Message ⇨ Forward As ⇨ Inline) or as an attachment (Message ⇨ Forward As ⇨ Attachment).

In each case, a mail Compose window appears, in which you compose your e-mail message. As you compose your message in the Compose window, you can use the following:

- **Address book** — Add e-mail addresses from your personal address book (or from one of several different directory servers) by selecting Tools ⇨ Address Book. Click the Contacts button to select recipients for your missive.

- **Attachments** — Add attachments such as a word processing file, image, or executable program by clicking the Attach button (or choosing File ⇨ Attach ⇨ File) and then selecting a file from your file system to attach. (You can also choose File ⇨ Attach ⇨ Web Page to choose the URL of a Web page that you want to attach.)

- **Certificates** — Add certificates or view security information about your mail message by selecting View ⇨ Message Security Info.

When you are finished composing the message, click Send to send the message. If you prefer, queue the message to be sent later by choosing File ⇨ Send Later. (Send Later is useful if you are not currently online.)

Tip
If you want to quit and finish the e-mail message later, choose File ⇨ Save As ⇨ Draft, and then click the X in the upper-right corner to close the window. When you are ready to resume work on the message, open the Draft folder in the Thunderbird window and double-click the message. ∎

Filtering Mail and Catching Spam

Thunderbird can do more with incoming messages than just place them in your Inbox. You can set up filters to have Thunderbird check each message first and then take an action you define when a message matches the rules you set up.

For example, your filter can contain a rule that checks the subject, sender, text body, date, priority, status, recipients, or age (in days) of the message for a particular word, name, or date, as appropriate. If there is a match, you can have Thunderbird put that message in a particular folder, label it with a selected phrase, change its priority, or set its junk mail status. You can add as many rules as you like. For example, you can

- Have all messages sent from a particular address sorted into a separate mail folder. For example, I direct some mailing lists to a separate folder so that important mail doesn't get lost when there's a lot of activity on the mailing lists to which I subscribe.

- Mark incoming messages from important clients as having highest priority.
- Have messages from particular people or places that are being mistakenly marked as spam change their junk status to Not Junk.

To set up filter rules in Thunderbird, select Tools ⇨ Message Filters. The Message Filters pop-up appears. If you have multiple mail accounts, select the account you want to filter. Then click New. From the Filter Rules pop-up window, choose the following:

- **For incoming messages that** — There are different ways to check parts of a message. For example, you can check whether the sender is in the address book. You can check what the priority is: low, medium, or high. You can create multiple rules for a filter (click More to add another rule), and then choose whether you want to match all or any of the rules to continue to the action.
- **Perform these actions** — The information in this section describes what to do with a message that matches the rules you've set. You can have the message moved to any existing folder, or label the message. With labels, the message appears in a different color depending on the label: important (red), work (orange), personal (green), to do (blue), or later (purple). You can also change the message priority.

Figure 4-4 shows a rule I created to have a star attached to mail from my friend Tweeks when it comes in.

A nice feature of Thunderbird's filtering rules is that you can apply the rules after the fact as well. If you decide you want to move all messages in your Inbox from a particular person to a different folder, for example, you can open the Message Filters window, create a rule to move the selected messages, select Inbox, and click Run Now.

For junk mail, with a mail message selected, click the Junk button in the toolbar. The message is marked as junk. Your selection helps teach Thunderbird what you think is junk mail. Click Tools ⇨ Run Junk Mail Controls on Folder, and Thunderbird looks for other messages that look like junk mail. (You can take the junk marker off of any message you think is not junk.) Then select Tools ⇨ Delete Mail Marked as Junk in Folder, and the junk mail is deleted. To open a window to configure how you handle junk mail, select Tools ⇨ Junk Mail Controls.

Managing E-mail in Evolution

If you are using Fedora, Ubuntu, or Debian, Evolution is the e-mail client that you can start right from the GNOME desktop (look for the envelope icon on the panel). Evolution is a groupware application, combining several types of applications that help groups of people communicate and work together. The features of Evolution include

- **Mail** — A complete set of features for getting, reading, managing, composing, and sending e-mail on one or more e-mail accounts.

- **Contacts** — Create contact information such as names, addresses, and telephone numbers for friends and associates. A Categories feature helps you remember who gets birthday and anniversary gifts.

- **Calendar** — Create and manage appointments on your personal calendar. You can e-mail appointment information to others and do keyword searches of your calendar.

- **Memos** — Write public, private, or confidential memos.

- **Tasks** — Organize ongoing tasks into folders.

FIGURE 4-4

Create filter rules to sort or highlight your e-mail messages.

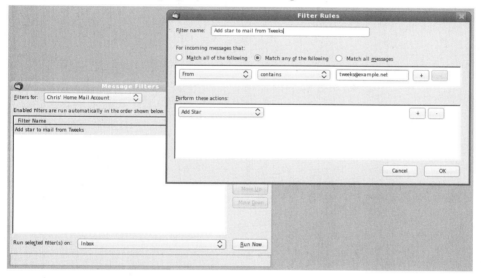

Coming from Windows

Evolution provides a default interface that looks a lot like that of Microsoft Outlook, making it easy for new users to make a smooth transition to a Linux system. ∎

Additional features recently added to Evolution include improved junk mail handling and Search Folders (for managing multiple physical folders as one folder).

Receiving, Composing, and Sending E-mail

Evolution offers a full set of features for sending, receiving, and managing your e-mail. Figure 4-5 shows an example of an Evolution window with the Inbox selected and ready to manage, compose, send, and receive e-mail.

FIGURE 4-5

Manage your e-mail from the Evolution Inbox.

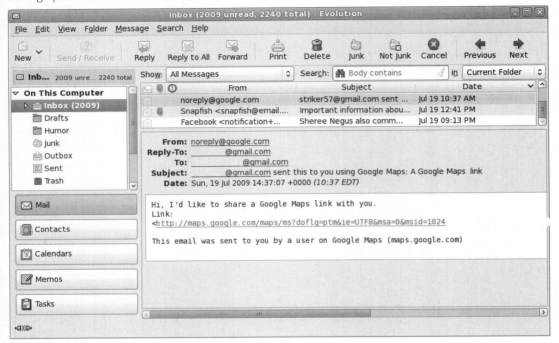

Here's a quick rundown of common e-mail tasks:

- **Read e-mail** — Click Inbox in the left column. Your messages appear to the right. Message headers are in the upper right; the current message is displayed in the lower pane. Double-click a message header to display it in a separate window.

- **Delete e-mail** — After you have read a message, select it and press the Delete key. Click View ➪ Hide Deleted Messages to toggle whether you can see deleted messages. Click Folder ➪ Expunge to permanently remove all messages marked for deletion in the current folder.

- **Send and receive** — Click the Send/Receive button to send any e-mail queued to be sent and receive any e-mail waiting for you at your mail server. (You may not need to do this if Evolution is configured to download your messages every few minutes. Select Edit ➪ Preferences, and then double-click on your mail account. The Receiving Options tab indicates whether automatic mail checking is being done.)

- **Compose e-mail** — Click New ➪ Mail Message. A Compose a Message window appears. Type your recipient's e-mail address, enter a subject line, and fill in the body of the message. Click Send when you are finished. Buttons on the Compose window enable you to add attachments, cut and paste text, choose a format (HTML or plain text), and sign the message (if you have set up appropriate keys).

- **Use address books** — Click the Contacts button (or View ➪ Window ➪ Contacts menu choice) to see a list of names, addresses, and other contact information for the people in your address book. When you compose a message, click the To or CC buttons to select addresses from the book to add as recipients for your message.

- **Create folders** — If you like to keep old messages, you may want to save them outside your Inbox (so it won't get too junked up). To create a folder in which to keep them, right-click on the Inbox and select New Folder. You can choose to store the new folder as a subfolder to any existing folder. Type a folder name and click OK.

- **Move messages** — With new folders created, you can easily move messages from your Inbox to another folder. The easiest way is to simply drag-and-drop each message (or a set of selected messages) from the message pane to the new folder.

- **Search messages** — Type a keyword in the search box over your e-mail message pane and select whether to search your message subject lines, sender, recipient, or message body. Click Find Now to search for the keyword. After viewing the messages, click Clear to have the other messages reappear.

Managing e-mail with Search Folders

Managing large amounts of e-mail can become difficult when the messages you want to refer to span several folders, dates, or senders. With Search Folders (also called virtual folders or vFolders), you can identify criteria to group together messages from all your mail folders so you can deal with them in one Search Folder.

Note

Where have vFolders gone? Search Folders used to be called vFolders. If you are familiar with older versions of Evolution, note that the name changed to Search Folders. ■

Here's a procedure for creating a Search Folder:

1. With Evolution open to read mail (click Inbox to get there), select Search ➪ Create Search Folder from Search. A New Search Folder pop-up appears.

2. Type a rule name.

3. Click Add Condition and select criteria for including a message in your Search Folder. At first you should see an entry that says "Sender contains," after which you can type a term to search on. Otherwise, you can change Message Body to Sender, Recipient, Subject, Expression, Date Sent, or other criteria to search on. Click Add Condition if you want to add more criteria.

4. If you want to search only specific folders, click Add in the Search Folder Sources box and select the folder you want to search. You can repeat the Add to choose more than

one. Otherwise, you can select to search all local folders, all active remote folders, or all local and active remote folders. Then click OK.

5. Make sure the folder bar is visible (select View ⇨ Layout ⇨ Show Side Bar). The folder you just created is listed under the Search Folders heading. Click that folder to see the messages you gathered with this action.

At this point, you can work with the messages you gathered in the Search Folder. Although it appears that there are multiple versions of each message across your mail folders, there is really only one copy of each. So deleting or moving the message from a Search Folder actually causes it to be deleted or moved from the original folder in which the real message resides.

Filtering E-mail Messages

You can take action on an e-mail message before it even lands in your Inbox. Click Message ⇨ Create Rule, and then select the type of filter to create. Evolution shows a Filters window to enable you to add filters to deal with incoming or outgoing messages. Click Add to create criteria and set actions.

For example, you can have all messages with a particular sender, subject, date, status, or size sorted to a selected folder. Or you can have messages matching your criteria deleted or assigned a color, or play a sound clip.

Evolution also supports many common features, such as printing, saving, and viewing e-mail messages in various ways. The help system that comes with Evolution (click the Help menu) includes a good manual and FAQs.

Reading E-mail with SeaMonkey Mail

The SeaMonkey Mail client program is a full-featured mail and newsgroup reader that comes with the SeaMonkey suite on many Linux systems. In general, the SeaMonkey suite is based on the older Mozilla suite, which was replaced by Thunderbird e-mail and Firefox Web browser clients. Thunderbird and Firefox were split from the large Mozilla suite and each now runs as a separate application. If you are used to the older Mozilla suite, now called SeaMonkey, you should consider upgrading to Thunderbird.

In most respects, SeaMonkey Mail works like Thunderbird, described previously. The major difference is that SeaMonkey Mail, because it is an older application, doesn't have all the features of the latest Thunderbird. This is a big change. In the last year or so, Thunderbird has all but replaced SeaMonkey Mail.

In many Linux distributions you can simply install the SeaMonkey package to get the entire SeaMonkey suite (Web browser, mail client, composer, address book, and IRC chat client). If SeaMonkey is not available with your Linux distribution, you can download the Mozilla SeaMonkey suite from www.mozilla.org/projects/seamonkey. Figure 4-6 shows an example of the SeaMonkey mail window.

FIGURE 4-6

Manage mail and newsgroups with SeaMonkey.

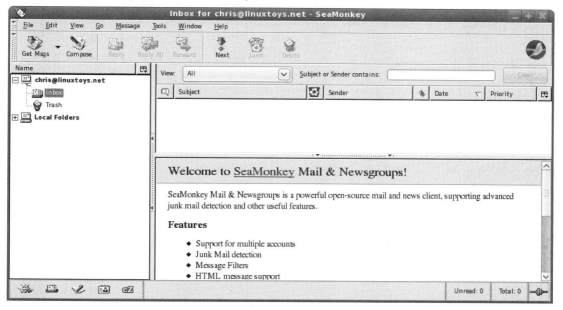

Working with Text-Based E-mail Readers

The first text-based mail clients could be configured quite simply. Mail clients such as mutt, mail, or pine were often run with the user logged in to the computer that was acting as the mail server. So instead of downloading the messages, using POP3 or IMAP, the mail client simply opened the mailbox (often under the user's name in /var/spool/mail) and began working with mail.

Today, some of these text-based e-mail clients have been enhanced to support more modern features. For example, you can point the mutt e-mail client at a remote mail server and access mail from both insecure (IMAP and POP3) and secure (IMAPS and POP3S) mail access services.

Many text-based mail programs are available for reading, sending, and working with your mail. Many of these programs have been around for a long time, so they are full of features and have been well debugged. As a group, however, they are not very intuitive.

Note
Mail readers described in the following sections are text-based and use the entire Terminal window (or other shell display). Although some features are different, menu bars show available options right on the screen. ∎

Mutt Mail Reader

The `mutt` command is a text-based, full-screen mail user agent for reading and sending e-mail. The interface is quick and efficient. Type **mutt** to start the program. Move arrow keys up and down to select from your listed messages. Press Enter to see a mail message and type **i** to return to the Main menu.

The menu bar indicates how to mark messages for deletion, undelete them, save messages to a directory, and reply to a message. Type **m** to compose a new message and it opens your default editor (`vi`, for example) to create the message. Type **y** to send the message. If you want to read mail without having your fingers leave your keyboard, mutt is a nice choice. (It even handles attachments!)

Mail Reader

The `mail` command was the first mail reader for UNIX. It is text-based, but not screen-oriented. Type **mail** to see the messages in your mailbox. You get a prompt after message headings are displayed — you are expected to know what to do next. (You can use the Enter key to step through messages.) Type **?** to see which commands are available.

While in mail, type **h** to see mail headings again. Simply type a message number to see the message. Type **d#** (replacing # with a message number) to delete a message. To create a new message, type **m**. To respond to a message, type **r#** (replacing # with the message number).

Choosing a Web Browser

Many Web browsers available in Linux are based on the Mozilla Web browser engine, called Gecko. Web browsers that might come with your Linux distribution include

- **Firefox** — This is the leading Web browser for Linux and other open source software systems. There are versions of Firefox available for Linux, Mac OS X, and Windows. Firefox has made inroads into the Mac and Windows worlds as well. This next generation browser from the Mozilla project is designed to be fast, efficient, and safe for Web browsing.

- **SeaMonkey Web browser** — Offered as part of the SeaMonkey suite, this Web browser is based on Mozilla Navigator, which was once the most popular open source Web browser. Although no longer actively developed by the Mozilla project, the SeaMonkey suite remains available with many Linux systems. Some people still install SeaMonkey for its easy-to-use HTML composer window.

- **Konqueror** — Comes as the default browser with many KDE desktop environments. Konqueror is a file manager as well as a Web browser and helps bring together many features of the KDE desktop. In recent KDE releases, some of Konqueror's file manager features have been moved to the Dolphin file manager, helping to make Konqueror run more efficiently as a Web browser.

- **Opera** — A commercial application that runs on many small devices such as mobile phones or the Nokia Linux–based Internet Tablet, this browser is available for free on Mac OS X, Microsoft Windows, and Linux. Because it is not open source, however, it is not redistributed with most major Linux systems.

- **links, lynx, and w3m** — If you are in a text-based environment (operating from the shell), these are among several text-based Web browsers you can try out.

Note

Some streamlined Linux versions, such as Damn Small Linux, include a very lightweight Web browser called dillo (www.dillo.org). Although its small size (only about 350KB binary) comes with some limitations (such as limited font and internationalization support), dillo is a good choice for displaying basic HTML on handheld devices and mini Linux distributions. ∎

The following sections describe SeaMonkey, Firefox, and some text-based Web browsers that are available with many Linux systems.

Exploring the SeaMonkey Suite

During the early 1990s, Netscape Navigator was the most popular Web browser. When it became apparent that Netscape was losing its lead to Microsoft Internet Explorer, its source code was released to the world as open source code.

Mozilla.org (www.mozilla.org) was formed to coordinate the development of a new browser from that code. The result was the Mozilla browser, which was included with most Linux distributions. The fact that Mozilla was available on multiple platforms was great, especially if you needed to switch between Linux and Windows, for example, using Windows at work and Linux at home. Mozilla looked and acted the same on many platforms.

With the focus of Mozilla project development turning to Firefox and Thunderbird, as mentioned earlier, the suite changed its name to SeaMonkey. In addition to viewing Web pages, you can also manage e-mail, newsgroups, IRC, and address books, and even create your own Web pages with SeaMonkey Composer.

Note

Slackware kept SeaMonkey so that the project could offer the SeaMonkey Composer. The Slackware project noted that SeaMonkey Composer is a WYSIWYG HTML editor that is still used by many open source enthusiasts as an alternative to Microsoft FrontPage for ease-of-use Web page development. ∎

In addition to the SeaMonkey browser, the SeaMonkey suite also includes the following features:

- **Mail and Newsgroups** — A full-featured program for sending, receiving, and managing e-mail, as well as for using newsgroups. (The SeaMonkey RPM or deb package must be installed.) SeaMonkey Mail has mostly been replaced by the Thunderbird application, covered previously.

- **IRC Chat** — An Internet Relay Chat (IRC) window, called ChatZilla, for participating in online, typed conversations. (The Mozilla-chat package must be installed.)

- **Composer** — A Web page (HTML) composer application.

- **Address Book** — A feature to manage names, addresses, telephone numbers, and other contact information. This is also part of Thunderbird.

Figure 4-7 shows examples of the Browser and Composer windows available with the SeaMonkey suite.

FIGURE 4-7

SeaMonkey includes a browser, composer, and other Internet clients from the old Mozilla suite.

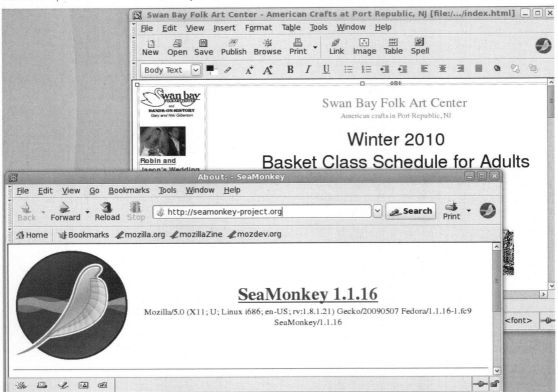

Using Firefox

Many Linux distributions ship Firefox as the default browser. In many desktop Linux distributions, you start the Firefox Web browser from an icon on the top panel or on an Applications menu. For example, in Fedora, select Applications ⇨ Internet ⇨ Firefox . If you don't see it on a menu, you can start Firefox by simply typing **firefox** from a Terminal window. (Some distributions, such as Debian, have rebranded Firefox as Iceweasel, although typing **firefox** can also be used to launch iceweasel.)

The version of Firefox described in this chapter (Firefox 3.6) includes some extraordinary features for ease of use, security, and performance. Many of those features are described in the following section. The Firefox project page (www.mozilla.com/en-US/firefox/) is shown in a Firefox browser in Figure 4-8.

The latest release of Firefox has many new features you may find interesting. Inside Firefox is the Gecko 1.9 Web rendering platform, with thousands of features to improve performance, rendering, and stability. You should notice improvements in color management and fonts.

FIGURE 4-8

Firefox is the leading open source Web browser, with thousands of improvements over earlier versions.

Improvements to the location box connect several features in Firefox. Figure 4-9 shows several location box examples that illustrate new ways of dealing with the Web sites you request.

In Figure 4-9, the example on the left shows what happens when you click on the icon on the left side of the location box when visiting a secured site. You can see that VeriSign verifies the authenticity of the site and that communications are encrypted. In the example on the right, by selecting the star on the right side of the location box, you can work with bookmark information for a page and modify that information. Other icons that might appear in the location box include a variety of security warnings, such as warnings for possible forged or dangerous content.

Firefox has all the basic features you need in a Web browser, plus a few special features. The following sections describe how to get the most out of your Firefox Web browser.

Coming from Windows

For help transitioning from Internet Explorer to Firefox, see the Firefox site at `www.mozilla.org/products/firefox/switch.html`. ∎

FIGURE 4-9

Do site verification and bookmarks from the location box.

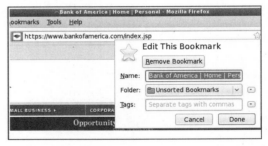

Setting Up Firefox

You can do many things to configure Firefox to run like a champ. The following sections describe some ways to customize your browsing experience in Firefox.

Setting Firefox Preferences

You can set your Firefox preferences in the Preferences window (see Figure 4-10). To open Firefox preferences, select Edit ➪ Preferences.

Tip

If you are upgrading from the Mozilla suite or an earlier Firefox release, you will notice the Preferences window looks completely different. Don't despair, however; the browser preferences have not changed much. The latest Firefox just has a simpler window layout. ∎

FIGURE 4-10

Change settings for navigating the Web from Firefox's Preferences window.

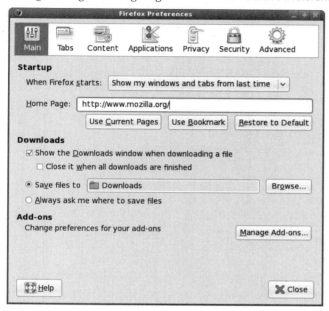

The following are some Firefox preferences that you might want to change:

- **General** — Lets you choose which pages to display when you start Firefox. It also lets you choose how to handle downloads and change add-on preferences.

- **Tabs** — Use these selections to control how Firefox uses tabs, one of the most useful features of this browser.

- **Content** — Set Content preferences to control how Firefox should deal with requests for different types of Web content. These options include

  - **Pop-up Windows** — Choose whether or not to block pop-up windows.

  - **Java and JavaScript** — You can control whether these languages are enabled.

  - **Images** — Choose whether or not to load images automatically (useful for small screens or low-bandwidth network connections).

  - **Fonts and Colors** — Select the default font type and size, as well as the colors used for text, background, visited links, and unvisited links.

  - **Language** — For Web pages that can appear in multiple languages, this sets the order in which you would prefer languages to be displayed. For example, you might choose English/United States, English, French, and German. Then Firefox tries to display a Web page you open in each of those languages successively, until one is matched. You can set other advanced features on this tab.

- **Applications** — View, search, and change which applications are used to display different types of content that might be encountered during browsing.

- **Privacy** — Choose how long to store a history of addresses of the sites you have typed in your location bar. (These addresses appear in the History tab on the Firefox sidebar.) Set Privacy preferences to control how Firefox caches private data and allows Web sites to find out information about you in cookies. These preferences include

  - **Cookies** — The Web content you choose can try to open, move, resize, raise, and lower windows. It can request to change your images, status bar text, or bits of information stored in what are called *cookies*. These preferences enable you to restrict what the content you request can do.

  - **Private Data** — Storing your history of browsing and downloading, forms and searches, visited pages, cookies, passwords, and authenticated sessions can simplify your browsing experience. However, if you are working on someone else's machine or otherwise don't want to leave a record of your browsing behind, you can clear that information by selecting Tools, then selecting Clear Recent History.

- **Security** — Firefox 3 has a great new feature from the Security preferences tab that lets you choose to be warned if a site you are visiting is a suspected attack site or forgery. You can also choose to be warned when a site tries to install add-ons. Other settings on this tab let you choose to remember passwords you enter for sites (so you don't have to type them every time you visit) or choose to keep a master password.

- **Advanced** — Several tabs within the Advanced tab include many features that you probably won't use every day. General features let you set accessibility features and browsing features. The Network tab lets you set up special network connections to use with Firefox (such as proxy settings) or configure an offline storage cache. From the Update tab, you can automatically check for Firefox updates. On the Encryption tab, you can choose the security protocols (SSL and TLS) and personal certificates to use when a site requests that information.

Adding Add-Ons and Plug-Ins

Add-ons extend the features in Firefox to personalize how you use your browser. Dozens of add-ons are available to help you manage and search your Web content more efficiently, handle downloads, work with news feeds, and interact with social networks. Plug-ins are special applications you can add to handle data that Firefox can't work with by default (such as special image or audio files).

To find out about available add-ons and plug-ins, select Tools ➪ Add-ons from the Firefox window to see the Add-ons pop-up window. Figure 4-11 shows an example of that window.

FIGURE 4-11

Select Add-ons to Firefox to manage content in different ways.

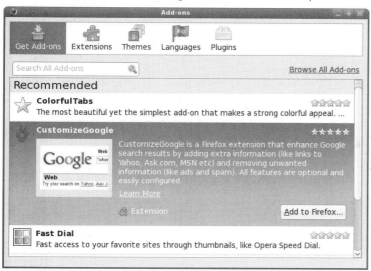

Select the link to see recommended add-ons from the Firefox Add-ons page. You can see reviews of each add-on, ratings, how often they are downloaded, and screenshots of how the add-on appears. Here are a few examples of popular Firefox add-ons:

- **FoxyTunes** — With FoxyTunes (www.foxytunes.com) installed, you can use any of more than a dozen music players to play music as you browse the Web. It also helps you find covers, videos, lyrics, biographies, and other information about the artists you play.

- **FireGestures** — With FireGestures, you can map different mouse gestures to launch scripts or perform actions that you set.

- **ColorfulTabs** — The ColorfulTabs add-on lets you set your Firefox browser tabs to different colors. Colors can be set in a variety of ways (such as at random or by domain name). Change settings from the Extensions tab on the Add-on window.

- **Noscript** — With Noscript, you can disable javascript, annoying pop-ups, and other features that annoy you.

- **Flashblock** — This add-on blocks flash content from running automatically.

- **Ad block plus** — Use this to remove advertisements.

- **WOT** — This add-on marks untrustworthy sites.

- **It's all text** — Enabling this add-on lets you open text boxes using your favorite text editor (such as vi).

After you have installed an add-on, you need to restart Firefox for it to take effect. In some cases, a change to an extension's options will also require you to restart Firefox. If you want to uninstall an add-on or change an add-on's options, select Tools ⇨ Add-On, then click Extensions from Firefox. Select the Extensions tab. This displays the add-ons you have installed and offers buttons to disable, uninstall, or change preferences.

Plug-ins are applications you add to your browser to play particular types of content. Usually you do this because either Firefox doesn't include the feature you want or you want to use a different application to play the content (such as your own music player).

Firefox Plug-ins

Many plug-ins are available for use in most Linux versions of Firefox. To see a list of plug-ins that are already installed in your browser, enter **about:plugins** in the address box where you normally type URLs.

Go to `https://addons.mozilla.org/` and select Plugins to view and download the most popular plug-ins, and look at `plugindoc.mozdev.org/linux.html` for links to other plug-ins. Some of the most popular plug-ins are

- **Adobe Reader Plug-in** (`http://get.adobe.com/reader`) — Displays files in Adobe Systems' PDF (Portable Document Format) format.

- **DjVuLibre Plug-in** (`djvu.sourceforge.net`) — Displays images in DjVu image compression technology. This plug-in is from AT&T.

- **Real Player** (`www.real.com/linux`) — Plays RealAudio and Video content. Real Networks and its open source Helix project have recently made RealVideo codecs available to the Linux community.

- **Adobe Flash Plug-in** (`http://get.adobe.com/flashplayer`) — Flash is the most popular player for playing video on the Web. Some Linux systems come with an open source Flash player installed, but most agree that the Adobe version works better so far.

- **CrossOver Plugin** (`www.codeweavers.com`) — Linux plug-ins are not yet available for some of the more interesting and popular plug-ins. QuickTime movies, Shockwave Director multimedia content, and various Microsoft movie, file, and data formats simply will not play natively in Firefox. Using software built on WINE for Linux on x86-based processors, CodeWeavers created the CrossOver Plugin. Although no longer offered as a separate product (you must buy the entire Crossover Linux product for $39.95 US), the CrossOver Plugin lets you play some content that you could not otherwise use in Linux. (Download a demo from `www.codeweavers.com/site/products/download_trial` and choose CrossOver Linux.)

  After you install the CrossOver Plugin, you see a nice Plugin Setup window that lets you selectively install plug-ins for QuickTime, Windows Media Player, Shockwave, Flash, iTunes, and Lotus Notes, as well as Microsoft Word, Excel, and PowerPoint viewers. (Support for later versions of these content formats may be available by the time you read this.) You can also install other multimedia plug-ins, as well as a variety of fonts to use with those plug-ins.

Many plug-ins are already packaged by their creators or by third-party repositories for popular Linux distributions. For example, some multimedia plug-ins for Fedora are available from the rpm-fusion.org repository, while Ubuntu and Debian might have the same plug-ins packaged in repositories labeled as non-free. The "Firefox Plug-ins" sidebar describes some popular plug-ins for Firefox.

Changing Firefox Themes

Several themes are available for changing the look and feel of your Firefox window. From the Firefox Add-ons site (`http://addons.mozilla.org`), select Themes. When you download a theme for Firefox, it knows that it is a Firefox theme and, in the download window, it gives you the option to install the theme by clicking the Use Theme button.

To change a theme later or get more Themes, select Tools ➪ Add-ons and select the Themes tab. After you have installed a new theme, you need to restart Firefox for the new theme to take effect.

Securing Firefox

Security has been one of the strongest reasons for people to switch to Firefox. By prohibiting the most unsafe types of content from playing in Firefox, and by warning you of potentially dangerous or annoying content before displaying it, Firefox has become the Web browser of choice for many security-conscious people. Here are some ways that Firefox helps make your Web browsing more secure:

- **ActiveX** — Because of major security flaws found in ActiveX, Firefox will simply not play ActiveX content. Although there have been projects to try to provide ActiveX support in Mozilla, none of those projects are being actively developed.

- **Pop-ups** — When pop-up windows are encountered as you browse with Firefox, a message (by default) tells you that "Firefox prevented this site from opening a popup window." By clicking on that message, you have an opportunity to allow all pop-ups from that site, just allow the requested pop-up, or edit your pop-up settings.

- **Privacy preferences** — From the Privacy window in Firefox (select Edit ➪ Preferences, and then click the Privacy button), you can clear stored private information from your browser in a single click. This is a particularly good feature if you have just used a computer that is not yours to browse the Web. You can select to individually clear your History, information saved in forms you might have filled in, any passwords saved by the browser, the history of what you have downloaded, cookies, and cached files. As an alternative, you can click Tools, then select Clear Recent History.

- **Web Forgeries** — The latest Firefox release helps you block forged Web sites by displaying a "Suspected Web Forgery" pop-up message when it encounters a page that has been reported as forged. You can choose to not display the page or ignore the warning. If you suspect a forged page that doesn't display that message, select Help ➪ Report Web Forgery to try to add the page to the Google Web Forgery list.

- **Certificates** — In Firefox, you can install and manage certificates that can be used for validating a Web site and safely performing encryption of communications to that site. Using the Preferences window (select Edit ➪ Preferences and then click the Advanced button), you can manage certificates under the Encryption tab, Certificates heading. Select View Certificates to display a window that lets you import new certificates or view certificates that are already installed. Firefox will check that certificates you encounter are valid (and warn you if they are not).

Along with all the excellent security features built into Firefox, it's important that you incorporate good security practices in your Web browsing. Here are some general tips for safe Web browsing:

- Download and install software only from sites that are secure and known by you to be safe.

- For any online transactions, make sure you are communicating with a secure site (look for the `https` protocol in the location box and the closed lock icon in the lower-right corner of the screen).

- Be careful about being redirected to another Web site when doing a financial transaction. An IP address in the site's address or misspellings on a screen where you enter credit card information are warning signs that you have been directed to an untrustworthy site.

Because new exploits are being discovered all the time, it's important that you keep your Web browser up-to-date. That means that, at the least, you need to get updates of Firefox from the Linux distribution you are using or directly from Mozilla.org. To keep up on the latest security news and information about Firefox and other Mozilla products, refer to the Mozilla Security Center (`www.mozilla.org/security/`).

Tips for Using Firefox

There are so many nice features in Firefox, it's hard to cover all of them. Just to point you toward a few more fun and useful features, here are some tips for using Firefox:

- **Add smart keywords** — Many Web sites include their own search boxes to enable you to look for information on their sites. With Firefox, you can assign a smart keyword to any search box on the Web, and then use that keyword from the location bar in the Firefox browser to search that site.

   For example, go to the Linux Documentation Project site (`http://tldp.org`). Right-click in the Search/Resources search box. Select Add a Keyword for this Search from the menu that appears. Add a name (Linux Documentation) and a keyword (tldp) and select Add to add the keyword to your Bookmarks.

   After you have added the keyword, you can use it by simply entering the keyword and one or more search terms to the Firefox location box (on the navigation toolbar). For example, I entered `tldp Lego Mindstorms` and came up with a list of How-tos for using Lego Mindstorms in Linux.

- **Check config** — Firefox has hundreds of configuration preferences available to set as you please. You can see those options by typing **about:config** into the location box.

Casual users should look at these settings, but not change them (because you can do irreparable harm to Firefox if you make a wrong selection).

If you feel secure about making changes, for true/false options, you can click on the preference name to toggle it between the two values. For other preferences, click the preference to enter a value into a pop-up box. Although many of these values can be changed through the Preferences menu (Edit ➪ Preferences), some technical people prefer to look at settings in a list like the one shown on the about:config page.

- **Multiple home pages** — Instead of just having one home page, you can have a whole set of home pages. When you start Firefox, a separate tab opens in the Firefox window for each address you identify in your home page list. To do this, create multiple tabs (File ➪ New Tab) and enter the address for each page you want in your list of home pages. Then select Edit ➪ Preferences ➪ General and click the Use Current Pages button. The next time you open Firefox, it will start with the selected tabs open to the home pages you chose. (Clicking the Home icon opens new tabs for all the home pages.) You can also manually enter multiple URLs into the text box. Separate each URL with a pipe character (|).

Using Firefox Controls

If you have used a Web browser before, the Firefox controls are probably as you might expect: location box, forward and back buttons, file and edit menus, and so on. There are a few controls with Firefox, however, that you might not be used to seeing:

- **Display Sidebar** — Select View ➪ Sidebar to toggle the bookmarks or history sidebars on and off. The sidebar is a left column on your Firefox screen for allowing quick access to Bookmarks and History. Use the Bookmarks tab to add your own bookmarks and the History tab to return to pages on your history list.

- **Send Web Content** — You can send an e-mail containing the URL of the current Web page (File ➪ Send Link) to selected recipients. Firefox will load your default e-mail client, such as Thunderbird or Evolution, to send the e-mail message.

- **Search the Internet** — You can search the Internet for a keyword phrase in many different ways. Choose Tools ➪ Web Search to start a search. Selecting this menu choice moves the mouse cursor to the search box, where you can enter search terms. Click the icon on the left side of this box to choose search engines such as Google, Yahoo!, and others. Select Manage Search Engines to select other search sites to use. Press the Enter key to search.

- **View Web Page Info** — You can view information about the location of a Web page, the location of each of its components, the dates the page was modified, and other information by clicking the right mouse button over a Web page and then choosing View Page Info. In the Page Info window, click the Links tab to see links on that page to other content on the Web. Click the Security tab to see information about verification and encryption used on the page.

Improving Firefox Browsing by Adding a Preferences Toolbar

Not every Web site you visit with Firefox is going to play well. Some sites don't follow standards: They use unreadable fonts, choose colors that make it hard to see, or demand that you use a particular type of browser to view their content. To improve your browsing experience, there are several things you can add to Firefox. One in particular is adding a preferences toolbar.

Note

If you encounter a problem with Firefox that you can't overcome, I recommend that you refer to the Mozilla Bugzilla database (www.mozilla.org/bugs/). This site is an excellent place to search for bugs others have found (many times you can get workarounds to your problems) or enter a bug report yourself. ∎

Did you ever run into a Web page that required you to use a particular type or version of a browser or had fonts or colors that made a page unreadable? The Firefox preferences toolbar called PrefBar4 enables you to try to spoof Web sites into thinking you are running a different browser. It also lets you choose settings that might improve colors, fonts, and other attributes on difficult-to-read pages.

You can install the neat little toolbar from the Mozdev.org site (http://prefbar.mozdev.org). Click the Install link, and after it is installed, restart Firefox.

The default set of buttons enables you to do the following:

- **Colors** — Change between default colors and those set on the Web page.
- **Images** — Toggle between having images loaded or not loaded on pages you display.
- **JavaScript** — Allow or disallow JavaScript content to play in Firefox.
- **Flash** — Allow or refuse all embedded Flash content on the current page.
- **Clear Cache** — Delete all cached content from memory and disk.
- **Save Page** — Save the current page and, optionally, its supporting images and other content, to your hard disk.
- **Real UA** — Choose to have your browser identified as itself (current version of Firefox) or any of the following: Mozilla 1.0 (in Windows 98), Netscape Navigator 4.7 (in Macintosh), Netscape 6.2 (in Linux), Internet Explorer 5.0 (in Macintosh), Internet Explorer 6.0 (in Windows XP), or Lynx (a text-based Web browser).

The user agent (UA) setting is very useful when dealing with Web sites that require Internet Explorer (IE) (and usually IE on Windows, not Mac OS). The IE 6.0 WinXP setting is good enough to allow Firefox to log on to the Microsoft Exchange Webmail service, which is usually set up to require IE. If you want to run Linux in a mostly Windows organization, install the Preferences toolbar.

Click the Customize button to add other buttons to the toolbar. You can add buttons to clear your History or location bar entries. You can even add a Pop-ups button to prevent a page from opening a pop-up window from Firefox.

Many of the preferences take effect immediately. Others may require you to restart Firefox.

Doing Cool Things with Firefox

Some neat bells and whistles are built into Firefox that can make your browsing more pleasant. The following sections explore a few of those features.

Blocking Pop-Ups

You can block annoying pop-up windows using the Firefox Preferences window. Here's how:

1. Click Edit ➪ Preferences. The Preferences window appears.
2. Click Block Pop-up Windows under the Content category.

By blocking all pop-ups you might keep some Web sites from working properly. Click the Exceptions button to allow pop-ups on certain sites that you choose.

Using Tabbed Browsing

If you switch back and forth among several Web pages, you can use the tabbed browsing feature to hold multiple pages in your browser window at once. You can open a new tab for browsing by simply selecting File ➪ New Tab or by pressing Ctrl+T. You can open any link into a new tab by right-clicking over the link and then selecting Open Link in New Tab.

You can also tailor how Tabbed Browsing works from a Web page or from the location box. Here's how:

1. Click Edit ➪ Preferences. The Preferences window appears.
2. Click the Tabs tab.
3. Click the tab-related options you desire.

A tab for each tabbed page appears at the top of the Firefox pane. To close a tab, create a new tab, bookmark a group of tabs, or reload tabs, right-click one of the tabs and choose the function you want from the drop-down menu.

One of the easiest ways to open a link in a tab is to right-click over a link on an HTML page. Select the Open Link in New Tab choice. Or you can simply middle-click on a link to open it in a new tab.

Resizing Web Page Text

There is a nice keyboard shortcut that lets you quickly resize the text on most Web pages in Firefox. Hold the Ctrl key and press the plus (+) or minus (–) key. In most cases, the text on the Web page gets larger or smaller, respectively. That page with the insanely small type font is suddenly readable.

There are many more things you can do with Firefox than I have covered in this chapter. If you have questions about Firefox features or you just want to dig up some more cool stuff about Firefox, I recommend checking out the MozillaZine forum for Firefox support:

```
http://forums.mozillazine.org/viewforum.php?f=38
```

This page has a sticky link to Miscellaneous Firefox Tips and a good FAQ post.

Using Text-Based Web Browsers

If you become a Linux administrator or power user, over time you will inevitably find yourself working on a computer from a remote login or where there is no desktop GUI available. At some point while you are in that state, you will want to check an HTML file or a Web page. To solve the problem, many Linux distributions include several text-based Web browsers.

With text-based Web browsers, any HTML file available from the Web, your local file system, or a computer where you're remotely logged in can be accessed from your shell. There's no need to fire up your GUI or read pages of HTML markup if you just want to take a peek at the contents of a Web page. In addition to enabling you to call up Web pages, move around with those pages, and follow links to other pages, some browsers even display graphics right in a Terminal window!

Which browser you use is a matter of which you are more comfortable with. Browsers that are available include

- **links** — You can open a file or a URL, and then traverse links from the pages you open. Use search forward (/string) and back (?string) features to find text strings in pages. Use up and down arrows to go forward and back among links. Press Enter to go to the current link. Use the right and left arrow keys to go forward and back among pages you have visited. Press Esc to see a menu bar of features from which to select.

- **lynx** — The lynx browser has a good set of help files (press the ? key). Step through pages using the spacebar. Although lynx can display pages containing frames, it cannot display them in the intended positioning. Use the arrow keys to display the selected link (right arrow), go back to the previous document (left arrow), select the previous link (up arrow), and select the next link (down arrow).

- **w3m** — This browser can display HTML pages containing text, links, frames, and tables. It even tries to display images (although it is a bit shaky). Both English and Japanese help files are available (press H with w3m running). You can also use w3m to page through an HTML document in plain text (for example, cat index.html | w3m -T text/html). Use the Page Up and Page Down keys to page through a document. Press Enter on a link to go to that link. Press B to go back to the previous link. Search forward and back for text using the / (slash) and ? (question mark) keys, respectively.

The w3m seems the most sophisticated of these browsers. It features a nice default font selection and seems to handle frames neatly; its use of colors also makes it easy to use. The links browser lets you use the mouse to cut and paste text.

You can start any of these text-based Web browsers by entering a filename, or if you have an active connection to the network, a Web address as an option to the command name. For example, to read the w3m documentation (which is in HTML format) with a w3m browser, type the following from a Terminal window or other shell interface:

```
$ w3m /usr/share/doc/w3m*/doc/MANUAL.html
```

An HTML version of the w3m manual is displayed. Or you can give w3m a URL to a Web page, such as the following:

```
$ w3m www.handsonhistory.com
```

After a page is open, you can begin viewing the page and moving around to links included in it. Start by using the arrow keys to move around and select links. Use the Page Up and Page Down keys to page through text.

Summary

A number of high-quality applications are available to fulfill your needs for a Web browser and e-mail client in Linux. Most Web browsers are based on the Mozilla Gecko engine (which came originally from Netscape Navigator). Firefox has become the main Linux Web browser. The combination of security, ease-of-use features, and extensions has made Firefox an extremely popular Web browser for both Linux and Windows users.

Graphical and text-based e-mail clients include Evolution, SeaMonkey Mail, and KMail. Thunderbird has become the next generation e-mail client to replace SeaMonkey Mail. Text-based mail clients include mail, mutt, and pine.

Playing Music, Video, Photos, and Games

## 5

L inux doesn't have to be just work, work, work all the time. There are
lots of ways to use Linux that are just plain fun.

Over the years, Linux software has become available for playing music,
video, images, and games. With improved multimedia players and tools
for storing and managing content, Linux has become a great platform for
storing, playing, and managing everything from your favorite songs to your
precious videos.

Despite improvements in multimedia and gaming software for Linux,
however, Linux desktop users still face some challenges in playing their
movies, music, and games. Proprietary codecs needed to play DVD movies, MP3 music, and Advanced Audio Coding (AAC) files from your iPod
are not delivered with most Linux systems because they are "non-free."
Many popular PC games don't play natively in Linux.

Even though not all of your favorite multimedia content will run natively
in Linux, there are ways to get software to do almost anything you want
from your desktop Linux systems. This chapter will help you do nearly
everything you want with multimedia files in Linux, plus a few things you
probably haven't thought of yet. Topics covered in this chapter include the
following:

- **Play music** — Using popular music players such as Totem,
  Amarok, and Rhythmbox, you'll learn to play music files and CDs,
  as well as manage your music collection.

- **Add multimedia support** — Learn where to find codecs for playing proprietary movies and music and understand legal issues surrounding those codecs.

IN THIS CHAPTER

**Playing, recording, and ripping
music**

Watching movies and videos

Working with images

Playing games in Linux

- **Bring over your content from Windows** — Get to the multimedia content you store on Windows systems by mounting it from local hard disks or transferring it over the network.

- **Manage your photos** — Use tools like GIMP to manipulate your digital images.

- **Find games** — Find challenging games that run natively in Linux and learn how to make games that were created to run in Windows play in Linux.

Note

Because many devices holding multimedia content are removable (CDs, DVDs, USB flash drives, digital cameras, Webcams, and so on), recent features in Linux to automatically handle removable hardware and media have greatly improved the Linux desktop experience. Try connecting your USB devices to Linux. In most cases, an appropriate application starts up to access the device or play content stored on it. ■

Some Linux distributions are more multimedia-friendly right after the install than others. An example of this is Ubuntu, which gives you the opportunity to enable "non-free" repositories from which you can get software that cannot be freely distributed. You also have the option of purchasing "non-free" software from the Ubuntu store (http://shop.canonical.com). This can save you a great deal of time tracking down licensing issues and resolving problems.

Running Multimedia Servers

Before launching into the individual applications for playing audio, video, and other multimedia content, I want to mention a few applications that are available for centrally managing your multimedia content. Here are a couple of software projects that can help you store and manage all of your multimedia content in one place:

- **MythTV** (www.mythtv.org) — Although it started out as just an open source digital video recorder (DVR) that is similar to Tivo, MythTV has expanded beyond that. Besides being able to watch TV and schedule recording, MythTV can be used to manage all of your movies, music, and photos as a home media center hub. It also includes friendly features, with an Internet connection, for displaying news, weather, and other types of content.

- **Media Tomb** (www.mediatomb.org) — You can use Media Tomb to manage your multimedia content through a web-based interface. From a Media Tomb server you can stream your multimedia content to UPnP devices around your house. Features in Media Tomb let you import content, move it around, and search it with an easy-to-use graphical interface.

There are many other open source projects that allow you to manage and play your multimedia content through one server. Examples include GMediaServer (http://www.gnu.org/software/gmediaserver/) and Enna Media Center (http://enna.geexbox.org/). The next few sections in this chapter describe individual applications for playing and managing your multimedia content.

Using Totem for Audio and Video

Open an audio or video file from the GNOME desktop, and chances are that Totem Movie Player (http://projects.gnome.org/totem) will start up and try to play it. Totem includes visualization features, so you have something to look at as your music plays. Figure 5-1 shows an example of Totem as it plays music.

FIGURE 5-1

Totem launches to play most audio files in GNOME.

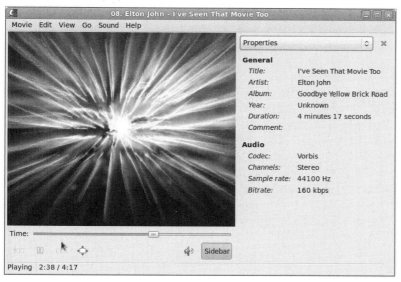

Adding Audio/Video Support to Totem

Despite the fact that Totem can play nearly every popular audio and video format used on computers, the codecs required to play many proprietary formats are not delivered with most Linux distributions that include Totem. Among those formats that won't work out-of-the-box are MP3 and Apple Audio Coding.

Because Totem is based on the GStreamer multimedia framework (see www.gstreamer.net), you need to add plug-ins created for that framework to play some of these "non-free" audio formats. For example, here is the set of gstreamer-plugin software packages available with Fedora that provide the codecs needed to play the full range of multimedia content:

- **gstreamer-plugin-base and gstreamer-plugin-good** — Totem should always include these two plug-in packages. The packages have plug-ins needed to play audio and video formats that can be freely distributed. Open source Ogg Vorbis and FLAC audio formats,

Theora video format, as well as WAV, AU, and other common audio formats, are included with these packages.

- **gstreamer-plugin-ugly** — Although these plug-in packages contain audio software that is as good quality as that which is included with base and good packages, software in this package may have patent or license restrictions. This package includes code from the LAME project (`http://lame.sourceforge.net/`) for playing MP3-formatted audio.

- **gstreamer-plugin-bad-free and gstreamer-plugin-bad-nonfree** — Software in these packages are not thought to be up to the standards of the base, good, and ugly plug-ins. This may mean they have not been thoroughly tested, debugged, or documented. Installing the bad-nonfree plug-in package (and the dependencies it pulls in) will get you the software needed to play music from your iPod (in AAC format).

You can purchase fully legal copies of the plug-ins just described from Fluendo SA (`www.fluendo.com`). Or you can enable the rpmfusion-free and rpmfusion-nonfree repositories in Fedora (as described in Chapter 2). Then either use PackageKit to install the gstreamer-plugin packages just mentioned or type the following as root user from the shell (again, assuming that you have enabled rpmfusion.org repositories):

```
# yum install gstreamer-plugin-ugly
# yum install gstreamer-plugin-bad gstreamer-plugin-bad-nonfree
```

At this point, you should be able to play a wide range of audio and video content through Totem from your Linux desktop.

Using Totem as a Movie Player

Totem will play Theora video and Ogg Vorbis audio formats out-of-the-box, so some videos you get from open source projects will just play. Many other video formats will not play without adding extra packages.

Software needed to play commercial DVD movies is the most contentious (see the discussion of libdvdcss later in this chapter before you install it). The libdvdcss package is available from the Livna.org repository. Other software needed to play DVD movies (as well as other video content) is available by installing the xine-lib-extras-nonfree package.

In Fedora, enable the Livna.org and rpmfusion.org repositories (as described in Chapter 2); then type the following as root user from a Terminal window:

```
# yum install libdvdcss xine-lib-extras-nonfree
```

Insert a commercial DVD into your computer's DVD drive. Select the default Movie Player presented by the pop-up window. Figure 5-2 shows an example of Totem playing a DVD movie.

Besides common controls you would expect with a movie player (play, pause, skip forward, skip backwards, and so on), Totem lets you create playlists, take a snapshot of the current frame, and adjust the volume. You can change preferences, which let you add proprietary plug-ins, select your DVD device, and balance color.

FIGURE 5-2

Play movies on the GNOME desktop with Totem.

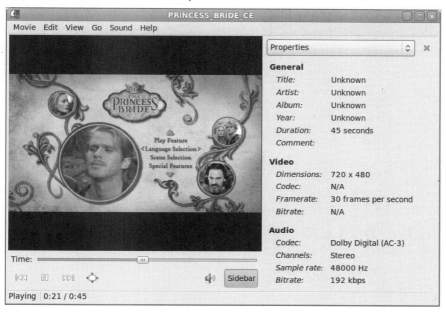

Playing Music in Linux

Totem Movie Player automatically launches to play most audio and video content from the GNOME desktop. Rhythmbox, which is also typically installed with GNOME, provides a more full-featured approach to playing and managing your music. However, there is also a variety of other audio players available for Linux distributions. Most of these applications can play CDs, downloaded files, and even streaming music.

Here is a cross-section of choices for playing audio with Linux:

- **Rhythmbox** (rhythmbox) — Import and manage your CD collection with Rhythmbox music management and playback software for GNOME. It uses GStreamer on the audio backend and can rip and compress music using Ogg Vorbis or other audio formats. In addition to enabling you to create playlists of your music library, Rhythmbox also has features for playing Internet radio stations. Links to free music stores in Rhythmbox let you play free music from Jamendo (www.jamendo.com/en/) and Magnatune (www.magnatune.com), and possibly purchase CDs or license use of that music for commercial projects.

117

- **KsCD player** (kscd) — The KsCD player comes with the KDE desktop. To use it, the kdemultimedia package must be installed. From the main menu on the KDE desktop, select Multimedia ⇨ KsCD (or type **kscd** in a Terminal window). This player lets you get title, track, and artist information from the CD database. KsCD, however, also lets you submit information to a CD database (if your CD isn't found there).

- **Amarok** (amarok) — With Amarok, you get a nice graphical interface where you can manage music by moving elements around with your mouse. Amarok uses SQLite (or other databases) to store your music. It also supports playlists and streaming audio playback from online radio stations.

- **gtkpod** (gtkpod) — Graphical application for managing your music on a wide range of Apple iPod, iPhone, and iPad products.

Because the Totem Movie Player is the application that opens automatically to play most movie and music files you open from the GNOME desktop, I start with a short description of Totem to begin the section on Linux audio players.

Playing Music with Rhythmbox

Rhythmbox provides the GNOME music player that lets you play music from CDs, local file systems, or network locations. Like Totem, Rhythmbox is built on the GStreamer framework for developing media players, video editors, and streaming media. However, it provides many more features for managing your music.

With Rhythmbox, you can play music files, import music from CDs, play podcasts, and play Internet radio stations, all from one interface. Other features enable you to play podcasts and custom radio stations from the Last.fm music service. Plug-ins for Rhythmbox enable you to display album covers, view lyrics, or show visual effects with the music.

To start Rhythmbox, insert a CD from a GNOME desktop (Rhythmbox is the default music player) or select Applications ⇨ Sound & Video ⇨ Rhythmbox Music Player. Figure 5-3 shows an example of Rhythmbox.

Here are some facts about using Rhythmbox as your music player:

- **Configuring your music collection** — Select Edit ⇨ Preferences. On the Music tab, tell Rhythmbox where you store your music files and how it should organize and store your music (including how folders are named, how songs are titled, and the format in which music is stored). If you carry your music on a USB flash drive, just plug it in. To set its location, browse to the /media directory and select the folder containing your music.

- **Adding MP3 support** — If your distribution does not include support for MP3 playback with Rhythmbox, fear not — there is hope! In Fedora, you can use the gstreamer-ffmpeg package available from the rpmfusion.org repository. For Ubuntu, when you try to play MP3 files or other content not supported out-of-the-box, Ubuntu opens a link to allow you to download the software needed to play that content. If you are unsure about patent issues surrounding open source multimedia codecs, you can purchase multimedia support from http://shop.canonical.com (select Software).

Support for Windows media, MPEG2, MPEG4, and other proprietary codecs is available from the store as well.

- **Ripping CDs** — Just insert the CD you want to rip, right-click the CD when it appears under the Devices heading in the left column, and click Extract to Library. The CD will be ripped and stored with your Rhythmbox music collection folder.

- **Playing Internet radio** — Without adding more codecs, you can play Ogg Vorbis Internet radio audio streams. Many more streams are available in MP3 format, however. To connect to an Internet radio account from `http://Last.fm`, select Last.fm in the left column and configure your account. To add a particular Internet radio station to Rhythmbox, right-click Radio, then New Internet Radio Station. Fill in the stream location (such as `http://wknc.sma.ncsu.edu:8000/wknchq.ogg.m3u`).

- **Playing podcasts** — Right-click Podcasts and type the podcast's URL (such as `http://www.osnews.com/files/oggcast.php`) into the pop-up that appears. Wait for it to download, and then double-click to play it. To add an image to your podcast, just download an appropriate image to your computer and drag-and-drop it onto the lower-left corner of the Rhythmbox window while your podcast is selected. Figure 5-4 shows Rhythmbox playing the OSNews podcast.

FIGURE 5-3

Playing music with Rhythmbox

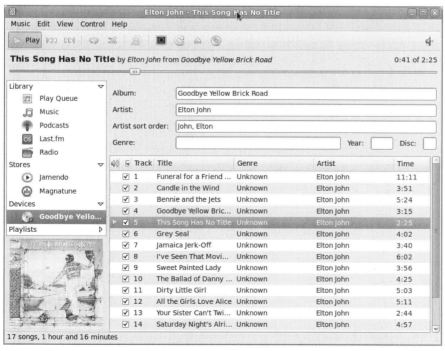

FIGURE 5-4

Rhythmbox playing a podcast feed

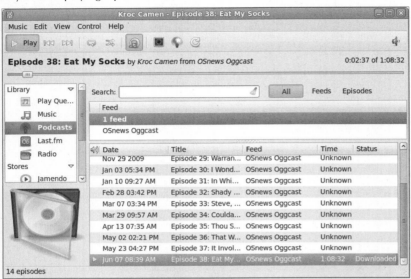

Playing Music with the XMMS Multimedia Player

The XMMS (X Multimedia System) multimedia player provides a compact, graphical interface for playing music files in MP3, Ogg Vorbis, WAV, and other audio formats. XMMS has some nice extras, too, including an equalizer, a playlist editor, and the capability to add more audio plug-ins. One of its greatest attributes is that XMMS is easy to use. If the player looks familiar to you, that's because it is styled after the Windows Winamp program.

- To add XMMS to your Fedora system, type **yum install xmms-*** as root user. This command gets you the player and some nice skins to use with it as well. To play MP3 audio with XMMS, you need to add the MPEG Layer 1/2/3 Player plug-in. In Fedora, you can get the xmms-mp3 package from the `http://rpmfusion.org` free repository.

- Start the XMMS audio player by selecting Sound & Video ➪ XMMS or by typing **xmms** from a Terminal window. Figure 5-5 shows the XMMS audio player. The skin I selected (right-click XMMS and select Options ➪ Skin Browser) is called GTK+.

As noted earlier, you can play several audio file formats. Supported formats include

- MP3 (with added plug-in)
- Ogg Vorbis
- WAV
- AU

- CD Audio
- CIN Movies

FIGURE 5-5

Play Ogg Vorbis, MP3, and other audio files from the XMMS player.

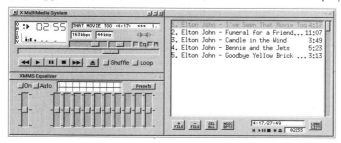

Note

If XMMS is not able to find a configured sound card, it redirects its output to the Disk Writer plug-in. This causes the files you play to be written to hard disk as WAV files. ■

You can get many more audio plug-ins from www.xmms.org. The XMMS audio player can be used in the following way:

1. Obtain music files by ripping songs from a CD or copying them from the Web so that they are in an accessible directory.

2. From the Applications menu, select Sound & Video ➪ XMMS. The X Multimedia System player appears.

3. Click the Eject button. The Load Files window appears.

4. Double-click the music file, and it starts to play.

5. With a file selected and playing, here are a few actions you can take:

   - **Control play** — Buttons for controlling play are what you would expect to see on a standalone CD player. From left to right, the buttons let you go to a previous track, play, pause, stop, go to the next track, and eject the CD. The Eject button opens a window, enabling you to load the next file.

   - **Adjust sound** — Use the left slider bar to adjust the volume. Use the right slider bar to change the right-to-left balance.

   - **Display time** — Click in the elapsed time area to toggle between elapsed time and time remaining.

   - **View file information** — Click the button in the upper-left corner of the screen to see the XMMS menu. Then select View File Info. You can often find out a lot of information about the file: title, artist, album, comments, and genre. For an Ogg Vorbis file, you can see specific information about the file itself, such as the format, bit rate, sample rate, frames, file size, and more. You can change or add to the tag information and click Save to keep it.

6. When you are done playing music, click the Stop button to stop the current song. Then click the X in the lower-right corner of the display to close the window.

Special features of the XMMS audio player enable you to adjust frequencies using a graphic equalizer, and gather and play songs using a playlist editor. Click the button marked EQ next to the balance bar on the player to open the Equalizer.

Using the Equalizer

The Equalizer lets you use slider bars to set different levels to different frequencies played. Bars on the left adjust lower frequencies, and those on the right adjust higher frequencies. Click the EQ button to open the Equalizer window. Here are tasks you can perform with the Equalizer:

- If you like the settings you have for a particular song, you can save them as a preset. Set each frequency as you like it and click the Preset button. Then choose Save ⇨ Preset. Type a name for the preset and click OK.

- To reload a preset you created earlier, click the Preset button and select Load ⇨ Preset. Select the preset you want and click OK.

The small window in the center/top of the Equalizer shows the sound wave formed by your settings. You can adjust the Preamp bar on the left to boost different levels in the set range.

Using the Playlist Editor

The Playlist Editor lets you put together a list of audio files that you want to play. You can add and delete files from this list, save them to a file, and use them again later. Click the PL button in the XMMS window to open the Playlist Editor.

The Playlist Editor enables you to

- **Add files to the playlist** — Click the Add button. The Load Files window appears. Select the directory containing your audio files (it's useful to keep them all in one place) from the left column. Then either select a file from the right column and click Add Selected Files or click Add All Files in the Directory. Click OK. The selected file or files appear(s) in the playlist. You can also add music files by dragging them from the Nautilus file manager onto the playlist window.

- **Select files to play** — To select from the files in the playlist, use the Previous Track and Next Track buttons in the main XMMS window. The selected file is highlighted. Click the Play button to play that file. Alternatively, you can double-click any file in the Playlist to start it playing.

- **Delete files from the playlist** — To remove files from the playlist, select the file or files you want to remove (use the Next Track and Previous Track buttons), right-click the Playlist window, and click Remove ⇨ Selected. The selected files are removed.

- **Save the playlist** — To save the current playlist, hold the right mouse button down on the List button and then select Playlist ⇨ Save List from the pop-up menu. Browse to the directory you want, and then type the name you want to assign to the playlist and click OK. The filename should end with a `.m3u` extension, such as `monkees_hits.m3u`.

- **Load the playlist** — To reload a saved playlist, click the List button. Select a playlist from the directory in which you saved it and click OK.

There is also a tiny set of buttons on the bottom of the Playlist Editor screen. These are the same buttons as those on the main screen used for selecting different tracks or playing, pausing, stopping, or ejecting the current track.

One of the most fun aspects of XMMS is that you can change the skin, or the look, of the user interface. XMMS skins allow you to see wildly different interfaces, even though the application remains the same. Not only can you control the look of XMMS, you can also use skins to adjust for any issues in the XMMS interface. For example, the current song in the playlist window may not be highlighted enough, especially if you have a high-resolution monitor. You can select a skin that provides better highlighting. You can also choose skins that make XMMS look like Winamp on Windows, or like the Mac OS X interface.

XMMS supports Windows .wsz Winamp skins, so you can download those skins and see your favorite musician or animated characters for your music player. Just download and copy the skin to your `/usr/share/xmms/Skins` directory to add it to your skins list.

Managing Music on Your iPod with gtkpod

Whether you have a first generation iPod, a Mini, a Shuffle, or the newest fifth generation Nano, the gtkpod player lets you manage (and possibly play) your Apple music player content in Linux. Install the gtkipod software and plug in your iPod. If all goes well (the device is detected and auto-mounted), you can be accessing your iPod content in just a few seconds.

Older devices (possibly Firewire or USB) typically mount your iPod content as a vfat (DOS) file system, while newer devices (usually USB) typically mount them as hfsplus file system types. Advanced Audio Coding (AAC) is the standard audio format for Apple devices, but requires special codecs (available from `http://www.rpmfusion.org`).

Installing and Starting gtkpod iPod Manager

To install the gtkpod software in most Linux distributions that include it, you must install the gtkpod package. In Fedora, you could type the following as the root user from a Terminal window: `yum install gtkpod`

Once it's installed, here's how to start with gtkpod iPod Manager:

1. Attach a cable from the iPod to your computer. A file manager window should open, displaying the content of your iPod. Close the window and go on to the next step. (If the file manager doesn't open, your Linux system may not have hfsplus file system support.)

123

2. Start the application by selecting Applications ➪ Sound and Video ➪ gtkpod iPod Manager (see Figure 5-6).

3. Choose your iPod player from the pop-up box that appears. You should see the name of your iPod player in the left column; you can select it to see your music.

FIGURE 5-6

Manage your iPod in Linux with gtkpod.

Using gtkipod iPod Manager

With your iPod content displayed, you can begin playing and managing it. Here are a couple of things you can do to get started:

- **Select music** — In the two lower-right panes, select the music you want to play or move around base on Artist, Album, Genre, Composer, Title, Year, or special features (such as rating, play count, or time most recently played, modified, or added).

- **Play music** — Right-click an audio file in the top-right panel and select Play Now. If you have configured Totem to play audio files as described earlier in this chapter (in particular, Apple Audio Codec format), Totem opens and begins playing your selected file.

- **Export tracks** — Select music from your iPod by artist, album, or some other means. With the songs highlighted that you want to export to a folder in Linux, select Music ➪ Export Tracks from Database ➪ Selected Tracks. A pop-up window asks you to select where on the local hard disk or other storage media you want to save the files.

If you run gtkpod from your desktop menu, that application will run with your user permission, but writing to the iPod will require root user permission. If you want to be able to upload or modify content on your iPod, you must run gtkpod as the root user. At that point, you will be able to create playlists, add files or folders, or synchronize data between your iPod and your Linux system.

Recording and Ripping Music

Writable CD-ROM drives are standard devices on computers. Where once you had to settle for a floppy disk (1.44MB) or a Zip disk (100MB) to store personal data, a CD-ROM burner lets you store more than 600MB of data in a format that can be exchanged with most computers. On top of that, you can create CD music discs!

Both graphical and command-line tools exist for creating audio and data CDs on Linux. The cdrecord command enables you to create audio and data CDs from the command line, writing to CD-recordable (CD-R) and CD-rewritable (CD-RW) drives. This command is discussed in the following section.

Creating an Audio CD with cdrecord

You can use the cdrecord command to create either data or music CDs. You can create a data CD by setting up a separate file system and copying the whole image of that file system to CD. Creating an audio CD consists of selecting the audio tracks you want to copy and copying them all at once to the CD.

This section focuses on using cdrecord to create audio CDs. cdrecord can use audio files in .au, .wav, and .cdr formats, automatically translating them when necessary. If you have audio files in other formats, you can convert them to one of the supported formats by using the sox command.

One way to create an audio CD is to use cdda2wav to extract (copy) the music tracks to a directory and then use cdrecord to write them from the directory to the CD. Here's an example:

Note

If you prefer a graphical tool for copying and burning CDs and DVDs, refer to Appendix A, which describes how to use the K3B CD/DVD Burning Facility for burning CD images. You can also use that tool for copying audio CDs. ∎

1. Create a directory to hold the audio files, and change to that directory. (Make sure the directory can hold up to 660MB of data — less if you are burning fewer songs.) For example:

```
# mkdir /tmp/cd
# cd /tmp/cd
```

2. Insert the music CD into your CD-ROM drive. (If a CD player opens on the desktop, close it.)

3. Extract the music tracks you want by using the cdda2wav command. For example:

```
# cdda2wav -D /dev/cdrom -B
```

This reads all the music tracks from the CD-ROM drive. The -B option says to output each track to a separate file. By default, the cdda2wav command outputs the files to the WAV audio format.

Instead of extracting all songs, you can choose a single track or a range of tracks to extract. For example, to extract tracks 3 through 5, add the -t3+5 option. To extract just track 9, add -t9+9. To extract track 7 through the end of the CD, add -t7.

Note

If you have a low-quality CD drive or an imperfect CD, cdda2wav might not be the best ripping tool. You might try cdparanoia -B to extract songs from the CD to hard disk instead. ■

4. When cdda2wav is done, remove the music CD and insert a blank CD into your writable CD drive.

5. Use the cdrecord command to write the music tracks to the CD. For example:

```
# cdrecord -v dev=/dev/cdrom -audio *.wav
```

The options for cdrecord tell the command to create an audio CD (-audio) on the writable CD device located at /dev/cdrom. The cdrecord command writes all .wav files from the current directory. The -v option causes verbose output.

6. If you want to change the order of the tracks, you can type their names in the order you want them written (instead of using *.wav). If your CD writer supports higher speeds, you can use the speed option to double (speed=2) or quadruple (speed=4) the writing speed.

After you have created the music CD, indicate the contents of the CD on its label side. It's now ready to play on any standard music CD player.

Ripping CDs with Grip

The Grip application (grip package) provides a more graphical method of copying music from CDs to your hard disk so that you can play the songs directly from your hard disk or burn them back onto a blank CD. Besides just ripping music, you can also compress each song as you extract it from the CD.

You can open Grip from the GNOME desktop Applications menu in Ubuntu, Fedora, and other Linux systems by selecting Sound & Video ⇨ Grip (or by typing grip from a Terminal window). Figure 5-7 shows an example of the Grip window.

To rip audio tracks from a CD with grip, do the following:

1. With the Grip window open, insert a music CD into your CD drive. If you have an active connection to the Internet and the CD is known to the CD database, the title, artist, and track information appear in the window.

2. Click each track that you want to rip (that is, copy to your hard disk). A check mark appears in that track's Rip column.

FIGURE 5-7

Rip and play songs from the Grip window.

3. Click the Config tab at the top of the page, and then select Encode.

4. You can choose the type of encoder used to compress the music by clicking the Encoder box and selecting an encoder (by default, oggenc compresses files in Ogg Vorbis, assuming that Ogg Vorbis was installed on your Linux distribution). If you have the LAME package installed (available from non-free repositories for some Linux distributions), you can encode your music to MP3 format.

5. Click the Rip tab at the top of the page. From the Ripper subtab, indicate the location and format of the ripped files. (I use ~/Music/%x/%A/%d/%n.wav to hold the ripped WAV files in subdirectories of my Music folder.)

6. Click one of the following:

- **Rip+Encode** — This rips the selected songs and (if you left in the default oggenc compression in Step 4) compresses them in Ogg Vorbis format. You need an Ogg Vorbis player to play the songs after they have been ripped in this format (many Ogg Vorbis players are available for Linux).

- **Rip only** — This rips the selected songs in WAV format. You can use a standard CD player to play these songs. (When I tried this, the same song ripped in WAV was 12 times larger than the Ogg Vorbis file.)

Songs are copied to the hard disk in the format you selected. By default, the files are copied into a subdirectory of $HOME/ogg (such as /home/jake/ogg). The subdirectory is named for the artist and CD. For example, if the user jake were ripping the song called "High Life" by the artist Mumbo, the directory containing the ripped songs would be /home/jake/ogg/mumbo/high_life. Each song file is named for the song (for example, fly_fly_fly.wav). Following the earlier example, I would use /home/ jake/Music to hold the ripped music, instead of the default ogg directory.

7. Now you can play any of the files using a player that can play WAV or Ogg files, such as XMMS. Or you can copy the files to a CD using cdrecord. Because the filenames are the song names, they don't appear in the same order as they appear on the CD, so if you want to copy them back to a writable CD in their original order, you may have to type each filename on the cdrecord command line. For example:

```
# cdrecord -v dev=/dev/cdrom -audio fly_fly.wav big_news.wav about_time.wav
```

The Grip window can also be used to play CDs. Use the buttons on the bottom of the display to play or pause, skip ahead or back, stop, and eject the CD. The Toggle Track Display button lets you shrink the size of the display so it takes up less space on the desktop. Click Toggle Disc Editor to see and change the title, artist, and track information.

Playing Videos

There are several fairly high-quality video players available for Linux. Totem was described at the beginning of this chapter as the default audio and video player on GNOME desktops in Linux. Other players include MPlayer (www.mplayerhq.hu), VLC (http://www.videolan.org/vlc), Ogle (www.dtek.chalmers.se/groups/dvd), and xine (http://www.xine-project.org/) video players.

One of the biggest obstacles to playing video, however, is obtaining the codecs needed to play video. With the necessary software installed, DVD playing works quite well. Currently Blu-ray support is hit-or-miss. The issue of getting codecs is covered below, followed by descriptions of the xine video player.

Exploring Codecs

If you want to play a video or audio file, you need the appropriate codec installed and ready for use by your media player. A *codec* is a software-based encoder-decoder used to take existing digital audio/video data and decode the content. Often, codecs use compression technology to reduce the size of the data files while retaining the quality of the output.

If you encounter a media file that you know is a working, playable file and you cannot play the file, you might need to identify and install the proper codec. This often involves installing the proper playback application, such as DivX 5.0.5 for Linux, which installs the MPEG4 codec for video and audio playback.

Many codecs are available, so finding the ones you need is usually not difficult. Advances in codec technology have continued to increase the quality of the encoded content, while reducing file size. Fortunately, most widely distributed video and audio files (from news sites, for example) are created using a few commonly used codecs.

Although some commonly used encoding standards exist, a slew of proprietary codecs are also in use today. This situation is really a battleground of sorts, with each vendor/developer trying to produce the superior standard and obtain the spoils of market share that can follow. For the end user, this means you might have to spend time chasing a variety of playback utilities to handle multiple video and audio formats.

Another debate: Can digital media match the quality of analog formats? This hardly seems much of a question anymore because DVD has shown the potential for high-quality digital video, and MPEG codecs have made huge strides in digital audio fidelity. The quality of digital media files is very high and getting better all the time. Some of the key technologies that reflect improvements in how audio and video codecs have improved include

- **Ogg Vorbis and Theora** — This audio codec has been developed as a freely available tool — no patents restrict its use. Ogg is the "data container" portion of the codec, and Vorbis is the audio compression scheme. Other compression schemes can be used with Ogg, such as Ogg FLAC, which is used for archiving audio in a lossless format, and Ogg Speex, which is used specifically to handle encoding speech. The open video format associated with Ogg Vorbis is called Theora.

- **WMA** — Windows Media Audio is used to create high-quality digital audio. WMA is considered a *lossless* codec, which means the audio doesn't lose quality or data as a result of repeated compression-decompression cycles. Among its other benefits is that it's one of the first widely used codecs to support digital surround sound.

- **WMV** — Windows Media Video is used, not surprisingly, to encode and decode video. It is also a very high-quality encoder and is billed to produce a video that is half the size of an MPEG4-encoded video at a comparable quality level.

- **DivX** — This video codec revolutionized digital video. Extremely high-quality video can be stored with amazingly small file sizes when using this codec. DivX (Digital Video Express) is based on the MPEG4 video standard and can produce 640 × 480 video, about 15 percent of the size of the source DVD material.

- **WebM** — An up and coming video codec is WebM. WebM (www.webmproject.org) aims at developing a freely available, high-quality, open video format for the web.

Some of these codecs are integral parts of Digital Rights Management (DRM) scenarios. For example, WMA, WMV, and DivX have elements that support DRM. DRM is basically proprietary copy protection.

The term *DRM* applies to a wide range of technologies that use server-based activation, encryption, and other elements to control who can access content and what they can then do with the content after it has been accessed. Although it is very attractive to distributors of audio and video, who are trying to prevent unchecked digital piracy of their content, it can be a real stumbling block for the consumer.

Many DRM solutions require proprietary software and even hardware to work with the protected content. A prime example is the production of some DRM-protected audio CDs, particularly in Europe. Some of these discs will not play in older, standalone CD players, some will play only on a computer that supports the DRM application on the CD itself, and (especially frustrating) some will not play on a computer at all. In almost all cases, such DRM solutions do not support Linux. Most support only Windows and a few support Windows and Mac OS X.

Just to make things clear, although the codecs just discussed do not include built-in DRM features, some codecs are specifically designed to integrate with DRM solutions. In other words, all of these codecs can theoretically be used to play encoded content on a Linux system. If the content is protected by a DRM solution, the likelihood that the content is playable on a Linux system is fairly remote. Despite this fact, or perhaps because of it, Linus Torvalds has not excluded the possibility of including support for DRM in Linux. Likewise, several open source projects are working on Linux DRM solutions.

Watching Video with xine

The xine player is an excellent application for playing a variety of video and audio formats. You can get xine from `xine.sourceforge.net` or from software repositories associated with your Linux distribution.

For Fedora, xine-ui is in the main Fedora repository (`yum install xine-ui`). However, you also need to install `xine-lib-extras-freeworld` from the `rpmfusion.org` site. To play commercial DVDs, you also need to get the libdvdcss package (possibly available from the `rpm.livna.org` site). For Ubuntu, you can get xine from non-free repositories (`sudo apt-get install xine-ui libxine1-ffmpeg phonon-backend-xine`).

Note
When you try to install xine, it tells you if you need any additional packages. If your xine player fails to start, see the "xine Tips" section later in this chapter. ■

xine supports a bunch of video and audio formats, including

- MPEG (1, 2, and 4)
- QuickTime (see "xine Tips" if your QuickTime content won't play)
- WMV
- DVDs, CDs, and VCDs
- Motion JPEG
- MPEG audio (MP3)
- AC3 and Dolby Digital audio
- DTS audio
- Commercial movies (libdvdcss package is required)
- Ogg Vorbis audio

xine understands different file formats that represent a combination of audio and video, including .mpg (MPEG program streams), .ts (MPEG transport streams), .mpv (raw MPEG audio/video streams), .avi (MS AVI format), and .asf (Advanced Streaming format). Although xine can play video CDs and DVDs, it can't play encrypted DVDs or the Video-on-CD hybrid format (because of legal issues mentioned earlier related to decrypting DVDs).

Using xine

With xine started, right-click in the xine window to see the controls. The quickest way to play video is to click one of the following buttons, and then click the Play button (right arrow or Play, depending on the skin you are using):

- VCD (for a video CD)
- DVD (for a DVD in /dev/dvd)
- CD (for a music CD in /dev/cdaudio)

Next, you can use the Pause/Resume, Stop, Play, Fast Motion, Slow Motion, or Eject buttons to work with video. You can also use the Previous and Next buttons to step to different tracks. The controls are very similar to what you would expect on a physical CD or DVD player.

To select individual files, or to put together your own list of content to play, use the Playlist feature.

Creating Playlists with xine

Click the Playlist button on the left side of the xine control window. A Playlist Editor appears, showing the files on your current playlist. You can add and delete content and then save the list to call on later.

xine content is identified as media resource locators (MRLs). Each MRL is identified as a file, DVD, or VCD. Files are in the regular file path (/path/file) or preceded by file:/, fifo:/, or stdin:/. DVDs and VCDs are preceded by dvd and vcd, respectively (for example, vcd://01).

Table 5-1 shows what the xine Playlist Editor buttons do.

TABLE 5-1

Using the xine Playlist Editor

Button	Description
CD, DVB, DVD, VCD, or VCDO	All content from the selected medium is added to the playlist.
Add	See the browser window. From that window, click File to choose a file from your Linux file system, and then click Select to add that file to the Playlist Editor.
Move Up Selected MRL Move Down Selected MRL	Move up and down the playlist using these two buttons.

continued

TABLE 5-1	_(continued)_
Button	**Description**
Play	Play the contents of the playlist.
Delete Selected MRL	Remove the current selection.
Delete All Entries	Clear the whole playlist.
Save	Save the playlist to your home directory ($HOME/.xine/ playlist.tox).
Load	Read in your (saved) playlist.

xine Tips

Getting video and audio to work properly can sometimes be a tricky business. Here are a few quick tips if you are having trouble getting xine to work correctly (or at all):

- **xine won't start.** To work best, xine needs an X driver that supports xvid. If no xvid support exists for your video card in X, xine shuts down immediately when it tries to open the default Xv driver. If this happens to you, try starting xine with the X11 video driver (which is slower, but should work) as follows:

```
$ xine -VXSHM
```

- **xine playback is choppy.** If playback of files from your hard disk is choppy, you can check a couple of settings: 32-bit I/O and DMA, features that, if supported by your hard disk, generally improve hard disk performance. Here's how to check:

Caution

Improper disk settings can result in destroyed data on your hard disk. Perform this procedure at your own risk. This procedure is for IDE hard drives only (no SCSI)! Also, be sure to have a current backup and no activity on your hard disk if you change DMA or I/O settings as described in this section. ■

1. Test the speed of hard disk reads. To test the first IDE drive (/dev/hda), type

```
# hdparm -t /dev/hda
Timing buffered disk reads: 64 MB in
      19.31 seconds = 3.31 MB/sec
```

2. To see your current DMA and I/O settings, as root user type

```
# hdparm -c -d /dev/hda
/dev/hda:
 I/O support = 0 (default 16-bit)
 using_dma   = 0 (off)
```

3. This result shows that both 32-bit I/O and DMA are off. To turn them on, type

```
# hdparm -c 1 -d 1 /dev/hda
/dev/hda:
 I/O support = 1 (32-bit)
 using_dma   = 1 (on)
```

4. With both settings on, test the disk again:

```
# hdparm -t /dev/hda
Timing buffered disk reads: 64 MB in
      2.2 seconds = 28.83 MB/sec
```

In this example, buffered disk reads of 64MB went from 19.31 seconds to 2.2 seconds after changing the parameters described. Playback would be much better now.

- **xine won't play particular media.** Messages such as `no input plug-in` mean that either the file format you are trying to play is not supported or it requires an additional plug-in (as is the case with playing DVDs). If the message is that xyx may be a broken file, the file may be a proprietary version of an otherwise supported format. For example, I had a QuickTime video fail that required an SVQ3 codec (which is currently not supported under Linux), although other QuickTime files played fine.
- **Xine started with the control panel.** Right-click on the main xine window and choose Show Controls.

Working with Images

Tools for creating and manipulating graphics are becoming both more plentiful and more powerful in Linux systems as a whole. To first download images from your camera, you can use tools such as Shotwell Photo Manager (in Fedora) or F-Spot (in Ubuntu). Shotwell will become the default image management tool for later releases of Ubuntu.

For image editing, the GNU Image Manipulation Program (GIMP) enables you to compose and author images as well as retouch photographs and take screen shots. GIMP can replace a handful of other digital image applications that may only do one or two of the features just mentioned.

Managing Images in Shotwell Photo Manager

The GNOME Volume Manager mounts the contents of your USB camera, treating the memory of your camera as it would any file storage device. Plug in your camera or insert your camera's memory card into a slot on your computer and, typically, it makes the images accessible to your file system.

Along with mounting your camera's contents to your file system, if GNOME notices that the camera contains images, it will offer to open those images in an application. In Fedora, that application is Shotwell. Figure 5-8 shows an example of the Shotwell Photo Manager window displaying the images from a digital camera.

FIGURE 5-8

Work with images from digital cameras with the Shotwell image viewer.

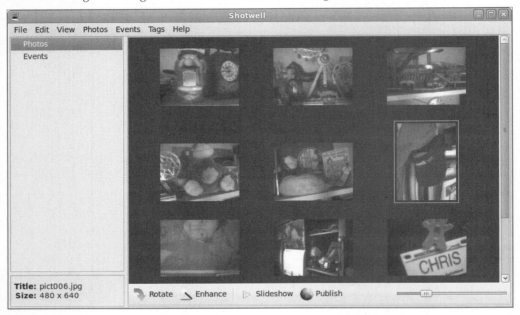

With your camera connected and the gThumb window open, here are some things you can do with the images on your camera:

- **Download images** — Click a single image or select Edit ⇨ Select All to highlight all images from the folder on your digital camera. Then select File ⇨ Import from Folder. From the Import from Folder window you can select the destination where you want the images to be downloaded.

- **View slideshow** — Select the Slideshow button. A full-screen slideshow appears on your display, with the images changing every few seconds. The toolbar that appears on the screen lets you go to the next photo, change the delay between slide changes, or exit the slideshow.

- **Manipulate images** — Double-click an image to open it. Buttons appear to offer a set of tools for enhancing, rotating, cropping, or otherwise transforming the image. You can also adjust the color balance or take out red eye.

After images are downloaded to your computer's hard disk, you can continue to work with them using Shotwell or use any of a number of tools available for manipulating digital images (GIMP, KView, or KuickShow, to name a few).

Note

If your camera saves images to SD or CF cards, you can purchase a USB card reader and view these files from Linux. Some PCs today come with card readers built in. ∎

Manipulating Images with GIMP

GIMP is a free software program for manipulating photographs and graphical images. To create images with GIMP, you can either import a drawing, photograph, or 3D image, or you can create one from scratch. You can start GIMP from the system menu by selecting Graphics ➪ GNU Image Manipulation Program or by typing gimp& from a Terminal window.

Figure 5-9 shows an example of GIMP.

GIMP is a powerful tool for graphic manipulation.

In many ways, GIMP is similar to Adobe Photoshop. Some people feel that GIMP's scripting features are comparable to, or even better than, Actions in Adobe Photoshop. One capability that GIMP lacks, however, is native support for CMYK (cyan-magenta-yellow-black) separations. If CMYK is not critical for your graphics needs, you will probably find GIMP to be just as powerful and flexible as Photoshop in many ways.

Tip

See `http://registry.gimp.org/node/471` for a CMYK plug-in for GIMP. This plug-in provides only rudimentary support for CMYK, according to its documentation. Even so, that may be enough for your needs. ∎

With an image open, you can select tools from the GIMP window to work on the image. When you select a tool, notice that options for that tool appear in tabs below. The following is a list of tools available in GIMP:

- **Path tool** — Use the path tool to create special types of rectangular, elliptical, or free-form shapes. Try creating a rectangle, with the final point ending on the first. Hold the Ctrl key and click on the first point to close the box. With the shape complete, select Stroke Path to define the shape with a solid or patterned line.

- **Color picker** — Use the color picker to select any color from your image as your foreground or background color.

- **Magnify** — Select this tool, and then click and drag to choose an area of your image. That area of your image will fill the screen. Or just click to zoom in or Ctrl+click to zoom out on the image.

- **Measure** — With measure selected, click and drag your mouse from one point to another. The status bar shows the distance (in pixels), angle, width, and height you just measured.

- **Select tools** — Use the select tools to select different areas of your image. You can select a rectangle, ellipse, or hand-drawn area, a region based on color, an edge of an element, or an area based on foreground objects. Once an area is selected, you can cut, copy, fill, paste, or do other things with it.

- **Text tool** — Select the text tool, click in the image, and begin typing to add text to that point in the image. You can change the font, size, color, justification, and other options relating to the text.

- **Paint tools** — Use these tools to add lines and colors to your image. The bucket tool fills a selected area or similar color with the current foreground color, background color, or pattern. The gradient tool lets you shade an area from one color to another. Use the pencil, brush, ink, or airbrush tools to draw lines. Paint over one part of an image from a sample taken from another part of an image or from a selected pattern using the clone tool. Use blur, smudge, and dodge/burn tools to blur and soften selected areas of the image. Erase (to transparency or to the layer below) using the erase tool.

- **Foreground and background colors** — The two color boxes show the foreground (upper right) and background (lower left) colors. Click to open a dialog to change either of those colors. Click the swap arrows to switch the two colors.

You can also access the tools just described from the Tools menu. Select the Dialogs menu to see a list of dialog boxes you can display to work with layers, channels, paths, patterns, fonts, and other elements you might need to work on your image.

GIMP also supports a variety of plug-ins. For example, the Cartoon plug-in gives an image a cartoon effect, Red Eye Removal lets you correct red eye, and Cubism lets you convert an image to randomly floating square blobs. Many of these plug-ins are available from the Filters menu in GIMP.

Tip
If you make a mistake, select Edit ⇨ Undo from the GIMP menu, or press the Ctrl+Z key combination to undo the most recent change. You can do multiple undos in this way as well. ■

Acquiring Screen Captures

Several screen capture tools are available with Linux systems. Using the GIMP program just described, you can take a screen shot by selecting File ⇨ Create ⇨ Screenshot. On GNOME desktops, select Applications ⇨ Accessories ⇨ Take Screenshot. From most KDE desktops, select Graphics ⇨ Ksnapshot. In either environment you can press the Print Screen button to take a screen shot.

Using the example of the GNOME Take Screenshot tool, a dialog box appears that lets you choose to grab the whole desktop or grab the current window. You can set a delay of several seconds if you need to set up something, such as opening a menu, before you take the shot. Then click Take Screenshot. Figure 5-10 shows an example of the Take Screenshot window after it has captured an image of the current desktop.

FIGURE 5-10

Grab a picture of your desktop or selected window with the Take Screenshot utility.

Select a folder to hold the screen shot and type a name for the image. Then click Save to save it.

After you are done working with your digital images, you might consider kicking back and having some fun. One way to do that is to look into some Linux gaming applications.

Playing Games on Linux

Every type of PC gaming is available now with Linux. Whether you are looking for a solitaire game to fill time or a full-blown online 3D gaming experience, you will have dozens (or hundreds) of choices on the Linux desktop.

Although some companies, such as ID Software (*Quake*) and Epic Games (*Unreal Tournament*) have done work to port their games to Linux, others have used third-party developers (such as RuneSoft) to port commercial games to Linux. Independent games developers, such as Frictional Games (http://frictionalgames.com) and Introversion Software (www.introversion.co.uk) are now producing high-quality gaming experiences in Linux. Linux clients for commercial online gaming, such as EVE Online (www.eve-online.com), are also available.

This section provides an overview of the state of Linux gaming today. It describes games that were created specifically to run in Linux, and explains how to find commercial games that run in Linux (either with a Linux version or running a Windows version along with Windows compatibility software, such as Cedega).

Jumping into Linux Gaming

Linux is a wonderful platform for both running and, perhaps more especially, developing computer games. Casual gamers have no shortage of fun games to try. Hardcore gamers face a few more challenges with Linux. Here are some of the opportunities and challenges as you approach Linux gaming:

- **3D acceleration** — If you are a more serious gamer, you will almost certainly want a video card that provides hardware acceleration. Open source drivers for some video cards are available from the DRI project. Video cards from NVIDIA and ATI often have binary-only drivers available. Fun open source games, such as *PenguinPlanet Racer*, *BZFlag,* and others that recommend hardware acceleration, will run much better if you get one of these supported cards and drivers.

- **Gaming servers** — Many commercial computer games that don't have Linux clients available do have Linux game servers associated with them. So Linux is a great operating system for hosting a LAN party or setting up an Internet gaming server.

- **Linux gaming development** — Some of the most advanced tools and application programming interfaces (APIs) for developing computer games run on Linux systems. If you are interested in developing your own games to run in Linux, check out the OpenGL (http://opengl.org) and Simple DirectMedia Layer (www.libsdl.org) projects. Blender (www.blender.org) is an open source project for doing animations, 3D models, post-production, and rendering that is being used today in commercial games and movie animations.

Although the development tools available for developing open source games are awesome, a primary goal of this book is to get you up and using Linux as quickly as possible. To that end, I want to give you details on how to get hold of games that already run well in Linux and then show you how to get games working in Linux that are intended for other platforms (particularly Windows and some classic gaming consoles).

Finding Linux Games

If you have a Linux system running and want to get started playing a game right now, here are some suggestions:

- **Check the Games menu** — Most Linux desktop systems come with a bunch of games already installed. If you are running either a GNOME or KDE desktop in Linux, select Applications ➪ Games from the panel. You should be able to select a variety of arcade, card, board, tactics, and other games to keep you busy for a while.

- **Games packaged for your Linux distribution** — Many of the most popular open source games are packaged to run on your Linux distribution. In Fedora, open the Add/Remove Software (PackageKit) window and select Games to see a list of more than 200 games you can download and play. In Ubuntu, the Add/Remove Applications window shows more than 300 games on the Games menu to download and play.

- **Other open source games** — If the open source game you want is not packaged for your distribution, try going to the game's project site to get the game. There are Internet sites that contain lists of games and links to each game's site. The Wikipedia Linux Gaming page (en.wikipedia.org/wiki/Linux_gaming) and the Linux Game Tome (http://happypenguin.org) are good places to start.

- **Commercial Windows games** — The latest commercial computer games are not all ported to run in Linux. Boxed commercial games for Linux include *Unreal Tournament 2003* and *2004*, as well as about 50 first-rate commercial games that have been ported to run in Linux. Using Cedega software from TransGaming Inc., you can get hundreds more commercial Windows games to run. Commercial Linux games are described in more depth later in this chapter.

Before you can play some of the more demanding 3D games, you need to check that your hardware can handle the games. Some games requiring support for 3D hardware acceleration need more RAM, faster processors, and particular video cards to run in Linux. Issues for setting up a gaming machine in Linux are described later in this chapter.

Here is a quick list of games that are available on Fedora and many other Linux distributions that you can try out. I've listed them in the order of simple-and-addicting to more-complex-and-addicting:

- **Frozen Bubble** (www.frozen-bubble.org) — *The Frozen Bubble* game is often mentioned as the most addictive Linux game. Shoot frozen bubbles and colored groups of bubbles as they slowly descend on you. Clear bubbles in sets of three or more until they are all gone (or come down and freeze you). The game can be played with multiple players. (Install the frozen-bubble package and select it from the Games menu.)

- **Gweled** (`http://sebdelestaing.free.fr/gweled`) — In this clone of the popular *Bejeweled* game, exchange two jewels on the board to match three or more jewels (vertically or horizontally). (Install the gweled package and select Gweled from the Games menu.)

- **Warzone 2100** (`http://wz2100.net`) — This 1999 real-time strategy game was released in open source in 2004. Build a base from which you design and build vehicles and weapons, set up structures, and research new technologies to fight a global war. (Install the warzone2100 package and select Warzone 2100 from the Games menu.)

- **Quake III Arena** (`ftp.idsoftware.com/idstuff/`) — Several first-person shooter games in the *Quake* series are available for download from id Software. In Fedora, install the quake3 package and select Quake III Arena. The application that starts up lets you download a demo version of the Quake III data files, which can be freely downloaded. Read and accept the licensing terms to download the data files and begin playing the Quake III Arena *demo*.

- **Vega Strike** (`http://vegastrike.sourceforge.net`) — Explore the universe in this 3D action, space simulation game. Accept missions to transport cargo, become a bounty hunter, or patrol space. In this 3D environment, you can chat with bartenders or watch news broadcasts to keep up with events in the universe. (To play this game in Fedora, install the vegastrike package and select Vega Strike from the Games menu.)

Note

Despite gains in gaming support in Linux, a lot of popular Windows games still don't run in Linux. For that reason, some PC gamers maintain a separate Windows partition on their computers so they can boot to Windows to play particular games. ■

Basic Linux Gaming Information

Many Web sites provide information about the latest games available for Linux, as well as links to download sites. Here are several to get you started:

- **TransGaming Inc.** (`www.transgaming.com`) — This company's mission is to bring games from other platforms to Linux. It is the provider of Cedega, formerly known as WineX, a powerful tool that enables you to play hundreds of PC games on your Linux system.

- **The Linux Game Tome** (`http://happypenguin.org`) — Features a database of descriptions and reviews of tons of games that run in Linux. You can do keyword searches for games listed at this site. It also has links to sites where you can get the different games and to other gaming sites.

- **LinuxGames** (`http://linuxgames.com`) — This site can give you some very good insight into the state of Linux gaming. There are links to HOWTOs and Frequently Asked Questions (FAQs), as well as forums for discussing Linux games. There are also links to Web sites that have information about specific games.

- **id Software** (`www.idsoftware.com`) — Go to the id Software site for information on Linux versions for *Quake* and *Return to Castle Wolfenstein*.

- **Linux Game Publishing** (`www.linuxgamepublishing.com`) — This site aims to be a one-stop shopping portal for native Linux games, as well as for ports of games from other platforms. At the time of this writing, it offers about a dozen games. To purchase games from this site, you must create a user account.

- **Loki Entertainment Software** (www.lokigames.com) — Loki provided ports of best-selling games to Linux but went out of business in 2001. Its products included Linux versions of *Civilization: Call to Power, Myth II: Soulblighter, SimCity 3000, Railroad Tycoon II*, and *Quake III Arena*. The Loki Demo Launcher is still available to see demo versions of these games, and some boxed sets are available for very little money. The Loki site also offers a list of commercial resellers for its games, which may or may not still carry those games.

- **Tux Games** (www.tuxgames.com) — The Tux Games Web site is dedicated to the sale of Linux games. In addition to offering Linux gaming news and products, the site lists its top-selling games and includes notices of games that are soon to be released.

- **Wikipedia** (http://en.wikipedia.org) — In the past few years, Wikipedia has become a wonderful resource for information on both commercial and open source games available for Linux. From the Wikipedia Linux games list (http://en.wikipedia.org/wiki/Linux_games) you can find links to free Linux games, commercial Linux games, and professionally developed Linux games.

- **Linux Gamers' FAQ** (http://icculus.org/lgfaq) — Contains a wealth of information about free and commercial Linux games. It lists gaming companies that have ported their games to Linux, tells where to get Linux games, and answers queries related to common Linux gaming problems. For a list of Linux games without additional information, see http://icculus.org/lgfaq/gamelist.php.

Although the sites just mentioned provide excellent information on Linux gaming, not all open source games have been packaged specifically for every version of Linux. Even though you can always nudge a game into working on your particular Linux distribution, it's probably easiest to start with games that are ready to run. The following list provides information about where to find out about games packaged for different Linux distributions:

- **Fedora** — Much of the recent increase in the number of Fedora games has come from the Fedora Games SIG (Special Interest Group). You can check out that SIG's activities for information on other games of interest that have not made it into Fedora at http://fedoraproject.org/wiki/SIGs/Games.

- **Debian** — Debian games resources are listed at the Debian wiki. Visit the games section at http://wiki.debian.org/Game.

- **Ubuntu** — The Games Community Ubuntu Documentation page offers some good information about available games and gaming initiatives related to Ubuntu (http://help.ubuntu.com/community/Games).

- **Slackware** — Though GNOME and KDE games run fine in Slackware, not a lot of gaming resources are particular to Slackware. However, because Slackware contains a solid set of libraries and development tools, many open source games will compile and run in Slackware if you are willing to get the source code for the game you want and build it yourself.

Getting Started with Commercial Games in Linux

How you get started with Linux gaming depends on how serious you are about it. If all you want to do is play a few games to pass the time, there are plenty of entertaining X Window games that come with Linux. If you want to play more powerful commercial games, you can choose from the following:

- **Games for Microsoft Windows (Cedega 6.0)** — Many of the most popular commercial games created to run on Microsoft operating systems will run in Linux using Cedega. To get RPM versions of Cedega, you must sign up for a Cedega subscription at www.transgaming.com. Make sure to check in with www.linuxgames.com to see if there is a relevant HOWTO for working with the particular game you have in mind. Many games are covered there, including *Half-Life* and *Unreal Tournament*. To see whether your favorite Windows game will run in Linux and Cedega, refer to the TransGaming.org Games database at www.cedega.com/gamesdb.

- **Games for Linux (id Software and others)** — Some older popular games have Linux versions available. Most notably, id Software offers its *DOOM* and *Return to Castle Wolfenstein* in Linux versions. Other popular games that run natively in Linux include *Unreal Tournament 2004* and *2005* from Atari (www.unrealtournament.com).

  Commercial games that run in Linux without Wine, Cedega, or some sort of Windows emulation typically come in a boxed version for Windows with a Linux installer included.

- **Independent Linux Game Developers** — Several small companies are currently producing games for Linux. Notable Linux game developers include Introversion Software (www.introversion.co.uk) and Frictional Games (www.frictionalgames.com). Introversion's games include *Uplink, Darwinia,* and *Defcon.* By the time you read this, *Multiwinia* will be available. Frictional games include *Penumbra: Overture* and *Penumbra: Black Plague,* both of which portray 3D horror stories.

Linux games that were ported directly to Linux from the now-defunct company Loki Software, Inc. are still available. Although you cannot purchase the titles directly from Loki, you can go online to one of Loki's resellers at www.lokigames.com/orders/resellers.php3. For example, Amazon.com (one of the listed resellers) shows titles, including *Quake III*, *Myth II: Soulblighter*, and *Heretic II* for Linux.

Playing TransGaming and Cedega Games

TransGaming Inc. brings to Linux some of the most popular games that currently run on Windows platforms. Working with Wine developers, TransGaming is developing Cedega, which enables you to run many different games on Linux that were originally developed for Windows. Although TransGaming is producing a few games that are packaged separately and tuned for Linux, in most cases it sells you a subscription service to Cedega instead of the games. That subscription service lets you stay up-to-date on the continuing development of Cedega so you can run more and more Windows games.

Coming from Windows

To get Windows games to run in Linux, Cedega particularly focuses its development on Microsoft DirectX features that are required by many of today's games. Issues related to CD keys and hooks into the Windows operating system also must be overcome (such as requiring Microsoft Active Desktop). A Cedega subscription has value, in part, because it lets you vote on which games you want to see TransGaming work on next. ■

A full list of games supported by TransGaming, as well as indications of how popular they are and how well they work, is available from the TransGaming site (www.cedega.com/gamesdb/). Browse games by category or alphabetically. An asterisk marks games that are officially supported by TransGaming. On each game description page is a link to a related WikiNode, when one exists, that gives you details about how well the game works under Cedega and tips for getting it to work better.

Note

Depending on your distribution, you may need to get the vanilla kernel from kernel.org and boot that on your system before running games with Cedega. TransGaming has added several new features to the Cedega GUI (formerly called Point2Play). The Cedega GUI provides a graphical window for installing, configuring, and testing Cedega on your computer. This application also lets you install and organize your games so you can launch them graphically. ■

Features in the Cedega GUI window include a new look and feel and tools for individually configuring how each game runs under Cedega. (If a game won't run from the GUI, try launching it from a Terminal window.) Here are some games that are known to run well in Cedega:

- *Day of Defeat: Source*
- *World of Warcraft*
- *Planescape*
- *Silkroad Online*
- *Half-Life 2*
- *Call of Duty 2*

To get binary copies of Cedega (ones that are already compiled to run), you need to subscribe to TransGaming. For details on how to become a "TransGamer," go to the TransGaming home page (www.transgaming.com). Benefits currently include

- Downloads of the latest version of Cedega
- Access to Cedega support forums
- Ability to vote on which games you want TransGaming to support next
- Subscription to the Cedega newsletter

Cedega used to be known as WineX. The source code for WineX may become available in the near future if you want to build your own WineX/Cedega package.

Summary

Getting up and running with digital media can take some doing, but once it's set up, you can play most audio and video content available today. This chapter takes you through the steps of setting up and using music players, video players, image manipulation applications, and games in Linux.

Every desktop Linux distribution comes with one or more ways of playing music from files or CDs. Popular music players include XMMS and Rhythmbox. Tools for ripping and recording CDs include grip and command-line utilities such as `cdda2wav` and `cdrecord`.

Image manipulation tools such as GIMP and Shotwell continue to improve. And though Linux has not taken over the computer gaming world, there are plenty of fun and challenging games that run natively in Linux, and ways of playing Windows games using emulators such as Cedega and Wine.

Part III

Learning System Administration Skills

Starting with System Administration

## 6

IN THIS CHAPTER

Doing graphical administration

Using the root login

Understanding administrative
commands, config files, and
log files

Linux, like other UNIX-based systems, was intended for use by more than one person at a time. *Multiuser* features enable many people to have accounts on a single Linux system, with their data kept secure from others. *Multitasking* enables many people to run many programs on the computer at the same time, with each person able to run more than one program. Sophisticated networking protocols and applications make it possible for a Linux system to extend its capabilities to network users and computers around the world. The person assigned to manage all of this stuff is called the *system administrator*.

Even if you are the only person using a Linux system, system administration is still set up to be separate from other computer use. To do most administrative tasks, you need to be logged in as the root user (also called the *superuser*) or temporarily get root permission. Users other than root cannot change, or in some cases even see, some of the configuration information for a Linux system. In particular, security features such as stored passwords are protected from general view.

Because Linux system administration is such a huge topic, this chapter focuses on the general principles of Linux system administration. In particular, it examines some of the basic tools you need to administer a Linux system for a personal desktop or on a small LAN. Beyond the basics, this chapter also teaches you how to work with file systems and monitor the setup and performance of your Linux system.

Graphical Administration Tools

Many Linux systems come with simplified graphical tools for administering Linux. If you are a casual user, these tools often let you do everything you need to administer your system without editing configuration files or running shell commands.

Let's examine some of the web-based administration tools available to use with most Linux systems.

Using Web-Based Administration

Web-based administration tools are available with many open source projects to make those projects more accessible to casual users. Often all you need to use those tools is a web browser (such as Firefox), the port number of the service, and the root password. Projects such as Samba and CUPS come with their own web administration tools. Webmin is a general-purpose tool for administering a variety of Linux system services from your web browser.

The advantages of web-based administration tools are that you can operate them from a familiar interface (your web browser) and you can access them remotely. Webmin includes graphical interfaces for configuring Apache web server, Sendmail mail server, and SSH server.

Note
Some Linux distributions come with their own set of graphical administration tools (such as SUSE's YaST or Red Hat's system-config tools). You should generally use those instead of any web-based interface that comes with a project because a distribution's own tools are usually better integrated with its features for starting and stopping services. ∎

Open Source Projects Offering Web Administration

Several major open source projects come with web-based interfaces for configuring those projects. Regardless of which Linux you are using, you can use your web browser to configure the following projects:

- **Samba** — To set up Samba for doing file and printer sharing with Microsoft Windows systems on your LAN, use the Samba SWAT web-based administration tools from any web browser. With SWAT installed and running, you can access your Samba server configuration from your web browser by typing the following URL in the location box:

  ```
  http://localhost:901
  ```

Note
If you get an `Unable to Connect` message, it may be because Samba or SWAT is not running. Or your firewall may be blocking access. ∎

  The Samba project also offers other graphical tools for administering Samba. You can check them out at `http://samba.org/samba/GUI`. For descriptions of these tools, see Chapter 18.

- **CUPS** — The Common UNIX Printing Service (CUPS) has its own web administration tool. With CUPS installed and configured, you can typically use CUPS web administration by typing the following URL in your web browser's location box:

  ```
  http://localhost:631
  ```

  You use the CUPS administration tool to manage printers and classes and do a variety of administration tasks. CUPS is described in Chapter 17.

Samba and CUPS are included with many Linux distributions. Other projects that offer web-based administration that may or may not be in your Linux distribution include SquirrelMail (a Webmail interface) and Mailman (a mailing list facility).

Because many web browser administrative interfaces send data in clear text, they are most appropriate for use on the local system. However, because they are web-based, you can also use these interfaces from your LAN or other network. If you plan to expose these administrative interfaces to an untrusted network, however, you should consider encrypting your communications.

The Webmin Administration Tool

The Webmin facility (www.webmin.com) offers more complete web-based Linux and UNIX administration features. Although Webmin isn't delivered with some Linux systems that offer their own graphical administration tools (such as Fedora and RHEL), the Webmin project has ported Webmin to run on more than 70 different operating systems. Supported Linux distributions include SUSE, Red Hat (Fedora and RHEL), Debian, Ubuntu, Gentoo, Slackware, Mandriva, Yellow Dog, and others (see www.webmin.com/support.html for a complete list).

After you get Webmin from Webmin.com and install it, you can use Webmin from your web browser. To start the Webmin interface, type the following in the web browser's location box:

```
http://localhost:10000
```

After you log in as root user, the main Webmin page displays, as shown in Figure 6-1.

FIGURE 6-1

Webmin offers a web browser interface for administering Linux.

Graphical Administration with Different Distributions

Some people fear that after they've left the familiar confines of their Microsoft Windows system for Linux, they'll be stuck doing everything from a command line. To gain a wider audience, commercial Linux distributions such as Red Hat Enterprise Linux and SUSE have their own sets of graphical tools to provide an easy entry point for new Linux users. The following sections describe the Fedora and Red Hat Enterprise Linux system-config and SUSE's YaST graphical administration tools.

Fedora/RHEL system-config Tools

A set of graphical tools that comes with Fedora and Red Hat Enterprise Linux systems can be launched from the Administration submenu of the System menu or from the command line. Most of the Fedora and RHEL tools that launch from the command line begin with the system-config string (such as system-config-network).

These system-config tools require root permission; if you are logged in as a regular user, you must enter the root password before the GUI application's window opens. Once you have typed the password, look for a yellow badge icon in the upper-right corner of the panel, indicating that you have root authorization. Click the badge to open a pop-up window that enables you to remove authorization. Otherwise, authorization goes away after a few minutes. While the badge is displayed, you can open any administrative GUI application without having to enter the password again.

The following list describes many of the graphical tools you can use to administer a Fedora or Red Hat Enterprise Linux system. Start these windows from the Administration submenu on the System menu. The name of the package that must be installed to get the feature is shown in parentheses:

Note

The availability of the selections described in the following list depends on which features you have installed. ■

- **Add/Remove Software** (PackageKit) — Launch the Add/Remove Software window for finding, adding, and removing software associated with software repositories configured for your system.
- **Server Settings** — Access the following server configuration windows from this submenu:
  - **Domain Name System (system-config-bind)** — Create and configure zones if your computer is acting as a DNS server.
  - **HTTP** (system-config-httpd) — Configure your computer as an Apache web server.
  - **NFS** (system-config-nfs) — Set up directories from your system to be **shared** with other computers on your network using the NFS service.
  - **Samba** (system-config-samba) — Configure Windows (SMB) file sharing. (To configure other Samba features, you can use the SWAT window.)

- **Services** (`system-config-services`) — Display and change which services are running on your Fedora system at different run levels from the Service Configuration window.

- **Authentication** (`authconfig-gtk`) — Change how users are authenticated on your system. Usually, Shadow Passwords and MD5 Passwords are selected. However, if your network supports LDAP, Kerberos, SMB, NIS, or Hesiod authentication, you can select to use any of those authentication types.

- **Bootloader** (`system-config-boot`) — If you have multiple operating systems on your computer, or multiple Linux kernels available to boot in Linux, you can use the Boot Configuration screen to choose which to boot by default. For example, you might have Fedora Linux, SUSE, and Windows XP all on the same hard disk. You could choose which would start automatically (after a set number of seconds), if one wasn't selected explicitly.

- **Date & Time** (`system-config-date`) — Set the date and time or choose to have an NTP server keep system time in sync.

- **Display** (`system-config-display`) — Change the settings for your X desktop, including color depth and resolution for your display. You can also choose settings for your video card and monitor.

- **Firewall and SELinux** (`system-config-firewall`) — Configure your firewall to allow or deny services to computers from the network.

- **Language** (`system-config-language`) — Select the default language used for the system.

- **Logical Volume Management** (`system-config-lvm`) — Manage your LVM partitions.

- **Network** (`system-config-network`) — Manage your current network interfaces and add interfaces.

- **Printing** (`system-config-printer`) — Configure local and network printers.

- **Root Password** (`system-config-rootpassword`) — Change the root password.

- **SELinux Management** (`system-config-selinux`) — Set SELinux enforcing modes and default policy.

- **SELinux Troubleshooter** (`setroubleshoot-server`) — Monitor and diagnose SELinux AVC denials.

- **Users & Groups** (`system-config-users`) — Add, display, and change user and group accounts for your Fedora system.

Other administrative utilities are available from the Applications menu on the top panel. Select the System Tools submenu to see some of the following options:

- **Configuration Editor** (`gconf-editor`) — Directly edit the GNOME configuration database.

- **Disk Usage Analyzer** (gnome-utils) — Display detailed information about your hard disks and removable storage devices.

- **Kickstart** (system-config-kickstart) — Create a kickstart configuration file that can be used to install multiple Fedora systems without user interaction.

Other applications that you add to Fedora or RHEL may also include administrative utilities that will appear in the System Tools submenu.

SUSE YaST Tools

The YaST administrative interface is one of the strongest features of SUSE Linux. From a SUSE desktop, open the YaST Control Center by selecting YaST from the Computer menu. Figure 6-2 shows an example of the YaST Control Center that appears.

FIGURE 6-2

Use the YaST Control Center to administer SUSE systems.

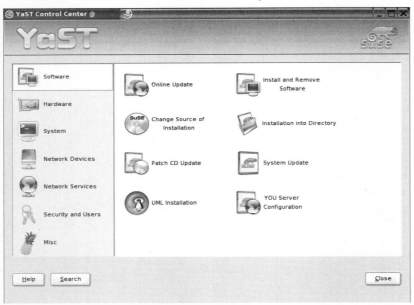

YaST has some useful tools in its Hardware section that enable you to probe your computer hardware. Selecting Hardware Information on my system, for example, enabled me to see that the CD-ROM drive that YaST detected was available through device /dev/cdrom and that it supported CD-R, CD-RW, and DVD media. I could also see detailed information about my CPU, network card, PCI devices, sound card, and various storage media.

YaST also offers interfaces for configuring and starting network devices, as well as a variety of services to run on those devices. In addition, you can use YaST to configure your computer as a client for file sharing (Samba and NFS), mail transfer agent (sendmail), and a variety of network services.

SUSE Linux Enterprise Server comes with a wide range of configuration tools that are specifically geared toward server setup, including tools for configuring a mail server, VPN tunnels, and full Samba 3. Although other distributions may include proprietary tools, YaST is in a class of its own.

Using the root Login

Every Linux system starts out with at least one administrative user account (the root user) and possibly one or more regular user accounts (given a name that you choose, or a name assigned by your Linux distribution). In most cases, you log in as a regular user and become the root user to do an administrative task.

The root user has complete control of the operation of your Linux system. That user can open any file or run any program. The root user also installs software packages and adds accounts for other people who use the system.

Tip
Think of the root user in Linux as similar to the Administrator user in Windows. ■

When you first install most Linux systems (although not all systems), you add a password for the root user. You must remember and protect this password — you will need it to log in as root or to obtain root permission while you are logged in as some other user. Other Linux systems (such as KNOPPIX) start you without an available root password, so you may want to add one when you first start up by typing the following from a Terminal window or other shell:

```
# passwd root
Changing password for user root.
New UNIX password: ********
Retype new UNIX password: ********
```

Note
Some bootable Linux distributions give you (as a regular user) the power to run commands as root. You simply have to ask for the privilege using the sudo command. For example, from a Terminal window, to open a shell as root, type the following:

```
$ sudo -i
#
```

You'll find out more about the sudo command later in this chapter. ■

The home directory for the root user is typically /root. The home directory and other information associated with the root user account are located in the /etc/passwd file. Here's what the root entry looks like in the /etc/passwd file:

```
root:x:0:0:root:/root:/bin/bash
```

This shows that for the user named root the user ID is set to 0 (root user), the group ID is set to 0 (root group), the home directory is /root, and the shell for that user is /bin/bash. (We're using a shadow password file to store encrypted password data, so the password field here contains an x.) You can change the home directory or the shell used by editing the values in this file. A better way to change these values, however, is to use the usermod command (see the "Modifying Users with usermod" section later in this chapter).

Note

By default, the root account is disabled in Ubuntu. This means that even though the account exists, you cannot log in using it or use su to become the root user. This adds an additional level of security to Ubuntu, and requires you to use sudo before each command you want to execute as the root user. ∎

Becoming root from the Shell (su Command)

Although you can become the superuser by logging in as root, sometimes that is not convenient. For example, you may be logged in to a regular user account and just want to make a quick administrative change to your system without having to log out and log back in. Or, you may need to log in over the network to make a change to a Linux system but find that the system doesn't allow root users in from over the network (a common practice in the days before secure shells were available).

The solution is to use the su command. From any Terminal window or shell, you can simply type the following:

```
$ su
Password: ******
#
```

When you are prompted, type in the root user's password. The prompt for the regular user ($) changes to the superuser prompt (#). At this point, you have full permission to run any command and use any file on the system. However, one thing that the su command doesn't do when used this way is read in the root user's environment. As a result, you may type a command that you know is available and get the message Command Not Found. To fix this problem, use the su command with the dash (-) option instead, like this:

```
$ su -
Password: ******
#
```

You still need to type the password, but after that, everything that normally happens at login for the root user happens after the su command is completed. Your current directory will be root's home directory (probably /root), and things such as the root user's PATH variable will be used. If you become the root user by just typing su, rather than su -, you won't change directories or the environment of the current login session.

You can also use the su command to become a user other than root. This is useful for troubleshooting a problem that is being experienced by a particular user, but not by others on the computer (such as an inability to print or send e-mail). For example, to have the permissions of a user named jsmith, you'd type the following:

```
$ su - jsmith
```

Even if you were root user before you typed this command, afterward you would have only the permissions to open files and run programs that are available to jsmith. As root user, however, after you type the su command to become another user, you don't need a password to continue. If you type that command as a regular user, you must type the new user's password.

When you are finished using superuser permissions, return to the previous shell by exiting the current shell. Do this by pressing Ctrl+D or by typing **exit**. If you are the administrator for a computer that is accessible to multiple users, don't leave a root shell open on someone else's screen — unless you want to let that person do anything he wants to the computer!

Allowing Limited Administrative Access

As mentioned earlier, when you run GUI tools as a regular user (from Fedora, SUSE, or some other Linux systems), you are prompted for the root password before you are able to access the tool. By entering the root password, you are given root privilege for that task. In the case of Fedora, after you enter the password, a yellow badge icon appears in the top panel, indicating that root authorization is still available for other GUI tools to run from that desktop session.

Gaining Administrative Access with sudo

A particular user can also be given administrative permissions for particular tasks without being given the root password. For example, a system administrator can add a user to particular groups, such as modem, disk, users, cdrom, ftp, mail, or www, and then open group permission to use those services. Or, an administrator can add a user to the wheel group and add entries to the /etc/ sudoers file to allow that user to use the sudo command to run individual commands as root.

Note
The wheel group does not exist in all distributions. In Ubuntu, for example, wheel is not created automatically. ■

The sudoers facility lets you give full or limited root privileges to any non-root user, which simply entails adding the user to /etc/sudoers and defining what privilege you want that user to have. Then the user can run any command he or she is privileged to use by preceding that command with the sudo command.

Here's an example of how to use the sudo facility to cause any users that are added to the wheel group to have full root privileges.

1. As the root user, edit the /etc/sudoers file by running the visudo command:

```
# /usr/sbin/visudo
```

By default, the file opens in vi, unless your EDITOR variable happens to be set to some other editor acceptable to visudo (for example, export EDITOR=gedit). The reason for using visudo is that the command locks the /etc/sudoers file and does some basic sanity checking of the file to ensure it has been edited correctly.

Note

If you are stuck here, refer to the vi tutorial in Chapter 8 for information on using the vi editor. ∎

2. Uncomment the following line to allow users in the wheel group to have full root privileges on the computer:

```
%wheel      ALL=(ALL)      ALL
```

Tip

If you look at the sudoers file in Ubuntu, you will see that this privilege exists, by default, for the admin group members. ∎

This line causes users in the wheel group to provide a password (their own password, not the root password) in order to use administrative commands. To allow users in the wheel group to have that privilege without using a password, uncomment the following line instead:

```
%wheel      ALL=(ALL)      NOPASSWD: ALL
```

3. Save the changes to the /etc/sudoers file (in vi, type **Esc**, and then **ZZ**).
4. Still as root user, open the /etc/group file using the vigr command and add to the wheel line any users you want to have root privilege. For example, if you were to add the users mary and jake to the wheel group, the line would appear as follows:

```
wheel:x:10:root,mary,jake
```

Now users mary and jake can run the sudo command to run commands, or parts of commands, that are normally restricted to the root user. The following is an example of a session by the user jake after he has been assigned sudo privileges:

```
[jake]$ sudo umount /mnt/win

    We trust you have received the usual lecture
    from the local System Administrator. It usually
    boils down to these two things:

        #1) Respect the privacy of others.
        #2) Think before you type.

Password: *********
 [jake]$ umount /mnt/win
mount: only root can mount /dev/sda1 on /mnt/win
[jake]$ sudo umount /mnt/win
[jake]$
```

In this session, the user jake runs the `sudo` command to unmount the `/mnt/win` file system (using the `umount` command). He is given a warning and asked to provide his password (this is jake's password, *not* the root password).

Even after jake has given the password, he must still use the `sudo` command to run subsequent administrative commands as root (the `umount` fails, but the `sudo umount` succeeds). Notice that he is not prompted for a password for the second `sudo`. That's because after entering his password successfully, he can enter as many `sudo` commands as he wants for the next 5 minutes without having to enter it again. (You can change the timeout value from 5 minutes to however long you want by setting the `passwd_timeout` value in the `/etc/sudoers` file.)

The preceding example grants a simple all-or-nothing administrative privilege to everyone you put in the wheel group. However, the `/etc/sudoers` file gives you an incredible amount of flexibility in permitting individual users and groups to use individual applications or groups of applications. Refer to the `sudoers` and `sudo` man pages for information about how to tune your sudo facility. Refer to the `pam_wheel` man page to see how the PAM facility affects members of the wheel group.

Exploring Administrative Commands, Configuration Files, and Log Files

You can expect to find many commands, configuration files, and log files in the same places in the file system, regardless of which Linux distribution you are using. The following sections give you some pointers on where to look for these important elements.

Coming from Windows

If GUI administrative tools for Linux have become so good, why do you need to know about administrative files? For one thing, while GUI tools differ among Linux versions, many underlying configuration files are the same. So, if you learn to work with them, you can work with almost any Linux system. Also, if a feature is broken or if you need to do something that's not supported by the GUI, when you ask for help, Linux experts almost always tell you how to change the configuration file directly. ■

Administrative Commands

Only the root user is intended to use many administrative commands. When you log in as root (or use `su -` from the shell to become root), your `$PATH` variable is set to include some directories that contain commands for the root user. These include the following:

- `/sbin` — Contains commands needed to boot your system, including commands for checking file systems (`fsck`) and changing system states (`init`).

- `/usr/sbin` — Contains commands for managing user accounts (such as `useradd`) and adding mount points for automounting file systems (`automount`). Commands that run as daemon processes are also contained in this directory. (Look for commands that end in d, such as `sshd`, `pppd`, and `cupsd`.)

Some administrative commands are contained in regular user directories (such as /bin and /usr/bin). This is especially true of commands that have some options available to everyone. An example is the /bin/mount command, which anyone can use to list mounted file systems, but only root can use to mount file systems. (Some desktops, however, are configured to let regular users use mount to mount CDs, DVDs, or other removable media by adding keywords to the /etc/fstab file.)

Note
See the section "Mounting File Systems" later in this chapter for instructions on how to mount a file system. ∎

To find commands intended primarily for the system administrator, check out the Section 8 manual pages (usually in /usr/share/man/man8). They contain descriptions and options for most Linux administrative commands.

Some third-party applications add administrative commands to directories that are not in your PATH. For example, an application may put commands in /usr/local/bin, /opt/bin, or /usr/local/sbin. Some Linux distributions automatically add those directories to your PATH, usually before your standard bin and sbin directories. In that way, commands installed to those directories are not only accessible, but can also override commands of the same name in other directories.

Administrative Configuration Files

Configuration files are another mainstay of Linux administration. Almost everything you set up for your particular computer — user accounts, network addresses, or GUI preferences — is stored in plain-text files. This has some advantages and some disadvantages.

The advantage of plain-text files is that it's easy to read and change them. Any text editor will do. The downside, however, is that as you edit configuration files, no error checking is going on. You have to run the program that reads these files (such as a network daemon or the X desktop) to find out whether you set up the files correctly. There are no standards for the structure of configuration files, so you need to learn the format of each file individually. A comma or a quote in the wrong place can sometimes cause a whole interface to fail.

Note
Some software packages offer a command to test the sanity of the configuration file tied to a package before you start a service. For example, the testparm **command is used with Samba to check the sanity of your** smb.conf **file. Other times, the daemon process providing a service offers an option for checking your config file. For example, run** httpd -t **to check your Apache web server configuration before starting your web server.** ∎

Throughout this book you'll find descriptions of the configuration files you need to set up the different features that make up Linux systems. The two major locations of configuration files are your home directory (where your personal configuration files are kept) and the /etc directory (which holds system-wide configuration files).

Following are descriptions of directories (and subdirectories) that contain useful configuration files. (Refer to Table 6-1 for some individual configuration files in /etc that are of particular interest.) Viewing the contents of Linux configuration files can teach you a lot about administering Linux systems.

- $HOME — All users store information in their home directories that directs how their login accounts behave. Most configuration files in $HOME begin with a dot (.), so they don't appear in a user's directory when you use a standard ls command (you need to type ls -a to see them). Likewise, dot files and directories won't show up in most file manager windows by default. There are dot files that define the behavior of each user's shell, the desktop look and feel, and options used with your text editor. There are even files such as those in each user's $HOME/.ssh directory that configure network permissions for each user. (To see the name of your home directory, type echo $HOME from a shell.)

- /etc — This directory contains most of the basic Linux system-configuration files. Table 6-1 shows some /etc configuration files of interest.

- /etc/cron* — Directories in this set contain files that define how the crond utility runs applications on a daily (cron.daily), hourly (cron.hourly), monthly (cron.monthly), or weekly (cron.weekly) schedule.

- /etc/cups — Contains files used to configure the CUPS printing service.

- /etc/default — Contains files that set default values for various utilities. For example, the file for the useradd command defines the default group number, home directory, password expiration date, shell, and skeleton directory (/etc/skel) that are used when creating a new user account.

- /etc/httpd — Contains a variety of files used to configure the behavior of your Apache web server (specifically, the httpd daemon process). (On some Linux systems, /etc/apache or /etc/apache2 is used instead.)

- /etc/init.d — Contains the permanent copies of System V–style run-level scripts. These scripts are often linked from the /etc/rc?.d directories to have each service associated with a script started or stopped for the particular run level. The ? is replaced by the run-level number (0 through 6). (Slackware puts its run-level scripts in the /etc/rc.d directory.)

- /etc/mail — Contains files used to configure your sendmail mail service.

- /etc/pcmcia — Contains configuration files that allow you to have a variety of PCMCIA cards configured for your computer. (PCMCIA slots are those openings on your laptop that enable you to have credit card–sized cards attached to your computer. You can attach devices such as modems and external CD-ROMs.)

- /etc/postfix — Contains configuration files for the postfix mail transport agent.

- /etc/ppp — Contains several configuration files used to set up Point-to-Point Protocol (PPP) so that you can have your computer dial out to the Internet.

- /etc/rc?.d — There is a separate rc?.d directory for each valid system state: rc0.d (shutdown state), rc1.d (single-user state), rc2.d (multiuser state), rc3.d (multiuser plus networking state), `rc4.d` (user-defined state), `rc5.d` (multiuser, networking, plus GUI login state), and `rc6.d` (reboot state). Some Linux distros, such as Slackware, put most of the startup scripts directly in `/etc/rc.d`, without the run-level notation.

- `/etc/security` — Contains files that set a variety of default security conditions for your computer. These files are part of the pam (pluggable authentication modules) package.

- `/etc/skel` — Any files contained in this directory are automatically copied to a user's home directory when that user is added to the system. By default, most of these files are dot (.) files, such as `.kde` (a directory for setting KDE desktop defaults) and `.bashrc` (for setting default values used with the bash shell).

- `/etc/sysconfig` — Contains important system configuration files that are created and maintained by various services (including `iptables`, `samba`, and most networking services). These files are critical for Linux distributions that use GUI administration tools but are not used on other Linux systems at all.

- `/etc/xinetd.d` — Contains a set of files, each of which defines a network service that the xinetd daemon listens for on a particular port. When the xinetd daemon process receives a request for a service, it uses the information in these files to determine which daemon processes to start to handle the request.

TABLE 6-1

/etc Configuration Files of Interest

File	Description
aliases	Can contain distribution lists used by the Linux mail service. (This file may be located in `/etc/mail`.)
bashrc	Sets system-wide defaults for bash shell users. (This may be called `bash.bashrc` on some Linux distributions.)
crontab	Sets times for running automated tasks and variables associated with the cron facility (such as the SHELL and PATH associated with cron).
csh.cshrc (or cshrc)	Sets system-wide defaults for csh (C shell) users
exports	Contains a list of local directories that are available to be shared by remote computers using the Network File System (NFS)
Fstab	Identifies the devices for common storage media (hard disk, floppy, CD-ROM, and so on) and locations where they are mounted in the Linux system. This is used by the `mount` command to choose which file systems to mount when the system first boots.
Group	Identifies group names and group IDs (GIDs) that are defined on the systems. Group permissions in Linux are defined by the second of three sets of rwx (read, write, execute) bits associated with each file and directory.

File	Description
gshadow	Contains shadow passwords for groups
host.conf	Used by older applications, sets the locations in which domain names (for example, redhat.com) are searched for on TCP/IP networks (such as the Internet). By default, the local hosts file is searched and then any name server entries in resolv.conf.
Hosts	Contains IP addresses and hostnames that you can reach from your computer. (Usually this file is used just to store names of computers on your LAN or small private network.)
hosts.allow	Lists host computers that are allowed to use certain TCP/IP services from the local computer
hosts.deny	Lists host computers that are *not* allowed to use certain TCP/IP services from the local computer (although this file will be used if you create it, it doesn't exist by default)
inittab	Contains information that defines which programs start and stop when Linux boots, shuts down, or goes into different states in between. This is the most basic configuration file for starting Linux.
modules.conf	Contains aliases and options related to loadable kernel modules used by your computer
mtab	Contains a list of file systems that are currently mounted
mtools.conf	Contains settings used by DOS tools in Linux
named.conf	Contains DNS settings if you are running your own DNS server
nsswitch.conf	Contains name service switch settings, for identifying where critical systems information (user accounts, host name-to-address mappings, and so on) comes from (local host or via network services)
ntp.conf	Includes information needed to run the Network Time Protocol (NTP)
passwd	Stores account information for all valid users for the system. Also includes other information, such as the home directory and default shell. (Rarely includes the user passwords themselves, which are typically stored in the /etc/shadow file.)
printcap	Contains definitions for the printers configured for your computer. (If the printcap file doesn't exist, look for printer information in the /etc/cups directory.)
profile	Sets system-wide environment and startup programs for all users. This file is read when the user logs in.
protocols	Sets protocol numbers and names for a variety of Internet services
rpc	Defines remote procedure call names and numbers
services	Defines TCP/IP and UDP services and their port assignments

continued

TABLE 6-1	*(continued)*
File	**Description**
shadow	Contains encrypted passwords for users who are defined in the passwd file. (This is viewed as a more secure way to store passwords than the original encrypted password in the passwd file. The passwd file needs to be publicly readable, whereas the shadow file can be unreadable by all but the root user.)
shells	Lists the shell command-line interpreters (bash, sh, csh, and so on) that are available on the system, as well as their locations
sudoers	Sets commands that can be run by users, who may not otherwise have permission to run the command, using the sudo command. In particular, this file is used to provide selected users with root permission.
syslog.conf	Defines what logging messages are gathered by the syslogd daemon and what files they are stored in. (Typically, log messages are stored in files contained in the /var/log directory.)
termcap	Lists definitions for character terminals, so that character-based applications know what features are supported by a given terminal. Graphical terminals and applications have made this file obsolete to most people. (Termcap was the BSD UNIX way of storing terminal information; UNIX System V used definitions in /usr/share/terminfo files.)
xinetd.conf	Contains simple configuration information used by the xinetd daemon process. This file mostly points to the /etc/xinetd.d directory for information about individual services. (Some systems use the inetd.conf file and the inetd daemon instead.)

Another directory, /etc/X11, includes subdirectories that each contains system-wide configuration files used by X and different X window managers available for Linux. The xorg.conf file (which makes your computer and monitor usable with X) and configuration directories containing files used by xdm and xinit to start X are in here.

Directories relating to window managers contain files that include the default values that a user will get if that user starts one of these window managers on your system. Window managers that may have system-wide configuration files in these directories include Twm (twm/) and Xfce (xdg/).

Note
Some files and directories in /etc/X11 are linked to locations in the /usr/X11R6 directory. ■

Administrative Log Files

One of the things that Linux does well is keep track of itself. This is a good thing, when you consider how much is going on in a complex operating system. Sometimes you are trying to get a new facility to work and it fails without giving you the foggiest reason why. Other times you want to monitor your system to see whether people are trying to access your computer illegally. In any of those cases, you can use log files to help track down the problem.

The main utilities for logging error and debugging messages for Linux are the syslogd and klogd daemons. (In some systems, rsyslogd and ksyslogd are replacing those daemons.)

General system logging is done by syslogd. Logging that is specific to kernel activity is done by klogd. Logging is done according to information in the /etc/syslog.conf file. Messages are typically directed to log files that are usually in the /var/log directory. Here are a few common log files:

- boot.log — Contains boot messages about services as they start up.
- messages — Contains many general informational messages about the system.
- secure — Contains security-related messages, such as login activity.
- XFree86.0.log or Xorg.0.log — Depending on which X server you are using, contains messages about your video card, mouse, and monitor configuration.

If you are using a Fedora or Ubuntu system, the System Log Viewer utility is a good way to step through your system's log files. From the Applications menu, select System ➪ Administration ➪ Log File Viewer. You not only can view boot, kernel, mail, security, and other system logs, but you can also use the viewing pane to select log messages from a particular date.

Using Other Administrative Logins

You don't hear much about other administrative logins (besides root) being used with Linux. It was a fairly common practice in UNIX systems to have several different administrative logins that allowed administrative tasks to be split among several users. For example, people sitting near a printer could have lp permissions to move print jobs to another printer if they knew a printer wasn't working.

In any case, administrative logins are available with Linux; however, logging in directly as those users is disabled by default. The accounts are maintained primarily to provide ownership for files and processes associated with particular services. Here are some examples:

- **lp** — This user account owns such things as the /var/log/cups printing log file and various printing cache and spool files. The home directory for lp is /var/spool/lpd.
- **uucp** — User owns various uucp commands (once used as the primary method for dial-up serial communications) as well as log files in /var/log/uucp, spool files in /var/spool, administrative commands (such as uuchk, uucico, uuconv, and uuxqt) in /usr/sbin, and user commands (uucp, cu, uuname, uustat, and uux) in /usr/bin. The home directory for uucp is /var/spool/uucp.

- **bin** — User owns many commands in /bin in traditional UNIX systems. This is not the case in some Linux systems (such as Fedora and Gentoo) because root owns most executable files. The home directory of bin is /bin.

- **news** — User could do administration of Internet news services, depending on how you set permission for /var/spool/news and other news-related resources. The home directory for news is /etc/news.

By default, the administrative logins in the preceding list are disabled. You would need to change the default shell from its current setting (usually /sbin/nologin or /bin/false) to a real shell (typically /bin/bash) to be able to log in as these users.

Summary

Getting started with system administration in Linux means understanding the concept of root user (or superuser). By logging in as the root user, or becoming root with the su or sudo command, you can control nearly every aspect of your Linux system.

As the superuser, you have a wide range of features available to you for administering your Linux system. This chapter described both graphical and command-line tools needed to administer Linux.

Other chapters in this part explore selected topics of system administration in depth. Administrative topics include installation, administering systems from the shell, adding user accounts, managing disks, setting up networking, and securing your systems.

Installing Linux

## 7

If someone hasn't already installed and configured a Linux system for you, this chapter is going to help you get started so you can try out the Linux features described in the rest of the book. With live CDs and improved installers, several of which are included with this book, getting your hands on a working Linux system is quicker and more solid than ever before.

If you are a first-time Linux user, I recommend that you

IN THIS CHAPTER

Choosing a Linux distribution

Getting a Linux distribution

Understanding installation issues

- **Try a bootable Linux** — This book's DVD includes several bootable Linux systems. The advantage of a bootable Linux is that you can try out Linux without touching the contents of your computer's hard drive. In particular, KNOPPIX is a full-featured Linux system that can give you a good feel for how Linux works. Using the DVD, you can try out several different live CDs, as described in Appendix A. Some of these live CDs also include features for installing Linux to your hard disk. Although live CDs tend to run slower than installed systems and often aren't set up to keep your changes after you reboot, they are good tools for starting out with Linux.

- **Install a desktop Linux system** — Choose one of the Linux distributions and install it on your computer's hard disk. Permanently installing Linux to your hard disk gives you more flexibility for adding and removing software, accessing and saving data to hard disk, and more permanently customizing your system. Installing Linux as a desktop system lets you try out some useful applications and get the feel for Linux before dealing with more complex server issues.

This chapter provides you with an overview of how to choose a Linux distribution, and then describes issues and topics that are common to installing most Linux distributions. Appendix A describes which Linux distributions are included on this book's DVD and how to run them live or use them to install Linux permanently. Each of the other chapters in this part of the book is dedicated to understanding and installing a particular Linux distribution.

After you've installed Linux, you'll want to understand how to get and manage software for your Linux system. These important topics are covered throughout the book, but this chapter describes the major packaging formats and tools to get you going.

Choosing a Linux Distribution

Dozens of popular Linux distributions are available today. Some are generalized distributions that you can use as a desktop, server, or workstation system; others are specialized for business or computer enthusiasts. One intention of this book is to help you choose which one (or ones) will suit you best.

Using the DVD that comes with this book, you can boot directly to KNOPPIX (or several other live CDs to try out Linux) or run an installer (to install one of several Linux distributions to your computer's hard disk). After you've tried out KNOPPIX and are ready to install Linux on your hard disk, I recommend you try Fedora or Ubuntu.

Because I know a lot of people who use Linux, both informally and at work, I want to share my general impressions of how different Linux distributions are being used in the United States. Many consultants I know who set up small office servers used to use Red Hat Linux. Some have continued to use Red Hat Enterprise Linux (RHEL), whereas others have moved to Fedora, CentOS (built from RHEL source code), Ubuntu, or Debian GNU/Linux.

Mandriva Linux (formerly Mandrake Linux) has been popular with people wanting a friendly Linux desktop, but Ubuntu and Fedora are also well liked. The more technically inclined like to play with Gentoo (highly tunable) or Slackware (Linux in a more basic form).

The agreement between Novell and Microsoft prompted some open source proponents to abandon SUSE. Whether this will result in a migration from SUSE in the enterprise space, however, has yet to play out. However, right now, Red Hat Enterprise Linux offers the best choice in the enterprise realm for those who object to the alliance.

As for the bootable Linuxes, everyone I know thinks they are great fun to try out and a good way to learn about Linux. For a bootable Linux containing desktop software that fits on a full CD (or DVD), KNOPPIX is a good choice, as is Ubuntu; for a bootable mini CD–size Linux, Damn Small Linux works well. However, you can also try out these live CDs from the media that comes with this book: INSERT, Puppy Linux, SystemRescueCD, or BackTrack.

Other notable Linux distributions include Sabayan, Arch Linux, and CentOS. Sabayon is a Gentoo-based desktop Linux system that contains multiple desktop interfaces (GNOME, KDE, Fluxbox, LXDE, and others). Arch Linux uses a simple, minimalist approach to its software packages. It features a "rolling release" system, which allows users to continuously update packages without full upgrades.

CentOS has become very popular among consultants who used to use Red Hat Linux. CentOS is a rebuild of the Red Hat Enterprise Linux source code. So, people use it for servers that require longer update cycles than you would get with Fedora. However, because CentOS and Red Hat Enterprise Linux are built from technology developed for Fedora, you can learn a lot about how to use those two distributions by using Fedora. The following sections explain how to look beyond the confines of this book for those and other Linux distributions.

This book exposes you to several different Linux distributions. It gives you the advantage of being able to see the strengths and weaknesses of each distribution by actually putting your hands on it. You can also try to connect to the growing Linux user communities because strong community support results a more solid software distribution and help when you need it (from such things as forums and online chats).

Getting Your Own Linux Distribution

By packaging a handful of Linux distributions with this book, I hope to save you the trouble of getting Linux yourself. If you have a DVD drive, perhaps you can use this opportunity to at least try KNOPPIX, so you'll better understand what's being discussed. If you have a CD drive only, you need to obtain a Linux distribution elsewhere.

If for some reason you can't use the software on the DVD, you may want to get your own Linux distributions to use with the descriptions in this book. Reasons you might want to get your own Linux distributions include

- **No DVD drive** — You need a bootable DVD drive on your computer to use the Linux distributions that come with this book.
- **Later distributions** — You may want a particular distribution that is more recent than the one that comes with this book.
- **Complete distributions** — Because there's limited space on the DVD and because some distributions require subscriptions or other fees, you may want to obtain your own, more complete distribution with which to work. However, keep in mind that in most cases, you can do a base system install, and then add software by downloading it from the Internet.

Today, there is no shortage of ways to get Linux.

Finding Another Linux Distribution

You can go to the Web site of each distribution (such as `http://fedoraproject.org/get-fedora` or `http://slackware.com/getslack`) to get Linux software. Those sites often let you download a complete copy of their distributions and give you the opportunity to purchase a boxed set.

However, one way to get a more complete view of available Linux distributions is to go to a Web site dedicated to spreading information about Linux distributions. Use these sites to connect to forums and download documentation about many Linux distributions. Here are some examples:

- **DistroWatch** (www.distrowatch.com) — The first place I go to find Linux distributions is DistroWatch.com. Go to the Major Distributions link to read about the top Linux distributions (most of which are included with this book). Links will take you to download sites, forums, home pages, and other sites related to each distribution.

- **Linux.com Download Directory** (www.linux.com/directory/Distributions) — Select Linux distributions from among several categories (desktop, enterprise, live CD, and so on). Descriptions, documentation, and download links are available for each distribution listed.

If you don't want to download and burn the CDs yourself, there are plenty of links on those sites from places willing to sell you Linux CDs or DVDs. Distribution prices are often only a little bit higher than the cost of the media and shipping. If you really like a particular Linux distribution, then purchasing it directly from the organization that makes it is a good idea. Doing so can ensure the health of the distribution into the future.

Books that come with software included can also be a good way to get a Linux distribution. Finding up-to-date documentation can be difficult when you have nothing but a CD to start out with. Standard Linux documentation (such as HOWTOs and man pages) is often out of date with the software. So, I would particularly recommend a book and distribution (such as this one or *Fedora Bible* from Wiley Publishing) for first-time Linux users.

Understanding What You Need

The most common media used to install Linux are CDs and DVDs that contain everything you need to complete the install. Another way to start a Linux installation is with a CD that includes an installation boot image, and then you can get the parts of Linux you need live from the network as you install Linux.

The images that are burned onto the CDs are typically stored in software repositories that are freely accessible on the Internet. You can download the images and burn them to CDs yourself. Alternatively, the software packages are usually also included separately in directories. Those separate software directories enable you to start an install process with a minimal boot disc that can grab packages over the network during the installation process. (Some of the installations I recommend with this book are done that way.)

When you follow links to Linux software repositories, here's what you look for:

- **Download directory** — You often have to step down a few directories from the download link that gets you to a repository. Look for subdirectories that describe the distribution, architecture, release, and medium format. For example, mirrors for the Fedora 14 Linux distribution might be named fedora/releases/14/Fedora/i386/iso. Other Linux distributions, such as Gentoo and Debian, have tools that will search out online repositories for you, so you don't have to find a mirror directory on your own.

(As an alternative, you can grab the Linux live CD or install images via BitTorrent, as described later in this chapter.)

- **ISO images** — The software images you are going to burn to CD are typically stored in ISO format. Some repositories include a README file to tell you what images you need (others just assume you know). To install a distribution, you want the set of ISOs containing the Linux distribution's binary files or a single live CD ISO.

Note

Although an ISO image appears as one file, it's actually like a snapshot of a file system. You can mount that image to see all the files the image contains by using the loop feature of the mount command. For example, with an image called abc.iso in the current directory, create an empty directory (mkdir myiso) and, as root, run the mount command: mount -o loop abc.iso myiso. Change to the myiso directory and you can view the files and directories the ISO image contains. When you are done viewing the contents, leave the directory and unmount the ISO image (cd .. ; umount myiso). ∎

- **MD5SUM** — To verify that you got the right CDs completely intact, after you download them look for a file named MD5SUM or ending in .md5 in the ISO directory. The file contains one or more MD5 (128-bit) checksums, representing the ISO files you want to check. Other distributions publish SHA1 checksums, which does 160-bit checksums. You can use that file to verify the content of each CD.

Downloading the Distribution

You can download each ISO image by simply clicking the link and downloading it to a directory in your computer when prompted. You can do this on a Windows or Linux system.

If you know the location of the image you want, with a running Linux system, the wget command is a better way to download than just clicking a link in your browser. The advantage of using wget is that you can restart a download that stops in the middle for some reason. A wget command to download a KNOPPIX CD image (starting from the directory you want to download to) might look like this:

```
$ wget -c kernel.org/pub/dist/knoppix/KNOPPIX_V6.0.1CD-2009-02-08-EN.iso
```

If the download stops before it is completed, run the command again. The -c option tells wget to begin where the download left off, so that if you are 690MB into a 696MB download when it stops, it just adds in the last 6MB.

A more "good citizen" approach to downloading your ISO images is to use a facility called BitTorrent (http://bittorrent.com). BitTorrent enables you to download a file to your computer by grabbing bits of that file from multiple computers on the network that are downloading the file at the same time. For the privilege, you also use your upload capacity to share the same file with others as you are downloading.

During times of heavy demand with a new Linux distribution, BitTorrent can be the best way to go. Some have portrayed BitTorrent as a tool for illegal activities, such as downloading copyrighted materials (movies, music, and so on). Because most Linux distributions contain only software covered under various open source licenses, there is no legal problem with using BitTorrent to distribute Linux distributions. Check out `http://linuxtracker.org` for a list of Linux distributions that you can download with BitTorrent.

If you are on a dial-up modem, you should seriously consider purchasing Linux CDs (or getting them from a friend) if you don't find what you want on the DVD with this book. You might be able to download an entire 700MB CD in under an hour on a fast DSL or cable modem connection. On a dial-up line, you might need an entire day or more per CD. For a large, multi-CD distribution, available disk space can also become a problem (although, with today's large hard disks, it's not as much of a problem as it used to be).

Burning the Distribution to CD

With the CD images copied to your computer, you can proceed to verify their contents and burn them to CD. All you really need is a CD burner on your computer.

With Linux running, you can use the `md5sum` or `sha1sum` commands to verify each CD.

Note

If you are using Windows to validate the contents of the Linux CD, you can get the MD5summer utility (`www.md5summer.org`) to verify each CD image. ∎

Assuming you downloaded the MD5 file associated with each CD image, and have it in the same directory as your CD images, run the `md5sum` command to verify the image. For example, to verify the KNOPPIX CD shown previously in the `wget` example, you can type the following:

```
$ md5sum KNOPPIX_V6.0.1CD-2009-02-08-EN.iso
d642d524dd2187834a418710001bbf82 KNOPPIX_V5.1.1CD-2007-01-04-EN.iso
```

The MD5SUM file I downloaded previously from the download directory was called `KNOPPIX_V6.0.1CD-2009-02-08-EN.iso`. It contained this content:

```
d642d524dd2187834a418710001bbf82  *KNOPPIX_V6.0.1CD-2009-02-08-EN.iso
```

As you can see, the checksum (first string of characters shown) that is output from the ISO image matches the checksum in the MD5 file, so you know that the image you downloaded is the image they put on the server. If the project uses sha1sum to verify its ISO images, you can test your downloaded images with the `sha1sum` command, as follows:

```
$ sha1sum FC-6-i386-DVD.iso
6722f95b97e5118fa26bafa5b9f622cc7d49530c FC-6-i386-DVD.iso
```

After you have verified the sha1sum or md5sum of the CD or DVD, as long as you got the image from a reliable site, you should be ready to burn the CD or DVD.

With your Linux distribution in hand (either the book's DVD or the set of CDs you got elsewhere), use commands such as `cdrecord` or `k3b` to burn your CD or DVD images to disk. You can find instructions for installing the distributions from the DVD in individual chapters devoted to each distribution (Chapters 19–24). Before you proceed, however, some information is useful for nearly every Linux system you are installing.

Exploring Common Installation Topics

Before you begin installing your Linux distribution of choice, you should understand some general Linux information. Reading over this information might help you avoid problems or keep you from getting stuck when you install Linux.

Knowing Your Computer Hardware

Every Linux distribution will not run on every computer. When installing Linux, most people use a Pentium-class PC. Linux systems exist that are compiled to run on other hardware, such as PowerPCs or 64-bit computers. However, the distributions provided with this book run on 32-bit Pentium-class PCs. Note that because new Mac computers are built from standard Intel components, installing Linux on those computers is possible as well (see the "Installing Linux on Intel Macs" sidebar).

Installing Linux on Intel Macs

Because of the popularity of MacBook and Mac mini computers, which are based on Intel architecture, several Linux projects have produced procedures for installing their systems to dual-boot with Mac OS X. Most of these procedures involve using the Apple BootCamp software (www.apple.com/support/bootcamp).

To install the Fedora Linux that comes with this book, refer to http://mactel-linux.source-forge.net/wiki/Main_Page or the Fedora on Mactel page (http://fedoraproject.org/wiki/FedoraOnMactel). For Ubuntu, refer to the Ubuntu MacBook page (https://help.ubuntu.com/community/MacBook). Another site to check out is http://refit.sourceforge.net.

Minimum hardware requirements from the Fedora Project are pretty good guidelines for most Linux systems:

- **Processor** — The latest version of Fedora recommends that you have at least a Pentium-class processor. For a text-only installation, a 200 MHz Pentium is the minimum, whereas a 400 MHz Pentium II is the minimum for a GUI installation.

Note

If you have a 486 machine (at least 100 MHz), consider trying Damn Small Linux or Slackware. The problem is that many machines that old have only floppy disks, so you can't use the CD or DVD that comes with this book. ∎

- **RAM** — You should have at least 64MB of RAM to install the smallest Linux distribution and run it in text mode. Slackware might run on 8MB of RAM, but 16MB is considered the minimum. If you are running in graphical mode, you will probably need at least 256MB. The recommended RAM for graphical mode in Fedora is 512MB. A GNOME environment generally requires a bit less memory to run than a KDE environment. If you are using a more streamlined graphical system (that runs X with a small window manager, such as Blackbox), you might get by with as little as 128MB. In that case, you might try Damn Small Linux or Slackware.

- **DVD or CD drive** — You need to be able to boot up the installation process from a DVD, CD, or USB drive. If you can't boot from a DVD or CD, there are ways to start the installation from a hard disk or USB drive or by using a PXE install. Some distributions, such as Slackware, let you use floppy disks to boot installation. After the install is booted, the software can sometimes be retrieved from different locations (over the network or from hard disk, for example).

- **Network card** — If you are doing an install of one of the distributions for which we provide a scaled-down boot disk, you might need to have an Ethernet card installed to get the software you need over the network. A dial-up connection won't work for network installs. You don't necessarily have to be connected to the Internet to do a network install. Some people download the necessary software packages to a computer on their LAN, and then use that as an install server.

- **Disk space** — You should have at least 3GB of disk space for an average desktop installation, although installations can range (depending on which packages you choose to install) from 600MB (for a minimal server with no GUI install) to 7GB (to install all packages). You can install the Damn Small Linux live CD to disk with only about 200MB of disk space.

If you're not sure about your computer hardware, there are a few ways to check what you have. If you are running Windows, the System Properties window can show you the processor you have, as well as the amount of RAM that's installed. As an alternative, you can boot KNOPPIX and let it detect and report to you the hardware you have.

Upgrading or Installing from Scratch

If you already have a version of the Linux you are installing on your computer, many Linux distributions offer an upgrade option. This lets you upgrade all packages, for example, from version 1 of the distribution to version 2. Here are a few general rules before performing an upgrade:

- **Remove extra packages** — If you have software packages you don't need, remove them before you do an upgrade. Upgrade processes typically upgrade only those packages that are on your system. Upgrades generally do more checking and comparing than clean installs do, so any package you can remove saves time during the upgrade process.

- **Check configuration files** — A Linux upgrade procedure often leaves copies of old configuration files. You should check that the new configuration files still work for you.

Tip
Installing Linux from scratch goes faster than an upgrade. It also results in a cleaner Linux system. So if you have the choice of backing up your data, or just erasing it if you don't need it, a fresh install is usually best. ■

Some Linux distributions, most notably Gentoo, have taken the approach of ongoing updates. Instead of taking a new release every few months, you simply continuously grab updated packages as they become available and install them on your system.

Dual Booting

Having multiple, bootable operating systems on the same computer is possible. You can do this using multiple partitions on a hard disk and/or multiple hard disks, then setting up to boot more than one operating system.

Caution

Although tools for resizing Windows partitions and setting up multiboot systems have improved in recent years, there is still some risk of losing data on Windows/Linux dual-boot systems. Different operating systems often have different views of partition tables and master boot records that can cause your machine to become unbootable (at least temporarily) or lose data permanently. Always back up your data before you try to resize a Windows (NTFS or FAT) file system to make space for Linux. ■

If the computer you are using already has a Windows system on it, quite possibly the entire hard disk is devoted to Windows. Although you can run a bootable Linux, such as KNOPPIX or Damn Small Linux, without touching the hard disk, to do a more permanent installation you'll want to find disk space outside of the Windows installation. There are a few ways to do this:

- **Add a hard disk** — Instead of messing with your Windows partition, you can simply add a hard disk and devote it to Linux.

- **Resize your Windows partition** — If you have available space on your Windows partition, you can shrink that partition so free space is available on the disk to devote to Linux. Commercial tools such as Partition Magic from Symantec (www.symantec.com) or Acronis Disk Director (www.acronis.com) are available to resize your disk partitions and set up a workable boot manager. Some Linux distributions (particularly bootable Linuxes used as rescue CDs) include a tool called Gparted that is an open source clone of Partition Magic (which includes software from the Linux-NTFS project for resizing Windows NTFS partitions).

Note

Type `yum install gparted` (in Fedora) or `apt-get install gparted` (in Ubuntu) to install GParted. Run `gparted` as root to start it. ■

Before you try to resize your Windows partition, you might need to defragment it. To defragment your disk on some Windows systems, so that all of your used space is put in order on the disk, open My Computer, right-click your hard disk icon (typically C:), select Properties, click Tools, and select Defragment Now.

Defragmenting your disk can be a fairly long process. The result of defragmentation is that all the data on your disk are contiguous, creating a lot of contiguous free space at the end of the partition. There are cases where you will have to do the following special tasks to make this true:

- If the Windows swap file is not moved during defragmentation, you must remove it. Then, after you defragment your disk again and resize it, you will need to restore the swap file. To remove the swap file, open the control panel, open the System icon, and then click the Performance tab and select Virtual Memory. To disable the swap file, click Disable Virtual Memory.

- If your DOS partition has hidden files that are on the space you are trying to free up, you need to find them. In some cases, you won't be able to delete them. In other cases, such as swap files created by a program, you can safely delete those files. This is a bit tricky because some files should not be deleted, such as DOS system files. You can use the attrib -s -h command from the root directory to deal with hidden files.

After your disk is defragmented, you can use the commercial tools described earlier (Partition Magic or Acronis Disk Director) to repartition your hard disk to make space for Linux. Or use the open source alternative GParted.

After you have cleared enough disk space to install Linux (see the disk space requirements in the chapter covering the Linux distribution you're installing), you can choose your Linux distribution and install it. As you set up your boot loader during installation, you will be able to identify the Windows, Linux, and any other bootable partitions so that you can select which one to boot when you start your computer.

Installing Linux to Run Virtually

Using virtualization technology such as VMware, VirtualBox, Xen, or KVM, you can configure your computer to run multiple operating systems simultaneously. Typically, you have a host operating system running (such as your Linux or Windows desktop), and then configure guest operating systems to run within that environment.

If you have a Windows system, you can use commercial VMware products to run Linux on your Windows desktop. Get a trial of VMware Workstation (www.vmware.com/tryvmware) to see if you like it. Then run your installed virtual guests with the free VMware Player. With a full-blown version of VMware Workstation, you can run multiple distributions at the same time.

Open source virtualization products that are available with Linux systems include VirtualBox (www.virtualbox.org), Xen (www.xen.org), and KVM (www.linux-kvm.org). VirtualBox was developed originally by Sun Microsystems. Xen has been popular with Red Hat systems, but Red Hat has recently begun moving toward KVM technology instead.

Using Installation Boot Options

Sometimes a Linux installation fails because the computer has some non-functioning or non-supported hardware. Sometimes you can get around those issues by passing options to the install process when it boots up. Those options can do such things as disable selected hardware (nousb, noscsi, noide, and so on) or not probe hardware when you need to select your own driver (noprobe).

Although some of these options are distribution-specific, others are simply options that can be passed to an installer environment that works from a Linux kernel.

Partitioning Hard Drives

The hard disk (or disks) on your computer provides the permanent storage area for your data files, applications programs, and the operating system itself. Partitioning is the act of dividing a disk into logical areas that can be worked with separately. In Windows, you typically have one partition that consumes the whole hard disk. However, with Linux there are several reasons why you may want to have multiple partitions:

- **Multiple operating systems** — If you install Linux on a PC that already has a Windows operating system, you may want to keep both operating systems on the computer. For all practical purposes, each operating system must exist on a completely separate partition. When your computer boots, you can choose which system to run.

- **Multiple partitions within an operating system** — To protect from having your entire operating system run out of disk space, people often assign separate partitions to different areas of the Linux file system. For example, if /home and /var were assigned to separate partitions, then a gluttonous user who fills up the /home partition wouldn't prevent logging daemons from continuing to write to log files in the /var/log directory.

  Multiple partitions also make doing certain kinds of backups (such as an image backup) easier. For example, an image backup of /home would be much faster (and probably more useful) than an image backup of the root file system (/).

- **Different file system types** — Different kinds of file systems have different structures. File systems of different types must be on their own partitions. Also, you might need different file systems to have different mount options for special features (such as read-only or user quotas). In most Linux systems, you need at least one file system type for the root of the file system (/) and one for your swap area. File systems on CD-ROM use the iso9660 file system type.

Tip

When you create partitions for Linux, you will usually assign the file system type as Linux native (using the ext2, ext3, or ext4 type on some Linux systems, and reiserfs on others). Reasons to use other types include needing a file system that allows particularly long filenames, large file sizes, or many inodes (each file consumes an inode).

For example, if you set up a news server, it can use many inodes to store news articles. Another reason for using a different file system type is to copy an image backup tape from another operating system to your local disk (such as one from an OS/2 or Minix operating system). ■

Coming from Windows

If you have used only Windows operating systems before, you probably had your whole hard disk assigned to C: and never thought about partitions. With many Linux systems, you have the opportunity to view and change the default partitioning based on how you want to use the system. ■

During installation, systems such as openSUSE and Fedora let you partition your hard disk using graphical partitioning tools. The following sections describe how to partition your disk during a Fedora installation or use fdisk to partition your disk. See the section "Tips for Creating Partitions" for some ideas.

Understanding Different Partition Types

Many Linux distributions give you the option of selecting different partition types when you partition your hard disk during installation. Partition types include:

- **Linux partitions** — Select this option to create a partition for an ext2, ext3, or ext4 file system type that is added directly to a partition on your hard disk (or other storage medium).

- **LVM partitions** — Create an LVM partition if you plan to create or add to an LVM volume group. LVMs give you more flexibility in growing, shrinking, and moving partitions later than regular partitions do.

- **RAID partitions** — Create two or more RAID partitions to create a RAID array. These partitions should be on separate disks to create an effective RAID array. RAID arrays can help improve performance, reliability, or both as those features relate to reading, writing, and storing your data.

- **Swap partitions** — Create a swap partition to extend the amount of virtual memory available on your system.

The following sections describe how to add regular Linux partitions, LVM, RAID, and swap partitions, using the Fedora graphical installer as an example.

Partitioning During Fedora Installation

During installation, Fedora gives you the opportunity to change how your hard disk is partitioned. If you select to do a custom layout (or review and modify the current partitioning), you have the opportunity to customize your disk partitioning. From the hard drives that appear on the installer screen, either select Free (to create a new partition using available disk space) or delete one or more partitions, and then select Free to reuse that space.

The following sections describe how to create different partition types:

Linux or Swap Partitions

Creating a standard Linux partition enables you to create the partition and apply the file system directly to it. Select Create ⇨ Standard Partition and click the Create button. Figure 7-1 shows an example of the screen that appears. Choose the mount point for the partition (such as / or /boot), the file system type (ext4 is the default), and the size (in MB). The partition can be a fixed size or simply fill up all available space.

To create a swap partition, you can follow the steps used to create a Linux partition. However, instead of selecting a file system type (ext3, ext4, and so on) you choose swap as the file system type. No mount point is needed.

FIGURE 7-1

Partition a regular Linux partition in Fedora.

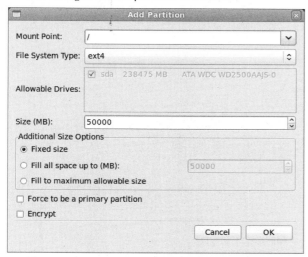

LVM Partitions

Logical Volume Manager (LVM) enables you to add a layer of abstraction and group disk space together that can be assigned to one or more logical volumes. Once logical volumes are created, you can add file systems to those volumes and mount them as you would regular Linux partitions. However, if you run out of space, you have much more flexibility when it comes to managing those partitions.

The steps outlined below detail how to create an LVM partition (referred to as an LVM physical volume), apply one or more LVM partitions to an LVM volume group, and then create logical volumes from that volume group:

1. Select Create ⇨ LVM Physical Volume and click the Create button. An Add Partition window appears.

2. Leave the File System type as "physical volume (LVM)" and choose how much space to devote to it. Some people apply all remaining space on their disk to the LVM partition, after creating any non-LVM partitions they want (such as a separate /boot partition and possibly a swap partition). Click OK to continue.

3. With one or more LVM physical volumes created, click Create, select LVM Volume Group, and click Create again. A "Make LVM Volume Group" window appears.

4. Select a volume group name (your hostname preceded by vg_ is used by default) and physical extent size (this is the smallest unit of space that can be added to or removed from a logical volume), and choose which partition to add to the group (use the LVM physical volume you created in a previous step).

5. Select Add and the Make Logical Volume window appears. This is where you create the actual logical volumes on which each file system will reside. Figure 7-2 shows the screens for creating the volume group and a logical volume. In most cases, you won't use all the space available, so you can grow your partitions later, as needed. In this example, the logical volume name is myhome, the group is vg_mygroup, and the resulting device representing the logical volume is /dev/mapper/vg_mygroup-myhome. If the file system type and size are correct, select OK to create the logical volume.

FIGURE 7-2

Create an LVM volume group and logical volume from an LVM physical volume.

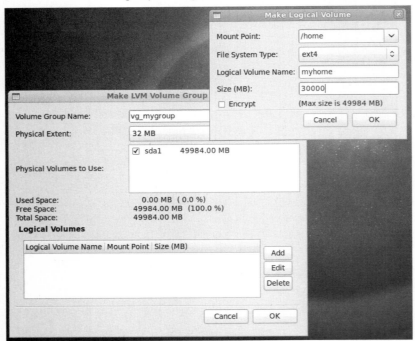

6. If space is still available from the volume group, you can create more logical volumes from that group by repeating the same steps. Click OK to return to the partitioning screen.

RAID Partitions

A RAID array lets you use multiple disks so that you can have multiple copies of your data or write data across multiple disks (to improve performance) or both. Execute the following steps to create the RAID partitions you need to create a RAID array:

1. Select Create ⇨ RAID Partition, and click Create. The Add Partition window appears.

2. Assuming you have multiple disks available, which you should to make a proper RAID array, choose the first disk, indicate the size of the RAID partition, and select OK.

3. Repeat Steps 1 and 2 for each disk to create each partition needed in the array. (The array size will be based on the smallest of the partitions you create, so generally you want them to be the same size.)

4. Select Create again, but this time select RAID Device and click Create. The Make Raid Device window appears, similar to the one shown in Figure 7-3.

FIGURE 7-3

Create a RAID device.

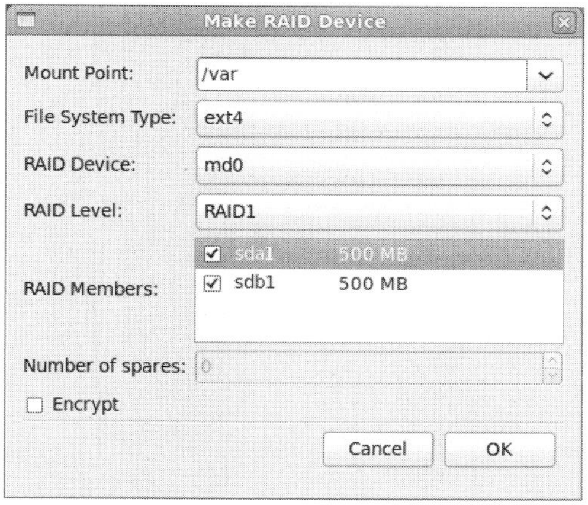

5. Select the mount point, file system type, and RAID device (typically md0 for the first RAID device). Then check the partitions to use as RAID Members, and select OK. The new raid array appears under the RAID Devices heading.

When you are finished partitioning your disk, select Next to save your partitioning and continue on through installation.

Reasons for Partitioning

Different opinions exist as to how to divide up a hard disk. Here are some issues to consider:

- **Do you want to install another operating system?** If you want Windows on your computer along with Linux, you need at least one Windows (Win95 FAT16, VFAT, or NTFS type), one Linux (Linux ext3), and one Linux swap partition.

- **Is it a multiuser system?** If you are using the system yourself, you probably don't need many partitions. One reason for partitioning an operating system is to keep the entire system from running out of disk space at once. That also serves to put boundaries on what an individual can use up in his or her home directory (although disk quotas are good for that as well).

- **Do you have multiple hard disks?** You need at least one partition per hard disk. If your system has two hard disks, you may assign one to / and one to /home (if you have lots of users) or /var (if the computer is a server sharing lots of data). With a separate / home partition, you can install another Linux system in the future without disturbing your home directories (and presumably all or most of your user data).

Partitioning with fdisk

The fdisk utility is available with almost every Linux system for creating and working with disk partitions in Linux. It does the same job as graphical partitioning tools, but runs in the shell.

Tip

During some Linux installation procedures that have virtual terminals running, you can switch to a shell (press Ctrl+Alt+F2) and use fdisk manually to partition your hard disk. ■

The following procedures are performed from the command line as root user.

Caution

Remember that any partition commands can easily make your disk inaccessible. Back up critical data before using any tool to change partitions! Then be very careful about the changes you do make. Keeping an emergency boot disk handy is a good idea, too. ■

The fdisk command is available on many different operating systems (although it looks and behaves differently on each). In Linux, fdisk is a text-based command. To use fdisk to list all your partitions, type the following (as root user):

```
# fdisk -1
Disk /dev/sda: 40.0 GB, 40020664320 bytes
255 heads, 63 sectors/track, 4865 cylinders
Units = cylinders of 16065 * 512 = 8225280 bytes

   Device Boot    Start      End    Blocks   Id  System
/dev/sda1    *        1       13    104391   83  Linux
/dev/sda2            14     4833  38716650   83  Linux
/dev/sda3          4834     4865    257040   82  Linux swap
```

To see how each partition is being used on your current system, type the following:

```
# df -h
Filesystem          Size  Used Avail Use% Mounted on
/dev/sda2            37G  5.4G   30G  16% /
/dev/sda1            99M  8.6M   86M  10% /boot
```

From the output of df, you can see that the root of your Linux system (/) is on the /dev/sda2 partition and that the /dev/sda1 partition is used for /boot.

Caution

Before using fdisk to change your partitions, I strongly recommend running the df -h command to see how your partitions are currently being defined. This helps reduce the risk of changing or deleting the wrong partition. ■

To use fdisk to change your partitions, you need to identify the hard disk you are partitioning. For example, the first SATA or SCSI hard disk is identified as /dev/sda. So, to partition your first hard drive, you can begin (as root user) by typing:

```
# fdisk /dev/sda
```

For different hard drive types or numbers, /dev/sda is replaced by the name of the device you want to work with. Table 7-1 shows some of your choices.

TABLE 7-1

Disk Device Names

Device	Description
/dev/sda	For the first SATA or SCSI hard disk; sdb, sdc, and so on for other disks.
/dev/hda	For the first IDE drive. (Some newer distributions use /dev/sda for IDE drives instead of /dev/hda.)
/dev/xvda	For the first Xen para virtualized disk.
/dev/vda	For the first Virtio virtual disk.

After you have started Fdisk, type **m** to see the options. Here is what you can do with fdisk:

- **Delete a partition** — Type **d** and a partition number, and then press Enter. For example, /dev/sda2 would be partition number 2. (The deletion won't take effect until you write the change — you can back out up to that point.)

- **Create a partition** — If you have free space, you can add a new partition. Type **n**; then choose **e** for an extended partition or **p** for a primary partition; then select a partition number from the available range. You can have only four primary partitions. However, after you have three primary partitions, make the fourth an extended partition (consuming all the remaining disk space). Then you can create many more logical partitions from the space in your extended partition.

  Next choose the first cylinder number from those available. (The output from fdisk -l shown earlier will show you cylinders being used under the Start and End columns.)

  After that, enter the cylinder number the partition will end with (or type the specific number of megabytes or kilobytes you want; for example, +50M or +1024K). You just created an ext3 Linux partition. Again, this change isn't permanent until you write the changes.

- **Change the partition type** — Press **t** to choose the type of file system. Enter the partition number for the partition you want to change. Type the number representing the file system type you want to use in hexadecimal code. (Type **L** at this point to see a list of file system types and codes.) For a Linux file system, use the number 83; for a Linux swap partition, use 82; and for a windows FAT32 file system, use the letter *b*.

- **Display the partition table** — Throughout this process, feel free to type **p** to display (print on the screen) the partition table as it now stands.

- **Quit or save** — Before you write your changes, display the partition table again and make sure that it is what you want it to be. If you don't like a change you made to your partitions, press **q** to exit without saving. Nothing changes on your partition table.

  If your changes are correct, write them to the partition table by pressing **w**. You are warned about how dangerous changing partitions can be, and you must confirm the change.

After you have changed your partition table, you must alert the kernel to the change. To do that, run the `partprobe` command as root, as follows:

```
# partprobe /dev/sda
```

An alternative to the menu-driven `fdisk` command is `sfdisk`, which is a command line–oriented partitioning tool. With `sfdisk`, you type the full command line to list or change partitions, instead of being taken through a set of prompts (as with `fdisk`). See the `sfdisk` man page for details. Linux experts often prefer `sfdisk` because it can be used in combination with other commands to take and output partitioning information.

Tips for Creating Partitions

Changing your disk partitions to handle multiple operating systems can be very tricky, in part because each operating system has its own ideas about how partitioning information should be handled, as well as different tools for doing it. Here are some tips to help you get it right:

- If you are creating a dual-boot system, particularly for Windows XP, try to install the Windows operating system first. Otherwise, the Windows installation may make the Linux partitions inaccessible. Choosing a VFAT instead of NTFS file system for Windows will also make sharing files between your Windows and Linux systems easier and more reliable. (Support for NTFS partitions from Linux has improved greatly in the past few years, but not all Linux systems include NTFS support.)

- The `fdisk` man page recommends that you use partitioning tools that come with an operating system to create partitions for that operating system. For example, the DOS fdisk knows how to create partitions that DOS will like, and the Linux fdisk will happily make your Linux partitions. After your hard disk is set up for dual boot, however, you should probably not go back to Windows-only partitioning tools. Use Linux fdisk or a product made for multi-boot systems (such as Partition Magic).

- You can have up to 63 partitions on an IDE hard disk. A SCSI hard disk can have up to 15 partitions. You typically won't need nearly that many partitions.

If you are using Linux as a desktop system, you probably don't need a lot of different partitions. However, some very good reasons exist for having multiple partitions for Linux systems that are shared by a lot of users or are public Web servers or file servers. Having multiple partitions within Fedora Linux, for example, offers the following advantages:

- **Protection from attacks** — Denial-of-service attacks sometimes take actions that try to fill up your hard disk. If public areas, such as /var, are on separate partitions, a successful attack can fill up a partition without shutting down the whole computer. Because /var is the default location for Web and FTP servers, and is expected to hold a lot of data, entire hard disks often are assigned to the /var file system alone.

- **Protection from corrupted file systems** — If you have only one file system (/), its corruption can cause the whole Linux system to be damaged. Corruption of a smaller partition can be easier to fix and often allows the computer to stay in service while the correction is made.

Table 7-2 lists some directories that you may want to consider making into separate file system partitions.

TABLE 7-2

Assigning Partitions to Particular Directories

Directory	Explanation
/boot	Sometimes the BIOS in older PCs can access only the first 1,024 cylinders of your hard disk. To make sure that the information in your /boot directory is accessible to the BIOS, create a separate disk partition (of about 100MB) for /boot and make sure that it exists below cylinder 1,024. The rest of your Linux system can exist outside of that 1,024-cylinder boundary if you like. Even with several boot images, there is rarely a reason for /boot to be larger than 100MB. (For newer hard disks, you can select the Linear Mode check box during installation. Then the boot partition can be anywhere on the disk.)
/usr	This directory structure contains most of the applications and utilities available to Linux users. Having /usr on a separate partition lets you mount that file system as read-only after the operating system has been installed. This prevents attackers from replacing or removing important system applications with their own versions that may cause security problems. A separate /usr partition is also useful if you have diskless workstations on your local network. Using NFS, you can share /usr over the network with those workstations.
/var	Your FTP (/var/ftp) and Web server (/var/www) directories are, by default, in many Linux systems, stored under /var. Having a separate /var partition can prevent an attack on those facilities from corrupting or filling up your entire hard disk.

continued

TABLE 7-2 *(continued)*	
Directory	**Explanation**
/home	Because your user account directories are located in this directory, having a separate /home account can prevent a reckless user from filling up the entire hard disk. It also conveniently separates user data from your operating system (for easy backups or new installs).
/tmp	Protecting /tmp from the rest of the hard disk by placing it on a separate partition can ensure that applications that need to write to temporary files in /tmp are able to complete their processing, even if the rest of the disk fills up.

Although people who use Linux systems casually rarely see a need for lots of partitions, those who maintain and occasionally have to recover large systems are thankful when the system they need to fix has several partitions. Multiple partitions can localize deliberate damage (such as denial-of-service attacks), problems from errant users, and accidental file system corruption.

Using LILO or GRUB Boot Loaders

A boot loader lets you choose when and how to boot the bootable operating systems installed on your computer's hard disks. Some Linux systems give you the opportunity to use GRUB or LILO boot loaders, although GRUB is used much more commonly these days. The following sections describe both GRUB and LILO boot loaders.

Note

SYSLINUX is another boot loader you will encounter with Linux systems. The SYSLINUX boot loaders are not typically used for installed Linux systems. However, SYSLINUX is commonly used as the boot loader for Linux CDs and DVDs. SYSLINUX is particularly good for booting ISO9660 CD images (isolinux), USB sticks (syslinux), for working on older hardware, or for PXE booting (pxelinux) a system over the network. ∎

Booting Your Computer with GRUB

With multiple operating systems installed and several partitions set up, how does your computer know which operating system to start? To select and manage which partition is booted and how it is booted, you need a boot loader. The boot loader that is installed by default with Fedora and other Linux systems is the GRand Unified Boot loader (GRUB).

GRUB is a GNU bootloader (www.gnu.org/software/grub) that replaced LILO as the default boot loader in many Linux systems, including Fedora and Ubuntu. GRUB offers the following features:

- Support for multiple executable formats
- Support for multi-boot operating systems (such as Fedora, FreeBSD, NetBSD, OpenBSD, and other Linux systems)
- Support for non–multi-boot operating systems (such as Windows 95, Windows 98, Windows NT, Windows ME, Windows XP, and OS/2) via a chain-loading function.

Chain-loading is the act of loading another boot loader (presumably one that is specific to the proprietary operating system) from GRUB to start the selected operating system.

- Support for multiple file system types
- Support for automatic decompression of boot images
- Support for downloading boot images from a network

For more information on how GRUB works, type **man grub** or **info grub**. The `info` command contains more details about GRUB.

Booting with GRUB

When you install Linux, you are typically given the option to configure the information needed to boot your computer (with one or more operating systems) into the default boot loader. With GRUB configured, when you boot your computer, the first thing you see after the BIOS loads is the GRUB boot screen (it says GRUB at the top and lists bootable partitions below it); do one of the following:

- **Default** — If you do nothing, the default operating system will boot automatically after a few seconds. (The timeout is set by the `timeout` value, in seconds, in the `grub.conf` file.)
- **Select an operating system** — Use the up and down arrow keys to select any of the titles, representing operating systems you can boot, that are shown on the screen. Then press Enter to boot that operating system.
- **Edit the boot process** — If you want to change any of the options used during the boot process, use the arrow keys to highlight the operating system you want and type **e** to select it. Follow the next procedure to change your boot options temporarily.

If you want to change your boot options so that they take effect every time you boot your computer, see the section on permanently changing boot options. Changing those options involves editing the `/boot/grub/grub.conf` file.

Temporarily Changing Boot Options

From the GRUB boot screen, you can select to change or add boot options for the current boot session. On some Linux systems, the menu is hidden, so you have to press a key (before a few seconds of timeout is exceeded) to see the menu. Then, select the operating system you want (using the arrow keys) and type **e** (as described earlier).

Three lines in the example of the GRUB editing screen identify the boot process for the operating system you chose. The first line (beginning with `root`) shows that the entry for the GRUB boot loader is on the fifth partition of the first hard disk (`hd0,4`). GRUB represents the hard disk as `hd`, regardless of whether it is a SCSI, IDE, or other type of disk. You just count the drive number and partition number, starting from zero (0).

The second line of the example (beginning with `kernel`) identifies the boot image (`/boot/vmlinuz-2.6.27.24-78.2.53.fc9.i686`) and several options. The options identify the partition as initially being loaded `ro` (read-only) and the location of the root file system on a partition with the label that begins `root=UUID`. The third line (starting with `initrd`) identifies the location of the initial RAM disk, which contains the minimum files and directories needed during the boot process.

If you are going to change any of the lines related to the boot process, you would probably change only the second line to add or remove boot options. Follow these steps to do just that:

1. Position the cursor on the `kernel` line and type **e**.
2. Either add or remove options after the name of the boot image. You can use a minimal set of bash shell command-line editing features to edit the line. You can even use command completion (type part of a filename and press Tab to complete it). Here are a few options you may want to add or delete:

   - **Boot to a shell** — If you forgot your root password or if your boot process hangs, you can boot directly to a shell by adding `init=/bin/sh` to the boot line. (If the root file system is mounted read-only, you can copy files out. You need to remount the root file system with read/write permission to be able to change files: `mount -o remount,rw /`)

   - **Select a run level** — If you want to boot to a particular run level, you can add the run level you want to the end of the kernel line. For example, to have Fedora Linux boot to run level 3 (multiuser plus networking mode), add 3 to the end of the kernel line. You can also boot to single-user mode (1), multiuser mode (2), or X GUI mode (5). Level 3 is a good choice if your GUI is temporarily broken. Level 1 is good if you have forgotten your root password.

3. Press Enter to return to the editing screen.
4. Type **b** to boot the computer with the new options. The next time you boot your computer, the new options will not be saved. To add options so they are saved permanently, see the next section.

Permanently Changing Boot Options

You can change the options that take effect each time you boot your computer by changing the GRUB configuration file. In Fedora and other Linux systems, GRUB configuration centers on the `/boot/grub/grub.conf` or `boot/grub/menu.lst` file.

The `/boot/grub/grub.conf` file is created when you install Linux. Here's an example of that file for Fedora:

```
# grub.conf generated by anaconda
#
# Note that you do not have to rerun grub after making changes to this file
# NOTICE:  You have a /boot partition.  This means that
#          all kernel and initrd paths are relative to /boot/, eg.
#          root (hd0,0)
#          kernel /vmlinuz-version ro root=/dev/mapper/vg_joke-lv_root
#          initrd /initrd-[generic-]version.img
#boot=/dev/sda
```

```
default=0
timeout=10
splashimage=(hd0,0)/grub/splash.xpm.gz
hiddenmenu
title Fedora (2.6.33.3-85.fc13.i686)
    root (hd0,0)
    kernel /vmlinuz-2.6.33.3-85.fc13.i686 ro root=/dev/mapper/vg_joke-lv_root
        rd_LVM_LV=vg_joke/lv_root rd_LVM_LV=vg_joke/lv_swap rd_NO_LUKS
        rd_NO_MD rd_NO_DM LANG=en_US.UTF-8 SYSFONT=latarcyrheb-sun16
        KEYBOARDTYPE=pc KEYTABLE=us rhgb quiet
    initrd /initramfs-2.6.33.3-85.fc13.i686.img

title Windows XP
    rootnoverify (hd0,1)
    chainloader +1
```

The default=0 line indicates that the first partition in this list (in this case Fedora) will be the one that is booted by default. The line timeout=10 causes GRUB to pause for 10 seconds before booting the default partition. (That's how much time you have to press **e** if you want to edit the boot line, or to press arrow keys to select a different operating system to boot.)

The splashimage line looks in the seventh partition on the first disk (hd0,4) for the boot partition (in this case /dev/sda5, which is the / partition). GRUB loads splash.xpm.gz as the image on the splash screen (/boot/grub/splash.xpm.gz). The splash screen appears as the background of the boot screen.

Note

GRUB indicates disk partitions using the following notation: (hd0,0). The first number represents the disk, and the second is the partition on that disk. So, (hd0,1) is the second partition (1) on the first disk (0). ■

The two bootable partitions in this example are Fedora and Windows XP. The title lines for each of those partitions are followed by the name that appears on the boot screen to represent each partition.

For the Fedora system, the root line indicates the location of the boot partition as the second partition on the first disk. So, to find the bootable kernel (vmlinuz-*) and the initrd initial RAM disk boot image that is loaded (initrd-*), GRUB looks in the root of hd0,0 (which is represented by /dev/sda1 and is mounted as /). Other options on the kernel line set the partition as read-only initially (ro) and set the root file system to the particular UUID set for the root partition.

For the Windows XP partition, the rootnoverify line indicates that GRUB should not try to mount the partition. In this case, Windows XP is on the second partition of the first hard disk (hd0,1) or /dev/sda2. Instead of mounting the partition and passing options to the new operating system, the chainloader +1 indicates to hand control the booting of the operating system to another boot loader. The +1 indicates that the first sector of the partition is used as the boot loader. (You could similarly set up to boot a Windows Vista or Windows 7 operating system.)

Note

Microsoft operating systems require that you use the `chainloader` to boot them from GRUB because GRUB doesn't offer native support for Windows operating systems. ∎

If you make any changes to the `/boot/grub/grub.conf` file, you do *not* need to load those changes. GRUB automatically picks up those changes when you reboot your computer. If you are accustomed to using the LILO boot loader, this may confuse you at first, as LILO requires you to rerun the `lilo` command for the changes to take effect.

Adding a New GRUB Boot Image

You may have different boot images for kernels that include different features. In most cases, installing a new kernel package will automatically configure `grub.conf` to use that new kernel. However, if you want to manually add a kernel, here is the procedure for modifying the `grub.conf` file to be able to boot that kernel:

1. Copy the new image from the directory in which it was created (such as `/usr/src/kernels/linux-2.6.25-11/arch/i386/boot`) to the `/boot` directory. Name the file something that reflects its contents, such as `bz-2.6.25-11`. For example:

```
# cd /usr/src/Linux-2.6.25.11/arch/i386/boot
# cp bzImage /boot/bz-2.6.25-11
```

2. Add several lines to the `/boot/grub/grub.conf` file so that the image can be started at boot time if it is selected. For example:

```
title Fedora (My own IPV6 build)
    root (hd0,4)
    kernel /bz-2.6.25-11 ro root=/dev/sda5
    initrd /initrd-2.6.25-11.img
```

3. Reboot your computer.

4. When the GRUB boot screen appears, move your cursor to the title representing the new kernel and press Enter.

The advantage to this approach, as opposed to copying the new boot image over the old one, is that if the kernel fails to boot, you can always go back and restart the old kernel. When you feel confident that the new kernel is working properly, you can use it to replace the old kernel or perhaps just make the new kernel the default boot definition.

Booting Your Computer with LILO

LILO stands for LInux LOader. Like other boot loaders, LILO is a program that can stand outside the operating systems installed on the computer so you can choose which system to boot. It also lets you give special options that modify how the operating system is booted. On Slackware and some other Linux systems, LILO is used instead of GRUB as the default boot loader.

If LILO is being used on your computer, it is installed in either the master boot record or the first sector of the root partition. The master boot record is read directly by the computer's BIOS. In general, if LILO is the only loader on your computer, install it in the master boot record. If another boot loader is already in the master boot record, put LILO in the /boot partition.

Note

If you are new to Linux and not familiar with boot loaders, I recommend you learn and use GRUB instead of LILO. Support for LILO — and inclusion in distributions — has been reduced in favor of GRUB. ■

Using LILO

When your computer boots with a graphical version of LILO installed in the master boot record, a graphical boot screen appears, displaying the bootable partitions on the computer. Use the up and down arrow keys on your keyboard to select the one you want and press Enter. Otherwise, the default partition that you set at installation will boot after a few seconds.

If you want to add any special options when you boot, press Ctrl+X. You will see a text-based boot prompt that appears as follows:

```
boot:
```

LILO pauses for a few seconds and then automatically boots the first image from the default bootable partition. To see the bootable partitions again, quickly press Tab. You may see something similar to the following:

```
LILO boot:
linux linux-up dos
boot:
```

This example shows that three bootable partitions are on your computer, called linux, linux-up, and dos. The first two refer to two different boot images that can boot the Linux partition. The third refers to a bootable DOS partition (presumably containing a Windows operating system). The first bootable partition is loaded if you don't type anything after a few seconds. Or you can use the name of the other partition to have that boot instead.

If you have multiple boot images, press Shift, and LILO asks you which image you want to boot. Available boot images and other options are defined in the /etc/lilo.conf file.

Setting Up the /etc/lilo.conf File

The /etc/lilo.conf file is where LILO gets the information it needs to find and start bootable partitions and images. By adding options to the /etc/lilo.conf file, you can change the behavior of the boot process. The following is an example of some of the contents of the /etc/lilo.conf file:

```
prompt
timeout=50
default=linux
boot=/dev/hda
```

```
map=/boot/map
install=/boot/boot.b
message=/boot/message
linear

image=/boot/vmlinuz-2.6.27.24-78.2.53.fc9.i686
        label=linux
        initrd=/boot/initrd-2.6.27.24-78.2.53.fc9.i686.img
        read-only
        root=/dev/hda5
        append="root=LABEL=/"

other=/dev/hda1
        optional
        label=dos
```

With `prompt` on, the boot prompt appears when the system is booted without requiring that any keys be pressed. The timeout value, in this case 50 tenths of a second (5 seconds), defines how long to wait for keyboard input before booting the default boot image. The boot line indicates that the bootable partition is on the hard disk represented by /dev/hda (the first IDE hard disk).

Note

Depending upon the distribution, "hda" may be "sda." If you are using LILO, the odds are good that you are using an older Linux implementation, so hda is shown in the example and used in this discussion. ∎

The `map` line indicates the location of the map file (/boot/map, by default). The map file contains the names and locations of bootable kernel images. The `install` line indicates that the /boot/boot.b file is used as the new boot sector. The `message` line tells LILO to display the contents of the /boot/message file when booting (which contains the graphical boot screen). The linear line causes linear sector addresses to be generated (instead of sector/head/cylinder addresses).

The sample file has two bootable partitions. The first (image=/boot/vmlinuz-2.6.27.24-78.2.53.fc9.i686) shows an image labeled linux. The root file system (/) for that image is on partition /dev/hda5. Read-only indicates that the file system is first mounted read-only, although it is probably mounted as read/write after a file system check. The `initrd` line indicates the location of the initial RAM disk image used to start the system.

The second bootable partition, which is indicated by the word *other* in this example, is on the /dev/hda1 partition. Because it is a Windows system, it is labeled a DOS file system. The table line indicates the device that contains the partition.

Other bootable images are listed in this file, and you can add another boot image yourself (such as one you create from reconfiguring your kernel, as discussed in the next section) by installing the new image and changing lilo.conf.

After you change `lilo.conf`, you then must run the `lilo` command for the changes to take effect. You may have different boot images for kernels that include different features. The following is the procedure for modifying the `lilo.conf` file:

1. Copy the new image from the directory in which it was created (such as `/usr/src/kernels/2.6.27.24-78.2.53.fc9/arch/i386/boot`) to the `/boot` directory. Name the file something that reflects its contents, such as `zImage-2.6.27.24-78.2.53.fc9.img`.

2. Add several lines to the `/etc/lilo.conf` file so that the image can be started at boot time if it is selected. For example:

   ```
   image=/boot/zImage-2.6.27.24-78.2.53.fc9.img
   label=new
   ```

3. Type the **lilo -t** command (as root user) to test that the changes were okay.

4. Type the **lilo** command (with no options) for the changes to be installed.

To boot from this new image, either select new from the graphical boot screen or type **new** and press Enter at the LILO boot prompt. If 5 seconds is too quick, increase the timeout value (such as 100 for 10 seconds).

Options that you can use in the `/etc/lilo.conf` file are divided into global options, per-image options, and kernel options. A lot of documentation is available for LILO. For more details on any of the options described here or for other options, you can see the `lilo.conf` manual page (type **man lilo.conf**) or any of the documents in `/usr/share/doc/lilo*/doc`.

Below are a few examples of global options that you can add to `/etc/lilo.conf`. Global options apply to LILO as a whole, instead of just to a particular boot image.

You can use the `default=label` option, where *label* is replaced by an image's label name, to indicate that a particular image should be used as the default boot image. If that option is excluded, the first image listed in the `/etc/lilo.conf` file is used as the default. For example, to start the image labeled new by default, add the following line to `lilo.conf`:

```
default=new
```

Change the delay from 5 seconds to something greater if you want LILO to wait longer before starting the default image. This gives you more time to boot a different image. To change the value from 5 seconds (50) to 15 seconds (150), add the following line:

```
delay=150
```

You can change the message that appears before the LILO prompt by adding that message to a file and changing the message line. For example, you could create a `/boot/boot.message` file and add the following words to that file: `Choose linux, new, or dos`. To have that message appear before the boot prompt, add the following line to `/etc/lilo.conf`:

```
message=/boot/boot.message
```

All per-image options begin with either an `image=` line (indicating a Linux kernel) or `other=` (indicating some other kind of operating system, such as a Windows system). The per-image options apply to particular boot images rather than to all images (as global options do). Along with the image or other line is a `label=` line, which gives a name to that image. The name is what you select at boot time to boot that image. Here are some of the options that you can add to each of those image definitions:

- `lock` — This enables automatic recording of `boot` command lines as the defaults for different boot options.
- `alias=name` — You can replace `name` with any name. That name becomes an alias for the image name defined in the label option.
- `password=password` — You can password-protect all images by adding a password option line and replacing `password` with your own password. The password would have to be entered to boot any of the images.
- `restricted` — This option is used with the password option. It indicates that a password should be used only if command-line options are given when trying to boot the image.

For Linux kernel images, there are specific options that you can use. These options let you deal with hardware issues that can't be autodetected, or provide information such as how the root file system is mounted. Here are some of the kernel image-specific options:

- `append` — Add a string of letters and numbers to this option that need to be passed to the kernel. In particular, these can be parameters that need to be passed to better define the hard disk when some aspect of that disk can't be autodetected (for example, `append="hd=64,32,202"`).
- `ramdisk` — Add the size of the RAM disk that you want to use in order to override the size of the RAM disk built into the kernel.
- `read-only` — Mount the root file system read-only. It is typically remounted read-write after the disk is checked.
- `read-write` — Mount the root file system read/write.

Changing Your Boot Loader

If you don't want to use the GRUB boot loader, or if you tried out LILO and want to switch back to GRUB, then changing to a different boot loader on Linux distributions that support both boot loaders is not hard. To switch your boot loader from GRUB to LILO, do the following:

1. Configure the `/etc/lilo.conf` file as described in the "Booting Your Computer with LILO" section.

2. As root user from a Terminal window, type the following:

   `# lilo`

3. The new Master Boot Record is written, including the entries in `/etc/lilo.conf`.

4. Reboot your computer. You should see the LILO boot screen.

To change your boot loader from LILO to GRUB, do the following:

1. Configure the `/boot/grub/grub.conf` file as described in the "Booting your computer with GRUB" section.

2. You need to know the device on which you want to install GRUB. For example, to install GRUB on the master boot record of the first disk, type the following as root user from a Terminal window:

   `# grub-install /dev/hda`

   The new Master Boot Record is written to boot with the GRUB boot loader.

3. Reboot your computer. You should see the GRUB boot screen.

If for some reason you don't see the GRUB boot screen when you reboot, you can use a rescue CD to reboot your computer and fix the problem. When the rescue CD boots up, mount the file system containing the `/boot/grub/grub.conf` file. Then use the `chroot` command to change to the root of that file system. Correct the `grub.conf` file and run `grub-install` again.

Configuring Networking

If you are connecting your computer to an Ethernet LAN that has a DHCP server available, you probably don't need to do anything to start up automatically on your LAN and even be connected to the Internet. However, if no DHCP server is on your LAN and you have to configure your TCP/IP connection manually, here is the information you will probably be prompted for during Linux installation:

- **IP address** — If you set your own IP address, this is the four-part, dot-separated number that represents your computer to the network. An example of a private IP address is 192.168.0.1.

- **Netmask** — The netmask is used to determine what part of an IP address represents the network and what part represents a particular host computer. An example of a netmask for a Class C network is 255.255.255.0. If you apply this netmask to an IP address of 192.168.0.1, for example, the network address would be 192.168.0 and the host address 1. Because 0 and 255 can't be assigned to a particular host, that leaves valid host numbers between 1 and 254 available for this local network.

- **Activate on boot** — Some Linux install procedures ask you to indicate whether you want the network to start at boot time (you probably do if you have a LAN).

- **Set the hostname** — This is the name identifying your computer within your domain. For example, if your computer is named "baskets" in the `handsonhistory.com` domain, your full hostname may be `baskets.handsonhistory.com`. You can either set the domain name yourself (manually) or have it assigned automatically, if that information is being assigned by a DHCP server (automatically via DHCP).

- **Gateway** — This is the IP number of the computer that acts as a gateway to networks outside your LAN. This typically represents a host computer or router that routes packets between your LAN and the Internet.

- **Primary DNS** — This is the IP address of the host that translates computer names you request into IP addresses. It is referred to as a Domain Name System (DNS) server. You may also have Secondary and Tertiary name servers in case the first one can't be reached. (Most ISPs will give you two DNS server addresses.)

Configuring Other Administrative Features

Depending on which Linux install you are using, you will be asked to enter other types of information. These might involve the following:

- **Firewall** — Most Linux distributions these days use iptables to configure firewalls. When you configure a default firewall, you typically choose which ports will be open to outside connections made to your system (although a firewall can be configured to do many other things as well).

- **Languages** — Although Linux itself doesn't include support for lots of different languages, some Linux distributions (such as Fedora) and desktop environments (such as KDE) do. Nearly all Linux distributions will let you configure language-specific keyboards.

- **Root password and additional user** — Most Linux systems that use passwords will have you add at least the root user's password when you install Linux. (Ubuntu is the notable exception, since it expects the first regular user to have root privilege via sudo.) Some distributions require that you add at least one additional non-root user as well.

Besides the features just mentioned, every distribution needs to have some initial configuration done before you have a fully functional Linux system.

Installing from the Linux Bible DVD

With the knowledge you've gained in this chapter, you're ready to select a Linux distribution to install. Read the descriptions of Linux distributions in the other chapters of this book.

If you need more information about the DVD that comes with this book, Appendix A describes the contents of that disc. It also tells you which Linux distributions you can run live or use to install Linux permanently to your hard disk from the DVD.

Summary

Although every Linux distribution includes a different installation method, you need to do many common activities, regardless of which Linux system you install. For every Linux system, you need to deal with issues of disk partitioning, network configuration, and boot loaders.

Linux Bible includes a DVD with several different Linux systems you can install. If you prefer, you can instead download and burn your own CDs or DVDs to install Linux. If you go the route of burning your own CDs, Appendix A helps you find Linux distributions you can download and describes tools you can use to verify their contents.

Running Commands from the Shell

efore icons and windows took over computer screens, you typed commands to interact with most computers. On UNIX systems, from which Linux was derived, the program used to interpret and manage commands was referred to as the *shell*.

No matter which Linux distribution you are using, you can always count on one thing being available to you: the shell. It provides a way to create executable script files, run programs, work with file systems, compile computer code, operate a system, and manage the computer. Although the shell is less intuitive than common graphic user interfaces (GUIs), most Linux experts consider the shell to be much more powerful than GUIs. Shells have been around a long time, and many advanced features have been built into them.

The Linux shell illustrated in this chapter is called the *bash shell,* which stands for Bourne Again Shell. The name is derived from the fact that bash is compatible with the one of the earliest UNIX shells: the Bourne shell (named after its creator, Stephen Bourne, and represented by the sh command).

Although bash is included with most distributions, and considered a standard, other shells are available. Other popular shells include the C shell (csh), which is popular among BSD UNIX users, and the Korn shell (ksh), which is popular among UNIX System V users. Linux also has a tcsh shell (a C shell look-alike) and an ash shell (another Bourne shell look-alike). Several different shells are introduced in this chapter.

Tip
The odds are strong that the Linux distribution you are using has more than one shell installed by default and available for your use. ■

IN THIS CHAPTER

Understanding the Linux shell

Using the Linux shell

Working with the Linux file system

Using the vi text editor in Linux

The following are a few major reasons to learn how to use the shell:

- You will know how to get around any Linux or other UNIX-like system. For example, I can log in to my Red Hat Enterprise Linux MySQL server, my bootable floppy router/firewall, or my wife's iMac and explore and use any of those computer systems from a shell.

- Special shell features enable you to gather data input and direct data output between commands and the Linux file system. To save on typing, you can find, edit, and repeat commands from your shell history. Many power users hardly touch a graphical interface, doing most of their work from a shell.

You can gather commands into a file using programming constructs such as conditional tests, loops, and case statements to quickly do complex operations that would be difficult to retype over and over. Programs consisting of commands that are stored and run from a file are referred to as *shell scripts*. Most Linux system administrators use shell scripts to automate tasks such as backing up data, monitoring log files, or checking system health.

The shell is a command language interpreter. If you have used Microsoft operating systems, you'll see that using a shell in Linux is similar to — but generally much more powerful than — the interpreter used to run commands in DOS or in the CMD command interface. You can happily use Linux from a graphical desktop interface, but as you grow into Linux you will surely need to use the shell at some point to track down a problem or administer some features.

How to use the shell isn't obvious at first, but with the right help you can quickly learn many of the most important shell features. This chapter is your guide to working with the Linux system commands, processes, and file system from the shell. It describes the shell environment and helps you tailor it to your needs. It also explains how to use and move around in the file system.

Starting a Shell

There are several ways to get to a shell interface in Linux. Three of the most common are the shell prompt, Terminal window, and virtual terminal. They're discussed in the following sections.

Using the Shell Prompt

If your Linux system has no graphical user interface (or has one that isn't working at the moment), you will most likely see a shell prompt after you log in. Typing commands from the shell will probably be your primary means of using the Linux system.

The default prompt for a regular user is simply a dollar sign:

```
$
```

The default prompt for the root user is a pound sign (also called a *hash mark*):

```
#
```

In most Linux systems, the $ and # prompts are preceded by your username, system name, and current directory name. For example, a login prompt for the user named jake on a computer named pine with /usr/share/ as the current working directory would appear as

```
[jake@pine share]$
```

You can change the prompt to display any characters you like — for example, you can use the current working directory, the date, the local computer name, or any string of characters as your prompt. To configure your prompt, see the "Setting your prompt" section later in this chapter.

Although a tremendous number of features are available with the shell, it's easy to begin by just typing a few commands. Try some of the commands shown in the remainder of this section to become familiar with your current shell environment.

In the examples that follow, the dollar ($) and pound (#) symbols indicate a prompt. While a $ indicates that the command can be run by any user, a # typically means you should run the command as the root user — many administrative tools require root permission to be able to run them. The prompt is followed by the command that you type (and then you press Enter or Return, depending on your keyboard). The lines that follow show the output resulting from the command.

Using a Terminal Window

With the desktop GUI running, you can open a terminal emulator program (sometimes referred to as a Terminal window) to start a shell. Most Linux distributions make it easy for you to get to a shell from the GUI. Here are two common ways to launch a Terminal window from a Linux desktop:

- **Right-click the desktop.** In the context menu that appears, if you see Shells, New Terminal, Terminal Window, Xterm, or some similar item, select it to start a Terminal window. (Many newer distributions have disabled this feature.)

- **Click on the panel menu.** Many Linux desktops include a panel at the top or bottom of the screen from which you can launch applications. For example, in some systems that use the GNOME desktop, you can select Applications ⇨ System Tools ⇨ Terminal to open a Terminal window. For Mandriva, select System ⇨ Terminals.

In all cases, you should just be able to type a command as you would from a shell with no GUI. Different terminal emulators are available with Linux. One of the following is likely to be the default used with your Linux system:

- **xterm** — A common terminal emulator for the X Window System. (In fact, I've never seen an X Window System for a major Linux distribution that didn't include xterm.) Although it doesn't provide menus or many special features, it is available with most Linux distributions that support a GUI.

- **gnome-terminal** — The default Terminal emulator window that comes with GNOME. It consumes more system resources than xterm does, and it has useful menus for cutting and pasting, opening new Terminal tabs or windows, and setting terminal profiles.

- **konsole** — The konsole terminal emulator that comes with the KDE desktop environment. With konsole, you can display multilanguage text encoding and text in different colors.

The differences in running commands within a Terminal window have more to do with the shell you are running than the type of Terminal window you are using. Differences in Terminal windows have more to do with the features each supports — for example, how much output is saved that can be scrolled back to, whether you can change font types and sizes, and whether the Terminal window supports features such as transparency or cut and paste.

Using Virtual Terminals

Most Linux systems that include a desktop interface start multiple virtual terminals running on the computer. Virtual terminals are a way to have multiple shell sessions open at once outside of the graphical interface you are using.

You can switch between virtual terminals much the same way that you would switch between workspaces on a GUI. Press Ctrl+Alt+F1 (or F2, F3, F4, and so on up to F7 on Fedora and other Linux systems) to display one of seven virtual consoles. The first virtual workspace in Fedora is where the GUI is and the next six virtual terminals are text-based virtual terminals. You can return to the GUI (if one is running) by pressing Ctrl+Alt+F1. (On some systems the GUI runs on the virtual terminal 7 or 5. So you'd return to the GUI by pressing Ctrl+Alt+F5 or Ctrl+Alt+F7.)

Choosing Your Shell

In most Linux systems, your default shell is the bash shell. To find out what your default login shell is, type the following command:

```
$ echo $SHELL
/bin/bash
```

In this example, it's the bash shell. There are many other shells, and you can activate a different one by simply typing the new shell's command (ksh, tcsh, csh, sh, bash, and so forth) from the current shell. For example, to change temporarily to the C shell, type the following command:

```
$ csh
```

Note

Most full Linux systems include all the shells described in this section. However, some smaller Linux distributions may include only one or two shells. The best way to find out whether a particular shell is available is to type the command and see whether the shell starts. ■

You might want to choose a different shell to use because

- You are used to using UNIX System V systems (often ksh by default) or Sun Microsystems and other Berkeley UNIX–based distributions (frequently csh by default), and you are more comfortable using default shells from those environments.

- You want to run shell scripts that were created for a particular shell environment, and you need to run the shell for which they were made so you can test or use those scripts from your current shell.

- You simply prefer features in one shell over those in another. For example, a member of my Linux Users Group prefers ksh over bash because he doesn't like the way aliases are used with bash.

Although most Linux users have a preference for one shell or another, when you know how to use one shell, you can quickly learn any of the others by occasionally referring to the shell's man page (for example, type **man bash**). Most people use bash just because they don't have a particular reason for using a different shell.

In Chapter 9, you learn how to assign a different default shell for a user. The following sections introduce several of the most common shells available with Linux.

Using bash (and Earlier sh) Shells

As mentioned earlier, the name bash is an acronym for Bourne Again Shell, acknowledging the roots of bash coming from the Bourne shell (sh command) created by Steve Bourne at AT&T Bell Labs. Brian Fox of the Free Software Foundation created bash, under the auspices of the GNU Project. Development was later taken over by Chet Ramey at Case Western Reserve University.

Bash includes features originally developed for sh and ksh shells in early UNIX systems, as well as some csh features. Expect bash to be the default shell in whatever Linux system you are using, with the exception of some specialized Linux systems (such as those run on embedded devices or run from a floppy disk) that may require a smaller shell that needs less memory and entails fewer features. Most of the examples in this chapter are based on the bash shell.

Tip
The bash shell is worth knowing, not only because it is the default in most installations, but because it is the one you will use with most Linux certification exams. ■

Bash can be run in various compatibility modes so that it behaves like different shells. It can be run to behave as a Bourne shell (bash +B) or as a POSIX-compliant shell (type **bash --posix**), for example, enabling it to read configuration files that are specific to those shells and run initialization shell scripts written directly for those shells, with a greater chance of success.

All the Linux distributions included with this book use bash as the default shell, with the exception of some bootable Linux distributions, which use the ash shell instead.

Using tcsh (and Earlier csh) Shells

The tcsh shell is the open source version of the C shell (csh). The csh shell was created by Bill Joy and used with most Berkeley UNIX systems (such as those produced by Sun Microsystems) as the default shell. Features from the TENEX and TOPS-20 operating systems (used on PDP-11s in the 1970s) that are included in this shell are responsible for the T in tcsh.

Many features of the original csh shell, such as command-line editing and its history mechanism, are included in tcsh as well as in other shells. Although you can run both csh and tcsh on most Linux systems, both commands actually point to the same executable file. In other words, starting csh actually runs the tcsh shell in csh compatibility mode.

Using ash

The ash shell is a lightweight version of the Berkeley UNIX sh shell. It doesn't include many of the sh shell's basic features, and is missing such features as command histories. Kenneth Almquist created the ash shell used with NetBSD. A port of ash, called dash, is available in Debian systems.

The ash shell is a good shell for embedded systems that have fewer system resources available. The ash shell is about one-seventh the size of bash (about 92KB versus 724KB for bash). Because of cheaper memory prices these days, however, many embedded and small bootable Linux systems have enough space to include the full bash shell.

Using ksh

The ksh shell was created by David Korn at AT&T Bell Labs and is the successor to the sh shell. It became the default and most commonly used shell with UNIX System V systems. The open source version of ksh was originally available in many rpm-based systems (such as Fedora and Red Hat Enterprise Linux) as part of the pdksh package. Now, however, David Korn has released the original ksh shell as open source, so you can look for it as part of a ksh software package in most Linux systems (see www.kornshell.com).

Using zsh

The zsh shell is another clone of the sh shell. It is POSIX-compliant (as is bash), but includes some different features, such as spell-checking and a different approach to command editing. The first Mac OS X systems used zsh as the default shell, although now bash is used by default.

Exploring the Shell

After you have access to a shell in Linux, you can begin by typing some simple commands. The "Using the Shell in Linux" section later in this chapter provides more details about options, arguments, and environment variables. For the time being, the following sections can help you poke around the shell a bit.

Note

If you don't like your default shell, simply type the name of the shell you want to try out temporarily. To change your shell permanently, use the chsh command. For example, to change to the csh shell for the current user, that user can type the following from a shell:

```
$ chsh
Changing shell for cnegus.

Password:
******
New shell [/bin/bash]:
/bin/csh ■
```

Checking Your Login Session

When you log in to a Linux system, Linux views you as having a particular identity, which includes your username, group name, user ID, and group ID. Linux also keeps track of your login session: It knows when you logged in, how long you have been idle, and where you logged in from.

To find out information about your identity, use the id command as follows:

```
$ id
uid=501(chris) gid=105(sales) groups=105(sales),4(adm),7(lp)
```

In this example, the username is chris, which is represented by the numeric user ID (uid) 501. The primary group for chris is called sales, which has a group ID (gid) of 105. The user chris also belongs to other groups called adm (gid 4) and lp (gid 7). These names and numbers represent the permissions that chris has to access computer resources. (Permissions are described in the "Understanding File Permissions" section later in this chapter.)

Note

Based on the distribution you are using, the uid numbering may be in the thousands. ■

You can see information about your current login session by using the who command. In the following example, the -u option says to add information about idle time and the process ID and -H asks that a header be printed:

```
$ who -uH
NAME       LINE    TIME          IDLE    PID    COMMENT
chris      tty1    Jan 13 20:57   .      2013
```

The output from this who command shows that the user chris is logged in on tty1 (which is the monitor connected to the computer), and his login session began at 20:57 on January 13. The IDLE time shows how long the shell has been open without any command being typed (the dot indicates that it is currently active). PID shows the process ID of the user's login shell. COMMENT would show the name of the remote computer the user had logged in from, if that user had logged in from another computer on the network, or the name of the local X display if the user was using a Terminal window (such as :0.0).

Checking Directories and Permissions

Associated with each shell is a location in the Linux file system known as the *current* or working directory. Each user has a directory that is identified as the user's home directory. When you first log in to Linux, you begin with your home directory as the current directory.

When you request to open or save a file, your shell uses the current directory as the point of reference. Simply provide a filename when you save a file, and it is placed in the current directory. Alternatively, you can identify a file by its relation to the current directory (relative path), or you can ignore the current directory and identify a file by the full directory hierarchy that locates it (absolute path). The structure and use of the file system is described in detail later in this chapter.

To find out what your current directory (the present working directory) is, type the pwd command:

```
$ pwd
/usr/bin
```

In this example, the current/working directory is /usr/bin. To find out the name of your home directory, type the echo command, followed by the $HOME variable:

```
$ echo $HOME
/home/chris
```

Here, the home directory is /home/chris. To get back to your home directory, just type the change directory (cd) command. (Although cd followed by a directory name changes the current directory to the directory that you choose, simply typing cd with no directory name takes you to your home directory):

```
$ cd
```

Note

Instead of typing $HOME, you can use the tilde (~) to refer to your home directory. So, to see your home directory, you could simply type echo ~. ∎

To list the contents of your home directory with the ls command, either type the full path to your home directory, or use the ls command without a directory name. Using the -a option to ls enables you to view the hidden files (known as *dot* files because they start with the dot character) as well as all other files. With the -l option, you can see a long, detailed list of information on each file. (You can put multiple single-letter options together after a single dash; for example, -la.)

```
$ ls -la /home/chris
total 158
drwxrwxrwx    2  chris   sales    4096  May 12 13:55 .
drwxr-xr-x    3  root    root     4096  May 10 01:49 ..
-rw-------    1  chris   sales    2204  May 18 21:30 .bash_history
-rw-r--r--    1  chris   sales      24  May 10 01:50 .bash_logout
-rw-r--r--    1  chris   sales     230  May 10 01:50 .bash_profile
-rw-r--r--    1  chris   sales     124  May 10 01:50 .bashrc
```

```
drw-r--r--      1    chris   sales    4096   May 10 01:50 .kde
-rw-rw-r--      1    chris   sales  149872   May 11 22:49 letter

      ^            ^       ^       ^       ^           ^               ^
   col 1      col 2   col 3   col 4   col 5      col 6           col 7
```

Displaying a long list (-l option) of the contents of your home directory shows you more about file sizes and directories. The `total` line shows the total amount of disk space used by the files in the list (158 kilobytes in this example). Directories such as the current directory (.) and the parent directory (..) — the directory above the current directory — are noted as directories by the letter d at the beginning of each entry (each directory begins with a d and each file begins with a -).

The file and directory names are shown in column 7. In this example, a dot (.) represents /home/chris and two dots (..) represent /home — the parent directory of /chris. Most of the files in this example are dot (.) files that are used to store GUI properties (.kde directory) or shell properties (.bash files). The only non-dot file in this list is the one named letter. Column 3 shows the directory or file owner. The /home directory is owned by root, and everything else is owned by the user chris, who belongs to the sales group (groups are listed in column 4).

In addition to the d or -, column 1 on each line contains the permissions set for that file or directory. (Permissions and configuring shell property files are described later in this chapter.) Other information in the listing includes the number of hard links to the item (column 2), the size of each file in bytes (column 5), and the date and time each file was most recently modified (column 6).

Here are a few other items related to file and directory listings:

- The number of characters shown for a directory (4096 bytes in these examples) reflects the size of the file containing information about the directory. Although this number can grow above 4096 bytes for a directory that contains a lot of files, this number doesn't reflect the size of files contained in that directory.

- The format of the time and date column can vary. Instead of displaying "May 12," the display can be "2011-05-12" depending upon the distribution and the language setting (LANG variable).

- On occasion, instead of seeing the execute bit (x) set on an executable file, you may see an s in that spot instead. With an s appearing within either the owner (-rwsr-xr-x) or group (-rwxr-sr-x) permissions, or both (-rwsr-sr-x), the application can be run by any user, but ownership of the running process is assigned to the application's user/group instead of that of the user launching the command. This is referred to as a *set UID* or *set GID* program, respectively. For example, the mount command has permissions set as -rwsr-xr-x. This allows any user to run mount to list mounted file systems (although you still have to be root to use mount to actually mount file systems, in most cases).

- If a t appears at the end of a directory, it indicates that the sticky bit is set for that directory (for example, drwxrwxr-t). By setting the sticky bit on a directory, the directory's owner can allow other users and groups to add files to the directory, but prevent users from deleting each other's files in that directory. With a set GID assigned to a directory, any files created in that directory are assigned the same group as the directory's group. (If you see a capital S or T instead of the execute bits on a directory, it means that the set GID or stick bit permission, respectively, was set, but for some reason the execute bit was not also turned on.)

- If you see a plus sign at the end of the permission bits (for example, -rw-rw-r--+), it means that extended attributes, such as Access Control Lists (ACLs) or SELinux, are set on the file.

Checking System Activity

In addition to being a multiuser operating system, Linux is also a multitasking system. *Multitasking* means that many programs can be running at the same time. An instance of a running program is referred to as a process. Linux provides tools for listing running processes, monitoring system usage, and stopping (or killing) processes when necessary.

The most common utility for checking running processes is the ps command. Use it to see which programs are running, the resources they are using, and who is running them. Here's an example of the ps command:

```
$ ps u
USER    PID %CPU %MEM  VSZ   RSS  TTY    STAT START  TIME COMMAND
jake   2147 0.0  0.7 1836  1020  tty1   S+   14:50  0:00 -bash
jake   2310 0.0  0.7 2592   912  tty1   R+   18:22  0:00 ps u
```

In this example, the u option asks that usernames be shown, as well as other information such as the time the process started and memory and CPU usage for processes associated with the current user. The processes shown are associated with the current terminal (tty1). The concept of a terminal comes from the old days, when people worked exclusively from character terminals, so a terminal typically represented a single person at a single screen. Now you can have many "terminals" on one screen by opening multiple virtual terminals or Terminal windows on the desktop.

On this shell session, there isn't much happening. The first process shows that the user named jake opened a bash shell after logging in. The next process shows that jake has run the ps u command. The terminal device tty1 is being used for the login session. The STAT column represents the state of the process, with R indicating a currently running process and S representing a sleeping process.

Note

Several other values can appear under the STAT column. For example, a plus sign (+) indicates that the process is associated with the foreground operations. ■

The USER column shows the name of the user who started the process. Each process is represented by a unique ID number referred to as a process ID (PID). (You can use the PID if you ever need to kill a runaway process or send another kind of signal to a process.) The %CPU and %MEM columns show the percentages of the processor and random access memory, respectively, that the process is consuming. VSZ (virtual set size) shows the size of the image process (in kilobytes), and RSS (resident set size) shows the size of the program in memory. START shows the time the process began running, and TIME shows the cumulative system time used. (Many commands consume very little CPU time, as is reflected by 0:00 for processes that haven't even used a whole second of CPU time.)

Many processes running on a computer are not associated with a terminal. A normal Linux system has many processes running in the background. Background system processes perform such tasks as logging system activity or listening for data coming in from the network. They are often started when Linux boots up and run continuously until it shuts down. To page through all the processes running on your Linux system for the current user, add the pipe (|) and the less command to ps ux, like this:

```
$ ps ux | less
```

To page through all processes running for all users on your system, use the ps aux command as follows:

```
$ ps aux | less
```

A pipe (above the backslash character on the keyboard) enables you to direct the output of one command to be the input of the next command. In this example, the output of the ps command (a list of processes) is directed to the less command, which lets you page through that information. Use the spacebar to page through and type **q** to end the list. You can also use the arrow keys to move one line at a time through the output.

Exiting the Shell

To exit the shell when you are done, type **exit** or press Ctrl+D.

You've just seen a few commands that can help you quickly familiarize yourself with your Linux system. There are hundreds of other commands that you can try. You'll find many in the /bin and /usr/bin directories, and you can use ls to see a directory's command list: ls /bin, for example, results in a list of commands in the /bin. Then use the man command (for example, man hostname) to see what each command does. Administrative commands are also in /sbin or /usr/sbin directories.

Using the Shell in Linux

When you type a command in a shell, you can include other characters that change or add to how the command works. In addition to the command itself, these are some of the other items that you can type on a shell command line:

- **Options** — Most commands have one or more options you can add to change their behavior. Options typically consist of a single letter, preceded by a dash. You can also often combine several options after a single dash. For example, the command ls -la lists the contents of the current directory. The -l asks for a detailed (long) list of information, and the -a asks that files beginning with a dot (.) also be listed. When a single option consists of a word, it is usually preceded by a double dash (--). For example, to use the help option on many commands, you enter --help on the command line.

Note

You can use the `--help` option with most commands to see the options and arguments that they support: for example, `hostname --help`. ∎

- **Arguments** — Many commands also accept arguments after certain options are entered or at the end of the entire command line. An argument is an extra piece of information, such as a filename, that can be used by the command. For example, `cat /etc/passwd` displays the contents of the `/etc/passwd` file on your screen. In this case, `/etc/passwd` is the argument.

- **Environment variables** — The shell itself stores information that may be useful to the user's shell session in what are called *environment variables*. Examples of environment variables include `$SHELL` (which identifies the shell you are using), `$PS1` (which defines your shell prompt), and `$MAIL` (which identifies the location of your mailbox). See the "Using shell environment variables" section later in this chapter for more information.

Tip

You can check your environment variables at any time. Type `env` to list the current environment variables. Or you can type echo $*VALUE,* where *VALUE* is replaced by the name of a particular environment variable you want to list. And because there are always multiple ways to do anything in Linux, you can also type `declare` to get a list of the current environment variables and their values along with a list of shell functions. ∎

- **Metacharacters** — These characters have special meaning to the shell. They can be used to direct the output of a command to a file (>), pipe the output to another command (|), and run a command in the background (&), to name a few. Metacharacters are discussed later in this chapter.

To save you some typing, there are shell features that let you store commands you want to reuse, recall previous commands, and edit commands. You can create aliases that enable you to type a short command to run a longer one. The shell stores previously entered commands in a history list, which you can display and from which you can recall commands. You'll see how this works a little later in the chapter.

Unless you specifically change to another shell, the bash shell is the one you use with most Linux systems. The bash shell contains most of the powerful features available in other shells. Although the description in this chapter steps you through many bash shell features, you can learn more about the bash shell by typing `man bash`; the sidebar "Getting Help Using the Shell" shows you a few other ways to learn about using the shell.

Locating Commands

If you know the directory that contains the command you want to run, one way to run it is to type the full, or absolute, path to that command. For example, you run the `date` command from the `/bin` directory by typing

```
$ /bin/date
```

Of course, this can be inconvenient, especially if the command resides in a directory with a long pathname. The better way is to have commands stored in well-known directories, and then add those directories to your shell's PATH environment variable. The path consists of a list of directories that are checked sequentially for the commands you enter. To see your current path, type the following:

```
$ echo $PATH
/usr/local/bin:/bin:/usr/bin:/usr/X11R6/bin:/home/chris/bin
```

The results show a common default path for a regular Linux user. Directories in the path list are separated by colons. Most user commands that come with Linux are stored in the /bin, /usr/bin, or /usr/local/bin directories. Although many graphical commands (that are used with GUIs) are contained in /usr/bin, some special X commands are in the /usr/X11R6/bin directory. The last directory shown is the bin directory in the user's home directory.

Tip

If you want to add your own commands or shell scripts, place them in the bin directory in your home directory (such as /home/chris/bin for the user named chris). This directory is automatically added to your path in some Linux systems, although you may need to create that directory or add it to your PATH on other Linux systems. So, as long as you add the command to your bin with execute permission (described in the "Understanding file permissions" section), you can begin using it by simply typing the command name at your shell prompt. To make commands available to all users, add them to /usr/local/bin. ■

Unlike some other operating systems, Linux does not, by default, check the current directory for an executable before searching the path. It immediately begins searching the path, and executables in the current directory are run only if they are in the PATH variable or you give their absolute (such as /home/chris/scriptx.sh) or relative address (for example ./scriptx.sh).

Getting Help Using the Shell

When you first start using the shell, it can be intimidating. All you see is a prompt. How do you know which commands are available, which options they use, or how to use advanced features? Fortunately, lots of help is available. Here are some places you can look to supplement what you learn in this chapter:

- **Check the PATH** — Type **echo $PATH**. You see a list of the directories containing commands that are immediately accessible to you. Listing the contents of those directories displays most standard Linux commands.

- **Use the** help **command** — Some commands are built into the shell, so they do not appear in a directory. The help command lists those commands and shows options available with each of them. (Type **help | less** to page through the list.) For help with a particular built-in command, type **help command**, replacing **command** with the name that interests you. The help command works with the bash shell only.

- **Use** --help **with the command** — Many commands include a --help option that you can use to get information about how the command is used. For example, type **date --help | less**. The

continued

continued

> output shows not only options, but also time formats you can use with the date command. Other commands simply use a -h option, such as fdisk -h.
>
> - **Use the** man **command** — To learn more about a particular command, type **man** *command*. (Replace *command* with the command name you want.) A description of the command and its options appears on the screen.
>
> - **Use the** info **command** — The info command is another tool for displaying information about commands from the shell. The info command can move among a hierarchy of nodes to find information about commands and other items. Not all commands have information available in the info database, but sometimes more information can be found there than on a man page.

The path directory order is important. Directories are checked from left to right. So, in this example, if there is a command called foo located in both the /bin and /usr/bin directories, the one in /bin is executed. To have the other foo command run, you either type the full path to the command or change your PATH variable. If you are the root user, directories containing administrative commands are also in your path. These directories include /sbin and /usr/sbin. (Changing your PATH and adding directories to it are described later in this chapter.)

Not all the commands that you run are located in directories in your PATH variable. Some commands are built into the shell. Other commands can be overridden by creating aliases that define any commands and options that you want the command to run. There are also ways of defining a function that consists of a stored series of commands. Here is the order in which the shell checks for the commands you type:

1. **Aliases** — Names set by the alias command that represent a particular command and a set of options. (Type **alias** to see what aliases are set.) Often, aliases enable you to define a short name for a long, complicated command.

2. **Shell reserved word** — Words reserved by the shell for special use. Many of these are words that you would use in programming-type functions, such as do, while, case, and else.

3. **Function** — A set of commands that are executed together within the current shell.

4. **Built-in command** — A command built into the shell. As a result, there is no representation of the command in the file system. Some of the most common commands you will use are shell built-in commands, such as cd (to change directories), echo (to echo text to the screen), exit (to exit from a shell), fg (to bring a command running in the background to the foreground), history (to see a list of commands that were previously run), pwd (to list the present working directory), set (to set shell options), and type (to show the location of a command).

5. **File system command** — This command is stored in and executed from the computer's file system. (These are the commands that are indicated by the value of the PATH variable.)

To find out where a particular command is taken from, you can use the type command. (If you are using a shell other than bash, use the which command instead.) For example, to find out where the bash shell command is located, type the following:

```
$ type bash
bash is /bin/bash
```

Try these few words with the type command to see other locations of commands: which, case, and return. If a command resides in several locations, you can add the -a option to have all the known locations of the command printed.

Tip

Sometimes you run a command and receive an error message that the command was not found or that permission to run the command was denied. If the command was not found, check that you spelled the command correctly and that it is located in your PATH variable. If permission to run the command was denied, the command may be in the PATH variable, but may not be executable. Adding execute permissions to a command is described later in this chapter. Also remember that case is important, so typing CAT or Cat will not find the cat **command.** ■

Rerunning Commands

After typing a long or complex command line, learning that you mistyped something is annoying. Fortunately, some shell features let you recall previous command lines, edit those lines, or complete a partially typed command line.

The *shell history* is a list of the commands that you have entered before. Using the history command in a bash shell, you can view your previous commands. Then, using various shell features, you can recall individual command lines from that list and change them however you please.

The rest of this section describes how to do command-line editing, how to complete parts of command lines, and how to recall and work with the history list.

Command-line Editing

If you type something wrong on a command line, the bash shell ensures that you don't have to delete the entire line and start over. Likewise, you can recall a previous command line and change the elements to make a new command.

By default, the bash shell uses command-line editing that is based on the emacs text editor. (Type **man emacs** to read about it, if you care to.) If you are familiar with emacs, you probably already know most of the keystrokes described here.

Tip

If you prefer the vi **command for editing shell command lines, you can easily make that happen. Add the line:**

```
set -o vi
```

to the .bashrc **file in your home directory. The next time you open a shell, you can use** vi **commands (as described in the tutorial later in this chapter) to edit your command lines.** ■

To do the editing, you can use a combination of control keys, meta keys, and arrow keys. For example, Ctrl+F means to hold the Ctrl key and type f. Alt+F means to hold the Alt key and type f. (Instead of the Alt key, your keyboard may use a Meta key or the Esc key. On a Windows keyboard, you can use the Windows key.)

To try out a bit of command-line editing, type the following:

```
$ ls /usr/bin | sort -f | less
```

This command lists the contents of the /usr/bin directory, sorts the contents in alphabetical order (regardless of case), and pipes the output to less. The less command displays the first page of output, after which you can go through the rest of the output a line (press Enter) or a page (press spacebar) at a time (press q when you are done). Now, suppose you want to change /usr/bin to /bin. You can use the following steps to change the command:

1. Press the up arrow to have the most recent command from your shell history appear.
2. Press Ctrl+A. This moves the cursor to the beginning of the command line.
3. Press Ctrl+F or the right arrow (~RA) key. Repeat this command a few times to position the cursor under the first slash (/).
4. Press Ctrl+D. Type this command four times to delete /usr from the line.
5. Press Enter. This executes the command line.

As you edit a command line, at any point you can type regular characters to add those characters to the command line. The characters appear at the location of your cursor. You can use right → and left ← arrows to move the cursor from one end to the other on the command line. You can also press the up ↑ and down ↓ arrow keys to step through previous commands in the history list to select a command line for editing. (See the discussion on command recall for details on how to recall commands from the history list.)

There are many keystrokes you can use to edit your command lines. Table 8-1 lists the keystrokes that you can use to move around the command line.

TABLE 8-1

Keystrokes for Navigating Command Lines

Keystroke	Full Name	Meaning
Ctrl+F	Character forward	Go forward one character.
Ctrl+B	Character backward	Go backward one character.
Alt+F	Word forward	Go forward one word.
Alt+B	Word backward	Go backward one word.
Ctrl+A	Beginning of line	Go to the beginning of the current line.

continued

TABLE 8-1 *(continued)*

Keystroke	Full Name	Meaning
Ctrl+E	End of line	Go to the end of the line.
Ctrl+L	Clear screen	Clear screen and leave line at the top of the screen.

The keystrokes in Table 8-2 can be used to edit command lines.

TABLE 8-2

Keystrokes for Editing Command Lines

Keystroke	Full Name	Meaning
Ctrl+D	Delete current	Delete the current character.
Backspace	Delete previous	Delete the previous character.
Ctrl+T	Transpose character	Switch positions of current and previous characters.
Alt+T	Transpose words	Switch positions of current and previous words.
Alt+U	Uppercase word	Change the current word to uppercase.
Alt+L	Lowercase word	Change the current word to lowercase.
Alt+C	Capitalize word	Change the current word to an initial capital.
Ctrl+V	Insert special character	Add a special character. For example, to add a Tab character, press Ctrl+V+Tab.

Use the keystrokes in Table 8-3 to cut and paste text on a command line.

TABLE 8-3

Keystrokes for Cutting and Pasting Text in Command Lines

Keystroke	Full Name	Meaning
Ctrl+K	Cut end of line	Cut text to the end of the line.
Ctrl+U	Cut beginning of line	Cut text to the beginning of the line.
Ctrl+W	Cut previous word	Cut the word located behind the cursor.
Alt+D	Cut next word	Cut the word following the cursor.
Ctrl+Y	Paste recent text	Paste most recently cut text.
Alt+Y	Paste earlier text	Rotate back to previously cut text and paste it.
Ctrl+C	Delete whole line	Delete the entire line.

Command-line Completion

To save you a few keystrokes, the bash shell offers several different ways of completing partially typed values. To attempt to complete a value, type the first few characters, and then press Tab. Here are some of the values you can type partially:

- **Variable** — If the text you type begins with a dollar sign ($), the shell completes the text with a variable from the current shell.
- **Username** — If the text you type begins with a tilde (~), the shell completes the text with a username. As a result, ~username indicates the home directory of the named user.
- **Command, alias, or function** — If the text you type begins with regular characters, the shell tries to complete the text with a command, alias, or function name.
- **Hostname** — If the text you type begins with an at (@) sign, the shell completes the text with a hostname taken from the /etc/hosts file.

Tip

To add hostnames from an additional file, you can set the HOSTFILE **variable to the name of that file. The file must be in the same format as** /etc/hosts. ■

Here are a few examples of command completion. (When you see *<Tab>*, it means to press the Tab key on your keyboard.) Type the following:

```
$ echo $OS<Tab>
$ cd ~ro<Tab>
$ fing<Tab>
```

The first example causes $OS to expand to the $OSTYPE variable. In the next example, ~ro expands to the root user's home directory (~root/). Next, fing expands to the finger command.

Pressing Tab twice offers some wonderful possibilities. There are times when several possible completions for the string of characters you have entered are available. In those cases, you can check the possible ways text can be expanded by pressing Tab twice at the point where you want to do completion.

This shows the result you would get if you checked for possible completions on $P.

```
$ echo $P<Tab><Tab>
$PATH $PPID $PS1 $PS2 $PS4 $PWD
$ echo $P
```

In this case, there are six possible variables that begin with $P. After possibilities are displayed, the original command line returns, ready for you to complete it as you choose.

Command-line Recall

After you type a command line, that entire command line is saved in your shell's history list. The list is stored in a history file, from which any command can be recalled to run again. After it is recalled, you can modify the command line, as described earlier.

To view your history list, use the `history` command. Type the command without options or followed by a number to list that many of the most recent commands. For example:

```
$ history 8
382 date
383 ls /usr/bin | sort -a | more
384 man sort
385 cd /usr/local/bin
386 man more
387 useradd -m /home/chris -u 101 chris
388 passwd chris
389 history 8
```

A number precedes each command line in the list. You can recall one of those commands using an exclamation point (!). Keep in mind that when using an exclamation point, the command runs blind, without presenting an opportunity to confirm the command you're referencing. There are several ways to run a command immediately from this list, including the following:

- *!n* — Run command number. Replace the *n* with the number of the command line, and that line is run. For example, here's how to repeat the `date` command shown as command number 382 in the preceding history listing:

```
$ !382
date
Fri Oct 29 21:30:06 PDT 2011
```

- `!!` — Run previous command. Runs the previous command line. Here's how you would immediately run that same `date` command:

```
$ !!
date
Fri Oct 29 21:30:39 PDT 2011
```

- `!?string?` — Run command containing string. This runs the most recent command that contains a particular *string* of characters. For example, you can run the `date` command again by just searching for part of that command line as follows:

```
$ !?dat?
date
Fri Oct 29 21:32:41 PDT 2011
```

Instead of just running a `history` command line immediately, you can recall a particular line and edit it. You can use the following keys or key combinations to do that, as shown in Table 8-4.

Another way to work with your history list is to use the `fc` command. Type **fc** followed by a history line number, and that command line is opened in a text editor. Make the changes that you want. When you exit the editor, the command runs. You can also give a range of line numbers (for example, `fc 100 105`). All the commands open in your text editor, and then run one after the other when you exit the editor.

The history list is stored in the .bash_history file in your home directory. Up to 1,000 history commands are stored for you by default.

Note

Some people disable the history feature for the root user by setting the HISTFILE to /dev/null or simply leaving HISTSIZE blank. This prevents information about the root user's activities from potentially being exploited. If you are an administrative user with root privileges, you may want to consider emptying your file upon exiting as well for the same reasons. Also, because shell history is stored permanently when the shell exits properly, you can prevent storing a shell's history by killing a shell. For example, to kill a shell with process ID 1234, you would type kill -9 1234 from any shell. ■

TABLE 8-4

Keystrokes for Using Command History

Key(s)	Function Name	Description
Arrow keys (~UA and ~DA)	Step	Press the up and down arrow keys to step through each command line in your history list to arrive at the one you want. (Ctrl+P and Ctrl+N do the same functions, respectively.)
Ctrl+R	Reverse Incremental Search	After you press these keys, you enter a search string to do a reverse search. As you type the string, a matching command line appears that you can run or edit.
Ctrl+S	Forward Incremental Search	Same as the preceding function but for forward search. (This may not work in all instances.)
Alt+P	Reverse Search	After you press these keys, you enter a string to do a reverse search. Type a string and press Enter to see the most recent command line that includes that string.
Alt+N	Forward Search	Same as the preceding function but for forward search. (This may not work in all instances.)

Connecting and Expanding Commands

A truly powerful feature of the shell is the capability to redirect the input and output of commands to and from other commands and files. To allow commands to be strung together, the shell uses metacharacters. As noted earlier, a metacharacter is a typed character that has special meaning to the shell for connecting commands or requesting expansion.

Piping Commands

The pipe (|) metacharacter connects the output from one command to the input of another command. This lets you have one command work on some data, and then have the next command deal with the results. Here is an example of a command line that includes pipes:

```
$ cat /etc/passwd | sort | less
```

This command lists the contents of the /etc/passwd file and pipes the output to the sort command. The sort command takes the usernames that begin each line of the /etc/passwd file, sorts them alphabetically, and pipes the output to the less command (to page through the output).

Pipes are an excellent illustration of how UNIX, the predecessor of Linux, was created as an operating system made up of building blocks. A standard practice in UNIX was to connect utilities in different ways to get different jobs done. For example, before the days of graphical word processors, users created plain-text files that included macros to indicate formatting. To see how the document really appeared, they would use a command such as the following:

```
$ gunzip < /usr/share/man/man1/grep.1.gz | nroff -c -man | less
```

In this example, the contents of the grep man page (grep.1.gz) are directed to the gunzip command to be unzipped. The output from gunzip is piped to the nroff command to format the man page using the manual macro (-man). The output is piped to the less command to display the output. Because the file being displayed is in plain text, you could have substituted any number of options to work with the text before displaying it. You could sort the contents, change or delete some of the content, or bring in text from other documents. The key is that, instead of all those features being in one program, you get results from piping and redirecting input and output between multiple commands.

Sequential Commands

Sometimes you may want a sequence of commands to run, with one command completing before the next command begins. You can do this by typing several commands on the same command line and separating them with semicolons (;):

```
$ date ; troff -me verylargedocument | lpr ; date
```

In this example, I was formatting a huge document and wanted to know how long it would take. The first command (date) showed the date and time before the formatting started. The troff command formatted the document and then piped the output to the printer. When the formatting was done, the date and time were printed again (so I knew how long the troff command took to complete).

Another useful command to add to the end of a long command line is the mail command. You could add

```
; mail -s "Finished the long command" chris@example.com
```

to the end of a command line. Then, for example, a mail message is sent to the user you choose after the command completes.

Background Commands

Some commands can take a while to complete. Sometimes you may not want to tie up your shell waiting for a command to finish. In those cases, you can have the commands run in the background by using the ampersand (&).

Text formatting commands (such as nroff and troff, described earlier) are examples of commands that are often run in the background to format a large document. You also might want to create your own shell scripts that run in the background to check continuously for certain events to occur, such as the hard disk filling up or particular users logging in.

Here is an example of a command being run in the background:

```
$ troff -me verylargedocument | lpr &
```

Other ways to manage background and foreground processes are described in the "Managing Background and Foreground Processes" section later in this chapter.

Expanding Commands

With command substitution, you can have the output of a command interpreted by the shell instead of by the command itself. In this way, you can have the standard output of a command become an argument for another command. The two forms of command substitution are $(command) and `command` (backticks, not single quotes).

The command in this case can include options, metacharacters, and arguments. Here is an example of using command substitution:

```
$ vi $(find /home | grep xyzzy)
```

In this example, the command substitution is done before the vi command is run. First, the find command starts at the /home directory and prints out all files and directories below that point in the file system. The output is piped to the grep command, which filters out all files except for those that include the string xyzzy in the filename. Finally, the vi command opens all filenames for editing (one at a time) that include xyzzy.

This particular example is useful if you want to edit a file for which you know the name but not the location. As long as the string is uncommon, you can find and open every instance of a filename existing beneath a point you choose in the file system. (In other words, don't use grep from the root file system or you'll match and try to edit several thousand files.)

Expanding Arithmetic Expressions

There may be times when you want to pass arithmetic results to a command. There are two forms you can use to expand an arithmetic expression and pass it to the shell: $[expression] or $(expression). Here is an example:

```
$ echo "I am $[2011 - 1957] years old."
I am 54 years old.
```

The shell interprets the arithmetic expression first [2011 - 1957], and then passes that information to the echo command. The echo command displays the text, with the results of the arithmetic (54) inserted.

Here's an example of the other form:

```
$ echo "There are $(ls | wc -w) files in this directory."
There are 14 files in this directory.
```

This lists the contents of the current directory (ls) and runs the word count command to count the number of files found (wc -w). The resulting number (14 in this case) is echoed back with the rest of the sentence shown.

Expanding Environment Variables

Environment variables that store information within the shell can be expanded using the dollar sign ($) metacharacter. When you expand an environment variable on a command line, the value of the variable is printed instead of the variable name itself, as follows:

```
$ ls -l $BASH
-rwxr-xr-x 1 root  root  625516 Dec 5 11:13 /bin/bash
```

Using $BASH as an argument to ls -l causes a long listing of the bash command to be printed. The following section discusses shell variables.

Creating Your Shell Environment

You can tune your shell to help you work more efficiently. Your prompt can provide pertinent information each time you press Enter. You can set aliases to save your keystrokes and permanently set environment variables to suit your needs. To make each change occur when you start a shell, add this information to your shell configuration files.

Configuring Your Shell

Several configuration files support how your shell behaves. Some of the files are executed for every user and every shell, whereas others are specific to the user who creates the configuration file. Table 8-5 shows the files that are of interest to anyone using the bash shell in Linux.

TABLE 8-5

Bash Configuration Files

File	Description
/etc/profile	Sets up user environment information for every user. It is executed when you first log in. This file provides values for your path, as well as setting environment variables for such things as the location of your mailbox and the size of your history files. Finally, /etc/profile gathers shell settings from configuration files in the /etc/profile.d directory.
/etc/bashrc	Executes for every user who runs the bash shell, each time a bash shell is opened. It sets the default prompt and may add one or more aliases. Values in this file can be overridden by information in each user's ~/.bashrc file.

continued

TABLE 8-5	(continued)
File	**Description**
~/.bash_profile	Used by each user to enter information that is specific to his or her use of the shell. It is executed only once, when the user logs in. By default, it sets a few environment variables and executes the user's .bashrc file. This is a good place to add environment variables because, once set, they are inherited by future shells.
~/.bashrc	Contains the information that is specific to your bash shells. It is read when you log in and also each time you open a new bash shell. This is the best location to add aliases so that your shell picks them up.
~/.bash_logout	Executes each time you log out (exit the last bash shell). By default, it simply clears your screen.

To change the /etc/profile or /etc/bashrc files, you must be the root user. Users can change the information in the $HOME/.bash_profile, $HOME/.bashrc, and $HOME/.bash_logout files in their own home directories.

The following sections provide ideas about items to add to your shell configuration files. In most cases, you add these values to the .bashrc file in your home directory. However, if you administer a system, you may want to set some of these values as defaults for all of your Linux system's users.

Setting Your Prompt

Your prompt consists of a set of characters that appear each time the shell is ready to accept a command. The PS1 environment variable sets what the prompt contains and is what you interact with most of the time. If your shell requires additional input, it uses the values of PS2, PS3, and PS4.

When your Linux system is installed, often a prompt is set to contain more than just a dollar sign or pound sign. For example, in Fedora or Red Hat Enterprise Linux, your prompt is set to include the following information: your username, your hostname, and the base name of your current working directory. That information is surrounded by brackets and followed by a dollar sign (for regular users) or a pound sign (for the root user). Here is an example of that prompt:

```
[chris@myhost bin]$
```

If you change directories, the bin name would change to the name of the new directory. Likewise, if you were to log in as a different user or to a different host, that information would change.

You can use several special characters (indicated by adding a backslash to a variety of letters) to include different information in your prompt. These can include your terminal number, the date, and the time, as well as other pieces of information. Table 8-6 provides some examples (you can find more on the bash man page).

Tip

If you are setting your prompt temporarily by typing at the shell, you should put the value of PS1 in quotes. For example, you could type export PS1="[\t \w]\$ " to see a prompt that looks like this: [20:26:32 /var/spool]$. ■

TABLE 8-6

Characters to Add Information to bash Prompt

Special Character	Description
\!	Shows the current command history number. This includes all previous commands stored for your username.
\#	Shows the command number of the current command. This includes only the commands for the active shell.
\$	Shows the user prompt ($) or root prompt (#), depending on which user you are
\W	Shows only the current working directory base name. For example, if the current working directory was /var/spool/mail, this value simply appears as mail.
\[	Precedes a sequence of nonprinting characters. This can be used to add a terminal control sequence into the prompt for such things as changing colors, adding blink effects, or making characters bold. (Your terminal determines the exact sequences available.)
\]	Follows a sequence of nonprinting characters
\\	Shows a backslash
\d	Displays the day name, month, and day number of the current date. For example: Sat Jan 23.
\h	Shows the hostname of the computer running the shell
\n	Causes a newline to occur
\nnn	Shows the character that relates to the octal number replacing nnn
\s	Displays the current shell name. For the bash shell, the value would be bash.
\t	Prints the current time in hours, minutes, and seconds (for example, 10:14:39)
\u	Prints your current username
\w	Displays the full path to the current working directory

To make a change to your prompt permanent, add the value of PS1 to your .bashrc file in your home directory (assuming that you are using the bash shell). There may already be a PS1 value in that file that you can modify. Refer to the Bash Prompt HOWTO (www.tldp.org/HOWTO/Bash-Prompt-HOWTO) for information on changing colors, commands, and other features of your bash shell prompt.

Adding Environment Variables

You may consider adding a few environment variables to your .bashrc file. These can help make working with the shell more efficient and effective:

- TMOUT — Sets how long the shell can be inactive before bash automatically exits. The value is the number of seconds for which the shell has not received input. This can be a nice security feature, in case you leave your desk while you are still logged in to Linux. So as not to be logged off while you are working, you may want to set the value to something like TMOUT=1800 (to allow 30 minutes of idle time). You can use any terminal session to close the current shell after a set number of seconds — for example, TMOUT=30.

- PATH — As described earlier, the PATH variable sets the directories that are searched for commands you use. If you often use directories of commands that are not in your PATH, you can permanently add them. To do this, add a PATH variable to your .bashrc file. For example, to add a directory called /getstuff/bin, add the following:

```
PATH=$PATH:/getstuff/bin ; export PATH
```

This example first reads all the current path directories into the new PATH ($PATH), adds the /getstuff/bin directory, and then exports the new PATH.

Caution

Some people add the current directory to their PATH by adding a directory identified simply as a dot (.), as follows:

```
PATH=.:$PATH ; export PATH
```

This enables you always to run commands in your current directory before evaluating any other command in the path (which people may be used to if they have used DOS). However, the security risk with this procedure is that you could be in a directory that contains a command that you don't intend to run from that directory. For example, a malicious person could put an ls command in a directory that, instead of listing the content of your directory, does something devious. Because of this, the practice of adding the dot to your path is highly discouraged. ■

- WHATEVER — You can create your own environment variables to provide shortcuts in your work. Choose any name that is not being used and assign a useful value to it. For example, if you do a lot of work with files in the /work/time/files/info/memos directory, you could set the following variable:

```
M=/work/time/files/info/memos ; export M
```

You could make that your current directory by typing cd $M. You could run a program from that directory called hotdog by typing $M/hotdog. You could edit a file from there called bun by typing vi $M/bun.

Understanding Common Shell Variables

Besides those that you set yourself, system files set variables that store things such as locations of configuration files, mailboxes, and path directories. They can also store values for your shell prompts, the size of your history list, and type of operating system.

To see the environment variables currently assigned to your shell, type the `env` command. (It will probably fill more than one screen, so type `env | more` .) You can refer to the value of any of those variables by preceding it with a dollar sign ($) and placing it anywhere on a command line. For example:

```
$ echo $USER
chris
```

This command prints the value of the USER variable, which holds your username (chris). Substitute any other value for USER to print its value instead.

When you start a shell (by logging in or opening a Terminal window), a lot of environment variables are already set. Table 8-7 shows some variables that are either set when you use a bash shell or that can be set by you to use with different features.

TABLE 8-7

Common Shell Environment Variables

Variable	Description
BASH	Contains the full pathname of the `bash` command. This is usually `/bin/bash`.
BASH_VERSION	A number representing the current version of the `bash` command
EUID	This is the effective user ID number of the current user. It is assigned when the shell starts, based on the user's entry in the `/etc/passwd` file.
FCEDIT	If set, this variable indicates the text editor used by the `fc` command to edit `history` commands. If this variable isn't set, the `vi` command is used.
HISTFILE	The location of your history file. It is typically located at `$HOME/.bash_history`.
HISTFILESIZE	The number of history entries that can be stored. After this number is reached, the oldest commands are discarded. The default value is 1000.
HISTCMD	This returns the number of the current command in the history list.
HOME	This is your home directory. It is your current working directory each time you log in or type the `cd` command with any options.
HOSTTYPE	A value that describes the computer architecture on which the Linux system is running. For Intel-compatible PCs, the value is i386, i486, i586, i686, or something like i386-linux. For AMD 64-bit machines, the value is x86_64.
MAIL	This is the location of your mailbox file. The file is typically your username in the `/var/spool/mail` directory.
OLDPWD	The directory that was the working directory before you changed to the current working directory

continued

TABLE 8-7	(continued)
Variable	**Description**
OSTYPE	A name identifying the current operating system. For Fedora Linux, the OSTYPE value is either linux or linux-gnu, depending on the type of shell you are using. (Bash can run on other operating systems as well.)
PATH	The colon-separated list of directories used to find commands that you type. The default value for regular users varies for different distributions, but typically includes the following: /bin:/usr/bin:/usr/local/bin:/usr/bin/X11:/usr/X11R6/bin:~/bin. You need to type the full path or a relative path to a command you want to run that is not in your PATH. For the root user, the value also includes /sbin, /usr/sbin, and /usr/local/sbin.
PPID	The process ID of the command that started the current shell (for example, the Terminal window containing the shell)
PROMPT_ COMMAND	Can be set to a command name that is run each time before your shell prompt is displayed. Setting PROMPT_COMMAND=date lists the current date/time before the prompt appears.
PS1	Sets the value of your shell prompt. There are many items that you can read into your prompt (date, time, username, hostname, and so on). Sometimes a command requires additional prompts, which you can set with the variables PS2, PS3, and so on.
PWD	This is the directory that is assigned as your current directory. This value changes each time you change directories using the cd command.
RANDOM	Accessing this variable causes a random number to be generated. The number is between 0 and 99999.
SECONDS	The number of seconds since the time the shell was started.
SHLVL	The number of shell levels associated with the current shell session. When you log in to the shell, the SHLVL is 1. Each time you start a new bash command (by, for example, using su to become a new user, or by simply typing bash), this number is incremented.
TMOUT	Can be set to a number representing the number of seconds the shell can be idle without receiving input. After the number of seconds is reached, the shell exits. This security feature makes it less likely for unattended shells to be accessed by unauthorized people. (This must be set in the login shell for it to actually cause the shell to log out the user.)

Adding Aliases

Setting aliases can save you even more typing than setting environment variables. With aliases, you can have a string of characters execute an entire command line. You can add and list aliases with the alias command. Here are some examples of using alias from a bash shell:

```
alias p='pwd ; ls -CF'
alias rm='rm -i'
```

In the first example, the letter p is assigned to run the command pwd, and then to run ls -CF to print the current working directory and list its contents in column form. The second example runs the rm command with the -i option each time you simply type rm. (This is an alias that is often set automatically for the root user. Instead of just removing files, you are prompted for each individual file removal. This prevents you from automatically removing all the files in a directory by mistakenly typing something such as rm *.)

While you are in the shell, you can check which aliases are set by typing the alias command. If you want to remove an alias, type unalias. (Remember that if the alias is set in a configuration file, it will be set again when you open another shell.)

Managing Background and Foreground Processes

If you are using Linux over a network or from a *dumb* terminal (a monitor that allows only text input with no GUI support), your shell may be all that you have. You may be used to a graphical environment where you have a lot of programs active at the same time so that you can switch among them as needed. This shell thing can seem pretty limited.

Although the bash shell doesn't include a GUI for running many programs, it does let you move active programs between the background and foreground. In this way, you can have a lot of stuff running, while selectively choosing the one you want to deal with at the moment.

There are several ways to place an active program in the background. One mentioned earlier is to add an ampersand (&) to the end of a command line. Another way is to use the at command to run commands in a way in which they are not connected to the shell.

To stop a running command and put it in the background, press Ctrl+Z. After the command is stopped, you can either bring it back into the foreground to run (the fg command) or start it running in the background (the bg command). Keep in mind that any command running in the background might spew output during commands that you run subsequently from that shell. For example, if output appears from a command running in the background during a vi session, simply press Ctrl+L to redraw the screen to get rid of the output.

Tip
To avoid having the output appear, you should have any process running in the background send its output to a file or to null. ∎

Starting Background Processes

If you have programs that you want to run while you continue to work in the shell, you can place the programs in the background. To place a program in the background at the time you run the program, type an ampersand (&) at the end of the command line, like this:

```
$ find /usr > /tmp/allusrfiles &
```

This example command finds all files on your Linux system (starting from /usr), prints those filenames, and puts those names in the file /tmp/allusrfiles. The ampersand (&) runs that command line in the background. To check which commands you have running in the background, use the `jobs` command, as follows:

```
$ jobs
[1]   Stopped (tty output)  vi /tmp/myfile
[2]   Running               find /usr -print > /tmp/allusrfiles &
[3]   Running               nroff -man /usr/man2/* >/tmp/man2 &
[4]-  Running               nroff -man /usr/man3/* >/tmp/man3 &
[5]+  Stopped               nroff -man /usr/man4/* >/tmp/man4
```

The first job shows a text-editing command (`vi`) that I placed in the background and stopped by pressing Ctrl+Z while I was editing. Job 2 shows the `find` command I just ran. Jobs 3 and 4 show `nroff` commands currently running in the background. Job 5 had been running in the shell (foreground) until I decided too many processes were running and pressed Ctrl+Z to stop job 5 until a few processes had completed.

The plus sign (+) next to number 5 shows that it was most recently placed in the background. The minus sign (-) next to number 4 shows that it was placed in the background just before the most recent background job. Because job 1 requires terminal input, it cannot run in the background. As a result, it is `Stopped` until it is brought to the foreground again.

Tip

To see the process ID for the background job, add a `-l` (the lowercase letter L) option to the jobs command. If you type `ps`, you can use the process ID to figure out which command is for a particular background job. ∎

Using Foreground and Background Commands

Continuing with the example, you can bring any of the commands on the jobs list to the foreground. For example, to edit `myfile` again, type

```
$ fg %1
```

As a result, the `vi` command opens again, with all text as it was when you stopped the `vi` job.

Caution

Before you put a text processor, word processor, or similar program in the background, make sure you save your file. It's easy to forget you have a program in the background and you will lose your data if you log out or the computer reboots later on. ∎

To refer to a background job (to cancel or bring it to the foreground), use a percent sign (%) followed by the job number. You can also use the following to refer to a background job:

- `%` — Refers to the most recent command put into the background (indicated by the plus sign when you type the `jobs` command). This action brings the command to the foreground.

- `%string` — Refers to a job where the command begins with a particular `string` of characters. The `string` must be unambiguous. (In other words, typing `%vi` when there are two `vi` commands in the background results in an error message.)

- %?string — Refers to a job where the command line contains a string at any point. The string must be unambiguous or the match will fail.

- %-- — Refers to the previous job stopped before the one most recently stopped.

If a command is stopped, you can start it running again in the background using the bg command. For example, take job 5 from the jobs list in the previous example:

```
[5]+ Stopped              nroff -man man4/* >/tmp/man4
```

Type the following:

```
$ bg %5
```

After that, the job runs in the background. Its jobs entry appears as follows:

```
[5]  Running              nroff -man man4/* >/tmp/man4 &
```

Working with the Linux File System

The Linux file system is the structure in which all the information on your computer is stored. Files are organized within a hierarchy of directories. Each directory can contain files, as well as other directories.

If you were to map out the files and directories in Linux, it would look like an upside-down tree. At the top is the root directory, which is represented by a single slash (/). Below that is a set of common directories in the Linux system, such as bin, dev, home, lib, and tmp, to name a few. Each of those directories, as well as directories added to the root, can contain subdirectories.

Figure 8-1 illustrates how the Linux file system is organized as a hierarchy. To demonstrate how directories are connected, the figure shows a /home directory that contains subdirectories for three users: chris, mary, and tom. Within the chris directory are subdirectories: briefs, memos, and personal. To refer to a file called inventory in the chris/memos directory, you can type the full path of /home/chris/memos/inventory. If your current directory is /home/chris/memos, you can refer to the file as simply inventory.

Some of the Linux directories that may interest you include the following:

- /bin — Contains common Linux user commands, such as ls, sort, date, and chmod.

- /boot — Has the bootable Linux kernel and boot loader configuration files (GRUB).

- /dev — Contains files representing access points to devices on your systems. These include terminal devices (tty*), floppy disks (fd*), hard disks (hd*), RAM (ram*), and CD-ROM (cd*). (Users typically access these devices directly through the device files.)

- /etc — Contains administrative configuration files.

- /home — Contains directories assigned to each user with a login account (with the exception of root).

- /media — Provides a standard location for mounting and automounting devices, such as remote file systems and removable media (with directory names of cdrecorder, floppy, and so on).

- /mnt — A common mount point for many devices before it was supplanted by the standard /media directory. Some bootable Linux systems still use this directory to mount hard disk partitions and remote file systems.

- /proc — Contains information about system resources.

- /root — Represents the root user's home directory. The home directory for root does not reside beneath /home for security reasons.

- /sbin — Contains administrative commands and daemon processes.

- /sys — A /proc-like file system, new in the Linux 2.6 kernel and intended to contain files for getting hardware status and reflecting the system's device tree as it is seen by the kernel. It pulls many of its functions from /proc.

- /tmp — Contains temporary files used by applications.

- /usr — Contains user documentation, games, graphical files (X11), libraries (lib), and a variety of other commands and files that are not needed during the boot process.

- /var — Contains directories of data used by various applications. In particular, this is where you would place files that you share as an FTP server (/var/ftp) or a Web server (/var/www). It also contains all system log files (/var/log) and spool files in /var/spool (such as mail, cups, and news).

The file systems in the DOS or Microsoft Windows operating systems differ from Linux's file structure, as the sidebar "Linux File Systems versus Windows-based File Systems" explains.

FIGURE 8-1

The Linux file system is organized as a hierarchy of directories.

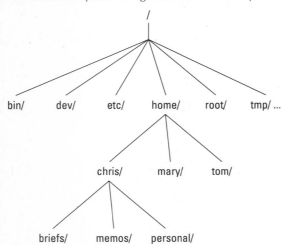

Linux File Systems versus Windows-based File Systems

Although similar in many ways, the Linux file system has some striking differences from file systems used in MS-DOS and Windows operating systems. Here are a few:

- In MS-DOS and Windows file systems, drive letters represent different storage devices (for example, A: is a floppy drive and C: is a hard disk). In Linux, all storage devices are connected to the file system hierarchy. So, the fact that all of /usr may be on a separate hard disk or that /mnt/rem1 is a file system from another computer is invisible to the user.

- Slashes, rather than backslashes, are used to separate directory names in Linux. So, C:\home\chris in an MS system is /home/chris in a Linux system.

- Filenames almost always have suffixes in DOS (such as .txt for text files or .doc for word-processing files). Although at times you can use that convention in Linux, three-character suffixes have no required meaning in Linux. They can be useful for identifying a file type. Many Linux applications and desktop environments use file suffixes to determine the contents of a file. In Linux, however, DOS command extensions such as .com, .exe, and .bat don't necessarily signify an executable (permission flags make Linux files executable).

- Every file and directory in a Linux system has permissions and ownership associated with it. Security varies among Microsoft systems. Because DOS and MS Windows began as single-user systems, file ownership was not built into those systems when they were designed. Later releases added features such as file and folder attributes to address this problem.

Creating Files and Directories

As a Linux user, most of the files you save and work with will probably be in your home directory. Table 8-8 shows commands to create and use files and directories.

TABLE 8-8

Commands to Create and Use Files

Command	Result
cd	Change to another directory.
pwd	Print the name of the current (or present) working directory.
mkdir	Create a directory.
chmod	Change the permission on a file or directory.
ls	List the contents of a directory.

The following steps lead you through creating directories within your home directory and moving among your directories, with a mention of setting appropriate file permissions:

1. Go to your home directory. To do this, simply type **cd**. (For other ways of referring to your home directory, see the "Identifying Directories" sidebar.)

2. To make sure that you're in your home directory, type **pwd**. When I do this, I get the following response (yours will reflect your home directory):

```
$ pwd
/home/chris
```

3. Create a new directory called test in your home directory, as follows:

```
$ mkdir test
```

4. Check the permissions of the directory:

```
$ ls -ld test
drwxr-xr-x  2 chris  sales   1024  Jan 24 12:17 test
```

This listing shows that test is a directory (d). The d is followed by the permissions (rwxr-xr-x), which are explained later in the "Understanding File Permissions" section. The rest of the information indicates the owner (chris), the group (sales), and the date that the files in the directory were most recently modified (Jan. 24 at 12:17 p.m.).

Note

In some Linux systems, such as Fedora, when you add a new user, the user is assigned to a group of the same name by default. For example, in the preceding text, the user chris would be assigned to the group chris. This approach to assigning groups is referred to as the user private group scheme. ∎

For now, type the following:

```
$ chmod 700 test
```

This step changes the permissions of the directory to give you complete access and everyone else no access at all. (The new permissions should read rwx------.)

5. Make the test directory your current directory as follows:

```
$ cd test
```

Identifying Directories

When you need to identify your home directory on a shell command line, you can use the following:

You can also use the tilde to identify someone else's home directory. For example, ~chris would be expanded to the chris home directory (probably /home/chris).

Other special ways of identifying directories in the shell include the following:

- **Use the** `help` **command** — Some commands are built into the shell, so they do not appear in a directory. The `help` command lists those commands and shows options available with each of them. (Type **help | less** to page through the list.) For help with a particular built-in command, type the **help *command***, replacing ***command*** with the name that interests you. The `help` command works with the bash shell only.

- **Use** `--help` **with the command** — Many commands include a `--help` option that you can use to get information about how the command is used. For example, type **date --help | less**. The output shows not only options, but also time formats you can use with the date command. Other commands simply use a `-h` option, such as `fdisk -h`.

- **Use the** `man` **command** — To learn more about a particular command, type **man *command***. (Replace **command** with the command name you want.) A description of the command and its options appears on the screen.

- **Use the** `info` **command** — The `info` command is another tool for displaying information about commands from the shell. The `info` command can move among a hierarchy of nodes to find information about commands and other items. Not all commands have information available in the info database, but sometimes more information can be found there than on a man page.

- In MS-DOS and Windows file systems, drive letters represent different storage devices (for example, A: is a floppy drive and C: is a hard disk). In Linux, all storage devices are connected to the file system hierarchy. So, the fact that all of /usr may be on a separate hard disk or that /mnt/rem1 is a file system from another computer is invisible to the user.

- Slashes, rather than backslashes, are used to separate directory names in Linux. So, C:\home\chris in an MS system is /home/chris in a Linux system.

- Filenames almost always have suffixes in DOS (such as .txt for text files or .doc for word-processing files). Although at times you can use that convention in Linux, three-character suffixes have no required meaning in Linux. They can be useful for identifying a file type. Many Linux applications and desktop environments use file suffixes to determine the contents of a file. In Linux, however, DOS command extensions such as .com, .exe, and .bat don't necessarily signify an executable (permission flags make Linux files executable).

- Every file and directory in a Linux system has permissions and ownership associated with it. Security varies among Microsoft systems. Because DOS and MS Windows began as single-user systems, file ownership was not built into those systems when they were designed. Later releases added features such as file and folder attributes to address this problem.

- `$HOME` — This environment variable stores your home directory name.

- `~` — The tilde (~) represents your home directory on the command line.

- `.` — A single dot (`.`) refers to the current directory.

- `..` — Two dots (`..`) refer to a directory directly above the current directory.

- `$PWD` — This environment variable refers to the current working directory.

- `$OLDPWD` — This environment variable refers to the previous working directory before you changed to the current one. (Typing `cd -` returns you to the directory represented by $OLDPWD.)

Using Metacharacters and Operators

To make efficient use of your shell, the bash shell lets you use certain special characters, referred to as metacharacters and operators. Metacharacters can help you match one or more files without typing each file completely. Operators enable you to direct information from one command or file to another command or file.

Using File-matching Metacharacters

To save you some keystrokes and to be able to refer easily to a group of files, the bash shell lets you use metacharacters. Anytime you need to refer to a file or directory, such as to list it, open it, or remove it, you can use metacharacters to match the files you want. Here are some useful metacharacters for matching filenames:

- `*` — Matches any number of characters.
- `?` — Matches any one character.
- `[...]` — Matches any one of the characters between the brackets, which can include a dash-separated range of letters or numbers.

Try out some of these file-matching metacharacters by first going to an empty directory (such as the test directory described in the previous section) and creating some empty files:

```
$ touch apple banana grape grapefruit watermelon
```

The touch command creates empty files. The next few commands show you how to use shell metacharacters with the ls command to match filenames. Try the following commands to see whether you get the same responses:

```
$ ls a*
apple
$ ls g*
grape
grapefruit
$ ls g*t
grapefruit
$ ls *e*
apple grape grapefruit watermelon
$ ls *n*
banana watermelon
```

The first example matches any file that begins with an a (apple). The next example matches any files that begin with g (grape, grapefruit). Next, files beginning with g and ending in t are matched (grapefruit). Next, any file that contains an e in the name is matched (apple, grape, grapefruit, watermelon). Finally, any file that contains an n is matched (banana, watermelon).

Here are a few examples of pattern matching with the question mark (?):

```
$ ls ????e
```

```
apple grape
$ ls g???e*
grape grapefruit
```

The first example matches any five-character file that ends in e (apple, grape). The second matches any file that begins with g and has e as its fifth character (grape, grapefruit).

Here are a couple of examples using braces to do pattern matching:

```
$ ls [abw]*
apple banana watermelon
$ ls [agw]*[ne]
apple grape watermelon
```

In the first example, any file beginning with a, b, or w is matched. In the second, any file that begins with a, g, or w and also ends with either n or e is matched. You can also include ranges within brackets. For example:

```
$ ls [a-g]*
apple banana grape grapefruit
```

Here, any filenames beginning with a letter from a through g is matched.

Using File-Redirection Metacharacters

Commands receive data from standard input and send it to standard output. Using pipes (described earlier), you can direct standard output from one command to the standard input of another. With files, you can use less than (<) and greater than (>) signs to direct data to and from files. Here are the file-redirection characters:

- < — Directs the contents of a file to the command. In most cases, this is the default action expected by the command and the use of the character is optional; using more bigfile is the same as more < bigfile.

- > — Directs the standard output of a command to a file, deleting the existing file.

- 2> — Directs standard error (error messages) to the file.

- &> — Directs both standard output and standard error to the file.

- >> — Directs the output of a command to a file, adding the output to the end of the existing file.

Here are some examples of command lines where information is directed to and from files:

```
$ mail root < ~/.bashrc
$ man chmod | col -b > /tmp/chmod
$ echo "I finished the project on $(date)" >> ~/projects
```

In the first example, the contents of the .bashrc file in the home directory are sent in a mail message to the computer's root user. The second command line formats the chmod man page (using the man command), removes extra back spaces (col -b), and sends the output to the file

/tmp/chmod (erasing the previous /tmp/chmod file, if it exists). The final command results in the following text being added to the user's project file:

```
I finished the project on Sat Jan 22 13:46:49 PST 2011
```

Another type of redirection referred to as *here documents* lets you type text that can be used as standard input for a command. Here documents involve entering two less-than characters (<<) after a command, followed by a word. All typing following that word is taken as user input until the word is repeated. Here is an example:

```
$ mail root cnegus rjones bdecker <<thetext
> I want to tell everyone that there will be a 10 am
> meeting in conference room B. Everyone should attend.
>
> -- James
> thetext
$
```

The example just shown sends a mail message to root, cnegus, rjones, and bdecker usernames. The text entered between <<thetext and thetext become the contents of the message. A common use of a here document is to use it with a text editor to create or add to a file from within a script:

```
/bin/ed /etc/resolv.conf <<resendit
a
nameserver 100.100.100.100
.
w
q
resendit
```

With these lines added to a script run by the root user, the ed text editor adds the IP address of a DNS server to the /etc/resolv.conf file.

Understanding File Permissions

After you've worked with Linux for a while, you are almost sure to get a Permission denied message. Permissions associated with files and directories in Linux were designed to keep users from accessing other users' private files and to protect important system files.

The nine bits assigned to each file for permissions define the access that you and others have to your file. Permission bits for a regular file appear as -rwxrwxrwx.

Note

For a regular file, a dash appears in front of the nine-bit permissions indicator. Instead of a dash, you might see a d (for a directory), l (for a link), b (for a block device), or c (for a character device). ■

Of the nine-bit permissions, the first three bits apply to the owner's permission, the next three apply to the group assigned to the file, and the last three apply to all others. The r stands for *read*, the w stands for *write*, and the x stands for *execute permissions*. If a dash appears instead of the letter, it means that permission is turned off for that associated read, write, or execute.

Because files and directories are different types of elements, read, write, and execute permissions on files and directories mean different things. Table 8-9 explains what you can do with each of them.

TABLE 8-9

Setting Read, Write, and Execute Permissions

Permission	File	Directory
Read	View what's in the file.	See what files and subdirectories it contains.
Write	Change the file's content, rename it, or delete it.	Add files or subdirectories to the directory. Remove files or directories from the directory.
Execute	Run the file as a program.	Change to that directory as the current directory, search through the directory, or execute a program from the directory. Access file metadata (file size, time stamps, etc.) of files in that directory.

You can see the permission for any file or directory by typing the `ls -ld` command. The named file or directory appears as those shown in this example:

```
$ ls -ld ch3 test
-rw-rw-r--  1 chris  sales   4983  Jan 18 22:13 ch3
drwxr-xr-x  2 chris  sales   1024  Jan 24 13:47 test
```

The first line shows that the ch3 file has read and write permission for the owner and the group. All other users have read permission, which means they can view the file but cannot change its contents or remove it. The second line shows the test directory (indicated by the letter d before the permission bits). The owner has read, write, and execute permissions while the group and other users have only read and execute permissions. As a result, the owner can add, change, or delete files in that directory, and everyone else can only read the contents, change to that directory, and list the contents of the directory.

If you own a file, you can use the chmod command to change the permission on it as you please. In one method of doing this, each permission (read, write, and execute) is assigned a number — r=4, w=2, and x=1 — and you use each set's total number to establish the permission. For example, to make permissions wide open for yourself as owner, you would set the first number to 7 (4+2+1), and then you would give the group and others read-only permission by setting both the second and third numbers to 4 (4+0+0), so that the final number is 744. Any combination of permissions can result from 0 (no permission) through 7 (full permission).

Here are some examples of how to change permission on a file (named file) and what the resulting permission would be:

```
# chmod 777 file      rwxrwxrwx
# chmod 755 file      rwxr-xr-x
# chmod 644 file      rw-r--r-
# chmod 000 file      ---------
```

You can also turn file permissions on and off using plus (+) and minus (-) signs, respectively. This can be done for the owner user (u), owner group (g), others (o), and all users (a). For example, start with a file that has all permissions open (rwxrwxrwx). Run the following chmod commands using minus sign options. The resulting permissions are shown to the right of each command:

```
chmod a-w file        r-xr-xr-x
chmod o-x file        rwxrwxrw-
chmod go-rwx file     rwx------
```

Likewise, here are some examples, starting with all permissions closed (---------) where the plus sign is used with chmod to turn permissions on:

```
chmod u+rw files      rw-------
chmod a+x files       --x--x--x
chmod ug+rx files     r-xr-x---
```

When you create a file, it's given the permission rw-r--r-- by default. A directory is given the permission rwxr-xr-x. These default values are determined by the value of umask. Type **umask** to see what your umask value is. For example:

```
$ umask
022
```

The umask value masks the permissions value of 666 for a file and 777 for a directory. The umask value of 022 results in permission for a directory of 755 (rwxr-xr-x). That same umask results in a file permission of 644 (rw-r--r--). (Execute permissions are off by default for regular files.)

Tip

Time saver: Use the -R options of chmod to change the permission for all the files and directories within a directory structure at once. For example, if you wanted to open permissions completely to all files and directories in the /tmp/test directory, you could type the following:

```
$ chmod -R 777 /tmp/test
```

This command line runs chmod recursively (-R) for the /tmp/test directory, as well as any files or directories that exist below that point in the file system (for example, /tmp/test/hat, /tmp/test/hat/caps, and so on). All would be set to 777 (full read/write/execute permissions). This is not something you would do on an important directory on a read/write file system. However, you might do this before you create a directory structure on a CD-ROM that you want to be fully readable and executable to someone using the CD-ROM later. ∎

Caution

The -R option of chmod works best if you are opening permissions completely or adding execute permission (as well as the appropriate read/write permission). If you were to turn off execute permission recursively, you would close off your capability to change to any directory in that structure. For example, chmod -R 644 /tmp/test turns off execute permission for the /tmp/test directory, and then fails to change any files or directories below that point. Execute permissions must be on for a directory to be able to change to that directory. ∎

Moving, Copying, and Deleting Files

Commands for moving, copying, and deleting files are fairly straightforward. To change the location of a file, use the mv command. To copy a file from one location to another, use the cp command. To remove a file, use the rm command. Here are some examples:

```
$ mv abc def
$ mv abc ~
$ cp abc def
$ cp abc ~
$ rm abc
$ rm *
```

Of the two move (mv) commands, the first moves the file abc to the file def in the same directory (essentially renaming it), whereas the second moves the file abc to your home directory (~). The first copy command (cp) copies abc to the file def in the same directory, whereas the second copies abc to your home directory (~). The first remove command (rm) deletes the abc file; the second removes all the files in the current directory (except those that start with a dot).

Note

For the root user, the mv, cp, and rm commands are aliased to each be run with the -i option. This causes a prompt to appear asking you to confirm each move, copy, and removal, one file at a time, and is done to prevent the root user from messing up a large group of files by mistake.

Another alternative with mv is to use the -b option. With -b, if a file of the same name exists at the destination, a backup copy of the old file is made before the new file is moved there. ■

Using the vi Text Editor

It's almost impossible to use Linux for any period of time and not need a text editor. This is because most Linux configuration files are plain-text files that you will almost certainly need to change manually at some point.

If you are using a GUI, you can run gedit, which is fairly intuitive for editing text. There's also a simple text editor you can run from the shell called nano. However, most Linux shell users will use either the vi or emacs command to edit text files. The advantage of vi or emacs over a graphical editor is that you can use it from any shell, a character terminal, or character-based connection over a network (using telnet or ssh, for example) — no GUI is required. They also each contain tons of features, so you can continue to grow with them.

This section provides a brief tutorial on the vi text editor, which you can use to manually edit a configuration file from any shell. (If vi doesn't suit you, see the "Exploring Other Text Editors" sidebar for other options.)

The vi editor is difficult to learn at first, but once you know it, you never have to use a mouse or a function key — you can edit and move around quickly and efficiently within files just by using the keyboard.

Exploring Other Text Editors

Dozens of text editors are available for use with Linux. Here are a few that might be in your Linux distribution, which you can try out if you find vi to be too taxing.

Text Editor	Description
Nano	A popular, streamlined text editor that is used with many bootable Linuxes and other limited-space Linux environments. For example, nano is available to edit text files during a Gentoo Linux install process.
gedit	The GNOME text editor that runs in the GUI.
jed	This screen-oriented editor was made for programmers. Using colors, jed can highlight code you create so you can easily read the code and spot syntax errors. Use the Alt key to select menus to manipulate your text.
joe	The joe editor is similar to many PC text editors. Use control and arrow keys to move around. Press Ctrl+C to exit with no save or Ctrl+X to save and exit.
Kate	A nice-looking editor that comes in the kdebase package. It has lots of bells and whistles, such as highlighting for different types of programming languages and controls for managing word wrap.
Kedit	A GUI-based text editor that comes with the KDE desktop.
mcedit	With mcedit, function keys help you get around, save, copy, move, and delete text. Like jed and joe, mcedit is screen-oriented.
nedit	An excellent programmer's editor. You need to install the optional nedit package to get this editor.

If you use ssh to log in to other Linux computers on your network, you can use any editor to edit files. A GUI-based editor will pop up on your screen. When no GUI is available, you will need a text editor that runs in the shell, such as vi, jed, or joe.

Starting with vi

Most often, you start vi to open a particular file. For example, to open a file called /tmp/test, type the following command:

```
$ vi /tmp/test
```

If this is a new file, you should see something similar to the following:

```
~
~
~
~
```

```
~
"/tmp/test" [New File]
```

The box at the top represents where your cursor is. The bottom line keeps you informed about what is going on with your editing (here you just opened a new file). In between, there are tildes (~) as filler because there is no text in the file yet. Now here's the intimidating part: There are no hints, menus, or icons to tell you what to do. On top of that, you can't just start typing. If you do, the computer is likely to beep at you. And some people complain that Linux isn't friendly.

The first things you need to know are the different operating modes: command and input. The vi editor always starts in command mode. Before you can add or change text in the file, you have to type a command (one or two letters and an optional number) to tell vi what you want to do. Case is important, so use uppercase and lowercase exactly as shown in the examples! To get into input mode, type an input command. To start out, type either of the following:

- **a** — The add command. After it, you can input text that starts to the *right* of the cursor.
- **i** — The insert command. After it, you can input text that starts to the *left* of the cursor.

Tip

When you are in insert mode, `-- INSERT --` will appear at the bottom of the screen. ∎

Type a few words and then press Enter. Repeat that a few times until you have a few lines of text. When you're finished typing, press Esc to return to command mode. Now that you have a file with some text in it, try moving around in your text with the following keys or letters:

Tip

Remember the Esc key! It always places you back into command mode. ∎

- **Arrow keys** — Move the cursor up, down, left, or right in the file one character at a time. To move left and right, you can also use Backspace and the spacebar, respectively. If you prefer to keep your fingers on the keyboard, move the cursor with h (left), l (right), j (down), or k (up).
- **w** — Moves the cursor to the beginning of the next word.
- **b** — Moves the cursor to the beginning of the previous word.
- **0** (zero) — Moves the cursor to the beginning of the current line.
- **$** — Moves the cursor to the end of the current line.
- **H** — Moves the cursor to the upper-left corner of the screen (first line on the screen).
- **M** — Moves the cursor to the first character of the middle line on the screen.
- **L** — Moves the cursor to the lower-left corner of the screen (last line on the screen).

The only other editing you need to know is how to delete text. Here are a few vi commands for deleting text:

- **x** — Deletes the character under the cursor.
- **X** — Deletes the character directly before the cursor.

- **dw** — Deletes from the current character to the end of the current word.
- **d$** — Deletes from the current character to the end of the current line.
- **d0** — Deletes from the previous character to the beginning of the current line.

To wrap things up, use the following keystrokes for saving and quitting the file:

- **ZZ** — Save the current changes to the file and exit from vi.
- **:w** — Save the current file but continue editing.
- **:wq** — Same as ZZ.
- **:q** — Quit the current file. This works only if you don't have any unsaved changes.
- **:q!** — Quit the current file and *don't* save the changes you just made to the file.

Tip

If you've really trashed the file by mistake, the `:q!` command is the best way to exit and abandon your changes. The file reverts to the most recently changed version. So, if you just did a `:w`, you are stuck with the changes up to that point. If you just want to undo a few bad edits, press u to back out of changes. ■

You have learned a few vi editing commands. I describe more commands in the following sections. First, however, here are a few tips to smooth out your first trials with vi:

- **Esc** — Remember that Esc gets you back to command mode. (I've watched people press every key on the keyboard trying to get out of a file.) Esc followed by ZZ gets you out of command mode, saves the file, and exits.
- **u** — Press u to undo the previous change you made. Continue to press u to undo the change before that, and the one before that.
- **Ctrl+R** — If you decide you didn't want to undo the previous command, use Ctrl+R for Redo. Essentially, this command undoes your undo.
- **Caps Lock** — Beware of hitting Caps Lock by mistake. Everything you type in vi has a different meaning when the letters are capitalized. You don't get a warning that you are typing capitals — things just start acting weird.
- **:!** *command* — You can run a command while you are in vi using `:!` followed by a command name. For example, type `:!date` to see the current date and time, type `:!pwd` to see what your current directory is, or type `:!jobs` to see whether you have any jobs running in the background. When the command completes, press Enter and you are back to editing the file. You could even use this technique to launch a shell (`:!bash`) from vi, run a few commands from that shell, and then type `exit` to return to vi. (I recommend doing a save before escaping to the shell, just in case you forget to go back to vi.)
- **Ctrl+G** — If you forget what you are editing, pressing these keys displays the name of the file that you are editing and the current line that you are on at the bottom of the screen. It also displays the total number of lines in the file, the percentage of how far you are through the file, and the column number the cursor is on. This just helps you get your bearings after you've stopped for a cup of coffee at 3 a.m.

Moving Around the File

Besides the few movement commands described earlier, there are other ways of moving around a vi file. To try these out, open a large file that you can't do much damage to. (Try copying /var /log/messages to /tmp and opening it in vi.) Here are some movement commands you can use:

- **Ctrl+F** — Page ahead, one page at a time.
- **Ctrl+B** — Page back, one page at a time.
- **Ctrl+D** — Page ahead one-half page at a time.
- **Ctrl+U** — Page back one-half page at a time.
- **G** — Go to the last line of the file.
- **1G** — Go to the first line of the file. (Use any number to go to that line in the file.)

Searching for Text

To search for the next or previous occurrence of text in the file, use either the slash (/) or the question mark (?) character. Follow the slash or question mark with a pattern (string of text) to search forward or backward, respectively, for that pattern. Within the search, you can also use metacharacters. Here are some examples:

- /hello — Searches forward for the word hello.
- ?goodbye — Searches backward for the word goodbye.
- /The.*foot — Searches forward for a line that has the word The in it and also, after that at some point, the word foot.
- ?[pP]rint — Searches backward for either print or Print. Remember that case matters in Linux, so make use of brackets to search for words that could have different capitalization.

After you have entered a search term, simply type n or N to search forward or backward for the same term again, respectively.

The vi editor was originally based on the ex editor, which didn't let you work in full-screen mode. However, it did enable you to run commands that let you find and change text on one or more lines at a time. When you type a colon and the cursor goes to the bottom of the screen, you are essentially in ex mode. Here is an example of some of those ex commands for searching for and changing text. (I chose the words Local and Remote to search for, but you can use any appropriate words.)

- :g/Local — Searches for the word Local and prints every occurrence of that line from the file. (If there is more than a screenful, the output is piped to the more command.)
- :s/Local/Remote — Substitutes Remote for the word Local on the current line.
- :g/Local/s//Remote — Substitutes the first occurrence of the word Local on every line of the file with the word Remote.

- `:g/Local/s//Remote/g` — Substitutes every occurrence of the word Local with the word Remote in the entire file.

- `:g/Local/s//Remote/gp` — Substitutes every occurrence of the word Local with the word Remote in the entire file, and then prints each line so that you can see the changes (piping it through `more` if output fills more than one page).

Using Numbers with Commands

You can precede most vi commands with numbers to have the command repeated that number of times. This is a handy way to deal with several lines, words, or characters at a time. Here are some examples:

- `3dw` — Deletes the next three words.
- `5cl` — Changes the next five letters (that is, removes the letters and enters input mode).
- `12j` — Moves down 12 lines.

Putting a number in front of most commands just repeats those commands. At this point, you should be fairly proficient at using the `vi` command. After you get used to using vi, you will probably find other text editors less efficient to use.

Note
When you invoke vi in many Linux systems, you're actually invoking the vim text editor, which runs in vi compatibility mode. Those who do a lot of programming might prefer vim because it shows different levels of code in different colors. vim has other useful features, such as the capability to open a document with the cursor at the same place as it was when you last exited that file. ∎

Learning More about vi

To learn more about the vi editor, try typing `vimtutor`. The `vimtutor` command opens a tutorial in your vi editor that steps you through common commands and features you can use in vi.

Summary

Working from a shell command line within Linux may not be as simple as using a GUI, but it offers many powerful and flexible features. This chapter explained how to find your way around the shell in Linux and provided examples of running commands, including recalling commands from a history list, completing commands, and joining commands.

The chapter described how shell environment variables can be used to store and recall important pieces of information. It also taught you how to modify shell configuration files to tailor the shell to suit your needs. Finally, this chapter showed you how to use the Linux file system to create files and directories, use permissions, and work with files (moving, copying, and removing them), and how to edit text files from the shell using the `vi` command.

Learning Basic Administration

Your system administrator duties don't end after you have installed Linux. If multiple people are using your Linux system, you, as administrator, must give each person his own login account. You'll use useradd and related commands to add, modify, and delete user accounts.

Configuring hardware is also on your duty list. When you add hardware to your Linux computer, that hardware is often detected and configured automatically. In some cases, however, the hardware may not have been set up properly, and you will use commands such as lsmod, modprobe, insmod, and rmmod to configure the right modules to get the hardware working.

Note

A module is object code that is loaded on demand. Most modules are device drivers that allow application programs to talk to a particular piece of hardware. The "Configure Hardware" section later in this chapter includes information about configuring modules. ∎

Your duties also include monitoring system performance. You may have a runaway process on your system or you may just be experiencing slow performance. Tools that come with Linux can help you determine how much of your CPU and memory are being consumed.

These tasks are explored in this chapter.

IN THIS CHAPTER

Creating user accounts

Configuring hardware

Monitoring system performance

Doing remote system administration

Creating User Accounts

Every person who uses your Linux system should have a separate user account. Having a user account provides each person with an area in which to securely store files, as well as a means of tailoring his or her user interface (GUI, path, environment variables, and so on) to suit the way that he or she uses the computer.

You can add user accounts to most Linux systems in several ways — Fedora and Red Hat Enterprise Linux systems use the system-config-users utility, for example, and SUSE offers a user setup module in YaST. This chapter describes how to add user accounts from the command line with useradd because most Linux systems include that command. (In some cases a Linux system will have a similar command called adduser.)

Adding Users with useradd

The most straightforward method for creating a new user from the shell is with the useradd command. After opening a Terminal window with root permission, you simply invoke useradd at the command prompt, with details of the new account as parameters.

The only required parameter is the login name of the user, but you probably want to include some additional information ahead of it. Each item of account information is preceded by a single letter option code with a dash in front of it. Table 9-1 lists the options available with useradd.

TABLE 9-1

useradd Command Options

Option	Description
-c comment -c "comment here"	Provide a description of the new user account. Often the person's full name. Replace comment with the name of the user account (-c jake). Use quotes to enter multiple words (-c "jake jackson").
-d home_dir	Set the home directory to use for the account. The default is to name it the same as the login name and to place it in /home. Replace home_dir with the directory name to use (for example, -d /mnt/homes/jake).
-D	Rather than create a new account, save the supplied information as the new default settings for any new accounts that are created.
-e expire_date	Assign the expiration date for the account in YYYY-MM-DD format. Replace expire_date with a date you want to use (-e 2011-05-06).
-f -1	Set the number of days after a password expires until the account is permanently disabled. The default, -1, disables the option. Setting this to 0 disables the account immediately after the password has expired. Replace -1 with the number to use.

Option	Description
-g *group*	Set the primary group (as listed in the /etc/group file) the new user will be in. Replace *group* with the group name (-g wheel).
-G *grouplist*	Add the new user to the supplied comma-separated list of groups (-G wheel,sales,tech,lunch).
-k *skel_dir*	Set the skeleton directory containing initial configuration files and login scripts that should be copied to a new user's home directory. This parameter can be used only in conjunction with the -m option. Replace *skel_dir* with the directory name to use. (Without this option, the /etc/skel directory is used.)
-m	Automatically create the user's home directory and copy the files in the skeleton directory (/etc/skel) to it.
-M	Do not create the new user's home directory, even if the default behavior is set to create it.
-n	Turn off the default behavior of creating a new group that matches the name and user ID of the new user. This option is available with Red Hat Linux systems. Other Linux systems often assign a new user to the group named users instead.
-o	Use with -u *uid* to create a user account that has the same UID as another username. (This effectively lets you have two different usernames with authority over the same set of files and directories.)
-p *passwd*	Enter a password for the account you are adding. This must be an encrypted password. Instead of adding an encrypted password here, you can simply use the passwd *user* command later to add a password for *user*.
-s *shell*	Specify the command shell to use for this account. Replace *shell* with the command shell (-s bash).
-u *user_id*	Specify the user ID number for the account (-u 474). Without the -u option, the default behavior is to automatically assign the next available number. Replace *user_id* with the ID number (-u).

For example, let's create an account for a new user named Mary Smith with a login name of mary. First, log in as root, and then type the following command:

```
# useradd -c "Mary Smith" mary
```

Tip

When you choose a username, don't begin with a number (for example, 26jsmith). Also, it's best to use all lowercase letters, no control characters or spaces, and a maximum of eight characters. The useradd command allows up to 32 characters, but some applications can't deal with usernames that long. Tools such as ps display UIDs instead of names if names are too long. Having users named Jsmith and jsmith can cause confusion with programs (such as Sendmail) that don't distinguish case. ■

Next, set Mary's initial password using the `passwd` command. You're prompted to type the password twice:

```
# passwd mary
Changing password for user mary.
New password: *******
Retype new password: *******
```

Note

Asterisks in this example represent the password you type. Nothing is actually displayed when you type the password. Also keep in mind that running `passwd` as root user lets you add short or blank passwords that regular users cannot add themselves. ∎

In creating the account for Mary, the `useradd` command performs several actions:

- Reads the `/etc/login.defs` and `/etc/default/useradd` files to get default values to use when creating accounts
- Checks command-line parameters to find out which default values to override
- Creates a new user entry in the `/etc/passwd` and `/etc/shadow` files based on the default values and command-line parameters
- Creates any new group entries in the `/etc/group` file. (Fedora creates a group using the new user's name; Gentoo adds the user to the users group; and SUSE adds it to every group you set for new users, such as dialout, audio, video, and other services.)
- Creates a home directory, based on the user's name, in the `/home` directory
- Copies any files located within the `/etc/skel` directory to the new home directory. This usually includes login and application startup scripts.

The preceding example uses only a few of the available `useradd` options. Most account settings are assigned using default values. You can set more values explicitly, if you want to; here's an example that uses a few more options to do so:

```
# useradd -g users -G wheel,apache -s /bin/tcsh -c "Mary Smith" mary
```

In this case, `useradd` is told to make `users` the primary group Mary belongs to (`-g`), add her to the wheel and apache groups, and assign tcsh as her primary command shell (`-s`). A home directory in `/home` under the user's name (`/home/mary`) is created by default. This command line results in a line similar to the following being added to the `/etc/passwd` file:

```
mary:x:502:100:Mary Smith:/home/mary:/bin/tcsh
```

Each line in the `/etc/passwd` file represents a single user account record. Each field is separated from the next by a colon (`:`) character. The field's position in the sequence determines what it is. As you can see, the login name is first. Again, the password field contains an x because we are using a shadow password file to store encrypted password data. The user ID selected by `useradd` is 502. The primary group ID is 100, which corresponds to the users group in the `/etc/group` file. The comment field was correctly set to Mary Smith, the home directory was automatically assigned as /home/mary, and the command shell was assigned as /bin/tcsh, exactly as specified with the useradd options.

By leaving out many of the options (as I did in the first useradd example), defaults are assigned in most cases. For example, by not using -g users or -G wheel,apache, in Fedora a group named mary would have been created and assigned to the new user. Other Linux systems assign users as the group name by default. Likewise, excluding -s /bin/tcsh causes /bin/bash to be assigned as the default shell.

The /etc/group file holds information about the different groups on your Linux system and the users who belong to them. Groups are useful for enabling multiple users to share access to the same files while denying access to others. Peek at the /etc/group file, and you find something similar to this:

```
bin:x:1:root,bin,daemon
daemon:x:2:root,bin,daemon
sys:x:3:root,bin,adm
adm:x:4:root,adm,daemon
tty:x:5:
disk:x:6:root
lp:x:7:daemon,lp
mem:x:8:
kmem:x:9:
wheel:x:10:root,joe,mary
apache:x:48:mary
     .
     .
     .
nobody:x:99:
users:x:100:
chris:x:500
sheree:x:501
```

Each line in the group file contains the name of a group, the group ID number associated with it, and a list of users in that group. By default, each user is added to his or her own group, beginning with GID 500. Note that Mary was added to the wheel and apache groups instead of having her own group.

It is actually rather significant that Mary was added to the wheel group. By doing this, you grant her the capability to use the sudo command to run commands as the root user (provided that sudo is configured as described in Chapter 6).

Setting User Defaults

The useradd command determines the default values for new accounts by reading the /etc/login.defs and /etc/default/useradd files. You can modify those defaults by editing the files manually with a standard text editor. Although login.defs is different on different Linux systems, here is an example containing many of the settings you might find in a login.defs file:

```
PASS_MAX_DAYS      99999
PASS_MIN_DAYS      0
PASS_MIN_LEN       5
PASS_WARN_AGE      7

UID_MIN                     500
UID_MAX                   60000
GID_MIN                     500
GID_MAX                   60000

CREATE_HOME  yes
```

All uncommented lines contain keyword/value pairs. For example, the keyword PASS_MIN_LEN is followed by some white space and the value 5. This tells useradd that the user password must be at least five characters. Other lines let you customize the valid range of automatically assigned user ID numbers or group ID numbers. (Fedora starts at UID 500; other Linuxes start with UID 100.) A comment section that explains that keyword's purpose precedes each keyword (which I edited out here to save space). Altering a default value is as simple as editing the value associated with a keyword and then saving the file.

If you want to view the defaults, you can find them in the /etc/default/useradd file. Another way is to type the useradd command with the -D option, as follows:

```
# useradd -D
GROUP=100
HOME=/home
INACTIVE=-1
EXPIRE=
SHELL=/bin/bash
SKEL=/etc/skel
```

You can also use the -D option to change defaults. When run with this flag, useradd refrains from actually creating a new user account; instead, it saves any additionally supplied options as the new default values in /etc/default/useradd. Not all useradd options can be used in conjunction with the -D option. You can use only the five options listed in Table 9-2.

To set any of the defaults, give the -D option first, and then add the defaults you want to set. For example, to set the default home directory location to /home/everyone and the default shell to /bin/tcsh, type the following:

```
# useradd -D -b /home/everyone -s /bin/tcsh
```

In addition to setting up user defaults, an administrator can create default files that are copied to each user's home directory for use. These files can include login scripts and shell configuration files (such as .bashrc).

TABLE 9-2

useradd Options for Changing User Defaults

Options	Description
-b *default_home*	Set the default directory in which user home directories are created. Replace *default_home* with the directory name to use (-b /garage). Usually this is /home.
-e *default_expire_date*	Set the default expiration date on which the user account is disabled. The *default_expire_date* value should be replaced with a date in the form YYYY-MM-DD (-e 2011-10-15).
-f *default_inactive*	Set the number of days after a password has expired before the account is disabled. Replace *default_inactive* with a number representing the number of days (-f 7).
-g *default_group*	Set the default group that new users will be placed in. Normally useradd creates a new group with the same name and ID number as the user. Replace *default_group* with the group name to use (-g bears).
-s *default_shell*	Set the default shell for new users. Normally this is /bin/bash. Replace *default_shell* with the full path to the shell that you want as the default for new users (-s /bin/ash).

Other commands that are useful for working with user accounts include usermod (to modify settings for an existing account) and userdel (to delete an existing user account).

Modifying Users with usermod

The usermod command provides a simple and straightforward method for changing account parameters. Many of the options available with it mirror those found in useradd. Table 9-3 lists the options that can be used with this command.

TABLE 9-3

usermod Options

Option	Description
-c *username*	Change the description associated with the user account. Replace *username* with the name of the user account (-c jake). Use quotes to enter multiple words (-c "jake jackson").
-d *home_dir*	Change the home directory to use for the account. The default is to name it the same as the login name and to place it in /home. Replace *home_dir* with the directory name to use (for example, -d /mnt/homes/jake).

continued

TABLE 9-3	*(continued)*
Option	**Description**
-e *expire_date*	Assign a new expiration date for the account in YYYY-MM-DD format. Replace *expire_date* with a date you want to use (-e 2011-10-15).
-f -1	Change the number of days after a password expires until the account is permanently disabled. The default, -1, disables the option. Setting this to 0 disables the account immediately after the password has expired. Replace -1 with the number to use.
-g *group*	Change the primary group (as listed in the /etc/group file) the user will be in. Replace *group* with the group name (-g wheel).
-G *grouplist*	Set the user's secondary groups to the supplied comma-separated list of groups. If the user is already in at least one group besides the user's private group, you must add the -a option as well. Otherwise, the user will only belong to the new set of groups and lose membership to any previous groups.
-l *login_name*	Change the login name of the account.
-m	Available only when -d is used, this causes the contents of the user's home directory to be copied to the new directory.
-o	Use only with -u uid to remove the restriction that UIDs must be unique.
-s *shell*	Specify a different command shell to use for this account. Replace shell with the command shell (-s bash).
-u *user_id*	Change the user ID number for the account. Replace user_id with the ID number (-u 474).

As an example, to change the shell to the csh shell for the user named chris, type the following as root user from a shell:

```
# usermod -s /bin/csh chris
```

Deleting Users with userdel

Just as usermod is used to modify user settings and useradd is used to create users, userdel is used to remove users. The following command will remove the user chris:

```
# userdel chris
```

The only option available with this utility is -r, which is used to remove not only the user, but also that user's home directory:

```
# userdel -r chris
```

Configuring Hardware

In a perfect world, after installing and booting Linux, all of your hardware is detected and available for access. Although many Linux systems are rapidly moving closer to that world, there are times when you must take special steps to get your computer hardware working. Also, the growing use of removable USB and FireWire devices (CDs, DVDs, flash drives, digital cameras, and removable hard drives) has made it important for Linux to

- Efficiently manage hardware that comes and goes
- Look at the same piece of hardware in different ways (for example, be able to see a printer as a fax machine, scanner, and storage device, as well as a printer)

If you are using a Linux system that includes the 2.6 kernel (as the latest versions of most major Linux systems do), new kernel features have made it possible to change drastically the way hardware devices are detected and managed. Features in, or closely related to, the kernel include Udev (to dynamically name and create devices as hardware comes and goes) and Hotplug and HAL (to pass information about hardware changes to user space).

If all this sounds a bit confusing, don't worry. It's actually designed to make your life as a Linux user much easier. The end result of features built on the 2.6 kernel is that device handling in Linux has become

- **More automatic** — For most common hardware, when a hardware device is connected or disconnected, it is automatically detected and identified. Interfaces to access the hardware are added, so it is accessible to Linux. Then the fact that the hardware is present (or removed) is passed to the user level, where applications listening for hardware changes are ready to mount the hardware and/or launch an application (such as an image viewer or music player).

- **More flexible** — If you don't like what happens automatically when a hardware item is connected or disconnected, you can change it. For example, features built into GNOME and KDE desktops let you choose what happens when a music CD or movie DVD is inserted, or when a digital camera is connected. If you prefer that a different program be launched to handle it, you can easily make that change.

This section covers several issues relating to getting your hardware working properly in Linux. First, it describes how to configure Linux to deal with removable media. Then it tells how to use tools for manually loading and working with drivers for hardware that is not detected and loaded properly.

Managing Removable Hardware

Linux systems such as SUSE, RHEL, Fedora, and others that support full KDE and GNOME desktop environments include simple graphical tools for configuring what happens when you attach popular removable devices to the computer. So, with a KDE or GNOME desktop running, you simply plug in a USB device or insert a CD or DVD, and a window may pop up to deal with that device.

Although different desktop environments share many of the same underlying mechanisms (in particular, Udev) to detect and name removable hardware, they offer different tools for configuring how they are mounted or used. Udev (using the udevd daemon) creates and removes devices (/dev directory) as hardware is added and removed from the computer. The Hardware Abstraction Layer (HAL) provides the overall platform for discovering and configuring hardware. Settings that are of interest to someone using a desktop Linux system, however, can be configured with easy-to-use desktop tools.

The following sections describe how removable hardware and media are configured, using a GNOME desktop in Fedora and a KDE desktop in SUSE.

Removable Media on a GNOME Desktop

The Nautilus file manager used with the GNOME desktop lets you define what happens when you attach removable devices or insert removable media into the computer from the File Management Preferences window. The descriptions in this section are based on GNOME 2.24.

From a Nautilus file manager window, select Edit ➪ Preferences, and then select the Media tab to see how your system is configured to handle removable media. Figure 9-1 shows an example of that window.

FIGURE 9-1

Change removable media settings in Nautilus.

The following settings are available from the Media tab on the File Management Preferences window. These settings relate to how removable media are handled when they are inserted or plugged in. In most cases, you are prompted how to handle a medium that is inserted or connected.

- **CD Audio** — When an audio CD is inserted, you can choose to be prompted for what to do (default), do nothing, open the contents in a folder window, or select from various audio CD players to be launched to play the content. Rhythmbox music player and Sound Juicer CD ripper are among the choices you have for handling an inserted audio CD.

- **DVD Video** — When a commercial video DVD is inserted, you are prompted for what to do with that DVD. You can change that default to launch Movie Player (Totem) or another media player you have installed (such as MPlayer).

- **Music Player** — When inserted media contains audio files, you are asked what to do. You can select to have Rhythmbox or some other music player begin playing the files by selecting that player from this box.

- **Photos** — When inserted media (such as a memory card from a digital camera) contains digital images, you are asked what to do with those images. You can select to do nothing. Or you can select to have the images opened in gThumb image viewer or F-Spot photo manager.

- **Software** — When inserted media contains an autorun application, an autorun prompt will open. To change that behavior (to do nothing or open the media contents in a folder), you can select that from this box.

- **Other Media** — Select the Type box under the Other Media heading to select how less commonly used media are handled. For example, you can select what actions are taken to handle blank Blu-Ray discs, CDs, or DVDs. You can select what applications to launch for Blu-Ray video, DVD audio, HD DVD videos, picture CDs, super video CDs, and video CDs.

Note that the settings described here are only in effect for the user who is currently logged in. If multiple users have login accounts, each can have his or her own way of handling removable media.

Note

The Totem movie player will not play movie DVDs unless you add extra software to decrypt the DVD. There are legal issues and other movie player options you should look into if you want to play commercial DVD movies from Linux. ■

If you have an earlier version of GNOME, you may see a Portable Music Players entry. A music player is started in Linux to play files from your portable iPod or other music player, if that is selected and you enter a player to use. The Banshee project (`http://banshee-project.org`) includes software for playing music from iPods in Linux. (From Fedora, type **yum install banshee** to install the software from the Fedora repository. Then add **ipod %d** to this field to use the player.) Other players with iPod support include gPodder (`http://gpodder.berlios.de/`) and gtkpod (`http://www.gtkpod.org/`).

Removable Media on a SUSE KDE Desktop

When you insert a removable medium (CD or DVD) or plug in a removable device (digital camera or USB flash drive) from a KDE desktop in openSUSE, a window opens to let you choose the type of action to take on it. If you want to add a different action, or change an existing action, click the Configure button.

Figure 9-2 shows an example of the window that appears when a 32MB USB flash drive is inserted, as well as the KDE Control Module that appears when Configure is selected.

FIGURE 9-2

Use the KDE Control Module to set how to respond to inserted media.

From the KDE Control Module, select the media type you want to change (in this case, Mounted Removable Medium). Click Add, and then select the type of action you would like to add as an option when that type of media is detected.

Working with Loadable Modules

If you have added hardware to your computer that isn't properly detected, you might need to manually load a module for that hardware. Linux comes with a set of commands for loading, unloading, and getting information about hardware modules.

If you have installed the Linux kernel source code, source code files for available drivers are stored in subdirectories of the /usr/src/linux*/drivers directory. You can find information about these drivers in a couple of ways:

- make xconfig — With /usr/src/linux* as your current directory (and Linux kernel source code installed), type **make xconfig** from a Terminal window on the desktop. Select the category of module you want and then click Help next to the driver that interests you. The help information that appears includes a description of the driver. (If your system is missing graphical libraries needed to run make xconfig, try make menuconfig instead.)

- **Documentation** — The /usr/src/linux*/Documentation directory contains lots of plain-text files describing different aspects of the kernel and related drivers.

After modules have been built, they are installed in the /lib/modules/ subdirectories. The name of the directory is based on the release number of the kernel that the modules were compiled for. Modules that are in that directory can then be loaded and unloaded as they are needed. Before building modules for a new kernel, or more important, a current kernel, it may be wise to add your initials to the kernel Makefile under the variable EXTRAVERSION at the top of the Makefile. This installs your new modules under /lib/modules/*kernel-version* with the EXTRAVERSION suffixed to the directory. If you completely wreck the module build, you haven't overwritten the current modules you may be running. It also makes it easier to identify custom kernel modules when debugging. To see your current kernel version, type

```
$ uname -r
```

Listing Loaded Modules

To see which modules are currently loaded into the running kernel on your computer, use the lsmod command. Here's an example:

```
# lsmod
Module                  Size  Used by
snd_seq_oss             38912  0
snd_seq_midi_event       9344  1 snd_seq_oss
snd_seq                 67728  4
snd_seq_oss,snd_seq_midi_event
snd_seq_device           8328  2 snd_seq_oss,snd_seq
.
.
.
autofs                  16512  0
ne2k_pci                 9056  0
8390                    13568  1 ne2k_pci
ohci1394                41860  0
ieee1394               284464  1 ohci1394
floppy                  65712  0
sg                      36120  0
```

```
scsi_mod            124600  1 sg
parport_pc          39724   0
parport             47336   1 parport_pc
ext3                128424  2
jbd                 86040   1 ext3
```

Note

If you don't have a Linux system installed yet, try booting KNOPPIX and using `lsmod` to list your loaded modules. If all your hardware is working properly, write down the list of modules. Later, when you permanently install Fedora or some other Linux system, if your CD drive, modem, video card, or other hardware doesn't work properly, you can use your list of modules to determine which module should have been used and load it, as described in the next section. ■

This output shows a variety of modules that have been loaded on a Linux system, including several to support the ALSA sound system, some of which provide OSS compatibility (`snd_seq_oss`).

To find information about any of the loaded modules, use the `modinfo` command. For example, you could type the following:

```
# /sbin/modinfo -d snd-seq-oss
"OSS-compatible sequencer module"
```

Not all modules have descriptions available and if nothing is available, no data will be returned. In this case, however, the `snd-seq-oss` module is described as an OSS-compatible sequencer module. You can also use the `-a` option to see the author of the module, or `-n` to see the object file representing the module. The author information often has the e-mail address of the driver's creator, so you can contact the author if you have problems or questions about it.

Loading Modules

You can load any module that has been compiled and installed (to a `/lib/modules` subdirectory) into your running kernel using the `modprobe` command. A common reason for loading a module is to use a feature temporarily (such as loading a module to support a special file system on a floppy you want to access). Another reason is to identify a module that will be used by a particular piece of hardware that could not be autodetected.

Here is an example of the `modprobe` command being used to load the parport module, which provides the core functions to share parallel ports with multiple devices:

```
# modprobe parport
```

After parport is loaded, you can load the `parport_pc` module to define the PC-style ports available through the interface. The `parport_pc` module lets you optionally define the addresses and IRQ numbers associated with each device sharing the parallel port. For example:

```
# modprobe parport_pc io=0x3bc irq=auto
```

In this example, a device is identified as having an address of 0x3bc, and the IRQ for the device is autodetected.

The modprobe command loads modules temporarily — they disappear at the next reboot. To permanently add the module to your system, add the modprobe command line to one of the startup scripts run at boot time. You can also add modules to the /etc/modules file to have them loaded at startup.

Note
An alternative to modprobe is the insmod command. The advantage of using modprobe, however, is that insmod loads only the module you request, whereas modprobe tries to load other modules that the one you requested is dependent on. For example, if we had not manually loaded parport, using modprobe to load parport_pc would have loaded it automatically. ■

Removing Modules

Use the rmmod command to remove a module from a running kernel. For example, to remove the module parport_pc from the current kernel, type the following:

```
# rmmod parport_pc
```

If it is not currently busy, the parport_pc module is removed from the running kernel. If it is busy, try killing any process that might be using the device. Then run rmmod again. Sometimes, the module you are trying to remove depends on other modules that may be loaded. For instance, the usbcore module cannot be unloaded while the USB printer module (usblp) is loaded, as shown here:

```
# rmmod usbcore
ERROR: Module usbcore is in use by wacom,usblp,ehci_hcd,ohci_hcd
```

Instead of using rmmod to remove modules, you could use the modprobe -r command. With modprobe -r, instead of just removing the module you request, you can also remove dependent modules that are not being used by other modules.

Monitoring System Performance

If your Linux system is a multiuser computer, sharing the processing power of that computer can be a major issue. Likewise, any time you can stop a runaway process or reduce the overhead of an unnecessary program running, your Linux server can do a better job serving files, web pages, or e-mail to the people who rely on it.

Some distributions of Linux include graphical utilities to simplify administration, such as System Monitor in Ubuntu (shown in Figure 9-3).

FIGURE 9-3

System Monitor, in Ubuntu, allows you to view processes, resources, and devices.

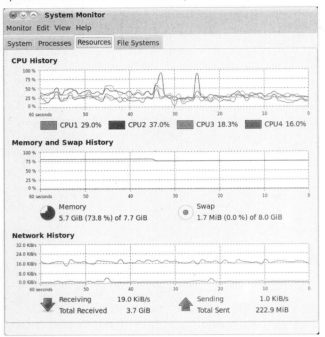

All Linux distributions include utilities that can help you monitor the performance of your Linux system. The kinds of features you want to monitor in Linux include CPU usage, memory usage (RAM and swap space), and overall load on the system. A popular tool for monitoring that information in Linux is the top command.

To start the top utility in a Terminal window, type **top**. The top command determines the largest CPU-consuming processes on your computer, displays them in descending order on your screen, and updates the list every five seconds.

By adding the -S option to top, the display shows you the cumulative CPU time for each process, as well as any child processes that may already have exited. If you want to change how often the screen is updated, you can add the -d secs option, where *secs* is replaced by the number of seconds between updates.

By default, processes are sorted by CPU usage. You can sort processes numerically by process identifier or PID (press N), by age (press A), by resident memory usage (press M), or by time (press T). To return to CPU usage, press P. To terminate a process, type **k** and enter the PID of the process you want to kill (listed in the left column). Be careful to kill only processes you are sure you don't need or want.

Doing Remote System Administration

Linux offers dozens of tools for administering remote systems. Among the most popular tools for doing remote system administration are those that come from the OpenSSH project. These include

- ssh — Command for doing remote login and remote execution
- scp — Command for copying files and directories to remote systems
- sftp — Command that includes an FTP client type of interface for traversing remote file systems and getting and putting files across the network connection

Although commands such as telnet and rlogin (for remote login) and rsh (for remote execution) have been around much longer, the ssh command is the preferred tool for remote logins and executions because ssh provides encrypted communication so you can use it securely over insecure, public networks between hosts that don't know each other.

Here is an example of ssh being used to log in to a computer named test.example.com. Because no user is specified, ssh tries to log in as the current user (which is the root user in this case).

```
# ssh test.example.com
root@test.example.com's password:
```

To log in as a different user, you could use the -l option. For example, to log in to the computer named maple as the user named jake, you could type the following:

```
# ssh jake@test.example.com
jake@test.example.com's password:
```

The ssh command can also be used to execute a command on the remote computer. For example, if you wanted to monitor the messages file on a remote computer for a minute, you could type the following command:

```
# ssh root@test.example.com "tail -f /var/log/messages"
root@test.example.com's password:
```

After you type the password, the last several lines of the /var/log/messages file on the remote computer are displayed. As messages are received, they continue to be displayed until you decide to exit (press Ctrl+C to exit the tail command).

A wonderful way to use remote ssh for remote execution is with the -X option. Using -X, ssh opens a tunnel to the remote system in which you can launch X Window system clients. So, for example, to log in to a remote system and launch a GUI tool for editing the remote system's network configurations, you could type the following:

```
# ssh -X root@test.example.com
root@test.example.com's password:
# system-config-network
```

The remote system's Network Configuration menu tool opens on your local desktop, ready to let you configure the remote system. In this same way, you can launch any remote X client to your local desktop.

The scp command is a simple yet secure way of copying files among Linux systems. It uses the underlying ssh facility, so if ssh is enabled, so is scp. Here is an example of using scp to copy a file from one computer to another:

```
# scp myfile toys.linuxtoys.net:/home/chris
root@toys.linuxtoys.net's password: ******
```

In this example, the file myfile is copied to the computer named toys.linuxtoys.net in the /home/chris directory. If you don't provide a username, scp assumes you are using the current username. Instead of myfile, you could indicate a directory name and add the -r option to recursively copy all files from that directory (and its subdirectories) to the remote system.

Unlike some tools that provide remote login, scp and ssh do allow you to log in as root user over the network, by default. (Many people turn off this feature for security reasons.)

The sftp command, which also communicates using secure ssh protocols, is a command for copying files from an FTP server. It is considered a more secure way of getting files from a remote system that has an sshd server running. The sftp command can be disabled on the server by commenting out the sftp line in the sshd_config directory.

If the SSH service doesn't seem to be running on a remote system, you may need to start the sshd daemon. In systems such as Fedora and RHEL, you could type the following:

```
# service sshd start
# chkconfig sshd on
```

Summary

Although you may be using Linux as a single-user system, many of the tasks you must perform to keep your computer running are defined as administrator tasks. A special user account called the root user is needed to do many of the things necessary to keep Linux working as you would like it to. If you are administering a Linux system used by lots of people, the task of administration becomes even larger. You must be able to add and support users, maintain the file systems, and ensure that system performance serves your users well.

To help the administrator, Linux comes with a variety of command-line utilities and graphical windows for configuring and maintaining your system. Tools such as top let you monitor system performance. Commands such as ssh and scp let you administer your system remotely.

Managing Disks and File Systems

File systems in Linux are organized in a hierarchy, beginning from root (/) and continuing downward in a structure of directories and subdirectories. As an administrator of a Linux system, it's your job to make sure that all the disk drives that represent your file system are available to the users of the computer. It is also your job to make sure there is enough disk space in the right places in the file system for users to store what they need.

Coming from Windows

File systems are organized differently in Linux than they are in Microsoft Windows operating systems. Instead of drive letters (for example, A:, B:, C:) for each local disk, network file system, CD-ROM, or other type of storage medium, everything fits neatly into the directory structure.

Some drives are connected (mounted) automatically into the file system. For example, a CD might be mounted on /media/cdrom. If the drive isn't mounted automatically, it is up to an administrator to create a mount point in the file system and then connect the disk to that point. ■

The organization of your file system begins when you install Linux. Part of the installation process is to divide your hard disk (or disks) into partitions. Those partitions can then be assigned to

- A part of the Linux file system
- Swap space for Linux
- Other file system types (perhaps containing other bootable operating systems)
- Free space (you can leave space unassigned so you can format it later as you need it)

Partitioning Hard Disks

Linux provides several tools for managing your hard disk partitions. This chapter focuses on partitions that are used for the Linux file system. To see what partitions are currently set up on partitions that the Linux kernel has detected, use the fdisk command:

```
# /sbin/fdisk -l
Disk /dev/sda:  40.0 GB, 40020664320 bytes
255 heads, 63 sectors/track, 4825 cylinders
Units = cylinders of 16065 * 512 bytes = 8225280 bytes

   Device Boot     Start        End      Blocks   Id  System
/dev/sda1    *         1         13         104    b  Win95 FAT32
/dev/sda2            84         89       48195   83  Linux
/dev/sda3            90        522    3478072+   83  Linux
/dev/sda4           523        554      257040    5  Extended
/dev/sda5           523        554     257008+   82  Linux swap
```

This output shows the disk partitioning for a computer capable of running both Linux and Microsoft Windows. You can see that the Linux partition on /dev/sda3 has most of the space available for data. There is a Windows partition (/dev/sda1) and a Linux swap partition (/dev/sda5). There is also a small /boot partition (46MB) on /dev/sda2. In this case, the root partition for Linux has 3.3GB of disk space and resides on /dev/sda3. The fdisk -l command displays partition information from the partition tables existing on all storage devices found on the system.

If you change a disk's partition table, it can get out of sync with the kernel. Type cat /proc/ partitions to see the kernel's current view of each disk's partition table. If the disk's and the kernel's views appear to be different, type partprobe to get them in sync.

Next use the mount command (with no options) to see what partitions are actually being used for your Linux system (which available disk partitions are actually mounted and where they are mounted):

```
# mount
/dev/sda3 on / type ext3 (rw)
/dev/sda2 on /boot type ext3 (rw)
/dev/sda1 on /mnt/win type vfat (rw)
/dev/proc on /proc type proc (rw)
/dev/sys on /sys type sysfs (rw)
/dev/devpts on /dev/pts type devpts (rw,gid=5,mode=620)
/dev/shm on /dev/shm type tmpfs (rw)
none on /proc/sys/fs/binfmt_misc type binfmt_misc (rw)
/dev/cdrom on /media/cdrecorder type iso9660 (ro,nosuid,nodev)
```

Although some of the file systems shown as mounted are for special purposes (/sys, /proc, and others), our concern here is with disk partition (/dev/hd*, /dev/sd*, and so on). The mounted Linux partitions in this case are /dev/sda2, which provides space for the /boot directory (contains data for booting Linux), and /dev/sda3, which provides space for the rest of the Linux file system beginning from the root directory (/).

This particular system also contains a Windows partition that was mounted in the /mnt/win directory and a CD that was mounted in /media/cdrecorder. (With most GUI interfaces, the CD is typically mounted automatically when you insert it. For 2.6 kernels, look in the /media directory; for 2.4 kernels, the /mnt directory is often used.)

After the word type, you can see the type of file system contained on the device. (See the description of different file system types in Table 10-1 in the following section.) Particularly on larger Linux systems, you may have multiple partitions for several reasons:

- **Multiple hard disks** — You may have several hard disks available to your users. In that case you would have to mount each disk (and possibly several partitions from each disk) in different locations in your file system.

- **Protecting different parts of the file system** — If the users on a system consume all the file system space, the entire system can fail. For example, there may be no place for temporary files to be copied (so the programs writing to temporary files fail), and incoming mail may fail to be written to mailboxes. With multiple mounted partitions, if one partition runs out of space, the others can continue to work.

- **Multiple operating systems** — You can configure your disk to contain multiple partitions that can each be used to hold a different operating system type. For example, if you started with a computer that had Windows on the hard disk, you could put Linux on a separate partition, and then set up the computer to boot either operating system.

- **Backups** — It is possible to back up data from your computer by copying the entire image of a disk or partition. If you want to restore that partition later, you can simply copy it back (bit by bit) to a hard disk. With smaller partitions, this approach can be done fairly efficiently.

- **Protecting from disk failure** — If one disk (or part of one disk) fails, having multiple partitions mounted on your file system may let you continue working and just fix the one disk that fails. Ghost for Linux (http://freshmeat.net/projects/g4l) is an example of a tool for backing up a hard disk partition in Linux.

- **Different mount options** — Certain tasks call for specific file system types or specific mount options. For example, some tasks require file systems that work well with many small files (a mail server) or a few very large files (a media server). Some tasks require special mount to enable or disable features (like Access Control Lists) or tune the way the file system updates timestamps on a file (which could dramatically increase performance on a development machine).

When a disk partition is mounted on the Linux file system, all directories and subdirectories below that mount point are stored on that partition. So, for example, if you were to mount one partition on / and one on /usr, everything below the /usr mount point would be stored on the second partition while everything else would be stored on the first partition. If you then mounted another partition on /usr/local, everything below that mount point would be on the third partition, while everything else below /usr would be on the second partition.

Tip

What happens if a remote file system is unmounted from your computer, and you go to save a file in that mount point directory? You will write the file to that directory and it will be stored on your local hard disk. When the remote file system is remounted, however, the file you saved will seem to disappear. To get the file back, you'll have to unmount the remote file system (causing the file to reappear), move the file to another location, remount the file system, and copy the file back there. ■

Mount points often mentioned as being candidates for separate partitions include /, /boot, /home, /usr, and /var. The root file system (/) is the catchall for directories that aren't in other mount points. The root file system's mount point (/) is the only one that is required. The /boot directory holds the images needed to boot the operating system. The /home file system is where all the user accounts are typically stored. Applications and documentation are stored in /usr. Below the /var mount point is where log files, temporary files, server files (Web, FTP, and so on), and lock files are stored (that is, items that need disk space for your computer's applications to keep running).

The fact that multiple partitions are mounted on your file system is invisible to people using your Linux system. It is an issue only when a partition runs out of space or if users need to save or use information from a particular device (such as a floppy disk or remote file system) that isn't mounted. Of course, any user can check this by typing the mount command.

Mounting File Systems

Most of your hard disk partitions are mounted automatically for you. When you install Fedora, Ubuntu, SUSE, and some other Linux systems, you are asked to create partitions and indicate the mount points for those partitions. (Other Linux installation procedures will expect you to know that you have to partition before beginning.) When you boot Linux, all Linux partitions residing on hard disk that are listed in your /etc/fstab file are typically mounted. For that reason, this section focuses mostly on how to mount other types of devices so that they become part of your Linux file system.

The mount command is used not only to mount devices but also to mount other kinds of file systems on your Linux system. This means that you can store files from other operating systems or use file systems that are appropriate for certain kinds of activities (such as writing large block sizes). The most common use of this feature for the average Linux user, however, is to enable that user to obtain and work with files from floppy disks, CD-ROMs, or other removable media.

Note

With the addition of automatic mounting features and changes in how removable media are identified with the Linux 2.6 kernel (using features such as Udev and Hardware Abstraction Layer), you no longer need to manually mount removable media for many Linux desktop systems. Understanding how to manually mount and unmount file systems on a Linux server, however, can be a very useful skill. ■

Supported File Systems

To see file system types that are currently loaded in your kernel, type **cat /proc/filesystems**. Table 10-1 shows the file system types that are supported in Linux, although they may not be in use at the moment or they may not be built into your current kernel (so they may need to be loaded as modules).

TABLE 10-1

Supported File System Types

Type	Description
adfs	Acorn disk file system, which is the standard file system used on RiscOS operating systems
befs	File system used by the BeOS operating system
cifs	Common Internet File System (CIFS), the virtual file system used to access servers that comply with the SNIA CIFS specification. CIFS is an attempt to refine and standardize the SMB protocol used by Samba and Windows file sharing.
ext4	Successor to the popular ext3 file system. It includes many improvements over ext3, such as support for volumes up to 1 exbibyte and file sizes up to 16 tebibytes. (This has replaced ext3 as the default file system used in Fedora.)
ext3	Ext file systems are the most common in most Linux systems. The ext3 file system, also called the third extended file system, includes journaling features that, compared to ext2, improve a file system's capability to recover from crashes.
ext2	The default file system type for earlier Linux systems. Features are the same as ext3, except that ext2 doesn't include journaling features.
ext	This is the first version of ext3. It is not used very often anymore.
iso9660	Evolved from the High Sierra file system (the original standard for CD-ROMs). Extensions to the High Sierra standard (called RockRidge extensions) allow iso9660 file systems to support long filenames and UNIX-style information (such as file permissions, ownership, and links). Data CD-ROMs typically use this file system type.
kafs	AFS client file system. Used in distributed computing environments to share files with Linux, Windows, and Macintosh clients.
minix	MINIX file system type, used originally with the MINIX version of UNIX. It supports filenames of up to only 30 characters.
msdos	An MS-DOS file system. You can use this type to mount floppy disks that come from Microsoft operating systems.
vfat	Microsoft extended FAT (VFAT) file system.
umsdos	An MS-DOS file system with extensions to allow features that are similar to UNIX (including long filenames).

continued

TABLE 10-1	*(continued)*
Type	**Description**
proc	Not a real file system, but rather a file system interface to the Linux kernel. You probably won't do anything special to set up a proc file system. However, the `/proc` mount point should be a proc file system. Many utilities rely on `/proc` to gain access to Linux kernel information.
reiserfs	ReiserFS journaled file system. ReiserFS was once a common default file system type for several Linux distributions. However, ext3 is now by far the most common file system type used with Linux.
swap	Used for swap partitions. Swap areas are used to hold data temporarily when RAM is currently used up. Data is swapped to the swap area and then returned to RAM when it is needed again.
squashfs	Compressed, read-only file system type. Squashfs is popular on live CDs, where there is limited space and a read-only medium (such as a CD or DVD).
nfs	Network File System (NFS) type of file system. NFS is used to mount file systems on other Linux or UNIX computers.
hpfs	File system used to do read-only mounts of an OS/2 HPFS file system.
ncpfs	This relates to Novell NetWare file systems. NetWare file systems can be mounted over a network.
ntfs	Windows NT file system. Depending upon the distribution you have, it may be supported as a read-only file system (so that you can mount and copy files from it).
affs	File system used with Amiga computers.
ufs	File system popular on Sun Microsystems operating systems (that is, Solaris and SunOS).
btrfs	New file system in development by Oracle to integrate RAID, snapshots, and other advanced features at the file system layer.
jfs	A 64-bit journaling file system by IBM that is relatively lightweight for the many features it has.
xfs	A high performance file system originally developed by Silicon Graphics that works extremely well with large files.
gfs2	A shared disk file system that allows multiple machines to use the same shared disk without going through a network file system layer such as CIFS, NFS, etc.

If you want to use a file system type that is not currently shown as available on your system (when you type `cat /proc/filesystems`), try using `modprobe` to load the module for that file system. For example, `modprobe ufs` adds the UFS file system type to the running kernel. Type **man fs** to see descriptions of Linux file systems.

Using the fstab File to Define Mountable File Systems

The hard disk partitions on your local computer and the remote file systems you use every day are probably set up to automatically mount when you boot Linux. The /etc/fstab file contains definitions for each partition, along with options describing how the partition is mounted. Here's an example of an /etc/fstab file:

```
LABEL=/         /                ext3           defaults              1 1
LABEL=/boot     /boot            ext3           defaults              1 2
/dev/devpts     /dev/pts         devpts         gid=5,mode=620        0 0
/dev/shm        /dev/shm         tmpfs          defaults              0 0
/dev/proc       /proc            proc           defaults              0 0
/dev/sys        /sys             sysfs          defaults              0 0
/dev/sda5       swap             swap           defaults              0 0
/dev/cdrom      /media/cdrecorder udf,iso9660   exec,noauto,managed   0 0
/dev/sda1       /mnt/win         vfat           noauto                0 0
/dev/fd0        /mnt/floppy      auto           noauto,owner          0 0
```

All partitions listed in this file are mounted at boot time, except for those set to noauto in the fourth field. In this example, the root (/) and boot (/boot) hard disk partitions are mounted at boot time, along with the /dev/pts, /dev/shm, /dev/sys, /dev/shm, and /proc file systems (which are not associated with particular storage devices). The CD drive (/dev/cdrom) and floppy disk (/dev/fd0) drives are not mounted at boot time. Definitions are put in the fstab file for floppy and CD drives so that they can be mounted in the future.

I also added one line for /dev/sda1, which enables me to mount the Windows (vfat) partition on my computer so I don't have to always boot Windows to get at the files on my Windows partition.

Coming from Windows

Most Windows systems today use the NTFS file system. Support for this system, however, is not delivered with every Linux system. NTFS support was added to the Fedora repository in Fedora 7 with the ntfs-3g package. Other NTFS support is available from the Linux-NTFS project (www.linux-ntfs.org/).

If your computer is configured to dual boot Linux and Windows, you can mount your Windows file system to make it available in Linux. To access your Windows partition, you must first create the mount point (in this example, by typing mkdir /mnt/win). Then you can mount it when you choose by typing (as root) mount /mnt/win. ■

Different Linux distributions will set up their fstab file differently. Some don't use labels and many others don't use a separate /boot partition by default. They will just have a swap partition and have all user data under the root partition (/).

Here is what's in each field of the fstab file:

- Field 1 — The name of the device representing the file system. This field can include the LABEL or UUID option, with which you can indicate a volume label or universally unique identifier (UUID) instead of a device name. The advantage to this approach is that because the partition is identified by volume name, you can move a volume to a different device name and not have to change the fstab file.

- Field 2 — The mount point in the file system. The file system contains all data from the mount point down the directory tree structure unless another file system is mounted at some point beneath it.

- Field 3 — The file system type. Valid file system types are described in the "Supported File Systems" section earlier in this chapter.

- Field 4 — Options to the mount command. In the preceding example, the noauto option prevents the indicated file system from being mounted at boot time, and ro says to mount the file system read-only (which is reasonable for a CD drive). Commas must separate options. See the mount command manual page (under the -o option) for information on other supported options.

Tip

Typically, only the root user is allowed to mount a file system using the mount command. However, to allow any user to mount a file system (such as a file system on a floppy disk), you could add the user option to Field 4 of /etc/fstab. In openSUSE, read/write permissions are given to specific devices (such as disk or audio devices) by specific groups (such as the disk or audio group) so that users assigned to those groups can mount or otherwise access those devices. ■

- Field 5 — The number in this field indicates whether the indicated file system needs to be dumped (that is, have its data backed up). A 1 means that the file system needs to be dumped, and a 0 means that it doesn't. (This field is not very useful anymore because most Linux administrators use more sophisticated backup options. Most often, a 0 is used.)

- Field 6 — The number in this field indicates whether the indicated file system needs to be checked with fsck: 1 means it needs to be checked first, 2 means to check after all those indicated by 1 have already been checked, and 0 means don't check it.

If you want to add an additional local disk or partition, you can create an entry for it in the /etc/fstab file. See Chapter 18 for information on mounting Samba, NFS, and other remount file systems from /etc/fstab.

Using the mount Command to Mount File Systems

Linux systems automatically run mount -a (mount all file systems) each time you boot. For that reason, you generally use the mount command only for special situations. In particular, the average user or administrator uses mount in two ways:

- To display the disks, partitions, and remote file systems currently mounted
- To temporarily mount a file system

Any user can type mount (with no options) to see what file systems are currently mounted on the local Linux system. The following is an example of the mount command. It shows a single hard disk partition (/dev/sda1) containing the root (/) file system, and proc and devpts file system types mounted on /proc and /dev, respectively. The last entry shows a floppy disk, formatted with a standard Linux file system (ext3) mounted on the /mnt/floppy directory.

```
$ mount
/dev/sda3 on / type ext3 (rw)
/dev/sda2 on /boot type ext3 (rw)
/dev/sda1 on /mnt/win type vfat (rw)
/dev/proc on /proc type proc (rw)
/dev/sys on /sys type sysfs (rw)
/dev/devpts on /dev/pts type devpts (rw,gid=5,mode=620)
/dev/shm on /dev/shm type tmpfs (rw)
none on /proc/sys/fs/binfmt_misc type binfmt_misc (rw)
/dev/cdrom on /media/cdrecorder type iso9660 (ro,nosuid,nodev)
/dev/fd0 on /mnt/floppy type ext3 (rw)
```

Traditionally, the most common devices to mount by hand are your floppy disk and your CD drive. However, depending on the type of desktop you are using, CDs and floppy disks may be mounted for you automatically when you insert them. (In some cases, the autorun program may also run automatically. For example, autorun may start a CD music player or software package installer to handle the data on the medium.)

Mounting Removable Media

With newer desktop features such as Udev and HAL, often USB drives, CDs, and DVDs are mounted automatically, so there is no need to manually run the mount command. Also, if the media has a volume name associated with it, that volume name is used as the directory name in /media on which the CD is mounted.

For these types of media, you simply insert the medium into the USB port or disc drive. No entry in the /etc/fstab file is needed. After the medium is mounted, a file manager window opens, displaying the contents of the medium.

Mounting a Disk Image in loopback

Another valuable way to use the mount command has to do with disk images. If you download a CD or floppy disk image from the Internet and you want to see what it contains, you can do so without burning it to CD or floppy. With the image on your hard disk, create a mount point and use the -o loop option to mount it locally. Here's an example:

```
# mkdir /mnt/mycdimage
# mount -o loop whatever-i386-disc1.iso /mnt/mycdimage
```

In this example, the /mnt/mycdimage directory is created, and then the disk image file (whatever-i386-disc1.iso) residing in the current directory is mounted on it. You can now change to that directory, view the contents of it, and copy or use any of its contents. This is useful for downloaded CD images from which you want to install software without having to burn the image to CD. You could also share that mount point over NFS, so you could install the software from another computer. When you are done, just type **umount /mnt/mycdimage** to unmount it.

Other options to mount are available only for specific file system types. See the mount manual page for those and other useful options.

Using the umount Command

When you are done using a temporary file system, or you want to unmount a permanent file system temporarily, use the umount command. This command detaches the file system from its mount point in your Linux file system. To use umount, you can give it either a directory name or a device name. For example:

```
# umount /mnt/floppy
```

This unmounts the device (probably /dev/fd0) from the mount point /mnt/floppy. You can also unmount using the form

```
# umount /dev/fd0
```

In general, it's better to use the directory name (/mnt/floppy) because the umount command will fail if the device is mounted in more than one location. (Device names all begin with /dev.)

If you get the message device is busy, the umount request has failed because either a process has a file open on the device or you have a shell open with a directory on the device as a current directory. Stop the processes or change to a directory outside the device you are trying to unmount for the umount request to succeed.

An alternative for unmounting a busy device is the -l option. With umount -l (a lazy unmount), the unmount happens as soon as the device is no longer busy. To unmount a remote NFS file system that's no longer available (for example, the server went down), you can use the umount -f option to forcibly unmount the NFS file system.

Tip
A really useful tool for discovering what's holding open a device you want to unmount is the lsof command. Type lsof with the name of the partition you want to unmount (such as lsof /mnt/floppy). The output shows you what commands are holding files open on that partition. The fuser command can be used in the same way. ■

Using the mkfs Command to Create a File System

You can create a file system for any supported file system type on a disk or partition that you choose. You do so with the mkfs command. Although this is most useful for creating file systems on hard-disk partitions, you can create file systems on USB flash drives, floppy disks, or rewritable CDs as well.

Before you create a new file system, make sure of the following:

- You have partitioned the disk as you want (using the fdisk command, as described in the "Adding a Hard Disk" section that follows).

- You get the device name correct, or you may end up overwriting your hard disk by mistake. For example, the first partition on the second SCSI or USB disk on your system would be /dev/sdb1 and the third would be /dev/sdc1.

- You unmount the partition if it's mounted before creating the file system.

Here is an example of using mkfs to create a file system on the first (and only) partition on a 2GB USB flash drive located as the third SCSI disk (/dev/sdc1):

```
# mkfs -t ext3 /dev/sdc1
mke2fs 1.40.8 (13-Mar-2008)
Warning: 256-byte inodes not usable on older systems
Filesystem label=
OS type: Linux
Block size=4096 (log=2)
Fragment size=4096 (log=2)
122160 inodes, 487699 blocks
24384 blocks (5.00%) reserved for the super user
First data block=0
Maximum filesystem blocks=503316480
15 block groups
32768 blocks per group, 32768 fragments per group
8144 inodes per group
Superblock backups stored on blocks:
        32768, 98304, 163840, 229376, 294912

Writing inode tables: done
Creating journal (8192 blocks): done
Writing superblocks and filesystem accounting information: done

This filesystem will be automatically checked every 39 mounts or
180 days, whichever comes first.  Use tune2fs -c or -i to override.
```

You can see the statistics that are output with the formatting done by the mkfs command. The number of inodes and blocks created are output, as are the number of blocks per group and fragments per group. You could now mount this file system (mkdir /mnt/myusb ; mount /mnt/myusb), change to it as your current directory (cd /mnt/myusb), and create files on it as you please.

Adding a Hard Disk

Adding a new hard disk to your computer so that it can be used by Linux requires a combination of steps described in previous sections. Here's the general procedure:

1. Install the new hard disk hardware.
2. Partition the new disk.
3. Create the file systems on the new disk.
4. Mount the file systems.

The easiest way to add a hard disk to Linux is to have the entire disk devoted to a single Linux partition. You can have multiple partitions, however, and assign them each to different types of file systems and different mount points, if you like. The following process takes you through adding a hard disk containing a single Linux partition. Along the way, it also notes which steps you need to repeat to have multiple file systems with multiple mount points.

Note

This procedure assumes that Linux is already installed and working on the computer. If this is not the case, follow the instructions for adding a hard disk on your current operating system. Later, when you install Linux, you can identify this disk when you are asked to partition your hard disk(s). ∎

1. Follow the manufacturer's instructions for physically installing and connecting the new hard disk in your computer. If this is a second hard disk, you may need to change jumpers on the hard disk unit itself to have it operate as a slave hard disk (if it's on the same cable as your first hard disk). You may also need to change the BIOS settings.

2. Boot your computer to Linux.

3. Determine the device name for the hard disk. As root user from a shell, type the following:

```
# dmesg | less
```

4. From the output, look for an indication that the new disk was found. For example, if it's a second IDE hard disk, you should see hdb: in the output. For a second SCSI or SATA drive, you should see sdb: instead. (The hd? and sd? drive letters are incremented as they are found by the kernel.) Be sure you identify the correct disk, or you will erase all the data from disks you probably want to keep!

5. Use the fdisk command to create partitions on the new disk. For example, if you are formatting the second SATA or SCSI disk (sdb), you can type the following:

```
# fdisk /dev/sdb
```

Now you are in fdisk command mode, where you can use the fdisk single-letter command set to work with your partitions. If the disk had existing partitions on it, you can change or delete those partitions now. Or, you can simply reformat the whole disk to blow everything away. Use p to view all partitions and d to delete a partition.

6. To create a new partition, type the letter **n**.

7. Choose an extended (e) or primary partition (p). To choose a primary partition, type the letter **p**.

8. Type in the partition number. If you are creating the first partition (or for only one partition), type the number **1**.

   Enter the first cylinder number (1 is the default). A range of cylinder numbers is displayed (for example, 1–4865 is the number of cylinders that appears for my 40GB hard drive).

9. To assign the new partition to begin at the first cylinder on the new hard disk, type the number **1**.

10. Enter the size of the partition. If you are using the entire hard disk, use the last cylinder number shown. Otherwise, type the plus sign and the number of megabytes you want to assign to the partition. For example, +1024M to create a 1024-megabyte partition.

11. To create more partitions on the hard disk, repeat Steps 6 through 10 for each partition (possibly changing the file system types as needed).

12. Type **w** to write changes to the hard disk and exit from the fdisk command. At this point, you should be back at the shell.

13. To create a file system on the new disk partition, use the mkfs command. By default, this command creates an ext2 file system, which is usable by Linux. However, in most cases you will want to use a journaling file system (such as ext3 or reiserfs). To create an ext3 file system on the first partition of the second hard disk, type the following:

```
# mkfs -t ext3 /dev/sdb1
```

If you created multiple partitions, repeat this step for each partition (such as /dev/sdb2, /dev/sdb3, and so on).

Tip

If you don't use -t ext3, an ext2 file system is created by default. Use other commands, or options to this command, to create other file system types. For example, use mkfs.vfat to create a VFAT file system, mkfs.msdos for DOS, or mkfs.reiserfs for Reiser file system type. The tune2fs command, described later in this section, can be used to change an ext2 file system to an ext3 file system. ■

14. After the file system is created, you can have the partition permanently mounted by editing the /etc/fstab and adding the new partition. Here is an example of a line you might add to that file:

```
/dev/sdb1    /abc          ext3    defaults      1 1
```

In this example, the partition (/dev/sdb1) is mounted on the /abc directory as an ext3 file system. The defaults keyword causes the partition to be mounted at boot time. The numbers 1 1 cause the disk to be checked for errors. Add one line like this example for each partition you created.

15. Create the mount point. For example, to mount the partition on /abc (as shown in the previous step), type the following:

```
# mkdir /abc
```

16. Create your other mount points if you created multiple partitions. The next time you boot Linux, the new partition(s) will be automatically mounted on the /abc directory.

After you have created the file systems on your partitions, a nice tool for adjusting those file systems is the tune2fs command. You can use it to change volume labels, the frequency with which the file system is checked, and error behavior. You can also use it to change an ext2 file system to an ext3 file system so the file system can use journaling. For example:

```
# tune2fs -j /dev/sdb1
tune2fs 1.40.4 (29-May-2008)
Creating journal inode: done
This filesystem will be automatically checked every 38 mounts or
180 days, whichever comes first. Use tune2fs -c or -i to override.
```

By adding the -j option to tune2fs, you can either change the journal size or attach the file system to an external journal block device (essentially turning a nonjournaling ext2 file system into a journaling ext3 file system). After you use tune2fs to change your file system type, you probably need to correct your /etc/fstab file to include the file type change (from ext2 to ext3). To see the current settings for your ext2/ext3 file system, type the following command:

```
# tune2fs -l /dev/sdb1
```

An ext3 file system is simply an ext2 file system with a journal, which means you can easily mount an ext2 file system as ext3 after adding a journal, or mount an ext3 file system as ext2 after dropping the journal. In newer distributions, ext4 has become the file system of choice that has more advanced features and lays out data on disk differently than ext2 or ext3. To convert an ext3 file system on /dev/sdb1 to ext4, unmount the file system and then type the following command:

```
# tune2fs -O extents,uninit_bg,dir_index /dev/sdb1
```

While it is easy to convert an ext3 file system to an ext4 file system, it is more difficult to do the reverse, so be careful and always make a backup.

Checking System Space

Running out of disk space on your computer is not a happy situation. You can use tools that come with Linux to keep track of how much disk space has been used on your computer, and you can keep an eye on users who consume a lot of disk space.

Displaying System Space with df

You can display the space available in your file systems using the df command. To see the amount of space available on all the mounted file systems on your Linux computer, type **df** with no options:

```
$ df
Filesystem    1k-blocks      Used  Available  Use%  Mounted on
/dev/sda3      30645460   2958356   26130408   11%   /
```

```
/dev/sda2         46668      8340      35919    19%   /boot
/dev/fd0           1412        13       1327     1%   /mnt/floppy
```

This example output shows the space available on the hard disk partition mounted on the / (root) partition (/dev/sda1) and /boot partition (/dev/sda2), and the floppy disk mounted on the /mnt/floppy directory (/dev/fd0). Disk space is shown in 1K blocks. To produce output in a more human-readable form, use the -h option:

```
$ df -h
Filesystem          Size  Used  Avail  Use%  Mounted on
/dev/sda3           29G   2.9G   24G   11%   /
/dev/sda2           46M   8.2M   25M   19%   /boot
/dev/fd0            1.4M  13k    1.2M   1%   /mnt/floppy
```

With the df -h option, output appears in a friendlier megabyte or gigabyte listing. Other options with df enable you to do the following:

- Print only file systems of a particular type (-t type)
- Exclude file systems of a particular type (-x type)
- Include file systems that have no space, such as /proc and /dev/pts (-a)
- List only available and used inodes (-i)
- Display disk space in certain block sizes (--block-size=#)

Checking Disk Usage with du

To find out how much space is being consumed by a particular directory (and its subdirectories), use the du command. With no options, du lists all directories below the current directory, along with the space consumed by each directory. At the end, du produces total disk space used within that directory structure.

The du command is a good way to check how much space is being used by a particular user (du /home/user1) or in a particular file system partition (du /var). By default, disk space is displayed in 1K block sizes. To make the output friendlier (in kilobytes, megabytes, and gigabytes), use the -h option as follows:

```
$ du -h /home/jake
114k    /home/jake/httpd/stuff
234k    /home/jake/httpd
137k    /home/jake/uucp/data
701k    /home/jake/uucp
1.0M    /home/jake
```

The output shows the disk space used in each directory under the home directory of the user named jake (/home/jake). Disk space consumed is shown in kilobytes (k) and megabytes (M). The total space consumed by /home/jake is shown on the last line. Add the -s option to see total disk space used for a directory and its subdirectories.

Finding Disk Consumption with find

The find command is a great way to find the file consumption of your hard disk using a variety of criteria. You can get a good idea of where disk space can be recovered by finding files that are over a certain size or were created by a particular person.

Note

You must be root user to run this command effectively, unless you are just checking your personal files. If you are not root user, there will be many places in the file system that you will not have permission to check. Regular users can usually check their own home directories but not those of others. ■

In the following example, the find command searches the root file system (/) for any files owned by the user named jake (-user jake) and prints the filenames. The output of the find command is organized in a long listing in size order (ls -ldS). Finally, that output is sent to the file /tmp/jake. When you view the file /tmp/jake (for example, less /tmp/jake), you will find all the files that are owned by the user jake listed in size order. Here is the command line:

```
# find / -xdev -user jake -print | xargs ls -ldS > /tmp/jake
```

Tip

The -xdev option prevents file systems other than the selected file system from being searched. This is a good way to cut out a lot of junk that may be output from the /proc file system. It can also keep large, remotely mounted file systems from being searched. ■

Here's another example, except that instead of looking for a user's files, we're looking for files larger than 100 kilobytes (-size +100k):

```
# find / -xdev -size +100k -print | xargs ls -ldS > /tmp/size
```

You can save yourself a lot of disk space by just removing some of the largest files that are no longer needed. In this example, you can see large files are sorted by size in the /tmp/size file.

Summary

Managing file systems is a critical part of administering a Linux system. Using commands such as fdisk, you can view and change disk partitions. File systems can be added to partitions using the mkfs command. Once created, file systems can be mounted and unmounted using the mount and umount commands, respectively.

Setting Up Networking

## 11

IN THIS CHAPTER

Connecting to the Internet

Connecting to the Internet with Ethernet

Connecting to the Internet with dial-up

Connecting to the Internet with wireless

You won't tap into the real power of Linux until you have connected it to a network — in particular, the Internet. Your computer probably has an Ethernet interface built in, so you can just plug a LAN (local area network) cable into it to connect to a LAN (typically a switch), DSL bridge or router, or cable modem. Some computers, particularly laptops, may have wireless Ethernet hardware built in.

Your computer also may have a dial-up modem. Although much more rare these days, there are still cases where someone has an older computer that has no Ethernet card. Or you may be in a situation in which you need to dial out over regular phone lines to reach your Internet service provider (ISP), and need to use this modem to get on the Internet.

This chapter describes how to connect your Linux system to the Internet. With broadband and wireless networks becoming more prevalent, Ethernet connections are the most common means of connecting to the Internet. For dial-up connections, you'll see how to use kppp (a dialer GUI that is often packaged with KDE desktops).

Sharing Internet connections with multiple desktop systems, or even your own mail or web server, is not that difficult to do from a hardware perspective. However, you need to consider some security and configuration issues when you set out to expand the way you use your Internet connection. Most Linux systems include software that lets you configure them as firewalls, routers, and a variety of server types to help you get this done.

Connecting to the Network

Linux supports a wide range of wired and wireless network devices, as well as a variety of network protocols to communicate over that media. As a home or small-office Linux user, you can start evaluating how to configure your connection to the Internet from Linux by considering the following:

- The type of Internet account you have with your ISP (dial-up or broadband). With broadband, you need to know if the ISP uses DHCP or PPPoE.
- Whether you are connecting a single computer, a bunch of desktops, and/or one or more server machines to the Internet

Connecting via Dial-Up Service

A few years ago, dial-up was the most common method for an individual to get on the Internet. Many computers had dial-up modems built into the motherboard or had serial ports where a modem could easily be connected. Many computers today do not include modems, but serial or USB modems can be purchased for just a few dollars if you need to use dial-up.

After you have a modem (56 Kbps speed is the standard today), the only other equipment you need is a regular telephone line. Essentially, you can use a dial-up modem anywhere you can connect to a phone line. Linux contains the tools you need to configure and complete a dial-up connection. Figure 11-1 shows the setup for the connection.

FIGURE 11-1

Connect a modem to a serial or USB port and dial out over regular phone lines.

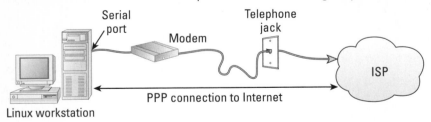

One difficulty with using modems in Linux is that many computers with built-in modems (especially laptops) come with what are referred to as *Winmodems*. With Winmodems, some of the processing normally done on the modem is actually implemented within the Windows system. Winmodems don't always look like real modems to Linux systems because, without the code that's inside Windows, they don't behave like real modems when they are connected to Linux systems.

Some Winmodems are supported in Linux, and those are sometimes referred to as *Linmodems*. If you find that Linux fails to detect your modem, check out the Linmodems Support Page (`http://linmodems.technion.ac.il`) or the Linmodems.org page (`www.linmodems.org`). These pages can help you determine whether you have a Winmodem and, if so, help you find the right Linmodem driver (if one is available).

Tip

If you find that you have a Winmodem, you are usually better off getting a real modem instead. An inexpensive external serial modem can save you the trouble of getting and loading a Linmodem driver that may or may not work. Most external modems or internal PCI modems described as being "controller-based" work well in Linux. ■

Connecting a Single Wired Ethernet Card

Today, most individuals and small businesses sign up for broadband Internet service with cable television providers or local telephone companies. These connections typically provide transmission speeds rated at least five times greater than you can get with a dial-up connection.

To make broadband connections from your home or small office, you typically need a cable modem or Digital Subscriber Line (DSL) modem. Cable modems share the bandwidth of the cable television line coming into your location. DSL uses existing house or office phone wires to connect to the Internet, sharing the wires with your phone service.

Because there are many ways that your ISP may be providing your Internet service, you should check with it to get the right hardware you need to connect. In particular, you should know that several incompatible DSL standards exist (ADSL, CDSL, HDSL, SDSL, and so on), so you can't just go out and buy DSL equipment without some guidance.

If you are using an external DSL or cable modem, chances are that a single connection from your Linux machine to that equipment requires only

- An Ethernet port on your computer
- A LAN cable (often provided with the ISP equipment)
- The DSL router/bridge or cable modem (often provided by ISP)

Figure 11-2 illustrates a Linux computer connected to a broadband cable modem.

Broadband equipment often supplies a service called Dynamic Host Configuration Protocol (DHCP). DHCP provides the Internet addresses and other information that a client computer needs to connect to the network. With the cable/DSL modem acting as a DHCP server, you can literally start using the Internet without doing any special configuration in Linux. Just plug in, boot Linux, and start browsing the web.

FIGURE 11-2

Connect an Ethernet card to broadband and start surfing.

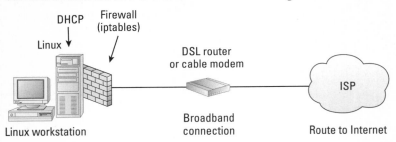

Note

The DSL or cable modem often acts as a router between the ISP and your computer. Usually that device also includes a firewall configured to do network address translation. Alternatively, some broadband equipment operates in a "bridging mode," in which it doesn't do routing, but simply passes data through as if your computer were on the same LAN as that of the ISP. In this setup, the public IP address is assigned to your computer instead of the DSL or cable modem. Because bridging mode exposes the IP addresses behind your firewall to the Internet, in most cases you should not set your DSL or cable modem to bridging mode. ■

Sharing a Network Connection with Other Computers

Instead of connecting your Linux computer directly to the cable modem or DSL equipment, you can join your machines together on a LAN and then connect the LAN to your ISP equipment so that everyone in the house or office can share the broadband connection.

It's fairly simple to add multiple machines to your home network — you can start by connecting your cable/DSL modem to your LAN instead of directly to your Linux box. Today, most DSL and cable modem hardware designed to connect your computers to your ISP provide many helpful features to access and secure your network connections. These might include the following:

- **Wired and wireless connections** — You may have several LAN ports on the equipment and may even have wireless support that you can configure.

- **Firewall support** — A well-configured firewall blocks access to all new connections on incoming ports, thereby minimizing the risks of intruders getting into your LAN. A firewall can also provide Network Address Translation (NAT), an IP Masquerading feature.

- **NAT or IP Masquerading** — For the most part, you don't want the computers behind your firewall that are simply desktop systems to be accessible to others from the Internet. By configuring your firewall to do NAT or IP Masquerading, your computers can be assigned private IP addresses. Your firewall then handles forwarding of messages between your LAN and the Internet. This is a good arrangement for several reasons. For one thing, the IP addresses of your private computers are not exposed to the outside world. Also, you can save the cost of paying your ISP for permanent IP addresses.

- **DHCP service** — Many firewall systems can act as a DHCP server. Those private IP addresses you can use with a NAT firewall can be assigned from the DHCP service running on your firewall system. When the client computer on your LAN starts up, besides its IP address, your DHCP service can tell the client the location of its DNS server, gateway to the Internet, or other information.

- **Routing** — In the home and small-office LAN environment illustrated in Figure 11-3, the firewall (which could be on your DSL/cable modem or even on a Linux system) often has two Ethernet interfaces: one connected to the LAN and the other to the DSL or cable modem that leads to the ISP. Because the Ethernet interfaces are viewed as being on separate subnetworks, the firewall/router must be configured to forward packets across the two interfaces.

FIGURE 11-3

A firewall provides a safeguard between your LAN and the Internet.

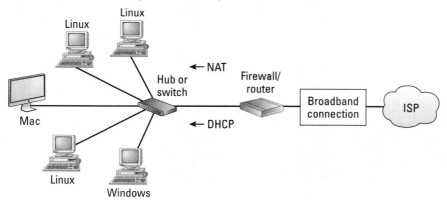

In this example, the equipment you need includes

- An Ethernet network interface card (NIC) on each computer, an Ethernet port on the firewall/router, and something connecting the firewall/router to the ISP
- A LAN cable for each computer (or wireless card, if your equipment supports wireless)
- A network switch
- The DSL or cable modem (acting as a firewall/router)

Note

Many devices provided by your ISP to connect you to the Internet actually have a version of Linux on the inside. You may have the ability to log in to the device and use it from the shell. If the device you have doesn't provide all the features you need in a firewall, you can take an old PC and install a Linux firewall distribution on it and use that between your ISP's equipment and your own network. ■

An alternative to a wired configuration is to replace the switch with a wireless access point. Then each computer equipped with a wireless LAN card can get on the network without wires.

Connecting Servers

So far you've seen configurations that let one or more computers from your home or small business browse the web. Allowing someone from the Internet to request services (web pages, file transfers, and so forth) from your computers requires some extra thought.

After you have TCP/IP (the primary set of protocols used on the Internet) configured to connect to your ISP, requests for data can pass in either direction between your computers and the Internet unless you use a firewall to restrict traffic. So the same connection you use for Internet browsing can be used to offer services to the Internet, with a few caveats:

- **Permanent IP address** — Each time you reboot your computer, your ISP's DHCP server dynamically assigns your DSL/cable modem's IP address. For that reason, your IP address could change at each reboot. If you want your servers to be reachable on a permanent basis, you usually need at least one permanent IP address at which people can reach your servers. You will have to ask your ISP about a permanent IP address, and it might cost you extra money to have one.

Note

A service called Dynamic DNS can be used in place of paying for a permanent IP address. With Dynamic DNS, you hire a service to constantly check whether your IP address has changed and assign your DNS hostname to the new address if it does. You can search the web for "Dynamic DNS" to find companies that offer that service. ■

- **ISP acceptable use policy** — Check that you are allowed to have incoming connections. Some ISPs, especially for inexpensive, home-use broadband service, will block incoming connections to web servers or mail servers.
- **DNS hostname** — Although typing an IP address into a browser location box works just fine, most people prefer to use names (such as www.linuxtoys.net) to reach a server. That requires you to purchase a DNS domain name and have an entry set up in a DNS server to resolve the name to the IP address of your server.

Although there is nothing magical about setting up an Internet server, given the few issues just mentioned, creating a public server can be a lot like opening up the doors of your house so that strangers can wander in. You want some policies in place to restrict where the strangers can go and what they can do.

For home or small-office locations that have a single Internet connection (represented by one public IP address), servers can be more exposed to the Internet than desktop systems by keeping them in one area that's referred to as the DMZ (demilitarized zone). In this configuration (illustrated in Figure 11-4), servers are directly behind the outside firewall. Desktop systems (that aren't to be accessible by people from the Internet) are behind a second, more restrictive firewall.

FIGURE 11-4

Add servers to a DMZ where they can be more publicly accessible than your desktop systems.

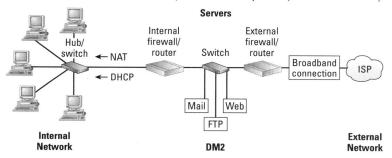

Whether you use Linux or dedicated firewall devices to provide firewall service, the outside firewall allows requests in for web services (port 80), simple mail transfer protocol (port 25), and possibly other services. The internal firewall blocks any requests for services from the outside and allows only Internet communications that were initiated from computers behind the inside firewall.

Cross-Reference

Chapters 15 though 18 explain how to configure different server types, and Chapter 13 contains some information on setting up Linux as a router/firewall. ■

Connecting Other Equipment

Although I've focused on basic Ethernet equipment and dial-up modems for configuring network connections, Linux supports many other types of network equipment as well as different protocols for communicating over that equipment. Here are a few examples:

- **ISDN** — Integrated Services Digital Network (ISDN) lines were the preferred method of high-speed data lines to small businesses in the United States before DSL became widespread. It is still popular in Europe, but is being supplanted by more affordable DSL equipment. ISDN4Linux drivers and tools (www.isdn4linux.de) are available in many Linux systems for connecting to ISDN networks.

- **USB cable modem** — Most cable modems offer an Ethernet port that you can connect to directly from your computer's own Ethernet port. However, if you don't have an Ethernet port, often you can connect to the cable modem through one of your USB ports. (You may need to manually load usbnet and cdc_ether drivers to get this to work.)

- **Token ring** — Support for token ring network cards is included in most Linux systems, although token rings are rarely used now. They were once popular at locations that had many IBM systems.

- **PLIP** — It's possible to connect two computers together from their parallel ports so that they can communicate using TCP/IP protocols. Parallel Line Internet Protocol (PLIP) requires only a special type of null modem cable (for the specs for that cable, refer to `http://tldp.org/HOWTO/NET3-4-HOWTO-9.html`). Most Linux systems have built-in software that enables you to log in, transfer files, and perform other activities over that connection.

- **DSL/PPPoE** — The point-to-point protocol (PPP) that is used for dial-up is also used by some ISPs over broadband Ethernet connections (PPPoE). By using PPPoE with broadband modems, an ISP can manage access to their service through user names and passwords. In essence, this allows the ISPs to have one infrastructure in place for both broadband and dial-up.

If your system has Linux source code installed, you can read about supported hardware devices in the documentation that comes with that source code. On Fedora and some other Linux systems, the location of kernel documentation for various networking hardware is `/usr/src/linux*/Documentation/networking`.

Using Ethernet Connections to Connect to the Internet

Most Linux systems today will either automatically detect or allow you to set up your Internet connection when you install Linux. Here's the general (default) method in which a network connection on a desktop system, with Linux installed, is started:

1. Check whether you have an Ethernet port on your computer (most recent computers have one). If so, connect your Ethernet card to the equipment that gets you to the Internet (cable modem, DSL router/bridge, or network hub/switch). If not, you can purchase an Ethernet card at any retailer that sells computer hardware.

2. Ensure that appropriate drivers are available for the card and bring up the interface (typically, the first wired Ethernet card is assigned to the eth0 interface). Usually, simply starting the computer causes the card to be detected and the appropriate driver loaded.

3. Get an IP address using DHCP if a DHCP server is available through the interface. Most ISPs and businesses expect you to connect to their networks using DHCP, so they will have provided a DHCP server to the equipment where you connect your computer to the network.

As long as your desktop system is connected to a network that has a DHCP server willing to give it an IP address, you can be up and browsing the web in no time.

If you find that the automatic method (DHCP) of connecting to your network doesn't work, then connecting to the Internet gets a bit trickier. Different Linux distributions offer different tools for manually configuring your Internet connection. The following sections describe a few graphical tools and some command-line and configuration-file approaches to configuring wired and wireless network connections.

Configuring Ethernet During Installation

Many Linux install processes ask you whether you want to configure your network connection for your Ethernet cards. This is typically just for your Ethernet cards and not for dial-up modems or other networking equipment. Information about what you'll need for that process (IP address, gateway, DNS server, and so on) is explained in Chapter 7.

When you boot Linux, you can check whether you have access to the Internet by opening a web browser (such as Firefox or Konqueror) and typing in a web address. If the web site doesn't appear in your browser, you'll need to do some troubleshooting. The "Understanding Your Internet Connection" section later in this chapter provides information on how to track down problems with your Internet connection.

Configuring Ethernet from the Desktop

Most major Linux distributions offer graphical tools for configuring network interfaces. These tools step you through the information you need to enter, and then start up the network interface (if you choose) to begin browsing the web.

Here is a list of tools for configuring network interfaces in a few different Linux distributions. Some of these are graphical tools and some are menu-based:

- **Red Hat Enterprise Linux/Fedora/Ubuntu** — For these and other Linux distributions, the NetworkManager facility automatically finds available wireless networks and tries to enable wired networks connected to your computer. If NetworkManager is running, an icon that looks like two terminals appears in your desktop panel. Click that icon to connect to available wireless networks. Right-click and select Edit Connections. From the dialog box that appears (see Figure 11-5), select the interface you are interested in and choose Edit.

- **SUSE Linux** — The YaST Control Center that comes with SUSE contains features for configuring your network. The YaST Control Center lets you configure a DSL, ISDN, Modem, or Network Card interface to the network. Select Network Card to configure your wired Ethernet interface to the Internet.

- **Gentoo Linux** — From a shell (as root user), type **net-setup eth0** to start a menu-driven interface to configure the network connection from your first Ethernet card (eth0). The tool lets you have the interface try to start using DHCP or use static address information that you provide yourself.

- **Ubuntu Linux** — In Ubuntu, you are encouraged to use the Network Connections window for NetworkManager.

FIGURE 11-5

Configuring a network interface in Ubuntu

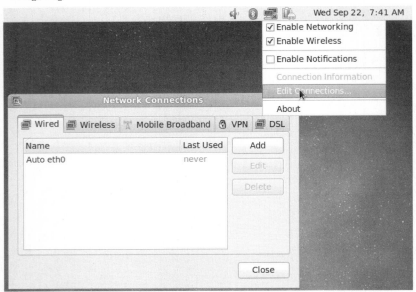

Using Network Configuration GUI in Fedora

As an alternative to NetworkManager, you can use the Network Configuration GUI that comes with Fedora and Red Hat Enterprise Linux systems. To install this feature, type `yum install system-config-network` as root user. If you did not configure your LAN connection during installation of Fedora or RHEL, you can do so at any time using the Network Configuration window. The IP address and hostnames can be assigned statically to an Ethernet interface or retrieved dynamically at boot time from a DHCP server.

Note
When accessing the Internet or a LAN, a computer typically has one IP address for each network interface. So if you have two Ethernet ports (eth0 and eth1), each usually has its own IP address. Also, the address 127.0.0.1 represents the local host and is not assigned to an Ethernet port. Through that address, users on the local computer can access services without those requests going out on the network. ■

Here's how to define the IP address for your Ethernet interface in Fedora or RHEL:

1. From the System menu, choose System ➪ Administration ➪ Network or, as root user from a Terminal window, type **system-config-network**. (If prompted, type the root password.) The Network Configuration window appears.

2. Click the Devices tab. A listing of your existing network interfaces appears.

3. Double-click the eth0 interface (representing your first Ethernet card). A pop-up window titled Ethernet Device appears (see Figure 11-6), enabling you to configure your eth0 interface.

FIGURE 11-6

Configure and activate Ethernet devices in Fedora.

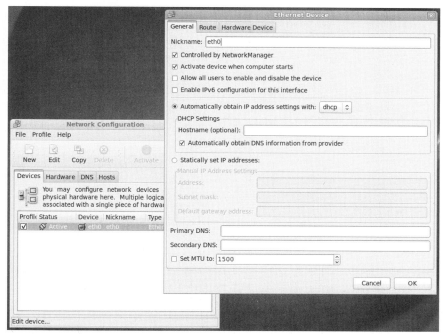

4. Select your preferences:

   - **Controlled by NetworkManager** — In the most recent versions of Fedora, NetworkManager controls your network interfaces. Unselect this box to manage your interfaces directly with the Network Configuration window.

   - **Activate device when computer starts** — Check here to have eth0 start at boot time.

- **Allow all users to enable and disable the device** — Check to let non-root users enable and disable the network interface.

- **Enable IPv6 configuration for this interface** — Check here if you are connected to an IPv6 network. (Most networks are still IPv4.)

5. You also must choose whether to get your IP addresses from another computer at boot time or enter the addresses yourself:

- **Automatically obtain IP address settings with** — Select this box if you have a DHCP or BOOTP server on the network from which you can obtain your computer's IP address, netmask, and gateway. DHCP is recommended if you have more than just a couple of computers on your LAN. Optionally, you can set your own hostname, which can be just a name (such as jukebox) or a fully qualified domain name (such as jukebox.linuxtoys.net).

- **Statically set IP addresses** — If no DHCP or other boot server exists on your LAN, add necessary IP address information statically by selecting this option and following these steps:

  a. Type the IP address of the computer into the Address box. This number must be unique on your network. For your private LAN, you can use private IP addresses.

  b. Enter the netmask in the Subnet Mask box. The netmask indicates the part of the IP address that represents the network.

  c. Type the IP address of the computer into the Default Gateway Address box if a computer or router connected to your LAN provides routing functions to the Internet or other network.

6. Click OK in the Ethernet Device window to save the configuration and close the window.

7. Click File ⇨ Save to save the information you entered.

8. Click Activate in the Network Configuration window to start your connection to the LAN.

Identifying Other Computers (Hosts and DNS)

Each time you use a name to identify a computer, such as when browsing the web or using an e-mail address, the computer name must be translated into an IP address. Typically, hostnames are translated to IP addresses by a Domain Name System (DNS) server. The locations (IP addresses) of the DNS servers your computer uses are stored in your /etc/resolv.conf file.

There are also other ways to add name-to-IP address mappings on your computer. For example, the nsswitch.conf file is configured to let you put that information to the /etc/hosts file or add additional services for gathering such information (such as an NIS service).

Again, for RHEL and Fedora systems, you can use the Network Configuration window to add

- **Hostnames** — You might do this to identify hosts on your LAN that are not configured on a DNS server.

- **DNS search path** — By adding domain names to a search path (such as `linuxtoys.net`), you can browse to a site by its hostname (such as `jukebox`) and have Linux search the domains you added to the search path to find the host you are looking for (such as `jukebox.linuxtoys.net`).

- **DNS name servers** — A DNS server can resolve addresses for the domains it serves and contact other DNS servers to get addresses for all other DNS domains.

Note

If you are configuring a DNS server, you can use that server to centrally store names and IP addresses for your LAN. This saves you the trouble of updating every computer's `/etc/hosts` file every time you add or change a computer on your LAN. ∎

To add hostnames, IP addresses, search paths, and DNS servers in Fedora, do the following:

1. **Start the Network Configuration tool.** As root user from a Terminal window, type **system-config-network** or from the top panel, click System ⇨ Administration ⇨ Network. The Network Configuration window appears.

2. **Click the Hosts tab.** A list of IP addresses, hostnames, and aliases appears.

3. **Click New.** An Add/Edit Hosts Entry pop-up window appears.

4. **Add address information.** Type in the IP address number, hostname, and, optionally, the host alias.

5. **Click OK.**

6. **Repeat this process** until you have added every computer on your LAN that cannot be reached by DNS.

7. **Click the DNS tab.**

8. **Type the IP address** of the computers that serve as your Primary and Secondary DNS servers. (You get these IP addresses from your ISP or, if you created your own DNS server, you can enter that server's IP address.)

9. **Type the name of the domain** (probably the name of your local domain) to be searched for hostnames into the DNS Search Path box.

10. **Click File ⇨ Save to save the changes.**

11. **Click File ⇨ Quit to exit.**

Now, when you use programs such as sftp, ssh, or other TCP/IP utilities, you can use any hostname that is identified on your local computer, exists in your search path domain, or can be resolved from the public Internet DNS servers. (Strictly speaking, you don't have to set up your `/etc/hosts` file. You could use IP addresses as arguments to TCP/IP commands. But names are easier to work with.)

Understanding Your Internet Connection

If your Ethernet interface to the Internet is not working, there are ways to check what's happening that will work on many Linux distributions. Use the following procedure to find out how your network interfaces are working:

1. Open a shell (if you are using a graphical interface, open a Terminal window).

2. Type the following right after you boot your computer to verify whether Linux found your card and installed the Ethernet interface properly:

```
dmesg | grep eth | less
```

The dmesg command lists all the messages that were output by Linux at boot time. The grep eth command causes only those lines that contain the word eth to be printed. Here are a couple of examples:

```
eth0: VIA Rhine II at 0xee001000, 00:0d:61:25:d4:17, IRQ 185.
eth0: MII PHY found at address 1, status 0x786d advertising
01e1 Link 45e1.
eth0: link up, 100Mbps, full-duplex, lpa 0x45E1
eth0: no IPv6 routers present
```

The first message appeared on my desktop computer with a VIA Rhine Ethernet controller. It shows that a card was found at software IRQ 185 with a port address of 0xee001000 and an Ethernet hardware address (MAC address) of 00:0d:61:25:d4:17. The other lines indicate that the link is up on the eth0 interface and running at 100 Mbps in full-duplex. In this case, IPv6 routing is not enabled.

Note

If the eth0 interface is not found, but you know that you have a supported Ethernet card, type lspci -vv | grep -i eth to see whether the Ethernet card is detected on the PCI bus. If it doesn't appear, check that your Ethernet card is properly seated in its slot. Here's what appeared for the preceding example:

```
00:12.0 Ethernet controller: VIA Technologies, Inc.
VT6102 [Rhine-II] (rev 74) ■
```

3. To view which network interfaces are up and running, type the following:

```
$ /sbin/ip addr
1: lo: <LOOPBACK,UP,LOWER_UP> mtu 16436 qdisc noqueue state UNKNOWN
    link/loopback 00:00:00:00:00:00 brd 00:00:00:00:00:00
    inet 127.0.0.1/8 scope host lo
    inet6 ::1/128 scope host
       valid_lft forever preferred_lft forever
2: eth0: <BROADCAST,MULTICAST,UP,LOWER_UP> mtu 1500 qdisc pfifo_fast
    state UNKNOWN qlen 1000
    link/ether 44:55:46:46:45:59 brd ff:ff:ff:ff:ff:ff
    inet 10.0.0.5/24 brd 10.0.0.255 scope global eth0
```

```
inet6 fe80::e2cb: 4455:4646:4559/64 scope link
```

```
valid_lft forever preferred_lft forever
```

The output shows a loopback interface (lo) and one Ethernet card (eth0). The Ethernet interface (eth0) is assigned the IP address of 10.0.0.5. Again, notice that the MAC address, which is a unique address related to the Ethernet card hardware, is noted after the HWaddr indicator (44:55:46:46:45:59).

4. Communicate with another computer on the LAN. The ping command can be used to send a packet to another computer and to ask for a packet in return. You can give ping either a hostname (butch) or an IP address (10.0.0.10). For example, to ping a computer on the network called butch, type the following command:

```
# ping butch
```

If the computer can be reached, the output will look similar to the following:

```
PING butch (10.0.0.10): 56(84) data bytes
64 bytes from butch (10.0.0.10): icmp_seq=1 ttl=255 time=0.351 ms
64 bytes from butch (10.0.0.10): icmp_seq=2 ttl=255 time=0.445 ms
64 bytes from butch (10.0.0.10): icmp_seq=3 ttl=255 time=0.409 ms
64 bytes from butch (10.0.0.10): icmp_seq=4 ttl=255 time=0.457 ms
64 bytes from butch (10.0.0.10): icmp_seq=5 ttl=255 time=0.401 ms
64 bytes from butch (10.0.0.10): icmp_seq=6 ttl=255 time=0.405 ms
64 bytes from butch (10.0.0.10): icmp_seq=7 ttl=255 time=0.443 ms
64 bytes from butch (10.0.0.10): icmp_seq=8 ttl=255 time=0.384 ms
64 bytes from butch (10.0.0.10): icmp_seq=9 ttl=255 time=0.365 ms
64 bytes from butch (10.0.0.10): icmp_seq=10 ttl=255 time=0.367 ms

--- butch statistics ---
10 packets transmitted, 10 packets received, 0% packet loss, time 9011ms
rtt min/avg/max/mdev = 0.351/0.402/0.457/0.042 ms
```

A line of output is printed each time a packet is sent and received in return. It shows how much data was sent and how long it took for each package to be received. Watch this for a while, and then press Ctrl+C to stop ping; you'll see statistics on how many packets were transmitted, received, and lost.

If the output doesn't show that packets have been received, there's no contact with the other computer. Verify that the names and addresses of the computers that you want to reach are in your /etc/hosts file or that your DNS server is accessible. Next, confirm that the names and IP addresses you have for the other computers you are trying to reach are correct (the IP addresses are the most critical).

5. If you are able to reach an IP address on your LAN with ping, but are unable to ping a host computer by name, you may not be communicating with your DNS server. Repeat the ping command with the IP address of your DNS server to see whether it is up and that you are able to communicate with it.

Using Dial-Up to Connect to the Internet

On the rare occasion that broadband is not available, you can still connect to the Internet using modems and telephone lines. The modem connects to a serial port (COM1, COM2, and so on) on your computer and then into a telephone jack. Your computer dials a modem at your Internet service provider or business that has a connection to the Internet.

The most common protocol for making dial-up connections to the Internet (or other TCP/IP network) is Point-to-Point Protocol (PPP). Take a look at how to use PPP to connect to the Internet.

Cross-Reference
See Chapter 21 for information on configuring a dial-up connection that is specific to Debian. ■

Getting Information

To establish a PPP connection, you need to get some information from the administrator of the network to which you are connecting. This is either your Internet service provider (ISP) when you sign up for Internet service, or the person in your workplace who walks around carrying cables, two or more cellular phones, and a couple of beepers. (When a network goes down, these people are in demand!) Here is the kind of information you need to set up your PPP connection:

- **Telephone number** — Gives you access to the modem (or pool of modems) at the ISP. If it is a national ISP, make sure that you get a local or toll-free telephone number (otherwise, you'll rack up long-distance fees on top of your ISP fees).

- **Account name and password** — Used to verify that you have an Internet account with the ISP. This is an account name when you connect to Linux or other UNIX system, but may be referred to as a system name when you connect to an NT server.

- **An IP address** — Most ISPs use Dynamic IP numbers, which means that you are assigned an IP number temporarily when you are connected. Your ISP assigns a permanent IP number if it uses Static IP addresses. If your computer or all the computers on your LAN need to have a more permanent presence on the network, you may be given one Static IP number or a set of Static IP addresses to use.

- **DNS Server IP addresses** — Your computer translates Internet hostnames to IP addresses by querying a domain name system (DNS) server. Your ISP should give you at least one IP address for a preferred (and possibly alternate) DNS server.

- **PAP or CHAP secrets** — You may need a PAP (Password Authentication Protocol) ID or CHAP (Challenge Handshake Authentication Protocol) ID and a secret, instead of a username and password, when connecting to a Windows NT system. These features are used with authentication on Microsoft and some other operating systems. Linux and other UNIX servers don't typically use this type of authentication, although they support PAP and CHAP on the client side. Your ISP will tell you whether you are using PAP or CHAP.

Your ISP typically provides services such as news and mail servers for use with your Internet connection. To configure these useful services, you need the following information:

- **Mail server** — If your ISP is providing you with an e-mail account, you must know the address of the mail server, the type of mail service (such as POP3 — Post Office Protocol; or IMAP — Internet Message Access Protocol), and the authentication password for the mail server so you can get your e-mail.

- **News server** — If your ISP provides the name of a news server so that you can participate in newsgroups, the server may require you to log on, so you need a password. The ISP provides that password, if required.

After you've gathered this information, you're ready to set up your connection to the Internet. To configure Linux to connect to your ISP, read on.

Setting Up Dial-Up PPP

PPP is used to create IP connections over serial lines. Most often, the serial connection is established over a modem; however, it also works over serial cables (null modem cables) or digital lines (including ISDN and DSL).

Although one side must dial out and the other side must receive the call to create the PPP connection over a modem, after the connection is established, information can flow in both directions. For the sake of clarity, however, I refer to the computer placing the call as the *client* and the computer receiving the call as the *server*.

To simplify the process of configuring PPP (and other network interfaces), most Linux systems include graphical tools to configure dial-up. Two such tools, available with Fedora and RHEL, are

- **Network Configuration window** — The same utility used to configure Ethernet cards can be used to configure modems. From the GNOME top panel in Fedora and RHEL systems, choose System ⇨ Administration ⇨ Network. When that window appears, select New. The Select Device Type pop-up that appears enables you to configure and test your modem for a dial-up PPP connection.

- **KDE PPP (KPPP) window** — From the KDE desktop, select Internet ⇨ KPPP, or from a Terminal window run the kppp command. From the KPPP window, you can set up and launch a PPP dial-up connection.

Before you begin either of these procedures, physically connect your modem to your computer, plug it in, and connect it to your telephone line. If you have an internal modem, you will probably see a telephone port on the back of your computer to which you need to connect. If your modem isn't detected, you can reboot your computer or run wvdialconf create (as described later in this chapter) to have it detected.

Creating a Dial-Up Connection with the Internet Configuration Wizard

If you are using a Fedora or RHEL system, you could use the Internet Configuration Wizard to set up dial-up networking. Here's how:

1. **Choose System ➪ Administration ➪ Network.** When the window appears, select New. (Type the root password, if prompted.) An Add New Device Type window appears (see Figure 11-7).

FIGURE 11-7

The Internet Configuration Wizard helps you set up a PPP Internet connection.

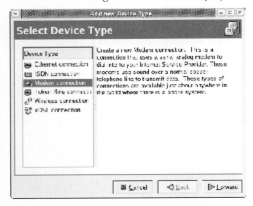

2. **Select Modem Connection and click Forward.** The wizard searches for a modem and then the Select Modem window appears. If you need to set up PPP over Ethernet (PPPoE), select xDSL Connection rather than Modem Connection, select your Ethernet device, and then skip to Step 4.

3. **Select the following modem properties:**

   - **Modem Device** — If the modem is connected to your first serial port (COM1) you can select /dev/ttyS0; for the second serial port (COM2) choose /dev/ttyS1. (By convention, the device is often linked to /dev/modem. Type **ls –l /dev/modem** to see whether it is linked to /dev/ttyS0, /dev/ttyS1, or another tty device.)

   - **Baud Rate** — The rate at which the computer talks to the modem (which is typically considerably faster than the modem can talk over the phone lines). The default is 115,200 bits per second, which is probably fine for dial-up connections.

   - **Flow Control** — Check the modem documentation to see whether the modem supports hardware flow control (CRTSCTS). If it doesn't, select software flow control (XON/XOFF). Flow control prevents more data than the modem can handle from being sent to it.

- **Modem Volume** — This is off by default because the noise can be annoying, but if you select medium while you're setting up the modem, the sound can give you a sense of where things are stopping if you can't get a connection. You can turn it off after everything's working.

- **Use Touch Tone Dialing** — Leave this check box selected in most cases. If for some reason your phone system doesn't support touch-tone dialing, you can turn it off.

4. **Click Forward.** The Select Provider window appears. Enter the following provider information:

   - **Internet Provider** — If you are using Internet service in any of the countries shown in the Internet Provider window, select the plus sign next to that country name. If your Internet service provider appears in the National list, select it. Information is automatically filled in for that provider. Otherwise, you need to fill in the rest of the dialog window.

   - **Phone Number** — The telephone number of the ISP you want to dial in to. An xDSL connection does not need a phone number. (An optional prefix is available in case you need to dial 9 or some other number to get an outside dial tone.)

   - **Provider Name** — The name of the Internet service provider. If there is only one ISP, I recommend you use it as the ppp0 provider name.

   - **Login Name** — The login name assigned to you by the ISP. The ISP may have called the login name a login ID or something similar.

   - **Password** — The password associated with the login name.

5. **Click Forward.** The IP Settings window appears. With a dial-up connection, you would typically select Automatically Obtain IP Address Settings. However, if the ISP has assigned a static IP address that you can use, select the Statically Set IP Addresses check box, and then enter your IP address, subnet mask, and default gateway address in the appropriate fields. Click Forward to continue. The Create Dialup Connection window appears, displaying the information you just entered.

6. **If all the information looks correct, click Apply** (otherwise, click the Back button, correct your information, and click Forward again to return to this window). The Network Configuration window appears, ideally with a new PPP connection of modem type appearing in the window.

7. **If the Network Configuration window doesn't appear, select System Settings ⇨ Network.**

8. **Select the new dial-up entry (so it is highlighted), and choose File ⇨ Save. This saves its new dial-up configuration.**

Now select the PPP device name and click the Activate button. The Internet dialer starts up and dials your ISP. (If you have sound turned on, you should hear your modem dialing out.) If everything is working properly, your login and password are accepted and the PPP connection is completed.

Try opening Firefox or another web browser to see whether you can access a web site on the Internet. If this doesn't work the first time, don't be discouraged. There are things to check to get your dial-up PPP connection working.

Launching Your PPP Connection

Your dial-up connection is now configured, but it is not set to connect automatically. One way to start the connection is to set it up to launch manually from the desktop panel. The following steps show you how.

From the GNOME desktop:

1. **Select Modem Lights.** Right-click the panel, and choose Add to Panel ⇨ Modem Lights, and then select Add. A Modem Lights icon appears on the panel.

2. **Select the new icon from the panel**. You are asked whether you want to start a connection with your modem.

3. **Select Connect** to start the connection.

From the KDE desktop:

1. **Select KPPP.** Right-click the panel and then choose Add Application to Panel ⇨ Internet ⇨ KPPP.

2. **Select the new icon from the panel** (type the root password, if prompted). A KPPP window appears.

3. **Select the dial-up interface you added** (probably ppp0) and click Connect to connect.

From this point forward, icons appear on your desktop that you can select to immediately connect to your ISP over the dial-up connection you configured.

Launching Your PPP Connection on Demand

Instead of starting a dial-up PPP connection manually each time you want to connect to the Internet, you can set your dial-up connection to start automatically when an application (such as a web browser or e-mail program) tries to use the connection. On-demand dialing is particularly useful if

- The dial-up connection on your Linux system is acting as the gateway for other computers in your home or office. You don't have to run over to your Linux box to start the connection when another computer needs the dial-up connection.

- Programs that you run during off hours, such as remote backups, require an Internet connection.

- You don't want to be bothered clicking an extra icon when you just want to browse the web a bit.

The risk of on-demand dialing is that because it gets going automatically, the dial-up connection can start up when you don't want it to. (Some people get worried when their computers start dialing by themselves in the middle of the night.)

For RHEL and Fedora systems, here is an example of settings you can add to your dial-up configuration file (probably /etc/sysconfig/network-scripts/ifcfg-ppp0) to configure on-demand dialing:

```
ONBOOT=yes
DEMAND=yes
IDLETIMEOUT=600
RETRYTIMEOUT=30
```

The ONBOOT=yes variable starts the pppd daemon (but doesn't immediately begin dialing because DEMAND is set to yes). Also, because of the setting DEMAND=yes, a dial-up connection attempt is made any time traffic tries to use your dial-up connection. With IDLETIMEOUT set to 600, the connection is dropped after 600 seconds (10 minutes) with no traffic on the connection. With RETRYTIMEOUT set to 30, a dropped connection is retried after 30 seconds (unless the connection was dropped by an idle timeout, in which case there is no retry). You can change the timeout values as it suits you.

Note
Because establishing dial-up connections can take a bit of time, operations may fail while dialing occurs. In particular, DNS requests can time out in 30 seconds, which may not be long enough to establish a dial-up connection. If you have three DNS servers configured for each client, you have a 90-second timeout period. As a result, the modem connection may be running before the request fails. ■

Checking Your PPP Connection

To debug your PPP connection or simply to better understand how it works, you can run through the following steps. They can help you understand where information is being stored and how to use tools to track this information.

Checking That Your Modem Was Detected

It is possible that your modem is not supported under Linux. If that is the case, your PPP connection might be failing because the modem was not detected at all. To scan your serial ports to see where your modem might be, type the following (as root user):

```
$ wvdialconf /etc/wvdial.conf.new
```

The wvdialconf command builds a configuration file (in this example, the /etc/wvdial .conf.new file) that is used by the dialer command (wvdial). (You need this file only if you use wvdial to do your dial-up.) Its first action, however, is to scan the serial ports on your computer and report where it finds modems. If it tells you that no modem was detected, it's likely that either your modem isn't connected properly or no driver is available to support the modem.

If the modem wasn't detected, you should determine whether it is a modem supported in Linux. You can do this by finding out what type of chip set is used in the modem. This is even more important than finding out the manufacturer of the modem because the same manufacturer can use chips from different companies. (This applies primarily to internal modems because most external serial modems and many USB modems are supported in Linux.)

After you have determined the chip set being used, check the Linmodems.org web site (www.linmodems.org). Search for the chip set on your modem from this site. In many cases, the site can tell you whether a driver is available for your modem.

A nice tool for determining what type of Winmodem you have and how to get it working is scan-Modem. If you have access to the Internet from another machine, you can download scanModem from this address:

```
http://linmodems.technion.ac.il/packages/scanModem.gz
```

Because you probably don't have a working Internet connection yet, find a way to copy scanModem.gz to your Linux system (maybe copy it to a flash drive or burn it to a CD). As root user from a Terminal window, type these commands, with that file in the current directory:

```
# gunzip scanModem.gz
# chmod 755 scanModem
# ./scanModem
```

The result is a Modem directory containing text files describing your modem and what you can do to configure it.

Note

If you are a new Linux user with a Winmodem and you are still baffled after referring to the linmodems.org site, you might consider getting a serial or USB modem. To get your Winmodem working, you might need to download, compile, and load a modem driver. Especially with some older Winmodems, drivers have not all been updated to work with the latest kernels. Picking up a cheap hardware modem (under $20) from a used computer store, which you can connect to a serial port, can save hours of frustration with a Winmodem that may ultimately not work anyway. ■

Connecting to the Internet with Wireless

Setting up a wireless network connection used to be one of the more challenging features to get working in Linux. In recent releases of Ubuntu, Fedora, and other major Linux distributions, that situation has changed for several major reasons:

- **Wireless drivers** — Because most wireless card manufacturers did not make source code available with their drivers, most Linux distributions resisted including those drivers in their distributions. Recently, most distributions have relented and included those binary-only drivers.

- **NetworkManager** — To use NetworkManager as the default tool for managing network interfaces in Fedora, Ubuntu, and others, simply click the NetworkManager icon on the top panel. This shows you a list of all wireless networks detected in your area.

As a result of the issues just described, in most cases Linux laptop or desktop users can simply log in to their systems and select the NetworkManager icon in the panel. From the menu that appears, a user can choose the desired wireless network interface from a list that appears and type any user and password information required to connect to that interface.

However, if your Linux system doesn't include the wireless drivers you need and isn't configured to automatically detect your network interfaces, here are a few open source projects you can look into to help get wireless working:

- **ndiswrappers** (`http://ndiswrapper.sourceforge.net`) — This project lets you use wireless drivers in Linux that were created to run in Windows.

- **madwifi** (`http://madwifi.org`) — Supports drivers for wireless chip sets from Atheros (`www.atheros.com`).

- **Intel PRO/Wireless for Linux** (`http://ipw2100.sourceforge.net`) — Several wireless driver projects support drivers for Intel PRO/Wireless hardware.

- **Linuxant Driver Loader** (`http://www.linuxant.com/driverloader`) — A commercial product that lets you use wireless drivers in Linux that were created to run in Windows.

Note

If you are using Red Hat Enterprise Linux and your wireless card isn't working, check the Drivers disc that comes with your RHEL boxed set. Many wireless drivers are included on that disc. ■

After the proper driver for your wireless card is installed and activated, different tools are available for configuring your wireless cards in different Linux releases. Here are examples:

- **Wireless in Fedora** — In Fedora, use the NetworkManager to configure your wireless network cards. It should be on by default. If it's not, however, as root you can type the following: `chkconfig NetworkManager on` so it is set to start at boot time. Next type `service NetworkManager start` to start it immediately. Then configure your wireless connection from a network icon that appears in the panel.

- **Wireless in KNOPPIX** — In KNOPPIX, try KWiFiManager. From the KDE menu, select KNOPPIX ⇨ Network/Internet ⇨ KWiFiManager.

For further information on configuring wireless devices in Linux, refer to the Wireless LAN resources for Linux page:

`http://hpl.hp.com/personal/Jean_Tourrilhes/Linux/Wireless.html`

If you find that you are unable to get the driver for your particular wireless card working at all, determine the type of card you have, using one of the following commands:

```
# dmesg |grep -i wireless
# lspci -vv |grep -i wireless
```

Then use some search tool, such as Google, to search for the name and model of your wireless card, along with the word "Linux" or the particular distribution of Linux you are using. Chances are, if your wireless device is at all popular, someone else has tried to get it working in Linux and has probably shared his or her experiences somewhere online.

Summary

Many different tools exist for configuring network connections in the various Linux distributions. Fedora and other Red Hat Enterprise Linux systems use a graphical network configuration tool. SUSE Linux uses its YaST administrative interface to configure network equipment. For dial-up networks, the KDE desktop includes the kppp GUI tool for configuring modems. If your network connection doesn't start up automatically (as it does in many cases), this chapter explains how to use some of these network configuration tools to configure it manually.

Using Network Tools

## 12

I n the time it takes to fire up a graphical FTP client, you could already
have downloaded a few dozen files from a remote server using command-line tools. Even when a GUI is available, commands for transferring files, web browsing, sharing directories, and reading mail can be quick
and efficient to use. When no GUI is available, they can be lifesavers.

This chapter covers commands for accessing resources (files, e-mail,
shared directories, and online chats) over the network. To use these commands, open a Terminal window (or use some other means to open a shell
interface).

Running Commands to Browse the Web

Text-mode web browsers provide a quick way to check that a web server is
working or to get information from a web server when a useable GUI isn't
available. The once-popular lynx text-based browser was supplanted in
most Linux systems by the links browser, which was later replaced by
elinks. To use a command-line browser, you need to install one of these
programs, with package names that match the command names: lynx,
links, w3m, or elinks. In most cases, if you want a command-line web
browser, install the elinks package.

The elinks browser runs in a Terminal window. Aside from not displaying
images in the terminal, elinks can handle most basic HTML content and
features: tables, frames, tabbed browsing, cookies, history, MIME types,
and simple cascading style sheets. You can even use your mouse to follow
links and select menu items.

IN THIS CHAPTER

Web browsing with elinks

**Wget, curl, lftp, and scp for file
transfers**

**Sharing directories with NFS,
Samba, and SSHFS**

IRC chats with irssi

Mail and mutt e-mail clients

Because elinks supports multiple colors, as long as the terminal you are using supports multiple colors, it's easy to spot links and headings in the text. (Colors may not work within a screen session.) Here are some examples of elinks command lines:

```
$ elinks                          Prompts for file name or URL
$ elinks www.handsonhistory.com   Opens file name or URL you request
```

If you have a mouse available, click near the top of the Terminal window to see the menu. Select the menu name or item you want. Select a link to go to that link. Table 12-1 shows elinks keyboard navigation keys.

TABLE 12-1

Control Keys for Using elinks

Keys	Description	Keys	Description
Esc (or F9/ F8)	Toggle menu on and off (then use arrow keys or mouse to navigate menus).	=	View page information.
Down arrow	Go to next link or editable field on page.	Ctrl+r	Reload page.
Up arrow	Go to previous link or editable field on the page.	A	Bookmark current page.
Right arrow or Enter	Go forward to highlighted link. Enter text in highlighted form field.	T	Open new browser tab.
Left arrow	Go back to previous page.	>	Go to next tab.
/	Search forward.	<	Go to previous tab.
?	Search backwards.	C	Close current tab.
n	Find next.	D	Download current link.
N	Find previous.	D	View downloads.
PageUp	Scroll one page up.	A	Add current link to bookmarks.
PageDown	Scroll one page down.	S	View bookmarks.
g	Go to a URL.	V	View current image.
q or Ctrl+c	Exit elinks.	H	View global history manager.

You can add global settings for elinks to /etc/elinks.conf. Per-user settings are stored in each user's $HOME/.elinks directory. Type **man elinkskeys** to see available settings.

Transferring Files

Commands in Linux for downloading files from remote servers (HTTP, HTTPS, FTP, or SSH) are plentiful and powerful. You might choose one command over another because of the specific options you need. For example, you may want to perform a download over an encrypted connection, resume an aborted download, or do recursive downloads. This section describes how to use wget, ftp, lftp, scp, and sftp.

Downloading Files With wget

Sometimes you need to download a file from a remote server using the command line. For example, you find a link to an RPM software package, but the link goes through several HTTP redirects that prevent rpm from installing straight from HTTP. Or you may want to script the automated download of a file, such as a log file, every night.

The wget command can download files from web servers (HTTP and HTTPS) and FTP servers. With a server that doesn't require authentication, a wget command can be as simple as the wget command and the location of the download file:

```
$ wget https://help.ubuntu.com/htdocs/ubuntunew/img/logo.png
```

If, for example, an FTP server requires a login and password, you can enter that information on the wget command line in the following forms:

```
$ wget ftp://user:password@ftp.abc.com/path/to/file
$ wget --user=user --password=pass ftp://ftp.abc.com/path/to/file
```

For example:

```
$ wget ftp://joe:mykuulpwd@ftp.linuxtoys.net/home/chris/image.jpg
$ wget --user=joe --password=mykuulpwd \
ftp://ftp.linuxtoys.net/home/chris/image.jpg
```

You can use wget to download a single web page as follows:

```
$ wget http://www.wiley.com          Download only the web page
```

If you open the resulting index.html, you'll have all sorts of broken links. To download all the images and other elements required to render the page properly, use the -p option:

```
$ wget -p http://www.wiley.com        Download page and other items
```

But if you open the resulting index.html in your browser, chances are you will still have all the broken links even though all the images were downloaded. That's because the links need to be translated to point to your local files. So instead, do this:

```
$ wget -pk http://www.wiley.com       Download pages, local file names
```

And if you'd like wget to create a backup of the original file before conversion, do the following:

```
$ wget -pkK http://www.wiley.com      Use local names, keep original
```

Sometimes an HTML file you download does not have a .html extension, but ends in .asp or .cgi instead. That may result in your browser not knowing how to open your local copy of the file. You can have wget append .html to those files using the -E option:

```
$ wget -E http://www.aspexamples.com      Append .html to files
```

With the wget command, you can recursively mirror an entire web site. While copying files and directories for the entire depth of the server's file structure, the -m option adds timestamping and keeps FTP directory listings. (Use this with caution because it can take a lot of time and space.)

```
$ wget -m http://www.linuxtoys.net
```

Using some of the options just described, the following command line results in the most usable local copy of a web site:

```
$ wget -mEkK http://www.linuxtoys.net
```

If you have ever had a large file download (such as a CD or DVD image file) disconnect before it completed, you may find the -c option to wget to be a lifesaver. Using -c, wget resumes where it left off, continuing an interrupted file download. For example:

```
$ wget http://example.com/DVD.iso      Begin downloading large file
...
95%[==========  ] 685,251,583 55K/s    Download killed before done
$ wget -c http://example.com/DVD.iso   Resume download where stopped
...
HTTP request sent, awaiting response... 206 Partial Content
Length: 699,389,952 (667), 691,513 (66M) remaining [text/plain]
```

Because of the continue feature (-c), wget can be particularly useful for those with slow Internet connections who need to download large files. If you have ever had a several-hour download get killed just before it finished, you'll know what I mean. (Note that if you don't use the -c when you mean to resume a file download, the file will be saved to a different file: the original name with a .1 appended to it.)

Transferring Files With curl

The curl command (which stands for client for URLs) provides similar features to wget for transferring files using web and FTP protocols. However, the curl command can also transfer files using other popular protocols, including SSH protocols (SCP and SFTP), LDAP, DICT, Telnet, and File.

Instead of supporting large, recursive downloads (as wget does), curl is designed for *single-shot file transfers*. It does, however, support more protocols (as noted) and some neat advanced features. To use this command, you need to install the curl package. Here are a few interesting examples of file transfers with curl:

```
$ curl -O ftp://kernelorg.mirrors.tds.net/pub/linux/kernel/v1.0/ \
    patch[6-8].sign
$ curl -OO ftp://kernelorg.mirrors.tds.net/pub/linux/kernel/v2.6/ \
    ChangeLog-2.6.{1,4}
$ curl -O ftp://joe:MyPasswd@ftp.example.com/home/chris/fileA \
    -Q '-DELE fileA'
$ curl -T install.log ftp://joe:MyPasswd@ftp.example.com/tmp/ \
    -Q "-RNFR install.log" -Q "-RNTO Xinstall.log"
$ curl ftp://ftp.kernel.org/pub//                     List /pub/ contents
```

The first two commands show how to use square brackets to indicate a range [6-8] and curly brackets for a list {1,4} of characters or numbers to match files.

The third command line illustrates how to use a username and password (joe:MyPasswd), download a file (fileA) from the server, and then delete the file on the server once the download is done (-Q '-DELE fileA').

The fourth example uploads (-T) the file install.log to an FTP server. Then it renames the remote file to Xinstall.log. The last example tells curl to list the contents of the /pub/ directory at ftp.kernel.org.

Transferring Files with FTP Commands

Most Linux distributions come with the standard FTP client (ftp command), which works the same way it does on most UNIX and Windows systems. We recommend you use the full-featured, user-friendly lftp instead. The lftp command offers features such as parallel downloads, bookmarks, job control, and command history editing, to name a few.

With these FTP clients, you open a session to the FTP server (as opposed to just grabbing a file, as you do with wget and curl). Then you navigate the server much as you would a local file system, getting and putting documents across the network connection. Here are examples of how to connect to an FTP server with lftp:

Note
When you enter the lftp command with a password, it may appear that the password has been accepted and you are connected to the server. However, the connection doesn't occur until you actually do something to access the server (such as by typing the ls command). This can sometimes confuse users who think they were authenticated and yet cannot view the contents of a site. ■

```
$ lftp mirrors.kernel.org                Anonymous connection
lftp mirrors.kernel.org:~>
$ lftp joe@example.com                   Authenticated connection
Password: ******
lftp example.com:~>
```

```
$ lftp -u joe example.com            Authenticated connection
Password: ******
lftp example.com:~>
$ lftp -u joe,Mypwd example.com      Authentication with password
lftp example.com:~>
$ lftp                               Start lftp with no connection
lftp :~> open mirrors.kernel.org     Open new connection in lftp
lftp mirrors.kernel.org:~>
```

Caution

The fourth example should be avoided in real life. Passwords that are entered in a command line end up stored in clear text in your ~/.bash_history. They may also be visible to other users in the output of ps auwx. ■

When a connection is established to an FTP server, you can use a set of commands during the FTP session. FTP commands are similar to shell commands. Just as in a bash shell, you can press Tab to autocomplete filenames. In a session, lftp also supports sending multiple jobs to the background (Ctrl+z) and returning them to the foreground (wait or fg). These are useful if you want to continue traversing the FTP site while files are downloading or uploading. Background jobs run in parallel. Type jobs to see a list of running background jobs. Type help to see a list of lftp commands.

The following sample lftp session illustrates useful commands when downloading:

```
$ lftp mirrors.kernel.org
lftp mirrors.kernel.org:~> pwd                Check current directory
ftp://mirrors.kernel.org
lftp mirrors.kernel.org:~> ls                 List current directory
drwxr-sr-x   8 400   400   4096 Jul 02 20:19 debian/
drwxr-xr-x   7 537   537     77 May 21 21:37 fedora/
      ...
lftp mirrors.kernel.org:~> cd fedora/releases/13/Live/i686 Change dir
lftp mirrors.kernel.org:...> get Fedora-13-Live-i686.iso     Download
Fedora-13-Live-i686.iso at 776398 (1%) 467.2K/s eta:26m [Receiving data]
lftp mirrors.kernel.org:...> <Ctrl+z>              Background download
lftp mirrors.kernel.org:...> mget /gnu/ed/*       Get all in /gnu/ed
lftp mirrors.kernel.org:...> !ls                  Run local ls
lftp mirrors.kernel.org:...> bookmark add Live    Bookmark location
lftp mirrors.kernel.org:...> quit                 Close lftp
```

This session logs in as the anonymous user at mirrors.kernel.org. After changing to the directory containing the ISO image I was looking for, I downloaded it using the get command. By pressing Ctrl+z, the download could continue while I did other activities. Next, the mget command (which allows wildcards such as *) downloaded all files from the /gnu/ed directory.

Any command preceded by an exclamation mark (such as !ls) is executed by the local shell. The bookmark command saves the current location (in this case, ftp://mirrors.kernel.org/fedora/releases/13/Live) under the name Live, so next time I can run lftp Live to return to the same location. The quit command ends the session.

Here are some useful commands during an authenticated lftp upload session. This assumes you have the necessary file permissions on the server:

```
$ lftp chris@example.com
Password: *******
lftp example.com:~> lcd /home/chris/songs      Change to a local dir
lftp example.com:~> cd pub/uploads             Change to server dir
lftp example.com:~> mkdir songs                Create dir on server
lftp example.com:~> chmod 700 songs            Change remote dir perms
lftp example.com:~> cd songs                   Change to the new dir
lftp example.com:~> put song.ogg tune.ogg      Upload files to server
3039267 bytes transferred
lftp example.com:~> mput /var/songs/*          Upload matched files
lftp example.com:~> quit                       Close lftp
```

The lftp session illustrates how you can use shell command names to operate on remote directories (provided you have permission). The mkdir and chmod commands create a directory and leave permissions open only to your user account. The put command uploads one or more files to the remote server. The mput command can use wildcards to match multiple files for download. Other commands include mirror (to download a directory tree) and mirror -R (to upload a directory tree).

lftp also provides a shell script for non-interactive download sessions: lftpget. The syntax of lftpget is similar to that of the wget command:

```
$ lftpget ftp://mirrors.kernel.org/ubuntu/dists/feisty/Release
```

Keep in mind that standard FTP clients are insecure because they do all their work in clear text. So your alternative, especially when security is a major issue, is to use SSH tools to transfer files.

Using SSH Tools to Transfer Files

SSH utilities are among the most important tools in a system administrator's arsenal of communications commands. In their most basic form, SSH utilities are the tools you should use most often for file transfer, remote login, and remote execution.

For file transfers, the scp command will do most of what you need to get a file from one computer to another, while making that communication safe by encrypting both the password stage and data transfer stage of the process. The scp command replaces the rcp command as the most popular tool for host-to-host file copies.

Caution
You do not get a warning before overwriting existing files with scp, so be sure that the target host doesn't contain any files or directories you want that are in the path of your scp file copies. ■

Copying Remote Files With scp

To use scp to transfer files, the SSH service (usually the sshd server daemon) must be running on the remote system. Here are some examples of useful scp commands:

```
$ scp myfile joe@server1:/tmp/          Copy myfile to server1
Password: ******
$ scp server1:/tmp/myfile .             Copy remote myfile to local dir
Password: ******
```

Use the -p option to preserve permissions and timestamps on the copied files:

```
$ scp -p myfile server1:/tmp/
```

If the SSH service is configured to listen on a port other than the default port 22, use -P to indicate that port on the scp command line:

```
$ scp -P 12345 myfile server1:/tmp/      Connect to a particular port
```

To do recursive copies, from a particular point in the remote file system, use the -r option:

```
$ scp -r mydir joe@server1:/tmp/         Copies all mydir to remote /tmp
```

Although scp is most useful when you know the exact locations of the file(s) you need to copy, sometimes it's more helpful to browse and transfer files interactively.

Copying Remote Files in sftp and lftp Sessions

The sftp command lets you use an FTP-like interface to find and copy files over SSH protocols. Here's an example of how to start an sftp session:

```
$ sftp chris@server1
chris@server1's password: *****
sftp>
```

Use sftp in the same manner as you use regular FTP clients. Type ? for a list of commands. You can change remote directories (cd), change local directories (lcd), check current remote and local directories (pwd and lpwd), and list remote and local contents (ls and lls). Depending on the permission of the user you logged in as, you may be able to create and remove directories (mkdir and rmdir), and change permissions (chmod) and ownership/group (chown and chgrp) of files and directories.

You can also use lftp (discussed earlier in this chapter) as an sftp client. Using lftp adds some user-friendly features such as *path completion* using the Tab key:

```
$ lftp sftp://chris@server1
Password: ********
lftp chris@server1:~>
```

Using Windows File Transfer Tools

In many cases, people need to get files from Linux servers using Windows clients. If your client operating system is Windows, you can use one of the following open source tools to get files from Linux servers:

- **WinSCP** (http://winscp.net) — Graphical scp, sftp, and FTP client for Windows over SSH1 and SSH2 protocols.

- **FileZilla** (http://filezilla.sourceforge.net) — Provides graphical client FTP and SFTP services in Windows, as well as offering FTP server features.

- **PSCP** (www.chiark.greenend.org.uk/~sgtatham/putty/) — Command-line scp client that is part of the PuTTY suite.

- **PSFTP** (www.chiark.greenend.org.uk/~sgtatham/putty/) — Command-line sftp client that is part of the PuTTY suite.

Sharing Remote Directories

Tools described to this point in the chapter provide atomic file access, where a connection is set up and files are transferred in one shot. In times where more persistent, ongoing access to a remote directory of files is needed, services for sharing and mounting remote file systems can be most useful. Such services include Network File System (NFS), Samba, and sshfs.

NFS and Samba file server configuration is covered in Chapter 18. Use the information here as a preview of commands you can use to access files on those servers.

Sharing Remote Directories with NFS

Assuming a server is already running the NFS service (part of the nfs-kernel-server package), you can use exportfs and showmount commands to see available and mounted shared directories. Mounting a shared directory is done with special options to the standard mount command. If you install the nfs-kernel-server package in Ubuntu or the nfs-utils package in Fedora, the NFS service will start automatically.

Viewing NFS Shares

From a client Linux system, you can use the showmount command to see what shared directories are available from a selected computer. For example:

```
$/usr/sbin/showmount -e server.example.com
/export/myshare client.example.com
/mnt/public     *
```

Mounting NFS Shares

Use the `mount` command to mount a remote NFS share on the local computer. Here is an example:

```
# mkdir /mnt/share
# mount server.example.com:/myshare /mnt/server-share
```

This example notes the NFS server (`server.example.com`) and the shared directory from that server (`/myshare`). The local mount point, which must exist before mounting the share, appears at the end of the command (`/mnt/share`).

Pass NFS-specific options to the `mount` command by adding them after the `-o` option:

```
# mount -o rw,hard,intr server.example.com:/myshare /mnt/share
```

The `rw` option mounts the remote directory with read-write permissions, assuming that permission is available. With `hard` set, someone using the share will see a `server not responding` message when a read or write operation times out. If that happens, having set the `intr` option lets you interrupt a hung request to a remote server (press Ctrl+c).

By default, NFS version 3 (nfs3) protocol is used to connect to the share. To use NFS version 4, which is designed to work over the Internet and through firewalls, indicate that protocol as the file system type on the command line as follows:

```
#mount -t nfs4 server.example.com:/ /mnt/share
```

Note

Depending on which version of Linux you are using, the implementation of NFS v4 may not be robust enough for production. It may be safer and/or more reliable to tunnel earlier versions of NFS over SSH. You can find more information on this topic with an Internet search for "nfs ssh," and go to www.howtoforge.com/nfs_ssh_tunneling. In addition, visit http://tldp.org/HOWTO/NFS-HOWTO/security.html for more on NFS security. ■

Sharing Remote Directories with Samba

Samba is the open source implementation of the Windows file and print sharing protocol originally known as *Server Message Block* (SMB) and now called Common Internet File System (CIFS). There is an implementation of Samba in Linux, as well as in many other operating systems. To use Samba, install the packages samba-client and samba-doc (in Fedora) or samba (in Ubuntu).

Graphical tools for sharing, querying, and mounting shared SMB directories from Windows include the Samba SWAT web-based administration tool. To use the SWAT tool in Linux, install the swat package. For an Ubuntu system, read the instructions at https://help.ubuntu.com/community/Swat for details on how you can start SWAT.

Commands for working with Samba shares can be used to query SMB servers, mount directories, and share directories.

Viewing and Accessing Samba Shares

To scan your network for SMB hosts, type the following:

```
$ findsmb
                              *=DMB
                              +=LMB
IP ADDR          NETBIOS NAME  WORKGROUP/OS/VERSION
-------------------------------------------------------------------
192.168.1.1    SERVER1    +[MYWORKGROUP] [Unix] [Samba 3.0.25a-3.fc7]
```

To view a text representation of your network neighborhood (shared directories and printers), use smbtree:

```
# smbtree

MYGROUP
    \\THOMPSON                Samba Server Version 3.5.4-68.el6.x86_64
        \\THOMPSON\hp2100  HP LaserJet 2100M Printer
        \\THOMPSON\IPC$    IPC Service (Samba  3.5.4-68.el6.x86_64)
    \\EINSTEIN                Samba Server
        \\EINSTEIN\hp5550  HP DeskJet 5550 Printer
        \\EINSTEIN\IPC$    IPC Service (Samba Server)
```

To add an existing Linux user as a Samba user, use the smbpasswd command:

```
# smbpasswd -a joe
New SMB password: ******
Retype new SMB password: ******
```

Note
You need to set up a Samba password to perform any of the commands that ask for a password. ∎

To list services offered by a server to an anonymous user, type the following:

```
$ smbclient -L server
Password: ******
Anonymous login successful
Domain=[MYGROUP] OS=[Unix] Server=Samba 3.5.4-68.el6.x86_64
tree connect failed: NT_STSTUS_LOGON_FAILURE
```

Here's the output from smbclient for a specific user named joe:

```
$ smbclient -L server -U joe
Password: ******
Domain=[MYGROUP] OS=[Unix] Server=[Samba 3.5.4-68.el6.x86_64]

    Sharename    Type    Comment
    ---------    ----    -------
    IPC$         IPC     IPC Service (Samba 3.5.4-68.el6.x86_64)
    hp5550       Printer HP DeskJet 5550 Printer
```

```
Server               Comment
---------            -------
THOMPSON             Samba Server Version 3.5.4-68.e16.x86_64

Workgroup            Master
---------            -------
MYGROUP              THOMPSON
```

To connect to a Samba share FTP-style, type the following:

```
$ smbclient //192.168.1.1/myshare -U joe
Password:
Domain=[MYWORKGROUP] OS=[Unix] Server=[Samba 3.5.4-68.e16.x86_64]
smb: \>
```

As with most FTP clients, type help or ? to see a list of available commands. Likewise, you can use common shell-type commands, such as cd, ls, get, put, and quit, to get around on the SMB host.

Mounting Samba (CIFS) Shares

You can mount remote Samba shares on your local file system much as you would a local file system or remote NFS file system. To mount the share:

```
# mount -t cifs -o username=joe,password=MySecret \
     //192.168.1.1/myshare /mnt/mymount/
```

Note

The Samba file system (smbfs) is deprecated and should no longer be used in some Linux distributions. The preferred method is to indicate CIFS (-t cifs) as the file system type when you mount a remote Samba share, as we do in the examples here. ∎

You can see the current connections and file locks on a server using the smbstatus command. This will tell you if someone has mounted your shared directories or is currently using an smbclient connection to your server:

```
# smbstatus
Samba version 3.5.4-68.e16.x86_64
PID     Username     Group     Machine
-------------------------------------------
 5466   joe          joe 10.0.0.55    (10.0.0.55)

Service     pid   machine     Connected at
-------------------------------------------
myshare     5644  10.0.0.55   Tue Jul 27 15:08:29 2010

No locked files
```

Looking Up Samba Hosts

NetBIOS names are used to identify hosts in Samba. You can determine the IP address of a computer using the nmblookup command to broadcast for a particular NetBIOS name on the local subnet as follows:

```
$ nmblookup thompson
querying thompson on 192.168.1.255
192.168.1.1 server1<00>
```

To find the IP address for a server on a specific subnet, use the -U option:

```
$ nmblookup -U 192.168.1.255 server1
querying server1 on 192.168.1.255
192.168.1.1 server1<00>
```

Checking Samba Server Configuration

If you are unable to use a Samba share or if you have other problems communicating with your Samba server, you can test the Samba configuration on the server. The testparm command can be used to check your main Samba configuration file (smb.conf):

```
$ testparm
Load smb config files from /etc/samba/smb.conf
Processing section "[homes]"
Processing section "[printers]"
Processing section "[myshare]"
Loaded services file OK.
Server role: ROLE_STANDALONE
Press Enter to see a dump of your service definitions
```

After pressing Enter as instructed, you can see the settings from your smb.conf file. Here's how an entry for the myshare shared directory, used earlier in an example, might appear in the smb.conf file:

```
[myshare]
          path = /home/joe
          username = joe
          valid users = joe
          hosts allow = einstein
          available = yes
```

This entry allows the Samba user joe to access the /home/joe directory (represented by the myshare share name) from the host computer named einstein. The share is shown as being currently available.

The previous example of testparm showed the entries you set in the smb.conf file. However, it doesn't show all the default entries you didn't set. You can view those using the -v option. Pipe it to the less command to page through the settings:

```
$ testparm -v | less
```

If you want to test a configuration file before it goes live, you can tell `testparm` to use a file other than `/etc/samba/smb.conf`:

```
$ testparm /etc/samba/test-smb.conf
```

Sharing Remote Directories with SSHFS

Another magical trick you can do over the SSH protocol is mount remote file systems. Using the SSH file system (`sshfs`), you can mount any directory from an SSH server that your user account can access from your local Linux system. `sshfs` provides encryption of the mount operation as well as of all the data being transferred. Another cool aspect of `sshfs` is that it requires no setup on the server side (other than having SSH service running).

Here is a quick procedure for mounting a directory of documents from a remote server to a local directory. Doing this requires that the remote server is running SSH, is accessible, and that the directory you want is accessible to your user account on the server. Also, you need to install the sshfs package in Ubuntu or the fuse-sshfs package in Fedora.

Here we are mounting a directory named `/var/docs` from the host at `10.0.0.50` to a mount point called `/mnt/docs` on the local system:

```
# mkdir /mnt/docs                                Create mount point
# sshfs chris@10.0.0.50:/var/docs /mnt/docs      Mount remote directory
```

When you are done using the remote directory, you can unmount it with the `fusermount` command (part of the fuse-utils package):

```
$ sudo fusermount -u /var/docs                   Unmount remote directory
```

Chatting with Friends in IRC

Despite the emergence of instant messaging, Internet Relay Chat (IRC) is still used by a lot of people today. Freenode.net has tons of chat rooms dedicated to supporting major open source software projects. In fact, many people stay logged into them all day and just watch the discussions of their favorite Linux projects scroll by. This is known as *lurking*.

The xchat utility is a good graphical, multi-operating-system IRC client. You can install just the xchat package or the GNOME bindings in the xchat-gnome package. But the elite way to do IRC is to run a text-mode client in `screen` on an always-on machine, such as an old server. Another similar option is to use an IRC proxy client, also known as a *bouncer*, such as `dircproxy` (part of the dircproxy package).

The original IRC client was `ircII`. It allowed the addition of scripts — in some ways similar to macros found in productivity suites — that automated some of the commands and increased usability. The most popular was PhoEniX by Vassago. Then came BitchX, which started as an ircII script and then became a full-blown client. Today, many people use irssi. To launch irssi, type the following:

```
$ irssi -n JayJoe199x
```

In this example, the username (nick) is set to JayJoe199x (you should choose your own). You should see a blue status bar at the bottom of the screen indicating that you are in Window 1, the status window. If this is the first time you've run irssi, the program will display help messages pointing you to the documentation. IRC commands are preceded with a / character. For example, to connect to the Freenode server, type the following:

```
/connect chat.freenode.net
```

If you didn't add your username on the command line, you are connected to chat.freenode. net with the username you are logged in under. On IRC, a chat room is called a *channel* and has a pound sign (#) in front of the name. Next, try joining the #centos IRC channel:

```
/join #centos
```

You are now in the channel in Window 2, as indicated in the status bar. Switch among the irssi windows by typing Alt+1, Alt+2, and so on (or Ctrl+n and Ctrl+p). Note that the Alt+1, Alt+2, and so on keys won't work inside a gnome-terminal window because the gnome-terminal eats those keystrokes. To get help at any time, type /help *command*, where *command* is the name of the command you want more information on. Help text will output in the status window, not necessarily the current window.

To add to the IRC chat, simply type a message and press Enter to send the message to those in the channel. Type /part to leave a channel. Type /quit to exit the program.

There is a lot more to irssi. You can customize it and improve your experience significantly. Refer to the irssi documentation (www.irssi.org/documentation) for more information about how to use irssi.

Using Text-Based E-mail Clients

Most mail user agents (MUAs) are GUI-based these days. So if you began using e-mail in the past decade or so, you probably think of Evolution, Kmail, Thunderbird, or (on Windows systems) Outlook when it comes to e-mail clients. On the first UNIX and Linux systems, however, e-mail was handled by text-based applications.

If you find yourself needing to check e-mail on a remote server or other text-based environment, venerable text-based mail clients are available and still quite useful. In fact, some hard-core geeks still use text-based mail clients exclusively, touting their efficiency and scoffing at HTML-based messages.

The mail clients described in this chapter use a local MBOX-formatted file by default. That means that you are either logged into the mail server or you have already downloaded the messages locally (for example, by using POP3 or similar).

Note

Text-based mail clients can be used to read mail already downloaded by other mail clients (if you were using a protocol that downloaded messages to your local system). For example, you could open your Evolution mail Inbox file by typing `mail -f $HOME/.evolution/mail/loc/Inbox`. ■

Managing E-mail with mail

The oldest command, and easiest to use when you just want a quick check for messages in the root user's mailbox on a remote server, is the `mail` command (`/bin/mail`), part of the mailx package. Although `mail` can be used interactively, it is often used for sending script-based e-mails. Here are some examples:

```
$ mail -s 'My Linux version' chris@example.com < /etc/lsb-release
$ ps auwx | mail -s 'My Process List' chris@example.com
```

The two `mail` examples just shown provide quick ways to mail off some text without having to open a GUI mail application. The first example sends the contents of the `/etc/lsb-release` file to the user `chris@example.com`. The subject (`-s`) is set to `'My Linux Version'`. In the second example, a list of currently running processes (`ps auwx`) is sent to the same user with a subject of `'My Process List'`.

Used interactively, by default the `mail` command opens the mailbox set by your current shell's `$MAIL` value. For example:

```
$ echo $MAIL
/var/spool/mail/chris
```

To read the mail for the root user, run the mail command as root:

```
# mail
Mail version 8.1 6/6/93.  Type ? for help.
"/var/spool/mail/root": 25 messages 25 new
>U  1 logwatch@ab.l  Fri Jun 15 20:03  44/1667   "Logwatch for ab "
 U  2 logwatch@ab.l  Sat Jun 16 04:32  87/2526   "Logwatch for ab "
    3 logwatch@ab.l  Sun Jun 17 04:32  92/2693   "Logwatch for ab "
 N  4 logwatch@ab.l  Fri Jun 22 09:28  44/1667   "Logwatch for ab "
 N  5 MAILER-DAEMON@ab  Fri Jun 22 09:28  93/3348   "Warning: could "
&
```

The current message has a greater-than sign (>) next to it. New messages have an N at the beginning, unread (but not new) messages have a U, and if there is no letter, the message has been read. The prompt at the bottom (&) is ready to accept commands.

At this point, you are in command mode. You can use simple commands to move around and perform basic mail functions in mail. Type ? to see a list of commands, or type the number of the message you want to see. Type v3 to open the third message in the vi editor. Type h18 to see a list of message headers that begins with message 18. To reply to message 7, type r7 (type your message, then put a dot on a line by itself to send the message). Type d4 to delete the fourth message (or d4-9 to delete messages 4 through 9). Type !bash to escape to the shell (then exit to return to mail).

Before you exit mail, know that any messages you view will be copied from your mailbox file to your $HOME/mbox file when you exit, unless you preserve them (pre*). To have all messages stay in your mailbox, exit by typing x. To save your changes to the mailbox, type q to exit.

You can open any file that is in MBOX format when you use mail. For example, if you are logged in as one user, but want to open the mailbox for the user chris, type this:

```
# mail -f /var/spool/mail/chris
```

Managing E-mail with mutt

If you want to use a command-line mail client on an ongoing basis, I recommend you use mutt instead of mail. The mail command has many limitations, such as not being able to send attachments without encoding them in advance (such as with the uuencode command), while mutt can easily send e-mail attachments and contains features for handling many other modern e-mail needs.

The mutt command is part of the mutt package, which you need to install to use this command. Configure mutt by editing /etc/Muttrc, ~/.muttrc or ~/.mutt/muttrc. You also need to configure sendmail to allow for sending e-mail or, as an alternative, add this line to your muttrc file:

```
set smtp_url="smtp://smtp.example.com/"
```

Like mail, mutt can also be used to pop off a message from a script. mutt also adds the capability to send attachments. For example:

```
$ mutt -s "My Linux Version" -a /etc/lsb-release \
    chris@example.com < email-body.txt
$ mutt -s "My Linux Version" -a /etc/lsb-release \
    chris@example.com < /dev/null
```

The first example just shown includes the file email-body.txt as the body of the message and attaches the file /etc/lsb-release as an attachment. The second example sends the attachment, but has a blank message body (< /dev/null).

You can begin your mutt mail session (assuming your default mailbox is $MAIL) by simply typing mutt:

```
$ mutt
/home/chris/Mail does not exist. Create it? ([yes]/no): y
```

```
q:Quit  d:Del  u:Undel  s:Save  m:Mail  r:Reply  g:Group  ?:Help

 1 0   Jun 16 logwatch@ab      (  69) Logwatch for ab (Linux)
 2 0   Jun 18 logwatch@ab      ( 171) Logwatch for ab (Linux)
 3 0   Jun 18 Mail Delivery S  ( 219) Warning: could not send
 4 0   Jun 19 logwatch@ab      (  33) Logwatch for ab (Linux)

--Mutt: /var/spool/mail/root [Msgs:22 New:2 Old:20 63K]--(date/date)
```

Because mutt is screen-oriented, it is easier to use than mail. As with mail, you use key commands to move around in mutt. As usual, type ? to get help. Hints appear across the top bar to help you with your mail. Use the up and down arrow keys to highlight the messages you want to read. Press Enter to view the highlighted message. Use PageUp and PageDown to page through each message. Press i to return to the message headers.

Search forward for text using slash (/) or backwards using Escape slash (Esc+/). Type **n** to search again. Press Tab to jump to the next new or unread message. Or go to the previous one using Esc+Tab. Type **s** to save the current message to a file. Type **d** to delete a message and **u** to undelete it.

To send a new mail message, type **m**. After adding the recipient and subject, a blank message opens in joe (or whatever you have your $EDITOR set to). After exiting the message body, type **a** to add an attachment, if you like. Type ? to see other ways of manipulating your message, headers, or attachments. Type **y** to send the message or **q** to abort the send.

When you are done, type **x** to exit without changing your mailbox; type **q** to exit and incorporate the changes you made (messages read, deleted, and so on).

Summary

Network access commands provide quick and efficient ways to get content you need over a network. The elinks web browser is a popular screen-oriented command for browsing the web or taking a quick look at any HTML file. Dozens of commands are available to download files over FTP, HTTP, SSH, or other protocols, including wget, curl, lftp, and scp.

For more ongoing access to remote directories of files, this chapter covered how to use NFS, Samba, and SSHFS command tools. You can do IRC chats, which are popular among open source projects, using the irssi command. For text-based e-mail clients, you have choices such as the mail and mutt commands.

Securing Linux

Since the dawn of interconnected networks, some users have been trying to break into other users' systems. As the Internet has grown and broadband Internet access has spread, the problem has only become more severe. A home computer running an insecure configuration can be used as a powerful mail relay, provide storage for traffic in pirated data, allow the user's personal information to become compromised, or any number of other such horrors.

Once upon a time, network attacks required some effort and skill on the part of the attacker. Today, automated tools can get even the most novice user up and compromising network-attached systems in an alarmingly short time. Additionally, worms have the capability to turn large numbers of insecure systems into an army of "zombies" usable for massive, coordinated, distributed denial-of-service (DDoS) attacks.

Why should you care about security? According to the Internet Storm Center (http://isc.sans.org), a computer connected to the Internet has an average of 16 minutes before it falls under some form of attack. Securing any computer system is not hugely difficult; it simply requires some common sense and careful application of good security practices.

In many cases, good practices for setting and protecting passwords, monitoring log files, and creating good firewalls will keep out many would-be intruders. Sometimes, more proactive approaches are needed to respond to break-ins.

Many tasks associated with securing your Linux system are common to desktop and server systems. However, because servers allow some level of access by outside clients, there are special considerations for protecting servers.

IN THIS CHAPTER

Linux security checklist

Using password protection

Monitoring log files

Communicating with secure shell tools

Understanding attack techniques

Protecting servers with certificates

Using special Linux security tools distributions

This chapter describes general tasks for securing Linux systems and techniques for securing desktop and server systems. It then describes some tools you can try out from a bootable Linux system to troubleshoot your computer and network.

Linux Security Checklist

Although most Linux systems offer all the tools you need to secure your computer, if you are reckless, someone can (and probably will) harm your system, take it over, or try to steal your data. Keep in mind that no security measures are 100 percent reliable and that, given physical access to a computer or an unlimited amount of time to try to break in, a skilled and determined cracker can break into any computer.

That said, however, you can take many safeguards to improve your chances of keeping your Linux system safe. The following checklist covers a range of security features to protect your Linux desktop or server.

- **Control physical access** — Keeping your computer behind locked doors is a good idea, especially if it contains critical data. You can limit what a person can do to your computer with physical access by enabling passwords in the BIOS (to prevent the computer from booting at all) and in the GRUB or LILO boot loader. You can also limit which devices can be booted in the BIOS.

- **Add users and passwords** — Creating separate user accounts (each with a good password) is your first line of defense in keeping your data secure. Users are protected from each other, as well as from an outsider who takes over one user account. Setting up group accounts can extend the concept of ownership to multiple users.

- **Set read, write, and execute permissions** — Every item in a Linux system (including files, directories, applications, and devices) can be restricted by read, write, and execute permissions for that item's owner and group, as well as by all others. In this way, for example, you can let other users run a command or open a file, without allowing them to change it.

- **Protect the root user** — In standard Linux systems, the root user (as well as other administrative user accounts such as apache) has special abilities to use and change your Linux system. Protect the root account's password and don't use the root account when you don't need to. An open shell or desktop owned by the root user can be a target for attack. Running graphical administration windows as a regular user (then entering the root password as prompted) and running administrative commands using sudo can reduce exposure to attacks on your root account.

Note
Some distributions, such as Ubuntu, simplify the protection of the root account because you are not required to set a root password. ■

- **Use trusted software** — Although no guarantees come with open source software, you have a better chance of avoiding compromised software by using an established Linux distribution (such as Fedora, Debian, or SUSE). Software repositories where you get add-on packages or updates should likewise be scrutinized. Using valid GPG public keys can help ensure that the software you install comes from a valid vendor. And, of course, always be sure of the source of data files you receive before opening them in a Linux application. If you download full ISO images of a distribution, check their integrity using MD5 or SHA1 checksums provided by their creators.

- **Get software updates** — As vulnerabilities and bugs are discovered in software packages, every major Linux distribution (including Debian, SUSE, Gentoo, and Red Hat) offers tools for getting and installing those updates. Be sure to get those updates as soon as they become available, especially if you are using Linux as a server. These tools include apt (for Debian and Ubuntu), yum (for Fedora and Red Hat Enterprise Linux), and emerge (for Gentoo).

- **Use secure applications** — Even with software that is valid and working, some applications offer better protection from attack or invasion than others. For example, if you want to log in to a computer over the Internet, the secure shell service (ssh) is considered more secure than rlogin or telnet services (which pass clear-text passwords). Also, some services that are thought to be insecure if you expose them on the Internet (such as Samba and NFS) can be used more securely over the Internet through VPN tunnels (such as IPSec).

- **Use restrictive firewalls** — A primary job of a firewall is to accept requests for services from a network that you want to allow and turn away requests that you don't (based primarily on port numbers requested). A desktop system should refuse most incoming requests for new services. A server system should allow requests for a controlled set of ports.

- **Enable only services you need** — To offer services in Linux (such as web, file, or mail services), a daemon process will listen on a particular port number. Don't enable services you don't need.

Note

A program that runs quietly in the background handling service requests (such as sendmail) is called a *daemon*. Usually, daemons are started automatically when your system boots up and they keep running until your system is shut down. Daemons may also be started on an as-needed basis by xinetd, a special daemon that listens on a large number of port numbers and then launches the requested process. ■

- **Limit access to services** — You can restrict access to a service you want to have on by allowing access only from a particular host computer, domain, or network interface. For example, a computer with interfaces to both the Internet and a local LAN might limit access to a service such as NFS to computers on the LAN, but not offer those same services to the Internet. Services may limit access in their own configuration files or using TCP/IP wrappers (described later in this chapter).

- **Check your system** — Linux has tons of tools available for checking the security of your system. After you install Linux, you can check access to its ports using nmap or watch network traffic using Wireshark. You can also add popular security tools, such as Nessus, to get a more complete view of your system security. Security tools included on the DVD with this book are described in this chapter.

- **Monitor your system** — You can log almost every type of activity on your Linux system. System log files, using the syslogd and klogd facilities, can be configured to track as much or as little of your system activity as you choose. Utilities such as logwatch provide easy ways to have the potential problem messages forwarded to your administrative e-mail account. Linux logging features are described later in this chapter.

Note
Remember that monitoring your system does not mean that you simply turn on logging — you must also carefully monitor those logs and react to what they tell you. ■

- **Use SELinux** — Security Enhanced Linux (SELinux) is an extraordinarily rich (and complex) facility that you can use to manage access to nearly every aspect of a Linux system. Red Hat systems offer a useful, limited set of SELinux policies that are turned on by default in Fedora and Red Hat Enterprise Linux systems. Other Linux distributions, such as openSUSE, are working on and including SELinux implementations as well. Figure 13-1 shows an example of the SELinux Administration tool included with Fedora (select System ➪ Administration ➪ SELinux Management), and Figure 13-2 shows the SELinux Troubleshooter (select Applications ➪ System Tools ➪ SELinux Troubleshooter).

FIGURE 13-1

SELinux utilities are included with Fedora.

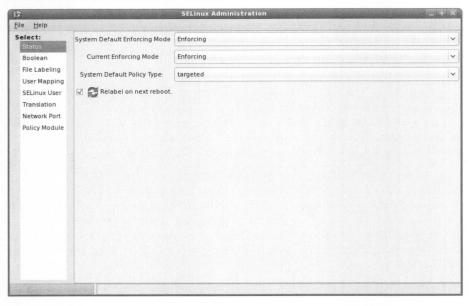

FIGURE 13-2

The SELinux Troubleshooter can identify areas of concern.

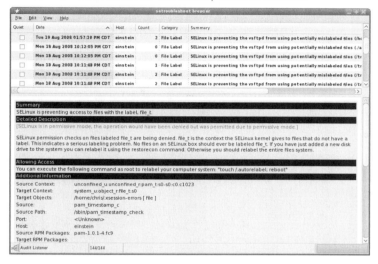

Finding Distribution-Specific Security Resources

Most major Linux distributions have resources devoted to helping you secure Linux and keep up with security information that is specific to that version of Linux. Here are a few online resources that focus on security for several Linux distributions:

- **Red Hat Enterprise Linux and Fedora security** — Check the Red Hat Security site (`www.redhat.com/security`) for RHEL security issues (that typically relate to Fedora systems as well). From here you can look for and read about available updates. You can also get information on security training and consulting from Red Hat, Inc. For Fedora security issues, see the Fedora Wiki (`http://fedoraproject.org/wiki/Security/Features`).

  Refer to the Red Hat Enterprise Linux Security Guide for an in-depth look at Linux security for Red Hat systems. You can access this guide online from the following address: `http://docs.redhat.com/docs/en-US/Red_Hat_Enterprise_Linux/6/html/Security_Guide/index.html`

- **Debian security** — The Debian Security Information page (`www.debian.org/security`) provides a central point for finding security advisories, answers to common Debian security questions, and links to security documents. You can find the Securing Debian online manual here: `www.debian.org/doc/manuals/securing-debian-howto`

- **Ubuntu security** — Find security guides and tools for Ubuntu on the Ubuntu security page (`https://help.ubuntu.com/community/Security`).

- **Gentoo security** — Included on the Gentoo Linux Security page (`www.gentoo.org/security`) are tools, announcements, and links to security policy and project documents associated with securing Gentoo systems. Find the Gentoo security handbook here: `www.gentoo.org/doc/en/security`

- **Slackware security** — To keep up with Slackware security issues, refer to the Slackware Security Advisories (`www.slackware.com/security`). You can also join the security mailing list (`www.slackware.com/lists`) for Slackware.

- **SUSE security** — Online security support for SUSE is provided by SUSE's parent company, Novell. Find links to a variety of SUSE security topics from this site: `www.novell.com/linux/security/securitysupport.html`

  For openSUSE visit this site: `www.novell.com/products/opensuse/security.html`

Finding General Security Resources

Many computer security web resources now offer information that is particularly useful to Linux system administrators. Here are a few sites you can check out:

- **CERT** (`www.cert.org`) — The CERT Coordination center follows computer security issues. Check its home page for the latest vulnerability issues. The site has many tips, including recommendations on what you should do if your computer has been compromised (`www.cert.org/tech_tips`).

- **SecurityFocus** (`www.securityfocus.com`) — In addition to offering news and information on general computer security topics, SecurityFocus also offers several Linux-specific resources. In particular, you can subscribe to receive a weekly Linux Security News newsletter.

- **LinuxSecurity** (`www.linuxsecurity.com`) — This site contains many news articles and features related to Linux security. It also tracks security advisories for more than a dozen Linux distributions.

Using Linux Securely

Getting and keeping your Linux system secure means not only making good decisions about how you initially set up your system but also how you use it going forward. Whether you are using your Linux system as a desktop or server system, good security practices related to choosing passwords, using secure applications, and monitoring log files are always important.

Setting up a secure firewall is critical to having a secure Linux system. There are also other security measures you should apply to Linux. This section describes some good practices for using passwords, keeping track of system activity by watching log files, and communicating with other systems using secure shell (ssh) applications.

Using Password Protection

Passwords are the most fundamental security tool of any modern operating system and, consequently, the most commonly attacked security feature. It is natural to want to choose a password that is easy to remember, but very often this means choosing a password that is also easy to guess. Crackers know that on any system with more than a few users, at least one person is likely to have an easily guessed password.

By using the "brute force" method of attempting to log in to every account on the system and trying the most common passwords on each of these accounts, a persistent cracker has a good shot of finding a way in. Remember that a cracker will automate this attack, so thousands of login attempts are not out of the question. Obviously, choosing good passwords is the first and most important step to having a secure system.

Here are some rules to follow when choosing a password:

- Do not use any variation of your login name or your full name. Even if you use varied case, append or prepend numbers or punctuation, or type it backwards, this will still be an easily guessed password.
- Do not use a dictionary word, even if you add numbers or punctuation to it.
- Do not use proper names of any kind.
- Do not use any contiguous line of letters or numbers on the keyboard (such as "qwerty" or "asdfg").

Choosing Good Passwords

A good way to choose a strong password is to take the first letter from each word of an easily remembered sentence. The password can be made even better by adding numbers, punctuation, and varied case. The sentence you choose should have meaning only to you, and should not be publicly available (choosing a sentence on your personal web page is a bad idea). Table 13-1 lists examples of strong passwords and the tricks used to remember them.

The passwords look like gibberish but are actually rather easy to remember. As you can see, I can place emphasis on words that stand for capital letters in the password. You set your password using the `passwd` command. Type the `passwd` command within a command shell, and it will enable you to change your password. First, it prompts you to enter your old password. To protect against someone "shoulder surfing" and learning your password, the password will not be displayed as you type.

TABLE 13-1

Examples of Good Passwords

Password	How to Remember It
Mrci7yo!	My rusty car is 7 years old!
2emBp1ib	2 elephants make BAD pets, 1 is better
ItMc?Gib	Is that MY coat? Give it back

Note

Several distributions include random password generators that can be used to conjure up secure passwords. Figure 13-3, for example, shows a password generator in the Users and Groups tool available in Ubuntu. ■

FIGURE 13-3

Generating random passwords

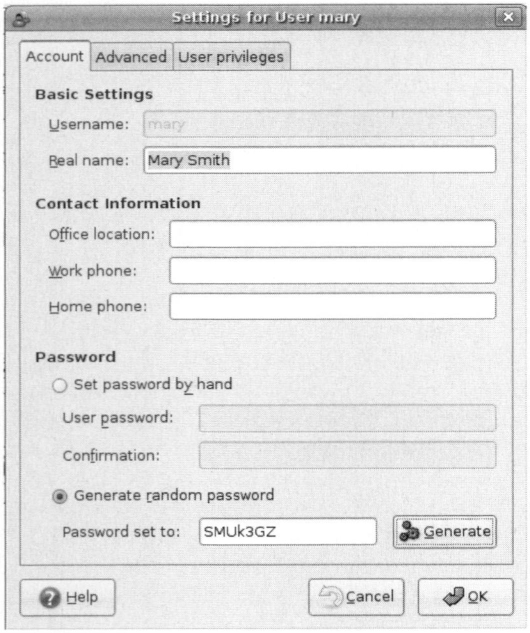

Assuming you type your old password correctly, the passwd command will prompt you for the new password. When you type in your new password, the passwd command checks the password against cracklib to determine whether it is a *good* or *bad* password. Non-root users will be required to try a different password if the one they have chosen is not a good password.

The root user is the only user who is permitted to assign bad passwords. After the password has been accepted by cracklib, the passwd command asks you to enter the new password a second time to make sure there are no typos (which are hard to detect when you can't see what you are typing). When running as root, changing a user's password is possible by supplying that user's login name as a parameter to the passwd command. For example

```
# passwd joe
Changing password for user joe.
New UNIX password: ********
Retype new UNIX password: ********
passwd: all authentication tokens updated successfully.
```

Here the passwd command prompts you twice to enter a new password for joe. It does not prompt you for his old password in this case. This allows root to reset a user's password when that user has forgotten it (an event that happens all too often).

Note
Many Linux systems incorporate the pluggable authentication modules (PAM) facility for controlling authentication. By modifying the /etc/pam.d/system-auth file, you can change how utilities on your system authenticate user logins. For example, you can change how many failed password attempts would be permitted and what to do if that number is reached. (Be careful modifying PAM files, however, because a misconfigured PAM facility can lock out all user login attempts.) ■

Using a Shadow Password File

In early versions of UNIX, all user account and password information was stored in a file that all users could read (although only root could write to it). This was generally not a problem because the password information was encrypted. The password was encrypted using an algorithm to encrypt the original password into a scrambled string of characters, but the string could not be translated back to the original password. In other words, the trapdoor implies that encryption only goes in one direction, so the encrypted password can't be used to go back to the original password.

How does the system check your password in this case? When you log in, the system encodes the password you entered, compares the resulting scrambled string with the scrambled string that is stored in the password file, and grants you access only if the two match. Have you ever asked a system administrator what the password on your account is only to hear, "I don't know" in response? If so, this is why: The administrator really doesn't have the password, only the encrypted version. The unencoded password exists only at the moment you type it.

Breaking Encrypted Passwords

There is a problem with allowing users other than the system administrator to be able to see encrypted passwords, however. Although reversing the encryption of a trapdoor algorithm may be difficult (or even impossible), encoding a large number of password guesses and comparing them to the encoded passwords in the password file is very easy. This is, in order of magnitude, more efficient than trying actual login attempts for each username and password. If a cracker can get a copy of your password file, the cracker has a much better chance of breaking into your system.

Fortunately, Linux and all modern UNIX systems support a shadow password file by default. The shadow file is a special version of the passwd file that only root can read. It contains the encrypted password information, so passwords can be left out of the passwd file, which any user on the system can read. Linux supports the older, single password file method as well as the newer shadow password file. You should always use the shadow password file (it is used by default).

Checking for the Shadow Password File

The password file is named passwd and is found in the /etc directory. The shadow password file is named shadow and is also located in /etc. If your /etc/shadow file is missing, it is likely that your Linux system is storing the password information in the /etc/passwd file instead. Verify this by displaying the file with the less command.

```
# less /etc/passwd
```

Something similar to the following should be displayed:

```
root:DkkS6Uke799fQ:0:0:root:/root:/bin/bash
bin:x:1:1:bin:/bin:
daemon:x:2:2:daemon:/sbin:/bin/sh
          .
          .
          .
mary:KpRUp2ozmY5TA:500:100:Mary Smith:/home/mary:/bin/bash
joe:OsXrzvKnQaksI:501:100:Joe Johnson:/home/joe:/bin/bash
jane:ptNoiueYEjwX.:502:100:Jane Anderson:/home/jane:/bin/bash
bob:Ju2vY7AOX6Kzw:503:100:Bob Reynolds:/home/bob:/bin/bash
```

Each line in this listing corresponds to a single user account on the Linux system. Each line is made up of seven fields separated by colon (:) characters. From left to right the fields are the login name, the encrypted password, the user ID, the group ID, the description, the home directory, and the default shell. Looking at the first line, you see that it is for the root account and has an encrypted password of DkkS6Uke799fQ. You can also see that root has a user ID of 0, a group ID of 0, and a home directory of /root, and root's default shell is /bin/bash.

All of these values are quite normal for a root account, but seeing that encrypted password should set off alarm bells in your head. It confirms that your system is not using the shadow password file. At this point, you should immediately convert your password file so that it uses /etc/shadow to store the password information. You do this by using the pwconv command. Simply log in as root (or use the su command to become root) and enter the pwconv command at a prompt. It will print no messages, but when your shell prompt returns, you should have a /etc/shadow file and your /etc/passwd file should now look like this:

```
root:x:0:0:root:/root:/bin/bash
bin:x:1:1:bin:/bin:
```

```
daemon:x:2:2:daemon:/sbin:
   .
   .
   .
mary:x:500:100:Mary Smith:/home/mary:/bin/bash
joe:x:501:100:Joe Johnson:/home/joe:/bin/bash
jane:x:502:100:Jane Anderson:/home/jane:/bin/bash
bob:x:503:100:Bob Reynolds:/home/bob:/bin/bash
```

Encrypted password data is replaced with an x. Password data has been moved to /etc/shadow.

You can also use an Authentication Configuration utility (available with Fedora and RHEL systems) to manage shadow passwords and other system authentication information. By default, this tool is enabled to work with MD5 passwords. However, you can also configure it to obtain user and password information from LDAP, NIS, or Kerberos 5 facilities. Select System ➪ Administration ➪ Authentication, and step through the screens to use it.

To work with passwords for groups, you can use the grpconv command to convert passwords in /etc/groups to shadowed group passwords in /etc/gshadow. If you change passwd or group passwords and something breaks (you are unable to log in to the accounts), you can use the pwunconv and grpunconv commands, respectively, to reverse password conversion.

So, now you are using the shadow password file and picking good passwords. You have made a great start toward securing your system. You may also have noticed by now that security is not just a one-time job. It is an ongoing process, as much about policies as programs. Keep reading to learn more.

Using Log Files

If you make use of good firewalling practices, you will be well prepared to mitigate and prevent most cracker attacks. If your firewall should fail to stop an intrusion, you must be able to recognize the attack when it is occurring. Understanding the various (and numerous) log files in which Linux records important events is critical to this goal. The log files for your Linux system are in the /var/log directory.

Most Linux systems make use of log-viewing tools, either provided with the desktop environment (such as GNOME) or as a command you can execute from a Terminal window. GNOME-based desktops often include a System Log Viewer window (gnome-system-log command) that you can use to view and search critical system log files from the GUI. To open the System Log Viewer window from the top panel in a Fedora GNOME desktop, select Applications ➪ System Tools ➪ Log File Viewer. Figure 13-4 shows an example of the System Log Viewer window.

FIGURE 13-4

Display system log files in the System Log Viewer window.

To view a particular log file, click the log name in the left column. Then scroll through the contents of that log.

Table 13-2 contains a listing of log files displayed in the System Log Viewer window, along with other files in the /var/log directory that may interest you. (Select File ⇨ Open to open a log file that doesn't appear in the left column.) Many of these files are included with most Linux systems and are viewable only by root. Also, some Linux systems may use different file or directory names (for example, /etc/httpd is /etc/apache on some Linux systems).

Because these logs are stored in plain-text files, you can view them using any text editor (such as vi or gedit) or paging command (such as the less command).

TABLE 13-2

Log Files in the /var/log Directory

System Log Name	Filename	Description
Boot Log	boot.log	Contains messages indicating which system services have started and shut down successfully and which (if any) have failed to start or stop. The most recent bootup messages are listed near the end of the file.
Cron Log	cron	Contains status messages from the crond, a daemon that periodically runs scheduled jobs, such as backups and log file rotation
Kernel Startup Log	dmesg	A recording of messages printed by the kernel when the system boots

System Log Name	Filename	Description
FTP Log	xferlog	Contains information about files transferred using the FTP service
Apache Access Log	httpd/access_log	Logs requests for information from your Apache web server
Apache Error Log	httpd/error_log	Logs errors encountered from clients trying to access data on your Apache web server
Mail Log	maillog	Contains information about addresses to which and from which e-mail was sent. Useful for detecting spamming.
MySQL Server Log	mysqld.log	Includes information related to activities of the MySQL database server (mysqld)
News Log	spooler	Directory containing logs of messages from the Usenet News server if you are running one
RPM Packages	rpmpkgs	Contains a listing of RPM packages that are installed on your system. (For systems that are not based on RPM packaging, look for a debian-installer or packages directory to find lists of installed packages.)
Security Log	secure	Records the date, time, and duration of login attempts and sessions
System Log	messages	A general-purpose log file to which many programs record messages
X.Org X11 Log	Xorg.0.log	Includes messages output by the X.Org X server
*	gdm/:0.log	Holds messages related to the login screen (GNOME display manager)
*	samba/log.smbd	Shows messages from the Samba SMB file service daemon
*	squid/access.log	Contains messages related to the squid proxy/ caching server
*	vsftpd.log	Contains messages relating to transfers made using the vsFTPd daemon (FTP server)
*	sendmail	Shows error messages recorded by the sendmail daemon
*	uucp	Shows status messages from the UNIX to UNIX Copy Protocol daemon

*Indicates a log file that is not contained in the System Log Viewer window. Access these files directly from /var/log.

The Role of syslogd

Most of the files in the /var/log directory are maintained by the syslogd service. The syslogd daemon is the system logging daemon. It accepts log messages from a variety of other programs and writes them to the appropriate log files. This is better than having every program write directly to its own log file because it enables you to centrally manage how log files are handled. Configuring syslogd to record varying levels of detail in the log files is possible. It can be told to ignore all but the most critical messages, or it can record every detail.

Note
Fedora now uses a multithreaded version of syslogd called rsyslogd. Although syslogd and rsyslogd are mostly compatible, the names of the daemon process (rsyslogd), configuration file (/etc/rsyslogd), and sysconfig file (/etc/sysconfig/rsyslog) are different. See www.rsyslog.com for details. ∎

The syslogd daemon can even accept messages from other computers on your network. This feature is particularly handy because it enables you to centralize the management and reviewing of the log files from many systems on your network. There is also a major security benefit to this practice.

If a system on your network is broken into, the cracker cannot delete or modify the log files because those files are stored on a separate computer. It is important to remember, however, that those log messages are not, by default, encrypted. Anyone tapping into your local network can eavesdrop on those messages as they pass from one machine to another. Also, although the cracker may not be able to change old log entries, he can affect the system such that any new log messages should not be trusted.

Running a dedicated loghost, a computer that serves no other purpose than to record log messages from other computers on the network, is not uncommon. Because this system runs no other services, it is unlikely that it will be broken into. This makes it nearly impossible for a cracker to erase his or her tracks, but it does not mean that all the log entries are accurate after a cracker has broken into a machine on your network.

Redirecting Logs to a Loghost with syslogd

To redirect your computer's log files to another computer's syslogd, you must make some changes to your local syslogd's configuration file, /etc/syslog.conf. Become root using the su - command and then open the /etc/syslog.conf file in a text editor (such as vi). You should see something similar to this:

```
# Log all kernel messages to the console.
# Logging much else clutters up the screen.
#kern.*                                   /dev/console

# Log anything (except mail) of level info or higher.
# Don't log private authentication messages!
*.info;mail.none;news.none;authpriv.none;cron.none  /var/log/messages
```

```
# The authpriv file has restricted access.
authpriv.*                              /var/log/secure

# Log all the mail messages in one place.
mail.*                                  /var/log/maillog

# Log cron stuff
cron.*                                  /var/log/cron

# Everybody gets emergency messages
*.emerg                                         *

# Save news errors of level crit and higher in a special file.
uucp,news.crit                          /var/log/spooler

# Save boot messages also to boot.log
local7.*                                /var/log/boot.log

#
# INN
#
news.=crit                              /var/log/news/news.crit
news.=err                               /var/log/news/news.err
news.notice                             /var/log/news/news.notice
```

The lines beginning with a # character are comments. Other lines contain two columns of information. The left field is a semicolon-separated list (spaces won't work) of message types and message priorities. The right field is the log file to which those messages should be written.

To send the messages to another computer (the loghost) instead of a file, start by replacing the log filename with the @ character followed by the name of the loghost. For example, to redirect the output normally sent to the messages, secure, and maillog log files, make these changes to the preceding file:

```
# Log anything (except mail) of level info or higher.
# Don't log private authentication messages!
*.info;mail.none;news.none;authpriv.none;cron.none  @loghost

# The authpriv file has restricted access.
authpriv.*                              @loghost

# Log all the mail messages in one place.
mail.*                                  @loghost
```

The messages will now be sent to the syslogd running on the computer named loghost. The name *loghost* was not an arbitrary choice. Creating such a hostname and making it an alias to the actual system acting as the loghost is customary. That way, if you ever need to switch the loghost duties to a different machine, you need to change only the loghost alias; you do not need to re-edit the syslog.conf file on every computer.

On the loghost side, that machine must run syslogd with the -r option, so it will listen on the network for log messages from other machines. In Fedora systems, that means adding a -r option to the SYSLOGD_OPTIONS variable in the /etc/sysconfig/syslog file and restarting the syslog service (service syslog restart). The loghost must also have UDP port 514 accessible to be used by syslogd (check the /etc/services file), so you might need to add a firewall rule to allow that.

Understanding the Messages Log File

Because of the many programs and services that record information to the messages log file, understanding the format of this file is important. You can get a good early warning of problems developing on your system by examining this file. Each line in the file is a single message recorded by some program or service. Here is a snippet of an actual messages log file:

```
Feb 25 11:04:32 toys network: Bringing up loopback interface:  succeeded
Feb 25 11:04:35 toys network: Bringing up interface eth0:  succeeded
Feb 25 13:01:14 toys vsftpd(pam_unix)[10565]: authentication failure;
     logname= uid=0 euid=0 tty= ruser= rhost=10.0.0.5  user=chris
Feb 25 14:44:24 toys su(pam_unix)[11439]: session opened for
     user root by chris(uid=500)
```

This is really very simple when you know what to look for. Each message is divided into five main parts. From left to right, they are

- The date and time that the message was logged
- The name of the computer from which the message came
- The program or service name to which the message pertains
- The process number (enclosed in square brackets) of the program sending the message
- The actual text message

Take another look at the preceding file snippet. In the first two lines, you can see that the network was restarted. The next line shows that the user named chris tried and failed to get to the FTP server on this system from a computer at address 10.0.0.5 (he typed the wrong password and authentication failed). The last line shows chris using the su command to become root user.

By occasionally reviewing the messages and secure files, it's possible to catch a cracking attempt before it is successful. If you see an excessive number of connection attempts for a particular service, especially if they are coming from systems on the Internet, you may be under attack.

Using Secure Shell Tools

The Secure Shell (ssh) tools are a set of client and server applications that allow you to do basic communications (remote login, remote copy, remote execution, and so on) between remote computers and your Linux system. Because communication is encrypted between the server (typically the sshd daemon process) and clients (such as `ssh`, `scp`, and `sftp`), these tools are inherently more secure than similar, older UNIX tools such as `telnet`, `rsh`, `rcp`, and `rlogin`.

Most Linux systems include secure shell clients, while many include the sshd server as well. If you are using the Fedora or Red Hat Enterprise Linux distribution, for example, the following client and server software packages include the ssh software: openssh, openssh-clients, and openssh-server packages.

Starting the ssh Service

Linux systems that come with the ssh service already installed often are configured for it to start automatically. In Fedora and RHEL systems, the sshd daemon is started from the `/etc/init.d` `/sshd` startup script. To make sure the service is set up to start automatically in Fedora, RHEL, and other RPM-based Linux systems, type the following (as root user):

```
# chkconfig --list sshd
sshd       0:off   1:off   2:on   3:on   4:on   5:on   6:off
```

This shows that the `sshd` service is set to run in system states 2, 3, 4, and 5 (normal bootup states) and set to be off in all other states. You can turn on the SSH service, if it is off, for your default run state, by typing the following as root user:

```
# chkconfig sshd on
```

This line turns on the ssh service when you enter run levels 2, 3, 4, or 5. To start the service immediately, type the following:

```
# service sshd start
```

Other Linux distributions may simply start the sshd daemon from an entry in the `/etc/rc.d` directory from a file named something like `rc.sshd`. In any case, you can find out whether the sshd daemon is currently running on your system by typing the following:

```
$ ps ax | grep sshd
1996 ?     Ss  0:00 /usr/sbin/sshd
```

The preceding example shows that the sshd daemon is running. If that is the case, and your firewall allows secure shell service (with TCP port 22 open), you should be able to use ssh client commands to access your system. (Any further configuration you want to do to restrict what the sshd daemon will allow is typically done in the `/etc/ssh/sshd_config` file.)

Using the ssh, sftp, and scp Commands

Three commands you can use with the SSH service are `ssh`, `sftp`, and `scp`. Remote users use the `ssh` command to log in to your system securely or remotely execute a command on your system. The `scp` command lets remote users copy files to and from a system. The `sftp` command provides a safe way to access FTP sites through the SSH service (for sites that offer SSH access to their FTP content).

Note

As with the normal remote shell services, secure shell looks in the /etc/hosts.equiv file and in a user's .rhost file to determine whether it should allow a connection. It also looks in the ssh-specific files /etc/shosts.equiv and .shosts. Using the shosts.equiv and the .shosts files is preferable because it avoids granting access to the unencrypted remote shell services. The /etc/shosts.equiv and .shosts files are functionally equivalent to the traditional hosts.equiv and .rhosts files, so the same instructions and rules apply. ■

Now you are ready to test the SSH service. From another computer on which SSH has been installed (or even from the same computer if another is not available), type the ssh command followed by a space and the name of the user and system you are connecting to. For example, to connect to the system ratbert.glaci.com, type:

```
# ssh jake@ratbert.glaci.com
```

If this is the first time ever you have logged in to that system using the ssh command, the system will ask you to confirm that you really want to connect. Type **yes** and press Enter when it asks this:

```
The authenticity of host 'ratbert.glaci.com (199.170.177.18)' can't be
established.
RSA key fingerprint is xx:xx:xx:xx:xx:xx:xx:xx:xx:xx:xx:xx:xx:xx:xx:xx.
Are you sure you want to continue connecting (yes/no)?
```

The ssh command should then prompt you for a password in the normal way. (If you don't type a username, ssh will assume you want to log in using your local username.) The connection will then function like a normal remote login connection (in other words, you can begin typing shell commands). The only difference is that the information is encrypted as it travels over the network. You should now also be able to use the ssh command to run remote commands from a shell on the remote system.

The scp command is similar to the rcp command for copying files to and from Linux systems. Here is an example of using the scp command to copy a file called memo from the home directory of the user named jake to the /tmp directory on a computer called maple:

```
$ scp /home/jake/memo jake@maple:/tmp
jake@maple's password: ********
memo          100%|****************|   153    0:00
```

Enter the password for your username (if a password is requested). If the password is accepted, the remote system indicates that the file has been copied successfully.

Similarly, the sftp command starts an interactive FTP-style session with a server that supports SSH connections (not an FTP server). Many security-conscious people prefer sftp to other ftp clients because it provides a secure connection between you and the remote host. Here's an example:

```
$ sftp jake@ftp.handsonhistory.com
Connecting to ftp.handsonhistory.com
jake@ftp.handsonhistory.com's password: ********
sftp>
```

At this point you can begin an interactive FTP session. You can use `get` and `put` commands on files as you would using any FTP client, but with the comfort of knowing that you are working on a secure connection.

Tip

The `sftp` command, as with `ssh` and `scp`, requires that the SSH service be running on the server. If you can't connect to a server using `sftp`, the SSH service may not be available. ∎

Using ssh, scp, and sftp without Passwords

For machines that you work with over a network all the time (particularly machines behind a firewall on your LAN), it can be useful to set them up so that you do not have to use a password to log in. The following procedure shows you how to do that.

These steps take you through setting up password-less authentication from one machine to another. In this example, the local user is named chester on a computer named host1. The remote user is also chester on a computer named host2.

1. Log in to the local computer (in this example, I log in as `chester` to `host1`).

Note

Run Step 2 only once as local user on your local workstation. Do not run it again unless you lose your ssh keys. When configuring subsequent remote servers, skip right to Step 3. ∎

2. Type the following to generate the ssh key:

```
$ ssh-keygen -t dsa
Generating public/private dsa key pair.
Enter file in which to save the key
(/home/chester/.ssh/id_dsa): <Enter>
Enter passphrase (empty for no passphrase): <Enter>
Enter same passphrase again: <Enter>
Your identification has been saved in /home/chester/.ssh/id_dsa.
Your public key has been saved in /home/chester/.ssh/id_dsa.pub.
The key fingerprint is:
3b:c0:2f:63:a5:65:70:b7:4b:f0:2a:c4:18:24:47:69 chester@host1
```

As shown in the example, press Enter to accept the filename where the key is stored. Then press Enter twice to accept a blank passphrase. (If you enter a passphrase, you will be prompted for that passphrase and won't be able to log in without it.)

Note

This example did not include a passphrase in order to demonstrate simplicity and to show off the core functionality of using ssh keys. In actual practice, you would most likely want to protect your private key with a passphrase, especially if your home directory is on a networked file system. Once you have a passphrase you can use an ssh agent so that you will only have to enter your passphrase once, at the beginning of your login session. ∎

3. You must secure the permissions of your authentication keys by closing permissions to your home directory, .ssh directory, and authentication files as follows:

```
$ chmod 700 $HOME $HOME/.ssh
$ chmod go-rwx $HOME/.ssh/*
```

4. Type the following to copy the key to the remote server (replace chester with the remote username and host2 with the remote hostname):

```
$ ssh-copy-id -i ~/.ssh/id_dsa.pub chester@host2
chester@host2's password: *******
```

5. For the sshd daemon to accept the key you copied to host2, the home directory and the authorized_keys file itself must have secure permissions. To secure that file and those directories, type the following:

```
$ ssh chester@host2 chmod 700 $HOME $HOME/.ssh
$ ssh chester@host2 chmod 600 $HOME/.ssh/authorized_keys2
```

It is important to note that after you have this working, it will work regardless of how many times the IP address changes on your local computer. The IP address has nothing to do with this form of authentication.

Securing Linux Servers

Opening up your Linux system as a server on a public network creates a whole new set of challenges when it comes to security. Instead of just turning away nearly all incoming requests, your computer will be expected to respond to requests for supported services (such as web, FTP, or mail service) by supplying information or possibly running scripts that take in data.

Entire books have been filled with information on how to go about securing your servers. Many businesses that rely on Internet servers assign full-time administrators to watch over the security of their servers. So, think of this section as an overview of some of the kinds of attacks to look out for and some tools available to secure your Linux server.

Controlling Access to Services with TCP Wrappers

Completely disabling an unused service is fine, but what about the services that you really need? How can you selectively grant and deny access to these services? For Linux systems that incorporate TCP wrapper support, the /etc/hosts.allow and /etc/hosts.deny files determine when a particular connection should be granted or refused for services such as sshd, vsftpd, rlogin, rsh, telnet, finger, and talk.

Most Linux systems that implement TCP wrappers do so for a set of services that are monitored by a single listening process called the Internet super server. For Fedora and RHEL systems, that server is the xinetd daemon, whereas in other systems (such as Debian) the inetd daemon is used. When a service that relies on TCP wrappers is requested from the server process, the hosts.allow and hosts.deny files are scanned and checked for an entry that matches the IP address of the connecting machine. These checks are made when connection attempts occur:

- If the address is listed in the hosts.allow file, the connection is allowed and hosts.deny is not checked.

- If the address is not matched in hosts.allow, but is in hosts.deny, the connection is denied.

- If the address is in neither file, the connection is allowed.

The service names you list refer to the daemon names (as opposed to the service name listed in the /etc/init.d directory, which may be different). To check whether or not a daemon is enabled to use TCP wrappers, run the strings or ldd command on the daemon and check for hosts_access or libwrap, respectively:

```
$ strings /usr/sbin/vsftpd |grep hosts
hosts_access
$ ldd /usr/sbin/sshd |grep libwrap
libwrap.so.0 => /lib/libwrap.so.0 (0x0012f000)
```

Keep in mind that the order in which hosts are evaluated is important. For example, you cannot deny access to a host in the hosts.deny file that has already been given access in the hosts.allow file.

Listing every single address that may try to connect to your computer is not necessary (or even possible). The hosts.allow and hosts.deny files enable you to specify entire subnets and groups of addresses. You can even use the keyword ALL to specify all possible addresses. You can also restrict specific entries in these files so they apply only to specific network services. Look at an example of a typical pair of hosts.allow and hosts.deny files. Here's the /etc/hosts.allow file:

```
#
# hosts.allow  This file describes the names of the hosts that are
#              allowed to use the local INET services, as decided
#              by the '/usr/sbin/tcpd' server.
#

sshd: 199.170.177.
in.telnetd: 199.170.177., .linuxtoys.net
vsftpd: ALL
```

Here's the /etc/hosts.deny file:

```
#
# hosts.deny This file describes names of the hosts which are
#            *not* allowed to use the local INET services, as
#            decided by the '/usr/sbin/tcpd' server.
#

ALL: ALL
```

The preceding example is a rather restrictive configuration. It allows connections to the sshd and telnet services from certain hosts, but then denies all other connections. It also allows connections to the FTP service (vsftp) to all hosts. Let's examine the files in detail.

As usual, lines beginning with a # character are comments and are ignored by the TCP wrappers library when it parses the file. Each noncomment line consists of a comma-separated list of daemons followed by a colon (:) character and then a comma-separated list of client addresses to check. In this context, a client is any computer that attempts to access a network service on your system.

A client entry can be a numeric IP address (such as 199.170.177.25) or a hostname (such as jukebox.linuxtoys.net), but is more often a wildcard variation that specifies an entire range of addresses. A client entry can take four different forms. The online manual page for the hosts .allow file describes them as follows:

- A string that begins with a dot (.) character. A hostname is matched if the last components of its name match the specified pattern. For example, the pattern .tue.nl matches the hostname wzv.win.tue.nl.

- A string that ends with a dot (.) character. A host address is matched if its first numeric fields match the given string. For example, the pattern 131.155. matches the address of (almost) every host on the Eindhoven University network (131.155.x.x).

- A string that begins with an at (@) sign is treated as an NIS netgroup name. A hostname is matched if it is a host member of the specified netgroup. Netgroup matches are not supported for daemon process names or for client usernames.

- An expression of the form *n.n.n.n/m.m.m.m* is interpreted as a *net/mask* pair. A host address is matched if *net* is equal to the bitwise *and* of the address and the mask. For example, the net/mask pattern 131.155.72.0/255.255.254.0 matches every address in the range 131.155.72.0 through 131.155.73.255.

The example host.allow contains the first two types of client specification. The entry 199.170.177. will match any IP address that begins with that string, such as 199.170.177.25. The client entry .linuxtoys.net will match hostnames such as jukebox.linuxtoys.net or picframe.linuxtoys.net.

Let's examine what happens when a host named jukebox.linuxtoys.net (with IP address 199.170.179.18) connects to your Linux system using the telnet protocol. In this case, the Linux system is Fedora, which uses the xinetd daemon to listen for service requests associated with TCP wrappers:

1. xinetd receives the connection request.

2. xinetd begins comparing the address and name of jukebox.linuxtoys.net to the rules listed in /etc/hosts.allow. It starts at the top of the file and works its way down the file until finding a match. Both the daemon (the program handling the network service on your Fedora box) and the connecting client's IP address or name must

match the information in the `hosts.allow` file. In this case, the second rule that is encountered matches the request:

```
in.telnetd: 199.170.177., .linuxtoys.net
```

3. The `jukebox` host is not in the `199.170.177` subnet, but it is in the `linuxtoys.net` domain. `xinetd` stops searching the file as soon as it finds this match.

How about if `jukebox` connects to your box using the tftp protocol (`in.tftpd` daemon)? In this case, it matches none of the rules in `hosts.allow`. The entry `ALL: ALL` in the `hosts.deny` file matches anything, so the TCP Wrappers library denies the connection.

The `ALL` wildcard was also used in the `hosts.allow` file for the `vsftpd` service. In this case, you are telling TCP Wrappers to permit absolutely any host to connect to the FTP service on the Linux box. This is appropriate for running an anonymous FTP server that anyone on the Internet can access. If you are not running an anonymous FTP site, you might not want to use the `ALL` flag.

A good general rule is to make your `hosts.deny` file as restrictive as possible and then explicitly enable only those services that you really need. Also, grant access only to those systems that really need access. Using the `ALL` flag to grant universal access to a particular service may be easier than typing a long list of subnets or domains, but better a few minutes spent on proper security measures than many hours recovering from a break-in.

Tip

For Linux systems that use the xinetd service, you can further restrict access to services using various options within the /etc/xinetd.conf file, even to the point of limiting access to certain services to specific times of the day. Read the manual page for `xinetd` (by typing man xinetd at a command prompt) to learn more about these options. ∎

Understanding Attack Techniques

Attacks on computing systems take on different forms, depending on the goal and resources of the attacker. Some attackers want to be disruptive, whereas others want to infiltrate your machines and utilize the resources for their own nefarious purposes. Still others are targeting your data for financial gain or blackmail. Here are three major categories of attacks:

- **Denial-of-service (DoS)** — The easiest attacks to perpetrate are denial-of-service attacks. The primary purpose of these attacks is to disrupt the activities of a remote site by overloading it with irrelevant data. DoS attacks can be as simple as sending thousands of page requests per second at a web site. These types of attacks are easy to perpetrate and easy to protect against. After you have a handle on where the attack is coming from, a simple phone call to the perpetrator's ISP will get the problem solved.

- **Distributed denial-of-service (DDoS)** — More advanced DoS attacks are called distributed denial-of-service attacks. DDoS attacks are much harder to perpetrate and nearly impossible to stop. In this form of attack, an attacker takes control of hundreds or even thousands of weakly secured, Internet-connected computers. The attacker then directs them in unison to send a stream of irrelevant data to a single Internet host. The result is that the power of one attacker is magnified thousands of times. Instead of an attack coming from one direction, as is the case in a normal DoS, it comes from thousands of directions at once. The best defense against a DDoS attack is to contact your ISP to see whether or not it can filter traffic at its border routers.

Many people use the excuse, "I have nothing on my machine anyone would want" to avoid having to consider security. The problem with this argument is that attackers have a lot of reasons to use your machine. The attacker can turn your machine into an agent for later use in a DDoS attack. More than once, authorities have shown up at the door of a dumbfounded computer user asking questions about threats originating from their computer. By ignoring security, the owners have opened themselves up to a great deal of liability.

- **Intrusion attacks** — To remotely use the resources of a target machine, attackers must first look for an opening to exploit. In the absence of inside information such as passwords or encryption keys, they must scan the target machine to see what services are offered. Perhaps one of the services is weakly secured and the attacker can use some known exploit to finagle his or her way in.

  A tool called nmap is generally considered the best way to scan a host for services (note that nmap is a tool that can be used for good and evil). When the attacker has a list of the available services running on his target, he needs to find a way to trick one of those services into letting him have privileged access to the system. Usually, this is done with a program called an *exploit*.

Although DoS attacks are disruptive, intrusion attacks are the most damaging. The reasons are varied, but the result is always the same. An uninvited guest is now taking up residence on your machine and is using it in a way you have no control over.

Protecting Against Denial-of-Service Attacks

As explained earlier, a denial-of-service attack attempts to crash your computer or at least degrade its performance to an unusable level. A variety of denial-of-service exploits exist. Most try to overload some system resource, such as your available disk space or your Internet connection. Some common attacks and defenses are discussed in the following sections.

Mailbombing

Mailbombing is the practice of sending so much e-mail to a particular user or system that the computer's hard drive becomes full. You have several ways to protect yourself from mailbombing, as described in the following sections. You can use the procmail e-mail filtering tool or, if you are using sendmail as your mail transport agent, configure your sendmail daemon.

Blocking Mail with procmail

The procmail e-mail filtering tool, installed by default with Fedora, RHEL, and many other Linux systems, is tightly integrated with the sendmail e-mail daemon; thus, it can be used to selectively block or filter out specific types of e-mail. You can learn more about procmail at the procmail web site at `www.procmail.org`.

To enable procmail for your user account, create a `.procmailrc` file in your home directory. The file should be mode 0600 (readable by you but nobody else). Type the following, replacing *evilmailer* with the actual e-mail address that is mailbombing you.

```
# Delete mail from evilmailer
:0
* ^From.*evilmailer
/dev/null
```

The procmail recipe looks for the `From` line at the start of each e-mail to see if it includes the string `evilmailer`. If it does, the message is sent to `/dev/null` (effectively throwing it away).

Blocking Mail with sendmail

The procmail e-mail tool works quite well when only one user is being mailbombed. If, however, the mailbombing affects many users, you should probably configure your sendmail daemon to block all e-mail from the mailbomber. Do this by adding the mailbomber's e-mail address or system name to the `access` file located in the `/etc/mail` directory.

Each line of the `access` file contains an e-mail address, hostname, domain, or IP address followed by a tab and then a keyword specifying what action to take when that entity sends you a message. Valid keywords are `OK`, `RELAY`, `REJECT`, `DISCARD`, and `ERROR`. Using the `REJECT` keyword will cause a sender's e-mail to be bounced back with an error message. The keyword `DISCARD` will cause the message to be silently dropped without sending an error back. You can even return a custom error message by using the `ERROR` keyword.

Thus, an example `/etc/mail/access` file may look similar to this:

```
# Check the /usr/share/doc/sendmail/README.cf file for a description
# of the format of this file. (search for access_db in that file)
# The /usr/share/doc/sendmail/README.cf is part of the sendmail-doc
# package.
#
# by default we allow relaying from localhost...
localhost.localdomain           RELAY
localhost                       RELAY
127.0.0.1                       RELAY
#
# Senders we want to Block
#
evilmailer@yahoo.com    REJECT
stimpy.glaci.com        REJECT
cyberpromo.com          DISCARD
199.170.176.99          ERROR:"550 Die Spammer Scum!"
199.170.177             ERROR:"550 Email Refused"
```

As with most Linux configuration files, lines that begin with a pound (#) sign are comments. The list of blocked spammers is at the end of this example file. Note that the address to block can be a complete e-mail address, a full hostname, a domain only, an IP address, or a subnet.

To block a particular e-mail address or host from mailbombing you, log in to your system as root, edit the /etc/mail/access file, and add a line to DISCARD mail from the offending sender.

After saving the file and exiting the editor, you must convert the access file into a hash-indexed database called access.db. The database is updated automatically the next time sendmail starts. On Fedora and other Red Hat systems, you can convert the database immediately, as follows:

```
# cd /etc/mail
# make
```

Sendmail should now discard e-mail from the addresses you added.

Spam Relaying

Your e-mail services can also be abused by having your system used as a spam relay. *Spam* refers to the unsolicited junk e-mail that has become a common occurrence on the Internet. Relay refers to the mail server feature that causes it to send mail it receives to another server. (Normally, only users with valid e-mail accounts on the server are allowed to use a mail server to relay messages on their behalf. A mail server configured as an open relay will allow anyone to forward e-mail messages through it and is, therefore, considered to be a very bad practice.)

Spammers often deliver their annoying messages from a low-bandwidth Internet service provider. They need some kind of high-capacity e-mail server to accept and buffer the payload of messages. They deliver the spam to the server all in one huge batch and then log off, letting the server do the work of delivering the messages to the many victims.

Naturally, no self-respecting Internet service provider will cooperate with this action, so spammers resort to hijacking servers at another ISP to do the dirty work. Having your mail server hijacked to act as a spam relay can have a devastating effect on your system and your reputation. Fortunately, open mail relaying is deactivated by default on Fedora and Red Hat Enterprise Linux installations. Open mail relaying is one security issue that you will not have to worry about.

You can allow specific hosts or domains to relay mail through your system by adding those senders to your /etc/mail/access file with keyword RELAY. By default, relaying is allowed from the local host only.

Tip

One package you might consider using to filter out spam on your mail server is SpamAssassin. SpamAssassin examines the text of incoming mail messages and attempts to filter out messages that are determined to be spam. SpamAssassin is described in Chapter 16. ∎

Smurf Amplification Attack

Smurfing refers to a particular type of denial-of-service attack aimed at flooding your Internet connection. It can be a difficult attack to defend against because tracing the attack to the attacker is not easy. Here is how smurfing works.

The attack makes use of the ICMP protocol, a service intended for checking the speed and availability of network connections. Using the `ping` command, you can send a network packet from your computer to another computer on the Internet. The remote computer will recognize the packet as an ICMP request and echo a reply packet to your computer. Your computer can then print a message revealing that the remote system is up and telling you how long it took to reply to the ping.

A smurfing attack uses a malformed ICMP request to bury your computer in network traffic. The attacker does this by bouncing a ping request off an unwitting third party in such a way that the reply is duplicated dozens or even hundreds of times. An organization with a fast Internet connection and a large number of computers is used as the relay. The destination address of the ping is set to an entire subnet instead of a single host. The return address is forged to be your machine's address instead of the actual sender. When the ICMP packet arrives at the unwitting relay's network, every host on that subnet replies to the ping! Furthermore, they reply to your computer instead of to the actual sender. If the relay's network has hundreds of computers, your Internet connection can be quickly flooded.

The best fix is to contact the organization being used as a relay and inform it of the abuse. Usually, they need only to reconfigure their Internet router to stop any future attacks. If the organization is uncooperative, you can minimize the effect of the attack by blocking the ICMP protocol on your router. This will at least keep the traffic off your internal network. If you can convince your ISP to block ICMP packets aimed at your network, it will help even more. (Note that some debate exists about whether or not blocking ICMP packets is a good idea because ICMP services can be useful for various administrative purposes.)

Protecting Against Distributed Denial-of-Service Attacks

DDoS attacks are much harder to initiate and extremely difficult to stop. A DDoS attack begins with the penetration of hundreds or even thousands of weakly secured machines. These machines can then be directed to attack a single host based on the whims of the attacker.

With the advent of DSL and cable modem, millions of people are enjoying Internet access with virtually no speed restrictions. In their rush to get online, many of those people neglect even the most basic security. Because the vast majority of these people run Microsoft operating systems, they tend to get hit with worms and viruses rather quickly. After the machine has been infiltrated, quite often the worm or virus installs a program on the victim's machine that instructs it to quietly *call home* and announce that it is now ready to do *the master's bidding*.

At the whim of the master, the infected machines can now be used to focus a concentrated stream of garbage data at a selected host. In concert with thousands of other infected machines, a *script kiddie* now has the power to take down nearly any site on the Internet.

Detecting a DDoS is similar to detecting a DoS attack. One or more of the following signs are likely to be present:

- Sustained saturated data link
- No reduction in link saturation during off-peak hours
- Hundreds or even thousands of simultaneous network connections
- Extremely slow system performance

To determine if your data link is saturated, the act of pinging an outside host can tell much of the story. Much higher than usual latency is a dead giveaway. Normal ping latency (that is, the time it takes for a ping response to come back from a remote host) looks like the following:

```
# ping www.example.com
PING www.example.com (192.0.34.166) from 10.0.0.11: 56(84) bytes of data
64 bytes from 192.0.34.166: icmp_seq=1 ttl=49 time=40.1 ms
64 bytes from 192.0.34.166: icmp_seq=2 ttl=49 time=42.5 ms
64 bytes from 192.0.34.166: icmp_seq=3 ttl=49 time=39.5 ms
64 bytes from 192.0.34.166: icmp_seq=4 ttl=49 time=38.4 ms
64 bytes from 192.0.34.166: icmp_seq=5 ttl=49 time=39.0 ms

--- www.example.com ping statistics ---
5 packets transmitted, 5 received, 0% loss, time 4035ms
rtt min/avg/max/mdev = 38.472/39.971/42.584/1.432 ms
```

In the preceding example, the average time for a ping packet to make the round trip was about 39 thousandths of a second.

A ping to a nearly saturated link looks like the following:

```
# ping www.example.com
PING www.example.com (192.0.34.166): from 10.0.0.11: 56(84)bytes of data
64 bytes from 192.0.34.166: icmp_seq=1 ttl=62 time=1252 ms
64 bytes from 192.0.34.166: icmp_seq=2 ttl=62 time=1218 ms
64 bytes from 192.0.34.166: icmp_seq=3 ttl=62 time=1290 ms
64 bytes from 192.0.34.166: icmp_seq=4 ttl=62 time=1288 ms
64 bytes from 192.0.34.166: icmp_seq=5 ttl=62 time=1241 ms

--- www.example.com ping statistics ---
5 packets transmitted, 5 received, 0% loss, time 5032ms
rtt min/avg/max/mdev = 1218.059/1258.384/1290.861/28.000 ms
```

In this example, a ping packet took, on average, 1.3 seconds to make the round trip. From the first example to the second example, latency increased by a factor of 31! A data link that goes from working normally to slowing down by a factor of 31 is a clear sign that link utilization should be investigated.

For a more accurate measure of data throughput, you can use a tool such as ttcp. To test your connection with ttcp you must have installed the ttcp package on machines inside *and* outside of your network. (The ttcp package is available with Fedora and other Linux systems.) If you are not sure whether the package is installed, simply type **ttcp** at a command prompt. You should see something like the following:

```
# ttcp
Usage: ttcp -t [-options] host [ < in ]
       ttcp -r [-options > out]
Common options:
       -l ##    length of bufs read from or written to network (default 8192)
       -u       use UDP instead of TCP
       -p ##    port number to send to or listen at (default 5001)
       -s       -t: source a pattern to network
                -r: sink (discard) all data from network
       -A       align the start of buffers to this modulus (default 16384)
       -O       start buffers at this offset from the modulus (default 0)
       -v       verbose: print more statistics
       -d       set SO_DEBUG socket option
       -b ##    set socket buffer size (if supported)
       -f X     format for rate: k,K = kilo{bit,byte}; m,M = mega; g,G = giga
Options specific to -t:
       -n##     number of source bufs written to network (default 2048)
       -D       don't buffer TCP writes (sets TCP_NODELAY socket option)
     -w ## number of microseconds to wait between each write
Options specific to -r:
       -B       for -s, only output full blocks as specified by -l (for TAR)
       -T       "touch": access each byte as it's read
    -I if Specify the network interface (e.g. eth0) to use
```

The first step is to start up a receiver process on the server machine:

```
# ttcp -rs
ttcp-r: buflen=8192, nbuf=2048, align=16384/0, port=5001  tcp
ttcp-r: socket
```

The -r flag denotes that the server machine will be the receiver. The -s flag, in conjunction with the -r flag, tells ttcp that you want to ignore any received data.

The next step is to have someone outside of your data link, with a network link close to the same speed as yours, set up a ttcp sending process:

```
# ttcp -ts server.example.com
ttcp-t: buflen=8192, nbuf=2048, align=16384/0, port=5001  tcp
    -> server.example.com
ttcp-t: socket
ttcp-t: connect
```

Let the process run for a few minutes and then press Ctrl+C on the transmitting side to stop the testing. The receiving side then takes a moment to calculate and present the results:

```
# ttcp -rs
ttcp-r: buflen=8192, nbuf=2048, align=16384/0, port=5001   tcp
ttcp-r: socket
ttcp-r: accept from 64.223.17.21
ttcp-r: 2102496 bytes in 70.02 real seconds = 29.32 KB/sec +++
ttcp-r: 1226 I/O calls, msec/call = 58.49, calls/sec = 17.51
ttcp-r: 0.0user 0.0sys 1:10real 0% 0i+0d 0maxrss 0+2pf 0+0csw
```

In this example, the average bandwidth between the two hosts was 29.32 kilobytes per second. On a link suffering from a DDoS, this number would be a mere fraction of the actual bandwidth for which the data link is rated.

If the data link is indeed saturated, the next step is to determine where the connections are coming from. A very effective way of doing this is with the `netstat` command, which is included as part of the base Fedora installation. Type the following to see connection information:

```
# netstat -tupn
```

Table 13-3 describes each of the `netstat` parameters used here.

TABLE 13-3

netstat Parameters

Parameter	Description
-t, --tcp	Show TCP socket connections.
-u, --udp	Show UDP socket connections.
-p, --program	Show the PID and name of the program to which each socket belongs.
-n, --numeric	Show numerical address instead of trying to determine symbolic host, port, or usernames.

The following is an example of what the output might look like:

```
Active Internet connections (w/o servers)
Proto Recv-Q Send-Q Local Address    Foreign Address       State        PID/Program name
tcp    0      0 65.213.7.96:22       13.29.132.19:12545    ESTABLISHED  32376/sshd
tcp    0    224 65.213.7.96:22       13.29.210.13:29250    ESTABLISHED  13858/sshd
tcp    0      0 65.213.7.96:6667     13.29.194.190:33452   ESTABLISHED  1870/ircd
tcp    0      0 65.213.7.96:6667     216.39.144.152:42709  ESTABLISHED  1870/ircd
tcp    0      0 65.213.7.96:42352    67.113.1.99:53        TIME_WAIT    -
tcp    0      0 65.213.7.96:42354    83.152.6.9:113        TIME_WAIT    -
```

```
tcp    0    0 65.213.7.96:42351 83.152.6.9:113      TIME_WAIT  -
tcp    0    0 127.0.0.1:42355   127.0.0.1:783       TIME_WAIT  -
tcp    0    0 127.0.0.1:783     127.0.0.1:42353     TIME_WAIT  -
tcp    0    0 65.213.7.96:42348 19.15.11.1:25       TIME_WAIT  -
```

The output is organized into columns defined as follows:

- **Proto** — Protocol used by the socket
- **Recv-Q** — The number of bytes not yet copied by the user program attached to this socket
- **Send-Q** — The number of bytes not acknowledged by the host
- **Local Address** — Address and port number of the local end of the socket
- **Foreign Address** — Address and port number of the remote end of the socket
- **State** — Current state of the socket. Table 12-4 provides a list of socket states.
- **PID/Program Name** — Process ID and program name of the process that owns the socket

TABLE 13-4

Socket States

State	Description
ESTABLISHED	Socket has an established connection.
SYN_SENT	Socket actively trying to establish a connection
SYN_RECV	Connection request received from the network
FIN_WAIT1	Socket closed and shutting down
FIN_WAIT2	Socket is waiting for remote end to shut down.
TIME_WAIT	Socket is waiting after closing to handle packets still in the network.
CLOSED	Socket is not being used.
CLOSE_WAIT	The remote end has shut down, waiting for the socket to close.
LAST_ACK	The remote end has shut down, and the socket is closed, waiting for acknowledgement.
LISTEN	Socket is waiting for an incoming connection.
CLOSING	Both sides of the connection are shut down, but not all of your data has been sent.
UNKNOWN	The state of the socket is unknown.

During a DoS attack, the foreign address is usually the same for each connection. In this case, it is a simple matter of typing the foreign IP address into the search form at ws.arin.net/whois/ so you can alert your ISP.

During a DDoS attack, the foreign address will likely be different for each connection. In this case, tracking down all the offenders is impossible because there will likely be thousands of them. The best way to defend yourself is to contact your ISP and see whether or not it can filter the traffic at its border routers.

Protecting Against Intrusion Attacks

Crackers have a wide variety of tools and techniques to assist them in breaking into your computer. Intrusion attacks focus on exploiting weaknesses in your security, so the crackers can take more control of your system (and potentially do more damage) than they could from the outside.

Fortunately, many tools and techniques exist for combating intrusion attacks. This section discusses the most common break-in methods and the tools available to protect your system. Although the examples shown are specific to Fedora and other Red Hat Linux systems, the tools and techniques are generally applicable to any Linux or UNIX-like operating system.

Evaluating Access to Network Services

Linux systems and their UNIX kin provide many network services, and with them many avenues for cracker attacks. You should know these services and how to limit access to them.

What do I mean by a network service? Basically, I am referring to any task that the computer performs that requires it to send and receive information over the network using some predefined set of rules. Routing e-mail is a network service. So is serving web pages. Your Linux box has the potential to provide thousands of services. Many of them are listed in the /etc/services file. Consider the following section from the /etc/services file:

```
# /etc/services:
# service-name    port/protocol   [aliases ...]    [# comment]
chargen           19/tcp          ttytst source
chargen           19/udp          ttytst source
ftp-data          20/tcp
ftp-data          20/udp
# 21 is registered to ftp, but also used by fsp
ftp               21/tcp
ftp               21/udp          fsp fspd
ssh               22/tcp                           # SSH Remote Login Protocol
ssh               22/udp                           # SSH Remote Login Protocol
telnet            23/tcp
telnet            23/udp
# 24 - private mail system
smtp              25/tcp          mail
```

After the comment lines, you will notice three columns of information. The left column contains the name of each service. The middle column defines the port number and protocol type used for that service. The rightmost field contains an optional alias or list of aliases for the service.

As an example, examine the last entry in the file snippet. It describes the SMTP (Simple Mail Transfer Protocol) service, which is the service used for delivering e-mail over the Internet. The middle column contains the text 25/tcp, which tells you that the SMTP protocol uses port 25 and uses the Transmission Control Protocol (TCP) as its protocol type.

What exactly is a *port number*? It is a unique number that has been set aside for a particular network service. It allows network connections to be properly routed to the software that handles that service. For example, when an e-mail message is delivered from some other computer to your Linux box, the remote system must first establish a network connection with your system. Your computer receives the connection request, examines it, sees it labeled for port 25, and thus knows that the connection should be handed to the program that handles e-mail (which happens to be sendmail).

I mentioned that SMTP uses the TCP protocol. Some services use UDP, the User Datagram Protocol. All you really need to know about TCP and UDP (for the purposes of this security discussion) is that they provide different ways of packaging the information sent over a network connection. A TCP connection provides error detection and retransmission of lost data. UDP doesn't check to ensure that the data arrived complete and intact; it is meant as a fast way to send non-critical information.

Disabling Network Services

Although hundreds of services (with official port numbers listed in /etc/services) could be available and subject to attack on your Linux system, in reality only a few dozen services are installed and only a handful of those are on by default. In Fedora and RHEL systems, most network services are started by either the xinetd process or by a startup script in the /etc/init.d directory. Other Linux systems use the inetd process instead of xinetd.

xinetd and inetd are daemons that listen on a great number of network port numbers. When a connection is made to a particular port number, xinetd or inetd automatically starts the appropriate program for that service and hands the connection to it.

For xinetd, the configuration file /etc/xinetd.conf is used to provide default settings for the xinetd server. The directory /etc/xinetd.d contains files telling xinetd what ports to listen on and what programs to start (the inetd daemon, alternatively, uses only the /etc/inetd.conf file). Each file in /etc/xinetd.d contains configuration information for a single service, and the file is usually named after the service it configures. For example, to enable the rsync service, edit the rsync file in the /etc/xinetd.d directory and look for a section similar to the following:

```
service rsync
{
    disable = yes
    socket_type      = stream
```

```
wait            = no
user            = root
server          = /usr/bin/rsync
server_args     = --daemon
log_on_failure  += USERID
}
```

Note that the first line of this example identifies the service as rsync. This exactly matches the service name listed in the /etc/services file, causing the service to listen on port 873 for TCP and UDP protocols. You can see that the service is off by default (disable = yes). To enable the rsync services, change the line to read disable = no instead. Thus, the disable line from the preceding example would look like this:

```
disable = no
```

Tip

The rsync service is a nice one to turn on if your machine is an FTP server. It allows people to use an rsync client (which includes a checksum-search algorithm) to download files from your server. With that feature, users can restart a disrupted download without having to start from the beginning. ■

Because most services are disabled by default, your computer is only as insecure as you make it. You can double-check that insecure services, such as rlogin and rsh (which are included in the rsh-server package in Fedora and RHEL systems), are also disabled by making sure that disabled = yes is set in the /etc/xinetd.d/rlogin and rsh files.

Tip

You can make the remote login service active but disable the use of the /etc/host.equiv and .rhosts files, requiring rlogin to always prompt for a password. Rather than disabling the service, locate the server line in the rsh file (server = /usr/sbin/in.rshd) and add a space followed by -L at the end. ■

You now need to send a signal to the xinetd process to tell it to reload its configuration file. The quickest way to do that in Fedora and RHEL systems is to reload the xinetd service. As the root user, type the following from a shell:

```
# service xinetd reload
Reloading configuration:         [ OK ]
```

You can also tell the xinetd process directly to reread the configuration file by sending it a SIGHUP signal. That works if you are using the inetd daemon instead (on systems such as Debian or Slackware) to reread the /etc/inetd.conf file. For example, type this (as root user) to have the inetd daemon reread the configuration file:

```
# killall -s SIGHUP inetd
```

That's it — you have enabled the rsync service. Provided that you have properly configured your FTP server, clients should now be able to download files from your computer via the rsync protocol.

Securing Servers with SELinux

Security Enhanced Linux (SELinux) is a project developed primarily by the National Security Agency to produce highly secure Linux systems. Although SELinux is available as add-on packages to openSUSE, Debian, Ubuntu, Gentoo, and Yellow Dog, SELinux is installed and turned on by default in Fedora and Red Hat Enterprise Linux systems.

Red Hat, Inc. did a clever thing when it took its first swipe at implementing SELinux in Red Hat systems. Instead of creating policies to control every aspect of your Linux system, it created a "targeted" policy type that focused on securing your system from attacks on those services that are most vulnerable to attacks. The company then set about securing those services in such a way that, if they were compromised, a cracker couldn't compromise the rest of the system as well.

After you have opened a port in your firewall so others can request a service, then started that service to handle requests, SELinux can be used to set up walls around that service. As a result, its daemon process, configuration files, and data can't access resources they are not specifically allowed to access. The rest of your computer, then, is safer.

As Red Hat continues to work out the kinks in SELinux, there has been a tendency for users to see SELinux failures and just disable the entire SELinux service. However, a better course is to find out whether SELinux is really stopping you from doing something that is unsafe. If it turns out to be a bug with SELinux, file a bug report and help make the service better.

If you are enabling FTP, web (HTTPD), DNS, NFS, NIS, or Samba services on your Fedora or RHEL system, you should consider leaving SELinux enabled and working with the settings from the Security Level Configuration window to configure those services. For information on SELinux that is specific to Fedora, refer to this site:

```
http://fedoraproject.org/wiki/SELinux
```

Protecting Web Servers with Certificates and Encryption

Previous sections told you how to lock the doors to your Linux system to deny access to crackers. The best deadbolt lock, however, is useless if you are mugged in your own driveway and have your keys stolen. Likewise, the best computer security can be for naught if you are sending passwords and other critical data unprotected across the Internet.

A savvy cracker can use a tool called a *protocol analyzer* or a *network sniffer* to peek at the data flowing across a network and pick out passwords, credit card data, and other juicy bits of information. The cracker does this by breaking into a poorly protected system on the same network and running software, or by gaining physical access to the same network and plugging in his or her own equipment.

You can combat this sort of theft by using encryption. The two main types of encryption in use today are symmetric cryptography and public-key cryptography.

Exporting Encryption Technology_____

Before describing how to use the various encryption tools, I need to warn you about an unusual policy of the United States government. For many years, the United States government treated encryption technology like munitions. As a result, anyone wanting to export encryption technology had to get an export license from the Commerce Department. This applied not only to encryption software developed within the United States, but also to software obtained from other countries and then re-exported to another country (or even to the same country you got it from).

Thus, if you installed encryption technology on your Linux system and then transported it out of the country, you were violating federal law! Furthermore, if you e-mailed encryption software to a friend in another country or let him or her download it from your server, you violated the law.

In January 2000, U.S. export laws relating to encryption software were relaxed considerably. However, often the U.S. Commerce Department's Bureau of Export Administration requires a review of encryption products before they can be exported. U.S. companies are still not allowed to export encryption technology to countries classified as supporting terrorism.

Symmetric Cryptography

Symmetric cryptography, also called *private-key cryptography*, uses a single key to both encrypt and decrypt a message. This method is generally inappropriate for securing data that will be used by a third party because of the complexity of secure key exchange. Symmetric cryptography is generally useful for encrypting data for one's own purposes.

A classic use of symmetric cryptography is for a personal password vault. Anyone who has been using the Internet for any amount of time has accumulated a quantity of usernames and passwords for accessing various sites and resources. A personal password vault lets you store this access information in an encrypted form. The end result is that you have to remember only one password to unlock all of your access information.

A few years ago, the United States government was standardized on a symmetric encryption algorithm called DES (Data Encryption Standard) to secure important information. Because there is no direct way to crack DES encrypted data, to decrypt DES encrypted data without a password you would have to use an unimaginable amount of computing power to try to guess the password. This is also known as the *brute force method of decryption.*

As personal computing power has increased nearly exponentially, the DES algorithm has had to be retired. In its place, after a very long and interesting search, the United States government has accepted the Rijndael algorithm as what it calls the AES (Advanced Encryption Standard). Although the AES algorithm is also subject to brute force attacks, it requires significantly more computing power to crack than the DES algorithm does.

For more information on AES, including a command-line implementation of the algorithm, you can visit `http://aescrypt.sourceforge.net/`.

Asymmetric Cryptography

Public-key cryptography does not suffer from key distribution problems, and that is why it is the preferred encryption method for secure Internet communication. This method uses two keys, one to encrypt the message and another to decrypt the message. The key used to encrypt the message is called the public key because it is made available for all to see. The key used to decrypt the message is the private key and is kept hidden.

Imagine that you want to send me a secure message using public-key encryption. Here is what we need:

1. I must have a public and private key pair. Depending on the circumstances, I may generate the keys myself (using special software) or obtain the keys from a key authority.

2. You want to send me a message, so you first look up my public key (or more accurately, the software you are using looks it up).

3. You encrypt the message with the public key. At this point, the message can be decrypted only with the private key (the public key cannot be used to decrypt the message).

4. I receive the message and use my private key to decrypt it.

Secure Socket Layer

Secure socket layer (SSL) communication offers a classic implementation of public-key cryptography. This is the technology that enables you to securely submit your credit card information to an online merchant. The elements of an SSL-encrypted session are as follows:

- SSL-enabled web browser (Mozilla, Internet Explorer, Opera, Konquerer, and so on)
- SSL-enabled web server (Apache)
- SSL certificate

To initiate an SSL session, a web browser first makes contact with a web server on port 443, also known as the HTTPS port (Hypertext Transport Protocol Secure). After a socket connection has been established between the two machines, the following occurs:

1. The server sends its SSL certificate to the browser.
2. The browser verifies the identity of the server through the SSL certificate.
3. The browser generates a symmetric encryption key.
4. The browser uses the SSL certificate to encrypt the symmetric encryption key.
5. The browser sends the encrypted key to the server.
6. The server decrypts the symmetric key with its private key counterpart of the public SSL certificate.

The browser and server can now encrypt and decrypt traffic based on a common knowledge of the symmetric key. Secure data interchange can now occur.

Creating SSL Certificates

To create your own SSL certificate for secure HTTP data interchange, you must first have an SSL-capable web server. The Apache web server, which comes with Fedora and other Linux systems, is SSL-capable. The following procedure for creating SSL certificates is done on a Fedora system that includes Apache from the httpd and mod_ssl packages. This procedure may be different for Apache on other Linux systems.

First install the necessary packages:

```
# yum install httpd mod_ssl openssl
```

Now create SSL certificates:

```
# cd /etc/pki/tls/certs
# make
This makefile allows you to create:
  o public/private key pairs
  o SSL certificate signing requests (CSRs)
  o self-signed SSL test certificates

To create a key pair, run "make SOMETHING.key".
To create a CSR, run "make SOMETHING.csr".
To create a test certificate, run "make SOMETHING.crt".
To create a key and a test certificate in one file, run "make SOMETHING.pem".

To create a key for use with Apache, run "make genkey".
To create a CSR for use with Apache, run "make certreq".
To create a test certificate for use with Apache, run "make testcert".

Examples:
  make server.key
  make server.csr
  make server.crt
  make stunnel.pem
  make genkey
  make certreq
  make testcert
```

The make command utilizes the makefile to create SSL certificates. Without any arguments the make command simply prints the information listed in the preceding example. The following defines each argument you can give to make:

- make server.key — Creates generic public/private key pairs
- make server.csr — Generates a generic SSL certificate service request
- make server.crt — Generates a generic SSL test certificate

- `make stunnel.pem` — Generates a generic SSL test certificate, but puts the private key in the same file as the SSL test certificate

- `make genkey` — Same as `make server.key` except it places the key in the `ssl.key` directory

- `make certreq` — Same as `make server.csr` except it places the certificate service request in the `ssl.csr` directory

- `make testcert` — Same as `make server.crt` except it places the test certificate in the `ssl.crt` directory

Using Third-Party Certificate Signers

In the real world, I know who you are because I recognize your face, your voice, and your mannerisms. On the Internet, I cannot see these things and must rely on a trusted third party to vouch for your identity. To ensure that a certificate is immutable, it has to be signed by a trusted third party when the certificate is issued and validated every time an end user taking advantage of your secure site loads it. The following is a list of the trusted third-party certificate signers:

- **GlobalSign** — `www.globalsign.com/`
- **GeoTrust** — `https://www.geotrust.com/`
- **VeriSign** — `https://www.verisign.com/`
- **RapidSSL** — `https://www.rapidssl.com/`
- **Thawte** — `www.thawte.com/`
- **EnTrust** — `www.entrust.com/`
- **ipsCA** — `www.ipsca.com/`
- **COMODO Group** — `www.comodogroup.com/`

Note

Because of the fluid nature of the certificate business, some of these companies may not be in business when you read this, while others may have come into existence. To get a more current list of certificate authorities, from your Firefox browser select Edit ⇨ Preferences. From the Preferences window that appears, select Advanced ⇨ Encryption, and then select the View Certificates button. From the Certificate Manager window that appears, refer to the Authorities tab to see Certificate Authorities from which you have received certificates. ∎

Each of these certificate authorities has gotten a chunk of cryptographic code embedded into nearly every web browser in the world. This chunk of cryptographic code allows a web browser to determine whether or not an SSL certificate is authentic. Without this validation, it would be easy for crackers to generate their own certificates and dupe people into thinking they are giving sensitive information to a reputable source.

Certificates that are not validated are called *self-signed certificates*. If you come across a site that has not had its identity authenticated by a trusted third party, your web browser will display a message similar to the one shown in Figure 13-5.

FIGURE 13-5

A pop-up window alerts you when a site is not authenticated.

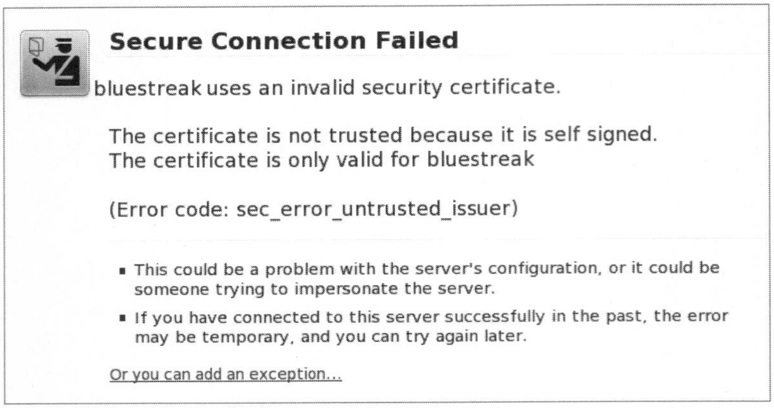

Secure Connection Failed

bluestreak uses an invalid security certificate.

The certificate is not trusted because it is self signed.
The certificate is only valid for bluestreak

(Error code: sec_error_untrusted_issuer)

- This could be a problem with the server's configuration, or it could be someone trying to impersonate the server.
- If you have connected to this server successfully in the past, the error may be temporary, and you can try again later.

Or you can add an exception...

This does not necessarily mean that you are encountering anything illegal, immoral, or fattening. Many sites opt to go with *self-signed* certificates, not because they are trying to pull a fast one on you, but because there may not be any reason to validate the true owner of the certificate and they do not want to pay the cost of getting a certificate validated. Some reasons for using a *self-signed* certificate include:

- **The web site accepts no input** — In this case, you, as the end user, have nothing to worry about. There is no one trying to steal your information because you aren't giving out any information. Most of the time this is done simply to secure the web transmission from the server to you. The data in and of itself may not be sensitive, but, being a good netizen, the site has enabled you to use an SSL connection (https) to provide basic security. A hacker can still sniff your traffic using a man-in-the-middle attack unless you manually verify that the certificate has not been modified.

- **The web site caters to a small clientele** — If you run a web site that has a very limited set of customers, such as an Application Service Provider, you can simply inform your users that you have no certificate signer. They can browse the certificate information and validate it with you over the phone or in person.

- **Testing** — Paying for an SSL certificate makes no sense if you are only testing a new web site or web-based application. Use a *self-signed* certificate until you are ready to go live.

Creating a Certificate Service Request

To create a third party–validated SSL certificate from a Fedora Linux system, you must first start with a certificate service request (CSR). To create a CSR, do the following on your web server:

```
# cd /etc/pki/tls/certs
# make certreq
umask 77 ; \
```

```
/usr/bin/openssl req -utf8 -new -key /etc/pki/tls/private/localhost.key
      -out /etc/pki/tls/certs/localhost.csr
    .
    .
    .
```

You will now be asked to enter a password to secure your private key. This password should be at least eight characters long, and should not be a dictionary word or contain numbers or punctuation. The characters you type will not appear on the screen, to prevent someone from shoulder surfing your password.

```
Enter pass phrase:
```

Enter the password again to verify.

```
Verifying - Enter pass phrase:
```

The certificate generation process now begins.

At this point, it is time to start adding some identifying information to the certificate that the third-party source will later validate. Before you can do this, you must unlock the private key you just created. Do so by typing the password you typed for your passphrase. Then enter information as you are prompted. The following is an example of a session for adding information for your certificate:

```
Enter pass phrase for /etc/pki/tls/private/localhost.key:  *******
You are about to be asked to enter information that will be incorporated
into your certificate request.
What you are about to enter is what is called
a Distinguished Name or a DN.
There are quite a few fields but you can leave some blank.
For some fields there will be a default value,
If you enter '.', the field will be left blank.
-----
Country Name (2 letter code) [GB]:US
State or Province Name (full name) [Berkshire]: Connecticut
Locality Name (eg, city) [Newbury]: Mystic
Organization Name (eg, company) [My Company Ltd]:Acme Marina, Inc.
Organizational Unit Name (eg, section) []:InfoTech
Common Name (eg, your name or your server's hostname) []:www.acmemarina.com
Email Address []: webmaster@acmemarina.com
```

To complete the process, you will be asked whether you want to add any extra attributes to your certificate. Unless you have a reason to provide more information, you should simply press Enter at each of the following prompts to leave them blank.

```
Please enter the following 'extra' attributes
to be sent with your certificate request
A challenge password []:
An optional company name []:
```

Getting your CSR Signed

After your CSR has been created, you need to send it to a signing authority for validation. The first step in this process is to select a signing authority. Each signing authority has different deals, prices, and products. Check out each of the signing authorities listed in the "Using Third-Party Certificate Signers" section earlier in this chapter to determine which works best for you. The following are areas where signing authorities differ:

- Credibility and stability
- Pricing
- Browser recognition
- Warranties
- Support
- Certificate strength

After you have selected your certificate signer, you have to go through some validation steps. Each signer has a different method of validating identity and certificate information. Some require that you fax articles of incorporation, whereas others require a company officer be made available to talk to a validation operator. At some point in the process you will be asked to copy and paste the contents of the CSR you created into the signer's web form.

```
# cd /etc/pki/tls/certs/
# cat localhost.csr
-----BEGIN CERTIFICATE REQUEST-----
MIIB6jCCAVMCAQAwgakxCzAJBgNVBAYTAlVTMRQwEgYDVQQIEwtDb25uZWN0aWN1
dDEPMA0GA1UEBxMGTX1zdG1jMRowGAYDVQQKExFBY21lIE1hcm1uYSwgSW5jLjER
MA8GA1UECxMISW5mb1RlY2gxGzAZBgNVBAMTEnd3dy5hY21lbWFyaW5hLmNvbTEn
MCUGCSqGSIb3DQEJARYYd2VibWFzdGVyQGFjbWVtYXJpbmEuY29tMIGfMA0GCSqG
SIb3DQEBAQUAA4GNADCBiQKBgQDcYH4pjMxKM1dyXRmcoz8uBVOvwlNZHyRWw8ZG
u2eCbvgi6w4wXuHwaDuxbuDBmw//Y9DMI2MXg4wDq4xmPi35EsO1Ofw4ytZJn1yW
aU6cJVQro46OnXyaqXZOPiRCxUSnGRU+OnsqKGjf7LPpXv29S3QvMIBTYWzCkNnc
gWBwwwIDAQABoAAwDQYJKoZIhvcNAQEEBQADgYEANv6eJOaJZGzopNR5h2YkR9Wg
18oB13mgoPH6OSccw3pWsoW4qbOWq7on8dS/++QOCZWZI1gefgaSQMInKZ1II7Fs
YIwYBgpoPTMC4bp0ZZtURCyQWrKIDXQBXw7B1U/3A25nvkRY7vgNL9Nq+7681EJ8
W9AJ3PX4vb2+ynttcBI=
-----END CERTIFICATE REQUEST-----
```

You can use your mouse to copy and paste the CSR into the signer's web form.

After you have completed the information validation, paid for the signing, and answered all the questions, you have completed most of the process. Within 48 to 72 hours you should receive an e-mail with your shiny new SSL certificate in it. The certificate will look similar to the following:

```
-----BEGIN CERTIFICATE-----
MIIEFjCCA3+gAwIBAgIQMI262Zd6njZgN97tJAVFODANBgkqhkiG9w0BAQQFADCB
ujEfMB0GA1UEChMWVmVyaVNpZ24gVHJ1c3QgTmV0d29yazEXMBUGA1UECxMOVmVy
aVNpZ24sIEluYy4xMzAxBgNVBAsTKlZlcm1TaWduIEludGVybmF0aW9uYWwgU2Vy
dmVyIENBIC0gQ2xhc3MgMzFJMEcGA1UrY2g0Dd3d3LmZlcm1zaWduLmNvbS9DUFMg
```

```
SW5jb3JwLmJ51FJ1Zi4gTE1BQk1MSVRZIExURC4oYyk5NyBWZXJpU21nbjAeFwOw
MzAxMTUwMDAwMDBaFwOwNDAxMTUyMzU5NT1aMIGuMQswCQYDVQQGEwJVUzETMBEG
A1UECBMKV2FzaG1uZ3RvHiThErE371UEBxQLRmVkZXJhbCBXYXkxGzAZBgNVBAoU
EklETSBTZXJ2aWMlcywgSW5jLjEMMAoGA1UECxQDd3d3MTMwMQYDVQQLFCpUZXJt
cyBvZiB1c2UgYXQgd3d3LnZlcm1zawduLmNvbS9ycGGEzKGMpMDAxFDASBgNVBAMU
C21kbXN1cnYuY29tMIGfMAOGCSqGS1b3DQEBAQUAA4GNADCBiQKBgQDaHSk+uzOf
7jjDFEnqT8UBa1L3yFILXFjhj3XpMXLGWzLmkDmdJjXsa4x7AhEpr1ubuVNhJVIO
FnLDopsx4pyr4n+P8FyS4M5grbcQzy2YnkM2jyqVF/7yOW2pD130t4eacYYaz4Qg
q9pTxhUzjEG4twvKCAFWfuhEoGu1CMV2qQ1DAQABo4IBJTCCASEwCQYDVROTBAIw
ADBEBgNVHSAEPTA7MDkGC2CGSAGG+EUBBxcDMCOwKAYIKwYBBQUHAgEWHGh0dHBz
Oi8vd3d3LnZlcm1zaWduLmNvbS9ycGGEwCwYDVRRPBAQDAgWgMCgGA1UdJQQhMB8G
CWCGSAGG+EIEMOOcOwIYBQUHAwEGCCsGAQUFBwmCMDQGCCsGAQUFBwEBBCgwJjAk
BggrBgEFBQcwAYYYaHROcDovL29jc2AudmVyaXNpZ24uY29tMEYGA1UdHwQ/MDOw
O6A5oDeGNWh0dHA6Ly9jcmwwudmVyaXNpZ24uY29tLONsYXNzM01udGGVybmF0aW9u
YWxxTZXJ2ZXIuY3JsMBkGCmCGSAgG+E+f4Nfc3zYJODA5NzMwMTEyMAOGCSqGSIb3
DQEBBAUAA4GBAJ/PsVttmlDkQai5nLeudLceb1F4isXP17B68wXLkIeRu4Novu13
81LZXnaR+acHeStRO1b3rQPjgv2y1mwjkPmC1WjoeYfdxH7+Mbg/6fomnK9auWAT
WFOiFW/+a8OWRYQJLMA2VQOVhX4znjpGcVNY9AQSHm1UiESJy7vtd1iX
-----END CERTIFICATE-----
```

Copy and paste this certificate into an empty file called server.crt, which should reside in the /etc/pki/tls/certs directory. Configure the SSLCertificateFile and SSLCertificateKeyFile values in the SSL file (/etc/httpd/conf.d/ssl.conf) and restart your web server:

```
# service httpd restart
```

Assuming your web site was previously working fine, you can now view it in a secure fashion by placing an "s" after the http in the web address. So if you previously viewed your web site at www.acmemarina.com, you can now view it in a secure fashion by going to https://www.acmemarina.com.

Creating Self-Signed Certificates

Generating and running a self-signed SSL certificate is much easier than having a signed certificate. To generate a self-signed SSL certificate on a Fedora system, do the following:

1. Remove the key and certificate that currently exist:

```
# rm /etc/pki/tls/private/localhost.key
# rm /etc/pki/tls/certs/localhost.crt
```

2. Create your own server key:

```
# cd /etc/pki/tls/certs
# make genkey
```

3. Create the self-signed certificate by typing the following:

```
# make testcert
umask 77 ; \
```

```
        /usr/bin/openssl genrsa -des3 1024 >
        /etc/pki/tls/private/localhost.key
        Generating RSA private key, 1024 bit long modulus
        ............................+++++
        ..........................................................+++++
        e is 65537 (0x10001)
        Enter pass phrase: *******
        Verifying - Enter pass phrase: *******
        Enter pass phrase for /etc/pki/tls/private/localhost.key: *******
           .
           .
           .
```

At this point, it is time to start adding some identifying information to the certificate. Before you can do this, you must unlock the private key you just created. Do so by typing the password you typed earlier. Then follow this sample procedure:

```
You will be asked to enter information that will be incorporated
into your certificate request.
What you are about to enter is called a Distinguished Name or DN.
There are quite a few fields but you can leave some blank.
For some fields there will be a default value,
If you enter '.', the field will be left blank.
-----
Country Name (2 letter code) [GB]: US
State or Province Name (full name) [Berkshire]: Ohio
Locality Name (eg, city) [Newbury]: Cincinnati
Organization Name (eg, company) [My Company Ltd]:Industrial Press, Inc.
Organizational Unit Name (eg, section) []:IT
Common Name (eg, your name or your server's hostname)
[]:www.industrialpressinc.com
Email Address []: webmaster@industrialpressinc.com
```

The generation process in this example creates the file named /etc/pki/tls/certs/localhost
.crt. Within the virtual host you created in the /etc/httpd/conf.d/ssl.conf file, identify the certificate file using the following directive:

```
SSLCertificateFile /etc/pki/tls/certs/localhost.crt
```

Then all you need to do is restart your web server and add https instead of http in front of your URL. Don't forget that you'll get a certificate validation message from your web browser, which you can safely ignore.

Restarting your Web Server

By now you've probably noticed that your web server requires you to enter your certificate password every time it is started. This is to prevent someone from breaking into your server and stealing your private key. Should this happen, you are safe in the knowledge that the private key is a jumbled mess. The cracker will not be able to make use of it. Without such protection, a cracker could get your private key and easily masquerade as you, appearing to be legitimate in all cases.

If you just cannot stand having to enter a password every time your web server starts, and are willing to accept the increased risk, you can remove the password encryption on your private key. Simply do the following:

```
# cd /etc/pki/tls/private
# /usr/bin/openssl rsa -in localhost.key -out  localhost.key
Enter pass phrase for localhost.key: *******
```

You should now be able to restart the server without entering a pass phrase.

Troubleshooting Your Certificates

The following tips should help if you are having problems with your SSL certificate:

- Only one SSL certificate per IP address is allowed. If you want to add more than one SSL-enabled web site to your server, you must bind another IP address to the network interface.

- Make sure you aren't blocking port 443 on your web server. All `https` requests come in on port 443. If you are blocking it, you will not be able to get secure pages.

- The certificate lasts for one year only. When that year is up, you have to renew your certificate with your certificate authority. Each certificate authority has a different procedure for doing this; check the authority's web site for more details.

- Make sure you have the mod_ssl package installed. If it is not installed, you will not be able to serve any SSL-enabled traffic.

Using Security Tools from Linux Live CDs

If you suspect your computers or networks have been exploited, a wide range of security tools is available for Linux that you can use to scan for viruses, do forensics, or monitor activities of intruders. The best way to learn about and use many of these tools is to use dedicated, bootable Linux distributions built specifically for security.

Advantages of Security Live CDs

One great advantage of using live CDs or DVDs to check the security of a system is that using a live CD separates the tools you use to check a system from the system itself. In other words, because the tools for finding problems on an installed system may themselves be compromised, a live CD of trusted software can be a good way to ensure that you are testing a potentially infected system with clean tools.

If, despite your best efforts (good passwords, firewalls, checking log files, and so on), you believe an intruder may have gained control of your system, you can use a live CD to check it out. Security live CDs such as System Rescue CD, INSERT, and BackTrack (all included on this book's DVD) are great tools for checking and fixing your system.

Cross-Reference
See Chapter 24 for more information on bootable security and rescue CDs. ∎

Using INSERT to Check for Rootkits

If an intruder gains access to your Linux system, to try to take over control of that system (and use it for more than just a hit-and-run), the intruder might install what is called a *rootkit*. A rootkit is a set of software that the intruder will use to do the following:

- Carry out his intent (such as hosting false web content from your server)
- Hide his activities from your view

Rootkits can employ different methods for hiding what they do. Often a rootkit will replace common system commands with its own version of those commands. So, for example, replacing ls and ps could be modified to not list the content added to your machine or not show certain processes running on your system, respectively.

The chkrootkit command is a good tool for checking for well-known rootkits, as well as for generally checking system files to see whether they have been infected or not. This tool will check for infections in disk-checking tools (such as du, find, and ls), process table tools (ps and pstree), login-related commands (login, rlogin, slogin), and many other tools. Here's how to run chkrootkit from INSERT:

1. Insert the CD that comes with this book into the CD drive and reboot.

2. From the boot screen, choose Insert. INSERT should boot to a desktop.

3. To be able to check the Linux system installed on your hard disk, you need to mount the partition representing your installed Linux system. Using the mount.app applet (displayed in the lower-right corner of the screen), click the arrows on that applet to click through the available storage media. If Linux was installed on the first partition of the first hard disk, select hda1. Then click the mount button to mount that partition.

4. Open a Terminal window by right-clicking the desktop and selecting Terminal Session ⇨ Aterm - super user. A Terminal window opens.

5. Run the chkrootkit command and save the output to a file. For example, run the following command to check the file system mounted on /mnt/hda1 and send the output to a file named chkroot-output.txt:

```
# chkrootkit -r /mnt/hda1 > /tmp/chkroot-output.txt
```

6. When the command completes, page through the output. For example:

```
# less /tmp/chkroot-output.txt
ROOTDIR is '/mnt/hda1/'
Checking 'amd' ... not found
Checking 'basename' ... not infected
  .
  .
  .
```

7. Press the spacebar to page through the output. The output should reveal the following:

   - If a rootkit has been planted on your system, some commands will likely come up as infected.

   - If any files or directories implanted by commonly known rootkits are detected, those will be noted. The command checks for more than 60 known rootkits.

   - If any suspicious-looking files appear, they will be listed so you can check them (although they might not represent the presence of a rootkit).

If the search turns up a rootkit, chances are that someone else has control of your machine. Often the best course of action is to reinstall the system. You may be able to just replace those commands that have been infected, but if you do, you first want to make sure that multiple backdoors have not already been placed on your system.

Summary

Securing your Linux system is something you need to do from the very beginning and continue as you use your Linux system. By implementing good security practices (such as practices described in the security checklist at the beginning of this chapter), you stand a better chance of keeping out intruders over the long haul.

Going forward, you can help keep your Linux system secure by using encrypted network applications (such as ssh), monitoring log files, and adhering to good password techniques. If your Linux system is being used as a server, you need to take particular care in narrowing the access to the server and protecting data. To that end, you can use such tools as TCP wrappers (to limit who can use your server) and certificates (to ensure that both ends of communications with your web server are authenticated).

Creating Useful Shell Scripts

You'd never get any work done if you typed every command that needs to be run on your Linux system when it starts. Likewise, you could work more efficiently if you grouped together sets of commands that you run all the time. Shell scripts can handle these tasks.

A *shell script* is a group of commands, functions, variables, or just about anything else you can use from a shell. These items are typed into a plain-text file. That file can then be run as a command. Most Linux systems use system initialization shell scripts during system startup to run commands needed to get services going. You can create your own shell scripts to automate the tasks you need to do regularly.

This chapter provides a rudimentary overview of the inner workings of shell scripts and how they can be used. You learn how shell scripts are responsible for the messages that scroll by on the system console during booting and how simple scripts can be harnessed to a scheduling facility (such as cron or at) to simplify administrative tasks.

Understanding Shell Scripts

Have you ever had a task that you needed to do over and over that took a lot of typing on the command line? Do you ever think to yourself, "Wow, I wish there was just one command I could type to do all this of this"? Maybe a shell script is what you're after.

Shell scripts are the equivalent of batch files in MS-DOS, and can contain long lists of commands, complex flow control, arithmetic evaluations, user-defined variables, user-defined functions, and sophisticated condition testing. Shell scripts are capable of handling everything from simple one-line commands to something as complex as starting up your Linux system.

In fact, as you will read in this chapter, Linux systems do just that. They use shell scripts to check and mount all your file systems, set up your consoles, configure your network, launch all your system services, and eventually provide you with your login screen. While there are dozens of different shells available in Linux, the default shell is called bash, the Bourne Again Shell.

Executing and Debugging Shell Scripts

One of the primary advantages of shell scripts is that they can be opened in any text editor to see what they do. A big disadvantage is that large or complex shell scripts often execute more slowly than compiled programs. There are two basic ways to execute a shell script:

- The filename is used as an argument to the shell (as in `bash myscript`). In this method, the file does not need to be executable; it just contains a list of shell commands. The shell specified on the command line is used to interpret the commands in the script file. This is most common for quick, simple tasks.

- The shell script may also have the name of the interpreter placed in the first line of the script preceded by #! (as in `#!/bin/bash`), and have its execute bit set (using `chmod +x`). You can then run your script just like any other program in your path simply by typing the name of the script on the command line.

When scripts are executed in either manner, options for the program may be specified on the command line. Anything following the name of the script is referred to as a *command-line argument*.

As with writing any software, there is no substitute for clear and thoughtful design and lots of comments. The pound sign (#) prefaces comments and can take up an entire line or exist on the same line after script code. It's best to implement more complex shell scripts in stages, making sure the logic is sound at each step before continuing. Here are a few good, concise tips to make sure things are working as expected during testing:

- In some cases, you can place an `echo` statement at the beginning of lines within the body of a loop and surround the command with quotes. That way, rather than executing the code, you can see what will be executed without making any permanent changes.

- To achieve the same goal, you could place dummy `echo` statements throughout the code. If these lines get printed, you know the correct logic branch is being taken.

- You could use `set -x` near the beginning of the script to display each command that is executed or launch your scripts using

```
bash -x myscript
```

- Because useful scripts have a tendency to grow over time, keeping your code readable as you go along is extremely important. Do what you can to keep the logic of your code clean and easy to follow.

Understanding Shell Variables

Often within a shell script, you want to reuse certain items of information. During the course of processing the shell script, the name or number representing this information may change. To store information used by a shell script in such a way that it can be easily reused, you can set variables. Variable names within shell scripts are case-sensitive and can be defined in the following manner:

```
NAME=value
```

The first part of a variable is the variable name, and the second part is the value set for that name. Be sure that the NAME and value touch the equal sign, without any spaces. Variables can be assigned from constants, such as text, numbers, and underscores. This is useful for initializing values or saving lots of typing for long constants. Here are examples where variables are set to a string of characters (CITY) and a numeric value (PI):

```
CITY="Springfield"
PI=3.14159265
```

Variables can contain the output of a command or command sequence. You can accomplish this by preceding the command with a dollar sign and open parenthesis, and following it with a closing parenthesis. For example, MYDATE=$(date) assigns the output from the date command to the MYDATE variable. Enclosing the command in backticks (`) can have the same effect.

Note

Keep in mind that characters such as dollar sign ($), backtick (`), asterisk (*), exclamation point (!), and others have special meaning to the shell, as you will see as you proceed through this chapter. To use one of those characters in an option to a command, and not have the shell use its special meaning, you need to precede that character with a backslash (\) or surround it in quotes. One place you will encounter this is in files created by Windows users that might include spaces, exclamation points, or other characters. In Linux, to properly interpret a file named my big! file!, **you either need to surround it in double quotes or type** my\ big\!\ file\!. ∎**

These are great ways to get information that can change from computer to computer or from day to day. The following example sets the output of the uname -n command to the MACHINE variable. Then I use parentheses to set NUM_FILES to the number of files in the current directory by piping (|) the output of the ls command to the word count command (wc -l).

```
MACHINE=`uname -n`
NUM_FILES=$(/bin/ls | wc -l)
```

Variables can also contain the value of other variables. This is useful when you have to preserve a value that will change so you can use it later in the script. Here, BALANCE is set to the value of the CurBalance variable.

```
BALANCE="$CurBalance"
```

Note

When assigning variables, use only the variable name (for example, BALANCE). When referenced, meaning you want the *value* of the variable, precede it with a dollar sign (as in $CurBalance). The result of the latter is that you get the value of the variable, and not the variable name itself. ∎

Special Shell Variables

There are special variables that the shell assigns for you. The most commonly used variables are called the *positional parameters* or command-line arguments and are referenced as $0, $1, $2, $3 ... $*n*. $0 is special and is assigned the name used to invoke your script; the others are assigned the values of the parameters passed on the command line. For instance, if the shell script named myscript were called as

```
myscript foo bar
```

the positional parameter $0 would be myscript, $1 would be foo, and $2 would be bar.

Another variable, $#, tells you how many parameters your script was given. In our example, $# would be 2. Another particularly useful special shell variable is $?, which receives the exit status of the last command executed. Typically, a value of 0 means everything is okay, and anything other than 0 indicates an error of some kind. For a complete list of special shell variables, refer to the bash man page.

Parameter Expansion in bash

As mentioned earlier, if you want the value of a variable, you precede it with a $ (for example, $CITY). This is really just shorthand for the notation ${CITY}; curly braces are used when the value of the parameter needs to be placed next to other text without a space. Bash has special rules that allow you to expand the value of a variable in different ways. Going into all the rules is probably overkill for a quick introduction to shell scripts, but Table 14-1 presents some common constructs that you're likely to see in bash scripts you find on your Linux system.

TABLE 14-1

Examples of bash Parameter Expansion

Construction	Meaning
${var:-value}	If variable is unset or empty, expand this to *value*.
${var#pattern}	Chop the shortest match for *pattern* from the front of *var*'s value.
${var##pattern}	Chop the longest match for *pattern* from the front of *var*'s value.
${var%pattern}	Chop the shortest match for *pattern* from the end of *var*'s value.
${var%%pattern}	Chop the longest match for *pattern* from the end of *var*'s value.

Try typing the following commands from a shell to test how parameter expansion works:

```
$ THIS="Example"
$ THIS=${THIS:-"Not Set"}
$ THAT=${THAT:-"Not Set"}
```

```
$ echo $THIS
Example
$ echo $THAT
Not Set
```

In the examples here, the THIS variable is initially set to the word Example. In the next two lines, the THIS and THAT variables are set to their current values or to Not Set, if they are not currently set. Notice that because I just set THIS to the string Example, when I echo the value of THIS it appears as Example. However, because THAT was not set, it appears as Not Set.

Note

For the rest of this section, I show how variables and commands may appear in a shell script. To try out any of those examples, however, you can simply type them into a shell, as shown in the previous example. ■

In the following example, MYFILENAME is set to /home/digby/myfile.txt. Next, the FILE variable is set to myfile.txt and DIR is set to /home/digby. In the NAME variable, the filename is cut down to simply myfile; then, in the EXTENSION variable, the file extension is set to txt. (To try these out, you can type them at a shell prompt as in the previous example, and then echo the value of each variable to see how it is set.)

```
MYFILENAME="/home/digby/myfile.txt"
FILE=${MYFILENAME##*/}          #FILE becomes "myfile.txt"
DIR=${MYFILENAME%/*}            #DIR becomes "/home/digby"
NAME=${FILE%.*}                 #NAME becomes "myfile"
EXTENSION=${FILE##*.}           #EXTENSION becomes "txt"
```

Performing Arithmetic in Shell Scripts

Bash uses *untyped* variables, meaning it normally treats variables as strings or text, but can change them on-the-fly if you want it to. Unless you tell it otherwise with declare, your variables are just a bunch of letters to bash. But when you start trying to do arithmetic with them, bash will convert them to integers if it can. This makes it possible to do some fairly complex arithmetic in bash.

Integer arithmetic can be performed using the built-in let command or through the external expr or bc commands. After setting the variable BIGNUM value to 1024, the three commands that follow would all store the value 64 in the RESULT variable. The last command gets a random number between 0 and 10 and echoes the results back to you.

```
BIGNUM=1024
let RESULT=$BIGNUM/16
RESULT=`expr $BIGNUM / 16`
RESULT=`echo "$BIGNUM / 16" | bc`
let foo=$RANDOM%10; echo $foo
```

Another way to incrementally grow a variable is using $(()) notation. Try typing the following:

```
$ I=0
$ echo The value of I after increment is $((++I))
$ echo The value of I before and after increment is $((I++)) and $I
```

Repeat either of those commands to continue to increment the value of $I.

Note

While most elements of shell scripts are relatively freeform (where white space, such as spaces or tabs, is insignificant), both let and expr are particular about spacing. The let command insists on no spaces between each operand and the mathematical operator, whereas the syntax of the expr command requires white space between each operand and its operator. In contrast to those, bc isn't picky about spaces, but can be trickier to use because it does floating-point arithmetic. ∎

To see a complete list of the kinds of arithmetic you can perform using the let command, type **help let** at the bash prompt.

Using Programming Constructs in Shell Scripts

One of the features that make shell scripts so powerful is that their implementation of looping and conditional execution constructs is similar to those found in more complex scripting and programming languages. You can use several different types of loops, depending on your needs.

The "if . . . then" Statements

The most commonly used programming construct is conditional execution, or the if statement. It is used to perform actions only under certain conditions. There are several variations, depending on whether you're testing one thing, or want to do one thing if a condition is true but another thing if a condition is false, or if you want to test several things one after the other.

The first if...then example tests if VARIABLE is set to the number 1. If it is, then the echo command is used to say that it is set to 1. The fi then indicates that the if statement is complete and processing can continue.

```
VARIABLE=1
if [ $VARIABLE -eq 1 ] ; then
echo "The variable is 1"
fi
```

Instead of using -eq, you can use the equal sign (=), as shown in the following example. The = works best for comparing string values, while -eq is often better for comparing numbers. Using the else statement, different words can be echoed if the criterion of the if statement isn't met ($STRING = "Friday"). Keep in mind that it's good practice to put strings in double quotes.

```
STRING="Friday"
if [ $STRING = "Friday" ] ; then
echo "WhooHoo.  Friday."
```

```
else
echo "Will Friday ever get here?"
fi
```

You can also reverse tests with an exclamation mark (!). In the following example, if STRING is not Monday, then "At least it's not Monday" is echoed.

```
STRING="FRIDAY"
if [ "$STRING" != "Monday" ] ; then
    echo "At least it's not Monday"
fi
```

In the following example, elif (which stands for "else if") is used to test for an additional condition (is filename a file or a directory).

```
filename="$HOME"

if [ -f "$filename" ] ; then
    echo "$filename is a regular file"
elif [ -d "$filename" ] ; then
    echo "$filename is a directory"
else
    echo "I have no idea what $filename is"
fi
```

As you can see from the preceding examples, the condition you are testing is placed between square brackets [ ]. When a test expression is evaluated, it will return either a value of 0, meaning that it is true, or a 1, meaning that it is false. Notice that the echo lines are indented. This is optional and done only to make the script more readable.

Table 14-2 lists the conditions that are testable and is quite a handy reference. (If you're in a hurry, you can type **help test** on the command line to get the same information.)

TABLE 14-2

Operators for Test Expressions

Operator	What Is Being Tested?
-a file	Does the file exist? (same as -e)
-b file	Is the file a special block device?
-c file	Is the file character special (for example, a character device)? Used to identify serial lines and terminal devices.
-d file	Is the file a directory?
-e file	Does the file exist? (same as -a)

continued

TABLE 14-2 *(continued)*

Operator	What Is Being Tested?
-f file	Does the file exist, and is it a regular file (for example, not a directory, socket, pipe, link, or device file)?
-g file	Does the file have the set-group-id bit set?
-h file	Is the file a symbolic link? (same as -L)
-k file	Does the file have the sticky bit set?
-L file	Is the file a symbolic link?
-n string	Is the length of the string greater than 0 bytes?
-O file	Do you own the file?
-p file	Is the file a named pipe?
-r file	Is the file readable by you?
-s file	Does the file exist, and is it larger than 0 bytes?
-S file	Does the file exist, and is it a socket?
-t fd	Is the file descriptor connected to a terminal?
-u file	Does the file have the set-user-id bit set?
-w file	Is the file writable by you?
-x file	Is the file executable by you?
-z string	Is the length of the string 0 (zero) bytes?
expr1 -a expr2	Are both the first expression and the second expression true?
expr1 -o expr2	Are either of the two expressions true?
file1 -nt file2	Is the first file newer than the second file (using the modification timestamp)?
file1 -ot file2	Is the first file older than the second file (using the modification timestamp)?
file1 -ef file2	Are the two files associated by a link (a hard link or a symbolic link)?
var1 = var2	Is the first variable equal to the second variable?
var1 -eq var2	Is the first variable equal to the second variable?
var1 -ge var2	Is the first variable greater than or equal to the second variable?

Operator	What Is Being Tested?
var1 -gt var2	Is the first variable greater than the second variable?
var1 -le var2	Is the first variable less than or equal to the second variable?
var1 -lt var2	Is the first variable less than the second variable?
var1 != var2	Is the first variable not equal to the second variable?
var1 -ne var2	Is the first variable not equal to the second variable?

There is also a special shorthand method of performing tests that can be useful for simple *one-command* actions. In the following example, the two pipes (||) indicate that if the directory being tested for doesn't exist (-d dirname), then make the directory (mkdir $dirname).

```
# [ test ] || {action}
# Perform simple single command {action} if test is false
dirname="/tmp/testdir"
[ -d "$dirname" ] || mkdir "$dirname"
```

Instead of pipes, you can use two ampersands to test if something is true. In the following example, a command is being tested to see if it includes at least three command-line arguments.

```
# [ test ] && {action}
# Perform simple single command {action} if test is true
[ $# -ge 3 ] && echo "There are at least 3 command line arguments."
```

You can combine the && and || operators to make a quick, one-line if-then-else statement. The following example tests that the directory represented by $dirname already exists. If it does, a message says the directory already exists. If it doesn't, the statement creates the directory:

```
# dirname=mydirectory
# [ -e $dirname ] && echo $dirname already exists || mkdir $dirname
```

The case Command

Another frequently used construct is the case command. Similar to a switch statement in programming languages, this can take the place of several nested if statements. A general form of the case statement is as follows:

```
case "VAR" in
    Result1)
        { body };;
    Result2)
        { body };;
    *)
        { body } ;;
esac
```

One use for the `case` command might be to help with your backups. The following case statement tests for the first three letters of the current day (`case ` `date +%a` ` in`). Then, depending on the day, a particular backup directory (`BACKUP`) and tape drive (`TAPE`) are set.

```
# Our VAR doesn't have to be a variable,
# it can be the output of a command as well
# Perform action based on day of week
case `date +%a` in
    "Mon")
            BACKUP=/home/myproject/data0
            TAPE=/dev/rft0
# Note the use of the double semi-colon to end each option
            ;;
# Note the use of the "|" to mean "or"
    "Tue" | "Thu")
            BACKUP=/home/myproject/data1
            TAPE=/dev/rft1
            ;;
    "Wed" | "Fri")
            BACKUP=/home/myproject/data2
            TAPE=/dev/rft2
            ;;
# Don't do backups on the weekend.
    *)

BACKUP="none"
            TAPE=/dev/null
            ;;
esac
```

The asterisk (*) is used as a catchall, similar to the `default` keyword in the C programming language. In this example, if none of the other entries are matched on the way down the loop, the asterisk is matched, and the value of `BACKUP` becomes `none`. Note the use of `esac`, or `case` spelled backwards, to end the case statement.

The "for . . . do" Loop

Loops are used to perform actions over and over again until a condition is met or until all data has been processed. One of the most commonly used loops is the `for...do` loop. It iterates through a list of values, executing the body of the loop for each element in the list. The syntax and a few examples are presented here:

```
for VAR in LIST
do
     { body }
done
```

The for loop assigns the values in LIST to VAR one at a time. Then for each value, the body in braces between do and done is executed. VAR can be any variable name, and LIST can be composed of pretty much any list of values or anything that generates a list.

```
for NUMBER in 0 1 2 3 4 5 6 7 8 9
do
    echo The number is $NUMBER
done

for FILE in `/bin/ls`
do
    echo $FILE
done
```

You can also write it this way, which is somewhat cleaner.

```
for NAME in John Paul Ringo George ; do
    echo $NAME is my favorite Beatle
done
```

Each element in the LIST is separated from the next by white space. This can cause trouble if you're not careful because some commands, such as ls -l, output multiple fields per line, each separated by white space. The string done ends the for statement.

If you're a die-hard C programmer, bash allows you to use C syntax to control your loops:

```
LIMIT=10
# Double parentheses, and no $ on LIMIT even though it's a variable!
for ((a=1; a <= LIMIT ; a++)) ; do
    echo "$a"
done
```

The "while . . . do" and "until . . . do" Loops

Two other possible looping constructs are the while...do loop and the until...do loop. The structure of each is presented here:

```
while condition     until condition
do                  do
    { body }            { body }
done                done
```

The while statement executes while the condition is true. The until statement executes until the condition is true — in other words, while the condition is false.

Here is an example of a while loop that will output the number 0123456789:

```
N=0
while [ $N -lt 10 ] ; do
```

```
        echo -n $N
        let N=$N+1
    done
```

Another way to output the number 0123456789 is to use an `until` loop as follows:

```
    N=0
    until [ $N -eq 10 ] ; do
        echo -n $N
        let N=$N+1
    done
```

Some Useful External Programs

Bash is great and has lots of built-in commands, but it usually needs some help to do anything really useful. Some of the most common useful programs you'll see used are `grep`, `cut`, `tr`, `awk`, and `sed`. As with all the best UNIX tools, most of these programs are designed to work with standard input and standard output, so you can easily use them with pipes and shell scripts.

The General Regular Expression Parser

The name *general regular expression parser* (grep) sounds intimidating, but `grep` is just a way to find patterns in files or text. Think of it as a useful search tool. Gaining expertise with regular expressions is quite a challenge, but many useful things can be accomplished with just the simplest forms.

For example, you can display a list of all regular user accounts by using `grep` to search for all lines that contain the text `/home` in the `/etc/passwd` file as follows:

```
    grep /home /etc/passwd
```

Or you could find all environment variables that begin with `HO` using the following command:

```
    env | grep ^HO
```

Note
The ^ in the preceding code is the actual caret character, ^, not what you'll commonly see for a backspace, ^H. Type ^, H, and O (the uppercase letter) to see what items start with the uppercase characters *HO*. ∎

To find a list of options to use with the `grep` command, type **man grep**.

Remove Sections of Lines of Text (cut)

The `cut` command can extract fields from a line of text or from files. It is very useful for parsing system configuration files into easy-to-digest chunks. You can specify the field separator you want to use and the fields you want, or you can break up a line based on bytes.

The following example lists all home directories of users on your system. Using an earlier example of the `grep` command, this line pipes a list of regular users from the `/etc/passwd` file and then displays the sixth field (-f6) as delimited by a colon (-d':'). The hyphen at the end tells cut to read from standard input (from the pipe).

```
grep /home /etc/passwd | cut -f6 -d':' -
```

Translate or Delete Characters (tr)

The tr command is a character-based translator that can be used to replace one character or set of characters with another or to remove a character from a line of text.

The following example translates all uppercase letters to lowercase letters and displays the words "mixed upper and lower case" as a result:

```
FOO="Mixed UPpEr aNd LoWeR cAsE"
echo $FOO | tr [A-Z] [a-z]
```

In the next example, the tr command is used on a list of filenames to rename any files in that list so that any tabs or spaces (as indicated by the [:blank:] option) contained in a filename are translated into underscores. Try running the following code in a test directory:

```
for file in * ; do
    f=`echo $file | tr [:blank:] [_]`
    [ "$file" = "$f" ] || mv -i -- "$file" "$f"
done
```

The Stream Editor (sed)

The sed command is a simple scriptable editor, and as such can perform only simple edits, such as removing lines that have text matching a certain pattern, replacing one pattern of characters with another, and other simple edits. To get a better idea of how sed scripts work, there's no substitute for the online documentation, but here are some examples of common uses.

You can use the sed command to essentially do what I did earlier with the grep example: search the /etc/passwd file for the word home. Here the sed command searches the entire /etc/passwd file, searches for the word home, and prints any line containing the word home.

```
sed -n '/home/p' /etc/passwd
```

In this example, sed searches the file somefile.txt and replaces every instance of the string Mac with Linux. Notice that the letter g is needed at the end of the substitution command to cause every occurrence of Mac on each line to be changed to Linux. (Otherwise, only the first instance of Mac on each line is changed.) The output is then sent to the fixed_file.txt file. The output from sed goes to stdout, so this command redirects the output to a file for safekeeping.

```
sed 's/Mac/Linux/g' somefile.txt > fixed_file.txt
```

You can get the same result using a pipe:

```
cat somefile.txt | sed 's/Mac/Linux/g' > fixed_file.txt
```

By searching for a pattern and replacing it with a null pattern, you delete the original pattern. This example searches the contents of the somefile.txt file and replaces extra blank spaces at the end of each line (s/ *$) with nothing (//). Results go to the fixed_file.txt file.

```
cat somefile.txt | sed 's/ *$//' > fixed_file.txt
```

Trying Some Simple Shell Scripts

Sometimes the simplest of scripts can be the most useful. If you type the same sequence of commands repetitively, it makes sense to store those commands (once!) in a file. Here are a couple of simple, but useful, shell scripts.

A Simple Telephone List

This idea has been handed down from generation to generation of old UNIX hacks. It's really quite simple, but it employs several of the concepts just introduced.

```
#!/bin/bash
# (@)/ph
# A very simple telephone list
# Type "ph new name number" to add to the list, or
# just type "ph name" to get a phone number

PHONELIST=~/.phonelist.txt

# If no command line parameters ($#), there
# is a problem, so ask what they're talking about.
if [ $# -lt 1 ] ; then
    echo "Whose phone number did you want? "
    exit 1
fi

# Did you want to add a new phone number?
if [ $1 = "new" ] ; then
    shift
    echo $* >> $PHONELIST
    echo $* added to database
    exit 0
fi

# Nope. But does the file have anything in it yet?
# This might be our first time using it, after all.
if [ ! -s $PHONELIST ] ; then
    echo "No names in the phone list yet! "
    exit 1
else
    grep -i -q "$*" $PHONELIST       # Quietly search the file
    if [ $? -ne 0 ] ; then          # Did we find anything?
```

```
            echo "Sorry, that name was not found in the phone list"
            exit 1
        else
            grep -i "$*" $PHONELIST
        fi
    fi
exit 0
```

So, if you created the file ph in your current directory, you could type the following from the shell to try out your ph script:

```
$ chmod 755 ph
$ ./ph new "Mary Jones" 608-555-1212
Mary Jones 608-555-1212 added to database
$ ./ph Mary
Mary Jones 608-555-1212
```

The chmod command makes the ph script executable. The ./ph command runs the ph command from the current directory with the new option. This adds Mary Jones as the name and 608-555-1212 as the phone number to the database ($HOME/.phone.txt). The next ph command searches the database for the name Mary and displays the phone entry for Mary. If the script works, add it to a directory in your PATH (such as $HOME/bin).

A Simple Backup Script

Because nothing works forever and mistakes happen, backups are just a fact of life when dealing with computer data. This simple script backs up all the data in the home directories of all the users on your Fedora or RHEL system.

```
#!/bin/bash
# (@)/my_backup
# A very simple backup script
#

# Change the TAPE device to match your system.
# Check /var/log/messages to determine your tape device.
# You may also need to add scsi-tape support to your kernel.
TAPE=/dev/rft0

# Rewind the tape device $TAPE
mt $TAPE rew
# Get a list of home directories
HOMES=`grep /home /etc/passwd | cut -f6 -d': '`
# Backup the data in those directories
tar cvf $TAPE $HOMES
# Rewind and eject the tape.
mt $TAPE rewoffl
```

Summary

Writing shell scripts gives you the opportunity to automate many of your most common system administration tasks. This chapter covered common commands and functions you can use in scripting with the bash shell. It also provided some concrete examples of scripts for doing backups and other procedures.

Part IV

Setting Up Linux Servers

## 15

Running a Linux Web Server

With the growing availability of broadband Internet connections and a popular desire to run personal web sites and weblogs (blogs), an increasing number of people are setting up web application servers on their home Internet connections. Web applications are also finding more popularity in business environments because web applications reduce the number of programs that need to be maintained on workstations.

One popular variety of web application server is known as a *LAMP server* because it brings together Linux, Apache, MySQL, and PHP. LAMP servers combine components from several open source projects to form a fast, reliable, and economical platform for other readily available applications.

This chapter helps you install and configure your own LAMP server. It begins with an introduction to the various components, guides you through the installation and configuration, and finishes with the installation of a sample web application.

The examples in this chapter are based on a system running Ubuntu but conceptually should work on other distributions, if you take into account that other Linux systems use different ways to install the software and start and stop services. Descriptions of how to set up web server configuration files, however, should work across multiple Linux distributions with only slight modifications. You can find more information about Ubuntu in Chapter 19.

Components of a Web Server (Apache, MySQL, and PHP)

You're probably familiar with Linux by this point, so this section focuses on the other three components — Apache, MySQL, and PHP — and the functions they serve within a LAMP system. (Sometimes the "P" in LAMP is used to indicate that the Perl or Python scripting language is used for the applications running on a LAMP server.)

Apache

Within a LAMP server, Apache HTTPD (also known as the Apache HTTPD Server) provides the service with which the client web browsers communicate. The daemon runs in the background on your server and waits for requests from clients. web browsers connect to the HTTP daemon and send requests, which the daemon interprets, sending back the appropriate data.

Apache HTTPD includes an interface that allows modules to tie into the process to handle specific portions of a request. Among other things, modules are available to handle the processing of scripting languages such as Perl or PHP within web documents and to add encryption to connections between clients and the server.

Apache began as a collection of patches and improvements from the National Center for Supercomputing Applications (NCSA), University of Illinois, Urbana-Champaign, to the HTTP daemon. The NCSA HTTP daemon was the most popular HTTP server at the time, but had started to show its age after its author, Rob McCool, left NCSA in mid-1994.

Note
Another project that came from NCSA is Mosaic. Most modern web browsers can trace their origins to Mosaic. ■

In early 1995, a group of developers formed the Apache Group and began making extensive modifications to the NCSA HTTPD code base. Apache soon replaced NCSA HTTPD as the most popular web server, a title it still holds today.

The Apache Group later formed the Apache Software Foundation (ASF) to promote the development of Apache and other free software. With the start of new projects at ASF, the Apache server became known as Apache HTTPD, although the two terms are still used interchangeably. Currently, ASF has more than 60 projects, including Jakarta (open source Java solutions), MyFaces (a web application framework), and SpamAssassin (an e-mail filtering program).

MySQL

MySQL is an open source DBMS (database management system) that has become popular among webmasters because of its speed, stability, and features. MySQL consists of a server that handles storage and access to data, and clients to handle interfacing with and managing the server. Client libraries are also included, and they can be used by third-party programs, such as PHP, to connect to the server.

In a LAMP server, MySQL is used for storing data appropriate to the web applications that are being used. Common uses include data such as usernames and passwords, entries in a journal, and data files.

Note

If you are not sure how a database works, refer to the sidebar "How MySQL Databases Are Structured" later in this chapter. In enterprise computing environments, Oracle database products are often used in place of MySQL. ■

MySQL was originally developed by Michael (Monty) Widenius of TcX (Sweden). In 1994, TcX needed a backend database for web applications and decided to use one supporting SQL, a standardized and widely recognized language for interacting with databases.

TcX investigated the free databases that were available at the time, plus some commercial databases, but could not find a system that supported the features it needed and could handle its large databases at the same time. Because it already had experience writing database programs, TcX decided that the best way to get what it wanted was to develop a new system that supported SQL.

In 1995, TcX released the source code for MySQL on the Internet. MySQL was not an open source program at that time (because of some of the restrictions in its license), but it still began to see widespread use. MySQL was later released under the GNU General Public License (GPL) and the company MySQL AB was formed to manage MySQL. In February 2008, Sun Microsystems acquired MySQL AB. After Oracle acquired Sun, it became owner of the MySQL project.

PHP

PHP is a programming language that was developed specifically for use in web scripts. It is preferred by many developers because it's designed to be embedded within HTML documents, making it simpler to manage web content and scripts within a single file.

PHP originated as a set of Perl scripts by Rasmus Lerdorf called *PHP/FI* (*Personal Home Page/ Forms Interpreter*). Over time, more features were implemented, and Rasmus rewrote PHP/FI in C.

In late 1997, Andi Gutmans and Zeev Suraski began working on a complete rewrite of PHP/FI. As the language evolved and more features were implemented, Gutmans and Suraski decided that it would be appropriate to rename the project to more accurately reflect these features. The name PHP Hypertext Preprocessor (PHP) was chosen, with Lerdorf's approval, to maintain familiarity for users of PHP/FI.

The core features of PHP are included within the PHP code itself, and additional features are implemented in the form of extensions. The latest stable version of PHP is 5.3.3, but several implementations still include the libapache-mod-php4 (PHP 4) package and PHP 6 is in development. Among the major changes offered in PHP 5 is enhanced security. This release improved the security features that have always been in PHP and fixed some possible holes. This made the language even more stable. You can find additional information about each release, and what it offers, at www.php.net/.

Setting Up Your Web Server

Before proceeding through the examples in this section, be sure that your Linux operating system is installed and configured. The specific instructions in this section were done on an Ubuntu system, using the version of Ubuntu included with this book's DVD. So go ahead and boot the DVD, select Ubuntu, and install Ubuntu to your hard disk.

The same procedure should work on other Debian-based systems with few or no differences. If you try this on a different Linux system, understand that such things as software packaging, the location of startup scripts and configuration files, and other features may be different.

When you install your Linux system, you typically choose whether to install a set of software packages that are appropriate for a workstation or a server. For the sake of simplicity, in this example, you set up a server on a system that has been configured using the layout and software packages intended for a workstation.

For a professional-quality web server, I recommend that you start with a basic server install and add on what you need from there. In fact, once you are comfortable working from the command line, you should seriously consider starting with a server install that doesn't even have the X Window System and other GUI components installed on it.

Note
Another option to using the Apache package that comes with Ubuntu is to use a LAMPP server. LAMPP is an all-in-one LAMP server with PERL support added. The XAMPP project (www.apachefriends.org/en/xampp.html**) is one implementation of a LAMPP server (which is available as a Windows server as well). XAMPP is a really good quick and dirty way to get a LAMPP server running. It is also good for testing pages on your desktop system before publishing when you have only one machine. ■**

Installing Apache

The next step toward a functioning LAMP server is to install the Apache HTTP server, which can be found in the apache package. Use APT to update your packages (you'll need an Internet connection), and then retrieve and install the apache2 package:

```
$ sudo apt-get update
$ sudo apt-get install apache2
```

The server should automatically start after the installation is finished, which means that you're now ready to install PHP.

Installing PHP

Now you're ready to install and test the PHP module in Apache. This is the most common method for installing PHP but introduces some security concerns on multiuser systems because all PHP scripts are run as the same user as the Apache daemon. Be sure to read the Security section of the PHP manual at http://php.net/manual/en/security.php before granting other users access to manipulate PHP files on your server.

The PHP Apache module is contained in the php5 package, which is installed using APT. The following lines download and install the Apache php5 module and the MySQL extensions, configure Apache to load the module automatically, and instruct Apache to reload its configuration:

```
$ sudo apt-get install libapache2-mod-php5 php5-mysql php5-gd
$ sudo /etc/init.d/apache2 restart
```

Note

Just as the numbering and versions of Apache can sometimes be confusing, PHP presents similar challenges. As of this writing, there are active development versions in both 5.*x* and 4.4.*x* (and PHP 6 is under development). ■

At this point, Apache should be ready to process HTTP requests, complete with processing of PHP files. To test it, create a file named /var/www/info.php containing a call to the phpinfo() function:

```
$ sudo su -
# cat > /var/www/info.php
<?php
    phpinfo();
?>
^D
# chmod 644 /var/www/info.php
```

The ^D means that you should press Ctrl+D on your keyboard. This tells the cat command that you are at the end of the input. Now try opening the page by going to http://localhost/info.php. You should see a page full of information about your Apache and PHP installation, as shown in Figure 15-1.

FIGURE 15-1

The PHP information page

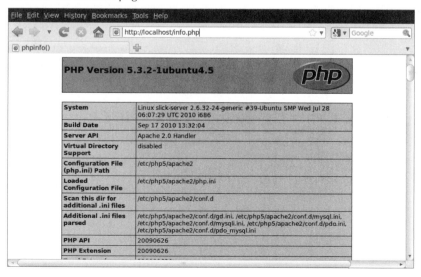

If, instead of an information page, you are prompted to download the file, check the appropriate PHP installation section (earlier in the chapter) to verify that all the steps were completed successfully.

After everything is tested and working, you should remove the `info.php` file so that it can't be used by potential attackers to gather specifics about your system:

```
$ sudo rm -f /var/www/info.php
```

Installing MySQL

The MySQL database system is divided into three main packages: the server, clients, and client libraries. The server is contained within the mysql-server package and requires the other two to function. APT is aware of this, which means the packages will be installed automatically when you install mysql-server:

```
$ sudo apt-get install mysql-server
```

Access to databases within MySQL is managed based on account information stored within the mysql database. As with UNIX systems, the superuser account is named `root`. The default installation asks you to set a password on this account. If you don't set it at this point, you can always set it later.

How MySQL Databases Are Structured

For those who aren't familiar with how a database system is structured, here's a quick introduction:

- Databases are the basic organizational block in a database system. Most database systems (including MySQL) are designed to support multiple databases from a single server. This allows separate databases to be created for different users or different functions.

- Tables are found within a database. A table is very much like a spreadsheet in that it has rows and columns. Columns define the different types of data that every entry can or must have, and every entry takes the form of a row. A database can hold multiple tables, allowing you to have many different data sets within a single database.

Operating Your Web Server

With the components of your web server installed and running, you are ready to configure Apache and try it out. For this example, Apache is set up to serve content for your own domain using a feature called *virtual hosting*, after which you'll see how to install the Coppermine Photo Gallery program, which enables you to create an online photo gallery on your LAMP server.

Editing Your Apache Configuration Files

The configuration files for Apache HTTPD are incredibly flexible, meaning that you can configure the server to behave in almost any manner you want. This flexibility comes at the cost of increased complexity in the form of a large number of configuration options (called *directives*), but in practice you'll need to be familiar with only a few directives.

Note

See `http://httpd.apache.org/docs/` **for a complete list of directives supported by Apache.** ■

In Ubuntu, the Apache configuration is stored in text files read by the Apache server, beginning with `/etc/apache2/apache2.conf`. Configuration is read from start to finish, with most directives being processed in the order in which they are read.

Additional files may also be read based on the `AccessConfig`, `ResourceConfig`, and `Include` directives. On modern installations, the `AccessConfig` and `ResourceConfig` options point to empty files, and the traditional contents of those files have been moved to the main `apache2.conf` file.

The `Include` directive is distinct from `AccessConfig` and `ResourceConfig` in that it can appear more than once and can include more than one file at a time. Files referenced by `Include` directives are processed as if their contents appeared at the location of the relevant `Include` statement. `Include` can point to a single file, to a directory in which all files are read, or to a wildcard that specifies a specific set of files within a directory. For example, virtual host files are included in `apache2.conf` by this line:

```
Include /etc/apache2/sites-enabled/
```

Note

Subdirectories are also processed when `Include` **points to a directory.** ■

The scope of many configuration directives can be altered based on context. In other words, some parameters may be set on a global level and then changed for a specific file, directory, or virtual host. Other directives are always global in nature, such as those specifying which IP addresses the server listens on, and some are valid only when applied to a specific location.

Locations are configured in the form of a start tag containing the location type and a resource location, followed by the configuration options for that location, and finishing with an end tag. This form is often called a *configuration block*, and looks very similar to HTML. A special type of configuration block, known as a *location block,* is used to override settings for specific files or directories. These blocks take the following form:

```
<locationtag specifier>
(options specific to objects matching the specifier go within this block)
</locationtag>
```

Different types of location tags exist and are selected based on the type of resource location that is being specified. The specifier that is included in the start tag is handled based on the type of location tag. The ones you generally use and encounter are `Directory`, `Files`, and `Location`.

Note

In this chapter, `Location` **refers specifically to the third type of tag, and** *location* **refers generically to any of the three.** ■

- `Directory` tags are used to specify a path based on the location on the file system. For instance, `<Directory />` refers to the root directory on the computer. Directories inherit settings from directories above them, with the most specific `Directory` block overriding less specific ones, regardless of the order in which they appear in the configuration files.

- `Files` tags are used to specify files by name. `Files` tags can be contained within `Directory` blocks to limit them to files under that directory. Settings within a `Files` block will override the ones in `Directory` blocks.

- `Location` tags are used to specify the URI used to access a file or directory. This is different from `Directory` in that it relates to the address contained within the request and not to the real location of the file on the drive. `Location` tags are processed last and override the settings in `Directory` and `Files` blocks.

Match versions of these tags — `DirectoryMatch`, `FilesMatch`, and `LocationMatch` — have the same function but can contain regular expressions in the resource specification. `FilesMatch` and `LocationMatch` blocks are processed at the same time as `Files` and `Location`, respectively. `DirectoryMatch` blocks are processed after `Directory` blocks.

Apache can also be configured to process configuration options contained within files with the name specified in the `AccessFileName` directive (which is generally set to `.htaccess`). Directives in access configuration files are applied to all objects under the directory they contain, including subdirectories and their contents. Access configuration files are processed at the same time as `Directory` blocks, using a similar "most specific match" order.

Note

Access control files are useful for allowing users to change specific settings without having access to the server configuration files. The configuration directives permitted within an access configuration file are determined by the `AllowOverride` **setting on the directory in which they are contained. Some directives do not make sense at that level and generally result in a "server internal error" message when trying to access the URI. The** `AllowOverride` **option is covered in detail at** `http://httpd.apache.org/docs/mod/core.html#allowoverride`. ■

Three directives commonly found in location blocks and access control files are `DirectoryIndex`, `Options`, and `ErrorDocument`:

- `DirectoryIndex` tells Apache which file to load when the URI contains a directory but not a filename. This directive doesn't work in `Files` blocks.

- `Options` is used to adjust how Apache handles files within a directory. The `ExecCGI` option tells Apache that files in that directory can be run as CGI scripts, and the `Includes` option tells Apache that server-side includes (SSI) are permitted. Also commonly used is the `Indexes` option, which tells Apache to generate a list of files if one of the filenames found in the DirectoryIndex setting is missing. An absolute list of options can be specified, or the list of options can be modified by adding + or - in front of an option name. See `http://httpd.apache.org/docs/mod/core.html#options` for more information.

- ErrorDocument directives can be used to specify which file to send in the result of an error. The directive must specify an error code and the full URI for the error document. Possible error codes include 403 (access denied), 404 (file not found), and 500 (server internal error). You can find more information about the ErrorDocument directive at `http://httpd.apache.org/docs/mod/core.html#errordocument`.

Another common use for location blocks and access control files is to limit access to a resource. The Allow directive can be used to permit access to matching hosts, and the Deny directive can be used to forbid it. Both of these options can occur more than once within a block and are handled based on the Order setting. Setting Order to Deny,Allow permits access to any host that is not listed in a Deny directive. A setting of Allow,Deny denies access to any host not allowed in an Allow directive.

As with most other options, the most specific Allow or Deny option for a host is used, meaning that you can Deny access to a range and Allow access to subsets of that range. By adding the Satisfy option and some additional parameters, you can add password authentication. For more information about access control, see `http://httpd.apache.org/docs/mod/mod_access.html`.

Location blocks (in the generic sense) can be enclosed within a VirtualHost block. Virtual hosts, which are described in greater detail in the next section, are a convenient (and almost essential) tool for altering server behavior based on the server address or name that a request is directed to. Most global configuration options are applied to virtual hosts but can be overridden by directives within the VirtualHost block.

Adding a Virtual Host to Apache

Apache supports the creation of separate web sites within a single server to keep content separate. Individual sites are configured on the same server in the form of virtual hosts, which also are useful when only a single site will be used. Here's how to configure a virtual host:

1. Create a file named /etc/apache2/sites-available/example.org.conf using this template:

```
NameVirtualHost *:80
<VirtualHost *:80>
    ServerName      www.example.org
    ServerAlias     web.example.org
    DocumentRoot    /home/username/public_html/
DirectoryIndex  index.php index.html index.htm
</VirtualHost>
```

This example includes the following settings:

- The `NameVirtualHost` line tells Apache to determine which virtual host to serve documents from based on the hostname provided by the HTTP client. The `*:80` means that requests to port 80 on any IP address will be treated in this manner.

- Similarly, the `*:80` specification in the `VirtualHost` block indicates what address and port this virtual host applies to. The port is optional for both the `NameVirtualHost` and `VirtualHost` specifications but should always be used to prevent interference with SSL virtual hosts.

- The `ServerName` and `ServerAlias` lines tell Apache which names this virtual host should be recognized as, so replace them with names appropriate to your site. You can leave out the `ServerAlias` line if you do not have any alternate names for the server, and you can specify more than one name per `ServerAlias` line or have multiple `ServerAlias` lines if you have several alternate names.

- The `DocumentRoot` specifies where the web documents for this site are stored. If you plan to have more than one site per user, you will need to modify this layout appropriately. Replace *username* with the name of the account that is administrating the web site. For this example, each web site must be administered by a different user account.

2. Having your virtual host file in the `sites-available` directory does not enable it. For it to be enabled, you must create a link to that file from the `/etc/apache2/sites-enabled` directory. In Ubuntu (and other Debian-based systems), you can use the `a2ensite` command as follows:

```
$ sudo a2ensite example.org.conf
Site example.org.conf installed; run /etc/init.d/apache2 reload to enable
```

3. With the host enabled, use `apache2ctl` to check the configuration, and then do a `graceful` restart:

```
$ sudo apache2ctl configtest
Syntax OK
$ sudo apache2ctl graceful
```

Note

Unless you have already created it, you will receive a warning about `public_html` **not existing. Run** `mkdir ~/public_html` **as the user that owns the web site in order to create it.** ■

Additional virtual hosts can be added by repeating the `VirtualHost` block and repeating the configuration test (`configtest`) and reload (`graceful`) steps.

Note

Keeping individual virtual hosts in separate files is a convenient way to manage virtual hosts. However, you should be careful to keep your primary virtual host in a file that will be read before the others because the first virtual host receives requests for site names that don't match any in your configuration. In a commercial web-hosting environment, it is common to make a special default virtual host that contains an error message indicating that no site by that name has been configured. ■

User Content and the UserDir Setting

In situations in which you do not have the ability to set up a virtual host for every user that you want to provide web space for, you can easily make use of the mod_userdir module in Apache. With this module enabled (which it is not by default), the public_html directory under every user's home directory is available to the web at http://servername/~username/. For example, a user named wtucker on www.example.org stores web content in /home/wtucker/public_html. That content would be available from http://www.example.org/~wtucker.

To enable the mod_userdir module, as well as other installed modules that are not enabled by default, you need to create links from the appropriate .load and .conf files in the /etc/apache2/mods-available directory to the mods-enabled directory. In Ubuntu, you can do this with the a2enmod command and restart the server as follows:

```
$ sudo a2enmod userdir
Module userdir installed; run /etc/init.d/apache2 force-reload to enable.
$ sudo apache2ctl graceful
```

Installing a Web Application: Coppermine Photo Gallery

After your web server is operational, you can begin installing or creating applications to run on it. One such application is Coppermine Photo Gallery (CPG), the installation of which is demonstrated in this section. CPG is a web-based photo gallery management system written in PHP. Through its web interface, you can upload pictures to your own photo galleries, which will be available on the web through your web server.

You can install CPG under a virtual host or under a user's home directory on your main host. A single server can easily support many CPG installations using either of these methods.

To install CPG on the Ubuntu system described in this chapter, follow these steps:

1. Install the unzip and imagemagick programs. Unzip is used to unpack the CPG program after downloading, and imagemagick is used to resize images and create thumbnails:

   ```
   $ sudo apt-get install unzip imagemagick
   ```

2. Create a MySQL database for CPG. You can use a database name other than cpg if you want. The database username (the part before the @'localhost' in the GRANT statement) and the database name do not need to match. Be sure to replace *mypassword* with something different:

   ```
   $ sudo mysql -u root -p
   Enter password:
   Welcome to the MySQL monitor.  Commands end with ; or \g.
   ```

```
Your MySQL connection id is 8
Server version: 5.0.41a-3ubuntu5.1 (Ubuntu)

Type 'help;' or '\h' for help.  Type '\c' to clear the
buffer.

mysql> CREATE DATABASE cpg;
Query OK, 1 row affected (0.00 sec)

mysql> GRANT ALL PRIVILEGES ON cpg.*
TO 'cpg'@'localhost' IDENTIFIED BY 'mypassword';
Query OK, 0 rows affected (0.00 sec)

mysql> \q
Bye
```

3. Open Firefox (or other web browser), select to download Coppermine from the following site, and save it to the /tmp directory:

   http://sourceforge.net/projects/coppermine

4. You can move the Coppermine zip file from the /tmp directory, and unpack it:

```
$ sudo su -
# cp /tmp/cpg1.5.8.zip /var/www
# cd /var/www
# unzip cpg1.5.8.zip
Archive:  cpg1.5.8.zip
  inflating: cpg15x/addfav.php
  inflating: cpg15x/addpic.php
[...]
  inflating: cpg15x/zipdownload.php
```

5. Rename the freshly unpacked cpg directory, and then set the permissions so that files can be uploaded from PHP:

```
# mv cpg15x photos
# cd photos
# chmod 777 include
# find albums -type d | xargs chmod 777
```

6. Go to a web browser on any machine that can reach your web server over the network and open the install.php script under your coppermine directory.

   If you're installing CPG under a user directory under your main host, the URL is http://servername/~username/photos/install.php.

   If you're installing CPG under a virtual host, the URL is http://virtualhostname/photos/install.php.

7. Click to view the classic install screen. Configure CPG to work with your installation by filling in the following fields and selecting Let's Go!:

- **Username and Password** — The administrative login and password that you will use to administer CPG

- **Email Address** — The administrator's (your) e-mail address

- **MySQL Host** — The server name that CGP will connect to for the database. In this case, you want to use localhost.

- **MySQL Database Name** — The name of the database that you created in Step 2. (In the example, I used cpg.)

- **MySQL Username and Password** — The username and password that you created in Step 2 for accessing the database. (In the example, I used cpg and mypassword, respectively.)

- **MySQL table prefix** — The prefix for the tables that will be used by CPG. The default value (cpg15x_) is fine.

- **ImageMagick path** — The directory containing the imagemagick binary. On Debian systems, this is /usr/bin.

8. You're now done installing CPG. At this point you can click Let's Continue to see the default Coppermine Photo Gallery page. You can use this CPG web interface to create photo galleries and upload photos. Figure 15-2 shows a sample gallery.

FIGURE 15-2

A sample Coppermine photo gallery

Although a complete description of the dozens of features of the Coppermine Photo Gallery is beyond the scope of this example, here are a few tips if you want to continue setting up a working photo gallery. To begin, go to the home page of the photo gallery you just created (`http://localhost/photos`) and log in with the administrative user and password you created. Then do the following:

- **Add an album** — Click the Albums button and then click New. Type a name for the album and select Apply modifications. Then select Continue as instructed.
- **Upload files** — Click the Upload file link at the top of the page. From the Upload file page, add either the full paths to file names (File Uploads) or web addresses (URI/URL Uploads) of the images you want to install. Then click Continue. If the uploads were successful, click Continue again.

  At this point, you can add information to be associated with each image you just uploaded. Select the Album each will go into, a file title, and a description, and then click Continue. After you have added information for all your uploaded images, click Continue again to return to the main photo gallery. There you can see your images sorted by album, as random files, or by latest additions.

If you installed Coppermine on a public server, you can give the web address of that server to your friends and family and they can begin viewing your photo albums. You can do a lot to customize your Coppermine Photo Gallery. You can begin by going through the settings on the Configuration page (click the Config link to get there). Click the Users or Groups links to create user or group accounts that give special access to upload or modify the content of your gallery.

Troubleshooting Your Web Server

In any complex environment, you occasionally run into problems. This section includes tips for isolating and resolving the most common errors that you may encounter.

Note

This section refers to the Apache HTTPD binary as `apache2`, which is what it is named on Ubuntu and other Debian-based systems. However, in many other distributions, the binary is named `httpd`. On different systems, you may need to substitute *httpd* for *apache* when it appears by itself, although not for commands such as `apache2ctl`. ■

Configuration Errors

You may occasionally run into configuration errors or script problems that prevent Apache from starting or that prevent specific files from being accessible. Most of these problems can be isolated and resolved using two Apache-provided tools: the `apache2ctl` program and the system error log.

When encountering a problem, first use the apache2ctl program with the configtest parameter to test the configuration. In fact, it's a good idea to develop the habit of running this every time you make a configuration change:

```
# apache2ctl configtest
Syntax OK
# apache2ctl graceful
/usr/sbin/apache2ctl graceful: httpd gracefully restarted
```

In the event of a syntax error, apache2ctl indicates where the error occurs and also does its best to give a hint about the nature of the problem. You can then use the graceful restart option (apache2ctl graceful) to instruct Apache to reload its configuration without disconnecting any active clients.

Note

The graceful **restart option in** apache2ctl **automatically tests the configuration before sending the reload signal to** apache**, but getting in the habit of running the manual configuration test after making any configuration changes is still a good idea.** ∎

Some configuration problems pass the syntax tests performed by apache2ctl but then result in the HTTP daemon exiting immediately after reloading its configuration. If this happens, use the tail command to check Apache's error log for useful information. On Debian systems, the error log is in /var/log/apache2/error.log. On other systems, the location can be found by looking for the ErrorLog directive in your Apache configuration.

An error message that you might encounter looks something like this:

```
[crit] (98)Address already in use: make_sock: could not bind to port 80
```

This error often indicates that something else is bound to port 80 (not very common unless you have attempted to install another web server), that another Apache process is already running (apache2ctl usually catches this), or that you have told Apache to bind the same IP address and port combination in more than one place.

You can use the netstat command to view the list of programs (including Apache) with TCP ports in the LISTEN state:

```
# netstat -nltp
Active Internet connections (only servers)
Proto  Local Address  Foreign Address  State   PID/Program name
tcp    0.0.0.0:80     0.0.0.0:*        LISTEN  2105/apache2
```

The output from netstat (which was shortened to fit here) indicates that an instance of the apache2 process with a process ID of 2105 is listening (as indicated by the LISTEN state) for connections to any local IP address (indicated by 0.0.0.0) on port 80 (the standard HTTP port). If a different program is listening to port 80, it is shown there. You can use the kill command to terminate the process, but if it is something other than apache2 (or httpd), you should also find out why it is running.

If you don't see any other processes listening on port 80, it could be that you have accidentally told Apache to listen on the same IP address and port combination in more than one place. Three configuration directives can be used for this: BindAddress, Port, and Listen:

- BindAddress — Enables you to specify a single IP address to listen on, or you can specify all IP addresses using the * wildcard. You should never have more than one BindAddress statement in your configuration file.

- Port — Specifies which TCP port to listen on but does not enable you to specify the IP address. Port is generally not used more than once in the configuration.

- Listen — Enables you to specify both an IP address and a port to bind to. The IP address can be in the form of a wildcard, and you can have multiple Listen statements in your configuration file.

Generally, using only one type of these directives is a good idea to avoid confusion. Of the three, Listen is the most flexible, so it is probably the one you want to use the most. A common error when using Listen is to specify a port on all IP addresses (*:80) as well as that same port on a specific IP address (1.2.3.4:80), which results in the error from make_sock.

Configuration errors relating to SSL (discussed later in this chapter) commonly result in Apache starting improperly. Make sure all key and certificate files exist and that they are in the proper format (use openssl to examine them, as shown later in this chapter).

For other error messages, try doing a web search to see whether somebody else has encountered the problem. In most cases, you can find a solution within the first few matches.

If you aren't getting enough information in the ErrorLog, you can configure it to log more information using the LogLevel directive. The options available for this directive, in increasing order of verbosity, are emerg, alert, crit, error, warn, notice, info, and debug. Select only one of these. Any message that is at least as important as the LogLevel you select will be stored in the ErrorLog. On a typical server, this is set to warn. You should not set it to any value lower than crit and should avoid leaving it set to debug because that can slow down the server and result in a very large ErrorLog.

As a last resort, you can also try running apache2 manually to check for crashes or other error messages:

```
# /usr/sbin/apache2 -d /etc/apache2 -F ; echo $?
```

The -d flag tells apache where to look for its configuration file, and the -F flag tells it to run in the foreground. The semicolon separates this command from the echo command, which displays the return code ($?) from Apache after it exits. In the event that apache crashes during this step, you can use tools such as gdb and strace to trace the problem.

Access Forbidden and Server Internal Errors

Two common types of errors that you may encounter when attempting to view specific pages on your server are permission errors and server internal errors. Both types of errors can usually be isolated using the information in the error log. After making any of the changes described in the following list to attempt to solve one of these problems, try the request again and then check the error log to see whether the message has changed (for example, to show that the operation completed successfully).

Note
"File not found" errors can be checked in the same way as "access forbidden" and "server internal errors." You may sometimes find that Apache is not looking where you think it is for a specific file. Generally, the entire path to the file shows up in the error log. Make sure you are accessing the correct virtual host, and check for any `Alias` settings that might be directing your location to a place you don't expect. ∎

- **File permissions** — A "file permissions prevent access" error indicates that the `apache` process is running as a user that is unable to open the requested file. Make sure that the account has execute permissions on the directory and every directory above it, as well as read permissions on the files themselves. Read permissions on a directory are also necessary if you want Apache to generate an index of files. See the manual page for `chmod` for more information about how to view and change permissions.

Note
Read permissions are not necessary for compiled binaries, such as those written in C or C++, but can be safely added unless a need exists to keep the contents of the program secret. ∎

- **Access denied** — A "client denied by server configuration" error indicates that Apache was configured to deny access to the object. Check the configuration files for `<Location>` and `<Directory>` sections that might affect the file you are trying to access. Remember that settings applied to a path are also applied to any paths below it. You can override these by changing the permissions only for the more specific path to which you want to allow access.

- **Index not found** — The "Directory index forbidden by rule" error indicates that Apache could not find an index file with a name specified in the `DirectoryIndex` directive and was configured to not create an index containing a list of files in a directory. Make sure your index page, if you have one, has one of the names specified in the relevant `DirectoryIndex` directive, or add an `Options Indexes` line to the appropriate `<Directory>` or `<Location>` section for that object.

- **Script crashed** — "Premature end of script headers" errors can indicate that a script is crashing before it finishes. On occasion, the errors that caused this also show up in the error log. When using `suexec` or `suPHP`, this error may also be caused by a file ownership or permissions error. These errors are indicated in `/var/log/apache2/suexec.log` or `/var/log/apache2/suphp.log`.

Securing Your Web Traffic with SSL/TLS

You want to add security for your server, including your own certificates. Your data is important, and so is your capability to pass it along your network or the Internet to others. Networks just aren't secure enough by themselves to protect your communications. This section examines ways in which you can help guard your communications.

Electronic commerce applications such as online shopping and banking are generally encrypted using either the Secure Socket Layer (SSL) or Transport Layer Security (TLS) specifications. TLS is based on version 3.0 of the SSL specifications, so they are very similar in nature. Because of this similarity — and because SSL is older — the SSL acronym is often used to refer to either variety. For web connections, the SSL connection is established first, and then normal HTTP communication is "tunneled" through it.

Note

Because SSL negotiation takes place before any HTTP communication, name-based virtual hosting (which occurs at the HTTP layer) does not work easily with SSL. As a consequence, every SSL virtual host you configure should have a unique IP address. You can use some tricks to get name-based virtual hosting to work with SSL, but they are outside the scope of this procedure. (See the Apache site for more information: `httpd.apache.org/docs/vhosts/name-based.html`.) ∎

During connection establishment between an SSL client and an SSL server, asymmetric (public key) cryptography is used to verify identities and establish the session parameters and the session key. A symmetric encryption algorithm such as DES or RC4 is then used with the negotiated key to encrypt the data that are transmitted during the session. The use of asymmetric encryption during the handshaking phase allows safe communication without the use of a preshared key, and the symmetric encryption is faster and more practical for use on the session data.

For the client to verify the identity of the server, the server must have a previously generated private key, as well as a certificate containing the public key and information about the server. This certificate must be verifiable using a public key that is known to the client.

Certificates are generally digitally signed by a third-party certificate authority (CA) that has verified the identity of the requester and the validity of the request to have the certificate signed. In most cases, the CA is a company that has made arrangements with the web browser vendor to have its own certificate installed and trusted by default client installations. The CA then charges the server operator for its services.

Commercial certificate authorities vary in price, features, and browser support, but remember that price is not always an indication of quality. Some popular CAs include InstantSSL (`www.instantssl.com`), Thawte (`www.thawte.com`), and VeriSign (`www.verisign.com`).

You also have the option of creating self-signed certificates, although these should be used only for testing or when a very small number of people will be accessing your server and you do not plan to have certificates on multiple machines. Directions for generating a self-signed certificate are included in the following section.

The last option is to run your own certificate authority. This is probably practical only if you have a small number of expected users and the means to distribute your CA certificate to them (including assisting them with installing it in their browsers). The process for creating a CA is too elaborate to cover in this book but is a worthwhile alternative to generating self-signed certificates. You can find guides on running your own CA at `http://sial.org/howto/openssl/ca/`.

The following procedure describes how to generate and use SSL keys with the web server (running on an Ubuntu system) configured in this chapter.

Generating Your SSL Keys

To begin setting up SSL, use the `openssl` command, which is part of the OpenSSL package, to generate your public and private key:

1. Use APT to verify that OpenSSL is installed. If it is not present, APT downloads and installs it automatically:

```
$ sudo apt-get install openssl
```

2. Generate a 1024-bit RSA private key and save it to a file:

```
$ sudo su -
# mkdir /etc/apache2/ssl.key/
# cd /etc/apache2/ssl.key/
# openssl genrsa -out server.key 1024
# chmod 600 server.key
```

Note

You can use a filename other than `server.key` and should do so if you plan to have more than one SSL host on your machine (which requires more than one IP address). Just make sure you specify the correct filename in the Apache configuration later. ■

In higher-security environments, encrypting the key by adding the `-des3` argument after the `genrsa` argument on the `openssl` command line is a good idea:

```
# openssl genrsa -des3 -out server.key 1024
```

3. You are asked for a passphrase, which is needed every time you start Apache.

Caution

Do not lose this passphrase because it cannot be easily recovered. ■

4. If you plan to have your certificate signed by a CA (including one that you run yourself), generate a public key and a certificate signing request (CSR):

```
# mkdir ../ssl.csr/
# cd ../ssl.csr/
# openssl req -new -key ../ssl.key/server.key -out server.csr

Country Name (2 letter code) [AU]:US
State or Province Name (full name) [Some-State]:Washington
Locality Name (eg, city) []:Bellingham
Organization Name (eg, company) [Internet Widgits Pty
Ltd]:Example Company, LTD.
Organizational Unit Name (eg, section) []:Network
Operations
Common Name (eg, YOUR name) []:secure.example.org
Email Address []:dom@example.org
```

```
Please enter the following 'extra' attributes
to be sent with your certificate request
A challenge password []:
An optional company name []:
```

The Common Name should match the name that clients will use to access your server. Be sure to get the other details right if you plan to have the CSR signed by a third-party CA.

5. When using a third-party CA, submit the CSR to it and then place the certificate it provides you into /etc/apache2/ssl.crt/server.crt (or a different file, as desired).

6. If you don't plan to have your certificate signed, or if you want to test your configuration, generate a self-signed certificate and save it in a file named server.crt:

```
# mkdir ../ssl.crt/
# cd ../ssl.crt/
# openssl req -new -x509 -nodes -sha1 -days 365 -key \
../ssl.key/server.key -out server.crt
Country Name (2 letter code) [AU]: .
State or Province Name (full name) [Some-State]: .
Locality Name (eg, city) []: .
Organization Name (eg, company) [Internet Widgits Pty
Ltd]:TEST USE ONLY
Organizational Unit Name (eg, section) []:TEST USE ONLY
Common Name (eg, YOUR name) []:secure.example.org
Email Address []:dom@example.org
```

Configuring Apache to Support SSL/TLS

After your keys have been generated, you need to enable the mod_ssl Apache module, which adds SSL/TLS support to Apache, and then configure it using the appropriate configuration directives. The mod_ssl module is installed with the basic apache2.2-common package. Here's how to enable it for your virtual hosts:

1. Run the a2enmod command to enable SSL:

```
$ sudo a2enmod ssl
Module ssl installed; run /etc/init.d/apache2 force-reload to enable.
```

2. Add an SSL-enabled virtual host to your Apache configuration files. Using the earlier virtual host as an example, your configuration will look something like this:

```
Listen *:443
<VirtualHost *:443>
    ServerName      secure.example.org
    ServerAlias     web.example.org
    DocumentRoot    /home/username/public_html/
    DirectoryIndex  index.php index.html index.htm
```

```
SSLEngine        On
SSLCertificateKeyFile /etc/apache2/ssl.key/server.key
SSLCertificateFile /etc/apache2/ssl.crt/server.crt
SSLCACertificateFile /etc/apache2/ssl.crt/ca.crt
</VirtualHost>
```

This example uses a wildcard for the IP address in the VirtualHost declaration, which saves you from having to modify your configuration file in the event that your IP address changes but also prevents you from having multiple SSL virtual hosts. In the event that you do need to support more than one SSL virtual host, replace * with the specific IP address that you assign to that host.

Note

See the "Troubleshooting Your web Server" section earlier in the chapter for more information about the `Listen` **directive.** ∎

A CA generally provides you with a certificate file to place in `ca.crt` and sometimes also provides you with a separate file that you will need to reference using a `SSLCertificateChainFile` directive.

3. Test the Apache configuration and then perform a full restart:

```
$ sudo apache2ctl configtest
Syntax OK.
$ sudo apache2ctl stop
$ sudo apache2ctl start
```

4. Browse to `https://servername/` and verify the SSL configuration. When using a self-signed certificate, or one signed by a CA, you are asked whether you want to accept the certificate.

Summary

Combining Linux with an Apache web server, MySQL database, and PHP scripting content (referred to as a LAMP server) makes it possible for you to configure your own full-featured web server. The instructions in this chapter showed you how to set up Apache to do virtual hosting, add content to a MySQL database, and allow PHP scripting in the content on your server. For added security, this chapter described how to add your own certificates and troubleshoot problems that might arise with your server.

Running a Mail Server

## 16

Electronic mail hardly requires an introduction. Communications made through the original forms of e-mail helped shape the Internet. Widespread availability of access to e-mail and enhancements such as MIME (Multipurpose Internet Mail Extensions, which allow for inclusion of attachments and alternate message formats) have helped to make e-mail the most popular application on the Internet.

With a Linux system and a suitable Internet connection, you can easily set up your own mail server for personal or business use. This chapter includes a description of how Internet mail works at the protocol level, and then guides you through the process of setting up a mail server, complete with spam and virus filtering. In the final section, you learn how to secure network communications between clients and your mail server through the use of SSL/TLS (Secure Sockets Layer and Transport Layer Security) protocols.

The examples in this chapter are based on an Ubuntu system. (See Chapter 19 for more information about Ubuntu.) However, much of the knowledge you gain from setting up a mail server in Ubuntu applies to other Linux systems as well.

IN THIS CHAPTER

Internet e-mail's inner workings

Understanding mail server software

Preparing your system

Installing and configuring the mail server software

Testing and troubleshooting

Configuring mail clients

Securing communications with SSL/TLS

Internet E-Mail's Inner Workings

E-mail messages are generated either by an automated process, such as a form processor on a web page or an automated notification system, or by an MUA (mail user agent) controlled by an end user. Messages are delivered through one of two methods to the software performing the MTA (mail transfer agent) function on a server:

- **SMTP** — The Simple Mail Transfer Protocol is a network-based protocol that allows for transmission of messages between systems.

- **Local IPC** — Interprocess communications are often used instead of SMTP when transferring a message between programs within a system.

Upon receiving a message, the MTA places it in a queue to be processed by an MDA (mail delivery agent). Mail delivery agents come in two varieties:

- **Local MDAs** — Deliver messages to mailboxes on the local server. Simple versions copy messages directly to a specified mailbox, whereas complex implementations can alter messages or delivery parameters based on user-specified rules.

- **Remote MDAs** — Deliver messages over the network to remote servers. Full remote MDAs use DNS (the Domain Name System) to determine the mail exchanger hosts for recipient addresses and deliver to the best one available for each. Simple remote MDAs (sometimes also called "null clients") forward messages to a central server to continue the delivery process. Most remote MDAs are capable of either method and will act as configured by the administrator who performed the configuration.

Note
You will often see the term MTA used in reference to the software that performs both MTA and MDA functions. This is a carry-over from older designs that did not separate the functions and is still fairly accurate, given the fact that most mail server implementations include a minimum of an MTA, remote MDA, and basic local MDA. ■

When a message reaches its destination server, it is written to the user's mailbox by the local MDA. From that point, the message may be viewed by the user using one of three methods:

- **Direct access to the mailbox** — An MUA (mail user agent) with access to the mailbox file, directly or through a network file system, can read messages from the disk and display them for the user. This is generally a console or webmail application running on the server.

- **Downloaded to a workstation for local viewing** — Most mail users use POP3 (Post Office Protocol, version 3) to download messages to their local computers and view them in applications such as Thunderbird, Evolution, Kmail, or Balsa. By default, messages are removed from the server as they are downloaded by the client.

- **Accessed interactively over the network** — Most clients also support viewing messages while they are still on the server, through IMAP (Internet Message Access Protocol). Unlike POP3, this protocol enables users to access multiple folders on their servers and also allows them to access their messages from anywhere. However, this also creates a heavier burden on the server because it must process (and store) everything that the user decides to keep. Most webmail applications use IMAP as their back-end protocol for accessing mailboxes; this eliminates the need for direct access to the mail files and makes it easier to split functions between server and client systems.

About the System and the Software Used

The mail server configuration described in this chapter is based on the Exim mail transfer agent. Along with Exim, several other components are added for managing the server and checking e-mail contents for spam and viruses:

- **Exim** (www.exim.org/) — An MTA written and designed by Philip Hazel at the University of Cambridge, with contributions from many people around the world. The version referred to in this chapter includes the Exiscan-ACL patch (http://duncanthrax.net/exiscan-acl/) from Tom Kistner. This patch allows content scanning from within Exim. Because this patch is integrated with Exim, its features are considered part of Exim for the purposes of this chapter.

- **Maildrop** (www.courier-mta.org/maildrop/) — A community-supported local MDA that is part of the Courier MTA package, but is also available as a standalone program. It is used in this configuration to allow the use of advanced features, such as mailbox quotas and server-side message sorting. Another MDA is procmail (which is officially supported in Ubuntu).

- **Courier IMAP and POP** (www.courier-mta.org/imap/) — Like Maildrop, these are parts of the Courier MTA that are also available separately. They were chosen for their easy installation, good performance, and compatibility with the Maildir format mail directories. This package is also community supported, and you can consider replacing it with the dovecot package.

- **ClamAV** (www.clamav.net) — An open source virus scanner that detects more than 20,000 viruses, worms, and Trojans. It uses a virus pattern database to identify viruses and includes a program named freshclam that handles updating the database automatically. Like SpamAssassin, ClamAV includes a daemon (clamd), a client (clamdscan), and a second command-line tool that does not use the daemon (clamscan).

- **SpamAssassin** (http://spamassassin.apache.org/) — A spam-filtering program written in Perl. It uses a large set of rules to help determine how "spammy" a message looks and assigns a score based on the total of the rule values. For performance reasons, SpamAssassin uses a background daemon called spamd to perform message analysis. Access to this daemon is performed through the spamc client. A spamassassin command that performs the analysis without using spamd is also installed but is not used by either of the example configurations in this chapter.

Preparing Your System

You will need a few common items for the mail server configuration covered in this chapter, starting with the proper hardware. A personal mail server can easily run on a Pentium-class computer, although you may notice occasional slowdowns while incoming messages are being scanned. Disk space requirements depend mostly on how much mail you want to have room for, so plan on having a few gigabytes for the operating system (which will leave you plenty of extra, just in case), plus the amount of mail you want to store.

If you don't have a spare system to act as a dedicated mail server, you can add the mail server to your workstation. Although this is obviously recommended only for personal use, the procedure in this chapter starts with an Ubuntu workstation install.

Your network settings should also be properly configured before you begin installing the mail software. The exact requirements depend on the method by which mail will be delivered to your server:

- Direct delivery is the method used by most traditional mail servers. Mail records (MX) on your DNS server tell remote servers that any mail addressed to your domain should be sent to your server via SMTP.

- Retrieval from a mail host is also possible using an MRA (mail retrieval agent) such as Fetchmail. This option can be used when you have a mailbox under a shared domain but want to access the mail on your own server. This can also be done in combination with direct delivery if you have both your own domain and mailboxes under shared domains.

Note
Configuration of Fetchmail is explained in the "Configuring Mail Clients" section of this chapter. ∎

Configuring DNS for Direct Delivery

For direct delivery to function, the SMTP service (TCP port 25) must be accessible to the outside world through a fixed name in DNS. This name will be in the form of an A (Address) record. "A" records allow DNS resolver processes to determine the IP address associated with a specific name and are used by most of the common protocols on the Internet. A typical DNS A record looks something like this:

```
bigserver.example.org.    IN    A    10.0.12.16
```

The first parameter, `bigserver.example.org.`, is the label, and the second parameter is the class (`IN` for Internet, which is where most DNS records are found). The `A` indicates the type, and the final parameter is the IP address associated with the label.

After you have your A record, you can direct mail to your server using an MX (Mail eXchanger) record. The A and MX records do not need to be part of the same domain, which allows for much greater flexibility. The following is a sample MX record:

```
widgets.test.      IN    MX    0    bigserver.example.org.
```

This MX record indicates that mail for *any address*@widgets.test should be sent through the server `bigserver.example.org`. The 0 indicates the numeric priority for this MX record. When more than one MX record exists for a given label, the MX with the lowest priority is tried first. If a temporary error is encountered, the next highest priority mail server is tried, and so on until the list is exhausted. At that point, the sending server will keep trying periodically until the message times out (generally five days). If multiple MX records exist with the same priority, they are tried in a random order.

Note

Most mail servers will also fall back on the IP address listed in the A record for a label in the event that no MX records exist. However, it is considered bad practice to rely on this feature. ■

In some cases, establishing an A record may be complicated because your IP address frequently changes. Obviously, this is not suitable for commercial purposes, but there is a workaround that is acceptably reliable for personal use. It is achieved through dynamic DNS services that are available (often at no charge) through a number of different companies. A list of these companies is maintained at `http://www.dmoz.org/Computers/Internet/Protocols/DNS/DNS_Providers/Dynamic_DNS/`. Two of the most popular are

- **ZoneEdit** (`www.zoneedit.com/`) — Supported by the ez-ipupdate package
- **No-IP** (`www.no-ip.com/`) — Supported by the no-ip package

Note

The ez-ipupdate package supports both of these, plus a number of others. View the package description (`apt-cache show ez-ipupdate`) for more information. ■

Most of these services will provide you with a hostname under a shared domain at no charge and can also provide a similar service for your own domain for a reasonable fee.

Configuring for Retrieval from a Mail Host

The configuration requirements when retrieving mail from a mail host are pretty limited. Your server should be ready to accept mail addressed to `localhost` and should generally have a name that is unique to it. In the event that a message sent to one of your mailboxes is rejected, the server will need to have a valid hostname by which to identify itself when sending out the DSN (Delivery Status Notification).

You must be able to access the server from clients, although you may need to do so only from clients within your network. In either case, you should be familiar with the information about DNS and A records in the previous section.

Installing and Configuring the Mail Server Software

After you have finished with the prerequisites, you are ready to begin the software installation. The software installation and configuration have been divided into two sections. The first section covers the installation of Exim and Courier. The second section covers the installation of ClamAV and SpamAssassin and configuring Exim to use them to filter incoming mail.

Installing Exim and Courier

Installing and configuring Exim and Courier are very straightforward, thanks to the quality of the packages that come with Ubuntu. For this procedure, I started by installing the version of Ubuntu on the DVD that comes with this book. Here are the installation steps:

1. Start by installing this Exim package:

   ```
   $ sudo apt-get install exim4-daemon-heavy
   ```

2. You need to change a few configuration options from the defaults. Run the following command:

   ```
   $ sudo dpkg-reconfigure --priority=medium exim4-config
   ```

   You are asked a number of questions. Here's how to answer them:

   - **General type** — Select "Mail sent by smarthost; received via SMTP or fetchmail" if you need to send all of your outgoing mail through a server at your Internet service provider. Otherwise, select "Internet site; mail is sent and received directly using SMTP."
   - **Mail name** — Enter the name of your mail server here.
   - **IP addresses** — Clear this box (or leave it empty if it already is) so that Exim will listen on all local IP addresses.
   - **Destinations to accept mail for** — Enter any domains that your server will be accepting mail for. Be sure to separate them with colons, and not commas or spaces.
   - **Domains to relay for** — Enter the names of any domains that your machine will relay mail for, meaning that it can receive mail from them but then passes it on. In most cases, you will not want to enter anything here.
   - **Machines to relay for** — Enter the IP address ranges of any client machines that you want your server to accept mail from. Another (safer) option is to leave this empty and require clients to authenticate using SMTP authentication. SMTP authentication is best performed over an encrypted connection, so this process is described in the security section at the end of this chapter.
   - **Rewrite headers** — Select Yes if you want to hide the local mail name in outgoing mail by rewriting the From, Reply-To, Sender, and Return-Path values to a selected system name in outgoing mail. If Yes, you must then set the visible domain name for local users.
   - **Split configuration into small files** — Selecting Yes causes Exim to split configuration files into about 50 smaller files (instead of one big one) in the `/etc/exim4/conf.d` directory. Otherwise, the `/etc/exim4/exim4.conf.template` file is used as a single, monolithic file.

3. This configuration uses Maildrop for local mail delivery. Maildrop can deliver messages to the Maildir-style folders that Courier is expecting, and can also handle basic sorting

and filtering (as described in the "Configuring Mail Clients" section). This package is not installed by default, so install it as follows:

```
$ sudo apt-get install maildrop
```

4. Create Maildir mail directories for every user already on the system. This step must be run as the user because running this command as root will result in Maildrop's being unable to write to the folders:

```
$ maildirmake.maildrop $HOME/Maildir
$ maildirmake.maildrop -f Trash $HOME/Maildir
```

5. Create mail directories under /etc/skel. The contents of /etc/skel will be copied to the home directories of any new accounts that you create after the setup is completed:

```
$ sudo maildirmake.maildrop /etc/skel/Maildir
$ sudo maildirmake.maildrop -f Trash /etc/skel/Maildir
```

6. Configure Maildrop to deliver to the Maildir folders instead of mbox files stored in /var/spool/mail. Use your favorite text editor to edit /etc/maildroprc and uncomment this line at the end of the file:

```
DEFAULT="$HOME/Maildir/"
```

7. Exim needs to be configured to deliver messages using Maildrop. Use your preferred text editor to open /etc/exim4/update-exim4.conf.conf and change the dc_localdelivery line at the end of the file to read as follows:

```
dc_localdelivery='maildrop_pipe'
```

8. Tell Exim to load the most recent configuration change:

```
$ sudo invoke-rc.d exim4 reload
```

9. Install Courier IMAP and Courier POP:

```
$ sudo apt-get install courier-imap courier-pop
```

Select No when asked whether or not the installer should create directories for web-based administration.

Your system should now be capable of receiving messages. You should also be able to connect to your server using a mail client such as Thunderbird or Evolution. This is a good time to test mail delivery, even if you're planning to follow the directions in the next section to enable virus and spam filters later. You can find more information about configuring a mail client to connect to your server in the "Configuring Mail Clients" section later in this chapter.

Installing ClamAV and SpamAssassin

Installing and configuring the virus and spam filtering mechanisms are more involved than installing Exim and Courier, but should still go smoothly as long as you follow the steps carefully. Keep in mind, however, that this filtering adds a lot of complexity to the system, so make sure the Exim mail server is working first so that you don't have as many things to check if the system doesn't work as expected.

Note

The version of ClamAV included with Ubuntu uses an older virus-scanning engine, as does the Debian system on which Ubuntu is based. Because the updated engine is not likely to make it into an update anytime soon because of the Debian upgrade policies, a group of Debian developers has created special sets of the ClamAV packages that are designed for easy installation. For more information about how to use these packages instead of the stock versions, see http://volatile.debian.net/. **You may choose to use these packages from the start, or to add the appropriate URIs to your APT configuration later and do an upgrade. In either case, the configuration process detailed in this section is about the same. You can also upgrade the database routinely using** clamav-freshclam **and** clamav-getfiles **to generate new** clamav-data **packages. ■**

Here's how to install ClamAV and SpamAssassin, and then configure Exim to use them for scanning messages:

1. Install the ClamAV and SpamAssassin packages:

```
$ sudo apt-get install clamav-daemon clamav-testfiles \
    spamassassin spamc
```

2. Add the clamav user to the Debian-exim group and restart the ClamAV daemon. This step allows the ClamAV daemon access to read the files in Exim's mail queue:

```
$ sudo gpasswd -a clamav Debian-exim
$ sudo invoke-rc.d clamav-daemon restart
```

3. Replace the report template used by SpamAssassin with one that will fit more easily in a message header. Use a text editor to add these lines to the end of the /etc/spamassassin/local.cf file:

```
clear_report_template
report _YESNO_, score=_SCORE_, required=_REQD_, summary=
report _SUMMARY_
```

4. Configure the SpamAssassin background daemon to run automatically and change the OPTIONS line to not attempt to create preference files for users. Change the following options in the /etc/default/spamassassin file:

```
ENABLED=1
OPTIONS="--max-children 5"
```

5. Start the SpamAssassin daemon:

```
$ sudo invoke-rc.d spamassassin start
```

6. Create the entries that will be included in Exim's ACL (Access Control List) for scanning message data. Use a text editor to create a file named /etc/exim4/acl_check_data_local that contains the following:

```
deny message = $malware_name detected in message
     demime = *
     malware = *

warn message = X-Spam-Score: $spam_score ($spam_bar)
     condition = ${if <{$message_size}{80k}{1}{0}}
     spam = nobody:true/defer_ok

warn message = X-Spam-Status: $spam_report
     condition = ${if <{$message_size}{80k}{1}{0}}
     spam = nobody:true/defer_ok

deny message = Spam score too high ($spam_score)
     condition = ${if <{$message_size}{80k}{1}{0}}
     spam = nobody:true/defer_ok
     condition = ${if >{$spam_score_int}{120}{1}{0}}
```

The first block rejects messages that contain viruses or other malware, and the second and third add headers to messages indicating whether or not SpamAssassin considers them spam. The final block checks $spam_score_int (the spam score multiplied by 10) and rejects the message if it is greater than 120.

The /defer_ok in the last three blocks tells Exim that it is okay to continue processing in the event that the SpamAssassin daemon could not be contacted. You can remove it if you would prefer to have the server return a temporary failure code in such cases. You can also add /defer_ok to the end of the malware = * line if you want processing to continue in the event that a message cannot be scanned by ClamAV.

7. Tell Exim which virus scanner to use and how to connect to SpamAssassin. Use a text editor to create a file named /etc/exim4/conf.d/main/10_exim4-exiscan_acl _options that contains the following:

```
av_scanner = clamd:/var/run/clamav/clamd.ctl
spamd_address = 127.0.0.1 783

CHECK_DATA_LOCAL_ACL_FILE = CONFDIR/acl_check_data_local
```

8. Tell Exim to load the new configuration:

```
$ sudo invoke-rc.d exim4 reload
```

415

All messages transmitted through your server should now be checked for viruses using ClamAV. Additionally, messages less than 80 kilobytes will also be checked using SpamAssassin. This is a good time to test the configuration again. You can find fixes for the problems that you are most likely to encounter in the next section.

Testing and Troubleshooting

This section contains some generic troubleshooting tips, plus specific information about some common errors and how to fix them.

Checking Logs

All logging information for Exim is written to three log files that can be found in `/var/log/exim4`: `mainlog`, `rejectlog`, and `paniclog`. The first of these, `mainlog`, contains log entries for all events, including normal events such as message deliveries. The second, `rejectlog`, contains entries for rejected messages. The third contains information about configuration or other errors, and is usually empty unless a serious problem has occurred. Every entry in these files generally starts with a timestamp.

Entries in the `mainlog` often include a string of characters, such as n7MJ123W002743. This is the message identifier for the message that the log entry is related to. Immediately after the message identifier there will generally be a two-character string. Table 16-1 details what those strings mean.

TABLE 16-1

Exim Log File Messages

Symbol	Description	Explanation
<--	Message arrival	These entries show messages coming into Exim, generally through SMTP or local IPC.
-->	Message delivery	These entries show message deliveries, whether they are to a local mailbox or to a remote host using SMTP or some other transport.
->	Additional addresses in message delivery	These entries show delivery to additional addresses for messages that have already been delivered to another recipient (and logged with an --> entry).
**	Delivery failure	These entries show permanent delivery errors. Errors such as these indicate that the message has been removed from the mail queue and in most cases a DSN (Delivery Status Notification) has been generated and sent to the original message sender.

Logging information for the Courier IMAP and POP daemons is saved to `/var/log/mail.log`. Normal entries include `LOGIN` and `LOGOUT` messages. `DISCONNECTED` messages generally indicate that a connection was broken before a normal logout was performed.

Note

The tail utility is useful for watching for new entries to a log. Use the `-f` switch to instruct tail to watch for new entries and display them to the screen as they are written to the log — for example, `tail -f /var/log/exim4/mainlog`. ∎

Common Errors (and How to Fix Them)

You will encounter two common types of problems with your server: messages being rejected or not delivered by Exim and login failures when connecting to Courier.

Messages Rejected by Exim

The first places to check when messages are rejected by Exim are the `mainlog` and `rejectlog` files. Here are examples of some common errors and tips for fixing them:

- **Relaying Denied** — The following error indicates that the client sending the message is not recognized as a client by Exim and that the recipient domain is not in the list of local or relay domains:

  ```
  H=sample.client [10.0.12.16] F=<sender@example.org> rejected
  RCPT <rcpt@remotesite.example.org>: relay not permitted
  ```

  If the client IP address will not change frequently or is in part of a trusted range of IP addresses, you can add it by running the following:

  ```
  $ sudo dpkg-reconfigure --priority=medium exim4-config
  ```

  The same command can also be used to add the recipient domain as a local or relay domain.

Caution

Do not add client IP ranges unless you trust all the users who can connect from those addresses. Likewise, do not add a domain as a relay domain unless you know the owner of the domain and have made arrangements to relay mail for him or her. Doing either of these incorrectly could open up your server as a relay that spammers can use to attack other sites. ∎

If the client IP address is likely to change frequently and is not part of a trusted range, you should either configure the client to use a mail server that is local to it or configure SMTP authentication in Exim. You can find more information about enabling SMTP authentication on your server in `/usr/share/doc/exim4-base/README.Debian .html` and `/etc/exim4/conf.d/auth/30_exim4-config_examples`.

Note

You can enable the Courier authdaemon examples in `30_exim4-config_examples`, **allowing Exim to use that facility for authentication and negating the need to set up a different mechanism. In order for it to work, however, you need to add the Debian-exim user to the daemon group (sudo** `gpasswd -a Debian-exim daemon`**) and restart Exim.** ■

- **ClamAV Misconfiguration** — The following error indicates that the ClamAV daemon could not read the temporary message file:

```
1E9PDq-0003Lo-BY malware acl condition: clamd: ClamAV
returned /var/spool/exim4/scan/1E9PDq-0003Lo-BY:
   Access denied. ERROR
```

Make sure you added clamav to the Debian-exim group and restarted ClamAV.

- **ClamAV Unavailable** — This error usually indicates that the ClamAV daemon is not running:

```
1E9PGL-0003MX-38 malware acl condition: clamd: unable to
connect to UNIX socket /var/run/clamav/clamd.ctl
   (No such file or directory)
```

Start the daemon using `invoke-rc.d clamav-daemon start`. You can also use the `clamdscan` program to test the daemon, as follows:

```
$ sudo clamdscan /usr/share/clamav-testfiles/clam.exe
/usr/share/clamav-testfiles/clam.exe: ClamAV-Test-File FOUND
----------- SCAN SUMMARY -----------
Infected files: 1
Time: 0.001 sec (0 m 0 s)
```

Messages Not Delivered by Exim

In some cases, messages will be accepted by the server but will not be deliverable. Some of these errors are considered temporary failures and do not generate a bounced message until the retry timer runs out. The error that you are most likely to see looks something like this in the `mainlog` file:

```
1E9PTu-0003jN-QY == user@example.org R=local_user T=maildrop_pipe defer (0):
Child process of maildrop_pipe transport returned 75 (could mean temporary
error) from command: /usr/bin/maildrop
```

This error indicates that Exim attempted to pass the message to Maildrop, but Maildrop returned an error code. The most likely causes are a missing Maildir directory, or a Maildir directory that is owned by the wrong user. The next section shows how to detect and fix these problems.

Login Failures When Connecting to Courier

Aside from genuine password errors (which can be remedied by entering the correct password in the mail client), a few other conditions can also result in login failures. Some of these conditions can also result in temporary delivery problems. A normal login failure results in a log entry that looks similar to this:

```
courierpop3login: LOGIN FAILED, ip=[::ffff:1.2.3.4]
```

In this case, a user from IP 1.2.3.4 entered the wrong username or password.

Several of the other errors that may occur will not be logged to the mail log, which means that you may have to test them by connecting manually to the POP3 service (from the mail server, or from a remote machine) and sending a valid username and password. This example shows how to connect to the POP3 service from a shell prompt on the mail server:

```
$ telnet localhost 110
Trying 127.0.0.1...
Connected to localhost.localdomain.
Escape character is '^]'.
+OK Hello there.
USER username
+OK Password required.
PASS password
```

The response you receive from the server should be similar to one of the following:

- +OK logged in — This response is normal and should mean that there are no problems with the service.

- -ERR Maildir: No such file or directory — This error indicates that the user's account does not have a Maildir directory. Use the maildirmake command to create it, as shown in the "Installing Exim and Courier" section.

- -ERR Maildir: Permission denied — This error indicates that the user's Maildir directory cannot be read or belongs to the wrong user. To remedy this, run this command as root:

  ```
  $ sudo chown -R username:groupname ~username/Maildir
  ```

  Be sure to replace *username* and *groupname* with the login name and primary group of the user. In a stock Ubuntu or Debian system, the primary group name will be the same as the username.

- -ERR Login failed — If you're certain that you are using the correct username and password, it could be that the Courier authdaemon service is not running. Try to start (or restart) it using this command:

  ```
  # invoke-rc.d courier-authdaemon restart
  ```

Configuring Mail Clients

Any mail client with support for POP3 or IMAP should be able to access mail from your server. Just use the name of your server in the mail server settings, and follow the troubleshooting steps in the previous section if something doesn't work.

Cross-Reference

You can find more information about mail clients for Linux in Chapter 4. ■

Configuring Fetchmail

Fetchmail is an MRA (mail retrieval agent) that you can use to pull mail from a remote account to your new server. It is configured in the $HOME/.fetchmailrc file and is very easy to set up. To pull mail to your server, log in as the user to whom the mail should go, and then configure and run it from there.

Note

Run Fetchmail as the user for whom the mail is being retrieved. You should never run it as root. If you're doing a complex setup in which you retrieve mail from a single mailbox that needs to be sorted out for multiple users, see the Fetchmail man page for information about multidrop mailboxes. ■

A .fetchmailrc file can be as simple as this:

```
poll mailserver.yourisp.example protocol pop3 username "foo"
```

If you have more than one mail server, you can add it as an additional line. If the server from which you are pulling mail supports IMAP, you can use imap instead of pop3. Other options that you can have are password=*your password* and ssl. Storing the password in the file enables you to run Fetchmail without entering a password, and the ssl option tells Fetchmail to use an SSL/TLS connection to the server.

Note

Your .fetchmailrc file should not be readable by others, and Fetchmail will generally complain if it is. To set the permissions so that only you can read it, run chmod 0600 $HOME/.fetchmailrc. ■

Running Fetchmail is as simple as typing

```
$ fetchmail
```

If you want to have Fetchmail run in the background, you can use the --daemon (or -d) flags with a parameter telling it how often (in seconds) to poll the servers:

```
$ fetchmail --daemon 300
```

To have Fetchmail automatically start when the system boots, add this to your crontab file:

```
@reboot    /usr/bin/fetchmail --daemon 300
```

Note
Fetchmail cannot prompt for passwords when run in this manner, which means that you must store the passwords in `.fetchmailrc` for this to work. ■

If you haven't configured a `crontab` file before, setting it up can be as easy as entering the following three commands:

```
$ cat > mycron
@reboot    /usr/bin/fetchmail --daemon 300
<Ctrl+D>
$ crontab mycron
```

Configuring Web-based Mail

If you're running an IMAP server, you can offer web-based access by installing SquirrelMail or Roundcube, found in the squirrelmail and roundcube packages, respectively. Start by configuring your system as a web server (see Chapter 15), and then install and configure the appropriate package.

Securing Communications with SSL/TLS

Because communication between mail clients and the server often contains sensitive information such as passwords, it is usually desirable to enable SSL/TLS encryption. Here's how to enable SSL/TLS in Exim and Courier:

1. Install the Courier daemons with SSL/TLS support:

   ```
   $ sudo apt-get install courier-imap-ssl courier-pop-ssl
   ```

2. Third-party CA certificates are provided on the ca-certificates package. This will be referenced in the configuration, so install it, too:

   ```
   $ sudo apt-get install ca-certificates
   ```

   Debconf asks you whether you want to trust the CA certificates by default. In most cases, you want to select Yes.

3. If you are going to be using a certificate from a CA that is not already recognized (generally only true if you are running your own CA), place the CA public certificate in its own file in `/etc/ssl/certs/` and update the certificate database:

   ```
   $ sudo update-ca-certificates
   ```

4. Generate the private key and certificate signing request, as described in Chapter 13. The best location for these files is in `/etc/ssl/private/`. Here's an example:

   ```
   $ sudo su -
   # cd /etc/exim4
   ```

```
# openssl genrsa -out mail.key 1024
# chmod 640 mail.key
# openssl req -new -key mail.key -out mail.csr
# chown root:Debian-exim mail.key
```

5. Get your CSR (Certificate Signing Request) signed and place the certificate in /etc/ mail/private/mail.crt. Or, to do a self-signed certificate, do the following:

```
# cd /etc/exim4
# openssl req -new -x509 -nodes -sha1 \
  -days 365 -key mail.key -out mail.crt
# chmod 640 mail.crt
# chown root:Debian-exim mail.crt
```

Caution

Some remote servers will refuse to send messages to your server if your certificate is not signed by a CA that they recognize. Also, make sure the common name (cn) attribute on your certificate matches the name of the server in DNS. ■

6. Concatenate the private key and certificate into a single file for Courier:

```
# cd /etc/courier
# cat /etc/exim4/mail.key /etc/exim4/mail.crt > mail.pem
# chmod 600 mail.pem
```

7. Enable SSL/TLS in the Courier IMAP and POP daemons by editing both /etc/courier/ imapd-ssl and /etc/courier/pop3d-ssl and replacing the values for TLS_CERTFILE and TLS_TRUSTCERTS with the following:

```
TLS_CERTFILE=/etc/courier/mail.pem
TLS_TRUSTCERTS=/etc/ssl/certs/ca-certificates.pem
```

8. Tell Exim where it can find the private key and certificate, and enable TLS. Create a file named /etc/exim4/conf.d/main/12_exim4-config_local_tlsoptions containing the following:

```
MAIN_TLS_CERTIFICATE = CONFDIR/mail.crt
MAIN_TLS_PRIVATEKEY = CONFDIR/mail.key
MAIN_TLS_ENABLE = 1
```

9. Restart Exim:

```
$ sudo invoke-rc.d exim4 restart
```

Your server should now support SSL/TLS when communicating with SMTP, POP, and IMAP clients.

Summary

Using Linux and a good Internet connection, you can set up and maintain your own mail server. Preparing your computer to become a mail server includes configuring your network connection, setting up delivery and retrieval methods, and adding required software packages.

This chapter describes how to install, configure, and troubleshoot the Exim MTA. Exim can be used in tandem with spam filtering software (such as SpamAssassin) and virus scanning software (such as ClamAV). Methods for securing your mail server include configuring support for SSL/ TLS encryption.

## 17

Running a Print Server

S haring printers is a good way to save money and make your printing more efficient. Very few people need to print all the time, but when they do want to print something, they usually need it quickly. Setting up a print server can save money by eliminating the need for a printer at every workstation. Some of those savings can be used to buy printers that can output more pages per minute or have higher-quality output.

You can attach printers to your Linux system to make them available to users of that system (standalone printing) or to other computers on the network as a shared printer. You can also configure your Linux printer as a remote Common UNIX Printing System (CUPS) or Samba printer. With Samba, you are emulating Windows printing services, which is pretty useful, given the abundance of Windows client systems.

This chapter describes configuring and using printers on Linux systems with various desktop environments in use. Some of the details may vary from one distribution to another, but the information included here should work well for the more commonly used distributions. This chapter focuses on CUPS, which is the recommended print service for the majority of Linux installations. Examples in this chapter use the printer configuration options GNOME and KDE.

After a local printer is configured, users on your system should easily be able to print web pages, documents, or images from desktop applications. From the command line, print commands such as lpr are available for carrying out printing. Commands also exist for querying print queues (lpq), manipulating print queues (lpc), and removing print queues (lprm). A local printer can also be shared as a print server for users on other computers on your network.

IN THIS CHAPTER

Understanding printing in Linux

Setting up printers

Using printing commands

Managing document printing

Sharing printers

Common UNIX Printing System

CUPS has become the standard for printing from Linux and other UNIX-like operating systems. It was designed to meet today's needs for standardized printer definitions and sharing on Internet Protocol–based networks (as most computer networks are today). Nearly every Linux distribution today comes with CUPS as its printing service. Here are some of the service's features:

- **IPP** — CUPS is based on the Internet Printing Protocol (`www.pwg.org/ipp`), a standard that was created to simplify the way printers can be shared over IP networks. In the IPP model, printer servers and clients who want to print can exchange information about the model and features of a printer using HTTP (that is, web content) protocol. A server can also broadcast the availability of a printer so a printing client can easily find a list of locally available printers.

- **Drivers** — CUPS also standardized the way printer drivers are created. The idea was to have a common format that could be used by printer manufacturers so that a driver could work across all different types of UNIX systems. That way, a manufacturer had to create the driver only once to work for Linux, Mac OS X, and a variety of UNIX derivatives.

- **Printer classes** — You can use printer classes to create multiple print server entries that point to the same printer or one print server entry that points to multiple printers. In the first case, multiple entries can each allow different options (such as pointing to a particular paper tray or printing with certain character sizes or margins). In the second case, you can have a pool of printers so that printing is distributed, decreasing the occurrence of congested print queues often caused by a malfunctioning printer or a printer that is dealing with very large documents. CUPS also supports *implicit classes*, which are print classes that are formed by merging identical network printers automatically.

- **Printer browsing** — With printer browsing, client computers can see any CUPS printers on your LAN with browsing enabled. As a result, clients can simply select the printers they want to use from the printer names broadcast on the LAN, without needing to know in advance what the printers are named and where they are connected. You can turn off this feature if you don't want others on the LAN to see your printer.

- **UNIX print commands** — To integrate into Linux and other UNIX environments, CUPS offers versions of standard commands for printing and managing printers that have been traditionally offered with UNIX systems.

Many Linux distributions come with simplified methods of configuring CUPS printers. Here are a few examples:

- In Fedora, CentOS, and Red Hat Enterprise Linux systems, the Printer Configuration window (`system-config-printer` command) enables you to configure printers that use the CUPS facility.

- In Ubuntu, the same Printer Configuration window (select System ➪ Administration ➪ Printing to open it) lets you add, delete, and manage printers.

- In SUSE, the YaST facility includes a printer configuration module. From the YaST Control Center, select Hardware ➪ Printer.

For distributions that don't have their own printer configuration tools, there are several ways to configure CUPS using tools that aren't specific to a Linux distribution. Here are a couple of them:

- **Configuring CUPS from a browser** — CUPS offers a web-based interface for adding and managing printers. You can access this service by typing **localhost:631** from a web browser on the computer running the CUPS service. (See the section "Using Web-Based CUPS Administration" later in this chapter.) The KDE desktop comes with a tool for managing CUPS server features.

- **Configuring CUPS manually** — You also can configure CUPS manually (that is, edit the configuration files and start the cupsd daemon manually). Configuration files for CUPS are contained in the /etc/cups directory. In particular, you might be interested in the cupsd.conf file, which identifies permission, authentication, and other information for the printer daemon, and printers.conf, which identifies addresses and options for configured printers. Use the classes.conf file to define local printer classes.

Coming from Windows

You can print to CUPS from non-UNIX systems as well. For example, you can use a PostScript printer driver to print directly from Windows XP to your CUPS server. You can use CUPS without modification by configuring the XP computer with a PostScript driver that uses http://printservername:631/printers/targetPrinter as its printing port.

You may also be able to use the native Windows printer drivers for the printer instead of the PostScript driver. If the native Windows driver does not work out-of-the-box on your CUPS print queue, you can create a Raw Print Queue under CUPS and use that instead. The Raw Print Queue will directly pass through the data from the Windows native print driver to the printer. ∎

To use CUPS, you need to have it installed. Most Linux distributions let you choose to add CUPS during the initial system install or will simply add CUPS by default. If CUPS was not added when you first installed your Linux distribution, check your original installation medium (DVD or CD) to see whether it is there for you to install now. Fedora, Slackware, Ubuntu, SUSE, and many other Linux distributions have CUPS on the first CD or DVD of their installation sets.

Setting Up Printers

Although using the printer administration tools specifically built for your distribution is usually best, many Linux systems simply rely on the tools that come with the CUPS software package. This section explores how to use CUPS web-based administration tools that come with every Linux distribution and then examines the printer configuration tool system-config-printer, which comes with Ubuntu, Fedora, and Red Hat Enterprise Linux systems to enable you to set up printers.

Using Web-Based CUPS Administration

CUPS offers its own web-based administrative tool for adding, deleting, and modifying printer configurations on your computer. The CUPS print service (using the cupsd daemon) listens on port 631 to provide access to the CUPS web-based administrative interface.

If CUPS is already running on your computer, you can immediately use CUPS web-based administration from your web browser. To see whether CUPS is running and to start setting up your printers, open a web browser on the local computer and type the following into its location box:

```
http://localhost:631/
```

A prompt for a valid login name and password may appear. If so, type the root login name and the root user's password, and then click OK. (For live CDs, you can often literally type **root** as the root password.) If you are using Ubuntu, a screen similar to the one shown in Figure 17-1 appears.

FIGURE 17-1

CUPS provides a web-based administration tool.

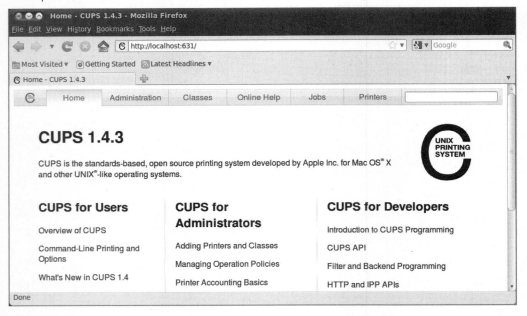

By default, web-based CUPS administration is available only from the local host. To access web-based CUPS administration from another computer, you must change the /admin section in the /etc/cups/cupsd.conf file. As recommended in the text of this file, you should limit access to CUPS administration from the web. The following example includes an Allow line to permit access from a host from IP address 10.0.0.5. You must also add a Listen line, so your CUPS service will listen for requests outside of the local host. In this example, a Listen line is configured to listen on your external interface to your LAN on address 10.0.0.1.

```
Listen localhost:631
Listen 10.0.0.1:631
<Location />
```

```
   Order allow,deny
   Allow From 10.0.0.5
</Location>
<Location /admin>
   Order allow,deny
   Allow From 10.0.0.5
</Location>
```

From the computer at address 10.0.0.5, you would type

```
http://localhost:631/admin
```

(substituting the CUPS server's name or IP address for *localhost*), and when prompted, enter the root username and password. For Ubuntu, you can enter your regular username and password (assuming the user has sudo privileges). You may be asked for that information later in the process of adding a printer.

Now, with the Admin screen displayed, here's how to set up a printer in Ubuntu:

1. Click the Add Printer button. The Add New Printer screen appears.
2. Select the device to which the printer is connected. The printer can be connected locally to a parallel, SCSI, serial, or USB port directly on the computer. Alternatively, you can select a network connection type for Apple printers (appSocket/HP JetDirect), Internet Printing Protocol (http or ipp), or a Windows printer (using Samba or SMB).
3. If prompted for more information, you may need to further describe the connection to the printer. For example, you may need to enter the baud rate and parity for a serial port, or you might be asked for the network address for an IPP or Samba printer.
4. Type a Name, Location, and Description for the printer and select if you want to share this printer. Then click Continue.
5. Select the make of the print driver (if you don't see the manufacturer of your printer listed, choose PostScript for a PostScript printer or HP for a PCL printer). For the manufacturer you choose, you will be able to select a specific model.
6. If you are asked to set options for your printer, you may do so. Then select Set Printer Options to continue.
7. If the printer is added successfully, click the name of your printer to have the new printer page appear; from it, you can select Maintenance or Administration to print a test page or modify the printer configuration.

With the basic printer configuration done, you can now do further work with your printers. Here are a few examples of what you can do:

- **List print jobs.** Click Show All Jobs to see what print jobs are currently active from any of the printers configured for this server. Click Show Completed Jobs to see information about jobs that are already printed.

- **Create a printer class.** Click the Administration tab and choose the Classes tab. Then click Add Class and identify a name, description, and location for a printer class. From the list of printers configured on your server, select the ones to go into this class.

- **Cancel a print job.** If you print a 100-page job by mistake or if the printer is spewing out junk, the cancel feature can be very handy. From the Administration tab, click Manage Jobs; then click Show Active Jobs to see what print jobs are currently in the queue for the printer. Select the Cancel Job button next to the print job you want to cancel.

- **View printers.** You can click the Printers link from the top of any of the CUPS web-based administration pages to view the printers you have configured. For each printer that appears, you can select Maintenance or Administrative tasks. Under Maintenance, click Pause Printer (to stop the printer from printing but still accept print jobs for the queue), Reject Jobs (to not accept any further print jobs for the moment), or Print Test Page (to print a page). Figure 17-2 shows the Printers page.

FIGURE 17-2

Print test pages or temporarily stop printing from the Printers page.

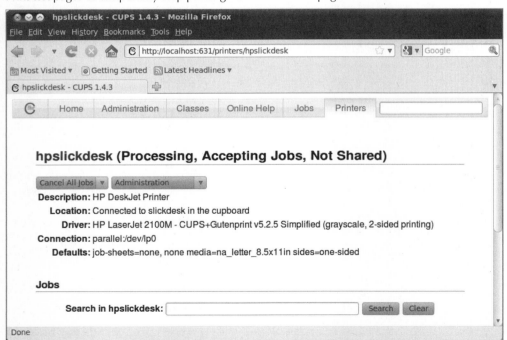

Using the Printer Configuration Window

If you are using Ubuntu, Fedora, RHEL, or other Red Hat–based systems, you can use the Printer Configuration window to set up your printers. In fact, I recommend that you use it instead of CUPS web administration because the resulting printer configuration files are tailored to work with the way the CUPS service is started on those systems.

To install a printer from your GNOME desktop in Ubuntu or Fedora, start the Printer Configuration window by selecting System ➪ Administration ➪ Printing or as root user by typing **system-config-printer**. This tool lets you add and delete printers and edit printer properties. It also lets you send test pages to those printers to make sure they are working properly.

The key here is that you are configuring printers that are managed by your print daemon (cupsd for the CUPS service). After a printer is configured, users on your local system can use it. You can refer to the "Configuring Print Servers" section to learn how to make the server available to users from other computers on your network.

The printers that you set up can be connected directly to your computer (as on a parallel port) or to another computer on the network (for example, from another UNIX system or Windows system).

Configuring Local Printers with the Printer Configuration Window

Add a local printer (in other words, a printer connected directly to your computer) with the Printer Configuration window using the following procedure. (See the sidebar "Choosing a Printer" if you don't yet have a printer.)

Tip

Connect your printer before starting this procedure. This enables the printer software to autodetect the printer's location and to immediately test the printer when you have finished adding it. If the printer is not yet connected, you can configure it anyway and begin queuing jobs to it. ■

Choosing a Printer

An excellent list of printers supported in Linux is available from the Linux Foundation site at `www.linux-foundation.org/en/OpenPrinting` (select the OpenPrinting Database link). I strongly recommend that you visit that site before you purchase a printer to work with Linux. In addition to showing supported printers, the site also has a page describing how to choose a printer for use with Linux:

```
www.linuxfoundation.org/en/OpenPrinting/Database/DatabaseIntro
```

In terms of general guidance when looking for a Linux printer, the PostScript language is the preferred format for Linux and UNIX printing and has been for many years. Every major word-processing product that runs on Fedora, SUSE, Debian, and UNIX systems supports PostScript printing on some level, so a printer that natively supports PostScript printing is sure to work in Linux.

continued

continued

If you get a PostScript printer and it is not explicitly shown in the list of supported printers, simply select the PostScript filter when you install the printer locally. No special drivers are needed. Your next best option is to choose a printer that supports PCL. In either case, make sure that the PostScript or PCL is implemented in the printer hardware and not in the Windows driver.

Avoid printers that are referred to as *Winprinters*. These printers use nonstandard printing interfaces (those other than PostScript or PCL). Support for these low-end printers is hit or miss. For example, some low-end HP DeskJet printers use the pnm2ppa driver to print documents in Printing Performance Architecture (PPA) format. Some Lexmark printers use the pbm217k driver to print. Although drivers are available for many of these Winprinters, many of them are not fully supported in Linux.

Ghostscript may also support your printer; if it does, you can use it to do your printing. Ghostscript (found at www.ghostscript.com) is a free PostScript-interpreter program. It can convert PostScript content to output that can be interpreted by a variety of printers. Both GNU and Aladdin Ghostscript drivers are available. Although the latest Aladdin drivers are not immediately released under the GPL, you can use older Aladdin drivers that are licensed under the GNU Public Licence.

Adding a Local Printer

To add a local printer from Ubuntu, Fedora, and several other Linux systems, follow these steps:

1. Select System ⇨ Administration ⇨ Printing from the Desktop menu or type the following as root user from a Terminal window:

   ```
   # system-config-printer &
   ```
   The Printing window appears.

2. Click Add. A New Printer window appears.

3. If the printer you want to configure is detected, simply select it and click Forward. If it is not detected, choose the device to which the printer is connected (LPT #1 and Serial Port #1 are the first parallel and serial ports, respectively) and click Forward. (Type **/usr/sbin/lpinfo -v | less** in a shell to see all available ports.) You are asked to identify the printer's driver.

4. To use an installed driver for your printer, choose Select Printer From Database, and then choose the manufacturer of your printer. As an alternative, you could select Provide PPD File and supply your own PPD file (for example, if you have a printer that is not supported in Linux and you have a driver that was supplied with the printer). PPD stands for PostScript Printer Description. Select Forward to see a list of printer models from which you can choose.

Coming from Windows

If you have a printer that works in Windows, but doesn't work in Linux, refer to the disk (probably a CD) that was included with the printer. Choose Provide PPD File, and then look for the PPD file on that disk to test that printer driver with Linux. ■

Tip

If your printer doesn't appear on the list but supports PCL (HP's Printer Control Language), try selecting one of the HP printers (such as HP LaserJet). If your printer supports PostScript, select PostScript printer from the list. Selecting Raw Print Queue enables you to send documents to the printer that are already formatted for that printer type. ■

5. With your printer model selected, click the driver you want to use with that printer. Click Forward to continue.

6. Add the following information and click Forward:

- **Printer Name** — Add the name you want to give to identify the printer. The name must begin with a letter, but after the initial letter, it can contain a combination of letters, numbers, dashes (-), and underscores (_). For example, an HP printer on a computer named maple could be named hp-maple.

- **Description** — Add a few words describing the printer, such as its features (an HP LaserJet 2100M with PCL and PS support).

- **Location** — Add some words that describe the printer's location (for example, "In Room 205 under the coffeepot").

7. When the printer is added, you may be prompted to print a test page (click No or Yes). The new printer entry appears in the Printing window, as shown in Figure 17-3.

FIGURE 17-3

Add printers connected locally or remotely with the Printing window.

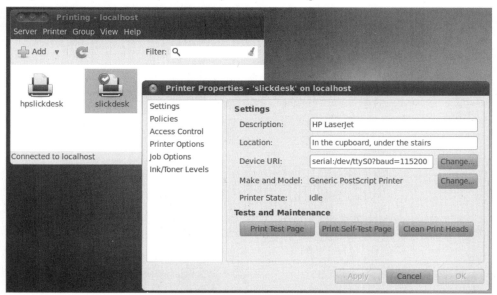

8. If you want the printer to be your default printer, right-click the printer and select Set As Default. As you add other printers, you can change the default printer by selecting the one you want and Set As Default again.

9. Printing should be working at this point. To make sure, open a Terminal window and use the lpr command to print a file (such as `lpr /etc/hosts`). (If you want to share this printer with other computers on your network, refer to the "Configuring Print Servers" section of this chapter.)

Editing a Local Printer

After selecting the printer you want to configure, choose from the following menu options to change its configuration:

- **Settings** — The Description, Location, Device URI, and Make and Model information you created earlier are displayed in this dialog.

- **Policies** — Click Policies to set the following items:

  - **State** — Select check boxes to indicate whether the printer will print jobs that are in the queue (Enabled), accept new jobs for printing (Accepting Jobs), or be available to be shared with other computers that can communicate with your computer (Shared). You also must select Server Settings and click the "Share published printers connected to this system" check box before the printer will accept print jobs from other computers.

  - **Policies** — In case of error, the stop-printer selection causes all printing to that printer to stop. You can also select to have the job discarded (abort-job) or retried (retry-job) in the event of an error condition.

- **Access Control** — If your printer is a shared printer, you can select this window to create a list that either allows users access to the printer (with all others denied) or denies users access to the printer (with all others allowed).

- **Printer Options** — Click Printer Options to set defaults for options related to the printer driver. The available options are different for different printers. Many of these options can be overridden when someone prints a document. Here are a few of the options you might (or might not) have available:

  - **Watermark** — Several Watermark settings are available to enable you to add and change watermarks on your printed pages. By default, Watermark and Overlay are off (None). By selecting Watermark (behind the text) or Overlay (over the text), you can set the other Watermark settings to determine how watermarks and overlays are done. Watermarks can go on every page (All) or only the first page (First Only).

    Select Watermark Text to choose what words are used for the watermark or overlay (Draft, Copy, Confidential, Final, and so on). You can then select the font type, size, style, and intensity of the watermark or overlay.

  - **Resolution Enhancement** — You can use the printer's current settings or choose to turn resolution enhancement on or off.

  - **Page Size** — The default is U.S. letter size, but you can also ask the printer to print legal size, envelopes, ISO A4 standard, or several other page sizes.

- **Media Source** — Choose which tray to print from. Select Tray 1 to insert pages manually.

- **Levels of Gray** — Choose to use the printer's current levels of gray or have enhanced or standard gray levels turned on.

- **Resolution** — Select the default printing resolution (such as 300, 600, or 1,200 dots per inch). Higher resolutions result in better quality but take longer to print.

- **EconoMode** — Either use the printer's current setting or choose a mode where you save toner or one where you have the highest possible quality.

- **Job Options** — Click Job Options to set common default options that will be used for this printer if the application printing the job doesn't already set them. These include Common Options (number of copies, orientation, scale to fit, and pages per side), Image Options (scaling, saturation, hue, and gamma), and Text Options (characters/inch, lines/inch, and margin settings).

- **Ink/Toner Levels** — Click Ink/Toner Levels to see information on how much ink or toner your printer has left. (Not all printers report these values.)

  Click Apply when you are satisfied with the changes you made to the local printer.

Configuring Remote Printers

To use a printer that is available on your network, you must identify that printer to your Linux system. Supported remote printer connections include Networked CUPS (IPP) printers, Networked UNIX (LPD) printers, Networked Windows (Samba) printers, and JetDirect printers. (Of course, both CUPS and UNIX print servers can be run from Linux systems as well as other UNIX systems.)

In each case, you need a network connection from your Linux system to the servers to which those printers are connected. To use a remote printer requires that someone set up that printer on the remote server computer. See the section "Configuring Print Servers" later in this chapter for information on how to do that on your Linux server.

Use the Printing window to configure each of the remote printer types. Here is how it is done in Ubuntu:

1. From the Desktop panel, select System ➪ Administration ➪ Printing.

2. Click Add. The New Printer window appears.

3. Depending on the type of ports you have on your computer, select one of the following:

   - **LPT #1** — For a printer connected to your parallel port.

   - **Serial Port #1** — For a printer connected to your serial port.

   - **AppleSocket/HP JetDirect** — For a JetDirect printer.

   - **Internet Printing Protocol (IPP)** — For a CUPS or other IPP printer.

   - **LPD/LPR Host or Printer** — For a UNIX printer.

   - **Windows Printer via SAMBA** — For a Windows system printer.

Continue with the steps in whichever of the following sections is appropriate.

Adding a Remote CUPS Printer

If you choose to add a CUPS (IPP) printer from the Printer Configuration window, you must add the following information to the window that appears:

- **Host** — Hostname of the computer to which the printer is attached (or otherwise accessible). This can be an IP address or TCP/IP hostname for the computer. The TCP/IP name is accessible from your /etc/hosts file or through a DNS name server.

- **Queue** — Printer name on the remote CUPS print server. CUPS supports printer instances, which allows each printer to have several sets of options. If the remote CUPS printer is configured this way, you are able to choose a particular path to a printer, such as hp/300dpi or hp/1200dpi. A slash character separates the print queue name from the printer instance.

Complete the rest of the procedure as you would for a local printer (see the "Adding a Local Printer" section earlier in this chapter).

Adding a Remote UNIX Printer

If you chose to add a UNIX printer (LPD/LPR) from the Printer Configuration window, you must add the following information to the window that appears:

- **Host** — Hostname of the computer to which the printer is attached (or otherwise accessible). This is the IP address or TCP/IP name for the computer (the TCP/IP name is accessible from your /etc/hosts file or through a DNS name server). Select the Probe button to search for the host.

- **Queue** — Printer name on the remote UNIX computer.

Complete the rest of the procedure as you would for a local printer (see the "Adding a Local Printer" section earlier in this chapter).

Tip

If the print job you send to test the printer is rejected, the print server computer may not have allowed you access to the printer. Ask the remote computer's administrator to add your hostname to the /etc/lpd .perms file. (Type lpq -P *printer* to see the status of your print job.) ∎

Adding a Windows (SMB) Printer

Enabling your computer to access an SMB printer (the Windows printing service) involves adding an entry for the printer in the Select Connection window.

When you choose to add a Windows printer to the Printer Configuration window (Windows Printer via Samba), select Browse to see a list of computers on your network that have been detected as offering SMB services (file and/or printing service). Here is how you can configure the printer from this window:

1. Type the URI of the printer, excluding the leading `smb://`. For example, `/host1/myprinter` or `/mygroup/host1/myprinter`.

2. Select either Prompt user if authentication is required or Set authentication details now.

3. If you chose to Set authentication details now, fill in the username and password needed to access the SMB printer. Click Verify to check that you can authenticate to the server.

4. Click Forward to continue.

Alternatively, you can identify a server that does not appear on the list of servers. Type the information needed to create an SMB URI that contains the following information:

- **Workgroup** — The workgroup name assigned to the SMB server. Using the workgroup name isn't necessary in all cases.

- **Server** — NetBIOS name or IP address for the computer, which may or may not be the same as its TCP/IP name. To translate this name into the address needed to reach the SMB host, Samba checks several places where the name may be assigned to an IP address. Samba checks the following (in the order shown) until it finds a match: the local `/etc/hosts` file, the local `/etc/lmhosts` file, a WINS server on the network, and responses to broadcasts on each local network interface to resolve the name.

- **Share** — Name under which the printer is shared with the remote computer. It may be different from the name by which local users of the SMB printer know the printer.

- **User** — Username is required by the SMB server system to give you access to the SMB printer. A username is not necessary if you are authenticating the printer based on share-level rather than user-level access control. With share-level access, you can add a password for each shared printer or file system.

- **Password** — Password associated with the SMB username or the shared resource, depending on the kind of access control being used.

Caution

When you enter a User and Password for SMB, that information is stored unencrypted in the `/etc/cups/printers.conf` file. Be sure that the file remains readable only by root. ∎

The following is an example of the SMB URI you could add to the SMB:// box:

```
jjones:my9passswd@FSTREET/NS1/hp
```

The URI shown here identifies the username (`jjones`), the user's password (`my9passswd`), the workgroup (`FSTREET`), the server (`NS1`), and the printer queue name (`hp`).

Complete the rest of the procedure as you would for a local printer (see the "Adding a Local Printer" section earlier in this chapter).

If everything is set up properly, you can use the standard `lpr` command to print the file to the printer. Using this example, employ the following form for printing:

```
$ cat file1.ps | lpr -P NS1-PS
```

Tip

If you are receiving failure messages, make sure that the computer to which you are printing is accessible. For the Printer NSI hp example, you can type smbclient -L NS1 -U jjones. Then type the password (my9passwd, in this case). The `-L` asks for information about the server; the `-U jjones` says to log in the user jjones. If you get a positive name query response after you enter a password, you should see a list of shared printers and files from that server. Check the names and try printing again. ■

Working with CUPS Printing

Tools such as CUPS web-based Administration and the Printer Configuration window effectively hide the underlying CUPS facility. There may be times, however, when you want to work directly with the tools and configuration files that come with CUPS. The following sections describe how to use some special CUPS features.

Configuring the CUPS Server (cupsd.conf)

The cupsd daemon process listens for requests to your CUPS print server and responds to those requests based on settings in the `/etc/cups/cupsd.conf` file. The configuration variables in the `cupsd.conf` file are in the same form as those in the Apache configuration file (`httpd.conf` or `apache2.conf`). Type **man cupsd.conf** to see details on any of the settings.

The Printer Configuration window adds access information to the `cupsd.conf` file. For other Linux systems, you may need to configure the `cupsd.conf` file manually. You can step through the `cupsd.conf` file to further tune your CUPS server. Most of the settings are optional or can just be left as the default. Let's take a look at some of the settings in the `cupsd.conf` file.

No classification is set by default. With the classification set to `topsecret`, you can have Top Secret displayed on all pages that go through the print server:

```
Classification topsecret
```

Other classifications you can substitute for `topsecret` include `classified`, `confidential`, `secret`, and `unclassified`.

The `ServerCertificate` and `ServerKey` lines (commented out by default) can be set up to indicate where the certificate and key are stored, respectively:

```
ServerCertificate /etc/cups/ssl/server.crt
ServerKey /etc/cups/ssl/server.key
```

Activate these two lines if you want to do encrypted connections. Then add your certificate and key to the files noted.

The term *browsing* refers to the act of broadcasting information about your printer on your local network and listening for other print servers' information. Browsing is on by default only for the local host (@LOCAL). You can allow CUPS browser information (BrowseAllow) for additional selected addresses. Browsing information is broadcast, by default, on address 255.255.255.255. Here's how these defaults appear in the cupsd.conf file:

```
Browsing On
BrowseProtocols cups
BrowseOrder Deny,Allow
BrowseAllow from @LOCAL
BrowseAddress 255.255.255.255
Listen *:631
```

To enable web-based CUPS administration, the cupsd daemon can be set to listen on port 631 for all network interfaces to your computer based on this entry: Listen *:631. By default, it only listens on the local interface (Listen localhost:631).

By turning on BrowseRelay (it's off by default), you can allow CUPS browse information to be passed among two or more networks. The source-address and destination-address can be individual IP addresses or can represent network numbers:

```
BrowseRelay source-address destination-address
```

This is a good way to enable users on several connected LANs to discover and use printers on other nearby LANs.

You can allow or deny access to different features of the CUPS server. An access definition for a CUPS printer (created from the Printer Configuration window) might appear as follows:

```
<Location /printers/ns1-hp1>
Order Deny,Allow
Deny From All
Allow From 127.0.0.1
AuthType None
</Location>
```

Here, printing to the ns1-hp1 printer is allowed only for users on the local host (127.0.0.1). No password is needed (AuthType None). To allow access to the administration tool, CUPS must be configured to prompt for a password (AuthType Basic).

Starting the CUPS Server

For Linux systems that use System V-style startup scripts (such as Fedora and RHEL), starting and shutting down the CUPS print service is pretty easy. Use the chkconfig command to turn on CUPS so it starts at each reboot. Run the cups startup script to have the CUPS service start immediately. In Fedora and RHEL, type the following as root user:

```
# chkconfig cupsd on
# service cups start
```

In Ubuntu, type the following:

```
$ sudo update-rc.d cups enable
$ sudo /etc/init.d/cups start
```

If the CUPS service is already running, you should use `restart` instead of `start`. Using the `restart` option is also a good way to reread any configuration options you may have changed in the `cupsd.conf` file.

Other Linux systems vary in how they start up the CUPS service. For example, in Slackware, you can turn on CUPS printing permanently by simply making the `rc.cups` script executable and then turning it on immediately by executing it (typing the following as root user):

```
# chmod 755 /etc/rc.d/rc.cups
# /etc/rc.d/rc.cups start
```

In Gentoo Linux, you use the `add` option of the `rc-update` command to have the CUPS service start at each reboot and run the `cupsd` run-level script to start it immediately. For example, type the following as root user:

```
# rc-update add cupsd default
# /etc/init.d/cupsd start
```

Most Linux systems have similar ways of starting the CUPS service. You may need to poke around to see how CUPS starts on the distribution you are using.

Configuring CUPS Printer Options Manually

If your Linux distribution doesn't have a graphical means of configuring CUPS, you can edit configuration files directly. For example, when a new printer is created from the Printer Configuration window, it is defined in the `/etc/cups/printers.conf` file. Here is what a printer entry looks like:

```
<DefaultPrinter printer>
Info HP LaserJet 2100M
Location HP LaserJet 2100M in hall closet
DeviceURI parallel:/dev/lp0
State Idle
Accepting Yes
Shared No
JobSheets none none
QuotaPeriod 0
PageLimit 0
KLimit 0
</Printer>
```

This is an example of a local printer that serves as the default printer for the local system. The `Shared No` value is set because the printer is currently available only on the local system. The most interesting information relates to DeviceURI, which shows that the printer is connected to parallel port /dev/lp0. The state is Idle (ready to accept printer jobs), and the Accepting value is Yes (the printer is accepting print jobs by default).

The DeviceURI has several ways to identify the device name of a printer, reflecting where the printer is connected. Here are some examples listed in the printers.conf file:

```
DeviceURI parallel:/dev/plp
DeviceURI serial:/dev/ttyd1?baud=38400+size=8+parity=none+flow=soft
DeviceURI scsi:/dev/scsi/sc1d6l0
DeviceURI socket://hostname:port
DeviceURI tftp://hostname/path
DeviceURI ftp://hostname/path
DeviceURI http://hostname[:port]/path
DeviceURI ipp://hostname/path
DeviceURI smb://hostname/printer
```

The first three examples show the form for local printers (parallel, serial, and scsi). The other examples are for remote hosts. In each case, *hostname* can be the host's name or IP address. Port numbers or paths identify the location of each printer on the host.

Tip

If you find that you are not able to print because a particular printer driver is not supported in CUPS, you can set up your printer to accept jobs in raw mode. This can work well if you are printing from Windows clients that have the correct print drivers installed. To enable raw printing in CUPS, uncomment the following line in the /etc/cups/mime.types file in Linux:

```
application/octet-stream
```

and uncomment the following line in the /etc/cups/mime.convs file:

```
application/octet-stream application/vnd.cups-raw 0 -
```

After that, you can print files as raw data to your printers without using the -oraw option to print commands. ■

Using Printing Commands

To remain backward compatible with older UNIX and Linux printing facilities, CUPS supports many of the old commands for working with printing. Most command-line printing with CUPS can be performed with the lpr command. Word processing applications such as StarOffice, OpenOffice, and AbiWord are set up to use this facility for printing.

You can use the Printer Configuration window to define the filters needed for each printer so that the text can be formatted properly. Options to the lpr command can add filters to properly process the text. Other commands for managing printed documents include lpq (for viewing the contents of print queues), lprm (for removing print jobs from the queue), and lpc (for controlling printers).

Printing with lpr

You can use the lpr command to print documents to both local and remote printers (provided the printers are configured locally). Document files can be either added to the end of the lpr command line or directed to the lpr command using a pipe (|). Here's an example of a simple lpr command:

```
$ lpr doc1.ps
```

When you specify just a document file with lpr, output is directed to the default printer. As an individual user, you can change the default printer by setting the value of the PRINTER variable. Typically, you add the PRINTER variable to one of your startup files, such as $HOME/.bashrc. Adding the following line to your .bashrc file, for example, sets your default printer to lp3:

```
export PRINTER=lp3
```

To override the default printer, specify a particular printer on the lpr command line. The following example uses the -P option to select a different printer:

```
$ lpr -P canyonps doc1.ps
```

The lpr command has a variety of options that enable lpr to interpret and format several different types of documents. These include -# num, where num is replaced by the number of copies to print (from 1 to 100) and -l (which causes a document to be sent in raw mode, presuming that the document has already been formatted). To learn more options to lpr, type **man lpr**.

Listing Status with lpc

Use the lpc command to list the status of your printers. Here is an example:

```
$ /usr/sbin/lpc status
hp:
                printer is on device 'parallel' speed -1
                queuing is enabled
                printing is disabled
                no entries
                daemon present
deskjet_5550:
                printer is on device '/dev/null' speed -1
                queuing is enabled
                printing is disabled
                no entries
                daemon present
```

This output shows two active printers. The first (hp) is connected to your parallel port. The second (deskjet_5550) is a network printer (shown as /dev/null). The hp printer is currently disabled (offline), although the queue is enabled so people can continue to send jobs to the printer.

Removing Print Jobs with lprm

Users can remove their own print jobs from the queue with the lprm command. Used alone on the command line, lprm removes all the user's print jobs from the default printer. To remove jobs from a specific printer, use the -P option, as follows:

```
$ lprm -P lp0
```

To remove all print jobs for the current user, type the following:

```
$ lprm -
```

The root user can remove all the print jobs for a specific user by indicating that user on the lprm command line. For example, to remove all print jobs for the user named mike, the root user types the following:

```
$ lprm -U mike
```

To remove an individual print job from the queue, indicate its job number on the lprm command line. To find the job number, type the lpq command. Here's what the output of that command may look like:

```
$ lpq
printer is ready and printing
Rank    Owner               Job Files                   Total Size Time
active  root                133 /home/jake/pr1              467
2       root                197 /home/jake/mydoc         23948
```

The output shows two printable jobs waiting in the queue. (The printer is ready and printing the job listed as active.) Under the Job column, you can see the job number associated with each document. To remove the first print job, type the following:

```
# lprm 133
```

Configuring Print Servers

You've configured a printer so that you and the other users on your computer can print to it. Now you want to share that printer with other people in your home, school, or office. Basically, that means configuring the printer as a print server.

The printers configured on your Linux system can be shared in different ways with other computers on your network. Not only can your computer act as a Linux print server (by configuring CUPS), but it can also appear as an SMB (Windows) print server to client computers. After a local printer is attached to your Linux system and your computer is connected to your local network, you can use the procedures in this section to share the printer with client computers using a Linux (UNIX) or SMB interface.

Configuring a Shared CUPS Printer

Making the local printer added to your Linux computer available to other computers on your network is fairly easy. If a TCP/IP network connection exists between the computers sharing the printer, you simply grant permission to all hosts, individual hosts, or users from remote hosts to access your computer's printing service.

To manually configure a printer entry in the /etc/cups/printers.conf file to accept print jobs from all other computers, make sure the Shared Yes line is set. The following example from a printers.conf entry earlier in this chapter demonstrates what the new entry would look like:

```
<DefaultPrinter printer>
Info HP LaserJet 2100M
Location HP LaserJet 2100M in hall closet
DeviceURI parallel:/dev/lp0
State Idle
Accepting Yes
Shared Yes
JobSheets none none
QuotaPeriod 0
PageLimit 0
KLimit 0
</Printer>
```

On Linux systems that use the Printer Configuration window described earlier in this chapter, it's best to set up your printer as a shared printer using that window. Here's how:

1. From the Desktop panel in GNOME, select System ➪ Administration ➪ Printing. The Printer Configuration window appears.

2. Double-click the name of the printer you want to share. (If the printer is not yet configured, refer to the "Setting Up Printers" section earlier in this chapter.)

3. Choose the Policies heading and select Shared so that a checkmark appears in the box.

4. If you want to restrict access to the printer to selected users, select the Access Control heading and choose one of the following options:

   - **Allow Printing for Everyone Except These Users** — With this selected, all users are allowed access to the printer. By typing usernames into the Users box and clicking Add, you exclude selected users.

   - **Deny Printing for Everyone Except These Users** — With this selected, all users are excluded from using the printer. Type usernames into the Users box and click Add to allow access to the printer for only those names you enter.

Now you can configure other computers to use your printer, as described in the "Setting Up Printers" section of this chapter. If you try to print from another computer and it doesn't work, here are a few troubleshooting tips:

- **Open your firewall.** If you have a restrictive firewall, it may not permit printing. You must enable access to port 513 (UDP and TCP) and possibly port 631 to allow access to printing on your computer.

- **Enable LPD-style printing.** Certain applications may require an older LPD-style printing service to print on your shared printer. To enable LPD-style printing on your CUPS server, you must turn on the cups-lpd service. Most Linux distributions that include CUPS should also have cups-lpd available. In Fedora and RHEL systems, type **yum install cups-lpd** as root user to install it. Then turn on the cups-lpd service:

```
# chkconfig cups-lpd on
```

- **Check names and addresses.** Make sure that you entered your computer's name and print queue properly when you configured it on the other computer. Try using the IP address instead of the hostname. (If that works, it indicates a DNS name resolution problem.) Running a tool such as Ethereal enables you to see where the transaction fails.

Access changes to your shared printer are made in the `cupsd.conf` and `printers.conf` files in your `/etc/cups` directory.

Configuring a Shared Samba Printer

Your Linux printers can be configured as shared SMB printers so they appear to be available from Windows systems. To share your printer as if it were a Samba (SMB) printer, simply configure basic Samba server settings as described in Chapter 18. All your printers should be shared on your local network by default. The next section shows what the resulting settings look like and how you might want to change them.

Understanding smb.conf for Printing

When you configure Samba, the `/etc/samba/smb.conf` file is constructed to enable all of your configured printers to be shared. Here are a few lines from the `smb.conf` file that relate to printer sharing:

```
[global]
    .
    .
    .
  load printers = yes
  cups options = raw
; printcap name = /etc/printcap
; printing = cups
    .
```

```
          .
          .
[printers]
        comment = All Printers
        path = /var/spool/samba
        browseable = yes
        writeable = no
        printable = yes
```

These example settings are the result of configuring Samba from the Samba Server Configuration window in Fedora. You can read the comment lines to learn more about the file's contents. Lines beginning with a semicolon (;) indicate the default setting for the option on a comment line. Remove the semicolon to change the setting.

The selected lines show that printers from /etc/printcap were loaded and that the CUPS service is being used. With cups options set to raw, Samba assumes that print files have already been formatted by the time they reach your print server. This allows the Linux or Windows clients to provide their own print drivers.

The last few lines are the actual printers' definitions. By changing the browseable option from no to yes, users can print to all printers (printable = yes).

It is also possible to store Windows native print drivers on your Samba server. When a Windows client uses your printer, the driver will automatically be available so you won't need to use a driver CD or download the driver from the vendor's web site. To enable the printer driver share, add a Samba share called print$ that looks like the following:

```
[print$]
comment = Printer Drivers
path = /var/lib/samba/drivers
browseable = yes
guest ok = no
read only = yes
write list = chris, dduffey
```

Once you have the share available you can start copying Windows print drivers to the share, as described in the Samba HOWTO:

```
http://www.samba.org/samba/docs/man/Samba-HOWTO-
    Collection/classicalprinting.html#id2626941
```

Setting Up SMB Clients

Chances are good that if you are configuring a Samba printer on your Linux computer, you want to share it with Windows clients. If Samba is set up properly on your computer and the client computers can reach you over the network, their finding and using your printer should be fairly straightforward.

The first place a client computer looks for your shared Samba printer is in Network Neighborhood (or My Network Places, for Windows 2000). From the Windows 9x desktop, double-click the

Network Neighborhood icon. (From Windows 2000 or XP, double-click the My Network Places icon.) With Windows Vista, you open the Network icon. The name of your host computer (the NetBIOS name, which is probably also your TCP/IP name) appears on the screen or within a work-group folder on the screen. Open the icon that represents your computer. The window that opens shows your shared printers and folders.

Tip

If your computer's icon doesn't appear in Network Neighborhood or My Network Places, try using the Search window. From Windows XP, choose Start ➪ Search ➪ Computer or People ➪ A Computer on the Network. Type your computer's name into the Computer Name box and click Search. Double-click your computer in the Search window results panel. A window displaying the shared printers and folders from your computer appears. ■

After your shared printer appears in the window, configure a pointer to that printer by opening (double-clicking) the printer icon. A message tells you that you must set up the printer before you can use it. Click Yes to proceed to configure the printer for local use. The Add Printer Wizard appears. Answer the questions that ask you how you intend to use the printer, and add the appropriate drivers. When you are done, the printer appears in your printer window.

Another way to configure an SMB printer from a Windows XP operating system is to go to Start ➪ Printers and Faxes. In the Printers and Faxes window that appears, click the Add a Printer icon in the upper-left portion of the window, and then select Network Printer from the first window. From there you can browse and/or configure your SMB printer.

Summary

Providing networked printing services is essential on today's business network. With the use of a few network-attached devices, you can focus your printer spending on a few high-quality devices that multiple users can share instead of numerous lower-cost devices. In addition, a centrally located printer can make it easier to maintain the printer, while still enabling everyone to get his or her printing jobs done.

The default printing service in nearly every major Linux distribution today is the Common UNIX Printing System (CUPS). Any Linux system that includes CUPS offers the CUPS web-based administrative interface for configuring CUPS printing. It also offers configuration files in the /etc/cups directory for configuring printers and the CUPS service (cupsd daemon).

In Ubuntu, Fedora, and other Linux systems, you can configure your printer with the printing configuration windows available in both KDE and GNOME desktops. A variety of drivers makes it possible to print to different kinds of printers, as well as to printers that are connected to computers on the network.

You can set up your computer as a Linux print server, and you can also have your computer emulate an SMB (Windows) print server. After your network is configured properly and a local printer is installed, sharing that printer over the network as a UNIX or SMB print server is not very complicated.

Running a File Server

## 18

Most networked computers are on the network in the first place so that users can share information. Some users need to collectively edit documents for a project, share access to spreadsheets and forms used in the daily operation of a company, or perform any number of similar file-sharing activities. It also can be efficient for groups of people on a computer network to share common applications and directories of information needed to do their jobs. A file server is an efficient way to share files over a network.

You can secure files on your file servers using standard Linux ownership and file permissions, as well as using more advanced features such as firewalls and SELinux to protect the data in your files. Some file servers also can require authentication to access or change the files you share.

Linux systems include support for each of the most common file server protocols in use today. Among these are the Network File System (NFS), which has always been the file-sharing protocol of choice for Linux and other UNIX systems, and Samba (SMB protocol), which is often used by networks with many Windows and OS/2 computers.

Coming from Windows

Samba allows you to share files with Windows PCs on your network, as well as access Windows file and print servers, making your Linux box fit in better with Windows-centric or mixed organizations. ■

This chapter describes how to set up file servers and clients associated with NFS and Samba.

Tip

When selecting file services to provide, keep in mind that less is more. If your clients and servers support multiple-file access capabilities (both NFS and SMB, for example), pick the service that lends itself to making the task less complicated for your organization. ■

Setting Up an NFS File Server

Instead of representing storage devices as drive letters (A, B, C, and so on), as they are in Microsoft operating systems, Linux systems invisibly connect file systems from multiple hard disks, floppy disks, CD-ROMs, and other local devices to form a single Linux file system. The Network File System (NFS) facility enables you to extend your Linux file system in the same way, to connect file systems on other computers to your local directory structure.

An NFS file server provides an easy way to share large amounts of data among the users and computers in an organization. An administrator of a Linux system that is configured to share its file systems using NFS has to perform the following tasks to set up NFS:

1. **Set up the network.** NFS is typically used on private LANs as opposed to public networks, such as the Internet.

2. **Choose what to share from the server.** Decide which file systems on your Linux NFS server to make available to other computers. You can choose any point in the file system and make all files and directories below that point accessible to other computers.

3. **Set up security on the server.** You can use several different security features to suit the level of security with which you are comfortable. Mount-level security lets you restrict the computers that can mount a resource and, for those allowed to mount it, lets you specify whether it can be mounted read/write or read-only. In NFS, user-level security is implemented by mapping users from the client systems to users on the NFS server (based on UID and not username) so that they can rely on standard Linux read/write/ execute permissions, file ownership, and group permissions to access and protect files.

4. **Mount the file system on the client.** Each client computer that is allowed access to the server's NFS shared file system can mount it anywhere the client chooses. For example, you may mount a file system from a computer called maple on the /mnt/maple directory in your local file system. After it is mounted, you can view the contents of that directory by typing ls /mnt/maple. Then you can use the cd command below the /mnt/maple mount point to see the files and directories it contains.

Figure 18-1 illustrates a Linux file server using NFS to share (export) a file system and a client computer mounting the file system to make it available to its local users.

In this example, a computer named oak makes its /apps/bin directory available to clients on the network (pine, maple, and spruce) by adding an entry to the /etc/exports file. The client computer (pine) sees that the resource is available and mounts the resource on its local file system at the mount point /oak/apps, after which any files, directories, or subdirectories from /apps/bin on oak are available to users on pine (given proper permissions).

FIGURE 18-1

NFS can make selected file systems available to other computers.

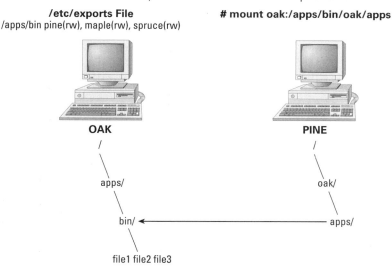

Although it is often used as a file server (or other type of server), Linux is a general-purpose operating system, so any Linux system can share file systems (export) as a server or use another computer's file systems (mount) as a client. Contrast this with dedicated file servers, such as NetWare, which can only share files with client computers (such as Windows workstations) and never act as a client.

Note

A file system is usually a structure of files and directories that exists on a single device (such as a hard disk partition or CD-ROM). A *Linux file system* refers to the entire directory structure (which may include file systems from several disks or NFS resources), beginning from root (/) on a single computer. A shared directory in NFS may represent all or part of a computer's file system, which can be attached (from the shared directory down the directory tree) to another computer's file system. ■

Getting NFS

Although nearly every Linux system supports NFS client and server features, NFS is not always installed by default. You'll need different packages for different Linux systems to install NFS. Here are some examples:

- **Fedora and Red Hat Enterprise Linux systems** — You need to install the nfs-utils package to use Fedora as an NFS server. There is also a graphical NFS configuration tool that requires you to install the system-config-nfs package. NFS client features are in the base operating system. After configuring NFS (via the /etc/exports file), turn on the NFS service by typing the following:

```
# service rpcbind start
# service nfs start
# chkconfig nfs on
```

- **Ubuntu and Debian** — To act as an NFS client, the nfs-common and portmap packages are required; for an NFS server, the nfs-kernel-server package must be added. The following apt-get command line (if you are connected to the Internet) installs them all. Then, after you add an exported file system to the /etc/exports file (as described later), you can start the nfs-common and nfs-kernel-server scripts, as shown here:

```
# apt-get install nfs-common portmap nfs-kernel-server
# /etc/init.d/nfs-kernel-server start
# /etc/init.d/nfs-common start
```

- **Gentoo** — With Gentoo, NFS file system and NFS server support must be configured into the kernel to use NFS server features. Installing the nfs-utils package (emerge nfs-utils) should get the required packages. To start the service, run rc-update and start the service immediately:

```
# emerge nfs-utils
# rc-update add portmap default
# rc-update add nfs default
# /etc/init.d/nfs start
```

The commands (mount, exportfs, and so on) and files (/etc/exports, /etc/fstab, and so on) for actually configuring NFS are the same on every Linux system I've encountered. So after you have NFS installed and running, just follow the instructions in this chapter to start using NFS.

Sharing NFS File Systems

To share an NFS file system from your Linux system, you need to export it from the server system. Exporting is done in Linux by adding entries into the /etc/exports file. Each entry identifies a directory in your local file system that you want to share with other computers. The entry also identifies the other computers that can share the resource (or opens it to all computers) and includes other options that reflect permissions associated with the directory.

Remember that when you share a directory, you are sharing all files and subdirectories below that directory as well (by default). So, you need to be sure that you want to share everything in that directory structure. There are still ways to restrict access within that directory structure; those are discussed later in this chapter.

Configuring the /etc/exports File

To make a directory from your Linux system available to other systems, you need to export that directory. Exporting is done on a permanent basis by adding information about an exported directory to the /etc/exports file.

The format of the /etc/exports file is

```
Directory    Host(Options...)  Host(Options...)  # Comments
```

where *Directory* is the name of the directory that you want to share, and *Host* indicates the client computer to which the sharing of this directory is restricted. *Options* can include a variety of options to define the security measures attached to the shared directory for the host. (You can repeat Host/Option pairs.) *Comments* are any optional comments you want to add (following the # sign).

As root user, you can use any text editor to configure /etc/exports to modify shared directory entries or add new ones. Here's an example of an /etc/exports file:

```
/cal    *.linuxtoys.net(rw)              # Company events
/pub    *(ro,insecure,all_squash)        # Public dir
/home   maple(rw,squash uids=0-99) spruce(rw,squash uids=0-99)
```

The /cal entry represents a directory that contains information about events related to the company. It is made accessible to everyone with accounts to any computers in the company's domain (*.linuxtoys.net). Users can write files to the directory as well as read them (indicated by the rw option). The comment (# Company events) simply serves to remind you of what the directory contains.

The /pub entry represents a public directory. It allows any computer and user to read files from the directory (indicated by the ro option) but not to write files. The insecure option enables any computer, even one that doesn't use a secure NFS port, to access the directory. The all_ squash option causes all users (UIDs) and groups (GIDs) to be mapped to the user ID 65534 (which is the nfsnobody user in Fedora and the nobody user in Ubuntu), giving them minimal permission to files and directories.

The /home entry enables a set of users to have the same /home directory on different computers. Say, for example, that you are sharing /home from a computer named oak. The computers named maple and spruce could each mount that directory on their own /home directories. If you gave all users the same username/UID on all machines, you could have the same /home/user directory available for each user, regardless of which computer they are logged into. The uids=0-99 is used to prevent any administrative login from another computer from changing any files in the shared directory.

These are just examples; you can share any directories that you choose, including the entire file system (/). Of course, there are security implications of sharing the whole file system or sensitive parts of it (such as /etc). Security options that you can add to your /etc/exports file are described throughout the sections that follow.

Hostnames in /etc/exports

You can indicate in the /etc/exports file which host computers can have access to your shared directory. If you want to associate multiple hostnames or IP addresses with a particular shared directory, be sure to have a space before each hostname. However, add no spaces between a host-name and its options. For example:

```
/usr/local maple(rw) spruce(ro,root_squash)
```

Notice that there is a space after (rw) but none after maple. You can identify hosts in several ways:

- **Individual host** — Enter one or more TCP/IP hostnames or IP addresses. If the host is in your local domain, you can simply indicate the hostname. Otherwise, use the full host.domain format. These are valid ways to indicate individual host computers:

```
maple
maple.handsonhistory.com
10.0.0.11
```

- **IP network** — Allow access to all hosts from a particular network address by indicating a network number and its netmask, separated by a slash (/). Here are valid ways to designate network numbers:

```
10.0.0.0/255.0.0.0 172.16.0.0/255.255.0.0
192.168.18.0/255.255.255.0
192.168.18.0/24
```

- **TCP/IP domain** — Using wildcards, you can include all or some host computers from a particular domain level. Here are some valid uses of the asterisk and question mark wildcards:

```
*.handsonhistory.com
*craft.handsonhistory.com
???.handsonhistory.com
```

The first example matches all hosts in the handsonhistory.com domain. The second example matches woodcraft, basketcraft, or any other hostnames ending in craft in the handsonhistory.com domain. The final example matches any three-letter host-names in the domain.

- **NIS groups** — You can allow access to hosts contained in an NIS group. To indicate an NIS group, precede the group name with an at (@) sign (for example, @group).

Access Options in /etc/exports

You don't have to just give away your files and directories when you export a directory with NFS. In the options part of each entry in /etc/exports, you can add options that allow or limit access by setting read/write permissions. These options, which are passed to NFS, are as follows:

- ro — Client can mount this exported file system read-only. The default is to mount the file system read/write.
- rw — Explicitly asks that a shared directory be shared with read/write permissions. (If the client chooses, it can still mount the directory as read-only.)

User Mapping Options in /etc/exports

In addition to options that define how permissions are handled generally, you can use options to set the permissions that specific users have to NFS shared file systems.

One method that simplifies this process is to have each user with multiple user accounts have the same username and UID on each machine. This makes it easier to map users so that they have the same permissions on a mounted file system that they do on files stored on their local hard disks. If that method is not convenient, user IDs can be mapped in many other ways. Here are some methods of setting user permissions and the /etc/exports option that you use for each method:

- **root user** — The client's root user is mapped by default into the nfsnobody username (UID 65534). This prevents a client computer's root user from being able to change all files and directories in the shared file system. If you want the client's root user to have root permission on the server, use the no_root_squash option.

Tip
There may be other administrative users, in addition to root, that you want to squash. I recommend squashing UIDs 0–99 as follows: squash_uids=0-99. Also, keep in mind that even though root is squashed, the root user from the client can still become any other user account and access files for those user accounts on the server. So be sure that you trust root with all your user data before you share it read/write with a client. ■

- **nfsnobody or nobody user/group** — By using the 65534 user ID and group ID, you essentially create a user/group with permissions that do not allow access to files that belong to any real users on the server, unless those users open permission to everyone. However, files created by the 65534 user or group are available to anyone assigned as the 65534 user or group. To set all remote users to the 65534 user/group, use the all_squash option.

  The 65534 UIDs and GIDs are used to prevent the ID from running into a valid user or group ID. Using anonuid or anongid options, you can change the 65534 user or group, respectively. For example, anonuid=175 sets all anonymous users to UID 175, and anongid=300 sets the GID to 300. (Only the number is displayed when you list file permission unless you add entries with names to /etc/password and /etc/group for the new UIDs and GIDs.)

- **User mapping** — If a user has login accounts for a set of computers (and has the same ID), NFS, by default, maps that ID. This means that if the user named mike (UID 110) on maple has an account on pine (mike, UID 110), he can use his own remotely mounted files on either computer from either computer.

  If a client user who is not set up on the server creates a file on the mounted NFS directory, the file is assigned to the remote client's UID and GID. (An ls -l on the server shows the UID of the owner.) Use the map_static option to identify a file that contains user mappings.

Exporting the Shared File Systems

After you have added entries to your /etc/exports file, run the exportfs command to have those directories exported (made available to other computers on the network). Reboot your computer or restart the NFS service, and the exportfs command runs automatically to export your directories. If you want to export them immediately, run exportfs from the command line (as root).

Tip

Running the exportfs command after you change the exports file is a good idea. If any errors are in the file, exportfs identifies them for you. ■

Here's an example of the exportfs command:

```
# /usr/sbin/exportfs -a -r -v
exporting maple:/pub
exporting spruce:/pub
exporting maple:/home
exporting spruce:/home
exporting *:/mnt/win
```

The -a option indicates that all directories listed in /etc/exports should be exported. The -r resyncs all exports with the current /etc/exports file (disabling those exports no longer listed in the file). The -v option says to print verbose output. In this example, the /pub and /home directories from the local server are immediately available for mounting by those client computers that are named (maple and spruce). The /mnt/win directory is available to all client computers.

Running the exportfs command temporarily makes your exported NFS directories available. To have your NFS directories available on an ongoing basis (that is, every time your system reboots), you need to set your nfs startup scripts to run at boot time. This is described in the next section.

Starting the nfs Daemons

If NFS has been disabled on your system (or is not active by default), you need to start the service. Different Linux distributions have different ways of turning on the NFS service, as you saw in the "Getting NFS" section earlier in the chapter. This section explores how the service is turned on in Fedora and Red Hat Enterprise Linux systems.

In Fedora, you can use the chkconfig command to turn on the NFS service so that your files are exported and the nfsd daemons are running when your system boots. There are two startup scripts you want to turn on for the service to work properly. The nfs service exports file systems (from /etc/exports) and starts the nfsd daemon that listens for service requests. The nfslock service starts the lockd daemon, which helps allow file locking to prevent multiple simultaneous use of critical files over the network.

To turn on the NFS service in Fedora, type the following as root user:

```
# chkconfig nfs on
# chkconfig nfslock on
```

The next time you start your computer, the NFS service will start automatically, and your exported directories will be available. If you want to start the service immediately, without waiting for a reboot, type the following:

```
# /etc/init.d/nfs start
# /etc/init.d/nfslock start
```

The NFS service should now be running and ready to share directories with other computers on your network.

Using NFS File Systems

After a server exports a directory over the network using NFS, a client computer connects that directory to its own file system using the `mount` command. That's the same command used to mount file systems from local hard disks, CDs, and floppies, but with slightly different options.

`mount` can automatically mount NFS directories added to the /etc/fstab file, just as it does with local disks. NFS directories can also be added to the /etc/fstab file in such a way that they are not automatically mounted (so you can mount them manually when you choose). With a `noauto` option, an NFS directory listed in /etc/fstab is inactive until the `mount` command is used, after the system is up and running, to mount the file system.

Manually Mounting an NFS File System

If you know that the directory from a computer on your network has been exported (that is, made available for mounting), you can mount that directory manually using the `mount` command. This is a good way to make sure that it is available and working before you set it up to mount permanently. Here is an example of mounting the /tmp directory from a computer named maple on your local computer:

```
# mkdir /mnt/maple
# mount maple:/tmp /mnt/maple
```

The first command (`mkdir`) creates the mount point directory (/mnt is a common place to put temporarily mounted disks and NFS file systems). The `mount` command identifies the remote computer and shared file system separated by a colon (`maple:/tmp`), and the local mount point directory (/mnt/maple) follows.

Note

If the mount fails, make sure the NFS service is running on the server and that the server's firewall rules don't deny access to the service. From the server, type ps ax | grep nfsd to see a list of nfsd server processes. If you don't see the list, try to start your NFS daemons as described in the previous section. To view your firewall rules, type iptables -L. By default, the nfsd daemon listens for NFS requests on port number 2049. Your firewall must accept udp requests on ports 2049 (nfs) and 111 (rpc). In some Linux systems, such as Fedora, you may need to set static ports for related services, then open ports for those services. To accomplish this, you can open the /etc/sysconfig/nfs file and set static port numbers for RQUOTAD_PORT, LOCKD_TCPPORT, LOCKD_UDPPORT, MOUNTD_PORT, STATD_PORT, and STATD_OUTGOING_PORT. ■

To ensure that the mount occurred, type **mount**. This command lists all mounted disks and NFS file systems. Here is an example of the mount command and its output (with file systems not pertinent to this discussion edited out):

```
# mount
/dev/sda3 on / type ext3 (rw)
...
...
...
maple:/tmp on /mnt/maple type nfs (rw,addr=10.0.0.11)
```

The output from the mount command shows the mounted disk partitions, special file systems, and NFS file systems. The first output line shows the hard disk (/dev/sda3), mounted on the root file system (/), with read/write permission (rw), with a file system type of ext3 (the standard Linux file system type). The just-mounted NFS file system is the /tmp directory from maple (maple:/tmp). It is mounted on /mnt/maple and its mount type is nfs. The file system was mounted read/write (rw), and the IP address of maple is 10.0.0.11 (addr=10.0.0.11).

This is a simple example of using mount with NFS. The mount is temporary and is not remounted when you reboot your computer. You can also add options for NFS mounts:

- -a — Mount all file systems in /etc/fstab (except those indicated as noauto).
- -f — This goes through the motions of (fakes) mounting the file systems on the command line (or in /etc/fstab). Used with the -v option, -f is useful for seeing what mount would do before it actually does it.
- -F — When used with -a, you tell mount to fork off a new incarnation of mount for each file system listed to be mounted in the /etc/fstab file. An advantage of using this option, as it relates to NFS shared directories, is that other file systems can be mounted if an NFS file system isn't immediately available. This option should not be used, however, if the order of mounting is important (for example, if you needed to mount /mnt/pcs and then /mnt/pcs/arctic).
- -r — Mounts the file system as read-only.
- -w — Mounts the file system as read/write. (For this to work, the shared file system must have been exported with read/write permission.)

The next section describes how to make the mount more permanent (using the /etc/fstab file) and how to select various options for NFS mounts.

Automatically Mounting an NFS File System

To set up an NFS file system to mount automatically each time you start your Linux system, you need to add an entry for that NFS file system to the /etc/fstab file. That file contains information about all different kinds of mounted (and available to be mounted) file systems for your system.

Here's the format for adding an NFS file system to your local system:

```
host:directory     mountpoint     nfs     options     0     0
```

The first item (host:directory) identifies the NFS server computer and shared directory. mountpoint is the local mount point on which the NFS directory is mounted. It's followed by the file system type (nfs). Any options related to the mount appear next in a comma-separated list. (The last two zeros configure the system to not dump the contents of the file system and not to run fsck on the file system.)

The following are examples of NFS entries in /etc/fstab:

```
maple:/tmp    /mnt/maple nfs    rsize=8192,wsize=8192  0 0
oak:/apps     /oak/apps  nfs    noauto,ro             0 0
```

In the first example, the remote directory /tmp from the computer named maple (maple:/tmp) is mounted on the local directory /mnt/maple (the local directory must already exist). The file system type is nfs, and read (rsize) and write (wsize) buffer sizes (discussed in the "Using Mount Options" section later in this chapter) are set at 8192 to speed data transfer associated with this connection. In the second example, the remote directory is /apps on the computer named oak. It is set up as an NFS file system (nfs) that can be mounted on the /oak/apps directory locally. This file system is not mounted automatically (noauto), however, and can be mounted only as read-only (ro) using the mount command after the system is already running.

Tip

The default is to mount an NFS file system as read/write. However, the default for exporting a file system is read-only. If you are unable to write to an NFS file system, check that it was exported as read/write from the server. ■

Mounting noauto File Systems

Your /etc/fstab file may also contain devices for other file systems that are not mounted automatically. For example, you might have multiple disk partitions on your hard disk or an NFS shared file system that you want to mount only occasionally. A noauto file system can be mounted manually. The advantage is that when you type the mount command, you can type less information and have the rest filled in by the contents of the /etc/fstab file. So, for example, you could type:

```
# mount /oak/apps
```

With this command, mount knows to check the /etc/fstab file to get the file system to mount (oak:/apps), the file system type (nfs), and the options to use with the mount (in this case ro for read-only). Instead of typing the local mount point (/oak/apps), you could have typed the remote file system name (oak:/apps) and had other information filled in.

Tip

When naming mount points, including the name of the remote NFS server in that name can help you remember where the files are actually being stored. This may not be possible if you are sharing home directories (/home) or mail directories (/var/spool/mail). For example, you might mount a file system from a machine called duck on the directory /mnt/duck. ■

Using Mount Options

You can add several `mount` options to the `/etc/fstab` file (or to a `mount` command line itself) to influence how the file system is mounted. When you add options to `/etc/fstab`, they must be separated by commas. For example, here, the `noauto`, `ro`, and `hard` options are used when `oak:/apps` is mounted:

```
oak:/apps    /oak/apps  nfs    noauto,ro,hard    0  0
```

The following are some options that are valuable for mounting NFS file systems:

- `hard` — If this option is used and the NFS server disconnects or goes down while a process is waiting to access it, the process will hang until the server comes back up. This is helpful if it is critical that the data you are working with not get out of sync with the programs that are accessing it. (This is the default behavior.)

- `soft` — If the NFS server disconnects or goes down, a process trying to access data from the server will time out after a set period of time when this option is on. An input/output error is delivered to the process trying to access the NFS server.

- `rsize` — The size of the blocks of data (in bytes) that the NFS client will request be used when it is reading data from an NFS server. The default is 1024. Using a larger number (such as 8192) will get you better performance on a network that is fast (such as a LAN) and is relatively error-free (that is, one that doesn't have a lot of noise or collisions).

- `wsize` — The size of the blocks of data (in bytes) that the NFS client will request be used when it is writing data to an NFS server. The default is 1024. Performance issues are the same as with the `rsize` option.

- `timeo=#` — Sets the time after an RPC timeout occurs that a second transmission is made, where # represents a number in tenths of a second. The default value is seventenths of a second. Each successive timeout causes the timeout value to be doubled (up to 60 seconds maximum). Increase this value if you believe that timeouts are occurring because of slow response from the server or a slow network.

- `retrans=#` — Sets the number of minor timeouts and retransmissions that need to happen before a major timeout occurs.

- `retry=#` — Sets how many minutes to continue to retry failed mount requests, where # is replaced by the number of minutes to retry. The default is 10,000 minutes (which is about one week).

- `bg` — If the first mount attempt times out, try all subsequent mounts in the background. This option is very valuable if you are mounting a slow or sporadically available NFS file system. By placing mount requests in the background, your system can continue to mount other file systems instead of waiting for the current one to complete.

- `fg` — If the first mount attempt times out, try subsequent mounts in the foreground. This is the default behavior. Use this option if it is imperative that the mount be successful before continuing (for example, if you are mounting `/usr`).

Note

If a nested mount point is missing, a timeout to allow for the needed mount point to be added occurs. For example, if you mount /usr/trip and /usr/trip/extra as NFS file systems and /usr/trip is not yet mounted when /usr/trip/extra tries to mount, /usr/trip/extra times out. If you're lucky, /usr/trip comes up and /usr/trip/extra mounts on the next retry. ∎

Using autofs to Mount NFS File Systems On Demand

Recent improvements to auto-detecting and mounting removable devices have meant that you can simply insert or plug in those devices to have them detected, mounted, and displayed. However, to make the process of detecting and mounting remote NFS file systems more automatic, you still need to use a facility such as autofs (short for automatically mounted file systems).

The autofs facility will mount network file systems on demand when someone tries to use the file systems. With the autofs facility configured and turned on, you can cause any NFS shared directories to mount on demand. To use the autofs facility, you need to have the autofs package installed. (For Fedora and RHEL, you can type yum install autofs, or for Ubuntu or Debian apt-get install autofs, to install the package from the network.)

With autofs enabled, if you know the hostname and directory being shared by another host computer, simply change (cd) to the autofs mount directory (/net or /var/autofs by default). This causes the shared resource to be automatically mounted and made accessible to you.

The following steps explain how to turn on the autofs facility in Fedora:

1. In Fedora, as root user from a Terminal window, open the /etc/auto.master file and look for the following line:

```
/net    -hosts
```

This causes the /net directory to act as the mount point for the NFS shared directories you want to access on the network. (If there is a comment character at the beginning of that line, remove it.)

2. Start the autofs service by typing the following as root user:

```
# service autofs start
```

3. On a Fedora system, set up the autofs service to restart every time you boot your system:

```
# chkconfig autofs on
```

Believe it or not, that's all you have to do. If you have a network connection to the NFS servers from which you want to share directories, try to access a shared NFS directory. For example, if you know that the /usr/local/share directory is being shared from the computer on your network named shuttle, you can do the following:

```
$ cd /net/shuttle
```

If that computer has any shared directories that are available to you, you can successfully change to that directory.

You also can type the following:

```
$ ls
usr
```

You should be able to see that the usr directory is part of the path to a shared directory. If there were shared directories from other top-level directories (such as /var or /tmp), you would see those as well. Of course, seeing any of those directories depends on how security is set up on the server.

Try going straight to the shared directory as well. For example:

```
$ cd /net/shuttle/usr/local/share
$ ls
info man music television
```

At this point, the ls should reveal the contents of the /usr/local/share directory on the computer named shuttle. What you can do with that content depends on how it was configured for sharing by the server.

This can be a bit disconcerting because you won't see any files or directories until you actually try to use them, such as changing to a network-mounted directory. The ls command, for example, won't show anything under a network-mounted directory until the directory is mounted, which may lead to a sometimes-it's-there-and-sometimes-it's-not impression. Just change to a network-mounted directory, or access a file on such a directory, and autofs will take care of the rest.

Unmounting NFS File Systems

After an NFS file system is mounted, unmounting it is simple. You use the umount command with either the local mount point or the remote file system name. For example, here are two ways you could unmount maple:/tmp from the local directory /mnt/maple:

```
# umount maple:/tmp
```

```
# umount /mnt/maple
```

Either form works. If maple:/tmp is mounted automatically (from a listing in /etc/fstab), the directory will be remounted the next time you boot Linux. If it was a temporary mount (or listed as noauto in /etc/fstab), it won't be remounted at boot time.

Tip

The command is umount, not unmount. This is easy to get wrong. ∎

If you get the message device is busy when you try to unmount a file system, it means the unmount failed because the file system is being accessed. Most likely, one of the directories in the NFS file system is the current directory for your shell (or the shell of someone else on your system). The other possibility is that a command (such as a text editor) is holding a file open in the NFS file system. Check your Terminal windows and other shells, and cd out of the directory if you are in it, or just close the Terminal windows.

If an NFS file system won't unmount, you can force it (umount -f /mnt/maple) or unmount and clean up later (umount -l /mnt/maple). The -l option is usually the better choice because a forced unmount can disrupt a file modification that is in progress. Another alternative is to run fuser -v *mountpoint*, to see what users are holding your mounted NFS share open, then fuser -k *mountpoint* to kill all of those processes.

Other Cool Things to Do with NFS

You can share some directories to make it convenient for a user to work on files from different Linux computers on your network as though the files were connected locally. Some examples of useful directories to share are:

- /var/spool/mail — By sharing this directory from your mail server and mounting it on the same directory on other computers on your network, users can access their mail from any of those other computers. This saves users from having to download messages to their current computers or from having to log in to the server just to get mail. There is only one mailbox for each user, no matter from where it is accessed.

- /home — This is a similar concept to sharing mail, except that all users have access to their home directories from any of the NFS clients. Again, you would mount /home on the same mount point on each client computer. When the user logs in, she has access to all of the startup files and data files contained in her /home/user directory.

Tip

If your users rely on a shared /home directory, you should make sure that the NFS server that exports the directory is fairly reliable. If /home isn't available, the user may not have the startup files to log in correctly, or any of the data files needed to get work done. One workaround is to have a minimal set of startup files (.bashrc, .Xdefaults, and so on) available in the user's home directory when the NFS directory is not mounted. This enables the user to log in properly at those times. ■

- /project — Although you don't have to use this name, a common practice among users on a project is to share a directory structure containing files that people on the project need to share so that everyone can work on original files and keep copies of the latest versions in one place. (Of course, a better way to manage a project is with CVS or some other version control–type software, but this is a poor person's way to do it.)

- /var/log — An administrator can keep track of log files from several different computers by mounting the /var/log file on the administrator's computer. (Each server may need to export the directory to enable root to be mapped between the computers for this to work.) If there are problems with a computer, the administrator can then easily view the shared log files live.

If you are working exclusively with Linux and other UNIX systems, NFS is probably your best choice for sharing file systems. You can mount NFS shares on a Windows client, but only if you have NFS client software for Windows, which does not come with Windows by default. If your network consists primarily of Microsoft Windows computers or a combination of systems, you may want to look into using Samba for file sharing.

Understanding NFS Security Issues

The NFS facility was created in a time when encryption and other security measures were not routinely built into network services (such as remote login, file sharing, and remote execution). Therefore, NFS (even up through version 3) suffers from some rather glaring security issues.

NFS security issues make it an inappropriate facility to use over public networks and even make it difficult to use securely within an organization. Some of these issues include:

- **Remote root users** — Even with the default root_squash (which prevents root users from having root access to remote shares), the root user on any machine to which you share NFS directories can gain access to any other user account. Therefore, if you are doing something like sharing home directories with read/write permission, the root user on any box you are sharing to will have complete access to the contents of those home directories.

- **Unencrypted communications** — Because NFS traffic is unencrypted, anyone sniffing your network will be able to see the data that is being transferred.

- **User mapping** — Default permissions to NFS shares are mapped by User ID. So, for example, a user with UID 500 on an NFS client will have access to files owned by UID 500 on the NFS server. This is regardless of the user names used.

That's the bad news. The good news is that most of these issues are addressed in NFSv4, but require some extra configuration. By integrating Kerberos support, NFSv4 lets you configure user access based on each user obtaining a Kerberos ticket. For you, the extra work is configuring a Kerberos server. See the Ubuntu NFSv4 HOWTO for details on how to do this in Ubuntu:

```
https://help.ubuntu.com/community/NFSv4Howto
```

Setting Up a Samba File Server

Samba is a software package that comes with Ubuntu, Fedora, and Red Hat Enterprise Linux systems and many other Linux systems. (You can obtain the Samba software package from www.samba.org if it is not included with your distribution.) Samba enables you to share file systems and printers on a network with computers that use the Server Message Block (SMB) or Common Internet File System (CIFS) protocols. SMB is the Microsoft protocol that is delivered with Windows operating systems for sharing files and printers. CIFS is an open, cross-platform protocol that is based on SMB. Samba contains free implementations of SMB and CIFS.

Note

In Windows file and printer sharing, SMB is sometimes referred to as CIFS (Common Internet File System), which is an Internet standard network file system definition based on SMB, or NetBIOS, which was the original SMB communication protocol. ■

The Samba software package contains a variety of daemon processes, administrative tools, user tools, and configuration files. To do basic Samba configuration, start with the Samba Server Configuration window, which provides a graphical interface for configuring the server and setting directories to share.

Most of the Samba configuration you do ends up in the /etc/samba/smb.conf file. If you need to access features that are not available through the Samba Server Configuration window, you can edit /etc/samba/smb.conf by hand or use SWAT (Samba Web Administration Tool), a Web-based interface, to configure Samba. Fedora and Red Hat Enterprise Linux offer the system-config-samba graphical interface.

Daemon processes consist of smbd (the SMB daemon) and nmbd (the NetBIOS name server). The smbd daemon makes the file-sharing and printing services you add to your Linux system available to Windows client computers. The Samba package supports the following client computers:

- Windows 9x
- Windows NT
- Windows ME
- Windows 2000
- Windows 2007
- Windows XP
- Windows Vista
- Windows 7
- Windows for workgroups
- MS Client 3.0 for DOS
- OS/2
- Dave for Macintosh computers
- Mac OS X
- Samba for Linux

Note

Mac OS X Server ships with Samba, so you can use a Macintosh system as a server. This chapter, however, discusses using a Linux system as a server. You can then have Macintosh, Windows, or Linux client computers. In addition, Mac OS X ships with both client and server software for Samba. ■

As for administrative tools for Samba, you have several shell commands at your disposal: testparm, with which you can check your configuration files; smbstatus, which tells you what computers are currently connected to your shared resources; and the nmblookup command, with which you can query computers.

Samba uses the NetBIOS service to share resources with SMB clients, but the underlying network must be configured for TCP/IP. Although other SMB hosts can use TCP/IP, NetBEUI, and IPX/SPX to transport data, Samba for Linux supports only TCP/IP. Messages are carried between host computers with TCP/IP and are then handled by NetBIOS.

Getting and Installing Samba

You can get Samba software in different ways, depending on your Linux distribution. Here are a few examples:

- **Gentoo** — With Gentoo, you need to have configured net-fs support into the kernel to use Samba server features. Installing the net-fs package (`emerge net-fs`) should get the required packages. To start the service, run `rc-update` and start the service immediately:

```
# emerge samba
# rc-update add samba default
# /etc/init.d/samba start
```

- **Fedora and Red Hat Enterprise Linux** — You need to install the samba, samba-client, samba-common, and optionally, the system-config-samba and samba-swat packages to use Samba in Fedora. You can then start Samba using the `service` and `chkconfig` commands as follows:

```
# service smb start
# chkconfig smb on
```

The commands and configuration files are the same on most Linux systems using Samba. The Samba project itself comes with a Web-based interface for administering Samba called Samba Web Administration Tool (SWAT). For someone setting up Samba for the first time, SWAT is a good way to get it up and running.

Note
If your Linux installation does not have help documents for Samba available, consult the documentation on the Samba project home page (`www.samba.org`). Also, check the extensive help information that comes with SWAT. ■

Configuring Samba with SWAT

In addition to offering an extensive interface to Samba options, SWAT also comes with an excellent help facility. And if you need to administer Samba from another computer, SWAT can be configured to be remotely accessible and secured by requiring an administrative login and password.

Turning on the SWAT Service

Before you can use SWAT, you must do some configuration. The first thing you must do is turn on the SWAT service, which is done differently in different Linux distributions.

Here's how to set up SWAT in Fedora and Red Hat Enterprise Linux systems:

1. Turn on the SWAT service by typing the following, as root user, from a Terminal window:

```
# chkconfig swat on
```

2. Pick up the change to the service by restarting the xinetd startup script as follows:

```
# service xinetd restart
```

Linux distributions such as Debian, Slackware, and Gentoo turn on the SWAT service from the inetd superserver daemon. After SWAT is installed, you simply remove the comment character from in front of the swat line in the /etc/inetd.conf file (as root user, using any text editor) and restart the daemon. Here's an example of what the swat line looks like in Ubuntu and Debian:

```
swat    stream    tcp    nowait.400    root    /usr/sbin/tcpd    /usr/sbin/swat
```

With the SWAT service ready to be activated, restart the inetd daemon so it rereads the inetd.conf file. To do that in Debian, type the following as root user:

```
# /etc/init.d/openbsd-inetd restart
```

The init.d script and xinetd services are the two ways that SWAT services are generally started in Linux. So if you are using a Linux distribution other than Fedora or Debian, look in the /etc/inetd.conf file or /etc/xinetd.d directory (which is used automatically in Fedora) for the location of your SWAT service.

When you have finished this procedure, a daemon process will be listening on your network interfaces for requests to connect to your SWAT service. You can now use the SWAT program, described in the next section, to configure Samba.

Starting with SWAT

You can run the SWAT program by typing the following URL in your local browser:

```
http://localhost:901/
```

Enter the root username and password when the browser prompts you. The SWAT window (see Figure 18-2) appears.

Tip

Instead of running SWAT from your local browser, you can run it from another computer on the network by substituting the server computer's name for localhost. (To allow computers besides localhost to access the SWAT service on Fedora systems, you must change or remove the only_from = 127.0.0.1 line from the /etc/xinetd.d/swat file and restart the xinetd service.) This is not necessary with Ubuntu systems. ■

FIGURE 18-2

Use SWAT from your browser to manage your Samba configuration.

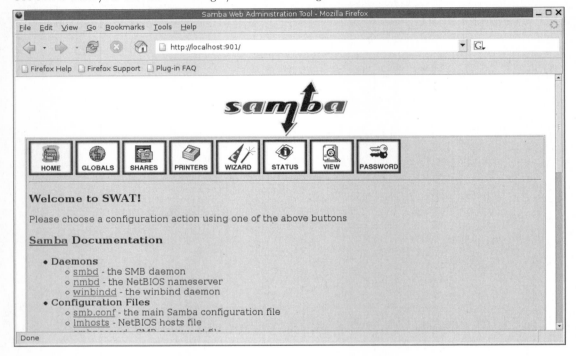

The following sections explain how to use SWAT to create your configuration entries (in /etc/samba/smb.conf) and to work with that configuration.

Caution

Any time you use a GUI to change a plain-text configuration file (as you do with SWAT), you may lose some of the information that you put in by hand. In this case, SWAT deletes comment lines and rearranges other entries. To protect changes you have made manually, make a backup copy of your /etc/samba/smb.conf file before you edit it with SWAT. ■

Creating global Samba settings in SWAT

A group of global settings affects how file and print sharing are generally accomplished on a Samba server. These settings appear under the [global] heading in the /etc/samba/smb.conf file. To view and edit global variables, click the GLOBALS button on the SWAT window.

Several types of options are available: base, security, logging, protocol, tuning, printing, browse, WINs, eventlog, and miscellaneous.

Note

Each option relates to the exact parameters used in the /etc/samba/smb.conf file. You can refer to the smb.conf man page (type man smb.conf) to get more information on these parameters. ∎

Base Options

The following options relate to basic information associated with your Samba server:

- **Workgroup** — The name of the workgroup associated with the group of SMB hosts. By default, the value for this field is WORKGROUP.

- **Realm** — If you are using Kerberos authentication, this value indicates the Kerberos realm to use. Typically, that is reflected by the hostname of the server providing the service.

- **NetBIOS name** — The name assigned to this Samba server. You can use the same name as your DNS hostname or make it blank, in which case the DNS hostname is used automatically. Your DNS hostname is filled in for you by default.

- **NetBIOS alias** — Enables you to set a way of referring to a host computer (an alias) that is different from the host's TCP/IP DNS name.

- **Server string** — A string of text identifying the server. This name appears in places such as the printer comment box. By default, it says Samba and the version number.

- **Interfaces** — Enables you to set up more than one network interface and let Samba browse several different subnetworks. The form of this field can be IP Address/ Subnetwork Mask. Or, you could identify a network interface (such as eth0 for the first Ethernet card on your computer). For example, a Class C network address may appear as

  192.168.24.11/255.255.255.0

Security Options

Of the security options settings, the first (security) is the most important one to get right. It defines the type of security used to give access to the shared file systems and printers to the client computers. (To see some of the fields described here, you need to click the Advanced view.)

- **Security** — Sets how password and user information is transferred to the Samba server from the client computer. As noted earlier, it's important to get this value right. Samba 2.0 and later has a different default value for security (security=user) than the earlier versions of Samba do (security=share). If you are coming from an earlier version of Samba and clients are failing to access your server, this setting is a good place to start. Here are your options:

  - user — The most common type of security used to share files and printers to Windows 95/98/2000/NT/XP clients. It is the default set with Samba in the current release. This setting is appropriate if users are doing a lot of file sharing (as opposed to a Samba server used mostly as a print server). It requires that a user provide a username/password before using the server. The easiest way to get this method working is to give a Linux user account to every client user who will use the Samba server, therefore providing basically the same file permissions to a user account through Samba as the same user would get if he or she were logged in directly to Linux.

- **share** — The share value for security works best for just print sharing or for providing file access that is more public (guest sharing). A client doesn't need to provide a valid username and password to access the server. However, the user typically has a guest level of permission to access and change files. See the "Assigning Guest Accounts" sidebar in this chapter for further information.

- **server** — From the client's point of view, this is the same as user security in that the client still has to provide a valid username/password combination to use the Samba server at all. The difference is on the server side. With server security, the username/password is sent to another SMB server for validation. If that fails, Samba tries to validate the client using user security.

- **domain** — From the client's point of view, this also looks the same as user security. This setting is used only if the Samba server has been added to a Windows NT domain (using the smbpasswd command). When a client tries to connect to the Samba server in this mode, its username and password are sent to a Windows NT Primary or Backup Domain controller. This is accomplished the same way that a Windows NT server would perform validation. Valid Linux user accounts must still be set up.

- **ads** — This security option causes Samba to act as a domain member in an ADS realm. Kerberos must be installed on the Samba machine to use this option. Samba must also join the ADS realm (see the net utility).

- **auth methods** — Sets the authentication method used by the Samba server (smbd). Leave the default in most cases. Authentication methods you can choose include anonymous access (guest), relay authentication through winbind (winbind), pre-winbind NT authentication (ntdomain), local lookups based on NetBIOS or domain name (sam), or remote DC authentication of trusted users (trustdomain).

- **Encrypt passwords** — Controls whether encrypted passwords can be negotiated with the client. This is on (Yes) by default. For domain security, this value must be Yes. Later versions of Windows NT (4.0 SP3 or later) and Windows 98 and Windows 2000 expect encrypted passwords to be on.

- **client schannel** — Choose if the client is to require the use of netlogin schannel (yes), offer schannel but not enforce it (auto), or not even offer schannel (no).

- **server schannel** — Choose if the server requires clients to use netlogin schannel (yes), offers schannel but doesn't enforce it (auto), or doesn't even offer schannel (no). If you set this to no, you must apply the Windows XP WinXP_SignOrSeal.reg patch available from the Samba project.

- **map to guest** — Lets you select to map clients into your guest account (minimal permissions) in selected situations. For example, you can map usernames that are not valid

(Bad User), users that provide the wrong password (Bad Password), or users with an invalid user ID (Bad UID). Or you can select Never to never map those users to guest.

- **Obey PAM restrictions** — Turn this on (Yes) if you want to use PAM for account and session management. Even if activated, PAM is not used if the encrypted passwords feature is turned on (encrypt passwords = yes). (PAM stands for *Pluggable Authentication Modules* and is used for authenticating host computers and users.)

- **PAM password change** — Indicates to use the PAM password change control flag for Samba. If this is on (Yes), SMB clients will use PAM instead of the program listed in the Password Program value for changing SMB passwords.

- **Passwd program** — Indicates which password program to use to change Linux user passwords. By default, /usr/bin/passwd is used, with the current username (%u) inserted.

- **Passwd chat** — Sets the chat that goes on between the Samba daemon (smbd) and the Linux password program (/usr/bin/passwd by default) when smbd tries to synchronize SMB passwords with Linux user passwords.

- **UNIX password sync** — With this on (Yes), Samba tries to update a user's Linux user password with his or her SMB password when the SMB password is changed. To do this, SMB runs the passwd command as the root user. This is on by default.

- **Guest account** — Specifies the username for the guest account. When a service is specified as Guest OK, the name entered here is used to access that service. The account is usually the nobody username.

Tip

Make sure that the guest account is a valid user. (The default of nobody should already be set up to work.) With an invalid user as the guest account, the IPC$ connection that lists the shared resources fails. ■

- **Hosts allow** — Contains a list of one or more hosts that are allowed to use your computer's Samba services. By default, users from any computer can connect to the Samba server (of course, they still have to provide valid usernames and passwords). Generally, you use this option to allow connections from specific computers (such as 10.0.0.1) or computer networks (such as 10.0.0.) that are excluded by the hosts deny option.

- **Hosts deny** — Contains a list of one or more hosts from which users are not allowed to use your computer's Samba services. You can make this option fairly restrictive, and then add the specific hosts and networks you want to use the Samba server. By default, no hosts are denied.

- **Preload modules** — You can add services that you want to add to the browse list to the preload option.

Logging Options

The following options help define how logging is done on your Samba server:

- **Log file** — Defines the location of the Samba smb log file. By default, Samba log files are contained in /var/log/samba (with filenames log.nmbd, log.smbd, and smb.log).

In this option, the %m is replaced by smb to set the smb log file as /var/log/samba/ smb.log.

- **Max log size** — Sets the maximum amount of space, in kilobytes, that the log files can consume. By default, the value is set to 0 (no limit).

Assigning Guest Accounts

Samba always assigns the permissions level of a valid user on the Linux system to clients who use the server. In the case of share security, the user is assigned a guest account (the nobody user account by default).

If the guest account value isn't set, Samba goes through a fairly complex set of rules to determine which user account to use. The result is that ensuring which user permissions will be assigned in each case can be hard. That's why user security is recommended if you want to provide more specific user access to your Samba server.

Protocol Options

Use the svcctl list option if you want to set a list of initialization scripts that the smbd daemon will use for starting and stopping UNIX services by way of the Win32 ServiceControl API. Using this feature, Windows administrators can use the Microsoft Management Console plug-ins to manage a UNIX server running Samba.

Tuning Options

Use the cluster addresses option to add additional addresses for nmbd to register with a WINS server.

Printing Options

The printing options are used to define how printer status information is presented. For the overwhelming majority of Linux systems, the printing value is set to cups. You can use printing styles from other types of operating systems, such as UNIX System V (sysv), AIX (aix), HP UNIX (hpux), and Berkeley UNIX (bsd), to name a few. LPRng (lprng), offered by many UNIX systems, is also included. Other printing options enable you to redefine the location of basic printing commands (lpq, lprm, and so on) and printing files (such as the name of the printcap file).

Browse Options

A browse list is a list of computers that are available on the network to SMB services. Clients use this list to find computers that are on their own LAN and also computers in their workgroups that may be on other reachable networks.

In Samba, browsing is configured by options described later in this section and implemented by the nmbd daemon. If you are using Samba for a workgroup within a single LAN, you probably don't need to concern yourself with the browsing options. However, if you are using Samba to provide services across several physical subnetworks, you might want to consider configuring Samba as a domain master browser. Here are some points to think about:

- Samba can be configured as a master browser, which allows it to gather lists of computers from local browse masters to form a wide-area server list. (Browse masters keep track of available shared directories and printers on the network of Samba systems and broadcast information about those resources as necessary.)

- If Samba is acting as a domain master browser, Samba should use a WINS server to help browse clients resolve the names from this list.

- Samba can be used as a WINS server, although it can also rely on other types of operating systems to provide that service.

- There should be only one domain master browser for each workgroup. Don't use Samba as a domain master for a workgroup with the same name as an NT domain.

If you are working in an environment that has a mix of Samba and Windows NT servers, use an NT server as your WINS server. If Samba is your only file server, choose a single Samba server (nmbd daemon) to supply the WINS services.

Note

A WINS server is basically a name server for NetBIOS names. It provides the same service that a DNS server does with TCP/IP domain names: It can translate names into addresses. A WINS server is particularly useful for allowing computers to communicate with SMB across multiple subnetworks where information is not being broadcast across the subnetworks' boundaries. ∎

To configure the browsing feature in Samba, you must have the workgroup named properly (described earlier in this section). Here are the global options related to SMB browsing:

- **OS level** — Set a value to control whether your Samba server (nmbd daemon) may become the local master browser for your workgroup. Raising this setting increases the Samba server's chance to control the browser list for the workgroup in the local broadcast area.

  If the value is 0, a Windows machine will probably be selected. A value of 60 ensures that the Samba server is chosen over an NT server. The default is 20.

- **Preferred master** — Set this to Yes if you want to force selection of a master browser and give the Samba server a better chance of being selected. (Setting Domain Master to Yes along with this option ensures that the Samba server will be selected.) This is set to Auto by default, which causes Samba to try to detect the current master browser before taking that responsibility.

- **Local master** — Set this to Yes if you want the Samba server to become the local browser master. (This is not a guarantee, but gives it a chance.) Set the value to No if you do not want your Samba server selected as the local master. Local Master is Auto by default.

- **Domain master** — Set this to Yes if you want the Samba server (nmbd daemon) to identify itself as the domain master browser for its workgroup. This list will then allow client computers assigned to the workgroup to use SMB-shared files and printers from subnetworks that are outside their own subnetwork. This is set to No by default.

Note

If browsing isn't working, check the nmbd log file (`/var/log/samba/log.nmbd`). To get more detail, increase the debug information level to 2 or 3 (described earlier in this section) and restart Samba. The log can tell you whether your Samba server is the master browser and, if so, which computers are on its list. ■

WINS options

Use the WINS options if you want to have a particular WINS server provide the name-to-address translation of NetBIOS names used by SMB clients:

- **WINS server** — If there is a WINS server on your network that you want to use to resolve the NetBIOS names for your workgroup, enter that server's IP address here. Again, you probably want to use a WINS server if your workgroup extends outside the local subnetwork.

- **WINS support** — Set this value to Yes if you want your Samba server to act as a WINS server. (It's No by default.) Again, this is not needed if all the computers in your workgroup are on the same subnetwork. Only one computer on your network should be assigned as the WINS server.

In addition to the values described here, you can access dozens more options by clicking the Advanced View button. When you have filled in all the fields you need, click Commit Changes on the screen to have the changes written to the `/etc/samba/smb.conf` file.

EventLog options

You can use the eventlog list option to create a list of log names for Samba to report to the Microsoft EventViewer utility.

Miscellaneous options

Two options in this category, usershare prefix allow and usershare prefix deny, let the administrator restrict which directories can be shared in user-defined shares. The deny list is defined first to allow the most restrictive interpretation of the list.

Configuring shared directories with SWAT

To make your shared directory available to others, add an entry to the SWAT window. To use SWAT to set up Samba to share directories, do the following:

Note

You may see one or more security warnings during the course of this procedure. These messages warn you that someone can potentially view the data you are sending to SWAT. If you are working on your local host or on a private LAN, the risk is minimal. ■

1. From the main SWAT window, click the SHARES button.

2. Type the name of the directory that you want to share in the Create Share box, and then click Create Share.

3. Add any of these options:

- **Comment** — A few words to describe the shared directory (optional).

- **Path** — The path name of the directory you are sharing.

- **Invalid users** — Lets you add a list of users who are not allowed to log in to the Samba service. Besides identifying usernames directly (from your /etc/passwd file), invalid users can be identified by Linux group or NIS netgroup, by adding a + or & in front of the name, respectively. Precede the name with @ to have Samba first check your NIS netgroup, then the Linux group for the name.

- **Valid users** — Add names here to identify which Linux user accounts can access the Samba service. As with invalid users, names can be preceded with +, &, or @ characters.

- **Admin users** — Lets you identify users who have administrative privilege on a particular share. This is available with security = share type of security only.

- **Read list** — Add users to this list if you want to grant read access to shares only (even if a share is available with read/write access). This is available with security = share type of security only.

- **Write list** — Add users to this list to grant write access by those users to shares, even if the share is available to all others with read-only access. This is available with security = share type of security only.

- **Guest account** — If Guest OK is selected, the username that is defined here is assigned to users accessing the file system. No password is required to access the share. The nobody user account (used only by users who access your computer remotely) is the default name used as the guest account. (The FTP user is also a recommended value.)

- **Read only** — If Yes, files can only be read from this file system, but no remote user can save or modify files on the file system. Select No if you want users to be allowed to save files to this directory over the network.

- **Hosts allow** — Add the names of the computers that will be allowed to access this file system. Separate hostnames by commas, spaces, or tabs. Here are some valid ways of entering hostnames:

  - localhost — Allows access to the local host.

  - 192.168.12.125 — IP address. Enter an individual IP address.

  - 192.168.12. — Enter a network address to include all hosts on a network. (Be sure to put a dot at the end of the network number or it won't work!)

- **pcren, pcstimpy** — Enables access to individual hosts by name.

- **EXCEPT** *host* — If you are allowing access to a group of hosts (such as by entering a network address), use EXCEPT to specifically deny access from one host from that group.

- **Hosts deny** — Denies access to specific computers by placing their names here. By default, no particular computers are excluded. Enter hostnames in the same forms you used for Hosts Allow.

- **Browseable** — Indicates whether you can view this directory on the list of shared directories. This is on (Yes) by default.

- **Available** — Enables you to leave this entry intact but turns off the service. This is useful if you want to close access to a directory temporarily. This is off (No) by default in Fedora. Select No to turn it off.

4. Select Commit Changes.

At this point, the shared file systems should be available to the Samba client computers (Windows 9x, Windows NT, Windows 2000, OS/2, Linux, and so on) that have access to your Linux Samba server. Before you try that, however, you can check your Samba configuration.

Checking your Samba setup with SWAT

From the SWAT window, select the STATUS button.

From this window, you can restart your smbd and nmbd processes. Likewise, you can see lists of active connections, active shares, and open files. (The preferred way to start the smbd and nmbd daemons is to set up the smb service to start automatically. Type **chkconfig smb on** to set the service to start at boot time.)

Working with Samba files and commands

Although you can set up Samba through the Samba Server Configuration window or SWAT, many administrators prefer to edit the /etc/samba/smb.conf directly. As root user, you can view the contents of this file and make needed changes. If you selected User security (as recommended), you will also be interested in the smbusers and smbpasswd files (in the /etc/samba directory). These files, as well as commands such as testparm and smbstatus, are described in the following sections.

Editing the smb.conf file

Changes you make using the Samba Server Configuration window or SWAT Web interface are reflected in your /etc/samba/smb.conf file. Here's an example of a smb.conf file (with comments removed):

```
[global]
workgroup = ESTREET
server string = Samba Server on Maple
hosts allow = 192.168.0.
printcap name = /etc/printcap
load printers = yes
printing = cups
log file = /var/log/samba/%m.log
```

```
max log size = 0
smb passwd file = /etc/samba/smbpasswd
security = user
encrypt passwords = Yes
unix password sync = Yes
passwd program = /usr/bin/passwd %u
passwd chat = *New*password* %n\n *Retype*new*password* %n\n *passwd:
        *all*authentication*tokens*updated*successfully*
pam password change = yes
obey pam restrictions = yes
socket options = TCP_NODELAY SO_RCVBUF=8192 SO_SNDBUF=8192
username map = /etc/samba/smbusers
dns proxy = no

[homes]
comment = Home Directories
browseable = no
writable = yes
valid users = %S
create mode = 0664
directory mode = 0775

[printers]
comment = All Printers
path = /var/spool/samba
browseable = no
guest ok = no
writable = no
printable = yes
```

I won't go through every line of this example, but here are some observations. In the [global] section, the workgroup is set to ESTREET, the server is identified as the Samba Server on Maple, and only computers that are on the local network (192.168.0.) are allowed access to the Samba service. You must change the local network to match your network.

Definitions for the local printers that will be shared are taken from the /etc/printcap file, the printers are loaded (yes), and the CUPS printing service is used.

Separate log files for each host trying to use the service are created in /var/log/samba/%m.log (with %m automatically replaced with each hostname). There is no limit to log file size (0).

This example uses the user-level security (security = user), which allows a user to log in once and then easily access the printers and the user's home directory on the Linux system. Password encryption is on (encrypt passwords = yes) because most Windows systems have password encryption on by default. Passwords are stored in the /etc/samba/smbpasswd file on your Linux system.

The dns proxy = no option prevents Linux from looking up system names on the DNS server (used for TCP/IP lookups).

The [homes] section enables each user to access his or her Linux home directory from a Windows system on the LAN. The user will be able to write to the home directory. However, other users will not be able see or share this directory. The [printers] section enables all users to print to any printer configured on the local Linux system.

Adding Samba Users

Performing user-style Samba security means assigning a Linux user account to each person using the Linux file systems and printers from his or her Windows workstation. (You could assign users to a guest account instead, but in this example, all users have their own accounts.) Then you need to add SMB passwords for each user. For example, this is how you would add a user whose Windows workstation login is chuckp:

1. Type the following as root user from a Terminal window to add a Linux user account:

   ```
   # useradd -m chuckp
   ```

2. Add a Linux password for the new user as follows:

   ```
   # passwd chuckp
   Changing password for user chuckp
   New UNIX password: ********
   Retype new UNIX password: ********
   ```

3. Repeat the previous steps to add user accounts for all users from Windows workstations on your LAN that you want to give access to your Linux system.

4. Add an SMB password for a user named chuckp as follows:

   ```
   # smbpasswd -a chuckp
   New SMB password: **********
   Retype new SMB password: **********
   ```

5. Repeat this step for each user. Later, each user can log in to Linux and rerun the passwd and smbpasswd commands to set private passwords.

Note

In the most recent version of Samba, options are available in the smb.conf file that cause SMB and Linux passwords to be synchronized automatically. See descriptions of the passwd program, passwd chat, and UNIX password sync options in the SWAT section of this chapter. ■

Starting the Samba Service

When you have your Samba configuration the way you want it, restart the Samba server as described earlier in the "Getting and Installing Samba" section. You can now check SMB clients on the network to see whether they can access your Samba server.

Testing Your Samba Permissions

You can run several commands from a shell to work with Samba. One is the `testparm` command, which you can use to check the access permissions you have set up. It lists global parameters that are set, along with any shared directories or printers.

Checking the Status of Shared Directories

The `smbstatus` command can view who is currently using Samba shared resources offered from your Linux system. The following is an example of the output from `smbstatus`:

```
# smbstatus

Samba version 3.5.2-60.fc13

PID      Username      Group         Machine
- - - - - - - - - - - - - - - - - - - - - - - - - - - - - - - - - - - - - - - - -
25770    chris         chris         booker        (10.0.0.50)
25833    chris         chris         10.0.0.50     (10.0.0.50)


Service      pid      machine       Connected at
- - - - - - - - - - - - - - - - - - - - - - - - - - - - - - - - - - - - - - -
IPC$         25729    booker        Wed Aug 25 12:06:29 2010
mytmp        25770    booker        Wed Aug 25 12:16:03 2010
mytmp        25833    10.0.0.50     Wed Aug 25 12:25:52 2010
IPC$         25730    booker        Wed Aug 25 12:06:29 2010


Locked files:
Pid   Uid DenyMode  Access   R/W  Oplock SharePath   Name    Time
- - - - - - - - - - - - - - - - - - - - - - - - - - - - - - - - - - - - - - - - -
- - - - - - - - - - - -
25833 501 DENY_NONE 0x12019f RDWR NONE   /tmp .b.txt.swp Wed Aug 25 12:26:18 2010
```

This output shows that from your Linux Samba server, the `mytmp` service (which is a share of the `/tmp` directory) is currently open by the computer named booker. PID 25833 is the process number of the smbd daemon on the Linux server that is handling the service. The file that is open is the `/tmp/.b.txt.swap` file, which was opened by a `vi` command. It has read/write access.

Using Samba Shared Directories

After you have configured your Samba server, you can try using the shared directories from a client computer on your network. The following sections describe how to use your Samba server from another Linux system or from various Windows systems.

Using Samba from Nautilus

To connect to a Samba share from a Nautilus file manager, use the Open Location box by clicking File ➪ Open Location. Then type **smb:** into your Nautilus file manager location box. As an alternative, you could select Places ➪ Network ➪ Windows Network from your GNOME top panel.

A list of SMB workgroups on your network appears in the window. You can select a workgroup, choose a server, and then select a resource to use. This should work for shares requiring no password.

The Nautilus interface seems to be a bit buggy when you need to enter passwords. It also requires you to either send clear-text passwords or type the username and password into your location box. For example, to get to my home directory (/home/chris) through Nautilus, I can type my username, password, server name, and share name as follows:

```
smb://chris:my72mgb@arc/chris
```

Mounting Samba Directories in Linux

Linux can view your Samba shared directories as it does any other medium (hard disk, NFS shares, CD-ROM, and so on). Use mount to mount a Samba shared file system so that it is permanently connected to your Linux file system.

Here's an example of the mount command in which a home directory (/home/chris) from a computer named toys on a local directory (/mnt/toys) is mounted. The command is typed, as root user, from a Terminal window:

```
# mkdir /mnt/toys
# mount -t cifs -o username=chris,password=a72mg //toys/chris /mnt/toys
```

The file system type for a Samba share is cifs (-t cifs). The username (chris) and password (a72mg) are passed as options (-o). The remote share of the home directory on toys is //toys/chris. The local mount point is /mnt/toys. At this point, you can access the contents of /home/chris on toys as you would any file or directory locally. You will have the same permission to access and change the contents of that directory (and its subdirectories) as you would if you were the user chris using those contents directly from toys.

To mount the Samba shared directory permanently, add an entry to your /etc/fstab file. For the example just described, you would add the following line (as root user):

```
//toys/chris   /mnt/toys    smbfs    username=chris,password=a72mg
```

Instead of putting username into the /etc/fstab file, which is readable by everyone, you could put username and password lines in a separate file. For example, you could add username and password lines to a cred.txt file. Then put the entry "credentials=/etc/samba/cred.txt" into the mount options file to have those options automatically used when the file system is mounted.

Troubleshooting your Samba Server

A lot can go wrong with a Samba server. If your Samba server isn't working properly, the descriptions in this section should help you pinpoint the problem.

Basic Networking in Place?

You can't share anything with other computers without a network. Before computers can share directories and printers from Samba, they must be able to communicate on your LAN.

Your Samba server can use the TCP/IP name as the NetBIOS name (used by Window networks for file and printer sharing), or a separate NetBIOS name can be set in the smb.conf file. It is critical, however, that the broadcast address be the same as the broadcast address for all clients communicating with your Samba server. To see your broadcast address, type the following (as root user):

```
# ifconfig -a
eth0       Link encap:Ethernet  HWadd 00:D1:B3:75:A5:1B
           inet addr:10.0.0.1  Bcast:10.0.0.255  Mask:255.255.255.0
```

The important information is the broadcast address (Bcast: 10.0.0.255), which is determined by the netmask (Mask:255.255.255.0). If the broadcast address isn't the same for the Samba server and the clients on the LAN, the clients cannot see that the Samba server has directories or printers to share.

Samba Service Running?

A basic troubleshooting check is to see whether the service is running. Try the smbclient command from your Linux system to see that everything is running and being shared as you expect it to be. The smbclient command is a great tool for getting information about a Samba server and even accessing shared directories from both Linux and Windows computers. While logged in as root or any user who has access to your Samba server, type the following:

```
$ smbclient -L localhost
Password: *********
Domain=[ESTREET] OS=[Unix] Server=[Samba 3.5.2-60]

    Sharename       Type        Comment
    ---------       ----        -------
    homes           Disk        Home Directories
    IPC$            IPC         IPC Service (Samba Server)
    ADMIN$          Disk        IPC Service (Samba Server)
    hp-ns1          Printer
Domain=[ESTREET] OS=[Unix] Server=[Samba 3.5.2-60]

    Server                  Comment
    ---------               -------
    PINE                    Samba Server
    MAPLE                   Windows XP
    NS1                     Samba Server

    Workgroup               Master
    ---------               -------
    ESTREET                 PINE
```

The Samba server is running on the local computer in this example. Shared directories and printers, as well as servers in the workgroup, appear here. If the Samba server is not running, you see Connection refused messages, and you need to start the Samba service as described earlier in this chapter.

Firewall Open?

If the Samba server is running, it should begin broadcasting its availability on your LAN. If you try to access the server from a Windows or Linux client on your LAN but get a `Connection refused` error, the problem may be that the firewall on your Linux Samba server is denying access to the NetBIOS service.

If you have a secure LAN, you can type the following (as root user) to flush your firewall filtering rules temporarily:

```
# iptables -F
```

Try to connect to the Samba server from a Windows or Linux client. If you find that you can connect to the server, turn the firewall back on:

```
# service iptables restart
```

You then need to open access to ports 137, 138, and 139 in your firewall so that the Samba server can accept connections for services. Keep in mind, however, that opening those ports can cause a host of security problems for Windows systems.

User Passwords Working?

Try accessing a shared Samba directory as a particular user (from the local host or other Linux system on your LAN). You can use the `smbclient` command to do this. Here is an example:

```
# smbclient //localhost/tmp -U chris
added interface ip=10.0.0.1 bcast=10.0.0.255 nmask=255.255.255.0
Password: *******
Domain=[ESTREET] OS=[Unix] Server=[Samba 3.5.2-60]
smb: \>
```

In this example, `smbclient` connects to the directory share named `tmp` as the Samba user named `chris`. If the password is accepted, you should see information about the server and an `smb:\>` prompt. If you cannot access the same shared directory from a Windows client, it's quite possible that the client is passing an improper username and password. Part of the problem may be that the Windows client is not providing encrypted passwords.

For certain Windows clients, using encrypted passwords requires that you change a Windows registry for the machine. One way to change the registry is with the Windows `regedit` command. Registry changes required for different Windows systems are contained within the `/usr/share/doc/samba-*/docs/Registry` directory.

Tip

The `smbclient` command, used here to list server information and test passwords, can also be used to browse the shared directory and copy files after you are connected. After you see the `smb:\>` prompt, type help to see the available commands. The interface is similar to any ftp client, such as sftp. ■

If your particular problem has not been addressed in this troubleshooting section, please refer to the user documentation that accompanies the Samba project. On Ubuntu systems, look in the `/usr/share/doc/samba-*/htmldocs` directory for some excellent documentation you can read from your Web browser. In particular, refer to the `Samba-HOWTO-Collection/diagnosis.html` file for help with troubleshooting.

Summary

By providing centralized file servers, an organization can efficiently share information and applications with people within the organization, with customers, or with anyone around the world. Several different technologies are available for making your Linux computer into a file-serving powerhouse.

The Network File System (NFS) protocol was one of the first file server technologies available. It is particularly well suited for sharing file systems among Linux and other UNIX systems. NFS uses standard `mount` and `umount` commands to connect file systems to the directory structures of client computers.

The Samba software package that comes with many Linux distributions (or can be easily installed if it doesn't) contains protocols and utilities for sharing files and printers among Windows and OS/2 operating systems. It uses SMB protocols that are included with all Microsoft Windows systems, and therefore provides a convenient method of sharing resources on LANs containing many Windows systems.

Part V

Choosing and Installing Different Linux Distributions

Running Ubuntu Linux

Ubuntu Linux (www.ubuntu.com) has experienced a meteoric rise in popularity since its first release at the end of 2004. Relying on a constantly expanding number of core developers and contributions from its growing legion of advocates and users, Ubuntu has become one of the most popular distributions around the world for Linux enthusiasts.

"Ubuntu" is an African word that means "humanity to others." The project pursues the meaning of its name by

- Making the distribution freely available; in fact, the project will even mail you pressed CDs without charge, although it can take up to 10 weeks to receive them (https://shipit.ubuntu.com).

- Providing support for many languages

- Offering features to make it usable by people with disabilities

Ubuntu is based on Debian GNU/Linux but offers more focused goals than Debian. The original goals of Ubuntu were to provide a tested, easy-to-use Linux distribution with a regular release schedule (every six months), to provide support and updates for those releases for an extended period of time, and to fit this easy-to-use desktop Linux on one CD. Ubuntu now offers Desktop and Server live/install CDs, as well as an Alternate install CD to help with automated deployments, partitioning, and low-resource system installs. There are also live CDs intended for use on netbook computers which, like the other CDs, can be copied and run from a USB disk.

Ubuntu offers its own repositories of freely available software on the Internet, providing a huge assortment of software organized in the traditional licensing-oriented Debian fashion. These packages can be installed using the familiar apt-get, aptitude, and synaptic software management tools.

This chapter describes some of the major features of Ubuntu. It also describes how to install Ubuntu on your computer or run the live CD version of Ubuntu.

Overview of Ubuntu

Although Ubuntu is primarily a Debian distribution on the inside, Ubuntu's focus on internationalization and general usability, its regular release schedule, and its simplified installation process are what make it different from Debian.

South African businessman, Internet entrepreneur, and long-time Debian advocate Mark Shuttleworth sponsors Ubuntu Linux through his organization, Canonical Limited (www.canonical.com). Some of the best and brightest open source developers (many originally from the Debian project) are on Canonical's team for producing Ubuntu. The organization's commitment to free distribution and rapid development has attracted a large and active user and development community for Ubuntu.

Ubuntu Releases

Coming into 2011, the Ubuntu project has produced 13 releases, which recently have followed Ubuntu's promised every-six-month release cycle. Each release carries a version number derived from the year and month in which it was released, and is named after a woodland creature:

- **Warty Warthog** — Released in October 2004 under Ubuntu version number 4.10
- **Hoary Hedgehog** — Released in April 2005 under Ubuntu version number 5.04
- **Breezy Badger** — Released in October 2005 under Ubuntu version number 5.10
- **Dapper Drake** — Released in June 2006 under Ubuntu version number 6.06
- **Edgy Eft** — Released in October 2006 under Ubuntu version number 6.10
- **Feisty Fawn** — Released in April 2007 under Ubuntu version number 7.04
- **Gutsy Gibbon** — Released in October 2007 under Ubuntu version number 7.10
- **Hardy Heron** — Released in April 2008 under Ubuntu version number 8.04
- **Intrepid Ibex** — Released in October 2008 under Ubuntu version number 8.10
- **Jaunty Jackalope** — Released in April 2009 under Ubuntu version number 9.04
- **Karmic Koala** — Released in October 2009 under Ubuntu version number 9.10
- **Lucid Lynx** — Released in April 2010 under Ubuntu version number 10.04
- **Maverick Meerkat** — Released in October 2010 under Ubuntu version 10.10

Note
In addition to releasing every six months, Ubuntu flags certain releases and LTS versions for Long Term Support for those who want reliability above features. The LTS version offers support for three years on desktop versions and five years on server versions. Ubuntu 10.04 is the most recent version offering LTS. ∎

If you are new to Linux, Ubuntu is designed with you in mind. The standard Ubuntu desktop installer provides a great set of defaults for most installation options. Ubuntu, however, also provides other installers that include many more choices for customization when you install it. If you are transitioning from Debian (or another Debian derivative, such as KNOPPIX), you will find it easy to work with Ubuntu. You install and remove packages and manage services with Ubuntu using the same methods as with Debian.

Beginning with the Dapper Drake release, the Ubuntu project offers each release as three different CDs or a single DVD. The CDs are as follows:

- **Desktop Install CD** — This boots directly to Ubuntu, where you can either experiment with Ubuntu (without changing anything on your existing system) or install Ubuntu to a hard drive. This is the equivalent of the live CD provided by many distributions, except that it also provides an easy way to install Ubuntu Linux permanently if you decide to do so. (This CD is included on the DVD that comes with this book.)

- **Server Install CD** — Enables you to install various server configurations, ranging from a basic server to a standard LAMP (Linux/Apache/MySQL/Perl) Web server.

- **Alternate Desktop CD** — Enables you to install an Ubuntu desktop system from the command line in a more complex fashion than that provided by the Desktop CD's graphical installer (such as using Logical Volume Management). It also supports OEM firms that want to customize and ship Ubuntu-based systems, and provides a custom server installation mechanism. It does not include the live CD.

Getting started with Ubuntu is easy because the Desktop Install CD boots to a fully functioning desktop system. The Ubuntu Desktop Install CD does a great job at detecting hardware, setting up your video card environment (mouse, keyboard, and video card), and booting right to a GNOME desktop without changing anything on your existing system. It includes an icon on the desktop that enables you to install Ubuntu to your computer's hard disk after walking through just a few simple configuration screens (discussed later in this chapter).

The following sections describe the desktop and server features in Ubuntu 10.04.1 (Lucid Lynx).

Ubuntu Installer

The Ubuntu installer has helped make Ubuntu a tremendously popular distribution, showing Ubuntu's commitment to usability right out of the gate. The desktop Ubuntu install process does an excellent job of detecting hardware and system configuration information. Ubuntu's Desktop Install CD "test-drive" needs only a few additional bits of information in order to install its whole set of software packages to your hard drive.

The other Ubuntu CDs feature a more traditional, text-based installer that should be familiar to users of any Debian-like system and are designed to work on almost any system with VGA graphics and at least 256MB of memory. This chapter focuses on the graphical Ubuntu installer, but the text-based installer on the Server and Alternate Install CDs is also quite easy to use.

Many ease-of-use features are built into the Ubuntu installer. For example, if you are not sure which type of keyboard you have, you have the option to type a few keys (as prompted by the installer) and have it try to figure out the type of keyboard you have. You also have the option to resize existing partitions on your disk during installation (a very handy feature if you have a hard disk with only one big Windows partition that you don't want to completely delete).

Ubuntu as a Desktop

As promised, Ubuntu 10.04 contains the latest desktop features available at the time it was released. Along with the latest desktop components you would expect (GNOME, OpenOffice.org, and so on), Ubuntu 10.04 also includes improved features for installing applications and customizing the desktop experience. Here are some of the features in Ubuntu 10.04:

- **GNOME Desktop** — GNOME 2.30 provides the desktop environment for this release of Ubuntu. Ubuntu's default desktop theme, Light, replaces the older brown Human theme. The entire look and feel is brighter and more colorful. New desktop features include a Me Menu that lets you get to your Facebook and Twitter accounts.

- **Firefox 3.6.8** — This Firefox release provides improved security, ease of use, and performance. (See Chapter 4 for details.)

- **Ubuntu One** — This online service, available from Ubuntu desktops, lets Ubuntu users register to get 2GB of free online storage. Associate machines with that account and you can sync those machines with your online storage. Besides syncing files, Ubuntu One can sync your Evolution contacts, Firefox bookmarks, and Tomboy notes. It also includes phone sync and a music store integrated into Rhythmbox.

- **Desktop productivity applications** — Ubuntu contains a broad range of open source applications suitable for the desktop. Leading the list are the latest versions of OpenOffice.org (popular office productivity suite), GIMP (image manipulation software), and Audacity (recording software). The PiTiVi application was added to let you edit your own videos.

- **Ubuntu Software Center** — In addition to offering thousands of open source software packages, the Ubuntu Software Center offers lots of information about available packages. For example, you can see user ratings of the software. There are also opportunities to purchase non-free software and music.

Many of the tools for configuring and setting preferences for the desktop that come with the GNOME project also fit well into the Ubuntu goals of accessibility and ease of use. GNOME's Removable Drives and Media Preferences window is set to immediately launch appropriate applications when you insert a CD or DVD, attach an external hard disk, or plug in a camera, printer, or scanner. The Assistive Technology Preferences window enables someone who is visually or physically impaired to use magnifiers and onscreen keyboards.

Figure 19-1 shows an example of an Ubuntu desktop.

FIGURE 19-1

Ubuntu 10.04 features the Light desktop theme.

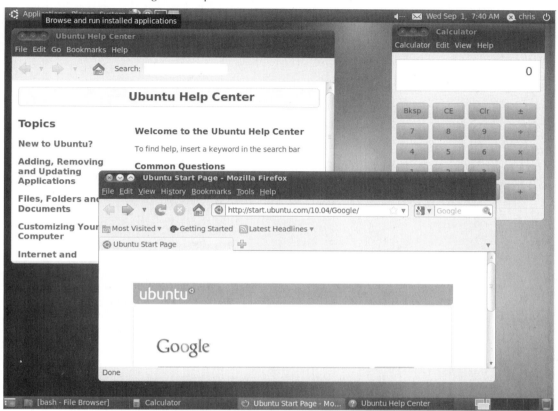

Ubuntu as a Server

Many features that are not useful for a desktop Linux system but are important to servers have been built into the Ubuntu default server installer, available on the Ubuntu Server Install CD (or the complete Ubuntu Install DVD).

As a central computing resource, servers tend to need to grow, and features such as the Ubuntu server installer's ability to create LVM partitions during installation make it easier for you to add disk space to your server on-the-fly in the places it is needed. Unlike the graphical Ubuntu Desktop installer described later in this chapter, the Ubuntu server installer is a non-graphical, terminal-oriented installer that is fast and easy to use regardless of the graphical capabilities of your server.

The default server installation supports up to 4GB of RAM on 32-bit PCs, and also provides kernel support for the GFS and OCFS2 cluster file systems. Although GFS and OCFS2 are still relatively new file systems, and therefore may not be ready for use on your production systems, they are available for you to try out in Ubuntu.

To use Ubuntu as a thin-client server, Linux Terminal Server Project software is included in the Ubuntu server. You can read about how to use LTSP on the Ubuntu Thin Client HOWTO (`https://help.ubuntu.com/community/UbuntuLTSP`).

Although LTSP is not part of the Server CD, you can download and install the package at any time. In fact, keep in mind that there are not separate repositories for desktop and server systems. So, regardless of whether you originally install a desktop or server system, you can later install any server or desktop package you choose.

The default server install takes up only about 400MB of disk space, although it is a very barebones system. Besides base system packages and core utilities, you get software for managing your network connections and file systems, but not much else. Luckily, however, you do get application management utilities (such as `apt-get`), so any open source software you want to add to your server is just an `apt-get` away with an Internet connection.

The most common type of server that many people install is a LAMP server system, which uses Linux to support an Apache Web server and provides the MySQL database. It also supports the Perl programming language, in which many Web applications are written. The Ubuntu Server Install CD provides a separate installer for this type of server system, highlighting Ubuntu's awareness of (and sensitivity to) the needs of its users, regardless of whether they are sitting in front of their desktop computer system or are cloistered in a machine room somewhere.

Ubuntu Spin-offs

Because no single CD set of software is going to please everyone, some spin-off projects have already been created from Ubuntu. The following are three partner projects associated with Ubuntu Linux:

- **Kubuntu** (`www.kubuntu.org`) — This project combines the latest version of the KDE desktop with each desktop Ubuntu release. KDE replaces the GNOME desktop, which is used by default with Ubuntu.

- **Xubuntu** (`www.xubuntu.org`) — This project blends the power and usability of Ubuntu with the lightweight Xfce desktop system, delivering a full-featured Ubuntu system that is less demanding of system and graphics resources. Xubuntu runs well on older or less powerful systems, and is ideal for laptops.

- **Edubuntu** (`www.edubuntu.org`) — This project focuses on producing a version of Ubuntu that is suitable for use in classrooms. Edubuntu combines Ubuntu with software geared toward education (such as KDE Edutainment software) and software used for creating inexpensive computer clusters (such as the Linux Terminal Server Project). As a result, Edubuntu can be used to fill a school's whole computer lab with working, educational workstations at very little cost.

Other Ubuntu spin-offs that have different levels of association with the main Ubuntu project include Mythbuntu (multimedia player spin centering on MythTV), Ubuntu Studio (multimedia-creator spin), Ubuntu Mobile (spin designed for Intel Mobile Internet devices), and Ubuntu Netbook Remix (like Ubuntu Mobile, but for subnotebooks). The Gobuntu spin (Ubuntu with no non-free software) has been abandoned to focus on installation tools that let you choose to only have free software during an install. Linux Mint is a user-friendly version of Ubuntu that includes many popular multimedia codecs. (A rolling Debian version of Linux Mint is also available.)

Because of Ubuntu's commitment to help people of different cultures, with support for many different languages and keyboard types, Ubuntu communities have grown to support users from all over the world. There's Ubuntu China (www.ubuntu.org.cn), Ubuntu Germany (www.ubuntuusers.de), Ubuntu Sweden (www.ubuntulinux.se), Ubuntu Indonesia (www.ubuntulinux.or.id), Ubuntu Portugal (www.ubuntu-pt.org), and many other international Ubuntu sites.

Challenges Facing Ubuntu

Despite its rise to stardom, Ubuntu is bound to suffer some growing pains. Some possible challenges Ubuntu faces include

- **Peaceful coexistence with Debian** — As a Debian-inspired distribution, Ubuntu was originally quite dependent on Debian and the work that project did related to licensing, usability, and stability issues. Some members of the Debian community initially saw Ubuntu as hijacking the hard work of the Debian project. The success of Ubuntu, however, speaks for both itself and the technical excellence and commitment of the Debian community. Ubuntu pushes its fixes and enhancements back to the Debian community, as well as to the developers who support individual open source packages. The two distributions need to continue to work together to improve both distributions and GNU/Linux in general.

- **Fast release cycles** — Ubuntu has set itself a pace of six-month release cycles. In terms of major free Linux distributions, only Fedora has stayed close to a six-month release cycle. Debian has certainly not been known to rush to release new versions — the slowness of Debian releases was one of the initial inspirations for Ubuntu.

- **Business model** — Although the Ubuntu project does offer shirts, hats, teddy bears, and other products you can purchase that carry the Ubuntu logo (https://shop.canonical.com/), proceeds from that and donations are clearly not going to be enough to support a long-term development effort. The project has made it clear that it intends to be committed to software that is "100% free of charge" going forward. Canonical, Ltd, and many other vendors around the world provide paid commercial support for Ubuntu releases, but "paid support" business models for Linux have rarely been successful. Only time (and a growing number of home, small, and medium business, and enterprise Ubuntu users) will tell whether Ubuntu can manage to succeed without adopting a free/paid community model such as those of Fedora/Red Hat and openSUSE/SUSE.

- **Commitment to open source** — Desktop computer users expect that their wireless cards will just work and their multimedia content will just play. Some of the software needed to do those things, however, is either encumbered by patent claims or not available in open source. To compete, Ubuntu has made some of this non-free software available to its users — sometimes from Ubuntu repositories and sometimes through for-pay software (offered through services such as `shop.ubuntu.com`). Whether this non-purist approach to the free software world will have long-term negative effects (some have already begun complaining about it) remains to be seen.

- **Freedom and responsibility** — Endeavors with goals such as freedom and equality can sometimes suffer from a lack of control. As philosophically inspired distributions become more popular, technical discussions can sometimes spin out of control to become almost religious discussions. Ubuntu seems to resist the response that some profit-oriented Linux projects ultimately resort to: "Because we say so," but the line between openness and determinism is a tough one to walk.

  Ubuntu's leadership has done a good job setting up a structure to make hard decisions in a free environment. For example, Ubuntu now has a Community Council (to create teams and projects, as well as leaders for each team) and a Technical Board (to guide the technical direction of Ubuntu). There is also now a Code of Conduct (`www.ubuntu.com/community/conduct`) presented to keep everyone participating in the project on the same path.

Ubuntu has prospered and increased in popularity far beyond the initial excitement inspired by being the new kid on the block. Ubuntu is holding up well under the pressure and continues to grow both in the size of its development and support communities and its popularity.

Installing Ubuntu

Installing Ubuntu to hard disk requires a computer with at least 128MB of RAM for an Ubuntu server and 256MB of RAM for an Ubuntu desktop installation. However, to use the live CD–based installer, you need at least 384MB of RAM. (If you have only the 384MB of RAM and no more, expect a slow install.)

As for hard disk space, you will need at least 4GB of space to install a desktop system or 500MB of disk space for a minimal server system. For the minimal server, you need to be able to work from the command line (no GUI is installed).

On the DVD
The Ubuntu 10.04.1 Desktop Install CD image is included on the DVD that comes with this book. Refer to Appendix A for information on using and installing from that image. ∎

If you are setting up Ubuntu to dual-boot on a desktop computer with a Windows system currently installed, you can resize your Windows partition during the installation process. It is easier, however, to first make sure that the free disk space exists outside of the Windows partition.

See Chapter 7 for information on resizing hard disk partitions to make space for a Linux installation. Of course, you should also back up any important data files at this point.

The following procedure describes how to boot and install Ubuntu:

1. Insert the Ubuntu Desktop Install CD and reboot your computer. (Or type **ubuntu** from the boot screen of the *Linux Bible* DVD.) You should see the Ubuntu CD's boot screen, as shown in Figure 19-2. (If your system doesn't boot from the CD or you don't see the Ubuntu splash screen, make sure your computer is capable of booting from a CD, as described in Chapter 7.)

FIGURE 19-2

The Ubuntu Desktop Install CD boot screen.

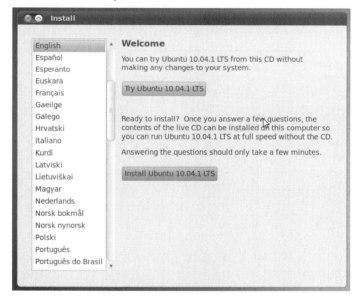

2. The boot screen for the Ubuntu Desktop Install CD lets you choose to boot Ubuntu live or install directly to hard disk (as shown in Figure 19-2). Select your language and click the Install Ubuntu button to continue. The time and time zone screen appears.

3. Configure your clock by entering your time and time zone. Then select Forward.

4. Select your keyboard type. To accept the selected value and proceed to the next screen, click Forward.

Caution

Changing or removing existing disk partitions, as described in the next steps, can lead to data loss. Consider your options carefully before selecting a partitioning method. ■

5. You are asked to begin partitioning your hard disk. Select one of the following choices for partitioning your hard disk.

- **Resize current operating system** — Select this choice if you want to take disk space from an existing partition to use for your Ubuntu installation. (You can use this if the entire hard disk is devoted to Windows and you want to be able to dual boot with Ubuntu.)

- **Erase and use the entire disk** — This erases your entire hard disk, and then repartitions it automatically. If you have more than one hard disk, it lets you choose which one to use. Choose this method if you are prepared to remove all the data on your hard disk. Ubuntu installer will repartition using common Linux file system types.

- **Specify partitions manually (advanced)** — This allows you to install Ubuntu with hard disk partitions that use encrypted file systems or other special features.

If you selected to manually edit the partition table, proceed to the next step. Otherwise, skip ahead past the partitioning steps.

6. During the manual partitioning phase, you can specify information about how you want to use partitions on the system where you are installing Ubuntu. You should define at least two partitions. One partition is used as swap space, which is a special partition format that Linux systems use for managing virtual memory. A second partition is used to hold the top-level directory of your Ubuntu Linux installation, known as the root directory and mounted as "/" on your Ubuntu system.

In the initial partitioning dialog, you select the free disk space in which you want to create a partition and click New Partition, which enables you to specify the type of file system that you want to use on the partition and whether it is a primary or extended partition. You can have only four primary partitions on a single disk drive — to create more than four partitions on a single disk drive, at least one of the four primary partitions must be defined as an extended partition, in which other (logical) partitions can then be defined.

7. To agree to the partitioning scheme, select Continue. You are asked to provide information about a user account that you want to create on this system.

8. Create a user account. This account will have administrative privileges, so you should create your own account at this point. Enter your full name (for example, John Smith), a username (for example, jsmith) that you will use to log in as this user, a password (twice) for the new user, and a name for this computer (which can be anything).

To accept the selected values and proceed to the next screen, click Forward. At this point you are asked to review the information you just entered. (You can also select the Advanced button to change the location of your boot loader and to identify a network proxy.)

9. If the installer finds user accounts from any partitions on your hard disk, it asks whether you want to import settings (such as from Firefox or Evolution) to your new

Ubuntu installation. Select any accounts for which you want to import information and click Forward.

10. You are asked whether you need a proxy server. If you need to indicate a proxy server to access the Internet, enter the location of that proxy server.

11. The confirmation screen summarizes the installation options that you have selected. To begin the installation, click Install. You can click Back to return to previous screens and change the values that you selected, or click Cancel to abort the installation process without changing anything on your system. If you select Forward, the Ubuntu installer begins the installation process. When the process is complete, the installer ejects the CD, reminds you to remove it from your system's CD drive, and asks you to press Return to reboot your system.

12. When installation is complete, the Desktop CD installer displays the Installation Complete dialog, which confirms a successful installation. When you see this dialog, you can either click Continue Using the live CD to continue experimenting with Ubuntu from the CD, or click Restart Now to reboot your system and begin running Ubuntu directly from your system's hard drive(s).

When you boot your system, Ubuntu displays a splash screen and progress dialog as it boots, followed by a graphical login screen. Congratulations — you're running Ubuntu Linux!

Ubuntu systems automatically run a graphical application called the Update Manager to notify you when system updates are available and to simplify retrieving and installing those updates. If updates to your system are available, the Update Manager displays a message to this effect and provides an icon at the right of the top panel that you can select to install those updates and keep your system current. You will need to provide your password in order to perform this (or any other) administrative operation. You can also check for updates manually at any time by selecting the System ➪ Administration ➪ Update Manager menu item.

To add other software packages, you can open the Synaptic Package Manager Window (select System ➪ Administration ➪ Synaptic Package Manager) or Add/Remove Applications window (select Applications ➪ Add/Remove Programs). Using Synaptic, you can add the software you want individually. Software not available on the CD will be downloaded from the Internet (provided you have an active Internet connection).

Getting Started with Ubuntu

On the surface, Ubuntu is not very different in appearance from other Linux desktop systems using GNOME. Underneath, the tools for managing your software packages are the same as you would expect with Debian systems. Many of the differences are subtle and do a lot to make using Linux easier for the end user.

Log in using the username and password you entered during installation. Figure 19-3 shows an example of an Ubuntu desktop with several applications started.

FIGURE 19-3

Manage software, take notes, configure printers, and do other tasks from Ubuntu.

Trying Out the Desktop

With the latest GNOME interface, menus are available on the top panel. You won't have all the applications you would expect from a full-featured desktop system. However, you can easily add lots of other applications from the Internet (as described later). A good way to familiarize yourself with the Ubuntu GNOME desktop is to check out some of the menus.

On the upper-left panel, the following categories of software are available from the Applications menu (I've added some notes about additional applications that you can grab from other locations):

- **Accessories** — From this menu, select some basic desktop utilities that are part of the GNOME project. Selecting gedit Text Editor starts the gedit graphical text editor (so you don't have to use the unintuitive vi editor to edit plain text documents). To go to a shell, you can launch the Terminal application from this menu. Other accessories include a calculator and a character map.

- **Games** — Under the Games menu, you have a selection of about a half-dozen GNOME games. Some are similar to ones you would find on a Windows desktop (for example, Mines and Aisleriot Solitaire). There are also Tetris-like games (Gnometris) and board games (Mahjongg). You don't get any of the more demanding open source games (such as Tux Racer) or networked games (such as the BZFlag networked tank battle game), but these can easily be installed using the Synaptic Package Manager.

- **Graphics** — The Ubuntu desktop install includes the F-Spot Photo Manager, for managing collections of digital photographs, and the gThumb Image Viewer. To import images from a scanner, Ubuntu includes the Simple Scan image scanning application. No document viewers are included here, but Evince (which can be used to view PostScript and PDF files) and the more traditional Adobe Acrobat viewer can be installed using Synaptic. For serious image manipulation, install the GNU Image Manipulation Program (GIMP).

- **Internet** — Popular, standard open source Internet clients can be launched from this menu. A social client called Gwibber is included. Firefox is the default Ubuntu Web browser and Empathy is used for instant messaging. This menu also includes a Terminal Server Client if you need to connect to Microsoft Windows Terminal servers (in the rare event that you still need access to a Microsoft Windows system). For e-mail, you could add the Thunderbird e-mail client (the Evolution e-mail client is available under the Office menu).

- **Office** — A full set of OpenOffice.org office productivity applications is available for Ubuntu, and several components are included with the initial live CD install. Initial selections include OpenOffice.org Calc (spreadsheet), Impress (presentations), and Writer (word processing). OpenOffice.org Database lets you create and access a database.

- **Sound & Video** — Ubuntu provides a movie player, the Rhythmbox Music Player for online audio, the Serpentine CD creator, and the Sound Recorder audio recording application. Like other commercial Linux distributions, Ubuntu doesn't include the software needed to play MP3 music out of the box. However, if you try to play MP3 music from Rhythmbox or some other music players, you are asked whether you want to add these capabilities from the Ubuntu repositories.

  The movie player included with Ubuntu (and other GNOME desktops) is the Totem Movie Player (identified simply as Movie Player). Additional non–open source codecs are needed to enable that video player to play commercial DVD movies. Movie players such as xine and MPlayer, whose use requires codecs that cannot be freely distributed, are not included with Ubuntu by default, but can also be added through the Ubuntu repositories.

The Places menu keeps track of places you want to go, lets you connect to remote servers, and lets you see (and, if you like, connect to) recently opened documents. There is also an option available to search your system for files.

The System menu provides selections for changing desktop preferences and doing system administration tasks.

Adding More Software

Although Ubuntu manages to install around 2GB of applications from a single Ubuntu CD, it's still only 2GB. By contrast, other implementations with multiple CDs in a set can install about 7GB of applications or more.

To add more software to Ubuntu, they created the Ubuntu Software Center. Older software installation tools, such as the common Debian packaging tools (apt-get, aptitude, and even dpkg) are still available. You can also use the Synaptic Package Manager for adding and removing software packages, which provides a friendly graphical interface, a handy search function to help you find packages, and many other usability improvements over the command-line tools.

To open the Ubuntu Software Center window, select Applications ➪ Ubuntu Software Center. Figure 19-4 shows the Ubuntu Software Center window.

FIGURE 19-4

Install thousands of packages from the Ubuntu Software Center.

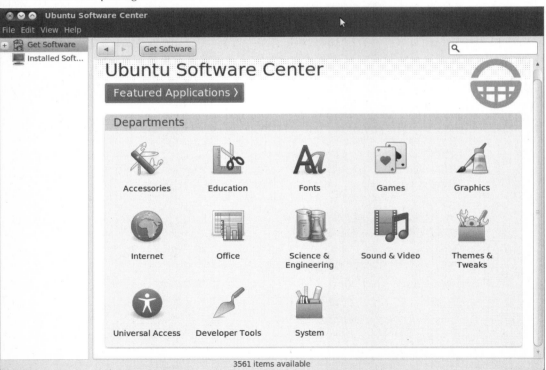

From the Ubuntu Software Center you can add software packages by selecting a category or by searching for packages. Here are some categories you can select to add more software:

- **Themes and Tweeks** — Packages in this category can help you spiff up your desktop. There are packages containing software that lets you enable advanced 3D effects on the desktop, such as the Compiz Configuration Settings Manager. You can also install themes to get a specific look and feel on your desktop.

- **Graphics** — The GNU Image Manipulation Program (GIMP) is one you almost surely want to have on your desktop. Also in this category are F-Spot (for organizing your images) and Gwenview (for viewing images).

- **Internet** — Add to the few Internet applications installed from the live CD with applications in this category. Besides a variety of tools for chatting, sharing files, doing e-mail, and browsing the Web, there are specialized applications for posting to your blog, monitoring bandwidth, adding a firewall, uploading images and videos, and running Google Gadgets.

You can also search to find the software packages you want. Figure 19-5 shows the results when I searched for first-person shooter games.

FIGURE 19-5

Find first-person shooter or other games to install from the Ubuntu Software Center.

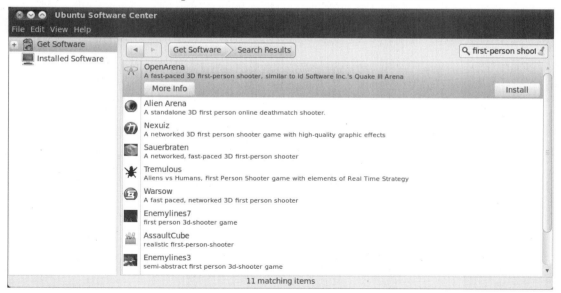

Getting More Information About Ubuntu

Because of Ubuntu's popularity many people have created online resources to support it. One of the best places to start learning more about Ubuntu or finding answers to specific questions is the Ubuntu Forums site (`www.ubuntuforums.org`). To begin participating in that site, I suggest you read the usage guidelines and policies in the Ubuntu Forums Code of Conduct at `http://ubuntuforums.org/index.php?page=policy`.

This document describes conduct rules and suggests the best ways of having your technical support questions answered. As with most forums, browsing through topics of interest and doing keyword searches are good ways to find the information you need.

A few resources from the Ubuntu forums are particularly useful for someone starting out with Ubuntu. I recommend the following:

- **FAQs, HowTo, Tutorials & Tips** (`http://ubuntuforums.org/forumdisplay.php?f=100`) — This forum lists common steps that many people do after installing Ubuntu, such as adding support for certain video cards or multimedia software.

- **Absolute Beginner Talk** (`http://ubuntuforums.org/forumdisplay.php?f326`) — Posts in this forum can help you understand what Linux is all about and whether or not Ubuntu will suit your needs. You can ask very basic questions here as well.

- **The Community Cafe** (`http://ubuntuforums.org/forumdisplay.php?f=11`) — To catch the spirit of the Ubuntu community, you can check out the Community Cafe forum and get a taste of what's on people's minds.

The Ubuntu community also has a wiki (`https://wiki.ubuntu.com`) that continues to gain useful content for people using Ubuntu. Currently, the wiki includes areas for Ubuntu documentation and community information, support for different languages and events, and much more. There are also specific areas devoted to each Ubuntu release.

Summary

Ubuntu continues to be the rising star of Linux distributions. Ubuntu started with Debian (one of the most respected but challenging distributions for beginners), simplifying the packaging and installation. It has demonstrated a commitment to frequent, well-designed, and supported releases. Today, Ubuntu is far more than a Debian spin-off, with its own community, advocates, and well-established development and maintenance groups.

Using a single installation CD, a user can install a set of useful desktop software or a streamlined server system. Ubuntu's graphical installer greatly simplifies the installation process by combining a graphical installer with a live distribution that you can run directly from the CD, which has made it easier than ever to test-drive and install Linux.

Along with the growth in popularity of Ubuntu has come an active community of developers and users. To become involved with Ubuntu, a good place to start is with community forums and the Ubuntu wiki.

Running Fedora and Red Hat Enterprise Linux

In September 2003, the world's leading Linux distribution, Red Hat Linux, disappeared.

Red Hat, Inc., the company that created Red Hat Linux, divided its development efforts in two directions: the Fedora Project, which produces the Fedora operating system (originally called Fedora Core), and Red Hat Enterprise Linux.

The split came from the desire to better serve two diverse groups with one operating system. Fedora focused on encouraging the open source development community interested in helping develop and test software that would one day go into Red Hat products. Red Hat Enterprise Linux focused on the needs of paying customers who needed enterprise computing solutions.

On the DVD

The Fedora 13 GNOME live/install CD is included on the DVD that comes with this book. You can try out the live version and then install a working Fedora desktop system from this DVD, using descriptions in Appendix A and the "Installing Fedora" section later in this chapter. If you don't have a DVD drive, you can get the software on CDs by downloading them from the Internet (http://fedoraproject.org/get-fedora) and burning them to CD, as described in Appendix A. ■

Both Fedora and Red Hat Enterprise Linux were developed using code from the original Red Hat Linux distribution. Fedora is a community-driven distribution that is intended to include the latest Linux technology and is used as the basis for Red Hat Enterprise Linux releases.

Although Fedora is primarily sponsored by Red Hat, Inc. and staffed by Red Hat employees, the Fedora Project encourages community leadership and involvement. The latest Fedora includes many more features than Red Hat

Enterprise Linux, but those features have less guarantee of stability and no guarantee of support. However, important decisions about the direction of Fedora are still very much under the control of Red Hat, Inc. Likewise, Red Hat owns Fedora trademarks and makes legal decisions for Fedora based on its own legal counsel. Nearly all financial support for Fedora comes from Red Hat.

Note

Fedora follows the legacy of Red Hat Linux. The final version of Red Hat Linux was version 9. Fedora Core 1 and Red Hat Enterprise Linux 3 followed Red Hat Linux 9. At the time of this writing, Fedora 13 (the "Core" having been dropped) and Red Hat Enterprise Linux 5.5 are the latest versions of those two operating systems. ∎

Red Hat Enterprise Linux (RHEL), which is actually represented by multiple products for desktop and server computer systems, is licensed commercially. Red Hat puts all its documentation, training, and support effort behind RHEL, which it sells to customers in the form of subscriptions. The intent is to have RHEL be a rock-solid Linux system that can be deployed across entire enterprises.

Despite the confusion it unleashed by dumping its flagship Red Hat Linux line and fears by some that Red Hat might become another Microsoft, Red Hat is still the dominant player when it comes to commercial Linux products. Many people have been happy to upgrade their critical Linux systems to Red Hat Enterprise Linux products.

In fact, when Microsoft announced its patent agreement with Novell, Red Hat reportedly turned down a similar offer of cooperation with Microsoft, calling such an arrangement an "innovation tax." So, Red Hat, which was once viewed by some in the free software community as a threat to the free software movement, is now being viewed more often as a great defender of free and open source software rights. In fact, Fedora has a reputation for its extraordinary commitment to remain freely redistributable and as free as possible from patent-encumbered software.

Note

One reflection of the quality of the source code that Red Hat releases into the world is the success of the CentOS project. With no affiliation to Red Hat, members of the CentOS project build their own binary distribution of the RHEL source code with a goal of 100 percent binary compatibility with RHEL. Today, many people who don't have the need for the support, certification, and other assurances that come with RHEL are using CentOS in their organizations. ∎

To its credit, Red Hat has managed to become a profitable venture while making some remarkable contributions to the open source effort. Releasing its installer (Anaconda) and software packaging tools (RPM Package Management) under the GNU Public License (GPL) has enabled other Linux distributions to use and enhance those features. Within Red Hat Linux and now Fedora, Red Hat, Inc. has worked hard to include only software that can be freely distributed (removing most software with patent and copyright issues).

Despite continued emphasis from Red Hat, Inc. that Fedora comes with no guarantees, Fedora is an excellent Linux distribution. I know of universities that have deployed hundreds of Fedora desktop systems in their computer labs and small companies that run their businesses exclusively with Fedora. Those organizations have simply accepted responsibility for maintaining those systems themselves and upgrading their systems more often.

Even if you prefer to bet your business on Red Hat Enterprise Linux, Fedora is a great way to evaluate and use technology that is in all Linux distributions from Red Hat. Features in the current Fedora system are those that are being prepared for a later release of RHEL. Both Fedora and RHEL are discussed in this chapter, so you can determine which distribution is right for you.

Digging into Features

There are many opinions on why Red Hat Linux and other distributions from the Red Hat Linux legacy have been so popular. The following sections describe some features of Red Hat Linux distributions commonly believed to have led to its success and that now add to the popularity of Fedora and Red Hat Enterprise Linux distributions.

Red Hat Installer (Anaconda)

When many Linux distributions still had you struggling from the command line to get the distribution installed, Red Hat created its own installer called Anaconda. Anaconda includes both graphical and text-based procedures for installing Linux, and is one of the oldest graphical installers continuously shipping. When you're done installing Fedora or Red Hat Enterprise Linux, you have the following:

- A set of software packages installed that suits how you want to use your computer (as a desktop, workstation, server, or some custom configuration)

- Configured online software repositories. By identifying Fedora and third-party repositories, you can choose from thousands of software packages to easily download and install.

- Standard information, such as date, time, time zone, and language set

- A configured mouse, keyboard, video card, and monitor

- An appropriately partitioned hard disk

- A configured network card and firewall, to immediately connect to a LAN

- A configured boot loader, to define how Linux starts up

In addition to being easy to use, Anaconda is loaded with features to make it easy to manage the installation of multiple RHEL or Fedora systems. For example, these power features are built into the Anaconda installer:

- **Network installs** — After booting the install process, the actual Fedora or RHEL distribution can be on a network server that is accessible via a Web server (http), FTP server (ftp), or UNIX file server (NFS).

- **Kickstart installs** — It's not so bad to sit there and click through the answers to run the installation of one Fedora system, but if you're doing dozens or hundreds of installs (especially on similar computers), automating that task can be a major time-saver. Anaconda supports kickstart installs, for which you use a preconfigured kickstart file to answer the questions that come up during a Fedora or RHEL installation. If you answer all the questions in the file, you can launch the installation and have it run from start to finish without you in attendance.

- **Upgrades** — With an existing Fedora system installed, Anaconda enables you to easily upgrade to a newer Fedora system. A lot of nice features for saving backups of configuration files and logging the upgrade activities are built into that process. During an upgrade, Anaconda takes into consideration any dependency issues, so the upgraded software packages will have all the libraries and commands that the features in those packages need.

Major enhancements to Anaconda have come with recent releases of Fedora. In particular, Anaconda now incorporates the yum facility for gathering, downloading, and installing packages. During initial installation, you can add multiple yum-enabled Fedora software repositories to install software from those repositories.

You'll find a detailed description of installing Fedora using the Anaconda installer at the end of this chapter.

Custom Spins, Install Sets, and Live CDs

By extending Anaconda installer features to tools such as `livecd-creator` and `pungi`, you can create your own software repositories, live CDs, and custom software install CDs/DVDs. So if you want to create your own software (or grab software from outside the Fedora repositories) and package it up with Fedora, the Fedora Project has easy-to-use tools to help you do that. The resulting CD or DVD ISO images are referred to as *custom spins*.

Using `livecd-creator`, you can select which software packages you want to use in your own live CD and which settings you want with it (user accounts, desktop settings, network configuration, and so on). With `pungi`, you create custom installation media, so your customers or friends can install exactly the system you offer them.

Both `livecd-creator` and `pungi` can run from the same type of kickstart file used with Anaconda, allowing you to save the packages and settings you choose. So it becomes easy to update your custom spin by rerunning the build command with the kickstart file as updated packages become available.

Custom spins created directly from the Fedora Project itself or from members of the community are already available. For example, there are Fedora live CDs featuring gaming, electronics tools, KDE desktops, and Creative Commons live content.

RPM Package Management

All Red Hat and Fedora distributions use the RPM Package Management (RPM) software packaging format to store and maintain software. Fedora and RHEL contain a set of tools for installing, upgrading, maintaining, and querying software packages in RPM format. Essentially, the RPM software packages that are installed are maintained in a local database, so you can list the contents of packages, view descriptions, and even check for tampering of the files in those packages you have installed.

Using RPM, add-on software can also be easily included in and maintained for Fedora systems. So users who once had to know how to deal with tarballs and makefiles to compile their own software can now simply install an RPM package to get the features they want. With other Linux distributions (such as SUSE and Mandrake) also using RPM packaging, your RPM tool skills can help you manage software on those distributions as well.

You can check out ongoing development of the RPM from the RPM project (`http://rpm.org`) site. Fedora 13 includes RPM 4.7. Improvements in RPM 4.7 include features to provide support for larger files, better compression, improved architecture dependency, and better cleanup of stale lock files. For end users, these improvements should result in better reliability, security, and performance.

Because of the popularity of Red Hat Linux systems, lots of software repositories and third-party software management tools have been created to further automate and simplify handling software in Red Hat systems. Tools such as yum (`http://yum.baseurl.org`) and apt-rpm (`http://fedoraproject.org/wiki/Tools/Apt`) are available for updating selected software.

As noted earlier, the yum facility forms the foundation for installing RPM packages in Fedora and RHEL. For several reasons, yum is usually preferred over the `rpm` command. First, it can be used to install from network repositories. Second, it can find and install dependent packages needed by the packages you request. And last, it is preferred because there are related tools for searching and managing repositories. Yum can also be used to install software from local media and, unlike rpm, resolve dependencies automatically.

Latest Desktop Technology

By keeping up with the latest technologies, the Fedora Project helps users discover the latest innovations in desktop technology. In the past year, Fedora releases have featured major new desktop technology such as KDE 4.4 and the recently developed Lightweight X11 Desktop Environment.

Fedora was the first major distribution to include KDE 4 as its default KDE environment. The most obvious new features include the ability of the new Plasma desktop to place widgets directly on the desktop. This allows mini-applications such as photo viewers, system monitors, and stock tickers to sit directly on the desktop. The Photon multimedia feature provides a single framework for KDE music and video applications. New Oxygen Artwork provides a whole new look to the KDE desktop. A lightweight file manager named Dolphin is now used as the default file manager.

The Lightweight X11 Desktop Environment (`www.lxde.org`) has been added recently to Fedora. LXDE was designed to perform well on low-RAM computers such as handhelds or on live CDs. (To use LXDE in Fedora, type **yum groupinstall LXDE** as root user. Then select LXDE as your desktop session when you log in.) Figure 20-1 shows an example of the LXDE desktop.

LXDE has its own set of efficient desktop applications. It uses PCMan as its file manager and GPicView to view images, as shown in Figure 20-1.

FIGURE 20-1

Fedora includes the new Lightweight X11 Desktop Environment (LXDE).

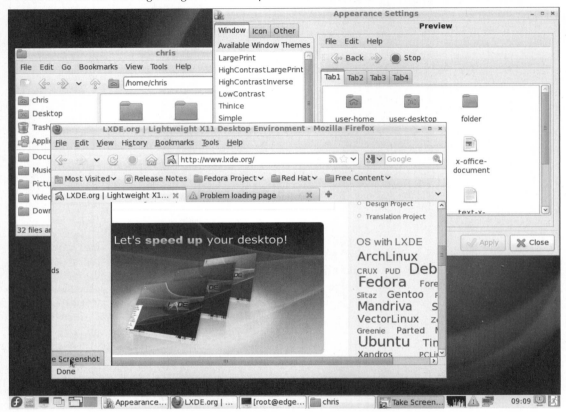

System Configuration Tools

Red Hat created a set of simplified, graphical tools for configuring and administering many basic administrative features in Red Hat systems. Using these tools, you can add printers, configure your network, add users, set up your sound card, and tune up your video card, to name a few of the features they cover.

Red Hat's graphical configuration tools can be launched from the Administration menu or from the command line.

Going Forward with Red Hat Enterprise Linux

Red Hat Enterprise Linux has become the de facto standard for Linux systems in the enterprise. There are large banks, stock exchanges, and highly secure government installations that rely on Red Hat Enterprise Linux for their most critical infrastructure applications.

Red Hat Enterprise Linux 6, Red Hat's first major release in three years, was completed in the fall of 2010. With that release, many features that have been refined in recent releases of Fedora (such as PackageKit and NetworkManager) are now being used by default in Red Hat Enterprise Linux. New initiatives in virtualization and cloud computing have become a reality.

Unlike Fedora, which offers no official support, RHEL has a full set of professional services built around it. For example:

- **Training** — Red Hat, Inc. offers training courses in system administration, software development, and other areas. (See www.redhat.com/courses.)
- **Certification** — Red Hat offers certifications for Red Hat Certified Technician and Engineer (RHCT and RHCE), Datacenter Specialist (RHCDS), Security Specialist (RHCSS), and Architect (RHCA). (See www.redhat.com/certification.)
- **Third-party hardware and software** — Through a variety of alliances with hardware vendors, software vendors, and resellers, you can be assured of finding certified hardware, certified software, and services to back up your Red Hat Enterprise Linux installations.

As for its future, Red Hat, Inc. is driving new initiatives to make Linux a critical component in large computing centers for a long time to come. Some of the features in Red Hat Enterprise Linux that make it easy to manage many systems (both physical and virtual) are described in the following sections.

Red Hat Network and Satellite Servers

Using Red Hat Network (RHN) you can install, upgrade, deploy, and manage your Red Hat Enterprise Linux systems. Red Hat Network is offered directly from Red Hat (http://rhn.redhat.com) or, for larger organizations, via your own Satellite server.

Typically, an organization using Satellite server will set up local repositories of Red Hat Enterprise Linux software and then install systems over the network. The install process can start from a boot CD, USB drive, or even from a computer's network interface card (using PXE boot and a tftp server).

With Red Hat Network you can also set up custom software channels, configure and deploy virtual host and guest systems, and manage custom configuration files and errata. For more on how RHN and Satellite servers work, see the RHN Architectural Overview (www.redhat.com/rhn/rhndetails/architecture).

Red Hat Enterprise Virtualization

In the past year, Red Hat has focused its efforts in virtualization toward a technology referred to as Red Hat Enterprise Virtualization (http://www.redhat.com/virtualization/rhev). Components of RHEV include Kernel Virtualization Module (KVM) and management tools for managing servers (RHEV for Servers) and desktops (RHEV for Desktops).

Unlike its earlier entry into virtualization, which relied on running a special kernel based on Xen, Red Hat uses KVM technology that includes virtualization support in the standard kernels delivered with all Red Hat Enterprise Linux systems. Other features in RHEV help you centrally manage all your virtual systems through a search interface.

Red Hat Cloud Computing

Red Hat has taken a leadership role in defining an open source framework for cloud computing. Red Hat Cloud Foundations Edition One (www.redhat.com/solutions/cloud/foundations) defines the tools needed to plan, create, and handle a private cloud.

Central to Red Hat's cloud initiative is recognition that enterprise customers need to be able to put together software and hardware components from many different vendors. Likewise, this initiative provides the foundation for being able to move virtual systems between private and public clouds.

Going Forward with Fedora

Fedora has done a particularly good job in serving the open source software development community and those who want to repackage Linux for different purposes. Fedora is particularly good if you want to use it in the following ways:

- **Personal desktop** — If you are on the technical side and want to have the latest Linux technology, Fedora can be a great choice. You may have to deal with more software updates and some less-complete features than with Red Hat Enterprise Linux. However, those negatives can be a small price for those who are always looking to try out the latest desktop features available.

- **Personal server** — Many people use Fedora for a personal file, print, or Web server with great results. Incorporating SELinux security can help make a Fedora server among the most secure server platforms available today, while still providing cutting edge server features.

- **Build your own Linux system** — By building your own live CD or install CD, you can repackage Fedora to have exactly the software you want. You can even build in your own software packages and repositories with Fedora tools. Because Fedora is made so that people can redistribute it, you have fewer concerns about potential copyright or patent infringements.

- **Develop software** — Many people use Fedora for developing their open source software projects. Using Fedora, software developers can test their own software on the latest systems. For enterprise software products, developers can test out features that will eventually make their way into Red Hat Enterprise Linux. Linus Torvalds himself uses Fedora to develop the latest Linux kernel technology, primarily because of its excellent support for PowerPC hardware.

If Fedora sounds interesting to you, the following sections describe some ways you can get involved. To become an official member of the Fedora community, you can go to the Join Fedora page (http://fedoraproject.org/wiki/join), which will lead you through opportunities with the Fedora Project and help you sign up.

Growing Community Support for Fedora

In the past few years, new initiatives and Web sites have popped up to support Fedora. Two of the best official assets of the Fedora Project are FedoraProject.org (the official Fedora Project site) and FedoraForum.org (which has been recognized as the official end-user forum of choice).

FedoraProject.org is the site for official information about schedules, goals, and initiatives that make up the Fedora Project. If you want to become involved in Fedora-related projects, such as Ambassadors, Marketing, Live CD, or Documentation, FedoraProject.org is the focal point for pursuing those initiatives.

FedoraForum.org features news, galleries, and (as you might guess) forums for sharing questions and information about Fedora. As of this writing, FedoraForum.org had more than 100,000 members.

The Unofficial Fedora FAQ (www.fedorafaq.org) has become an excellent resource for getting answers to the most constant, nagging questions about Fedora. This FAQ is a good place to start for learning how to get all those things you need (MP3 players, viewing DVD movies, instant messaging, video players, access to your Windows XP NTFS file system, and so on).

On the whole, the total amount of software available and greater stability among software repositories has meant that it's possible to get a much better total experience with Fedora than was possible even with Red Hat Linux.

Joining Fedora Special Interest Groups

People in the Fedora community join together into special interest groups (SIGs) to pursue common goals with Fedora. Some of the groups stay in touch using mailing lists, regular meetings on IRC chat channels, and Fedoraproject.org wiki pages. Here are a few Fedora SIGs you might find interesting:

- **One Laptop Per Child SIG** (http://fedoraproject.org/wiki/OLPC) — You may have heard of the OLPC project's (www.laptop.org) goal of bringing low-cost laptops to children around the world. But you may not know that the operating system inside those laptops is Fedora. The Fedora OLPC SIG explores ways for the Fedora Project to provide software and infrastructure support to OLPC.

- **Games SIG** (http://fedoraproject.org/wiki/SIGs/Games) — The Fedora Games SIG has done a great job packaging open source and liberated commercial games to run on Fedora. To participate, you can join the fedora-games-list mailing list,

chat on the #fedora-games channel on irc.freenode.net, or just check out the
Games SIG wiki page.

- **Artwork Team** (http://fedoraproject.org/wiki/Artwork) — The Fedora
  Artwork team provides an avenue for creative people to contribute to Fedora. While
  encouraging the use of open source tools, the Artwork team has created logos, backgrounds, promo banners, posters, and other art to support Fedora.

- **Education SIG** (http://fedoraproject.org/wiki/SIGs/Education) — The
  Fedora Education SIG is working to get more educational applications into Fedora and
  then produce a Fedora Education Spin to efficiently distribute that software.

- **Spins SIG** (http://fedoraproject.org/wiki/SIGs/Spins) — The Spins SIG was
  created to help people create their own custom spins of Fedora software. Anyone can
  create a spin and submit it for approval from the Spins SIG. If it meets Fedora Project
  requirements, the spin could be hosted by Fedora or simply have the instructions for
  producing the spin (typically a kickstart file) stored by Fedora for others to use.

Other interesting SIGs include the Fedora Robotics SIG, the Astronomy SIG, Embedded Systems
SIG, and Store SIG. There are also efforts you can join to improve documentation, the wiki, trans-
lations, marketing, and other areas.

Forums and Mailing Lists

If you want to get into the flow of the Fedora community, I recommend starting with the Fedora
Project's own mailing lists. You can choose the Fedora mailing list that interests you from the Red
Hat Mailing Lists page (http://lists.fedoraproject.org/mailman/listinfo). Start with
the Fedora-list or Fedora-announce-list mailing list.

Installing Fedora

The Linux operating system Fedora, sponsored by Red Hat, is included on this book's DVD. The
rest of this chapter leads you through its installation.

Fedora installation guides are available in several different languages. To download a tarball of an
installation guide or simply read it online, refer to this site:

    http://docs.fedoraproject.org/install-guide/

Beginning the Installation

This installation procedure is based on using the Fedora GNOME live CD that is included on the
DVD that comes with this book. Throughout most of the procedure, you can click Back to make
changes to earlier screens. However, after you are warned that packages are about to be written to
hard disk, there's no turning back. What was on the selected partitions will be gone and Fedora
will be installed. Most items that you configure can be changed after Fedora is installed.

Coming from Windows

It is quite possible that your entire hard disk is devoted to a Windows 95, 98, 2000, ME, NT, XP, Windows 7, or Vista operating system, and you may want to keep much of that information after Fedora is installed. Although there are installation choices that let you retain existing partitions, they don't let you take space from existing DOS or NTFS partitions without destroying them. If you like, you can try resizing your Windows partition using the gparted utility. You can run gparted by booting the Ubuntu or Fedora distributions that come on the DVD included with this book. Just be aware that, if used improperly, gparted (or any disk partitioning tool) can damage or erase important data from your hard disk. ■

Ready to install? (Have you backed up any data you want to keep safe?) Okay, then here's what to do:

1. **Insert the DVD into the DVD drive.** If you are not able to boot from the DVD, obtain an official Fedora installation CD set as described earlier in this chapter and continue with this procedure by inserting the first CD into the drive.

2. **Reboot your computer.** If you see the *Linux Bible* boot screen, continue to the next step.

Tip

If you don't see the installation screen, your DVD or CD-ROM drive may not be bootable. You may be able to make the drive bootable, however. Here's how: Restart the computer. Immediately, you should see a message telling you how to select the boot device, such as by pressing the F12 or Del key. From the list that appears, select the CD/DVD drive and press Enter. ■

3. **Boot the install medium.** From the *Linux Bible* DVD boot screen, type **fedora** and press Enter. The Fedora live CD boots up to a full-blown Fedora desktop (this may take several minutes).

4. **Run Install to Hard Drive.** From the desktop of the Fedora live CD, double-click the Install to Hard Drive icon to begin the installation.

5. **Continue.** When the welcome screen appears, click Next to continue.

6. **Choose an installation language.** If you are asked to choose an installation language, move the arrow keys to the language you want and then select Next. (Later, you will be able to add additional languages.)

7. **Enter hostname.** Identify the network name used by this computer. You may enter a fully qualified domain name (such as host.example.com).

8. **Choose a time zone.** Select the time zone. Either click a spot on the map or choose from the drop-down box. Before you click your exact location on the map, click on the area of the map that includes your continent or move the slider to zoom in. Then select the specific city. You can click "System clock uses UTC" to have your computer use Coordinated Universal Time (also known as Greenwich Mean Time). With multiple operating systems installed, you might want to uncheck this box because some operating systems expect the BIOS to be set to local time.

9. **Set root password.** You must choose a password for your root user at this point. The root password provides complete control of your Fedora system. Without it, and before you add other users, you will have no access to your own system. Enter the root password, and then type it again in the Confirm box. (Remember the root user's password and keep it confidential! Don't lose it!) Click Next to continue.

10. **Choose your partitioning strategy.** You have the following choices related to how your disk is partitioned for a Fedora installation:

Note

Instead of installing to a local hard disk, you can identify an iSCSI initiator as the storage device by selecting the Advanced Storage Configuration button and entering the IP address and iSCSI Initiator Name of the SCSI device. After that is identified, you can use that device for installing Fedora. ■

- **Use entire drive** — This erases the entire contents of the hard disks you select.
- **Replace existing Linux system** — This erases all Linux partitions, but leaves Windows partitions intact.
- **Shrink current system** — This allows you to resize the disk partitions for the currently installed Linux or Microsoft Windows system so you can then use the remaining space to install Linux.
- **Use free space** — This works only if you have enough free space on your hard disk that is not currently assigned to any partition. (You can choose this option if you resized your Windows partition to make space for Linux.)
- **Create custom layout** — Select this if you want to create your own custom partitioning.

   If you have multiple hard disks, you can select which of those disks should be used for your Fedora installation. Check the Encrypt system box if you want to have an encrypted file system. Check the Review and Modify Partitioning Layout check box to see how Linux is choosing to partition your hard disk. Click Next to continue.

11. **Review and modify partitioning layout.** If you chose to review or customize your partitioning, you will see the Disk Setup tool with your current partitioning layout displayed. You can change any of the partitions you choose, provided that you have at least one root (/) partition that can hold the entire installation and one swap partition. A small /boot partition (about 100MB) is also recommended (possibly using an ext3, rather than an ext4, file system type). Note that LVM partitions are assigned by default to your root partition and swap space. This will enable you to easily resize those partitions in the future.

12. **Configure boot loader.** All bootable partitions and default boot loader options that are detected are displayed. By default, the install process will use the GRUB boot loader, install the boot loader in the master boot record of the computer, and choose Fedora as your default operating system to boot.

Note

If you keep the GRUB boot loader, you have the option of adding a GRUB password. The password protects your system from having potentially dangerous kernel options sent to the kernel by someone without that password. This password can and should be different from the root password you are asked to enter later. ■

   The names shown for each bootable partition will appear on the boot loader screen when the system starts. Change a bootable partition name by clicking it and selecting Edit.

Caution

Before proceeding to the next step, you need to know that for the live CD install, the live CD image is simply copied to your hard disk when you continue. You won't get a chance to back out after this, so make sure you mean it. ∎

13. At this point, **the software from the live CD is simply copied to your hard disk.** When the install is complete, click the Close button. Then select System ⇨ Shut Down and choose Restart. Remove the live CD/DVD to reboot your installed system.

14. **Your computer restarts.** Remove the CD or DVD as the system is rebooting. If you installed GRUB, you will see a graphical boot screen that displays the bootable partitions. Press the up or down arrow key to choose the partition you want to boot, and press Enter. If Fedora is the default partition, you can simply wait a few moments and it boots automatically.

The first time your system boots after installation, the Fedora Setup Agent (Firstboot) runs to do some initial configuration of your system. The next section explains how Fedora Setup Agent works.

Running the Fedora Firstboot

The first time you boot Fedora after it is installed, the Fedora Firstboot runs to configure some initial settings for your computer.

The Welcome screen displays. From it, step through screens to read (and agree to) the license, create a regular user, set time and date, and view your hardware profile. Click the Finish button and you are ready to log in to Fedora.

Once you log in to your Fedora desktop, there are lots of great ways to configure your desktop to do everything you want it to do. Refer to Chapter 2 for information on adding extra software for such things as custom themes and support for playing different kinds of multimedia.

Summary

Since leaving its well-known Red Hat Linux name behind, Red Hat, Inc. has focused its development efforts on the free Fedora Project and commercial Red Hat Enterprise Linux.

Fedora and Red Hat Enterprise Linux distributions distinguish themselves from other Linux distributions with their simplified installer (Anaconda), graphical configuration tools, RPM Package Management tools, and a tenacious commitment to supporting open source software. Fedora is freely available, whereas Red Hat Enterprise Linux is available on a paid subscription basis.

Running Debian GNU/Linux

IN THIS CHAPTER

Inside Debian

Installing Debian

Managing your Debian system

Debian GNU/Linux is a creation of the Debian Project. Founded in 1993 by Ian Murdock, the Debian Project is an association of individuals who have made a common cause to create a free, coherent, and complete operating system.

Note

Ian Murdock later became associated with Sun (now owned by Oracle) and continues to be an outspoken visionary on Debian, Linux, and operating systems in general. You can still access his old blog at: `http://ianmurdock` `.com`**. The name Debian is a combination of Ian's wife's name (Deb) and his own.** ∎

The principles of the Debian Project are defined in the Debian Social Contract. This contract is a commitment to the free software community that basically states the following:

- All software within the Debian system will remain free, as defined in the Debian Free Software Guidelines (DFSG).

- The Debian Project will contribute to the free software community by licensing any software developed for the Debian system in accordance with the DFSG, developing the best system it can, and by sharing improvements and fixes with the original developers of any programs incorporated into Debian GNU/Linux.

- Problems will not be hidden from users, and any bug reports filed against Debian components will be made promptly available to the public through the Debian Bug Tracking System (BTS).

- The Debian Project will focus on the needs of its users and on the principles of free software.

- Provisions will be made for the support of programs that do not meet the standards in the DFSG because some users may depend on these programs to make effective use of the system. The bug tracking and support systems will always include mechanisms for handling these programs when they are provided with the Debian system.

Debian's commitment to free software distribution and openness has earned it a huge following in the technical community. More than any other Linux system, Debian has been used as the basis for other Linux distributions, including KNOPPIX, Ubuntu, Damn Small Linux, and many others.

The success of Debian has come despite the lack of large corporate sponsors, formal enterprise initiatives, or official certification and training programs. Debian enthusiasts will tell you that it is the most stable and reliable Linux system. It is thoroughly tested, and new versions aren't released until the Debian leadership believes that software is extraordinarily stable.

On the CD

A single Debian GNU/Linux network install CD image is contained on the DVD that comes with this book. You can install Debian directly from that DVD as described in this chapter. An Internet connection is needed to get additional components needed for a full install. ■

Inside Debian GNU/Linux

As with most modern operating systems, software programs in Debian GNU/Linux are bundled into packages for easy distribution and management. The package format and management tools used in Debian GNU/Linux were created by the Debian Project and are arguably the most sophisticated of their type. Additionally, careful adherence to packaging policies and quality-control measures ensure compatibility and help make upgrades go smoothly. Debian is one of the operating system distributions in which all components (except the kernel) can be upgraded without rebooting the system.

Debian Packages

Debian packages come in two forms: binary and source. Binary packages contain files that can be extracted directly onto the system by the package management tools. Source packages contain source code and build instructions that the Debian build tools use to create binary packages.

In addition to programs and their associated data files, Debian packages contain control data that enable the package management tools to support advanced features:

- A main `control` file contains version and package interrelationship data. The version can be compared to an installed version of the same package to determine whether an upgrade is needed. The interrelationship data tell the package management tools which packages must or cannot be installed at the same time as the package.

Note

Package interrelationship fields include Depends, Conflicts, Replaces, Provides, Recommends, Suggests, and Enhances. For a complete list of control file fields, see `www.debian.org/doc/debian-policy/ch-controlfields.html`. ■

- Optional `preinst`, `postinst`, `prerm`, and `postrm` files can instruct the package management tools to perform functions before or after package installation or removal. For example, most packages containing daemons (such as Apache HTTPD) include a `postinst` script that starts the daemon automatically after installation.

- A `conffiles` file can designate specific files in the package as configuration files, which are not automatically overwritten during upgrades. By default, all files under the `/etc/` directory are configuration files.

Two special package types, meta and virtual, also exist. Meta packages are standard binary packages that do not contain any files, but depend on a number of other packages. Installation of a meta package results in the automatic installation of all packages that they depend on. These can be used as a convenient method for installing a set of related packages.

Virtual packages do not actually exist as files but can be referenced in the package interrelationship fields. They are most commonly used in cases where more than one package fulfills a specific requirement. Packages with this requirement can reference the virtual package in their `Depends` field, and packages that satisfy this dependency reference it in their `Provides` field.

Because most programs providing a virtual package are mutually exclusive, they also include the virtual package in their `Conflicts` field to prevent the installation of conflicting packages. An example of this is the mail-transport-agent virtual package, which is required by most system programs in order to send mail.

Note

An easy way to browse the list of available packages is through the Debian web site at `www.debian.org/distrib/packages`. **The current release comes with more than 29,400 packages.** ■

Debian Package Management Tools

Perhaps the most interesting and well-known part of the Debian package management system is APT, the Advanced Package Tool. APT, through the `apt-get` utility, maintains a database of packages available in the repositories that it is configured to check and can handle automatically downloading new or upgraded packages. A program named `aptitude` has been added to simplify package management. `aptitude` acts as an interface for the command-line operations of `apt-get`.

When installing or upgrading packages, APT downloads the necessary files to a local cache directory and then instructs the `dpkg` tool to take the appropriate actions. Among other things, this allows the user to select programs for addition or removal without having to manually instruct the system to handle any package dependencies.

Most basic package management functions are performed by dpkg, although not always at the direct request of the user. This tool handles medium-level package installation and removal and also manages the package status database. That database contains information about every package known to dpkg, including the package meta information and two other important fields: the package state and selection state.

Note

You can find more information about how to determine the state of a package in the "Querying the Package Database" section of this chapter. ■

As its name suggests, the package state indicates the present state of the package, which is one of the following:

- **not-installed** — The package is known but is not installed on the system.
- **half-installed** — An attempt was made to install the package, but an error prevented it from finishing.
- **unpacked** — The files have been extracted from the package, but any post-extract configuration steps have not yet been performed.
- **half-configured** — The post-extract configuration was started, but an error prevented it from finishing.
- **installed** — The package is fully installed and configured.
- **config-files** — The package was removed, but the configuration files still exist on the system.

Note

If you have manually removed a configuration file and want to get it back by reinstalling the package, you can do so by passing the `--force-confmiss` option to dpkg. Doing so will not overwrite the other configuration files for that package. If you want to start over with all the original configuration files, you can also pass the `--force-confnew` option. ■

The package selection state indicates what state you want the package to be in. Changes to package status through dpkg happen immediately when using the `--install, --remove,` and `--purge` options on a package, but other uses and tools will instead set this flag and then process any pending changes in a batch. The package selection state is one of the following:

- **install** — The package should be installed.
- **deinstall** — The package files should be removed, with the exception of configuration files.
- **purge** — All package files and configuration files should be removed.
- **hold** — dpkg should not do anything with the package unless explicitly told to do so with the `--force-hold` argument.

Some packages are designed to enable you to select configuration options as they are being installed. This configuration is managed through the debconf utility. The debconf utility supports a number of different interfaces, including command-line, menu-based, and GUI-based interfaces. A database of configuration options is also maintained by debconf, allowing it to automatically answer repeated questions, such as those you might encounter while upgrading or reinstalling a package.

Examples of how to use these utilities are included in the section "Managing Your Debian System" later in this chapter.

Debian Releases

In Debian terms, a distribution is a collection of specific package versions. From time to time, a distribution is declared ready for release and becomes a release. In practice, these two terms are often used interchangeably when referring to Debian distributions that have reached the "stable" milestone.

Debian distributions are given code names (recent ones include potato, woody, sarge, etch, lenny, and squeeze, named for characters in the movie *Toy Story*) to identify their archive directory on the Debian servers. While a particular distribution release is active, it will be referenced by one of three release tags, each one pointing to one of the three active releases. The tags — unstable, testing, and stable — identify the state of the release within the release cycle. At the time of this writing, the current stable release is lenny, and the testing release is squeeze. The unstable release is special in that it is always named Sid (after the kid who broke all the toys).

New packages, and new versions of packages, are uploaded to the Debian archive and are imported into the unstable distribution. This distribution always contains the newest version of every package, which means that changes have not yet been thoroughly tested to verify that installing them will not cause unexpected behavior.

After a package has been assigned to the unstable area for a few days and testing shows that it has not had any significant bugs filed against it, it is imported into the testing distribution. The testing distribution remains open to changes (just as the unstable area was) until it is frozen in preparation for release as the next stable distribution. When testing is in the frozen state, only changes necessary to fix significant bugs are imported.

After all release-critical bugs have been fixed in the frozen testing distribution, the release manager declares the release ready and it replaces the stable distribution. When the previous stable version becomes obsolete (but remains on the Debian archive for a reasonable period of time), a new testing distribution is created from the changes that went into packages in the unstable area while testing was frozen, and the process begins again.

Getting Help with Debian

The Debian Project has a mature set of resources to support those who use, administer, and develop software for Debian systems. A place to begin learning more about Debian is the Debian

Support page (www.debian.org/support). Here are some of the resources you can connect to from that page:

- **Documentation** (www.debian.org/doc/) — From this page, you can find links to both Debian-specific and general Linux documentation. For specific Debian information, refer to the Release Notes, Installation Guide Debian GNU/Linux FAQ, and various user, administrator, and programming manuals. General Linux information includes manuals, HOWTOs, and FAQs.

- **Mailing lists** (www.debian.org/MailingLists) — Ways of accessing (and behaving on) a Debian mailing list are described on this page. A complete listing of the more than 200 Debian mailing lists is available from http://lists.debian.org/completeindex.html.

- **Bug tracking** (www.debian.org/Bugs) — If you are interested in following the bug tracking system for Debian, links from the support page can take you to the Bug Tracking System site. If you are having problems with any Debian software, you can search this site for bug reports and file a bug report, if your bug was not yet reported.

- **Help** (www.debianhelp.org) — This site offers connections to a range of information about Debian. In particular, you can find Debian forums from this site, containing literally thousands of posts. The Debian User Forums site (http://forums.debian.net) is another place you can go to post questions about Debian.

If you are interested in becoming a Debian developer, start at the Debian Developers' Corner (www.debian.org/devel). That site acts as a guide to ways in which you can enter the Debian development community. There are Debian developers all over the world. The largest concentrations of Debian developers are in Europe and the United States, as you can see from the Debian Developer Location map (www.debian.org/devel/developers.loc).

Installing Debian GNU/Linux

The Debian CD image included with this book is a minimal, network install of the Debian system. Additional packages can be downloaded and installed from the Internet after the base system has been installed and an Internet connection established. For information about how to obtain additional Debian packages on CD or DVD, see www.debian.org/distrib/.

Hardware Requirements and Installation Planning

To run Debian, you need at least a 386 processor and 48MB of RAM. For a server or a graphical workstation (running the X Window System), it is recommended that you have at least 256MB to 512MB of memory and a Pentium-class processor.

A minimal set of packages requires 250MB of disk space, and a normal installation of desktop applications can require at least 2–4 gigabytes. Additional space will be needed to store any data files that you want to keep on the system.

Most ISA and PCI network cards are supported under Linux, although ISA models are not usually detected automatically by the installer. Inexpensive cards based on RealTek 8139 chipsets can be found at most PC dealers and will work fine for low-demand applications. Intel PRO/100 and PRO/1000 adapters are supported in Linux and will work well in high-demand applications, as will cards based on the "tulip" chipsets and most 3com network cards.

Many other devices, such as sound and video capture cards, can also be used under Linux. For more information about hardware compatibility, see the Hardware Compatibility HOWTO at `http://tldp.org/HOWTO/Hardware-HOWTO/`.

Workstations

In most cases, workstation users will want to run the X Window System (X11). The ability to run X11 depends on compatibility with the video chipset on your video card or mainboard.

Servers

A Linux server installation generally consists of only the minimum set of packages required to provide the service for which it was designed. In particular, this means that servers do not usually have a graphical interface installed.

Server hardware is generally more expensive than workstation hardware, although you can still run smaller servers on less-expensive desktop hardware. If you are planning to store important data on your server, look into a RAID array for storage. A number of inexpensive ATA RAID controllers work well under Linux.

Note
More information about ATA RAID compatibility is available at the following sites: `http://linuxmafia.com/faq/Hardware/sata.html` and `http://ibiblio.org/pub/Linux/docs/HOWTO/other-formats/html_single/Hardware-HOWTO.html#IDERAID.` ■

Higher-end servers will, of course, require more expensive hardware. In applications such as mail servers where you will have a lot of disk activity, plan on splitting the disk-intensive tasks across multiple arrays. When it comes to CPU and RAM, more of both is good, but most applications benefit more from extra RAM than they do from multiple CPUs.

Running the Installer

The latest Debian installation process is done in one stage, where it used to require two stages (with a reboot in the middle of the process). During this procedure, you create the settings needed for your computer (time zone, language, keyboard, user accounts, and so on), partition your disk as needed, install a base system to disk, and download additional software needed.

Caution
Before you begin installing Debian to your hard disk, be sure to back up any data that is important to you. A simple mistake during partitioning can result in losing some or all of your data. ■

The following is the Debian installation procedure from the CD image included on the DVD that comes with this book:

Note
Because the Debian CD image included with this book is the network install image, the CD itself will provide software for installing only a minimal Debian system. You will need a network connection or other Debian software CDs to install, for example, a full desktop system. ∎

1. **Boot DVD** — Boot the DVD that comes with this book and type **debian** from the boot prompt to begin the Debian installer. (If you download an official copy of the Debian CD, type **linux** instead.)

Note
Some systems may require special parameters in order to boot. Other options are also available, such as the option to use a Linux kernel from the 2.6 series. Press F1 at the boot: **prompt for more information. ∎**

2. **Language, Region, Keyboard** — After the installer has finished booting, you are presented with the series of menus that make up the installation process. Use the arrow keys to navigate through the menus and select your language, region, and keyboard mapping.

3. **Network** — Configure the network connection. This step is skipped automatically if no network card is detected in your system.

   If a network card is detected in your system, the installer will attempt to automatically detect the network using the DHCP protocol. This involves the computer sending out requests on the network for configuration details from a DHCP server. Most networks and broadband routers support this service.

   If the DHCP configuration fails, you are presented with four options:

   - **retry** — Select this option if you suspect that a temporary problem prevented your computer from communicating with the DHCP server.

   - **retry with hostname** — Select this option if your network provider requires you to enter a DHCP hostname. This used to be common on cable modem networks, but is rarely seen anymore.

   - **manual configuration** — Select this option if you have static IP address information that must be entered for your Internet connection.

   - **do not configure at this time** — Select this option if you do not have an Internet connection, are using a dial-up connection, or have a broadband connection that requires the use of PPPoE. In the latter two cases, you'll want to establish the connection at the point that it is noted during stage 2 of the installation.

4. **Hostname** — Provide a hostname (a single-word name that you give to your system, such as debian, littlebeigebox, or yoda) and a domain name. If you do not have your own domain name, you can make one up, such as myhouse.local.

5. **Time zone** — Select your time zone and select Continue.

6. **Partitions** — Next, you will be asked to configure your disk partitions for Debian. If you haven't already done so, read Chapter 7 for more information about partitioning.

   If you already have partitions on your drive and have room for more, you are given the option to use this space for your Debian system. Another option is to erase the entire disk and use the whole thing for Debian. Either of these two options takes you through the guided partitioning, which is covered in this section. Besides the two options just mentioned, two other options enable you to use the entire disk and assign partitions to LVM or encrypted LVM. *LVM* stands for Logical Volume Manager. LVM partitions provide great flexibility when you need to resize, move, or remove file system partitions.

   The guided partitioning section presents three partitioning schemes. Each of the options includes a suitable amount of swap space but has different benefits based on your situation. You must select one from the list before you proceed. See the sidebar "Selecting a Partition Scheme" for more information.

Note

When installing to small disk drives (those under a few gigabytes in size), you should use ext2 file systems instead of ext3. The journaling feature in ext3 requires that a portion of the disk be set aside for the journal, but the feature is of limited usefulness on small file systems. You can change file system types by going into the partition properties. To do this, highlight the partition using the arrow keys and press Enter. ∎

Selecting a Partition Scheme

The guided partitioning feature allows you to select one of three templates to use to create your partitions. Use these guidelines to select the template that is correct for you.

- **All files in one partition** — Makes a single Linux partition for files. This is the easiest option to manage because you don't have to worry about balancing the sizes of your partitions. This can also be dangerous because users have the capability to fill up the entire disk, which can cause problems for the operating system. Do not use this option unless you are prepared to monitor disk space carefully.

- **Separate /home partition** — This option is recommended for a desktop system. It gives the operating system its own space and gives home directories their own space. This option is a good trade-off between the convenience of a single partition and the increased safety of the multiuser scheme. However, the /tmp/ directory is still part of the operating system partition, meaning that it is still fairly easy for people who habitually use that directory to fill up the operating system partition.

- **Separate /home, /usr, /var, and /tmp partitions** — Creates separate partitions for the root file system, /usr/, /var/, /tmp/, and /home/. You can choose this option when you are using this system as a server. It may also be a good choice for systems that will be used by more than just you, your relatives, and your close friends. The trade-off is that you may run out of room on a given partition even though the others have plenty of space, which means that you will need to plan carefully.

continued

continued

In some situations, you may need to adjust the partition sizes selected by the multiuser partitioning scheme to put more room where you are likely to need it:

- If you are planning to compile a lot of large software packages, you'll need to have plenty of space in the /usr/ partition.

- Active servers (especially web and mail servers) may need extra room in /var/ for log files. Mail servers also use this space for the mail queue, and the default mail system also stores incoming mail here (you may also want to consider making /var/mail/ a separate partition in these cases).

- Web browsers such as Mozilla use /tmp/ for storing files while they are downloaded. This file system must be big enough to hold any large files that you want to download through there, plus any other files that may be there at the same time.

Note that with the server-style partitioning scheme, the /home/ partition generally ends up receiving most of the space on larger disks. This usually makes it a good place to "borrow" space from when you want to make other partitions larger. However, because partman (the partitioning tool used by the Debian installer) has already mapped out the partitions, you actually need to delete /home/ and then re-add it after you increase the size of the other partition. If other partitions are between /home/ and the one that you are increasing in size, you also need to delete them, and then add them back in an appropriate order.

Caution

The next step modifies the contents of your hard disk. Check your partition settings carefully. You receive an additional confirmation before proceeding. ■

7. **Write Changes** — With your partition configuration chosen, select Finish Partitioning and Write Changes to Disk. This is your last chance to cancel changes that could cause damage to any other operating systems you may have on the disk, so check the screen carefully before proceeding!

   The installer writes the partitions to disk and creates the necessary file systems. After they have been prepared and mounted, the Debian base system is extracted from the CD and installed to the target partitions.

8. **Root password** — The base system includes an empty password for the root (super-user) account, which means that you want to set one here. Select a password that you can remember but that others will not be able to guess easily.

9. **User account** — Add a non-administrative account that you can use for your day-to-day tasks on the server. Enter a username (this should not contain any spaces or punctuation other than dashes, must not start with a number, and is generally all in lowercase), and a password for this account.

10. **Install from mirror** — You are asked to select your country so that Debian can locate a network mirror from which to get software over the Internet (using only the install CD that comes with this book, you will only get a minimal system).

11. **Choose mirror** — Select a mirror site that is close to your region and press Enter.

12. **Proxy** — If you need to use an HTTP proxy to reach the Internet, type the name or IP address of that system. Otherwise, just leave the field blank and press Enter.

13. **Survey** — You are asked to participate in a survey of the most popular packages in Debian. Select Yes if you don't mind submitting anonymous information about the packages you install and use, with information updated about every week. (You can see the results of this survey at `http://popcon.debian.org`.)

14. **Software selection** — Select the software categories you want to install. To start with a basic desktop system, you can use the Desktop Environment and Standard System categories that are selected by default. Highlight a category and press the spacebar to select or unselect a category. Press Enter to begin downloading and installing software. This could take 20 minutes or more.

15. **Package settings** — If any of the packages you just installed require extra settings, you are asked to enter them now. For example, if you installed file sharing, you are asked to enter the workgroup/domain name for your Samba server.

16. **Install boot loader** — The final step is to install GRUB, the boot loader. The default setting is to install to the master boot record (MBR), which is generally the best option. If other bootable operating systems are detected on the disk, you can add them to the boot loader as well. Once the boot loader is properly configured, select Continue. The installer ejects the CD and prompts you to remove the CD. Remove the CD and press Enter to continue. Your computer should restart from the Debian system installed on your hard disk.

You now have a functional Debian GNU/Linux system. If you left the default selection to install a desktop interface you will have a good, basic GNOME desktop to start with. Take some time, as needed, to browse through Chapter 8 and familiarize yourself with the command line before continuing with the next section.

Managing Your Debian System

Some of the basic tasks that you may encounter while running Debian GNU/Linux include package installation, configuration, and removal, as well as handling some special situations that you may come across.

All these steps require that you be logged in as the superuser (root). If you have just finished installing the system, you can log in as root from the login prompt.

Configuring Network Connections

Debian includes a set of tools for managing most types of network interfaces, including Ethernet, PPP, wireless, and even ATM. You may find that you need to add or change network settings after the system has been installed.

IP Networks: Ethernet and Wireless

On Debian systems, standard network connections are configured in the /etc/network/ interfaces file. If you have a network card configured to obtain an IP address automatically, this file will look like this:

```
# This file describes the network interfaces available on
# your system and how to activate them. For more information,
# see interfaces(5).

# The loopback network interface
auto lo
iface lo inet loopback

# The primary network interface
auto eth0
iface eth0 inet dhcp
```

Caution

Do not modify the loopback entry unless you are absolutely certain that you know what you are doing. ■

In some cases, such as when the system will be acting as a server, you want to configure your network interface with a fixed IP address. To do so, edit /etc/network/interfaces and replace the iface eth0 inet dhcp line. Use the following block as a template, replacing the parameters with the correct settings for your network:

```
iface eth0 inet static
    address 192.168.1.220
    netmask 255.255.255.0
    gateway 192.168.1.1
```

Note

You can obtain IP network settings from your ISP or network administrator. ■

Wireless interfaces can also be configured using the interfaces file but require that the wireless-tools package be installed. Use dpkg or apt-get to install the wireless-tools package. Then add the necessary parameters to the entry for your wireless network interface. This example shows the settings for a wireless network with an access point (managed mode) set to the ESSID Home, and operating on channel 11:

```
iface eth0 inet dhcp
    wireless_essid Home
    wireless_mode Managed
    wireless_channel 11
```

Note

If your wireless network is using encryption, you need to specify a wireless-key parameter. You can find a complete list of wireless options in the iwconfig man page and /usr/share/doc/wireless-tools/ README.Debian. ■

Dial-up PPP Connections

Dial-up connections can be managed using the pppconfig utility. After installing the pppconfig package, run `pppconfig`. You are provided with a menu from which you can create, modify, and delete dial-up connections. If you have not created a connection yet, you want to select that option from the menu. Otherwise, you can edit your existing connections instead.

The pppconfig utility asks a number of questions during the connection creation process. Start by selecting "Create a connection," and then enter the following information as prompted:

1. **Provider name** — Enter any name you like to identify this connection. For the dial-up entry to your primary ISP, you can simply leave the name `provider` as the Provider name.

2. **DNS server configuration method** — Here you can configure the connection to static DNS servers if needed. This is probably not necessary unless your service provider included the DNS server information in the information that it provided about the connection. If you aren't certain, select Dynamic DNS and change it later if needed.

3. **Authentication method** — This is the method that your computer will use to identify itself to the dial-up server. PAP is the most commonly used protocol, and some systems also support CHAP. The CHAP option should be used if the dial-up servers use text prompts to ask for the username and password. If in doubt, select PAP.

4. **Username and password** — Enter the username and password that will be recognized by the dial-up server.

5. **Speed** — This is the speed that your computer and your modem will communicate with one another. In most cases, this should be set to 115200.

6. **Dialing method** — If your telephone system requires pulse dialing, you can configure that here.

7. **Phone number** — Enter the number that you need to dial in order to reach the dial-up server, including any area codes and other codes that may be needed. For example, if you have to dial 9 in order to reach an outside line, use 9,*<number to dial>*. The comma tells your modem to pause before continuing the dialing process. You may also enter the appropriate numbers for disabling features such as call waiting through your telephone service.

8. **Modem configuration method** — Here, you can have pppconfig attempt to automatically find the port that your modem is on. If a modem is not found, you are then given the chance to enter the path to the modem device. You can find more information about what to enter here in the "Identifying and Configuring Your Modem" sidebar later in this chapter.

   Save your settings by selecting Finished from the menu, and then exit the pppconfig utility.

Dial a connection by using the `pon` command, by replacing *peer* with the name you assigned to your connection, or by leaving it out if your connection is named `provider`:

```
# pon peer
```

You can disconnect using the `poff` command and can view logs (for diagnosing problems or determining status) using the `plog` command. The user that was created during the base system configuration will automatically have access to run these commands. You will need to add any other users who need to run them to the dialout group through the use of the `gpasswd` utility:

```
# gpasswd -a <username> dialout
```

PPPoE Connections

Some DSL and cable modem providers require that you use PPPoE (PPP over Ethernet) to connect to their systems. PPPoE connections are managed using the `pppoeconf` program. (You may need to install `pppoeconf` because it is not installed by default.) As long as your computer is connected to the broadband connection, it should be able to detect most of the settings automatically.

Package Management Using APT

For most users, APT will be the primary tool for installing, removing, and upgrading packages. This section shows how to use the apt-get and apt-cache utilities. From the console, you can also use the aptitude utility, which acts as an interface to apt-get.

When you run aptitude with no options, you can manage packages in interactive mode. From the aptitude screen, you can get security updates or view new packages. You can work with installed packages or those that are not yet installed (or virtual packages that only exist to provide functions needed by other packages). Installing tasks, however, is one of the most useful features.

The Add/Remove Applications window is another popular application to install software from a GNOME desktop in Debian. Select this application from the System Administration menu. Figure 21-1 shows an example of the Add/Remove Applications window.

Select the Search box to type a term related to the package you want to install. Alternatively, you can select a category and scroll through available packages in that category. Select the check boxes of the applications and click Apply Changes. The packages, and any dependent packages needed by those packages, are downloaded and installed on your system.

An alternative to the Add/Remove Applications window is the Synaptic Package Manager. Synaptic includes features that enable you to:

- Edit software sources to choose which software repositories to use
- Search all packages, including dependencies, libraries, and other related packages, and not just applications
- Get information about packages
- Lock packages so they cannot be upgraded
- Do advanced package searches and filtering
- Get software updates

See Chapter 19 for information on how to use the Synaptic Package manager.

FIGURE 21-1

Use Add/Remove Applications interactively to view and install packages.

Managing the List of Package Repositories

The configuration file /etc/apt/sources.list contains a list of Debian package repositories that APT will use. As with most configuration files on a Linux system, you can view this plain-text file using any text editor or pager. To view its contents, run the following:

```
# pager /etc/apt/sources.list
#deb cdrom:[Debian GNU/Linux 5.0.1 Lenny Official i386]/ lenny main

deb http://ftp.us.debian.org/debian/ lenny main
deb-src http://ftp.us.debian.org/debian/ lenny main

deb http://security.debian.org/ lenny/updates main contrib
deb-src http://security.debian.org/ lenny/updates main contrib
```

Note

Depending on which pager is configured as your default, you may need to press the Q key in order to return to a prompt. ■

Your output will differ from this example's, of course, but the kind of information remains the same. The first part of each line indicates whether the repository is to be used for binary packages (indicated by the deb prefix) or source packages (deb-src). The rest of the line defines the method (in this case, cdrom or http), the location, the distribution (lenny), and the sections (main). The contrib section is also added. If you want to use software from the non-free section, you can use a text editor to add them after main and contrib.

Note
Run man sources.list on any Debian system for more information. ∎

If you aren't going to have your Debian CD available all the time, you may want to remove the cdrom: entry from the file (or comment out the line, as shown earlier). Use a text editor (as root user) to edit the file:

```
# editor /etc/apt/sources.list
```

Make any changes you need to the file, exit the editor, and then update the package database as described in the following section.

Note
Astute readers may notice that the pager and editor commands used in this section are not common UNIX commands. Both are pointers to programs and are managed using Debian's alternatives system, which is discussed later in this chapter. ∎

Updating the APT Package Database

Because the lists of packages available in the Debian package repositories may change from time to time, you need to instruct APT to download these lists and update its database occasionally. To perform this process, run the following command:

```
# apt-get update
```

You generally want to run this command before installing new packages so that you do not download an older version. Run it before checking for upgrades as well.

Finding and Installing Packages

When looking for new packages to install, you may not always know what package you want. The package database maintained by APT includes package descriptions and other fields that can be searched using the apt-cache utility:

```
# apt-cache search tetris
bsdgames — a collection of classic textual unix games
pytris — two-player networked console tetris clone
stax — collection of puzzle games similar to Tetris Attack.
...
```

Tip
Specifying multiple keywords in a search prevents apt-cache from listing packages that do not contain all the keywords you specify. This enables you to do very specific searches, such as word processor. ∎

You can also use this utility to find out more information about a specific package in the repositories:

```
# apt-cache show pytris
Package: pytris
Priority: optional
Section: games
Installed-Size: 96
Maintainer: Radovan Garabik <garabik@kassiopeia.juls.savba.sh>
Architecture: i386
Version: 0.98
Depends: python (>=2.1), libc6 (>= 2.3.5-1)
Filename: pool/main/p/pytris/pytris_0.98_i386.deb
Size: 16258
MD5sum: d08e8ed6cce5e7b78e2c799eb83d463b
SHA1: 8cca87b2689ab69b5d3a07fda7ef4a47f06d2042
SHA256:
   9353512ee65466fc72105d535453a55cdf3ba8f1b07aa8fd09818e5c65ffe095
Description: two-player networked console tetris clone
 two-player networked console based tetris clone, written
 in python, similar to xtet42.
Tag: game::tetris, implemented-in::python, interface::x11,
   role::program, use::gameplaying, x11::application
```

Note

To view information about a specific package that is already installed on your system, use dpkg, as discussed later in this chapter. ∎

After you know the name of the package you want to install, use the install method to download it and any packages on which it depends. For example, the ssh package is very useful for remotely accessing systems and is probably one of the first programs that you will want to install:

```
# apt-get install ssh
```

On this command, APT retrieves and installs the ssh package. If additional packages are required, a list of those packages is displayed by APT. If you choose to continue, APT will download and install those packages along with the package you requested.

Note

When installing packages that support automatic configuration through debconf, you're prompted to answer the appropriate configuration questions. Although the Debian package developers have gone to great lengths to ensure that the default options for these questions will work in most situations, it's best to read the questions thoroughly to be sure that the defaults work for you. ∎

Removing Packages

You can also use APT to remove packages from your system. Unlike dpkg, which removes only the package you tell it to remove, apt-get also removes any packages that depend on the package you are removing. This is best used in conjunction with the `-s` option to simulate what would happen if the removal were actually performed:

```
# apt-get -s remove python2.3
Reading Package Lists... Done
Building Dependency Tree... Done
The following packages will be REMOVED:
  bittornado python python2.3 python2.3-dev
0 upgraded, 0 newly installed, 4 to remove and 0 not upgraded.
Remv pytris (0.96 Debian:testing)
Remv python (2.3.4-1 Debian:testing)
Remv python2.3-dev (2.3.4-5 Debian:testing)
Remv python2.3 (2.3.4-5 Debian:testing)
```

In this example, several other packages depend on the python2.3 package and also need to be removed. To proceed with removing python2.3 and all packages that depend on it, run the command again without the `-s` flag.

Upgrading Your System

As new versions of packages become available, you can instruct APT to download and install them, automatically replacing the older versions. This is as simple as updating your package list, followed by a simple command:

```
# apt-get upgrade
```

APT begins by downloading the necessary packages, and then moves on to installing and configuring them. If necessary, you can abort the upgrade during the download process by pressing Control+C. APT may also be able to recover if you have to abort during the installation or configuration steps, but it is still best to let the process run without interruption after it has begun installing packages.

Note

When upgrading to a newer distribution, use `dist-upgrade` instead of `upgrade`. This changes the rules that APT uses when deciding which actions to take, making it expect major changes in dependencies and handle them appropriately. ■

Package Management Using dpkg

As mentioned earlier, the `dpkg` utility is the core package management tool in Debian. Most other package management tools within the system, including APT, use `dpkg` to perform the midlevel work, and `dpkg` in turn uses `dpkg-deb` and `dpkg-query` to handle a number of the low-level functions. In most cases, you will want to use APT or Aptitude for package management, and use `dpkg` in only a few situations.

Far too many commands associated with `dpkg` exist to list in this chapter, but the most common ones are explained in the following sections. In most cases, there are both short and long commands to perform the same function. Use whichever is easier for you to remember.

Installing and Removing Packages

You can install packages with dpkg using the `-i` or `--install` flags and the path to the `.deb` file containing the package. The path must be accessible as a file system path (HTTP, FTP, and other methods are not supported), and you can specify more than one package:

```
# dpkg --install /home/wayne/lsof_4.77.dfsg.1-3_i386.deb
```

Package removal through `dpkg` is also straightforward and is done with the `-r` or `--remove` commands. When configuration files are to be removed, you can use the `-P` or `--purge` command instead. Both commands can also be used to specify multiple packages to remove:

```
# dpkg --remove lsof
```

or . . .

```
# dpkg --purge lsof
```

Querying the Package Database

You often need to obtain more information about packages that are already installed on your system. Because these operations do not modify the package database, you can do them as a non-root user.

To list all packages known to dpkg, use the `-l` or `--list` commands:

```
$ dpkg --list
```

You can restrict the list by specifying a glob pattern:

```
$ dpkg --list "*lsof*"
```

Note

The quotes are used to prevent the shell from replacing the wildcard with a list of matching files in the current directory. For more information about wildcards, see Chapter 8 or type man 7 glob to see a list of wildcards. ■

To view detailed information about a specific package, use the `-s` or `--status` command:

```
$ dpkg --status lsof
Package: lsof
Status: install ok installed
Priority: standard
Section: utils
...
```

To determine the origin package for a file use the `-S` or `--search` command:

```
$ dpkg --search /bin/ls
coreutils: /bin/ls
```

To view the list of files in an installed package use the -L or --listfiles command:

```
$ dpkg --listfiles lsof
/.
/usr
/usr/sbin
/usr/bin
/usr/bin/lsof
...
```

Examining a Package File

You can examine package files before installing them using either the --info (-I) or the --contents (-c) command. You can use these options on packages in a local directory, as opposed to using them to examine packages on a remote server.

The following --info option shows the lsof package name, version information, and sizes of different parts of the package. Beyond that (although shortened here for space considerations) you would be able to see a list of packages lsof depends on and descriptive information about the package.

```
$ dpkg --info lsof_4.77.dfsg.1-3_i386.deb
new debian package, version 2.0.
size 205312 bytes: control archive= 1207 bytes.
    517 bytes,    15 lines       control
   1615 bytes,    22 lines       md5sums
Package: lsof
Version: 4.77.dfsg.1-3
...
Description: List open files
 Lsof is a Unix-specific diagnostic tool. Its name stands
 for LiSt Open Files, and it does just that. It lists
 information about any files that are open, by processes
 currently running on the system.
```

The following --contents option enables you to see the full contents of the package you choose as if you were listing the contents with an ls -l command. You can see the name and path to each file, its permission settings, and file/group ownership:

```
$ dpkg --contents lsof_4.77.dfsg.1-3_i386.deb
drwxr-xr-x root/root         0 2006-05-15 18:09 ./
drwxr-xr-x root/root         0 2006-05-15 18:09 ./usr/
drwxr-xr-x root/root         0 2006-05-15 18:09 ./usr/bin/
...
```

Installing Package Sets (Tasks) with tasksel

Some package sets are too large to be managed practically through meta packages, so tasks have been created as an alternative. You install and remove tasks with the tasksel utility. When run without any arguments, tasksel presents a menu from which you can select tasks to install or remove.

Additional options are available from the command line:

- To see a list of known tasks, run `tasksel --list-tasks`.
- To list the packages that are installed by a task, run `tasksel --task-packages` `<task name>`.

Refer to the `/usr/share/tasksel/debian-tasks.desc` file for a list of tasks that APT knows about, along with descriptions of those tasks.

Caution

When a task is removed, all programs associated with that task, whether installed manually or as part of that task, are removed! ∎

If you want to try a desktop other than the GNOME desktop installed by default, you can use `tasksel` to install a KDE or Xfce desktop. Use the `kde-desktop` task to install KDE or `xfce-desktop` to install the Xfce desktop. Note that the `kde-desktop` task takes a long time to download and install and requires several hundred megabytes of disk space to complete. To start the `kde-desktop` task, run the following:

```
# tasksel install kde-desktop
```

Alternatives, Diversions, and Stat Overrides

In cases where more than one installed program provides a specific function, package maintainers have the option of utilizing Debian's alternatives system. The alternatives system manages which program is executed when you run a specific command. For example, the ed, nano, and nvi packages each provide a text editor. An alternative maintained in the system guarantees that a text editor is accessible through the generic `editor` command, regardless of which combination of these packages is installed.

The system administrator can designate which program is referenced in the alternatives database through the use of the `update-alternatives` command:

```
# update-alternatives --config editor

These are alternatives that provide 'editor'.
  Selection    Alternative
-------------------------------------------------
        1       /bin/ed
*+      2       /bin/nano
        3       /usr/bin/nvi

Press enter to keep the default[*],
or type selection number: 2
```

You can also use the `--all` command with `update-alternatives` to configure every entry in the alternatives database, one at a time. You can find more details by typing the following: **man update-alternatives**.

Note

By default, all alternatives are in automatic mode, meaning that the system automatically selects a suitable program from the available candidates. Installing a new candidate program generally results in the automatic updating of the appropriate alternatives. Manually configuring an alternative disables automatic mode, preventing the system from changing these settings without prior knowledge of the system administrator. ■

The Debian package management tools also provide a mechanism for renaming specific files in a package and for overriding the ownership and permission settings on files. Unlike when these changes are made manually, using mv, chmod, or chown, changes made through the Debian tools remain in place across package upgrades and reinstallations.

For example, if you want to replace /usr/bin/users without modifying the coreutils package, you can divert it to /usr/bin/users.distrib:

```
# dpkg-divert --local --rename --add /usr/bin/users
Adding `local diversion of /usr/bin/users to /usr/bin/users.distrib'
```

Removing the diversion returns the original filename:

```
# dpkg-divert --remove /usr/bin/users
Removing `local diversion of /usr/bin/users to /usr/bin/users.distrib'
```

Stat overrides are useful when you want to disable access to a program, or when you want to make it set-UID. For example, to disable access to the wall program, type the following:

```
# dpkg-statoverride --update --add root root 0000 /usr/bin/wall
```

This sets the owner and group of /usr/bin/wall to root and disables all permissions on the file.

Note

You can find more information about file permissions in the section "Understanding File Permissions" in Chapter 8. ■

Unlike dpkg-divert, dpkg-statoverride does not keep track of the original file permissions. As a result, removing an override does not restore the old permissions. After removing the override, you need to either set the permissions manually or reinstall the package that contained the file:

```
# dpkg-statoverride --remove /usr/bin/wall
# apt-get --reinstall install bsdutils
Reading package lists... Done
Building dependency tree... Done
0 upgraded, 0 newly installed, 1 reinstalled, 0 to remove and 1 not upgraded.
Need to get 0B/68.5kB of archives.
After unpacking 0B of additional disk space will be used.
Do you want to continue? [Y/n]Y
(Reading database ... 16542 files and directories currently installed.)
Preparing to replace bsdutils 1:2.12r-19etch1 (using .../bsdutils_1%3a2.12r-
19etch1_i386.deb) ...
Unpacking replacement bsdutils ...
Setting up bsdutils (2.12r-19etch1) ...
```

Managing Package Configuration with debconf

All packages that include support for configuration management through debconf are configured as they are being installed. If you want to change a configuration option later, you can do so using the `dpkg-reconfigure` command. For example, you can change the configuration options for ssh using the following command:

```
# dpkg-reconfigure ssh
```

Every configuration parameter is assigned a priority by the package maintainer. This allows debconf to select the default values for settings below a specific priority. There are four levels of priorities for configuration items: low, medium, high, and critical. By default, you will be prompted to answer questions of only medium, high, or critical priority; low-priority questions are answered automatically. You can change this by reconfiguring the debconf package:

```
# dpkg-reconfigure debconf
```

Note

Advanced users maintaining multiple systems may want to create a database of configuration settings that can be distributed to every computer (or to sets of computers) to reduce the number of repeated steps. This process is documented in the `debconf` and `debconf.conf` man pages. It is also possible to configure debconf with a non-interactive front end so that it will not stop to ask any questions. ■

Summary

The reliability of Debian GNU/Linux, combined with the large number of high-quality packages available for it, make Debian a great choice for both workstations and servers. The carefully executed releases and the capability to upgrade most software without rebooting serve to further increase its suitability as a server operating system.

APT is a primary tool for installing, removing, and upgrading packages. This chapter explored how to use the `aptitude`, `apt-get`, and `apt-cache` utilities for package management. The chapter also covered the installation of package sets (tasks) using the `tasksel` utility and managing package configuration with the `dpkg-reconfigure` utility.

Running SUSE and openSUSE Linux

## 22

Once the most popular Linux distribution in Europe, SUSE was purchased by the U.S. networking company Novell, Inc. in November 2003. Since that time, SUSE Linux Enterprise (SLE) products have been positioned to challenge Red Hat to become the dominant Linux distribution for large enterprise computing environments worldwide.

Like Fedora and Red Hat Enterprise Linux, openSUSE and SUSE Linux Enterprise are excellent for people who are looking for a Linux system to use in large, enterprise environments. Because Novell's Linux product line is geared toward enterprise computing, the skills you gain using SUSE on your home Linux system will be useful in a business environment as well.

SUSE systems have a slick graphical installer that leads you through installation and intuitive administrative tools, consolidated under a facility called YaST. SUSE and its parent company, Novell, offer a range of Linux products and support plans that scale from free versions of openSUSE with community support, to supported SUSE distributions for enterprise desktop (SUSE Linux Enterprise Desktop, or SLED), all the way up to SUSE's Linux Enterprise Server (SLES) product.

In 2005, Novell refocused its development efforts to do as Red Hat does with its Red Hat Enterprise Linux product and Fedora Project: Novell formed the openSUSE Project, which, like the Fedora Project, produces a free community-driven Linux system with relatively frequent releases that feed into Novell's for-profit Linux systems.

On the DVD

The DVD that comes with this book contains the openSUSE 11.3 KDE live/ install CD. ■

IN THIS CHAPTER
Understanding SUSE
What's in SUSE
Installing openSUSE

This chapter describes the features and approach to Linux that sets SUSE Linux Enterprise apart from other Linux distributions. It also explains how to install the openSUSE Linux distribution that is included with this book.

The current version of openSUSE features the YaST installer, and the current versions of KDE 4.4 Desktop Environment, GNOME 2.30, Firefox 3.6.6, GIMP 2.6.8, Apache 2.2.15, MySQL 5.1, and OpenOffice.org 3.2.1. To see all the packages available with openSUSE, open the YaST Package Manager (as described later in this chapter).

Note

With the split between SUSE Linux Enterprise and openSUSE, Linux product names from Novell have changed significantly in the past few years. Most significantly, what was previously called SUSE Professional Linux is now called SUSE Linux Enterprise. ■

Running with the Enemy: The SUSE/Microsoft Deal

In November 2006, Novell announced that it had struck a deal with Microsoft to further collaboration and interoperability with Microsoft products. This deal includes indemnification against patent-related lawsuits, and has raised a fair amount of concern and controversy in the open source community. In reality, Novell hasn't admitted and doesn't see any evidence of the use of Microsoft's intellectual property (IP) in Linux, but indemnification against patent liabilities has become an important part of the Linux scene ever since The SCO Group (www.sco.com) launched its series of questionable IP lawsuits against Linux. Red Hat and Oracle already offer indemnification against this sort of thing.

Paranoia aside, this deal is important if for no other reason than that it is a statement by Microsoft that Linux is important to its customers and a viable enterprise operating system. As always, the long-term effects of this deal remain to be seen.

Understanding SUSE Linux Enterprise and openSUSE

If you are looking for a Linux system with the stability and support on which you can bet your business, SUSE offers impressive, stable Linux products backed by a company (Novell, Inc.) that has been selling enterprise solutions for a long time. SUSE Linux Enterprise products range from desktop systems to enterprise-quality servers.

SUSE (originally written as SuSE) began as a German version of Slackware in 1992, on 40 floppy disks, and was first officially released on CD (SUSE Linux 1.0) in 1994. Founded by Hubert Mantel, Burchard Steinbild, Roland Dyroff, and Thomas Fehr, SUSE set out as a separate distribution from Slackware to enhance the software in the areas of installation and administration.

Although SUSE had success and respect with its Linux distribution, it was not profitable, and Novell's $210 million offer for SUSE was seen as a good thing both for SUSE and for Linux in general. SUSE was running short on cash, and Novell was looking for a way to regain its stature as a growth company in the enterprise and network-computing arena.

In the 1980s and early 1990s, Novell was the world's number-one computer networking company. Before the Internet took hold, Novell's NetWare servers and IPX/SPX protocols were the most popular ways to connect PCs together on LANs. International training, support, and sales teams brought Novell products to businesses and organizations around the world.

Despite Novell's huge lead in the network computing market, file- and printer-sharing features in Microsoft Windows and late entry into the TCP/IP (Internet) arena caused Novell to lose its market dominance in the 1990s. Although its NetWare products contained excellent features for directory services and managing network resources, Novell didn't have end-to-end computing solutions and relied on Windows for client computers.

Novell's association with the UNIX operating system in the early 1990s makes an interesting footnote in the history of Linux. Novell purchased UNIX System V source code from AT&T and set out to make its resulting UnixWare product (a UNIX desktop product for x86 processors) a competitor to Microsoft's growing dominance on the desktop. The effort was half-hearted, and in the mid-1990s Novell gave the UNIX trademark to the Open Group and sold the UNIX source code to SCO.

Novell's purchase of SUSE marked its second major attempt to fill in its product line with a UNIX-like desktop and server product. In its first few years of supporting Linux, Novell is already doing a better job with Linux than it did with UNIX. However, it has still failed to make significant gains in market share from the leading enterprise Linux company: Red Hat, Inc.

What's in SUSE Distributions?

Unlike distributions geared toward more technical users, such as Gentoo and Slackware, you can configure and launch most major features of SUSE Linux by selecting menus on the desktop. New Linux users should find SUSE to be very comfortable for daily use and basic administration.

Like Red Hat Enterprise Linux, SUSE is made to have a more cohesive look and feel than most Linux distributions that are geared toward Linux enthusiasts. In other words, you aren't required to put together a lot of SUSE by hand just to get it working. Although SUSE is ultimately aimed more toward enterprise computing, it also works well as a home desktop system.

The following sections explore what openSUSE and SUSE Linux Enterprise offer you.

Installation and Configuration with YaST

A set of modules that you can use to configure your SUSE system is gathered together under the YaST facility. Because many of the features needed in a Linux installer are also needed to configure a running system (network, security, software, and other setup features), YaST does double duty as an installer and an administrative tool.

YaST (which stands for Yet Another Setup Tool) was originally proprietary code that was not available as open source. However, to gain wider acceptance for YaST among major computing clients as a framework for managing a range of computing services, Novell released YaST under the GNU Public License in March 2004.

YaST makes obvious what you need to do to install Linux. Hardware detection is done before your eyes. You can set up your disk partitions graphically (no need to remember options to the fdisk command). Setting up the GRUB boot loader is done for you, with the option to modify it yourself.

One of the nice features of YaST installation is that you can scan the configuration process without stepping through every feature. If you scan through the mouse, keyboard, installation mode, partitioning, and other information and they look okay, you can click Accept and just keep going. Or you can change any of those settings you choose. (The "Installing openSUSE" section later in this chapter details the installation process with YaST.)

Because YaST offers both graphical (QT) and text-based (ncurses) interfaces, you can use YaST as a configuration tool from the desktop or the shell. To start YaST from the KDE desktop, click the Computer tab on the openSUSE menu and select YaST from the menu that appears. Figure 22-1 shows the graphical YaST utility.

Launching the YaST utility actually involves running the /sbin/yast2 command. When you run /sbin/yast2, YaST starts in graphical mode by default. (An alternative is to run /sbin/yast as root user from a Terminal window, which starts YaST in text mode.) Figure 22-2 shows what YaST looks like when started in text mode from a Terminal window.

FIGURE 22-1

Configure common Linux features using the YaST control center.

FIGURE 22-2

Use the arrow and Tab keys to navigate YaST in text mode.

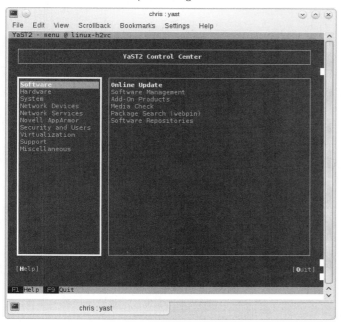

YaST offers you some intuitive tools for configuring your system and comes preconfigured so you start with a nice set of defaults. YaST also does a good job detecting your hardware, finding partitions, and the like, so a new user can often just accept the settings YaST chooses. Here are some examples of what YaST does for you:

- **Detects hardware** — You don't have to check through /etc configuration files or run lsmod, lspci, or hwinfo to see the drivers for your hardware or how your hardware has been configured in SUSE. From the Hardware section, you can select icons representing your graphics cards, printers, joysticks, scanners, sound cards, and mice. Click the Hardware information icon to see your full list of detected hardware.

- **Manages system configuration** — Like Red Hat Enterprise Linux, SUSE stores much of the information it uses to configure services at boot time in files in the /etc/sysconfig directory. The information in those files is in the form VARIABLE="VALUE".

  Under the YaST System heading (in the left-hand pane), you can select the sysconfig Editor, which lets you select each file and then view and possibly change each variable so that you don't have to guess what variables are available for each configuration. For more advanced system administrators, this is a great way to fine-tune the startup services for your system.

  SUSE also includes a Profile Manager applet, which lets you store and manage a collection of system settings so it can be used again later.

- **Configures network devices** — YaST detects your dial-up modem, Ethernet card, DSL modem, or ISDN hardware, and gives you the opportunity to configure each piece of hardware. SUSE also does a much better job than most distributions at getting Winmodems working in Linux, which is particularly useful for using dial-up features on laptops that have cheap, built-in modems.

- **Defines network services** — With a connection to your LAN or WAN, YaST provides some helpful graphical tools for configuring some services that can be unintuitive to configure from the command line. NetworkManager (which is enabled by default in openSUSE) tries to detect and configure your network interfaces automatically. However, to scan available network interfaces and manually override those settings from YaST, select Network Settings from the Network Devices category.

- **Changes security settings** — Security settings in Linux are often among the most unintuitive features to configure, but they are also among the most important. Although features such as iptables work great for most Linux gurus for setting up a firewall, people who are accustomed to graphical interfaces may find them challenging.

  From the YaST Security and Users selection, the Firewall icon enables you to step through your network interfaces and add access to those services you want by name (such as Web Server, Mail Server, and Other Services) or by port number. It even enables you to do initial setup of more complex firewall features, such as packet forwarding, IP Masquerading, and logging.

To make your way around the graphical YaST interface, you need only to click the mouse and use the Tab key to move between fields. For the text-based YaST interface, you can use the Tab and arrow keys to move among the selections and the Enter key to select the currently highlighted item.

RPM Package Management

Like Red Hat Enterprise Linux and Fedora, SUSE packages its software using the RPM Package Management file format and related tools. RPM contains a lot of features for adding, removing, and managing software in SUSE. Although software packages in the Red Hat and SUSE distributions are different, the tools you use for managing packages in those two distributions from the command line are very much the same.

In most cases, you will use the YaST Software Manager to find, install, and uninstall software packages in SUSE distributions. However, you also can run the rpm utility to work with RPM software packages from the command line.

- **Installing local or remote packages** — You can use the rpm command to add a software package to SUSE, and rpm doesn't care if the package is in the local directory, CD, or remote computer (providing you have network access to that computer). A remote package can be available on a Web server (http://) or FTP server (ftp://). Here's an example of using an rpm command to install a software package from an FTP server:

```
# rpm -iv ftp://ftp.linuxtoys.net/pub/suse/11/abc.i586.rpm
```

In this example, the -i option says to install the package, and the -v option says to give verbose output as the package is installed. The fictitious package (abc.i586.rpm) is installed from an FTP repository. If there are dependency or access issues, rpm informs you and fails. Otherwise, the package is installed. (The -U option is often used instead of the -i option to install RPMs because -U succeeds even if the package is already installed. The -U says to upgrade the package.)

- **Querying the RPM database** — One of the best features of the RPM facility is that you can find out a lot of information about the software packages that are installed. The query option (-q) lets you list package names, descriptions, and contents in various ways. Here are a few examples:

  ```
  # rpm -qa coreutils
  # rpm -ql coreutils| less
  # rpm -qi coreutils| less
  ```

  The first example (-qa) searches for the coreutils package and reports the current version of the package that is installed. In the second, -ql lists all files in the coreutils package and then pipes that output to the less command to page through it. And finally, -qi displays a description and other information about the coreutils package.

- **Verifying installed packages** — Use rpm to verify the contents of an RPM package. The -V option enables you to check whether any of the files in a package have been tampered with. Here is an example:

  ```
  # rpm -V aaa_base
  ..5....T c /etc/inittab
  S.5....T   /etc/profile.d/alias.ash
  ```

  The -V checks whether any of the files contained in the aaa_base package (which contains some basic system configuration files) have been modified since the package was installed. The output shows that the inittab and alias.ash files have been modified from the originals. The 5 indicates that the md5sum of the files differ, while the T indicates that the time stamp on the file differs. On the alias.ash file, the S shows that the size of the file is different.

The rpm command has many other options as well. To find out more about them, type man rpm or rpm --help from any shell.

Automated Software Updates

SUSE Linux includes an automatic update agent, referred to as the YaST Online Update (YOU) utility. This utility is built right into the YaST facility and offers an easy way to get updates, security patches, and bug fixes for SUSE Linux Enterprise or openSUSE by downloading and installing them from software repositories over the network. You can also execute YOU from the command line as root user, using the you command.

From within YaST, select Software ➪ Online Update. YaST uses software installation sources that have been defined in YaST's Installation Source module to enable you to begin retrieving software updates with a single click. It presents you with a list of patches from which you can choose. Security patches are in red, all recommended patches are selected, and optional patches are shown (unselected). It's easy to see all available patches and read their descriptions to determine whether you want them.

Installing openSUSE

The DVD that comes with this book includes the openSUSE 11.3 KDE live/install CD, remastered to coexist with other Linux systems on the DVD. If you like openSUSE and want a boxed set, you can purchase one from the openSUSE project. The boxed set of SUSE Linux includes installation support and hardcopy documentation.

The following are the steps for installing openSUSE Linux on your hard disk from the openSUSE live CD included on the DVD accompanying this book. This procedure has fewer steps than installing from install media. In particular, instead of letting you choose which software packages to install, the live CD media simply copies the exact live CD software to your hard disk.

1. **Insert the DVD that comes with this book in your drive.** Reboot the computer. The boot screen appears.

2. **Select suse from the boot screen.** You are offered the opportunity to boot openSUSE live or install directly.

3. **Start installing.** Select Installation. A Welcome screen appears, offering you the chance to view the software license and change the language and keyboard.

4. **License, language, and keyboard.** You can change the default language and keyboard from English (US) if you need to on this screen. Then read the Novell Software License Agreement. If you agree, select the check box and click Next. (Selecting No ends the install process.) The system is probed to make sure minimum hardware requirements are met. If more drivers are needed than are available on the installation medium, they will be downloaded from the Internet.

5. **Clock and time zone.** Select the geographic region and time zone in which you're located. If the time is wrong, click Change, and type your new date and/or time and click Accept. Note that other operating systems may not expect the Hardware Clock (in the BIOS) to be set to UTC (Coordinated Universal Time). If you dual-boot, you may want to consider setting this to Local time so it does not conflict with other operating systems. Linux works with either mode. Select Next to continue.

6. **Partitioning.** Partitioning is very important, especially if you want to protect any data currently on your hard disk. The openSUSE install screen recommends a partitioning scheme. (If your disk is already partitioned, openSUSE tries to use that scheme.) You can simply accept that scheme (just click Next) or select the Edit Partitions button.

   The partitioning screen enables you to use a partitioning interface that is very similar to the partition screen used when installing Fedora.

7. **Create new user.** You are asked to add a user account, as prompted, for your computer. Add your full name; a short, one-word login name; and a password to protect that account.

   You can choose to have the same password for your regular user and the root user. If you want to have this user automatically logged in on the system whenever you restart, leave the Automatic Login check box selected. Otherwise, deselect it to see a standard login prompt whenever you boot your system. You can also check the Receive System Mail check box to ensure that the user account that you have just created automatically receives a copy of any mail sent to the root user on your system, which is often sent by administrative applications. To proceed, click Next.

8. **Installation Settings.** Installation headings are displayed for System, Partitioning, Booting, Keyboard Layout, Time Zone, and Default run level. Review those settings and click on the heading representing any settings you want to change

9. **Start the install.** If the Installation settings all look okay, click Install to begin the install process. Remember that this is your last chance to back out! When the confirmation dialog box appears, click Back to return to the installer so that you can modify or abort the install process, or click Install to start the installation.

   If you select Install, openSUSE formats your hard disk and installs the entire contents of the openSUSE live CD. After installation finishes, a message tells you to reboot.

10. **Reboot your computer.** When installation is done, reboot the computer (select Shut down and Restart from the computer menu). Remove the CD or DVD before the computer boots up again. After your system starts up (this time from hard disk), openSUSE probes for information about your video card, printers, and network. It then tries to automatically configure those devices.

At this point you should have a working openSUSE system. You can go ahead and start using openSUSE as described in the next section.

Starting with openSUSE

If you created a user account during the preceding installation and left Automatic Login selected when you created that account, openSUSE should automatically log you in as that user and present you with the KDE desktop. (If you are presented with a graphical login screen instead, log in as that user now.) Here are a few things to help you get started using openSUSE:

- **Desktop applications** — The default openSUSE install is configured as a desktop system that includes a set of easily accessible desktop applications. Select the Application Launcher and the Applications tab to see icons for starting popular desktop applications: Firefox (Web browser), Amarok Media Player, GIMP (image editor), KMail (mail client), OpenOffice.org Writer (word processor), and Nautilus (file browser).

- **Home folder** — The Home folder on the desktop gives you access to your desktop, as well as folders for Documents and Music, and other content folders in a file manager window.

- **Reconfigure your computer** — Get to the YaST administration tool by selecting Computer ⇨ YaST from the openSUSE menu. Reconfigure your system hardware and software from the YaST Control Center that appears.

If you want to configure your desktop (change backgrounds, screen savers, or themes), just right-click the desktop and select Desktop Settings. A Desktop Activity Settings window is also available from the openSUSE menu, to further configure your system.

Summary

SUSE Linux Enterprise is generally considered to be the next best choice for enterprise-quality Linux systems in the United States, after Red Hat Enterprise Linux. However, SUSE Linux Enterprise is very popular in Europe.

The openSUSE distribution on which SUSE Linux Enterprise is based is recommended for home users and enthusiasts. Both distributions offer graphical installation and administrative tools (implemented in a facility called YaST) that help set them apart from other Linux distributions geared more toward technical users.

Running PCLinuxOS

## 23

With many commercial Linux distributions focusing on large enter-prise server systems, other distributions have stepped up to go the last mile for desktop users. PCLinuxOS (www.pclinuxos.com) is one such desktop-oriented Linux system.

PCLinuxOS is a Linux distribution that makes it easy for desktop users to be able to run the kind of applications they need and play the type of content they want without jumping through hoops. It's distributed on a live CD, so you can try it first and then, if you like it, follow a simple install procedure that starts from an icon on the desktop.

By offering many popular applications that are lacking in other Linux desktop distributions and adding some great remastering and customization tools, PCLinuxOS has gained a large and enthusiastic following of desktop Linux users. PCLinuxOS makes it easy to leave behind your Windows desktop system for Linux without leaving behind your music, videos, or documents.

In addition to playing MP3 and Flash content from the get-go, PCLinuxOS makes it easy to get software for playing commercial DVD movies, Windows media content, and other content types where it is legal to do so. It is set up so that with just a few quick downloads you can play the content you care about most.

Adding to the stability of the PCLinuxOS desktop experience is the fact that PCLinuxOS doesn't always just include the latest, and often unstable, versions of open source software available. By offering stable versions of KDE, Firefox, and other critical desktop components, your desktop might provide more reliable performance than you'll get with the latest Ubuntu or Fedora desktops.

IN THIS CHAPTER

Starting with PCLinuxOS

Installing PCLinuxOS

Remastering PCLinuxOS

This chapter tells you how to use PCLinuxOS as a desktop system. It also describes some of the many PCLinuxOS remasters you can use for special applications or particular desktop environments. Then it shows how you can create your own remastered PCLinuxOS.

Starting with PCLinuxOS

PCLinuxOS is often recommended for first-time users because its developers have hidden many of the intricacies of Linux. They have taken the time to set up an easy-to-use desktop so you don't have to do a lot of tricks from the command line to have the features you want. Many things that don't work out-of-the box with other Linux distributions just work with PCLinuxOS.

Boot up PCLinuxOS from a live CD, open a browser, and go to YouTube.com to immediately begin playing Flash content. Java content is ready to run as well. Open a media player, such as Kaffeine, and start listening to your MP3 music right now. Kaffeine will even warn you about content you can't currently play (DVD movies and Windows media) and what you can do to remedy that (if it's legal to do so where you are).

On the DVD
A PCLinuxOS live CD is included on the DVD that comes with this book. See Appendix A for information on how to use that live CD. ■

To start using PCLinuxOS, simply insert the CD or DVD you have containing PCLinuxOS. From the DVD supplied with this book, just select PCLinuxOS from the boot screen.

User accounts for a regular user (guest) and administrative user (root) are preconfigured for PCLinuxOS. Select which user you want to log in as (guest is recommended) and enter the password (shown on the screen) for the associated user. After a few moments, a desktop should appear that is similar to the one shown in Figure 23-1.

Discovering What's in PCLinuxOS

A lot of applications are available on the PCLinuxOS live CD and you can install many more later. But what sets PCLinuxOS apart is how many applications have so many features enabled by default. With PCLinuxOS running, try a few things:

- **Get on the Internet.** Open the Firefox icon on the desktop and type a URL into the location box. If your computer has an available Internet connection, you should be able to browse the web. If not, select PC ⇨ More Applications ⇨ Configuration ⇨ Network Center and configure your networking as required.

- **Try out web content.** Plug-ins added to Firefox in PCLinuxOS should allow you to play Flash, Java, MP3, PDF, and other content without any additional software. Some content, such as Microsoft Word files, appear when the browser automatically launches an external application.

FIGURE 23-1

Boot PCLinuxOS to the default desktop.

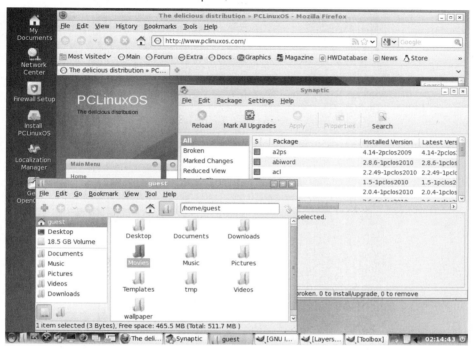

- **Configure your system.** You can perform lots of other configuration on your system from the Control Center. Select System ⇨ Configuration ⇨ Control Center.

- **Try other applications.** Select the PC ⇨ More Applications ⇨ Configuration ⇨ Configure Your Computer icon in the lower-left corner of the screen. From the menu that appears, you can select to play games, connect to other systems (e-mail, IM, file sharing, news, and BitTorrent), do word processing, or configure your system.

Adding More Applications

If the content you want to play or display cannot be interpreted by your browser or other application (such as those on the PCLinuxOS menus), use Synaptic to install additional software over the Internet. From the bottom panel, select the Package Manager icon. After you type the root password, the Synaptic package manager appears as shown in Figure 23-2.

If this is the first time using Synaptic for this installation, you should reload package information. Select Edit ⇨ Reload Package Information. With an active Internet connection, your system will download updated package information to your system.

FIGURE 23-2

Add more software with Synaptic Package Manager.

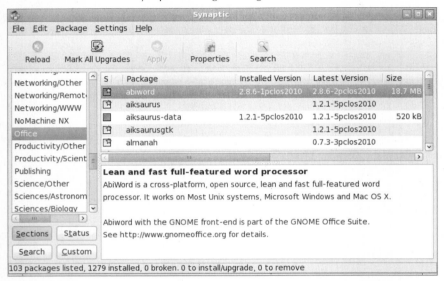

Every repository that contains software you want may not be immediately enabled. Select Settings ➪ Repositories and check for repositories that you may want to enable. For example, you need to click Get OpenOffice to set up the repository entries for OpenOffice.org office productivity applications.

With that information updated, you can begin adding the software that you want to your PCLinuxOS installation. Here are some examples:

- **Commercial DVD software** — Because of contention about the legality of open source software for decrypting commercial DVD movies, it is not delivered by default in PCLinuxOS.

- **Win32 codec binaries** — In the non-free repository are also packages containing codec binaries to play a variety of multimedia content. The win32-codecs-all package includes many such binaries.

- **Office productivity software** — The OpenOffice.org office productivity suite is available for PCLinuxOS (as it is for other Linux distributions). It is not included on the live CD, but you can download it from Synaptic with the OpenOffice.org repository enabled. For U.S. English, select the task-openoffice3-en-US package. (You need about 440MB of disk space for all the packages associated with that metapackage.)

If you miss some other Windows applications, you can try running them using WINE (WINE Is Not an Emulator) software. Install the wine package to give it a try. WINE has been well tested for running many popular Microsoft Windows applications, including Microsoft Office, Internet Explorer, and Outlook. (See Chapter 2 for more information about WINE.)

Installing PCLinuxOS

You can install PCLinuxOS to your computer either directly from the medium (DVD or CD) containing PCLinuxOS or by first booting the PCLinuxOS live CD and installing from an icon on the desktop. The following procedure describes how to install from a running live CD.

Warning

If there is any data on your computer that you want to keep, be sure to back it up before starting this procedure. Although you can choose to not erase selected partitions, you should back up any important data just to be safe. ■

Starting the Install

To begin installing PCLinuxOS, you need a PC and the DVD that comes with this book. The following are steps you can follow to begin the installation process.

1. **Boot PCLinuxOS.** Insert the DVD that comes with this book (or otherwise get a copy of PCLinuxOS live CD) and reboot your computer.

2. **Select to boot PCLinuxOS.** From the *Linux Bible 2011 Edition* DVD, select the entry for booting PCLinuxOS. If PCLinuxOS is unable to boot, refer to the boot options described earlier in this chapter. If it boots properly, a desktop similar to the one shown earlier in Figure 23-1 appears.

3. **Select to install PCLinuxOS.** With PCLinuxOS running on your computer, you can double-click on the Install PCLinuxOS icon to start the installation process.

    Figure 23-3 shows an example of the PCLinuxOS installation icon.

FIGURE 23-3

Select the Install PCLinuxOS icon to begin hard disk installation.

4. **Enter root password.** When prompted, type **root** as the root password. (This step will happen several times in this procedure.) The PCLinuxOS Installer wizard appears.

5. **Continue installation.** Click Next. A dialog asks you to select your partitioning scheme.

6. **Partitioning.** Select one of these choices for partitioning your computer's hard disk:

Warning

As soon as you make your selection, PCLinuxOS is installed, erasing any data that exists on the selected disk partitions. ■

- **Use existing partitions** — Choose this option to keep your disk partitions as they are and then pick how you want directories on your system assigned (or not assigned) to those partitions. Don't assign a directory to any partition that you don't want to be erased and reused!

- **Use free space** — Assign space from disk space that is not currently assigned to any partition.

- **Erase and use entire disk** — All data on all partitions will be erased and reused for the new installation.

- **Custom disk partitioning** — Set up disk partitioning yourself.

After you make your partitioning selections, the installer begins writing PCLinuxOS to your computer's hard disk.

7. **Bootloader.** Choose whether you want to use the GRUB boot loader (graphical or text-based), which device you want to boot from, and how long to delay before booting the default boot entry if no selection is made (10 seconds by default). If PCLinuxOS is the only operating system installed, you will probably want the bootloader installed to the master boot record (MBR) of the first hard disk (usually /dev/sda). Alternatively, you can install to the root partition where PCLinuxOS is installed and manually add the boot information to the boot loader for another operating system installed on your system.

If you choose to install the bootloader on a partition, the installer will ask you which drive you are booting from. If that is the case, you are prompted to add, modify, or remove any boot entries you choose. PCLinuxOS will be added to your existing boot loader by default and set as the default entry to boot. Click Next to continue.

At this point, installation is done. As instructed, remove the live CD and restart the computer to run your new PCLinuxOS installation.

Configuring After Installation

The first time you start PCLinuxOS after installation to hard disk, it prompts you to do some basic configuration for your system. Here is what you are asked to do:

- Add a password for the root (administrative) user
- Add a full name, username, and password for a user account for everyday use

After that configuration, you can log in to your PCLinuxOS system, using the information you just entered, and begin using your installed system.

Remastering PCLinuxOS

Offering tools for remastering PCLinuxOS has encouraged users to create their own custom versions of PCLinuxOS. Using these tools, you can create a PCLinuxOS system that includes the exact applications you want and the settings that work best for you. Once you have configured the system you like, run the mylivecd command to create a complete image of that system that you can burn to a CD or DVD and boot as your own live CD or DVD.

The DVD that comes with this book includes an official version of the PCLinuxOS live CD that offers an LXDE desktop. That and other remasters are available from official PCLinuxOS download sites such as the following:

```
http://ibiblio.org/pub/linux/distributions/texstar/pclinuxos
```

Official remasters include:

- **pclinuxos** — Includes a KDE desktop (about 689MB)
- **pclinuxos-gnome** — Includes the GNOME desktop (about 698MB)
- **pclinuxos-lxde** — Includes the Lightweight X11 Desktop Environment (about 587MB)
- **pclinuxos-minime** — Includes a stripped-down KDE desktop (about 454MB)

Whether you use one of these live CDs or build your own, it's easy to configure PCLinuxOS to get the Linux system you want.

Summary

The great popularity of PCLinuxOS stems from the desire of many people to replace their current desktop operating systems with an easy-to-use Linux system. PCLinuxOS is often recommended to first-time Linux users because so many features are enabled by default.

To start with PCLinuxOS, you just run one of several available live CD versions. An icon on the PCLinuxOS desktop lets you install your running system to hard disk. After that, adding more applications to do everything you might expect from a full-featured desktop system is easy.

Another feature of PCLinuxOS is the set of tools it offers to remaster your current PCLinuxOS system to an ISO image. You can then use that ISO image to replicate your system to run live, without your having to reinstall the software.

People in the PCLinuxOS community have created custom remasters of PCLinuxOS. These remasters do such things as offer different desktop environments (GNOME, LXDE, and others) or special application sets (such as a set of business tools).

Running Bootable Linux Distributions

A *bootable* Linux distribution refers to an entire Linux system that is contained on a removable medium (such as a CD, DVD, or USB flash drive). Because the first full bootable Linux systems were contained on CDs, the common name for this type of Linux system is a live CD.

Here are some reasons to use a live CD for your first experience with a new Linux system:

- **Doesn't need to be installed** — As its name implies, the live CD runs live (and immediately) from the removable medium. You don't need to take the time or commandeer the disk space needed to install Linux to your hard disk. Just insert the medium into your computer and reboot to bypass your hard disk and run the CD.

- **Lets you test your computer** — With the live CD, you can check that your hardware is supported before committing to a Linux system. So you will know in advance whether your printer, video card, network card, or other component will just work with your selected Linux system, or whether you might need to do some extra tweaking.

- **Doesn't disrupt your installed computer system** — Because the entire operating system is on a CD or DVD, and uses your computer's RAM to hold temporary data, you can run the live system without touching the contents of your hard disk.

Huge improvements to live CD technology in recent years mean you can do the following tasks with some live CDs:

- **Fix your computer** — If there is a problem with your installed system or a hardware component on your computer, you can often

IN THIS CHAPTER

Exploring bootable Linuxes

Choosing bootable Linux
   distributions

Booting rescue distributions

Booting multimedia
   distributions

Booting tiny desktop
   distributions

Building or customizing a
   bootable Linux

use tools to check and possibly fix the problems. Likewise, if you want to prepare to install Linux on your system, some live CDs come with tools for such tasks as backing up data and partitioning your hard disk.

- **Install to hard disk** — If you like the live CD, check the live CD's desktop or menus for a selection that enables you to immediately install the contents of that live CD to hard disk. You will then be able to boot the Linux as you would any operating system from hard disk.

- **Keep your data (persistency)** — A downside of the first live CDs was that, once you rebooted, you would lose any changes you made during the live CD session. Many Linux live CDs now include persistency features that enable you to save desktop settings, data files, or installed software to an alternate medium (such as a USB flash drive or even your hard disk) so the data are available the next time you boot your live CD.

With improvements to live CD technology have also come better tools for building your own live CDs. Those tools range from manual commands for gathering, installing, packaging, and burning live media to single-click GUI tools that can do all that in a single step.

This chapter describes several different Linux live CD distributions (some of which are included on the DVD that comes with this book) that you can use to try out different types of Linux systems. It also tells you how to use tools that come with various Linux distributions for customizing or building your own live CDs.

Note

If you haven't already done so, I recommend you try the KNOPPIX distribution included with this book and described in this chapter. You can also check out Appendix A for a list of other bootable Linux distributions that come on the DVD included with this book. ■

Overview of Bootable Linux Distributions

By stuffing removable media (CDs, DVDs, floppies, and even USB flash drives) with a select mix of open source software, bootable Linuxes enable you to bypass the hard disk completely (if you like) and have a special Linux distribution running on almost any computer within minutes.

A bootable Linux distribution can offer you some amazing opportunities. On a removable medium, you can take the following with you:

- Your favorite operating system
- As many of your favorite applications as will fit on your medium
- As much of your music, video, documents, or other data as will fit on your medium
- A fully customized set of features and configuration settings

In other words, if you are willing to build your own custom bootable distribution, the concept of bootable Linux distributions can be extended any way you like. Your bootable business card (mini-CD) or CD can carry all the applications you are used to having, so you can use them anywhere from a handy PC. But it can also hold your presentations, documents, mail-server settings, address books, favorite backgrounds and screensavers, personal photos, and any other kinds of data you want as well.

Most bootable Linux distributions that are created primarily as live CDs are based on established Linux distributions that are typically installed to hard disk. For example, KNOPPIX is based on Debian, as is Damn Small Linux. SLAX is based on Slackware. The SystemRescueCD is based on Gentoo. So if, for example, you want to choose a bootable Linux to customize as a personal desktop or server, you might choose one based on a Linux system you are familiar with.

In recent years, Linux distributions such as Fedora, Ubuntu, openSUSE, and Gentoo have begun producing their own live CDs to showcase their distributions. Tools such as the Fedora Project's livecd-creator greatly simplify the task of building live CDs based on packages from the Fedora software repository.

If you don't have a preference regarding which distribution your live CD is based on, however, you will likely want to choose a bootable Linux because it contains a specialized set of tools (such as a security toolkit) or is built to provide a specific function (such as playing multimedia). For example, tools that are included with the BackTrack Network Security Suite live CD are focused on securing, checking, and recovering computers and networks. BackTrack's menus are organized based on the security tools it provides. Components in GeeXboX include those geared toward playing movies, music, and images.

Trying a Bootable Linux

Whether you choose a bootable Linux to do a special job (security, multimedia playback, gaming, and so on) or as a way of trying Linux before doing a permanent install, several bootable Linux distributions are included with this book for you to try out. For descriptions of those, and other bootable Linux distros, I recommend you visit the following sites:

- **FrozenTech LiveCD List** — More than 300 Linux live CD distributions are listed at this site (www.livecdlist.com). You can sort that list by size, name, primary function, and most votes. This is also a great place to see lists of live CDs based on computer architectures other than x86 (x86-64, PPC, PPC64, Xbox, Alpha, MIPS, and so on). Click the links to each live CD to see reviews and helpful tips.

- **Wikipedia List of LiveDistros** — Live CDs based on Linux and other operating systems are listed at http://en.wikipedia.org/wiki/List_of_LiveDistros.

- **LinuxLinks.com** — This site has a list of mini-distributions, many of which are bootable Linux systems. The page that contains this list is www.linuxlinks.com/ Distributions/Mini_Distributions/.

- **DistroWatch.com** — DistroWatch keeps a list of CD-based Linux distributions and live Linux CDs (http://distrowatch.com/dwres.php?resource=cd). Its site also contains information and links to hundreds of distributions.

- **KNOPPIX Customizations** — The KNOPPIX Customizations page (www.knoppix.net/wiki/Knoppix_Customizations) lists about 100 distributions based on KNOPPIX. Before live CD creation tools were widely available, simply remastering KNOPPIX was a popular way to create new live CDs.

If you have trouble running any bootable Linux distributions, try adding options to the boot prompt. Because so many of the distributions are based on KNOPPIX, refer to the KNOPPIX boot options (also called *cheat codes*) described later in this chapter to help get your Linux distribution to start up the way you would like. View these codes online at www.knoppix.net/wiki/Cheat_Codes.

This book comes with several bootable Linux distributions, which you can find out about in Appendix A. You can get more recent versions of distributions that interest you (some are updated quite often) by following links from the sites just mentioned.

Caution

Many bootable Linux distributions are created by individuals and should still be considered experimental in nature. The quality can vary widely and often the controls are not as stringent as they would be for commercial Linux systems, such as Red Hat Enterprise Linux. You can limit your risks by doing such things as mounting all hard disk partitions as read-only (as is usually, but not always, done by default), but remember that this software is distributed with no warranty. ■

The following sections describe interesting bootable Linux distributions, based on the type of content they contain.

Starting with KNOPPIX

KNOPPIX is a bootable Linux that includes a nice selection of open source software. Originally, there was just a CD version of KNOPPIX (about 700MB image). Now, there is also a DVD version (about 4GB image). It is the KNOPPIX CD image that is included on the DVD that comes with this book.

KNOPPIX was the trailblazer of Linux live CDs. In fact, for a long time KNOPPIX was used as the basis for creating many specialized Linux live CDs, including Gnoppix (featuring GNOME instead of LXDE), KNOPPIX STD (security), KnoppMyth (MythTV media player), Damn Small Linux (mini desktop), and KnoppiXMAME (console game player), to name a few. To try out the latest features, however, you should start with the most recent version of KNOPPIX, as described here.

Looking Inside KNOPPIX

After automatically detecting and configuring your computer hardware, KNOPPIX boots right up to a fast, lightweight desktop system with a handful of ready-to-use desktop applications (no login required). It includes some powerful server and power user features.

The latest KNOPPIX release (6.2) marks a departure from earlier KNOPPIX releases (such as 5.1.1). Instead of including a boatload of applications, it includes a good set of standard applications and seems to otherwise focus on making the desktop rock solid and blazing fast.

If you have used earlier versions of KNOPPIX, the first thing you'll notice is how quickly it boots up to a desktop. Then you'll notice that the KDE desktop is gone and is replaced by the Lightweight X11 Desktop Environment (www.lxde.org). So you lose a few dozen KDE utilities (including applications such as Konqueror), but you gain tremendous efficiency, even with desktop effects enabled by default. (Compiz is the default window manager!)

Take a look at the following list of some of KNOPPIX's major components:

- **LXDE** — A lightweight, efficient desktop environment that runs well, even with cool desktop effects (screen wobble, deleted windows bursting into flames, and so on).

- **OpenOffice.org** — The OpenOffice.org suite of office productivity tools that you can use to create documents, graphics, presentations, spreadsheets, and most anything you expect to be able to do with office applications. With KNOPPIX, you can give a presentation created in OpenOffice.org software anywhere that you have access to a PC.

- **Internet tools** — web browser (Iceweasel, which is a streamlined version of Firefox), e-mail clients (Icedove and mutt), an instant messaging client (Pidgin), Linphone webphone, and several other applications for using the Internet. (See Chapter 6 for descriptions of popular web browsers and mail clients.)

- **Multimedia software** — Applications for playing music and video (Mplayer), working with graphics (GIMP), and displaying images (GPicView).

- **Administrative tools** — Under the Preferences menu you can find tools for installing KNOPPIX to hard disk or USB flash disk, setting up special network connections, and editing your desktop configuration. Select the Synaptic Package Manager, select to update your packages list, and, provided you have an Internet connection, you can download and install from thousands of packages available from the Debian software repository.

- **Servers** — Only a few server packages have been retained in the latest version of KNOPPIX. However, you can still configure KNOPPIX as an NFS or a DHCP server.

Booting KNOPPIX

If you have a PC in front of you, get started by following these steps:

1. Insert the *Linux Bible* DVD into the appropriate drive.
2. Reboot the computer. After a few moments, the boot screen appears.
3. Press Enter. If all goes well, you should see the KNOPPIX desktop, and you can start using KNOPPIX. If KNOPPIX doesn't boot up properly or if you want to tune it further before it boots, continue on to the next section. In particular, you might want to use some of the boot options shown in Table 24-1.

Note

Although the boot screens look different for the *Linux Bible 2011 Edition* DVD and a regular KNOPPIX CD, you can proceed with the boot process the same way. ∎

Correcting Boot Problems

By understanding a bit about the boot process you can, in most cases, overcome any problems you might have installing KNOPPIX. You can apply many of these same principles to other live Linux systems. Here are some things you should know:

- **Check boot order** — Your computer's BIOS has a particular order in which it looks for bootable operating systems. A typical order would be floppy, CD or DVD, and hard disk. If your computer skips over the KNOPPIX boot disk and boots right from hard disk, make sure that the boot order in the BIOS is set to boot from CD or DVD. To change the BIOS, restart the computer, and as it first boots the hardware enter Setup (quickly) as instructed (usually by pressing F1, F2, or DEL). Look for a selection to change the boot order so that your CD or DVD boots before the hard disk. Instead, you can usually change the boot order temporarily by selecting a function key (often F12) and choosing a boot device.

- **Add boot options** — Instead of just letting the boot process autodetect and configure everything about your hardware, you can add options to the boot prompt that will override what KNOPPIX autoconfiguration might do. Many of those boot options are described in the rest of this section.

Some boot options are available with which you can try to overcome different issues at boot time. KNOPPIX refers to these options as *cheat codes*. For a more complete list, refer to the file `knoppix-cheatcodes.txt`, which you'll find in the KNOPPIX directory on the KNOPPIX CD or DVD. (With KNOPPIX booted, you can find the cheat codes in `/mnt-system/KNOPPIX/`.)

Note

Many boot options can be used with different Linux systems. So if you are having trouble installing or booting a different Linux distribution, you can try any of these options to see if they work. Instead of the word "knoppix," you will probably use a different word to launch the install or boot process for other distributions (such as "dsl" for Damn Small Linux or "ubuntu" for an Ubuntu live CD, depending on the distribution). See Appendix A for information on how to start each Linux distribution. ∎

After booting the *Linux Bible* DVD or a KNOPPIX CD, you will see a `boot:` prompt at the bottom. The following tables provide boot prompt options that can help you get KNOPPIX running the way you like. Table 24-1 shows options to use when you want specific features turned on that may not be turned on by default when you boot.

If hardware is being improperly detected or configured, you can have KNOPPIX skip over that hardware. Table 24-2 contains options for skipping or turning off various hardware features.

TABLE 24-1

Boot Options to Select Features

Option	Feature
knoppix lang=??	Choose a specific language/keyboard. Replace ?? with one of the following: cn, de, da, es, fr, it, nl, pl, ru, sk, tr, tw, uk, or us.
knoppix blind	Start BrailleTerminal (running without X). (Note that there is a special version of KNOPPIX called Adriane KNOPPIX that contains special accessibility features.)
knoppix brltty=type,port,table	Add parameters to use for the Braille device.
knoppix wheelmouse	For a wheel mouse, enable IMPS/2 protocol.
knoppix nowheelmouse	For a regular PS/2 mouse, force PS/2 protocol.
knoppix keyboard=us xkeyboard=us	Assign different keyboard drivers to use with text (shell) and graphical (X).
knoppix dma	Turn on DMA acceleration for all IDE drives.
knoppix gmt	Use time that is based on Greenwich Mean Time. You can use utc instead of gmt to get the same result.
knoppix tz=country/city	Specify a particular time zone, based on country and city.
knoppix noeject	Don't eject the CD after KNOPPIX has stopped.
knoppix noprompt	Don't prompt to remove CD after KNOPPIX stops.

TABLE 24-2

Boot Options to Turn Off or Debug Hardware

Option	Result
knoppix debug	Run KNOPPIX with verbose kernel messages.
knoppix atapicd	No SCSI-Emulation for IDE CD-ROMs
knoppix noagp	No detection of AGP graphics card
knoppix noapic	Disable Advanced Programmable Interrupt Controller (can overcome some problems on SMP computers).
knoppix acpi=off	Disable Advanced Configuration and Power Interface (ACPI).

continued

TABLE 24-2   *(continued)*

Option	Result
knoppix noapm	No Advanced Power Management support. (With a working acpi, apm will be off by default. Only one can be active at a time.)
knoppix noaudio	No sound support
knoppix nodhcp	Don't try to start your network connection automatically via DHCP.
knoppix fstab	Don't read the fstab file to find file systems to mount or check.
knoppix nofirewire	No detection of Firewire devices
knoppix nopcmcia	No detection of PCMCIA card slots
knoppix noscsi	No detection of SCSI devices
knoppix noswap	No detection of swap partitions
knoppix nousb	No detection of USB devices
knoppix nousb2	Disable extensions for USB 2.0.
knoppix pnpbios=off	Don't initialize plug-and-play (PnP) in the BIOS.
knoppix failsafe	Do almost no hardware detection.

Table 24-3 lists options that may help if you are having trouble with your video card. Several of these options are particularly useful if you are having trouble with X on a laptop.

TABLE 24-3

Boot Options to Fix Video Problems

Option	Result
knoppix screen=??	Pick X screen resolution. Replace ?? with 640×480, 800×600, 1024×768, 1280×1024, or any other resolution supported by your video card.
knoppix xvrefresh=60	Set vertical refresh rate to 60 Hz for X (or other value as specified by your monitor's manual).
knoppix xhrefresh=80	Set horizontal refresh rate to 80 Hz for X (or other value as specified by your monitor's manual).
knoppix xmodule=??	Select the specific driver to use for your video card. Replace ?? with one of the following: ati, fbdev, i810, mga, nv, radeon, savage, s3radeon, svga, or i810.

Option	Result
knoppix 2	Runlevel 2, Text mode only
knoppix vga=normal	No-framebuffer mode, but X
knoppix fb1280x1024	Use fixed framebuffer graphics (1).
knoppix fb1024x768	Use fixed framebuffer graphics (2).
knoppix fb800x600	Use fixed framebuffer graphics (3).

Customizing KNOPPIX

Several boot options exist that tell KNOPPIX to run in special ways. For example, you can tell KNOPPIX to run entirely from RAM or tell it to install KNOPPIX to hard disk instead of running live. Table 24-4 describes some of these special boot options.

TABLE 24-4

Special Boot Options

Option	Result
knoppix mem=???M	Make the specified amount of memory available to KNOPPIX (for example, 128MB).
knoppix toram	Copy the contents of the CD to RAM and run it from there. (For a live CD, you should have at least 1GB of RAM available to use toram.)
knoppix tohd=/dev/????	Copy the contents of the CD to a hard disk partition and run it from there. Replace ???? with the device name, such as hda1 or sda1. The partition must be ext2 or VFAT to use this feature.
knoppix fromhd	Look for KNOPPIX to run on hard disk, instead of the CD.
knoppix fromhd=/dev/????	Look for KNOPPIX to run from a particular partition on hard disk, instead of the CD. Replace ???? with the device name, such as hda1 or sda1.
knoppix bootfrom=/dev/????	If the KNOPPIX image is on an NTFS or ReiserFS file system, use this option to boot the image from there.
knoppix bootfrom=/dev/????/KNX.iso	Select a particular image name to boot from, when the image exists on an NTFS or ReiserFS file system on the selected hard disk. The kernel versions on the CD and hard disk image must match.

Special Features and Workarounds

Other boot options are described in the `knoppix-cheatcodes.txt` file that comes on the KNOPPIX CD (open the KNOPPIX folder from the KNOPPIX icon on the desktop to find the file). Things you can do with boot options include changing the splash screen when KNOPPIX boots, running in expert mode so you can load your own drivers, testing your computer's RAM, and trying to overcome special problems with laptop computers.

- **Testing the CD** — If you suspect that you have a bad KNOPPIX CD, I recommend running this from the boot prompt:

  ```
  knoppix testcd
  ```

  If you are still not able to boot KNOPPIX at this point, it might be that your hardware is either not supported or is broken in some way. To further pursue the problem, check out an appropriate forum at `www.knoppix.net`.

- **Running KNOPPIX from RAM** — To improve performance, KNOPPIX offers a way to run the entire KNOPPIX distribution from RAM (provided you have enough available) or install it on hard disk and run it from there. Provided that you have more than 1GB of RAM, you can run KNOPPIX entirely from RAM (so you can remove the KNOPPIX DVD or CD and use that drive while you run KNOPPIX) by typing the following from the boot prompt:

  ```
  knoppix toram
  ```

- **Installing KNOPPIX to hard disk** — You can run KNOPPIX entirely from hard disk if your hard disk is either a FAT or ext2 file system type and contains at least 800MB of space. To do this, you must know the name of the hard disk partition you are installing on. For example, to use the first partition on the first IDE drive you would use `/dev/hda1`. In that case, to copy KNOPPIX to that disk partition, you would type this at the boot prompt:

  ```
  knoppix tohd=/dev/hda1
  ```

  You can watch as KNOPPIX is copied to your hard disk partition and then boots automatically from there. The next time you want to boot KNOPPIX, you can boot it from hard disk again by inserting the KNOPPIX medium and typing the following:

  ```
  knoppix fromhd=/dev/hda1
  ```

With KNOPPIX running from your hard disk, you can safely eject your CD or DVD and use the drive for other things (type **eject /dev/cdrom**). Refer to the `knoppix-cheatcodes.txt` file for information on other things you can do from the KNOPPIX boot prompt.

Showcasing Linux from a Live CD

Although KNOPPIX was designed primarily as a live CD, most major Linux distributions were created to install to hard disk. To get you started, however, most Linux distributions also offer live CD versions of their systems. You can use those live CDs to try that Linux before installing. Then, often, you can install the contents of the live CD directly to hard disk from the live CD itself.

Here are descriptions of live CDs that are available from major Linux distributions:

- **Ubuntu live CDs** — Official live CDs from Ubuntu (`www.ubuntu.com/getubuntu`) include desktop and server editions that are available on both x86 and 64-bit AMD (amd64) versions. Both server and desktop (GNOME) editions are available. There are also live CDs for related Kubuntu (KDE desktop) and Edubuntu (education-oriented) projects. By selecting a desktop icon, you can install the live CD to hard disk.

- **Fedora live CDs** — GNOME and KDE desktop live CDs are offered by the Fedora Project (`www.fedoraproject.org/get-fedora`). Fedora also offers a collection of what they call live *spins* (`www.fedoraproject.org/wiki/CustomSpins`). Specialty live CDs that are built using live CD creation tools include a games spin, electronic lab spin, developer spin, and Xfce spin. An install icon is available on the desktop.

- **Gentoo live CDs** — Gentoo (`www.gentoo.org/main/en/where.xml`) offers desktop live CDs and DVDs. Builds of those media are available on eight different computer architectures. Each CD and DVD includes an installer.

- **Mepis live CDs** — The Mepis Project (`www.mepis.org/mirrors`) offers SimplyMEPIS live CDs that can also be used to install a desktop Mepis system. An offshoot project of Mepis called AntiX also offers a live CD that is tailored to run well on low-end computers.

- **OpenSUSE live CDs** — You can get GNOME and KDE live CDs and DVDs from the openSUSE Project (`software.opensuse.org`) for x86, x86-64, and PowerPC architectures. These media also include tools for installing their contents to hard disk.

As you use these live CDs, you can install additional software packages over the Internet to try out other features. Keep in mind, however, that because running the live CD requires more RAM than the same system would need when running from hard disk, many of these Linux distributions will run better after you have installed their contents to hard disk.

On the DVD
Ubuntu, Fedora, Gentoo, AntiX, PCLinuxOS, and openSUSE live CDs are all available from the DVD that comes with this book. Check Appendix A for details on each of those live CDs. ∎

Security and Rescue Bootables

Rescuing broken systems and diagnosing network problems are among the most popular uses of bootable Linuxes. At a point where your hard disk might be inaccessible, bootable rescue CDs or DVDs can literally save damaged or infected computers. Some rescue CDs are touted as complete security toolkits, offering a wide range of tools for monitoring Linux or Windows systems, scanning for viruses, debugging networks, and doing forensics.

Most bootable Linux systems will boot up on your network if a wired or wireless DHCP server is available. (If there isn't one, many include the netcardconfig utility to let you set up a wired Ethernet card manually.) So, with your computer booted and connected to a network with a bootable Linux, you could proceed to check, fix, back up, and otherwise control the local computer as well as other computers on your network.

Note
Some live CDs were designed primarily to check or fix the security of installed systems. Some of those projects note that the tools their live CDs include were chosen, in part, from the Insecure.org "Top 100 Network Security Tools" list (http://sectools.org). The list was put together from more than 3,200 responses to a survey on the nmap-hackers mailing list. While the list is a few years old now, most of the tools and descriptions are valid today. ∎

The following are suggestions for ways to use Linux security/rescue CDs, along with descriptions of the tools included with these live CDs:

- **Assessing vulnerability** — Tools for assessing vulnerabilities of your computer include those to let you scan shared Windows SMB folders (nbtscan), CGI scripts (nikto and screamingCobra), and the computer's ports (nmap), as well as scan for viruses (clamAV). You can also check whether someone has used a rootkit to replace critical system files (chkrootkit), or you can use a scanner dispatch (warscan) to test any exploit you like across lots of machines.

- **Running forensics on Windows machines** — If you believe a Windows system has been compromised, there are many tools you can use to find problems and correct them. Boot a security CD, such as Knoppix-STD, and you can recover Internet Explorer cookies (galleta), convert Outlook Express dbx files to mbox format (readdbx and readoe), check system integrity (ftimes), and check the Windows recycle bin (rifiuti).

- **Recovering data** — If a Windows or other operating system won't boot or is otherwise impaired, you can get data off that computer. You can copy files over the network (using rsync, scp, or others) or back up to local CD or tape (cpio, tar, or others). You can selectively recover file types from disk images (foremost) or check and recover lost partitions (testdisk).

- **Dealing with intruders** — Tools such as Snort (www.snort.org) enable you to analyze network traffic in real time, as well as log and analyze data as attacks are happening. Honeypots enable you to watch intruders' moves as the honeypots lead intruders to believe they've compromised your system. Honeypots in security-related Linux CDs include honeyd (http://honeyd.org). Kill zombies from DDoS attacks with zz (zombie zapper).

- **Using and analyzing encryption techniques** — Many tools enable you to use encryption techniques to protect your data and find when others have tried to compromise it. GNU privacy guard (gpg) is used for verifying the authenticity of computers and people. For setting up virtual private networks, there are stunnel and OpenVPN. You can find images (giffshuffle, stegbreak, and stegdetect) and music (mp3stego) that contain hidden messages using a technique called *stegonography*.

- **Managing a firewall** — Bring a firewall up quickly or assess what's happening on a running firewall. The blockall script can block all inbound TCP traffic, flushall flushes your firewall rules, and fwlogwatch can monitor firewall logs. The firestarter and floppyfw utilities offer quick ways to start up a firewall. Tools for managing iptables firewalls include gtk-iptables and shorewall.

Popular Linux rescue CDs that illustrate very well how many tools you can get on a single CD include System Rescue CD, BackTrack, Knoppix-STD, and the Inside Security Rescue Toolkit (INSERT) rescue CDs.

Caution

When you use a rescue CD to change a master boot record, fix partition tables, or clean viruses from a system, you risk doing irreparable damage to your computer system. Remember that GPL software comes with no warranty, so you use that software at your own risk. ■

BackTrack Network Security Suite

A wide range of powerful, well-organized security tools is on the BackTrack Network Security Suite (`http://www.backtrack-linux.org/`) live CD. BackTrack is based on two live Linux distributions used to test whether your computer system has been compromised: Whax and Auditor.

BackTrack offers a good combination of GUI and command-line security tools. The BackTrack menus (shown in Figure 24-1) organize all of those tools together, enabling you to look in one place for all similar tools. When you select a command from a menu, the command runs with the help (`-h`) option so you can see how it works. It's up to you to then type the command and add the options you want.

On the DVD

The BackTrack CD is included on the DVD that comes with this book. Refer to Appendix A for information on running BackTrack. ■

SystemRescueCd

The SystemRescueCd (`www.sysresccd.org`) is aimed squarely at recovering crashed systems. Tools included on this distribution include those specifically designed for repairing and saving your data, such as the following:

- **Disk partitioning tools** — You can check, add, remove, move, and resize disk partitions with tools such as `parted` and `gparted`.

- **Logical Volume Management tools** — For file systems with LVM, there are `lvm` tools. (Logical volume management allows you to add space to areas of a file system without changing the physical partitions.)

- **Security tools** — Check whether the data on your system has been compromised with tools such as `chkrootkit` (to check for software installed by hackers to let them access your system), as well as `clamav` and `clamd` (to scan for existing and incoming viruses). Use `nmap` (scan network computers for open ports) and `nc` (the Netcat utility for checking connections to remote hosts) to check network security.

- **Backup tools** — As you might expect, this distribution contains standard Linux tools for archiving data (`tar`, `cpio`, `dump`, `rar`, and so on) and compressing data (such as `bzip2`, `gzip`, and `compress`). Likewise, it contains standard tools for copying your data over the network (`scp`, `sftp`, `ftp`, and so on).

FIGURE 24-1

BackTrack organizes graphical and command-line security tools.

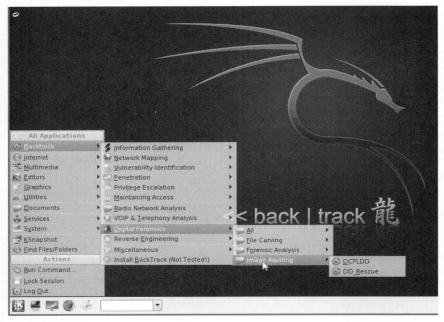

Because SystemRescueCd doesn't include a graphical interface, it can get a lot of commands into about 190MB of disk space. Some of the tools, however, such as the midnight commander (`mc` command) file manager, provide a GUI-like interface from a regular Linux shell via the ncurses libraries.

On the DVD

The SystemRescueCd image is included on the DVD that comes with this book. Refer to Appendix A for information on running the SystemRescueCD. ■

KNOPPIX Security Tools Distribution

The Knoppix-STD goes lightweight on the window manager to go heavyweight on the diagnostic tools. The distribution contains hundreds of tools that can be used for repairing and assessing computer and network security (see `http://s-t-d.org/`).

Instead of a full GNOME desktop, Knoppix-STD uses the Fluxbox window manager. It will run on lesser machines, but you'll get a usable GUI on almost any Pentium-class machine with at least 64MB of RAM. With at least 640MB of RAM, you can run the entire distribution from RAM (type **knoppix toram** to boot it to run entirely from RAM). With Knoppix-STD running in RAM, the system operates faster and your CD or DVD drive is available for other purposes.

Go to the project's Tools page (`http://s-t-d.org/tools.html`) to find out about more features in the project. Or go to the download page (`http://s-t-d.org/download.html`) to download and try it yourself.

The Inside Security Rescue Toolkit

Another KNOPPIX derivative that includes features from Damn Small Linux is INSERT (Inside Security Rescue Toolkit). INSERT bills itself as a disaster recovery and network analysis system. It contains a more compact set of tools to fit on a bootable business card (about 50MB). Check it out at `www.inside-security.de/insert_en.html`.

On the DVD

INSERT is included on the DVD that comes with this book. Refer to Appendix A for information on using INSERT. ■

The Fluxbox window manager offers some docked system monitors for monitoring CPU, network traffic, memory and swap use, and battery (if you are on a laptop). Another applet displays the Matrix screensaver (double-click it to launch a Terminal window). The mount applet enables you to step through the CD, floppy, and hard disk partitions on your computer. Click the key button on that applet (so it turns green), and you can double-click it to mount and open that device or partition.

Right-click the desktop to see a menu that allows you to select from a handful of graphical tools for troubleshooting your computer and network, most of which will run from the shell. Figure 24-2 shows the INSERT desktop.

You can find what tools are included on the INSERT live CD from the List of Applications page on the Inside Security site (`www.inside-security.de/applicationlist.html`).

FIGURE 24-2

Use INSERT to troubleshoot computers and networks.

Demonstration Bootables

Individuals and organizations that want to promote their businesses or software projects can create custom live CDs to incorporate their own content or display their wares. And software developers can rest assured that the project they want to show off will work because it can be adapted to an entire operating system. An organization that wants to demonstrate what it's about can boot up to play any content (images, presentations, movies, music, and so on) on any existing open source player.

Here are some examples of bootable CDs that are used for demonstration purposes:

- **Software Projects** — There are open source projects that produce a live CD to let people try out their projects. The GNOME Live Media project (http://live.gnome.org/GnomeLiveMedia) offers a live CD that can be used to try the features of GNOME.

- **Sugar on a Stick** — The innovative Sugar desktop (used with the One Laptop per Child Project) runs on a Fedora Linux system. Its creators at Sugar Labs offers a bootable version of this software that you can put on a USB drive:

  ```
  http://wiki.sugarlabs.org/go/Sugar_on_a_Stick
  ```

- **Any Content You Choose** — Live CDs are becoming a popular medium to hold and play specific content. GeeXboX Generator is an example of a project for creating live CDs to play any video you include (see the following section). Boxee Live (`http://boxee-live.sourceforge.net/site/`) is a live CD that runs a Boxee Media Center.

  Because Linux can act as both client and server, it is a great medium to demo custom web applications. The book *Ajax Construction Kit* by Michael Morrison (Prentice Hall, 2008) includes a live CD that contains all the Ajax web applications described in the book. Because a complete LAMP server package is also on the live CD, that disc is all you need to run the sample projects, display them in a web browser, and modify them in an HTML editor.

Because open source software can be manipulated as you choose and redistributed, live CDs are becoming an increasingly popular method of demonstrating software projects and content.

Multimedia Bootables

Some bootable Linuxes are tailored specifically to let you play movies, music, and images. Most let you play whatever content you have on your hard disk or can point to from the Internet. Many run in a small enough amount of memory to let you remove the bootable DVD or CD containing Linux and insert your own content (such as a music CD or movie DVD) to play.

MoviX

With MoviX (`http://sourceforge.net/projects/movix/`), you run a multimedia player that disregards the operating systems (Windows, Linux, or otherwise) installed on your system. Because MoviX is small enough to run in your system memory, after it has booted you can remove it and insert the CD or DVD containing the content you want to run. With MoviX, you can play

- **Videos** — You can play video from many different formats, including DivX/XVID, MPEG 1 and 2, and MPEG 4. So that MoviX can be freely distributed, it does not include the capability to play most DVD movies.

Caution
The U.S. Digital Millennium Copyright Act (DCMA) prohibits the creation or distribution of software that is made to circumvent encryption that protects copyrighted material. The libdvdcss library, needed to decrypt DVD movies (even if only for playback), has been the subject of much discussion. Although this library is available on the Internet, most Linux systems in the U.S. have chosen not to distribute this library because using it may be illegal under the DCMA. You should research this issue yourself if you plan to add libdvdcss to MoviX or any other Linux distribution that includes MPlayer or xine media players. ∎

- **Music** — You can play audio files in AVI, MP3, Ogg Vorbis, and other formats.
- **Images** — You can run a slide show using the Linux Frame Buffer Image (fbi) viewer that displays images in JPEG, PNG, and a variety of other image formats.

The MoviX player itself doesn't include any video, music, or images for you to play. Instead, it enables you to choose the location of your content. Here are the possibilities, depending on what is available from your computer:

- **DVDs** — If you have a DVD drive on your computer, you can play supported content from there. (As previously stated, that doesn't include most commercial movies, by default.)
- **VCDs and SVCDs** — These are video formats that can be put on standard CDs.
- **Audio CDs** — You can play standard music CDs (including AVI, MP3, and other formats).
- **Hard disk files** — Any supported content on the local hard disk can also be played from MoviX. As with KNOPPIX, MoviX detects hard disk partitions and then mounts them as you request files from those partitions. The mounts are done read-only, by default, so you can play your content without any risk of deleting or otherwise damaging it.
- **Network** — MoviX boots onto the network if a DHCP server is detected. Although the friendly user interface doesn't appear to support it yet, software in MoviX should enable you to get content from your LAN or the Internet to play back using an NFS (UNIX file sharing) or FTP (standard Internet file sharing facility) file server.

MoviX boots right up to MPlayer, so you can eject the MoviX disk; insert a CD, DVD, or VCD into your drive; and play any supported content. Right-click the desktop to see your choices for selecting content.

If you are comfortable moving around in Linux, you can go to different virtual terminals while you are using MoviX. Press Ctrl+Alt+F2 to view a sound mixer or Ctrl+Alt+F3 to go to a Linux shell. Then press Ctrl+Alt+F4 to get back to the main screen (with MPlayer). Select Switch to MoviX from the menu, and you can choose to run your audio player, slide show, or TV viewer (the latter if you have a television card installed).

If you think MoviX is cool, you'll really like the idea of the eMoviX project. With eMoviX, you put a mini-MoviX2 distribution on a CD or DVD with your video, so that your video content comes with its own bootable player! (See http://movix.sourceforge.net/Docs/eMoviX for details.)

Note
Both eMovix and MoviX are described in the book *Linux Toys II* by Christopher Negus (Wiley, 2006), in a project devoted mainly to creating your own bootable movies. Newer multimedia live distributions include XBMC (http://xmbc.org) and Boxee (http://www.boxee.tv). ∎

GeeXboX
GeeXboX (www.geexbox.org) is another bootable multimedia player distribution. From the screen that appears after GeeXboX boots, you can use your cursor to select the location of the

content you want to choose. As with MoviX, you can play a variety of audio and video content. It also boots up on your network, so you can get audio and video content from it.

Because GeeXboX is so small (just a few megabytes), you can fit it easily on a mini-CD, bootable business card, or even a pen drive (provided your computer can be booted from those media). There is no graphical interface; you just use the keyboard to select content and simple controls from menus.

Use arrow keys to move among the few GeeXboX selections (Open, Controls, Options, Help, and Quit). Press Enter to make a selection. You can open a file from hard disk, a music playlist, directory of images, or removable media (DVD, VCD/XCD, or audio CD) containing video content. Press M to show or hide menus and use P to pause.

KnoppMyth

KnoppMyth (`http://mysettopbox.tv/knoppmyth.html`) represents a new and interesting class of bootable Linux distributions. MythTV is a fairly complex set of software used to configure an entertainment center that can include a personal video recorder (complete with downloaded local TV listings and tools for managing recording and playback), music player, weather center, and tools for getting news and other information.

KnoppMyth is a CD distribution based on KNOPPIX that is intended to help simplify getting a MythTV installation up and running. Boot up KnoppMyth, answer a few questions, and MythTV is installed on your hard disk.

KnoppMyth also includes another nice feature: a MythTV front end. With MythTV configured on a computer on your LAN, you can use the KnoppMyth disk to boot up a MythTV front end. That way you can use your MythTV entertainment center from any TV on your local area network. If you prefer other Linux distributions, there are also MythTV versions for Fedora (Mythdora) and Ubuntu (Mythbuntu).

Tiny Desktops

A small CD, shaped in the form of a business card, can fit in your wallet. A USB pen drive can hang from your keychain. There are whole bootable Linux distributions that let you boot up a desktop with which you can connect to the Internet, browse the web, play music, send and receive e-mail, do instant messaging, write documents, and work with spreadsheets. And they can do all that in about 50MB of space on a removable medium.

Note

CD business cards are really just regular CDs that have been cut into the shape of a business card. Depending on the CD business card you choose, it can hold from 40MB to 52MB of data. A mini-CD can hold about 180MB of data. You can purchase these CDs in bulk from many locations that sell regular CDs, and you can play them in any CD drive. (However, it's best to use these CDs in trays that have a mini-CD inset because they have been known to fly loose and break CD drives.) ∎

Although the small media size is fun, perhaps the best attribute of these tiny desktop systems is how efficient they are. With their small footprint and scaled-down applications, small desktop live CDs will usually perform fast — even on older, less powerful machines.

Many of the first bootable Linuxes were either based on KNOPPIX or the Bootable Business Card project (www.lnx-bbc.com/). These days, bootable Linux distributions tend to be built on major Linux distributions, such as Debian, Fedora, Gentoo, or Ubuntu. Reasons for the shift from simply modifying an existing live CD is that Linux distributions have improved on tools for creating live CDs and offer massive software repositories to make customizing CDs much easier.

Two examples of tiny desktop Linux distributions are Damn Small Linux and Puppy Linux.

Damn Small Linux

If you want your desktop Linux distribution to fit in your wallet, Damn Small Linux is one of your best choices. Damn Small is one of the first distributions based on KNOPPIX to fit on a bootable business card (about 48MB currently).

On the DVD

Damn Small Linux is included on the DVD that accompanies this book. You can use it as described in Appendix A. ∎

With KNOPPIX inside, you have many of the features you get with KNOPPIX: excellent hardware detection and bootup to a desktop with network connectivity (provided you have an Ethernet connection with DHCP). Many features specific to Damn Small, however, are there to let you get a workable desktop system on a small CD (mini-CD) or small USB drive and low RAM. Figure 24-3 shows an example of the DSL desktop.

FIGURE 24-3

Damn Small Linux fits a lot of features in under 50MB.

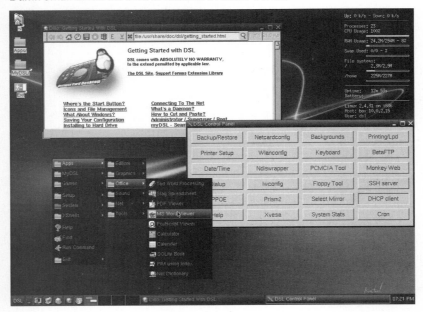

Damn Small's default desktop is pretty simple. The window manager is the powerful, yet efficient Fluxbox window manager (based on BlackBox). Right-click the desktop to see a menu of features you can select. Here are a few things you want to do when you first boot up Damn Small:

- **Change desktop theme** — Right-click to see the Damn Small menu, and then select System ➪ Control Panel. Select Backgrounds, choose a different background from the list, and select the TryIt button to display the new background.

- **Get a network connection** — If you don't automatically get on the Internet at boot time, select Setup ➪ Net Setup from the Damn Small menu. Then you can choose to configure your Ethernet card, DSL connection, dial-up modem, or wireless card.

- **Browse the web** — Damn Small comes with the Firefox and Dillo web browsers. Select Apps ➪ Net ➪ Browsers, and then choose either Firefox or Dillo to start browsing. The Dillo browser is small and fast, and can run on any X window manager because it doesn't require GNOME libraries.

- **Configure and read e-mail** — The Sylpheed e-mail client is also very compact and runs fast. Select Apps ➪ Net ➪ Sylpheed to open it. Configure it and you can be up and reading your e-mail within a few minutes.

- **Try out other applications** — Right-click and look through the menu for applications that interest you. To see descriptions of those applications, visit `http://damnsmalllinux .org/applications.html`.

- **Get other applications** — Select the MyDSL icon on the desktop to see a selection of application categories you can choose from. If you are connected to the Internet, you can see lists of applications in each category to choose for downloading and installing.

Note

You can get other DSL files that will let you download other applications from your desktop as well. Visit `www.damnsmalllinux.org` and select the link to packages to see the myDSL repository. ■

Damn Small Linux has recently added some excellent customization features. For example, packages you download, desktop settings, and configuration information can be saved across reboots. By creating a list of files and packages you want to save, those files and packages can be saved to a backup file that is stored on your hard disk or any removable medium. The next time you reboot, you can tell Damn Small Linux where to find that backup file and all settings and applications will be inserted into your current Damn Small Linux session.

More information about using Damn Small Linux is available at the project FAQ page, `www.damnsmalllinux.org/faq.html`.

Puppy Linux

The other heavyweight contender for lightweight Linux bootables is Puppy Linux (`www.puppylinux.com/`). The Puppy Linux ISO image is about 130MB. So, for example, you can install and boot Puppy Linux on a 256MB flash drive and still have another 120+ megabytes of space left for data.

On the DVD

Puppy Linux is included on the DVD that accompanies this book. You can use it as described in Appendix A. ∎

Puppy Linux is built for speed, small size, and ease of use. To emphasize the ease-of-use aspects, Puppy Linux tends to lean more toward open and easy than closed and secure. Here are some examples:

- **Backs up data** — Puppy Linux lets you save files and configuration settings to memory the first time you use it. When you are done with your session, you are asked whether you want to save that information permanently to a USB flash drive, Zip drive, floppy drive, or hard disk partition. If you choose to save your information, it will be backed up to a single archive file (named `pup_save.3fs` in ext3 format) on the permanent storage location you selected. You can choose the size of that archive as well. The next time you boot Puppy Linux on that computer, it will find your archive and restore its contents to your Puppy Linux session.

- **Loads to RAM** — When you load Puppy Linux, it will, by default, run in RAM. So you should get excellent performance, provided your machine has at least 128MB of RAM available. With Puppy Linux in RAM, that also frees up your CD/DVD drive. So you can pop in a CD or DVD and play it without disturbing the running Puppy Linux system.

- **Sets no firewall rules** — Because Puppy Linux uses a Linux 2.6 kernel, the iptables firewall is built in. However, no firewall rules are set by default. So, if you are think-ing of expanding Puppy Linux to offer some services (web server, mail server, and so on), keep in mind that it is intended for a desktop system and not built to securely offer services.

Every major category of desktop applications is represented in Puppy Linux. For word process-ing, you have AbiWord. You can play music and video with Gnome-MPlayer. Midora is included for web browsing. Sylpheed is there for mail and news. For other Internet client applications, you have Ayttm (instant messaging), Gftp (FTP client), and several remote login and remote execution tools (secure shell and telnet).

Other personal productivity tools that come with Puppy Linux include calendar (Osmo Calendar), spreadsheet (Gnumeric), contacts (Gabby and SeaMonkey Addressbook), finance manager (Home Bank finance management), and personal information (DidiWiki) applications. Most of these applications are lightweight but serviceable utilities.

Puppy Linux is still a relative newcomer to bootable Linuxes, but it seems to have a good fol-lowing and fairly active forums and development effort. Tools for configuring your network and detecting devices seem to work better in KNOPPIX derivatives, such as Damn Small Linux, at the moment. But look for these areas to improve as Puppy Linux develops.

Special-Purpose Bootables

As people begin learning about and playing with customizing bootable Linux distributions, I believe more special-purpose distributions will begin to emerge. The eMoviX2 distribution (part of the MoviX project) is an example of a distribution geared specifically toward a particular function (in that case, playing video content that you package yourself with the distribution).

A firewall is a very good application for a bootable Linux distribution. Using almost any PC and a CD (or even a floppy disk) Linux distribution, you can protect your LAN from intruders and provide a route for multiple computers to the Internet. Popular firewall distributions include Devil-Linux (`www.devil-linux.org`) and Smoothwall (`www.smoothwall.org`).

There are also bootable Linux distributions that are suited for education and for the visually impaired. There are bootable Linux distributions that are suited to be run as a server or to centralize management of clusters. The cool thing is that if there isn't the exact kind of bootable Linux available for you to use, you can start with an existing bootable Linux and customize it yourself.

Customizing a Bootable Linux

A Linux live CD is like a Linux system running from a hard disk, with a few significant differences. It has to be tailored to run from a read-only medium, it usually doesn't (by default) save information across reboots, and it needs to be able to detect and configure hardware each time it starts. Many live CD distributions have created ways of working around these limitations, including allowing you to customize the CD and to save your customizations across reboots.

If you are setting out to create your own customized live CD, or simply save your own custom settings to go with an existing live CD, you have a few ways to go about it:

- **Customizing data** — Live CD distributions, including KNOPPIX and Damn Small Linux, enable you to save your settings, data files, and even installed applications in a couple of different ways. One approach is to save all your changes to a single archive file to any available writable medium (hard disk, pen drive, and so on), and then restore that archive the next time you boot the CD. Another approach is to create a "persistent desktop" that assigns your home directory and possibly other directories to a writable, mounted file system on your hard disk or other medium. The latter saves your data as you go along.

  Live CDs such as Slax and Damn Small Linux have their own packaging format that consists of tarballs you can store to be added to the live CD. At boot time, you just point the live CD to the Damn Small MyDSL files or Slax Modules and the archive containing the application is distributed to its proper location in the file system. (See Installing_MyDSL_Extension from the `damnsmalllinux.org/wiki` or `www.slax .org/modules.php`.)

- **Remastering** — You can make many more changes to a live CD by remastering it. Remastering is typically done by copying the contents of a live CD to a directory on your hard disk (uncompressing the compressed file system), opening that directory in a chroot environment, adding and deleting software as you please, and then packaging it back up into an ISO image. This approach lets you start with a CD that is basically working, while allowing you to fix problems, update software, and add any data you like so it is included on the CD.

- **Remastersys** — To remaster an Ubuntu live CD, you can use Remastersys scripts (`http://www.geekconnection.org/remastersys/`). Using these scripts, you will be able to set up a remastering environment from an Ubuntu live CD, make the modifications you want, and create a new ISO image in one process.

- **Live CD Projects** — Several projects also focus on building live CDs from the ground up. The Linux From Scratch project has its own tools and procedures for building live CDs (`www.linuxfromscratch.org/livecd`). Linux Live CD/USB scripts (`www.linux-live.org`) enable you to make a live CD from an existing installed Linux system. (The Slax distribution is made using Linux Live CD scripts.)

Here are links to information about how to customize several popular live Linux distributions:

- **KNOPPIX** — A very extensive KNOPPIX remastering HOWTO is available for those who want to create their own custom KNOPPIX distributions. You can find that document here:

  `www.knoppix.net/wiki/Knoppix_Remastering_Howto`

  To remaster a KNOPPIX CD, you should have at least 3GB of disk space on a Linux (ext2, ext3, xfs, or other) file system along with at least 1GB of available memory (combining RAM and swap space). It's also a good idea to have an active Internet connection during any remastering because there is almost surely some software you will want to download in the process.

- **Damn Small Linux (DSL)** — This is the Linux distribution I have used the most when I want one that runs efficiently on older computer hardware. DSL does good hardware detection and has a good selection of working desktop applications. I can start with the 48MB ISO image, and then add lots of software and customized features to fill up a CD. In fact, the CD that comes with the book *Linux Toys II* (Wiley, 2006) is a remastered version of DSL that includes software for building *Linux Toys* projects as well.

  If you simply want to install DSL to a pen drive or other media, DSL offers an automated feature for doing that. After DSL is on a rewritable pen drive, you can easily add applications (using the MyDSL feature) and customize desktop features in a way that persists across reboots.

- **Puppy Linux** — The project uses its own package management system (called PupGet) that now offers more than 400 packages you can add to Puppy Linux. By adding and deleting these packages, you can create a customized version of Puppy Linux. To see available packages, check out a `pet_packages` directory from a Puppy Linux mirror site, such as the following:

  `ftp.ibiblio.org/pub/linux/distributions/puppylinux`

- **Gentoo** — Tools for building a potentially more finely tuned live CD are available with the Gentoo distribution. Although creating a Gentoo live CD is supported through the livecd-ng tool, there is currently no complete document describing a simple way to use this, or other tools, to create a custom Gentoo live CD. Here is a link, however, that can get you started:

```
en.gentoo-wiki.com/wiki/Build_Your_Own_LiveCD_or_LiveDVD
```

Of the projects I've just mentioned, I'd recommend starting with a KNOPPIX or Damn Small Linux distribution for your first attempt at remastering. Because a lot of people are using those, or other distributions based on Debian/KNOPPIX technology, mature procedures and forums are available to help you get over any bumps in the road.

Building a Live CD with Fedora

For the first few years after KNOPPIX was released in 2003, many Linux live CDs were created by simply remastering KNOPPIX. Remastering usually entailed copying the contents of KNOPPIX to hard disk on a running Linux system, setting up a chroot environment to modify the content, and then repackaging it all into a new ISO image. Today more tools are available for creating live CDs and there are more ways to go about it.

If you want to build Linux live CDs from scratch, the Fedora Project offers some powerful tools for creating a live CD in much the same way you install a Linux system. You can create a live CD or DVD image with the livecd-creator command, a kickstart file, and access to a Fedora software repository. The kickstart file tells livecd-creator which software packages to install and how to set such things as language, keyboard, time zone, authentication, services, and other information needed to run the live CD.

Here is a quick procedure for using livecd-creator to create your own Fedora live CD or DVD. Start with a computer that has a Fedora system running with disk space available that is at least three times the amount of disk space of the CD or DVD created. For a live CD, I would start with at least 5GB of disk space, so there is room for a few live CDs and local downloads of the packages you want.

1. Install the livecd-tools package (other dependent packages will install automatically).

2. Create a kickstart file that contains the packages and settings you want. Look in the /usr/share/livecd-tools directory to choose a sample kickstart file to begin with.

3. Run the livecd-creator command. Here is an example of a livecd-creator command line you can run as root user from a Terminal window:

```
# livecd-creator -c mylivecd-fedora-13.ks \
    -f F13liveCD \
    -t ~/cache
```

The command just shown uses a kickstart file in the current directory named mylivecd-fedora-13.ks. It stores temporary files in a directory named cache in the user's home directory. The resulting live CD is in the form of an ISO image file named F13liveCD.iso. Within the image, it is assigned a volume name of F13liveCD.

After you have created the live CD, you can test it using a processor emulator program, such as qVirtualBox. Then you can burn the image to a CD or DVD using the cdrecord, k3b, or other CD-burning tool.

Summary

Dozens of bootable Linux distributions have appeared in the past few years. Those distributions can contain anywhere from 1.4MB of data on a bootable firewall to many gigabytes of data on a bootable DVD. Without needing to touch the computer's hard disk, these distributions can offer full-featured systems that are tailored to be desktop systems, multimedia players, rescue systems, or many other types of systems.

Many bootable Linuxes are based on KNOPPIX, so they feature very fine hardware detection and strong network connectivity. If you want to try out a mini-bootable Linux distribution, try Damn Small Linux or Puppy Linux. For a Linux distribution that fits on a floppy disk, try Coyote Linux (described in Appendix A).

Nearly all bootable Linux distributions offer ways to access data from the hard disks of the computers on which they are running. Although many bootable Linuxes are still experimental in nature, you can have lots of fun playing with them. Also, with the extraordinary improvements in custom features, you can create your own customized bootable Linux distribution to take with you on a floppy, CD, DVD, or USB flash drive (also referred to as pen drives, thumb drives, or other names).

Part VI

Programming in Linux

Programming Environments and Interfaces

## 25

Y ou can slice and dice the topic of Linux programming tools, environments, and programming interfaces in a variety of ways. For example, a list of the programming languages known to have compilers that target or run on Linux easily runs to three single-spaced, typewritten pages. You could also examine the literally hundreds of programming libraries that exist for Linux. Alternatively, you can organize the discussion of programming tools by dividing everything into three categories: graphically oriented applications, command-line applications, and complete programming environments.

To some readers, a "programming environment" means a graphical, point-and-click integrated development environment (IDE) such as that provided by ActiveState Komodo or IBM's Eclipse. Yet another way to approach the subject is to look at Linux's development support for certain academic and computing subjects, such as graphics, databases, mathematics, engineering, chemistry, text processing, physics, biology, astronomy, networking, and parallel computing.

Unfortunately, there's no single definitive taxonomy on which everyone agrees, so this chapter takes the easy way out and divides things into environments and interfaces. For the purposes of this chapter, a *programming environment* refers to the setting in which programming takes place. Individual tools (both graphical and text based) can be used in lieu of full-blown environments to perform software development tasks. Whereas, by *interfaces* I'm usually referring to application programming interfaces (APIs) that allow programmers to create certain types of applications.

IN THIS CHAPTER

Developing applications for Linux

Using graphical programming tools

Using command-line programming tools

Programming for GUI interfaces

Programming for command-line interfaces

Using application programming interfaces

Understanding Programming Environments

Conventionally understood, a programming environment is either graphically or command line–oriented. However, the Linux programming environment also consists of the services and capabilities provided by the system itself; that is, by the kernel and the core system components. Whether you use a mouse-driven IDE or a text editor and `make`, Linux imposes certain requirements and provides a number of capabilities that determine what the code you write in an IDE or text editor must do and can do.

In this chapter, the term *programming interface* refers to the rules or methods followed to accomplish a particular task. As with programming environments, programming interfaces are usually thought of as graphical or command line:

- **Graphical interface** — Uses the X Window System, or X, to receive and process user input and display information.
- **Command-line interface** — A strictly text-based affair that does not require a windowing system to run.

For example, Firefox, a web browser, has a graphical interface; it won't work if X isn't running. Mutt, a popular e-mail client, has a command-line interface; it works whether X is running or not.

There is a third type of interface, however — an *application programming interface*, or API. An API provides a structured method to write a program that performs a certain task. For example, to write a program that plays sounds, you use the sound API; to write a program that communicates over a TCP/IP network, you use the socket API. Neither playing a sound nor communicating over a TCP/IP network necessarily requires a graphical user interface or command-line interface; both graphical and command-line programs can play sounds or use TCP/IP, provided they use the proper API.

Using Linux Programming Environments

Linux boasts arguably the richest set of programming tools of any operating system currently available.

This section looks first at the fundamental services and capabilities that inform and constrain programming on a Linux system. Next, you examine a few of the most popular graphical IDEs for creating programs on a Linux system. The section closes with a look at some of the command-line tools used for writing programs.

Note

A number of tools are available that simplify cross-platform programming. One such tool is SlickEdit. This interface runs on 7 platforms, supports 40 languages, and emulates 13 editors. More information on it can be found at www.slickedit.com. ■

As you will discover, some of the graphical IDEs provide comfortable editors for writing code, drawing dialog boxes, and navigating the file system, but use the command-line tools to do the work of compiling the code, hiding the command-line tools beneath an attractive interface.

The Linux Development Environment

The Linux development environment consists of the services and capabilities provided by the kernel and core system components, including libraries of prebuilt functions that ship with each Linux distribution. These services and capabilities both define and limit how to write programs that run on a Linux system.

Consider files and the file system. Linux, like the UNIX systems on which it is modeled, is built on the key idiom that "everything is a file." This is a powerful metaphor and model that dramatically simplifies writing application programs to communicate with all sorts of devices. How? You can use the same function, the write() system call, to write data to a text file; to send data to a printer; to send keystrokes to an application; and, if you have one, to tell your network-connected coffee pot to brew another pot of coffee.

The file metaphor works this way because Linux treats all devices, such as modems, monitors, CD-ROM drives, disc drives, keyboards, mice, and printers as if they were files. Device drivers, which are part of the kernel, sit between a device and the user and application trying to access it. A device driver translates an application's write() call into a form that the device can understand.

So, if an application uses the write() system call to write data to a text file on an ext3 file system, the ext3 driver writes the necessary bytes to a file on the disk, but if the application later uses the write() system call to write that same data to a printer, the printer driver transmits that data out the parallel port (or across the network) to the printer in a manner that the printer can understand and interpret. This is one way in which the Linux development environment informs, or defines, writing programs on a Linux system.

The catch? If the device you want to use doesn't have a driver (also called a kernel module), you can't use the write() call to do anything with that device. You simply do not have a way to communicate with the device. This is how the Linux development environment constrains programming on a Linux system.

What, then, in addition to the file idiom already discussed, are the key features of Linux that characterize its development environment? In no particular order:

- The process model
- CPU and memory protection
- The security model
- Preemptive multitasking
- Its multiuser design
- Interprocess communication
- The building blocks approach

Let's take a closer look at each of these features.

The Process Model

The process model is the way that Linux creates and manages running processes. Provided that a process has the necessary privileges, it can create (or spawn) other processes, referred to as child processes. The parent process can also exchange data with child processes. Of course, the capability to create child processes is not unique to Linux, but the particular way in which Linux does so is characteristic of all UNIX-like systems.

When a process calls the fork() system call, it creates an exact copy of itself. After being created by the fork() call, the child process typically calls one of a family of functions collectively known as exec(), providing a program to execute and any options or arguments to that program. Listing 25-1 illustrates the fork()/exec() process in a short program in the C language.

Note

Actually, the child process created when a process fork()s isn't an *exact* duplicate of the parent. The process ID (PID) of the child process is different, as is the parent PID (PPID); any file locks held by the parent are reset, and any signals pending for the parent are cleared in the child. ■

LISTING 25-1

Simple fork() and exec() sequence

```
/*
 * forkexec.c - illustrate simple fork/exec usage
 */
#include <stdio.h>
#include <unistd.h>
#include <sys/types.h>
#include <sys/wait.h>

int main(int argc, char *argv[])
{
        pid_t child;
        int status;

        child = fork();
        if (child == 0) {
                printf("in child\n");
                execl("/bin/ls", "/bin/ls", NULL);
        } else {
                printf("in parent\n");
                waitpid(child, &status, 0);
        }

        return 0;
}
```

Don't worry about what all the code means. The key points to understand are

- The `child = fork()` statement creates a new (child) process.
- The code between `if (child == 0)` and the `else` statements is executed in the child process. In particular, the child uses the `execl()` function call to execute the `/bin/ls` program, which creates a directory listing of the current directory.
- The `waitpid()` statement is executed in the parent process, which means that the parent process will wait for the child process to terminate before continuing execution.

You can compile this program with the following command (if you have the GCC compiler installed):

```
$ gcc forkexec.c -o forkexec
```

and then execute it like this:

```
$ ./forkexec
in parent
in child
28.doc  a.out  forkexec  forkexec.c
```

Your output might be slightly different. The point to take away from this example is that Linux makes it very easy to create new processes programmatically. Because it is so easy, it is a common and powerful programming technique and a characteristic of the Linux programming model. Linux is hardly alone in providing a mechanism by which one program can start another, but the `fork()`/`exec()` technique is unique to Linux (and the UNIX systems on which Linux is based).

CPU and Memory Protection

Another fundamental component of programming on Linux systems is that the operating system itself, which consists of the Linux kernel, is almost entirely insulated from all application programs. The kernel runs in a protected CPU mode known variously as ring 0, kernel mode, or, more prosaically, kernel space. User programs, such as web browsers, e-mail clients, graphics programs, and games run outside of kernel mode in what is colloquially referred to as *user space*.

The distinction between kernel space and user space is important. The kernel has raw, uncontrolled access to system resources such as the CPU, RAM, and attached peripherals. The kernel mediates all access from user space programs to system resources, funneling it through the *system call*, or syscall, interface. The syscall interface carefully checks the data passed in from user programs before passing that data on to other parts of the kernel. As a result of this careful gatekeeping, it is extremely rare for even the most poorly written user space program to crash the kernel.

The strict division between kernel and user space code is what contributes to Linux's reliability and stability and why you hardly ever see the familiar Windows "Blue Screen of Death" on a Linux system (except in a screensaver).

In addition to the distinction between kernel and user mode code, the kernel and user programs also have their own distinct memory regions. Each process, each instance of a running program, has a virtual memory space, known more formally as the process address space, of 4GB (under most 32-bit processor architectures, as 4GB is 2^{32}, or two raised to the 32nd power). Under most circumstances, the kernel gets 1GB of this space, while user space gets the other 3GB. (There are other options for the layout of memory in Linux — this is just the most common.)

User space programs are not permitted to access kernel memory directly. As with CPU and peripheral protection, the motivation for strict memory partitioning is to prevent ill-behaved (or even deliberately malicious) programs from modifying kernel data structures, which can create system instability or even crash the system.

The distinction between kernel and user space is another fundamental feature of the Linux development environment that gives developers considerable flexibility to write almost any code they want with reasonable assurance that if their program crashes, it won't also crash the system. At the same time, the syscall interface that serves as the gateway between user mode and kernel mode code enables user mode programs to access kernel features and services in a safe, controlled manner.

Moreover, the kernel can perform tasks that ordinarily might be executed by user space programs without needing a different programming model. For example, if you implement some sort of user space functionality, such as providing a basic HTTP server, in the kernel, the same syscall interface makes it possible to interact with the HTTP server; there is no need to use a new or different programming interface.

On the downside, the sharp delineation between kernel and user space creates some disadvantages for normal users. For example, user space programs do not have direct access to hardware devices. For user space programs to access a sound card, for example, the system administrator must take steps to permit this sort of access. However, this inconvenience is small when you consider the increased stability for which Linux systems are known.

The Security Model

As you learned earlier in this book, all users are not created equal. Some users, such as the root user, are effectively omnipotent and can do anything on a system. Most users have more limited access. The user (and group) IDs of these less privileged users control what programs they can execute and the files they can access. The same restrictions apply to the development environment. For example, if you write a program, you might not be able to access a certain feature, such as locking memory with the mmap() system call, unless your program runs with root permissions.

If your program creates files, the default file permissions are controlled by the umask of the user executing the program and/or a umask that you might specifically set at runtime using the umask() system call. Naturally, your program cannot create, delete, or modify files or directories if it doesn't have the necessary privileges. The Linux development environment also makes it possible for a program to drop or add privileges at runtime by calling functions that change its UID or GID.

The impact of the Linux security model on programming is two-fold. First, the same rules and restrictions that affect running programs and other elements of normal system usage also affect the process of creating programs and what those programs can do. This effect is no more than the logical consequence of the Linux security model itself. Programmatically, however, you have more ways, or perhaps more finely grained ways, to interact with the security subsystem than you do as a normal user of the system.

The second effect of the Linux security model for programmers is that writing a program imposes significant burdens on programmers to program securely. An e-mail program, for example, that stores usernames and passwords in a text file that is unencrypted and/or readable by any user (oftentimes called world-readable) is just as insecure as a program that fails to check user input for buffer overflow.

To use a subtler example, when faced with a problem that seems to require root privileges, such as access to a sound card, the initial impulse is usually to run the program as root. However, there are often user space solutions that can accomplish the same goal and that do not require root access. In the case of writing programs that access a sound card, for example, the ALSA (Advanced Linux Sound Architecture) libraries give application programmers access to a rich interface for emitting squeaks and squawks without needing to rely on running a program as the root user.

Preemptive Multitasking

Perhaps the easiest way to express the preemptive multitasking characteristic of programming in a Linux environment is simply to write, "You don't own the CPU; it only seems like you do."

In imprecise terms, the CPU (actually, the CPU scheduler, which is part of the kernel) allocates a quantum of time (on the order of 50 milliseconds) to execute your program and then preempts it (interrupts or suspends it) to spend another 50 millisecond quantum executing another program. It then preempts the second program to execute the third, and so on until the scheduler returns to your program, when (under normal circumstances) the round robin starts again.

The context switch between programs happens so rapidly that you have the illusion that your program is running all the time.

Task preemption happens automatically and unavoidably; very few processes escape preemption. What you might not realize, however, is that a process can voluntarily yield its quantum of CPU time. That is, while a process cannot request additional CPU time, it can voluntarily give it up. The implication of this for a developer is that you can delay executing certain blocks of code if they are either non-critical or rely on input from other processes that are still running. The function that makes this possible is named `sched_yield()`.

Multitasking, while a boon for computer users, poses (at least) three potential problems for programmers: deadlocks, livelocks, and races:

- **Deadlocks** — A deadlock occurs when two or more processes are unable to proceed because each is waiting for one of the others to do something. Deadlocks can happen in several ways. For example, suppose an e-mail client is communicating with a mail server, waiting on the server to send a message. A deadlock occurs if the mail server is waiting for input from the e-mail client before sending the message. This type of deadlock is sometimes referred to as a *deadly embrace*.

A *starvation deadlock* occurs when one or more low-priority processes never get time on the CPU because they are crowded out by higher-priority processes. A third common type of deadlock occurs when two processes are trying to send data to each other but can't because each process's input buffers are full because they are so busy trying to send data that they never read any data sent by the other process. This type of deadlock is colorfully referred to as *constipation*.

- **Livelocks** — A livelock occurs when a task or process, usually a server process, is unable to finish because its clients continue to create more work for it to do before the server can clear its queue. The difference between a livelock and a deadlock is that a deadlocked process doesn't have any work queued; it is blocked or waiting for something to happen. A livelocked process, on the other hand, has too much work to do and never empties its work queue.

- **Races** — A race occurs when the result of a computation depends on the order in which two events occur. Say, for example, that two processes are accessing a file. The first process writes data to the file and the second process reads data from the file to calculate and display a summary value. If the reader process reads the file after the writer completes, the reader calculates and returns the correct value. If the reader process reads the file before the writer completes, the reader will calculate and return an incorrect summary value.

The likelihood of deadlocks, livelocks, or races occurring increases dramatically on multitasking (and multiuser) systems because the number of processes that are potentially competing for access to a finite number of resources is greater. Good design, careful analysis, and the judicious use of locks, semaphores, and other mutual exclusion (or *mutex*) mechanisms, which mediate access to shared resources, can prevent or reduce their occurrence.

Multiuser by Design

Linux is multiuser by design, an element of the Linux development model that has far-reaching consequences for developers. A program cannot assume, for example, that it has sole access to any resource such as a file, memory, peripheral devices, or CPU time; multiple programs might be attempting to print simultaneously or trying to allocate memory.

Similarly, a program cannot be written with the assumption that only one copy of the program is running at a time. So, if you are writing a program that creates temporary working files in /tmp, you need to ensure that the temporary files created by one user's copy of the program are distinct from the temporary files created by another user's instance of the program. If you don't, hilarity will ensue (if not hilarity, at least confusion and consternation).

Another common need is for programs to honor per-user configurations. At start-up time, a program might apply reasonable global defaults and then read a user's configuration file to apply, say, a custom color scheme.

There are also a number of per-user settings, such as environment variables, that programs need to know how to accommodate. For example, the $MAIL environment variable identifies where the user's mail spool file is kept and the $VISUAL environment variable defines the user's preferred full screen editor (which all true Linux users know is vi). The $PRINTER environment variable stores the name of the user's default printer and, of course, $HOME identifies the user's home directory.

In a pervasively multiuser system such as Linux, programs and programmers must always take into account that most resources a program might want to use are usually shared. Likewise, they must also take into account that most real-world usage scenarios (more formally known as *use cases*) assume that multiple instances of the program are running at the same time.

Interprocess Communication

Interprocess communication (IPC) enables programs to share data and resources with a minimum amount of overhead and is used extensively on all Linux systems. It is especially common with daemons and server processes that spawn child processes to handle client connections. IPC comes in three varieties: shared memory, semaphores, and message queues.

- **Shared memory** — Shared memory is just what the name suggests: a region or segment of memory specifically set aside for use by multiple processes. Because shared memory is never paged out to disk, it is an extremely fast way for two processes to exchange data.

- **Semaphores** — Semaphores, briefly mentioned in the "Preemptive Multitasking" section, serve as flags that indicate a condition controlling the behavior of processes. For example, one process can set a semaphore to indicate a specific file is in use. Before other processes attempt to access that file, they check the semaphore's status and don't (or shouldn't) attempt to access the file if the flag is set.

- **Message queues** — Message queues are first-in-first-out (FIFO) data structures that make it possible for processes to exchange short messages in a structured, orderly manner.

Note

Message queues are not necessarily accessed in FIFO data structures. System V UNIX-style message queues are, but POSIX message queues enable readers to pull messages out of a queue in an arbitrary order. ∎

Shared memory, semaphores, and message queues are idiomatic in the Linux development environment. They solve three distinct domains of problems that arise when multiple processes need to exchange data or share resources without having to resort to slow disk files or network connections. All of which is to say that you don't always need IPC, but it sure is nice to have when you do need it.

The Building Blocks Philosophy

The building blocks philosophy that characterizes the Linux development is best expressed as a short series of rules or principles:

- Do one thing very well.
- Whenever possible, accept input data from standard input and send output data to standard output.
- Keep individual programs as self-contained as possible.
- Remember that someone will use your program in ways you didn't intend and for purposes that you never imagined.

The first rule simply means that programs should not try to be all things to all people: A text editor doesn't need to be able to send e-mail messages and a drawing program doesn't also need to be able to function as a web browser. Although it is less true today than it used to be, the best Linux programs don't have every imaginable feature (also known as *featuritis*). Rather, developers spend time perfecting the program's intended purpose and making it possible for programs to interoperate.

The second rule allows you to create chains of commands, each of which uses the output of the previous command as its input. A typical use of this behavior is a command pipeline, such as the following rather contrived example:

```
$ cat /etc/passwd | cut -f 1 -d: | tr [:lower:] [:upper:] | sort | head -5
```

The first part of the command pipeline, `cat /etc/passwd`, writes the contents of the `/etc/passwd` file to standard output. The second part, `cut -f 1 -d:`, cuts out the first field of its standard input (the contents of `/etc/passwd`), using the colon character (`:`) as the field delimiter. (The first field of `/etc/passwd` is the user name field.)

The third part, `tr [:lower:] [:upper:]`, translates all lowercase characters in the standard input to uppercase characters. The next element, `sort`, performs an alphabetic sort on the first letter of its input before sending the sorted list to standard output. The final component, `head -5`, displays only the first five lines of its standard input to standard out. The output of this pipeline might resemble the following:

```
ADM
APACHE
AVAHI
AVAHI-AUTOIPD
BIN
```

The following command pipeline should prove more useful: It e-mails the current uptime and load average to the root user:

```
$ uptime | mailx -s "System Usage" root
```

The third rule, keeping programs self-contained, is related to the second. The concept behind it is that programs intended for use in command pipelines should make no assumptions about what their input might look like or do any massaging of the output.

Consider the `cut` command shown in the first command pipeline. It takes arbitrarily formatted input and allows the user to specify on what piece of data to operate (the fifth field in the example, where fields are colon-delimited) and then just displays the requested data on standard output. `cut` doesn't do any post-processing of the output, allowing the user to do with it as she pleases, probably using another tool.

The fourth rule is really more a philosophical observation that you can't really predict all the ways in which your program might be put to use. Indeed, as S. C. Johnson once noted, "A successful [software] tool is one that was used to do something undreamed of by its author."

The point is that the Linux toolkit, for both developers and end users, is full of small tools and utilities that are building block programs routinely used to create larger programs and tools that, together, perform complex tasks that no single program can do, or can do efficiently. Another element of the building blocks approach is that it enables tasks to be performed in batch mode, without active user intervention or participation. This building block philosophy is another characteristic feature of the Linux development environment, one that can make your life a lot simpler once you grasp the idea. It also helps you to stand on the shoulders of those who have come before because you can build on existing building blocks instead of having to create everything anew.

Graphical Programming Environments

If you are sitting in front of a Linux system, chances are pretty good that:

- It is running some version of the X Window System.
- Several terminal (or shell) windows (terminal emulators) are running on top of X's graphical interface.
- One or more graphical programs are also running, such as a web browser.

Linux programming environments can be divided into two broad categories, graphical IDEs and discrete collections of command line–based tools. Developers and users coming from a predominantly Windows background will be familiar with IDEs; the 800-pound gorilla in the Windows world is Microsoft's Visual Studio product.

This section looks at some of the full-featured graphical IDEs that collect and merge all the constituent components necessary for the development task, such as an editor, compiler, linker, debugger, class browser, and project manager, in a single, unified interface. The examples discussed include the open source Eclipse environment, KDevelop, Anjuta environment, and Code Crusader environment.

Eclipse: The Universal Tool Platform

Eclipse is a large, Java-based development platform. In principle and in practice, Eclipse is a universal IDE that is used to create applications as diverse as web sites, C, C++, and Java programs, and even plug-ins that extend Eclipse itself. Eclipse is amply capable of handling every aspect of Linux development in an astonishing variety of languages. Figure 25-1 shows Eclipse with the "Hello, World" example program, written in Java, on the screen.

Figure 25-1 illustrates a number of characteristics typical of IDEs. The project view on the left side of the screen provides a project file browser that enables you to see at a glance the contents of the programming project. You can see the primary project folder, HelloWorld, and some of the associated files necessary to support Java projects, such as the default package for Java projects and a folder containing the necessary JRE (Java Runtime Environment) files.

FIGURE 25-1

The Eclipse IDE

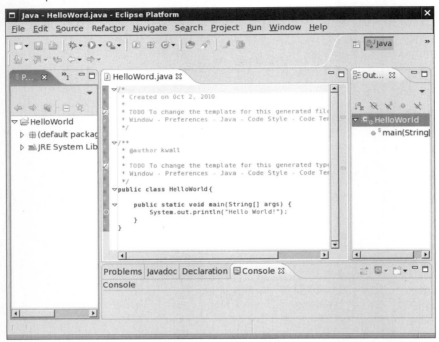

The code editor view in the center of the screen shows the code for the HelloWorld.java program. Although it isn't visible in the black-and-white figure produced for this book, the code editor performs on-the-fly syntax highlight using color and font-style changes. Java keywords are purple; plain comments appear in green; javadoc-style comments appear in a pale blue; strings are colored blue; and normal code is black. This is all quite customizable to your liking as well.

The right side of Eclipse displays another feature common among IDEs, a class browser. Class browsers enable developers to see the structure of their programs from the point of view of the code modules that make up the program rather than as mere files in a directory. This feature is not terribly useful for a small program such as HelloWorld.java, but larger programs that consist of dozens of classes or code modules are much easier to navigate using a code or class browser.

The bottom of the screen shows various information and status windows. For example, the Problems view shows problems that might have occurred while compiling the program. Eclipse, like many other IDEs, allows you to double-click on an error in the Problems view to jump right to the error in the associated code file (see Figure 25-2).

FIGURE 25-2

Eclipse's Problems view

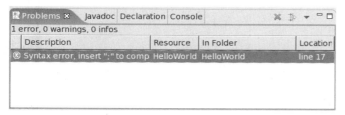

The Javadoc view, which is unique to the Eclipse Java development plug-in, enables you to view the output of Javadoc, a tool that creates documentation from specially formatted Java source code comments. The Declaration view works in combination with the class browser to show you the complete declaration of methods and data types. The Console view shows the actual output of the Java program.

Although much of Eclipse was designed to support developing applications in the Java language, plug-ins provide support for C, C++, Perl, Python, and other languages.

Note

For more information about Eclipse, including download information, visit the Eclipse home page at www.eclipse.org. ■

KDevelop: KDE's IDE

KDevelop, another open source IDE licensed under the GPL, was originally created to provide an IDE that interoperated seamlessly with KDE and the Qt framework (a large C++ application framework) on which KDE is based. Over the years, however, KDevelop has evolved into an attractive, feature-rich development environment supporting a number of languages other than C++. Today, KDevelop is a general-purpose IDE, although it works best when used to create Qt-based applications written in C++. Figure 25-3 shows a representative screenshot of KDevelop.

If you compare KDevelop's appearance to Eclipse's appearance, you will see that both have the same type of components. In Figure 25-3, the class browser is located on the left side of the screen, the project window is located in the upper-right portion of the screen, and KDevelop's version of the Declaration view is displayed in the lower-right portion of the screen.

The log view that occupies the bottom of the KDevelop interface in Figure 25-3 shows the compilation process. As with Eclipse, KDevelop's toolbars and menus are stuffed with buttons and menu items that cater to the needs of developers, just as a word processor is customized with buttons and menu items specific to the task of writing and formatting documents.

FIGURE 25-3

The KDevelop IDE

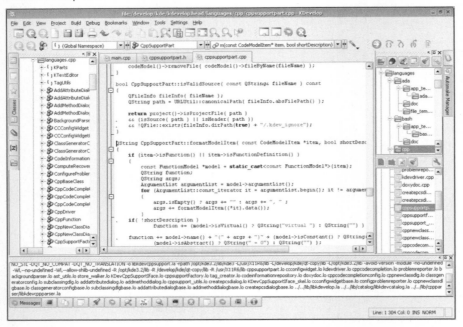

Note

For more information about KDevelop, including download information, visit the KDevelop home page at http://kdevelop.kde.org/. The language status support page (www.kdevelop.org/HEAD/doc/api/html/LangSupportStatus.html) shows the current status of programming languages supported. KDevelop is available with most Linux distributions that include the K Desktop Environment. (For example, type yum install kdevelop to install KDevelop from Fedora.) ■

Anjuta: An IDE for GTK/GNOME

To develop C and C++ applications for GTK/GNOME desktop environments, you can use the Anjuta Integrated Development Environment (http://projects.gnome.org/anjuta). With Anjuta, you can use editors such as GtkSourceView or Scintilla to view and modify code. You can edit files in the main Documents window, and then select to see a tree view in the Project window or open the Symbols window to see a tree of the project's available symbols generated from a ctags parser.

The Anjuta Project Manager plug-in can help you manage most projects based on automake and autoconf. You can create a new project, change its structure, configure build flags and other settings, compile and link source code, and execute your programs. By not adding any Anjuta-specific files to a project, Anjuta allows you to work with your project in environments outside of Anjuta.

Anjuta comes with most major Linux distributions. In Fedora, type **yum install anjuta*** as root user to install Anjuta. To open the Anjuta window, select Applications ➪ Programming ➪ Anjuta IDE. Figure 25-4 shows an example of the Ajuntu window.

The Anjuta IDE for GTK/GNOME

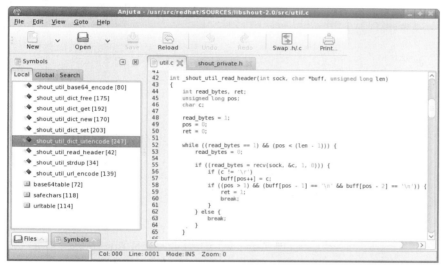

Code Crusader

Code Crusader is a commercially available and supported IDE written in C++ and specifically targeted at the Linux developer; it is not available for Windows. You can use Code Crusader to write Java, FORTAN, C++, and, of course, C programs. Unlike the IDEs discussed so far, Code Crusader does not include a built-in debugger. Rather, New Planet Software, developer of Code Crusader, makes its debugger application, Code Medic, available separately (although you can buy the two together as an IDE bundle). Figure 25-5 shows Code Crusader with the forkexec.c program from Listing 25-1 open in an editor window.

As you can see in Figure 25-5, Code Crusader has a much simpler, cleaner interface than the other IDEs mentioned so far. Another significant difference between Code Crusader and the larger IDEs such as Eclipse and KDevelop is that each IDE component, such as the project browser, the class browser, editor windows, and the log viewer, open in their own, independent windows rather than being part of a single-document interface (SDI).

Having multiple windows is more consistent with traditional Linux and UNIX windowing conventions, but developers coming from a Windows background might find Code Crusader's multiple-document interface (MDI) a little jarring at first. On the other hand, programmers who prefer a leaner, cleaner interface might prefer Code Crusader to the rather overstuffed-looking interfaces that Eclipse and KDevelop offer.

FIGURE 25-5

The Code Crusader IDE

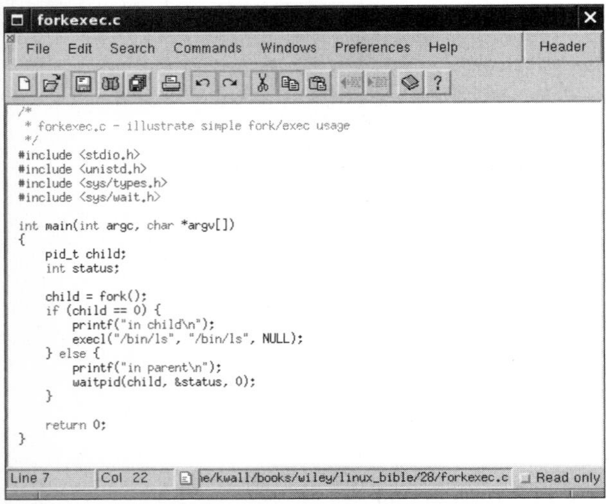

Note

For more information about Code Crusader, including download information, visit the Code Crusader home page at www.newplanetsoftware.com/jcc/. ∎

There are many more IDEs than the three discussed in this section. Some are less mature or still in beta stage. Others are special-purpose IDEs, such as the Quanta HTML editor or the Glade interface designer for GNOME. If Eclipse, KDevelop, and Code Crusader don't appeal to you, a quick search at Freshmeat (use http://freshmeat.net/tags/integrated-development-environments-ide to get right to the IDE category) should turn up many options from which to choose. There's something available for everyone. This is Linux, after all, so you are free to choose the IDE that appeals to you the most. As you'll learn in the next section, however, not everyone wants (or needs) a GUI IDE.

The Command-line Programming Environment

The Linux command-line programming environment or CLI (command-line interface) stands in sharp contrast to the GUI IDEs described in the previous section. It often shocks developers who have only a Windows development background and who aren't accustomed to using a CLI.

To be fair, it must be intimidating to find yourself in front of a command prompt without anything to double-click to start and not the faintest clue how to proceed. That said, while a CLI might seem Spartan to the newcomer, programming at the command line is surprisingly powerful and allows you to mix and match best-of-breed tools in a way that most IDEs cannot begin to approach. The CLI programming environment can match the environment provided by GUIs feature for feature, with the single exception of the graphical interface itself.

The inconvenience, if inconvenience it is, arises from the fact that the CLI programming environment relies on separate tools. For example, assuming you are working in the X Window System, you might be running one or more text editors, such as vi, pico, nano, joe, or emacs, each in its own Terminal window. You might use another Terminal window for compiling your program, either by invoking the compiler gcc (the GNU compiler collection) directly, or by using the make utility. In still another window you might be running a debugger such as gdb (the GNU debugger). If you are unfamiliar with the library you are using, you might have a web browser open to view some sort of online documentation, or you might be using a program such as xman that displays Linux manual (man) pages in a graphical format.

It is not a given, however, that graphical IDEs are better than using discrete tools. Rather, it is a matter of which model developers feel most comfortable using, which method makes developers the most productive, and which approach best fits each developer's personal working style. Many long-time UNIX and Linux developers feel more comfortable with and work more productively using command-line tools: vi or emacs for writing and editing code, gcc and make for compilation, and gdb and kgdb for debugging.

In any event, the lines are not so sharply drawn. Emacs, for example, has the facility to invoke both compilation and debugging facilities, has an extremely rich code-editing interface (syntax highlighting and automatic indentation, for example), and also supports other code development features. Emacs also includes features such as source code control, symbol and class browsing, and built-in support for at least three different online help facilities.

If you prefer vi, it also can be configured to support symbol and class browsing using the ctags program, it has basic syntax highlighting (depending on the implementation), and it can also work with the error messages produced by failed compilation.

Perhaps the GUI versus CLI debate boils down to this distinction: CLI-oriented programming environments give developers direct access to the tools and utilities they need, don't consume system resources to draw an attractive GUI, and don't provide so-called point-and-click programming. GUI-oriented programming environments hide the tools and utilities underneath a consistent, unified interface; provide a convenient dashboard or instrument panel for access to the necessary programming tools; and let developers take advantage of some of the conveniences associated with graphical environments.

Linux Programming Interfaces

As defined at the beginning of this chapter, a programming interface refers to the rules or methods followed to accomplish a particular task. As with programming environments, programming interfaces are usually thought of as either graphical or command line.

Graphical interfaces use the X Window System to receive and process user input and display information. Command-line interfaces, sometimes referred to as text-mode user interfaces (TUIs), are strictly text-based and do not require a windowing system to run. Thanks to the X Window System, however, you can also execute CLI-based programs in terminal emulators running on top of X.

As also mentioned at the beginning of the chapter, there is a third type of interface: an *application programming interface*, or API. This section of the chapter looks at the ncurses library used to create text-mode user interfaces, examines some of the popular graphical interfaces in use today, and describes a small set of the most popular APIs used by Linux programmers.

Creating Command-line Interfaces

There are three primary means of creating programs that interact with users at the command line. Two use libraries of screen manipulation routines, S-Lang and ncurses, to create TUIs, and the third just uses standard input and standard output, conventionally known as stdin and stdout, respectively. Using stdin and stdout is trivially simple. Input and output occur one line at a time; users type input using the keyboard or pipe input in from a file, and output is displayed to the screen or redirected to a file. Listing 25-2 shows such a program, readkey.c.

LISTING 25-2

Reading and Writing to stdin and stdout

```
/*
 * readkey.c - reads characters from stdin
 */
#include <stdio.h>

int main(int argc, char *argv[])
{
        int c, i = 0;

        /* read characters until newline read */
        printf("INPUT: ");
        while ((c = getchar()) != '\n') {
                ++i;
                putchar(c);
        }
        printf("\ncharacters read: %d\n", i + 1);

        return 0;

}
```

In this program, the ++i syntax is used to increment the variable i by one each time through the while loop.

To compile this program, use the following command:

```
$ gcc readkey.c -o readkey
```

In the preceding code listing, readkey.c reads input from stdin until it encounters a newline (which is generated when you press the Enter key). Then it displays the text entered and the number of characters read (the count includes the newline) and exits.

Here's how it works:

```
$ ./readkey
INPUT: There are three primary means of creating programs that interact with
users at the command line
There are three primary means of creating programs that interact with users at
the command line
characters read: 96
```

The text wraps oddly because of this book's formatting constraints. You can also feed readkey.c input from stdin using the cat command:

```
$ cat /etc/passwd | ./readkey
INPUT: root:x:0:0::/root:/bin/bash
characters read: 28
```

In this case, you see only the first line of /etc/passwd because each line of the file ends with a newline. It should be clear that programmatically interacting with the command line is simple, but not terribly user-friendly or attractive.

Creating Text Applications with ncurses

Screen manipulation libraries such as S-Lang and ncurses create more attractive programs, but, as you might expect, the tradeoff for a nicer-looking interface is more complicated code. ncurses, which stands for *new curses*, is a free reimplementation of the classic curses UNIX screen-handling library. The term "curses" derives from the phrase *cursor optimization*, which succinctly describes what the curses library does: compute the fastest way to redraw a text-mode screen and place the cursor in the proper location.

ncurses provides a simple, high-level interface for screen control and manipulation. It also contains powerful routines for handling keyboard and mouse input; creating and managing multiple windows; and using menus, forms, and panels. ncurses works by generalizing the interface between an application program and the screen or terminal on which it is running.

Given the literally hundreds of varieties of terminals, screens, and terminal emulation programs available, and the different features they possess (not to mention the different commands to use these features and capabilities), UNIX programmers quickly developed a way to abstract screen manipulation. Rather than write a lot of extra code to take into account the different terminal types, ncurses provides a uniform and generalized interface for the programmer. The ncurses API insulates the programmer from the underlying hardware and differences between terminals.

ncurses gives to character-based applications many of the same features found in graphical X Window applications — multiple windows, forms, menus, and panels. ncurses windows can be managed independently, may contain the same or different text, scroll or not scroll, be visible or hidden. Forms enable the programmer to create easy-to-use data entry and display windows, simplifying what is usually a difficult and application-specific coding task. Panels extend ncurses' capability to deal with overlapping and stacked windows. Menus provide, well, menus, again with a simpler, generalized programming interface. The ncurses library even provides support for mouse input.

To give you an idea of how ncurses works and what is involved in writing code to use it, Listing 25-3 shows the readkey.c program (now named nreadkey.c) introduced in Listing 25-2, adapted here to work with ncurses.

LISTING 25-3

Reading Input and Writing Output with ncurses

```
/*
 * nreadkey.c - reads characters from stdin
 */
#include <stdio.h>
#include <curses.h>

int main(int argc, char *argv[])
{
        int c, i = 0;
        int maxx, maxy;
        int y, x;

        /* start ncurses */
        initscr();

        /* draw a purty border */
        box(stdscr, ACS_VLINE, ACS_HLINE);
        mvwaddstr(stdscr, 1, 1, "INPUT: ");
        refresh();

        /* read characters until newline read */
        noecho();
        while ((c = getch()) != '\n') {
                ++i;
                getyx(stdscr, y, x);
                /* at the right margin */
                if (x == 79) {
                        mvaddch(y + 1, 1, c);
                } else {
                        waddch(stdscr, c);
                }

                refresh();
```

```
}
echo();
refresh();

/* print the character count */
getmaxyx(stdscr, maxy, maxx);
mvwprintw(stdscr, maxy - 2, 1, "characters read: %d\n", i);
curs_set(0);
refresh();

/* time to look at the screen */
sleep(3);

/* shutdown ncurses */
endwin();

return 0;

}
```

One of the first things you notice is that nreadkey.c is about twice as long as readkey.c. The additional code addresses the need to set up the screen, position the cursor, and so forth. To see whether the additional code is worth it, compile nreadkey.c using the following command:

```
$ gcc nreadkey.c -lncurses -o nreadkey
```

To run the program, type **./nreadkey**. Figure 25-6 shows the result after typing the same text as typed for readkey.c earlier.

FIGURE 25-6

An ncurses-based TUI

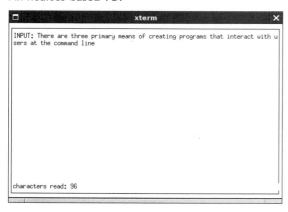

ncurses-based programs can also read input piped from stdin. Figure 25-7 shows the results of the command `cat /etc/passwd | ./nreadkey`.

FIGURE 25-7

Displaying input piped to an ncurses-based program

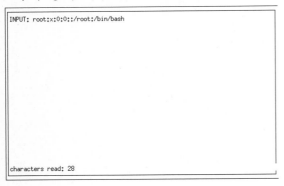

```
INPUT: root:x:0:0::/root:/bin/bash




characters read: 28
```

As you saw with the command pipeline used with the `readkey.c` program (shown in Listing 25-2), the input is truncated at the end of the first line because each line in `/etc/passwd` ends with the newline character, and `readkey.c` uses the newline character to signal the end of input.

Note

For more information about ncurses, including download information, visit the ncurses FAQ at `http://invisible-island.net/ncurses/ncurses.faq.html`. Also, using the dialog command and examples in the /usr/share/doc/dialog*/samples directory, you can try some powerful examples of ncurses features. ■

Creating Text Applications with S-Lang

S-Lang, created by John Davis, is an alternative to ncurses for creating TUIs. In addition to providing screen manipulation and cursor control routines, S-Lang also consists of an embeddable S-Lang interpreter, a large library of built-in (intrinsic) routines that simplify certain parts of programming, and a variety of predefined data types and data structures. Listing 25-4 shows the same program as Listing 25-3, with appropriate updates to reflect use of S-Lang instead of ncurses.

LISTING 25-4

Reading Input and Writing Output with S-Lang

```
/*
 * sreadkey.c - simple S-Lang-based UI
 */
```

```c
#include <stdio.h>
#include <string.h>
#include <slang/slang.h>

int main(int argc, char *argv[])
{
        int i = 0;
        unsigned int ch;

        /* start s-lang */
        SLtt_get_terminfo();
        SLang_init_tty(-1, 0, 1);
        SLsmg_init_smg();

        /* draw a purty border */
        SLsmg_draw_box(0, 0, 24, 80);
        SLsmg_gotorc(1, 1);
        SLsmg_write_nchars("INPUT: ", 7);
        SLsmg_refresh();

        /* read characters until newline read */
        while(1) {
                ++i;
                ch = SLang_getkey();
                if (ch == 13)
                        break;
                if (SLsmg_get_column() == 79)
                        SLsmg_gotorc(2, 1);
                SLsmg_write_char(ch);
                SLsmg_refresh();
        }

        /* print the character count */
        SLsmg_gotorc(22, 1);
        SLsmg_write_nchars("characters read: ", 17);
        SLsmg_printf("%d", i);
        SLsmg_refresh();

        /* time to look at the screen */
        sleep(3);

        /* shutdown s-lang */
        SLsmg_reset_smg();
        SLang_reset_tty();

        return 0;

}
```

To compile this program, use the following command:

```
$ gcc sreadkey.c -lslang -o sreadkey
```

You will need the slang, slang-devel, ncurses, and ncurses-devel packages to compile and run this program. In Ubuntu, the package is libslang2-devel.

To run the program, type **./sreadkey**. Figure 25-8 shows the result after typing the same text as typed for readkey.c earlier.

FIGURE 25-8

An S-Lang–based TUI

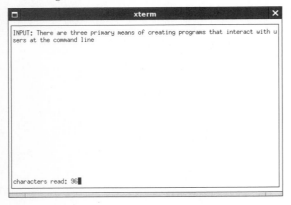

As you can see from Figure 25-8, the basic appearance and functionality of sreadkey.c is the same as nreadkey.c. The differences between the two, which have to do with the TUI framework used to create sreadkey.c, are invisible to the user. S-Lang–based programs can also read input piped from stdin.

From a developer's perspective, there are significant differences between ncurses and S-Lang in program structure and the actual library usage, but the output is almost identical.

Note

For more information about S-Lang, including download information, visit the S-Lang web page at www.s-lang.org. ■

Creating Graphical Interfaces

When it comes to creating GUIs, Linux programmers have more options available than they do for creating TUIs. Probably the most popular and certainly the best known toolkits used to create graphical applications are Qt and GTK+. Qt is the C++ application framework that powers

KDE, the K Desktop Environment. GTK+ is the toolkit underneath GNOME, the GNU Network Object Model Environment. GTK+ is written largely in C, but it has language bindings available for many other programming languages, such as Perl, C++, and Python, so you can use GTK+ features in many programming environments. Because of the limited space available, this chapter does not show examples of Qt and GTK+ applications.

Note

For more information about GTK+, visit the GTK+ web site at `www.gtk.org`. You can find information about the Qt framework at `http://qt.nokia.com/`. ∎

Although Qt and GTK+ are the big hammers of Linux graphical development, you can use many other toolkits, frameworks, and libraries to develop GUI-based applications for Linux. The following list, arranged alphabetically, describes some of the available toolkits. Most of these toolkits and frameworks describe widget sets, which are implemented in one or more programming libraries. *Widget* is the term applied to a user interface abstraction, such as a scrollbar or a button, created using the toolkit.

Note

Nearly every programming toolkit described in the following list is available with the major Linux distributions (Fedora, Ubuntu, openSUSE, Debian, and so on) included with this book. Use the appropriate packaging tools that come with your Linux system to find and install the programming tools that interest you. ∎

- **Athena** — The Athena library was one of the earliest (think ancient) widget libraries available for the X Window System. It was a thin layer of abstraction on top of raw Xlib calls that made it slightly less painful to create scrollbars, text entry boxes, and other typical GUI elements. It is part of the standard X11 distribution.

- **3D Athena Toolkit** — The 3D Athena Toolkit was a 3D version of the original Athena toolkit. It gave Athena a 3D look and was a considerable visual improvement over plain vanilla Athena. The 3D Athena toolkit, although no longer widely used, is still available on the web at `http://directory.fsf.org/project/xaw3d`.

- **FLTK** — FLTK, which is pronounced "full tick," is an acronym for the Fast Light Toolkit. FLTK is a GUI for X, Mac OS X, and Microsoft Windows. Written in C++, FLTK makes it possible to write GUIs that look almost identical regardless of the platform on which the GUI runs. FLTK also supports OpenGL graphics. You can find more information about FLTK on the web at `www.fltk.org`.

- **XForms** — XForms is a GUI toolkit based on Xlib. It isn't highly configurable like the other GUI toolkits discussed in this section, but its simplicity makes XForms easier to use than the other graphical toolkits. It comes with a GUI builder that makes it fast and easy to get working applications up and running. More information about XForms can be found on the web at `http://savannah.nongnu.org/projects/xforms/`.

- **OpenGL** — OpenGL is the industry standard 3D graphics toolkit. It provides the most realistic and lifelike graphics currently available for the X Window System. It is generally available as part of XFree86. More information about OpenGL is available on the web at `www.opengl.org`.

- **Motif** — Motif was one of the first widget or interface toolkits available for the X Window System that combined both an interface toolkit and a window manager. Originally available only as a commercial product, it is now available in an open source version as OpenMotif from the MotifZone at `www.openmotif.org`.

- **Xlib** — Xlib is shorthand for the X library, a low-level, C-based interface to the raw X Window System protocol. If you want to write as close to the X graphics core as possible, you write Xlib-based programs. Indeed, most window managers, widget libraries, and GUI toolkits are written using Xlib function. Although using straight Xlib gives you the best performance, it is extremely code intensive. Xlib is an essential ingredient of the standard X distribution. You can learn more about Xlib from the HTML manual page, available on the web at `http://tronche.com/gui/x/xlib`.

- **Xt** — Xt Intrinsics are a very thin layer of functions and data structures on top of Xlib. Xt Intrinsics create an object-oriented interface that C programs can use to create graphical elements. Without other widget sets, the Intrinsics are not especially useful. Xt, like Xlib, is a part of the standard X distribution and is not available separately.

Application Programming Interfaces

Application programming interfaces, or APIs, provide programmers with libraries of code for performing certain tasks. There are many APIs, probably as many as there are types of programming problems that need to be solved. The ncurses library, for example, provides an API that you can use to create text-mode user interfaces. In turn, ncurses works by using either the terminfo or termcap API to perform the actual screen updates in a manner consistent with the underlying type of display device in use.

Developers keep having to perform a specific type of programming task, such as updating a database, communicating over a network, getting sound out of a sound card, or performing complicated mathematical calculations. As a result, there is at least one database API, socket API, sound API, or mathematical API already in existence that they can use to simplify those tasks.

Note

This section discusses APIs for use in C and C++ programming. You can also make use of these libraries in other programming languages, but you may need to write software to adapt to the C-based API. For example, Perl, Python, and Java all have a means to call on C functions or APIs, but you will need to write the code needed to adapt the actual C library to your programming language. ∎

APIs consist of three components:

- **Header file** — Declares the interface (the function calls, macros, and data structures) the developers can use in their own programs.

- **One or more library files** — Implement(s) the interfaces declared in the header files and against which programs must be linked.

- **API documentation** — Describes how to use the API and often provides example code. The documentation might be provided in manual pages, text files, HTML files, GNU TeXinfo files, or some combination of all of these formats.

Table 25-1 describes many popular or widely used APIs, but the list provided here is far from complete.

TABLE 25-1

Common Linux APIs

API	Category	Description
atk	Accessibility	atk is a library of accessibility functions used by GNOME.
audiofile	Audio	audiofile, used by the esound daemon (Enlightened Sound Daemon), is a library for processing various audio file formats. You can also use it to develop your own audio file–based applications.
db-4	Database	The Berkeley Database (Berkeley DB) library enables developers to create applications with database support.
dbus	Messaging	D-Bus is a library used to send messages between applications.
expat	XML	Expat is a stream-oriented C library for parsing XML. It is used by Python, GNOME, Xft2, and other applications.
freeglut	3D Graphics	Completely open source alternative to the OpenGL Utility Toolkit (GLUT). It is a 3D graphics library based on the OpenGL API. It provides a higher-level interface for creation of OpenGL-based graphics.
gdbm	Database	The GNU Database Manager (GDBM) is a set of database routines that work similarly to the standard UNIX dbm routines.
gdk_pixbuf	2D Graphics	GdkPixbuf is an API for loading, scaling, compositing, and animating images. GdkPixBuf is required by many GTK+ programs.
gmp	Mathematics	The GNU Multiple Precision (GMP) API implements a library for arbitrary precision arithmetic, such as operations on signed integers, rational numbers, and floating-point numbers.
gnet	Network	GNet is an object-oriented library of network routines. Written in C and based on the GLib library, GNet is used by gnomeicu and Pan.
imlib	Graphics	ImLib (image library) is an image loading and rendering API designed to simplify and speed up the process of loading images and obtaining X Window System.
libao	Audio	libao is a cross-platform audio library used by other libraries and programs that use audio, including ogg123, GAIM, and the Ogg Vorbis libraries.
libart_lgpl	2D Graphics	Libart is a library for high-performance 2D graphics used by KDE and GNOME.

continued

TABLE 25-1 *(continued)*

API	Category	Description
libexif	Graphics	This library provides an API allowing programs to read, parse, edit, and save Exchangeable Image File Format (EXIF) data in image files. EXIF is a format used to store extra information in images, such as the JPEG files produced by digital cameras.
libglade	Graphics	The Glade library, used heavily in GNOME programs, allows programs to load user interfaces from definitions stored in external files. This allows the interface to be changed without recompiling the program.
libid3tag	Audio	libid3tag is a library for reading ID3 tags. ID3 tags allow extra information to be embedded in audio files.
libieee1284	Hardware	libieee1284 enables applications that need to communicate with (or at least identify) devices that are attached via IEEE1284–compliant parallel ports, such as scanners.
libjpeg	Graphics	The JPEG library provides a rich API for manipulating JPEG-format images, including reading, writing, converting, compressing, and decompressing images.
libmad	Audio	libmad provides a high-quality MPEG audio decoder API. libmad provides full 24-bit PCM output, so applications using this API can produce high-quality audio.
libmng	Graphics	libmng implements the Multiple-image Network Graphics (MNG) API. MNG provides multi-image animation capabilities similar to animated GIFs, but free of patent encumbrances.
libogg	Audio	Libogg is a library for reading and writing ogg format bitstreams. libogg is needed to use the Ogg Vorbis audio format.
libpng	Graphics	The Portable Network Graphics (PNG) standard is an extensible file format for the lossless, portable, well-compressed storage of images. PNG provides a patent-free replacement for GIF. (As of this writing, the GIF compression patent should have expired.)
libtermcap	Hardware	libtermcap implements the GNU termcap library API, a library of C functions that enable programs to send control strings to terminals in a way that is independent of the terminal type.
libtiff	2D Graphics	The TIFF library provides an API for working with images stored in the Tag Image File Format (TIFF), a widely used format for storing high-quality, high-resolution images.
libungif	2D Graphics	libungif provides an API unencumbered by patents for loading and saving images in GIF format.
libusb	Hardware	libusb allows user space application access to USB devices.

API	Category	Description
libvorbis	Audio	This library supports the Vorbis General Audio Compression Codec, commonly known as Ogg Vorbis. Ogg Vorbis is an open, patent- and royalty-free, general-purpose compressed audio format for audio and music.
libwmf	Graphics	libwmf provides an API for interpreting, displaying, and converting metafile images to standard image formats such as PNG, JPEG, PS, EPS, and SVG.
libxml2	XML	libxml2 is the XML parser library used by GNOME and KDE.
pango	Text layout	Pango is a library for layout and rendering of text, with an emphasis on internationalization. Pango forms the core of text and font handling in GTK+-2.0.
pcre	Regular expressions	The Perl-compatible regular expression (PCRE) library implements an API for regular expression pattern matching that uses the same syntax and semantics as Perl 5. The PCRE library is used by many programs.
pilot-link	PalmOS	pilot-link implements a library for communicating with Palm handheld devices and with other devices that adhere to the PalmOS interface standard. gnome-pilot and KPilot use pilot-link.
popt	General	popt is a C library for parsing command-line parameters. popt was heavily influenced by the `getopt()` and `getopt_long()` functions, but improves on them by allowing more powerful argument expansion and allows command-line arguments to be aliased via configuration files.
sdl	Multimedia	The Simple DirectMedia Layer (SDL) provides a generic, cross-platform API for low-level access to audio, keyboards, mice, joysticks, 3D hardware via OpenGL, and 2D framebuffers. This is a popular API for many Linux games (see `www.libsdl.org`).
t1lib	Graphics	t1lib provides an API for generating character and string glyphs from Adobe Type 1 fonts.
taglib	Audio	taglib is a library for reading and editing the metadata stored in ID3v1 and ID3v2 (MP3 files) and Ogg Vorbis comments and ID3 tags (Ogg Vorbis files).
zlib	Data Compression	zlib provides a general-purpose, thread-safe data compression library that implements the data formats defined by RFC1950, RFC1951, and RFC1952 (see `www.ietf.org/rfc.html` to find any of the RFCs just mentioned).

As you can see, a wide variety of APIs exists for performing an equally wide variety of programming tasks. Chances are pretty good that if you need to perform some sort of programming task, someone has written a library that you can use to do it.

Summary

The phrase "Linux programming environments and interfaces" is shorthand that masks a rich set of features, which, taken together, only partially characterize the activity of programming on a Linux system.

This chapter looked at both graphical programming IDEs and the less visually attractive but just as powerful command-line or text-mode programming environments. You also learned some of the characteristics of Linux and of Linux systems that define and shape programming and programs on, and for, Linux.

The second part of the chapter looked at the variety of programming interfaces and the methods available for getting particular programming tasks done. You learned that you can create text-mode or command-line interfaces and that you can choose from a variety of graphical interfaces for structuring user interaction with your program. Finally, you took a fast-paced look at some of the many APIs that make it possible to do a variety of things, such as manipulate or create images or interact with a database.

Programming Tools and Utilities

## 26

The preceding chapter provided a high-level view of Linux programming, focusing on the overall development environment and introducing the idioms that give programming on a Linux system its distinctive character. This chapter goes into greater detail and describes some of the tools and toys found on a typical Linux development system.

The goal of this chapter is not to turn you into a developer in 30 pages or less, but simply to explore some of the variety of tools developers use so you will at least know what they are and what they do. You'll also learn how to use some of the programs and utilities.

IN THIS CHAPTER

Using the GCC compiler

Automating builds with make

Examining library utilities

Exploring source code control

Debugging with GDB

The Well-Stocked Toolkit

Whether you prefer a graphical development environment or the classic command-line environment, you need a good set of tools if you want to write, compile, and debug programs for Linux. The good news is that Linux has plenty of editors, compilers, and debuggers from which to choose. The bad news is that Linux has plenty of editors, compilers, and debuggers from which to choose.

The range of programming tool options is good news for developers because they can pick the best and most appropriate tools for the development task at hand. The proliferation of choices is bad news for system administrators who need to install and maintain the tools and for people who evaluate the tools. Too many choices make choosing the right one a difficult task.

This chapter discusses the most popular programs and utilities of each type. In most cases, alternatives (and sometimes multiple alternatives) exist, but I cover only one to keep the discussion simple. (I try to mention the others just so you're familiar with their names.)

What constitutes a well-stocked Linux development toolkit? The basics include an editor to write the code, one or more compilers to turn source code into binaries, and a debugger to track down the inevitable bugs. Most people have a favorite editor, and you'd have a difficult time trying to persuade them to try a new one. Most editors support some set of programming-related functionality (some more than others, to be sure). There are too many to cover in this space, so suffice it to say: You'll need an editor.

Perhaps the most popular console editors are vi and emacs. An improved version of vi called vim is often used instead of the standard vi editor. If you prefer graphical editors, gedit in GNOME and kedit in KDE also provide basic programming support, as does nedit, a Linux and UNIX-based programmer's editor.

Cross-Reference
Chapter 8 has a short tutorial on using the vi editor, as well as short descriptions of several other popular open source text editors. ■

When it comes to compilers, GCC is the compiler of choice, or, if you will, the choice of the GNU generation, so this chapter discusses only GCC. Other compilers are available for Linux, such as Intel's C and C++ compiler and a very powerful (and expensive) offering from the Portland Compiler Group. Similarly, GDB, the GNU debugger, is the only debugger described in this chapter.

In Chapter 25, you examined the role that programming interfaces play in simplifying the development task. Interfaces usually include one or more libraries that implement the functionality that interfaces define. Because you need to be able to work with programming libraries, utilities for creating, examining, and manipulating libraries also occupy the well-stocked programming toolkit.

To this list, most developers would add a build automation tool, such as make, because most non-trivial projects need some sort of utility that handles building and rebuilding complicated, multifile projects with a minimum of effort and time.

Another challenge for large projects is tracking source code changes and maintaining a record of what code changed, when it changed, how it changed, and who changed it. This task is the province of source code control systems, and this chapter looks at two: RCS and CVS.

Using the GCC Compiler

The GNU Compiler Collection (GCC) is by far the most dominant compiler (rather, the most dominant *collection* of compilers) used on Linux systems. It compiles programs written in C, C++, Objective-C, Fortran, Java, and Ada. This chapter focuses on the C compiler.

GCC gives programmers extensive control over the compilation process. That process includes up to four stages: preprocessing, compilation, assembly, and linking. You can stop the process after any of these stages to examine the compiler's output at that stage. GCC can also handle the various C dialects, such as ANSI C or traditional (Kernighan and Ritchie) C. You can control the amount and type of debugging information, if any, to embed in the resulting binary. And as with most compilers, GCC also performs code optimization.

The gcc command invokes the C compiler. To use it, provide it the name of a C source file and use its -o option to specify the name of the output file. gcc will preprocess, compile, assemble, and link the program, generating an executable, often called a binary. Here's the simplest syntax:

```
gcc infile.c [-o outfile]
```

infile.c is a C source code file and -o says to name the output file outfile. The [] characters indicate optional arguments throughout this book. If the name of the output file is not specified, gcc names the output file a.out by default. Not all steps need to be handled by the gcc program itself, as gcc can hand off processing tasks such as linking to ld, the GNU linker.

The following example uses gcc to create the hello program from the source file hello.c. First, the source code:

```
/*
 * hello.c - canonical hello world program
 */
#include <stdio.h>

int main(int argc, char *argv[])
{
        printf("Hello, Linux programming world!\n");
        return 0;
}
```

Now, to compile and run this program, type the following:

```
$ gcc hello.c -o hello
```

If all goes well, gcc does its job silently and returns to the shell prompt. It compiles and links the source file hello.c (gcc hello.c), creating a binary named hello, as specified using the -o hello argument.

If you run the program, here's the output you get:

```
$ ./hello
Hello, Linux programming world!
```

Caution

The command that executed the hello program specifically included the current directory, denoted with a period (.) because having the current directory in your path is a security risk. That is, instead of a $PATH environment variable that resembles /bin:/usr/bin:/usr/local/bin:., it should be /bin:/usr/bin:/usr/local/bin so that a cracker cannot put a dangerous command in your current directory that happens to match the name of the more benign command you really want to execute. ∎

With GCC (and any other C compiler), the preprocessing stage handles constructs such as the #include <stdio.h> as well as #define macros. After these are handled, normal processing begins.

GCC relies on file extensions to determine what kind of source code file it is — that is, in which programming language the source code is written. Table 26-1 lists the most common extensions and how GCC interprets them.

TABLE 26-1

GCC's Filenaming Conventions

Extension	Type
.a, .so	Compiled library code
.c	C language source code
.C, .cc	C++ language source code (these may also have .cpp, .cxx, .CPP, .cp, and .c++ as an extension)
.i	Preprocessed C source code
.ii	Preprocessed C++ source code
.m	Objective-C source code
.o	Compiled object code
.S, .s	Assembly language source code

Compiling Multiple Source Code Files

Most non-trivial programs consist of multiple source files, and each source file must be compiled to object code before the final link step. To do so, pass gcc the name of each source code file it has to compile. GCC handles the rest. The gcc invocation might resemble the following:

```
$ gcc file1.c file2.c file3.c -o progname
```

The gcc command will compile file1.c, file2.c, and file3.c to object code and then link them all together to create progname. As an alternative, you can use gcc's -c option on each file individually, which creates object files from each file. Then in a second step, you link the object files together to create an executable. Thus, the single command just shown becomes:

```
$ gcc -c file1.c
$ gcc -c file2.c
$ gcc -c file3.c
$ gcc file1.o file2.o file3.o -o progname
```

One reason to do this is to avoid recompiling files that haven't changed. If you change the source code only in file3.c, for example, you don't need to recompile file1.c and file2.c to recreate progname. Another reason to compile source code files individually before linking them to create the executable is to avoid long-running compilation. Compiling multiple files in a single gcc invocation can take a while if one of the source code modules is really lengthy.

Let's take a look at an example that creates a single binary executable from multiple source code files. The example program named newhello comprises a C source code file, main.c (see Listing 26-1); a header file, msg.h (see Listing 26-2); and another C source code file, msg.c (see Listing 26-3).

LISTING 26-1

Main Program for newhello

```
/*
 * main.c  driver program
 */
#include <stdio.h>
#include "msg.h"

int main(int argc, char *argv[])
{
        char msg_hi[] = { "Hi there, programmer!" };
        char msg_bye[] = { "Goodbye, programmer!" };

        printf("%s\n", msg_hi);
        prmsg(msg_bye);
        return 0;
}
```

LISTING 26-2

Header File for newhello Helper Function

```
/*
 * msg.h - header for msg.c
 */

#ifndef MSG_H_
#define MSG_H_

void prmsg(char *msg);

#endif /* MSG_H_ */
```

LISTING 26-3

Definitions for newhello Helper Function

```
/*
 * msg.c - function declared in msg.h
```

continued

LISTING 26-1   *(continued)*

```
*/
#include <stdio.h>
#include "msg.h"

void prmsg(char *msg)
{
        printf("%s\n", msg);
}
```

The command to compile these programs to create newhello is

```
$ gcc msg.c main.c -o newhello
```

The gcc command finds the header file msg.h in the current directory and automatically includes that file during the preprocessing stage. The stdio.h file resides in a location known to the gcc command, so this file also gets included. You can add directories to search for such files, called *include* files, with the -I command-line option.

To create the object files individually, you might use the following commands:

```
$ gcc -c msg.c
$ gcc -c main.c
```

Then, to create newhello from the object files, use the following command:

```
$ gcc msg.o main.o -o newhello
```

When you run this program, the output is as follows:

```
$ ./newhello
Hi there, programmer!
Goodbye, programmer!
```

Before it creates the newhello binary, gcc creates object files for each source file. Typing long commands such as this does become tedious, however. The section "Automating Builds with make" later in this chapter shows you how to avoid having to type long, involved command lines.

GCC Command-line Options

The list of command-line options GCC accepts runs to several pages, so Table 26-2 describes only the most common ones. (Type **man gcc** to see a more complete list of options available with GCC.)

As mentioned earlier, -o file tells GCC to place output in the file file regardless of the output being produced. If you do not specify -o, for an input file named file.suffix, the defaults are to name the executable a.out, the object file file.o, and the assembly language file file.s. Preprocessor output goes to stdout.

TABLE 26-2

GCC Command-line Options

Option	Description
-ansi	Supports the ANSI/ISO C standard, turning off GNU extensions that conflict with the standard
-c	Compiles without linking, resulting in an object file but not an executable binary
-Dfoo=bar	Defines a preprocessor macro foo with a value of bar on the command line
-g	Includes standard debugging information in the binary
-ggdb	Includes lots of debugging information in the binary that only the GNU debugger (GDB) can understand
-Idirname	Prepends dirname to the list of directories searched for include files
-Ldirname	Prepends dirname to the list of directories searched for library files. By default, gcc links against shared libraries.
-lfoo	Links against libfoo
-MM	Outputs a make-compatible dependency list
-o file	Creates the output file file (not necessary when compiling object code). If file is not specified, the default is a.out.
-O	Optimizes the compiled code
-On	Specifies an optimization level n, 0<=n<=3
-pedntic	Emits all warnings required by the ANSI/ISO C standard
-pedantic-errors	Emits all errors required by the ANSI/ISO C standard
-static	Links against static libraries
-traditional	Supports the Kernighan and Ritchie C syntax. (If you don't understand what this means, don't worry about it.)
-v	Shows the commands used in each step of compilation
-W	Suppresses all warning messages
-Wall	Emits all generally useful warnings that gcc can provide. Specific warnings can also be flagged using Wwarning, where *warning* is replaced by a string identifying an item for which you want to list warnings.
-werror	Converts all warnings into errors, stopping the compilation

Automating Builds with make

The make utility is a tool to control the process of building and rebuilding software. make automates what software gets built, how it gets built, and when it gets built, freeing programmers to concentrate on writing code. It also saves a lot of typing because it contains logic that invokes GCC compiler-appropriate options and arguments. Furthermore, it helps you to avoid errors in typing all the complicated commands to build an application; instead, you just type one or two make commands. Use this section to familiarize yourself with the look and layout of makefiles.

For all but the simplest software projects, make is essential. In the first place, projects composed of multiple source files require long, complex compiler invocations. The make utility simplifies this by storing these difficult command lines in the makefile, a text file that contains all of the commands required to build software projects.

The make utility is convenient for both the developer and the user who want to build a program. As developers make changes to a program, whether to add new features or incorporate bug fixes, make makes it possible to rebuild the program with a single, short command. make is convenient for users because they don't have to read reams of documentation explaining in excruciating, mind-numbing detail how to build a program. Rather, they can simply be told to type **make** followed by **make test** followed by **make install**. Most users appreciate the convenience of simple build instructions.

Finally, make speeds up the edit-compile-debug process. It minimizes rebuild times because it is smart enough to determine which files have changed, and recompiles only files that have changed.

So, how does make accomplish its magical feats? By using a makefile, which contains rules that tell make what to build and how to build it. A rule consists of the following:

- **Target** — The "thing" make ultimately tries to create
- **Dependencies** — A list of one or more dependencies (usually files) required to build the target
- **Commands** — A list of commands to execute to create the target from the specified dependencies

Makefiles constitute a database of dependency information for the programs they build and automatically verify that all the files necessary for building a program are available.

When invoked, GNU make looks for a file named GNUmakefile, makefile, or Makefile, in that order. For some reason, most developers use the last form, Makefile. Makefile rules have this general form:

```
target : dependency dependency [...]
        command
        command
        [...]
```

In this syntax, target is usually the file, such as a binary or object file, to create. dependency is a list of one or more files required as input to create target. Each command is a step such as a compiler invocation or a shell command that is necessary to create *target*. Unless specified otherwise, make does all of its work in the current working directory.

Caution

The first character in a command must be the tab character; eight spaces will not suffice. This often catches people unaware, and can be a problem if your preferred editor "helpfully" translates tabs to eight spaces. If you try to use spaces instead of a tab, make displays the message Missing separator and stops. ■

Listing 26-4 shows a sample makefile for building a text editor imaginatively named editor.

LISTING 26-4
___

A Sample Makefile

```
editor : editor.o screen.o keyboard.o
        gcc -o editor editor.o screen.o keyboard.o

editor.o : editor.c
        gcc -c editor.c

screen.o : screen.c
        gcc -c screen.c

keyboard.o : keyboard.c
        gcc -c keyboard.c

clean :
        rm -f *.o core *~

realclean : clean
        rm -f editor
```

To compile editor, you simply type **make** in the directory that contains the makefile. It's that simple.

This example makefile has six rules. The first defines how to create the target named editor. The first target in every makefile is the default target (unless you specifically define one using the .DEFAULT directive, which is not covered in this chapter). The default target is the one that make builds if no target is specified as an argument to make. editor has three dependencies: editor.o, screen.o, and keyboard.o; these three files must exist to build editor. The second line in the first rule is the command that make must execute to create editor: gcc -o editor editor.o screen.o keyboard.o. It builds the executable from the three object files: editor.o, screen.o, and keyboard.o.

The next three rules tell make how to build the individual object files. Each rule consists of one object file target (editor.o, screen.o, keyboard.o); one source code file dependency (editor.c, screen.c, keyboard.c); and a rule that defines how to build that target.

The fifth rule defines a target named clean with no dependencies. When a target has no dependencies, its commands are executed whenever the target is invoked. In this case, clean deletes the constituent object files (*.o), plus any core files (core) as well as any emacs backup files (*~) from previous builds.

The sixth rule defines a target named realclean. It uses the fifth rule as one of its dependencies. This causes make to build the clean target and then to remove the editor binary.

Here is where make's value becomes evident: Ordinarily, if you tried to build editor using the command from the second line, gcc would complain loudly and ceremoniously quit if the dependencies did not exist. make, on the other hand, after determining that editor requires these files, first verifies that they exist and, if they don't, executes the commands to create them.

After creating the dependencies, make returns to the first rule to create the editor executable. Of course, if the dependencies for the components editor.c, screen.c, or keyboard.c don't exist, make gives up because it lacks targets named, in this case, editor.c, screen.c, or keyboard.c (that is, no rules are defined in the makefile for creating editor.c, screen.c, and keyboard.c).

All well and good, you are probably thinking, but how does make know when to build or rebuild a file? The answer is simple: If a specified target does not exist in a place where make can find it, make builds or rebuilds it. If the target does exist, make compares the timestamp on the target to the timestamps on the dependencies. If one or more of the dependencies is newer than the target, make rebuilds that target, assuming that the newer dependency implies some code change that must be incorporated into the target.

Tip
You can force make to think that a file has changed by using the touch command. The touch command changes the modified date for a file without altering the file's contents. ■

Library Utilities

Programming libraries are collections of code that can be reused across multiple software projects. Libraries are a classic example of software development's ardent goal: code reuse. They collect frequently used programming routines and utility code into a single location.

The standard C libraries, for example, contain hundreds of frequently used routines, such as the output function printf() and the input function getchar() that would be wearisome to rewrite each time you create a new program. Beyond code reuse and programmer convenience, however, libraries provide a great deal of thoroughly debugged and well-tested utility code, such as routines for network programming, graphics handling, data manipulation, and system calls.

You need to know the tools at your disposal for creating, maintaining, and managing programming libraries. The two types of libraries are static and shared, as follows:

- **Static libraries** — Static libraries are specially formatted files that contain object files, called modules or members, of reusable, precompiled code. They are stored in a special format along with a table or map that links symbol names to the members in which the symbols are defined. The map speeds up compilation and linking. Static libraries are typically named with the extension .a, which stands for archive.

- **Shared libraries** — As with static libraries, shared libraries are files that contain other object files or pointers to other object files. They are called shared libraries because the code they contain is not linked into programs when the programs are compiled. Rather, the dynamic linker/loader links shared library code into programs at runtime.

Shared libraries have several advantages over static libraries. For example, they require fewer system resources. They use less disk space because shared library code is not compiled into each binary but linked and loaded from a single location dynamically at runtime. They use less system memory because the kernel shares the memory the library occupies among all the programs that use the library.

Note

There can be advantages to static libraries as well, if you want to build an application that does not depend on anything on the host system, or special-purpose commands where you are not sure of the deployment environment. In general, however, shared libraries are recommended. ■

The dynamic linker/loader, ld.so, links symbol names to the appropriate shared library in which they are defined at runtime. Shared libraries have a special name, the *soname*, which consists of the library name and the major version number. The full name of the C library on one of my systems, for example, is libc-2.3.4.so. The library name is libc.so; the major version number is 2; the minor version number is 3; and the release or patch level is 4. For historical reasons, the C library's soname is libc.so.6. Minor version numbers and patch level numbers change as bugs are fixed, but the soname remains the same and newer versions are usually compatible with older versions.

I emphasize the soname because applications link against it. How does linking work? The ldconfig utility creates a symbolic link from the actual library, say libc-2.3.2.so, to the soname, libc.so.6, and stores this information in /etc/ld.so.cache. At runtime, ld.so scans the cache file, finds the required soname and, because of the symbolic link, loads the actual library into memory and links application function calls to the appropriate symbols in the loaded library.

The nm Command

The nm command lists all the symbols encoded in an object or binary file. It's used to see what function calls a program makes or to see whether a library or object file provides a needed function. nm has the following syntax:

```
nm [options] file
```

The nm command lists the symbols stored in *file*, which must be a static library or archive file, as described in the preceding section. *options* controls nm's behavior. Symbols are things such as functions referenced in the code, global variables from other libraries, and so on. You can use the nm command as a tool when you have to track down a missing symbol needed by a program.

Table 26-3 describes useful options for nm.

nm Command-Line Options

Option	Description
-C	Converts symbol names into user-level names. This is especially useful for making C++ function names readable.
-l	Uses debugging information to print the line number where each symbol is defined, or the relocation entry if the symbol is undefined
-s	When used on archive (.a) files, prints the index that maps symbol names to the modules or members in which the symbol is defined
-u	Displays only undefined symbols, symbols defined externally to the file being examined

Here's an example that uses nm to show some of the symbols in /usr/lib/libdl.a:

```
$ nm /usr/lib/libdl.a | head

dlopen.o:
00000040 T __dlopen_check
         U _dl_open
         U _dlerror_run
00000040 W dlopen
00000000 t dlopen_doit

dlclose.o:
         U _dl_close
```

The ar Command

The ar command creates, modifies, or extracts archives. It is most commonly used to create static libraries, which are files that contain one or more object files. This command also creates and maintains a table that cross-references symbol names to the members in which they are defined. The ar command has the following syntax:

```
ar {dmpqrtx} [options] [member] archive file [...]
```

The ar command creates the archive named *archive* from the file(s) listed in file. At least one of d, m, p, q, r, t, and x is required. You will usually use r. Table 30-4 lists the most commonly used ar options.

TABLE 26-4

ar Command-Line Options

Option	Description
-c	Suppresses the warning ar would normally emit if the archive doesn't already exist
-q	Adds files to the end of archive without checking for replacements
-r	Inserts files into archive, replacing any existing members whose names match those being added. New members are added at the end of the archive.
-s	Creates or updates the map linking symbols to the member in which they are defined
-d	Deletes files that are in the archive
-m	Moves files within the archive
-p	Prints files from the archive
-t	Lists the contents of the archive
-x	Extracts files that are in the archive

Tip

Given an archive created with the ar **command, you can speed up access to the archive by creating an index to the archive.** ranlib **does precisely this, storing the index in the archive file itself.** ranlib's **syntax is as follows:**

```
ranlib file
```

This generates a symbol map in file. **It is equivalent to** ar -s file. ■

The ldd Command

Although nm lists the symbols defined in an object file, unless you know what library defines which functions, it is not terribly helpful. That is ldd's job. It lists the shared libraries that a program requires to run. Its syntax is

```
ldd [options] file
```

The ldd command prints the names of the shared libraries file requires. Two of ldd's most useful options are -d, which reports any missing functions, and -r, which reports missing functions *and* missing data objects. For example, the following ldd reports that the mail client mutt (which may or may not be installed on your system) requires eight shared libraries.

```
$ ldd /usr/bin/mutt
        libncursesw.so.5 => /lib/libncursesw.so.5 (0x40021000)
        libssl.so.0 => /usr/lib/libssl.so.0 (0x40066000)
        libcrypto.so.0 => /usr/lib/libcrypto.so.0 (0x40097000)
```

```
libc.so.6 => /lib/libc.so.6 (0x40195000)
libgpm.so.1 => /lib/libgpm.so.1 (0x402c5000)
libdl.so.2 => /lib/libdl.so.2 (0x402cb000)
/lib/ld-linux.so.2 => /lib/ld-linux.so.2 (0x40000000)
libncurses.so.5 => /lib/libncurses.so.5 (0x402ce000)
```

The output might be different on your system.

The ldconfig Command

The ldconfig command determines the runtime links required by shared libraries that are located in /usr/lib and /lib, specified in libs on the command line, and stored in /etc/ld.so.conf. It works in conjunction with ld.so, the dynamic linker/loader, to create and maintain links to the most current versions of shared libraries available on a system. It has the following syntax:

```
ldconfig [options] [libs]
```

Running ldconfig with no arguments simply updates the cache file, /etc/ld.so.cache. options controls ldconfig's behavior. The -v option tells ldconfig to be verbose as it updates the cache. The -p option says to print without updating the current list of shared libraries about which ld.so knows. To see what ldconfig is doing when updating the cache, the -v option will print out a display of directories and symlinks ldconfig has found.

Environment Variables and Configuration Files

The dynamic linker/loader ld.so uses a number of environment variables to customize and control its behavior. These variables include

- $LD_LIBRARY_PATH — This variable contains a colon-separated list of directories in which to search for shared libraries at runtime. It is similar to the $PATH environment variable.

- $LD_PRELOAD — This variable is a white space–separated list of additional, user-specified shared libraries to load before all other libraries. It is used selectively to override functions in other shared libraries.

The ld.so utility also uses two configuration files whose purposes parallel those environment variables:

- /etc/ld.so.conf — Contains a list of directories that the linker/loader should search for shared libraries in addition to the standard directories, /usr/lib and /lib, as well as /lib64 on 64-bit architecture systems.

- /etc/ld.so.preload — Contains a disk-based version of the $LD_PRELOAD environment variable, including a white space–separated list of shared libraries to be loaded prior to executing a program.

You can use $LD_PRELOAD to override installed versions of a library with a specific version; this is often useful when you are testing a new (or different) library version but don't want to install the replacement library on your system. In general, use the environment variables only while you create your programs. Don't depend on these environment variables in production, as they have created security issues in the past, so you may not be able to control the values of the variables.

Source Code Control

Version control is an automated process for keeping track of and managing changes made to source code files. Why bother? Because:

- One day you *will* make that one fatal edit to a source file, delete its predecessor, and forget exactly which line or lines of code you "fixed."
- Simultaneously keeping track of the current release, the next release, and eight bug fixes manually *will* become mind-numbing and confusing.
- Frantically searching for the backup tape because one of your colleagues overwrote a source file for the fifth time *will* drive you over the edge.
- One day, over your morning chai, you will say to yourself, "Version control, it's the Right Thing to Do."

Source Code Control Using RCS

The Revision Control System (RCS) is a common solution to the version control problem. RCS, which is maintained by the GNU Project, is available on almost all UNIX systems, not just on Linux. Two alternatives to RCS are the Concurrent Version System (CVS), which also is maintained by the GNU Project, and the Source Code Control System (SCCS), a proprietary product.

More modern version control software projects include Subversion (http://subversion .apache.org) and Git (http://git-scm.com). In fact, if you are starting a new software project, I would recommend investigating those projects to possibly use for your source code control system instead of the RCS and CVS projects described in this section.

Before you proceed, however, Table 26-5 lists a few terms that will be used throughout the chapter. Because they are used so frequently, I want to make sure you understand their meaning insofar as RCS and version control in general are concerned.

RCS manages multiple versions of files, usually (but not necessarily) source code files. It automates file version storage and retrieval, change logging, access control, release management, and revision identification and merging. As an added bonus, RCS minimizes disk space requirements because it tracks only file changes.

TABLE 26-5

Version Control Terms

Term	Description
Lock	A working file retrieved for editing such that no one else can edit it simultaneously. A working file is locked by the first user against edits by other users.
RCS file	Any file located in an RCS directory, controlled by RCS, and accessed using RCS commands. An RCS file contains all versions of a particular file. Typically, an RCS file has a ,v extension.
Revision	A specific, numbered version of a source file. Revisions begin with 1.1 and increase incrementally, unless forced to use a specific revision number.
Working file	One or more files retrieved from the RCS source code repository (the RCS directory) into the current working directory and available for editing

One attraction of RCS is its simplicity. With only a few commands, you can accomplish a great deal.

Checking Files In and Out

You can accomplish a lot with RCS using only two commands (ci and co) and a directory named RCS. ci stands for "check in," which means storing a working file in the RCS directory; co means "check out" and refers to retrieving an RCS file from the RCS repository.

To get started, you need to create an RCS directory. All RCS commands will use this directory, if it is present in your current working directory. The RCS directory is also called the *repository*. When you check a file in, RCS asks for a description of the file, copies it to the RCS directory, and deletes the original. "Deletes the original?" Ack! Don't worry, you can retrieve it with the check out command, co.

Here's how to create an RCS directory:

```
$ mkdir RCS
```

Next, create the following source file (naming it howdy.c) in the same directory in which you created the RCS directory.

```
/*
 * $Id$
 * howdy.c - Sample to demonstrate RCS Usage
 */
#include <stdio.h>

int main(void)
{
    fprintf(stdout, "Howdy, Linux programmer!");
    return EXIT_SUCCESS;
}
```

Now, use the command `ci howdy.c` to check the file into the repository:

```
$ ci howdy.c
RCS/howdy.c,v  <--  howdy.c
enter description, terminated with single '.' or end of file:
NOTE: This is NOT the log message!
>> Simple program to illustrate RCS usage
>> .
initial revision: 1.1
done
```

With the file safely checked into the repository, you can check it out and modify it. To check a file out for editing, use the `co` command. Here's an example:

```
$ co -l howdy.c
RCS/howdy.c,v  -->  howdy.c
revision 1.1 (locked)
done
```

The working file you just checked out is editable. If you do not want to edit it, omit the `-l` option.

Making Changes to Repository Files

To see version control in action, make a change to the working file. If you haven't already done so, check out and lock the `howdy.c` file. Change anything you want, but I recommend adding `\n` to the end of `fprintf()`'s string argument because Linux (and UNIX), unlike DOS and Windows, does not automatically add a newline to the end of console output.

Next, check the file back in and RCS will increment the revision number to 1.2, ask for a description of the change you made, incorporate the changes you made into the RCS file, and (annoyingly) delete the original. To prevent deletion of your working files during check-in operations, use the `-l` or `-u` option with `ci`. Here's an example:

```
$ ci -l howdy.c
RCS/howdy.c,v  <--  howdy.c
new revision: 1.2; previous revision: 1.1
enter log message, terminated with single '.' or end of file:
>> Added newline
>> .
done
```

The messages shown in the preceding code may differ depending on whether you modified the file or did not lock the file during check out.

When used with `ci`, both the `-l` and `-u` options cause an implied check out of the file after the check-in procedure completes. `-l` locks the file so you can continue to edit it, whereas `-u` checks out an unlocked or read-only working file.

Additional Command-line Options

In addition to -l and -u, ci and co accept two other very useful options: -r (for revision) and -f (force). Use -r to tell RCS which file revision you want to manipulate. RCS assumes you want to work with the most recent revision; -r overrides this default. The -f option forces RCS to overwrite the current working file. By default, RCS aborts a check-out operation if a working file of the same name already exists in your working directory. So if you really botch your working file, use the -f option with co to get a fresh start.

RCS's command-line options are cumulative, as you might expect, and RCS does a good job of disallowing incompatible options. To check out and lock a specific revision of howdy.c, you would use a command such as co -l -r2.1 howdy.c. Similarly, ci u r3 howdy.c checks in howdy.c, assigns it revision number 3.1, and deposits a read-only revision 3.1 working file back into your current working directory.

The following example creates revision 2.1 of howdy.c. Make sure you have checked out and changed howdy.c somehow before executing this command.

```
$ ci -r2 howdy.c
RCS/howdy.c,v  <--  howdy.c
new revision: 2.1; previous revision: 1.2
enter log message, terminated with single '.' or end of file:
>> Added something
>> .
done
```

This command is equivalent to ci -r2.1 howdy.c.

The next example checks out revision 1.2 of howdy.c, disregarding the presence of higher-numbered revisions in the working directory.

```
$ co -r1.2 howdy.c
RCS/howdy.c,v  -->  howdy.c
revision 1.2
done
```

The handy command shown next discards all the changes you've made to version 1.2 (above) and lets you start over with a known good source file.

```
$ co -l -f howdy.c
RCS/howdy.c,v -->  howdy.c
revision 2.1 (locked)
done
```

When used with ci, -f forces RCS to check in a file even if it has not changed.

Source Code Control with CVS

You may have noticed that RCS has some shortcomings that make it inadequate for use on large projects. First, without some sophisticated wrapper scripts to provide the directory handling machinery, RCS doesn't work very well with a single, centralized repository. And you need such a repository for a programming team with more than a few members.

An RCS repository is always the current directory unless you exert yourself to use a directory located elsewhere. More pertinent for Linux and other open source projects, RCS is utterly unsuitable for distributed development because it doesn't support network protocols. (That is, it doesn't work over the Internet.)

Furthermore, RCS suffers from programmers forgetting commands. If you forget to check out a file with a certain option, you may regret it later. Even if you work alone, you may find CVS a better option.

The Concurrent Versions System (CVS) supports both centralized repositories and network-based access. It is well suited for use by multiple programmers, and a single CVS repository can support multiple projects. To keep the discussion simple, however, the example in this chapter deals only with a repository accessed locally. The following steps resemble the process described earlier for RCS, but they are slightly more involved and obviously use CVS concepts:

1. Create a CVS repository:

   ```
   $ mkdir /space/cvs
   $ export CVSROOT=/space/cvs
   $ cvs init
   ```

   The first command creates a directory named /space/cvs in which to establish the repository. The second command defines the environment variable $CVSROOT with this directory. Defining $CVSROOT makes using CVS much simpler. The third command initializes the repository, which creates some administrative directories CVS needs to work properly.

2. Create a top-level working directory in which to store your various projects and then change into this directory:

   ```
   $ mkdir projects
   $ cd projects
   ```

3. Check out a copy of the CVS root directory into the directory you just created:

   ```
   $ cvs -d $CVSROOT co -l .
   cvs checkout: Updating .
   ```

   The -d option tells cvs the directory containing the CVS repository ($CVSROOT, or /space/cvs); co means check out (just as with RCS); the -l option, which stands for local, means to work only in the current directory rather than recursing through subdirectories; and the . indicates the current directory.

4. Create a directory to hold a project and add it to the repository:

```
$ mkdir newhello
$ cvs add newhello
Directory /space/cvs/newhello added to the repository
```

5. Change into the new directory, copy your project files into it (fill in the your_new _hello_code with the name of the directory where you have the actual source code files for the new project), and then add those files (and any directories that might be present) to the repository:

```
$ cd newhello
$ cp /your_new_hello_code/* .
$ cvs add *c *h
cvs add: scheduling file `hello.c' for addition
cvs add: scheduling file `msg.c' for addition
cvs add: scheduling file `main.c' for addition
cvs add: scheduling file `showit.c' for addition
cvs add: use 'cvs commit' to add these files permanently
```

6. Do as the instructions recommend: Execute the command cvs commit to make the added files and directories permanent. You'll first see a screen (which is actually a vi editor session) asking you to enter a log message. If you don't want to enter a log message, press Esc, and type **ZZ** to save and exit. After you close the vi session, the output you see should resemble the following:

```
$ cvs commit
cvs commit: Examining .
RCS file: /space/cvs/newhello/hello.c,v
done
Checking in hello.c;
/space/cvs/newhello/hello.c,v  <--  hello.c
initial revision: 1.1
done
RCS file: /space/cvs/newhello/msg.c,v
done
Checking in msg.c;
/space/cvs/newhello/msg.c,v  <--  msg.c
initial revision: 1.1
done
RCS file: /space/cvs/newhello/showit.c,v
done
Checking in main.c;
/space/cvs/newhello/main.c,v  <--  main.c
initial revision: 1.1
done
```

Notice that CVS uses RCS filenaming conventions to work with files in the repository because CVS was built on top of RCS and retains compatibility with the basic RCS feature set.

CVS handles checking files in and out slightly differently than RCS. When checking a file out, it isn't necessary to specifically request a lock to get a writable copy of the file. To work on a file, you do need to use the checkout or co command:

```
$ cd projects
$ cvs -d /space/cvs co newhello
cvs checkout newhello
U newhello/hello.c
U newhello/msg.c
U newhello/main.c
```

The checkout command used in this example specifies the path to the repository using the -d option. This is unnecessary if you set the $CVSROOT environment variable. After you have made changes to files such as main.c, you can check them in using the cvs commit command (commit is comparable to RCS's ci command):

```
$ cd projects/newhello
$ cvs commit .
cvs commit: Examining .
[editor session]
Checking in main.c;
/space/cvs/newhello/main.c,v <-- main.c
new revision: 1.2; previous revision: 1.1
done
```

When you check in a modified file, CVS opens an editor session to enable you to enter a log message that describes the changes you made. The editor used is the editor defined in the $EDITOR environment variable or compiled-in default (usually vi text editor) if $EDITOR is undefined. This example did not use the -d option because the $CVSROOT environment variable is set.

To check out a specific version, or revision, of a file, use the -r option following the checkout or co command, followed by a revision number. For example, to check out revision 1.1 of the main.c file, use the following command:

```
$ cvs checkout -r 1.1 main.c
U main.c
```

To see the differences between two revisions, use the diff command, using the -r m.n, where m.n indicates the revision number you want to check. If you specify -r only once, the indicated version will be compared against the working file (using the diff option). If you specify -r twice, the two versions will be compared against each other. The following example compares revision 1.2 of showit.c to the current working revision (the revision currently in the working directory):

```
$ cvs diff -r 1.2 main.c
Index: main.c
===================================================================
```

```
RCS file: /space/cvs/newhello/main.c,v
retrieving revision 1.2
retrieving revision 1.3
diff -r1.2 -r1.3
9,10c9,10
<         char msg_hi[] = { "Hi there, programmer!" };
<         char msg_bye[] = { "Goodbye, programmer!" };
---
>         char msg_hi[] = { "Hi there, programmer!\n" };
>         char msg_bye[] = { "Goodbye, programmer!\n" };
12c12
<         printf("%s\n", msg_hi);
---
>         printf("%s", msg_hi);
```

The diff output is easier to understand than you might expect. Lines that begin with < appear in the first file (revision 1.2 of main.c) but not in the second (revision 1.3 of main.c). Similarly, lines beginning with > appear in the second file, but not in the first. Each section of diff output begins with an alphanumeric sequence such as 9,10c9,10 or 12c12.

The numeric values of the diff output indicate the lines in the first and second files to which an operation must be applied to get the second file from the first. The operation to perform, such as inserting, deleting, or changing lines, is specified by the alphabetic character. So, for example, the sequence 9,10c9,10 means that to create the second file from the first, you have to change (c) lines 9 and 10 of the first file to lines 9 and 10 of the second file.

Finally, if you totally botch all of your changes to your working files and want to revert to the most recent versions, use the update command. It updates the specified directory with the most recent versions stored in the repository, as shown in the following example:

```
$ cd ~/projects/newhello
$ cvs update .
cvs update: Updating .
U showit.c
U msg.c
U hello.c
```

There's much more to CVS than the few examples presented here. For additional information, visit the CVS home page on the web at www.nongnu.org/cvs.

Although CVS improves a lot on the limitations of RCS, CVS has its own limitations. Subversion is a newer source code control system that aims to solve many of the limitations of CVS. See subversion.tigris.org for more on SVN.

Debugging with GNU Debugger

Software is buggy, and some programs have more bugs than other programs. Although debugging sessions will never be aggravation-free, the advanced features of GNU Debugger (GDB) lighten the load and enable you to be more productive in squashing bugs. A debugger runs a program in a special mode that allows you to view the inner workings of the programs, especially the value of variables at a given point in the code. The theory is that by exposing the inner workings of the program, you can more easily determine what is not correct in the program's source code — that is, where the bug is located.

Time and effort invested in learning GDB is well spent if you can track down and fix a serious bug in just a few minutes. GDB can make this happen. Most of what you will need to accomplish with GDB can be done with a surprisingly small set of commands. The rest of this chapter explores GDB features and shows you enough GDB commands to get you going.

Effective debugging requires that your source code be compiled with the -g option to create a binary with an extended symbol table. For example, the following command

```
$ gcc -g file1 file2 -o prog
```

causes prog to be created with debugging symbols in its symbol table. If you want, you can use GCC's -ggdb option to generate still more (GDB-specific) debugging information. However, to work most effectively, this option requires that you have access to the source code for every library against which you link. Although this can be very useful in certain situations, it can also be expensive in terms of disk space. In most cases, you can get by with the plain -g option.

Starting GDB

To start a debugging session, simply type **gdb** *progname*, replacing *progname* with the name of the program you want to debug. Using a core file is optional but will enhance GDB's debugging capabilities. Of course, you'll need a program on which to try out GDB debugging, so Listing 26-5 provides one: debugme.c.

LISTING 26-5

A Buggy Program

```
/*
 * debugme.c - poorly written program to debug
 */
#include <stdio.h>

#define BIGNUM 5000
#define SZ 100
void index_to_the_moon(int ary[]);

int main(int argc, char *argv[])
{
        int intary[100];

        index_to_the_moon(intary);
```

continued

LISTING 26-5   *(continued)*

```
        return 0;
}

void index_to_the_moon(int ary[])
{
        int i;
        for (i = 0; i < BIGNUM; ++i)
                ary[i] = i;
}
```

Compile this program using the command gcc -g debugme.c -o debugme. Then, execute the program using the command ./debugme.

```
$ ./debugme
Segmentation fault (core dumped)
$ file core
core: ELF 32-big LSB core file Intel 80386, version 1 (SYSV
), SVR4-style, SVR4-stylee, from 'debugme'
```

On most systems, when you execute ./debugme, it immediately causes a segmentation fault and dumps core, as shown in the previous output listing. The following output listing shows the same commands run on a 64-bit system:

```
$ file core
core: ELF 64-bit LSB core file x86-64, version 1 (SYSV
), SVR4-style, from 'debugme'
```

Note

A *core dump* refers to an application failing and copying all data stored in memory for the application into a file named core in the current directory. That file can be used to help debug a problem with the application. The file output may be called core, or have a numeric extension, such as core.12345 (usually the process ID of the program that died). ∎

If you don't see the core dumped message, try executing the shell command ulimit -c unlimited, which allows programs to drop a memory dump in their current working directory.

The program has a bug, so you need to debug it. The first step is to start GDB, using the program name, debugme, and the core file, core, as arguments:

```
$ gdb debugme core
```

After GDB initializes, the screen should resemble Figure 26-1.

As you can see near the middle of the figure, GDB displays the name of the executable that created the core file: ` + ,'. Obviously, the displayed name is wrong; it should be debugme. The odd characters and the incorrect program name would give an experienced developer an immediate clue that the program has a significant memory bug. The next line in the figure, the text that reads Program terminated with signal 11, Segmentation fault, explains why the program terminated. A segmentation fault occurs anytime a program attempts to access memory that doesn't explicitly belong to it. GDB also helpfully displays the function it was executing, `index_to_the_moon`.

GDB's startup screen

Tip

If you don't like the licensing messages (they annoy me), use the `-q` (or `--quiet`) option when you start GDB to suppress them. Another useful command-line option is `-d dirname`, where `dirname` is the name of a directory, which tells `gdb` where to find source code (it looks in the current working directory by default). ■

After you load the program and its core dump into the debugger, run the program in the debugger. To do so, type the command `run` at the GDB command prompt, `(gdb)`, as the following example shows:

```
(gdb) run
Starting program: /home/kwall/code/debugme

Program received signal SIGSEGV, Segmentation fault.
0x0804483db in index_to_the_moon (ary=0xbffff4b0) at debugme.c:24
24                      ary[i] = i;
```

This short output listing shows that the segmentation fault occurred in the function `index_to_the_moon` at line 24 of `debugme.c`. Notice the last line of the output; GDB displays the line of code, prefixed with the line number (24), where the segmentation fault occurred. It also shows the memory address (in hexadecimal format) at which the fault occurred: `0xbffff4b0`.

You can pass any arguments to the run command that your program would ordinarily accept. GDB also creates a full shell environment in which to run the program. Ordinarily, GDB uses the value of the environment variable $SHELL to create the simulated environment. If you want, however, you can use GDB's set and unset commands to set or unset arguments and environment variables before you use the run command to run the program in the debugger.

To set command-line arguments to pass to the program, type **set args** *arg1 arg2*, where *arg1* and *arg2* (or any number of arguments) are options and arguments the program being debugged expects. Use **set environment** *env1 env2* to set environment variables (again, *env1* and *env2* are placeholders for the environment variables you want to set or unset).

Inspecting Code in the Debugger

What is happening in the function index_to_the_moon that's causing the error? You can execute the backtrace (or bt or back) command to generate the function tree that led to the segmentation fault. The backtrace doesn't usually show you *what* the problem is, but it does show you more precisely *where* the problem occurred. Here's how the function trace for the example looks on my system:

```
(gdb) backtrace
#0  0x080483db index_to_the_moon (ary=0x7ffffc90) at debugme.c:24
#1  0x080483a6 in main (argc=104,argv=0x69) at debugme.c:15
```

A backtrace shows the chain of function calls that resulted in the error. The backtrace starts with the most recently called function — index_to_the_moon() in this case — which resides at the hexadecimal memory address shown in the second column of the display (0x0800483db). The function index_to_the_moon() was called by the main() function. As you can see from the output, the most recently called function was index_to_the_moon(), so, somewhere in the function, the segmentation fault occurred. Incidentally, the backtrace also shows that index_to_the_moon() was called from line 15 of the main() function in debugme.c.

Tip

It's not necessary to type complete command names while using GDB. Any sufficiently unique abbreviation works. For example, back suffices for backtrace. ∎

It would be helpful, however, to have some idea of the context in which the offending line(s) of code exist. For this purpose, use the list command, which takes the general form, list [m,n], where m and n are the starting and ending line numbers you want displayed. For example:

```
(gdb) list 10,24
```

would display code lines 10 through 24.

A bare list command displays 10 lines of code, including the line where the error was first detected, as illustrated here:

```
(gdb) list
15              index_to_the_moon(intary);
16
```

```
17              exit(EXIT_SUCCESS);
18      }
19
20      void index_to_the_moon(int ary[])
21      {
22              int i;
23              for (i = 0; i < BIGNUM; ++I {
24                      ary[i] = i;
```

Examining Data

One of GDB's most useful features is its ability to display both the type and the value of almost any expression, variable, or array in the program being debugged. It can print the value of any legal expression in the language in which your program is written. The command is, predictably enough, print. Here are a couple of print commands and their results:

```
(gdb) print i
$1 = 724
(gdb) print ary[i]
Cannot access memory at address 0xc0000000.
```

This example continues the earlier examples of debugging debugme.c because you are still trying to identify where and why debugme crashed. Although in this example, the program crashed at the point when the counter variable i equaled 724 (the expression $1 refers to an entry in GDB's value history, explained in a moment), where it crashes on your system depends on several variables. Those variables could include the system's memory layout, the process's memory space (especially the kernel's stack space), the amount of available memory on your system, and other factors.

The result of the second command (print ary[i]) makes it pretty clear that the program does not have access to the memory location specified, although it does have legal access to the preceding one.

The expression $1 is an alias that refers to an entry in GDB's value history. GDB creates value history entries for each command you type that produces computed results. The alias numbers increment sequentially each time you execute a command that produces some sort of computed output. As a result, you can access these computed values using aliases rather than retyping the command. For example, the command $1-5 produces the following:

```
(gdb) print $1-5
$2 = 719
```

Notice that the alias incremented to $2. If you later need to use the value 719, you can use the alias $2. The value history is reset each time you start GDB and the values are not accessible outside of GDB.

You are not limited to using discrete values because gdb can display the addresses of data stored in an arbitrary region of memory. For example, to print the first 10 memory locations associated with ary, use the following command:

```
(gdb) print ary@10
$3 = {0xbffffc90, 0x40015580, 0x400115800, 0x0, 0x1, 0x2, 0c3, 0x4, 0x5}
```

The notation @10 means to print the 10 values that begin at ary. Say, on the other hand, that you want to print the five values stored in ary beginning with the first element. The command for this would be the following:

```
(gdb) print ary[1]@5
$4 = {1, 2, 3, 4, 5}
```

Why go to the trouble of printing variable or array values? Although it isn't necessary in this particular example because you know where the trouble occurs, it is often necessary to see the value of a variable at a particular point in a program's execution so you monitor what is happening to variables. It's pretty clear in this case that the index_to_the_moon() function is suspect, but depending on experience, some people may not see the exact problem within the function.

In the case of arrays, a command that prints the values in an array, such as print ary[1]@5 in the preceding example, enables you to confirm at a glance that the values are what you expect them to be. If the values don't match up with your expectations, however, that is a clue that some code is altering the array in a way you didn't intend. As a result, you can focus your bug hunting on a specific section of code.

GDB also can tell you the types of variables using the whatis command. GDB's whatis command is comparable to the man -f command, which searches the whatis database of system commands for short descriptions of those system commands (the manual page whatis database is totally separate from the whatis command used by GDB). Although man's whatis database works on system commands, GDB's whatis command describes the types of variables and other data structures used in a program.

```
(gdb) whatis i
type = int
(gdb) whatis ary
type = int *
(gdb) whatis index_to_the_moon
type = void (int *)
```

This feature may seem rather useless because, of course, you know the types of all the variables in your program (yeah, right!). But, you will change your mind the first time you have to debug someone else's code or have to fix a multifile project for which you haven't seen the source files for a couple of months. The whatis command can also help you track down bugs that result from assigning an inappropriate value to a variable.

Setting Breakpoints

As you debug problematic code, halting execution at some point is often useful. Perhaps you want to stop execution before the code enters a section that is known to have problems. In other cases, you can set breakpoints so you can look at the values of certain variables at a given point in the execution flow. In still other situations, you might find it useful to stop execution so you can step through the code one instruction at a time.

GDB enables you to set breakpoints on several different kinds of code constructs, including line numbers and function names, and also enables you to set conditional breakpoints, where the code stops only if a certain condition is met. To set a breakpoint on a line number, use the following syntax:

```
(gdb) break linenum
```

To stop execution when the code enters a function, use the following:

```
(gdb) break funcname
```

In either case, GDB halts execution before executing the specified line number or entering the specified function. You can then use `print` to display variable values, for example, or use `list` to review the code that is about to be executed. If you have a multifile project and want to halt execution on a line of code or in a function that is not in the current source file, use the following forms:

```
(gdb) break filename:linenum
(gdb) break filename:funcname
```

Conditional breakpoints are usually more useful. They enable you to temporarily halt program execution if or when a particular condition is met. The correct syntax for setting conditional breakpoints is as follows:

```
(gdb) break linenum if expr
(gdb) break funcname if expr
```

In the preceding code, `expr` can be any expression that evaluates to true (non-zero). For example, the following `break` command stops execution at line 24 of `debugme` when the variable i equals 15:

```
(gdb) break 24 if i == 15
Breakpoint 1 at 0x80483cb: file debugme.c, line 24.
(gdb) run
Starting program: /home/kwall/code/debugme

Breakpoint 1, index_to_the_moon (ary=0xbffff4b0) at debugme.c:24
24                      ary[i] = i;
```

Tip

Verify the line numbers as seen by gdb. In this case, gdb has line 24 as the assignment of ary[i] to the value of i, as shown in the preceding code. Use the gdb list command to verify the line numbers used by gdb. ■

Stopping when i equals 15 is an arbitrary choice to demonstrate conditional breaks. As you can see, gdb stopped on line 24. A quick `print` command confirms that it stopped when the value of i reached the requested value:

```
(gdb) print i
$1 = 15
```

To resume executing after hitting a breakpoint, type **continue**. If you have set many breakpoints and have lost track of what has been set and which ones have been triggered, you can use the `info breakpoints` command to refresh your memory.

Working with Source Code

Locating a specific variable or function in a multifile project is a breeze with GDB, provided you use the -d switch to tell it where to find additional source code files. This option is particularly helpful when not all of your source code is located in your current working directory or in the program's compilation directory (which GCC recorded in its symbol table).

To specify one or more additional directories containing source code, start GDB using one or more -d dirname options, as this example illustrates:

```
$ gdb -d /source/project1 -d /oldsource/project1 \
     -d /home/bubba/src killerapp
```

To locate the next occurrence of a particular string in the current file, use the search string command. Use reverse-search string to find the previous occurrence of string. If you want to find the previous occurrence of the word "return" in debugme.c (refer to Listing 26-5), for example, use the command reverse-search return. GDB obliges and displays the text:

```
(gdb) reverse-search return
17              return ret;
```

The search and reverse-search commands are especially helpful in large source files that have dozens or hundreds of lines. One common use of the reverse-search command is to find the file and/or line in which a variable is first used or in which it is defined. The search command similarly enables you to locate with relative ease each location in which a program symbol (variable, macro, or function) is used, perhaps to find the use that changes a variable unexpectedly or the place where a function is called when it shouldn't be.

Summary

This chapter took you on a whirlwind tour of a few of the most common programs and utilities used by Linux programmers. You learned how to use GCC to compile programs, how to use make to automate compiling programs, and how to find information about programming libraries using programs such as ldd, nm, and ldconfig. You also learned enough about the source code control systems RCS and CVS to be comfortable with the terminology and how to use their most basic features. Finally, you learned how to use the GNU debugger (GDB) to figure out why, or at least where, a program fails.

Part VII

Appendix and License

Media

The DVD that accompanies *Linux Bible 2011 Edition* contains a variety of Linux systems that you can use. You can boot and run some of these Linux systems live, whereas you can use others to install a Linux system permanently to hard disk. Some can do both.

Most of the Linux systems included here are slightly remastered versions of official live and installation CDs that come from different Linux projects. Changes made to those CDs were made exclusively to allow each to be booted from a single boot screen on the DVD. After you have selected a Linux to start up, however, it should behave exactly as the original CD from the selected Linux project.

General information on running live or installing the various Linux distributions on the DVD is in Chapter 7. You can find specific instructions for using and installing some of the Linux distributions in Chapters 19 through 24.

Caution

The software contained on the DVD is covered under the GNU Public License (GPL) or other licenses included on the medium for each software distribution. Use the software on the DVD (as you would any GPL software) at your own risk. Refer to README, RELEASE-NOTES, and any licensing files delivered with each distribution, and be sure that you agree with the terms they spell out before using the software. ∎

IN THIS APPENDIX

Understand how to use the book's DVD

Learn which Linux distributions are installed on the DVD

Finding Linux Distributions on the DVD

The following sections describe the Linux distributions on the DVD that accompanies this book. All except one of these distributions are immediately bootable from the DVD, although some are made to run as live CDs and others are used to install to hard disk. (The exception is Coyote Linux, which comes in a form that allows you to create a Linux-based firewall system that runs from a floppy disk.)

Fedora Linux

The DVD that comes with this book includes the Fedora 13 Desktop live/install CD distribution that normally comes on a single CD. Fedora is used as the example for many of the procedures and applications in this book. You can boot Fedora as a live CD directly from the DVD, and then use that live CD to install the same Fedora desktop system permanently to your hard disk.

To begin installing Fedora to your hard disk, insert the DVD into your PC's DVD drive, reboot, and select `fedora`.

Details on installing and using Fedora are in Chapter 20. If any application that you want is not available as described, use the PackageKit window or the `yum` command to install the package containing that application from the Internet.

Note
If you find that you like Fedora, consider getting *Fedora Bible* (Wiley Publishing, 2010) to learn more about that distribution. Although some of the material overlaps with this book's, you will get more complete coverage of installation and different kinds of servers available with Fedora, along with the official Fedora DVD. ∎

KNOPPIX Linux

The KNOPPIX 6.2.1 live CD Linux distribution is configured to boot by default from the DVD that comes with this book. KNOPPIX was one of the first popular live CD Linux distributions and offers some unique features to set it apart from other bootable Linux distributions.

To boot KNOPPIX directly from the DVD, insert the DVD into your PC's DVD drive, reboot, and select `knoppix`.

Information on using KNOPPIX and configuring it in various ways is in Chapter 24.

Slackware Linux

The DVD that comes with this book contains software compiled from CD images of the Slackware 13.1 distribution. Slackware is the oldest surviving Linux system and continues to have a loyal following among Linux enthusiasts. To begin installing Slackware to your hard disk, insert the DVD into your PC's DVD drive, reboot, and select `slackware`.

You can find instructions on how to install Slackware from this book's DVD in the /docs directory on the DVD that comes with this book. Chapter 3 describes how to configure a simple window manager for use with Slackware.

Ubuntu Linux

The Ubuntu 10.04.1 (Lucid Lynx) installation and live CD is contained on the DVD that comes with this book. You can use that image to run live, and then install, a minimal desktop system. You can do further software installation from the Internet, after the basic install is done.

To boot the Ubuntu live CD image from the DVD that comes with this book, insert the DVD into your PC's DVD drive, reboot, and select ubuntu.

Your computer will boot a live CD version of Ubuntu that is intended to be used as a desktop system. An icon on the desktop lets you install the contents of the CD image to your computer's hard disk. The procedure for booting and installing Ubuntu is in Chapter 19.

AntiX Linux

AntiX is a lightweight, desktop-oriented live CD that is suitable for older, less powerful computers. It can run on machines with as little as 64MB of RAM (although 128MB is recommended). AntiX is based on MEPIS. AntiX release 8.5 is included on the DVD.

To start AntiX from the DVD, insert the DVD into your computer's DVD drive, reboot the computer, and select antix.

BackTrack 3 Linux Security Suite

BackTrack 3 is a live CD that contains a set of tools for testing, repairing, and otherwise securing Linux systems, Windows systems, and networks. Use the BackTrack menu on the main menu of this live CD to select from dozens of security-related tools. BackTrack is discussed in Chapter 24.

To boot the BackTrack live CD image from the DVD that comes with this book, insert the DVD into your PC's DVD drive, reboot, and select backtrack. (Although a later version of BackTrack, BackTrack 4, is now available, it was too large to fit on the DVD that comes with this book. You can download it yourself from http://http://www.backtrack-linux.org/downloads.)

Gentoo Linux

The DVD that comes with this book includes a Gentoo minimal install CD (dated 9/21/2010). With the Gentoo CD, you build a minimal system and then add any of the nearly 7,000 software packages that are available with Gentoo. You can obtain those packages over a network connection or from a local CD, DVD, or hard disk.

To boot the Gentoo minimal install CD image from the DVD that comes with this book, insert the DVD into your PC's DVD drive, reboot, and select gentoo.

Documents in the /doc directory of the DVD that comes with this book describe how to build most of the Gentoo operating system from scratch, specifically for your computer hardware. During the procedure, you will download packages as you need them from the Internet.

openSUSE Linux

The openSUSE Linux 11.3 live/install CD lets you boot an openSUSE desktop live, and then install it to your hard drive from software downloaded over the network. openSUSE Linux is developed and supported by Novell and a community of software developers. Novell also offers the commercial SUSE Linux Enterprise system as part of a wider range of Enterprise-ready Linux and NetWare software.

To begin installing openSUSE to your hard disk, insert the CD into your PC's CD drive, reboot, and select suse.

To install openSUSE from this DVD, follow the installation instructions in Chapter 22. This version of openSUSE offers a quick way to try out a KDE desktop.

PCLinuxOS

PCLinuxOS is a popular desktop Linux distribution. PCLinuxOS makes it easy to get support for common multimedia content that isn't always so easy to find with other Linux distributions.

To run PCLinuxOS 2010.10 live, insert the DVD into your PC's DVD drive, reboot, and select pclinuxos. Chapter 23 contains descriptions of PCLinuxOS. This version of PCLinuxOS provides a great way to try out an LXDE desktop.

Inside Security Rescue Toolkit

Inside Security Rescue Toolkit (INSERT) is a small, bootable Linux distribution that contains a variety of useful tools for checking, repairing, and recovering computers and networks. INSERT is small enough to fit on a bootable business card CD or mini-CD. Although many of its tools are text-based, INSERT includes a simple graphical interface (using X and FluxBox window manager) and a few graphical tools.

To run INSERT live, insert the DVD that comes with this book into your PC's DVD drive, reboot, and select insert.

Refer to Chapter 24 for descriptions of what's inside INSERT.

Puppy Linux

This mini live CD contains a desktop Linux system that you can use for creating documents, playing multimedia content, accessing the Internet, and many other functions. Puppy Linux 5.1.1 contains many features for configuring your desktop and saving your features across reboots. Chapter 24 describes Puppy Linux.

To run Puppy Linux live, insert the DVD into your PC's CD drive, reboot, and select `puppy`.

Debian GNU/Linux

The network install ISO image of Debian GNU/Linux distribution (506) is contained on the DVD. Debian offers thoroughly tested releases that many Linux consultants and experts use because of Debian's excellent software packaging and stability.

You can start a Debian installation directly from the DVD that comes with this book. With a basic install done from this Debian CD image, to add the components you need for a desktop or server system, you must have a connection to the Internet.

To begin installing Debian to your hard disk, insert the DVD into your PC's DVD drive, reboot, and select `debian`.

The procedure for installing Debian is in Chapter 21.

Damn Small Linux

Damn Small Linux 4.4.10 is set up to boot from the DVD that accompanies this book. This distribution illustrates how a useful desktop Linux distribution, which includes full network connectivity and some useful productivity applications, can fit in a very small space.

To run Damn Small Linux live, insert the DVD into your PC's DVD drive, reboot, and select `dsl`.

See Chapter 24 for information on using Damn Small Linux.

SystemRescueCd

Like INSERT, SystemRescueCd is a bootable Linux that includes a variety of tools for checking and fixing your installed computer systems. It includes tools for managing and fixing file systems, checking for viruses, monitoring the network, and checking whether a machine has been cracked. You can boot the SystemRescueCd version 1.6.1 image directly from the DVD that comes with this book.

To run SystemRescueCd live, insert the DVD into your PC's DVD drive, reboot, and select `rescue`.

Refer to Chapter 24 for further information about SystemRescueCd.

Coyote Linux

Although not considered a major Linux distribution, Coyote Linux 2.24 is an excellent illustration of a useful Linux distribution that fits on a floppy disk (1.4MB). You can copy the tar file of Coyote Linux on the DVD that comes with this book to a Linux system, configure Coyote Linux to suit your needs, and copy the resulting boot image to floppy disk.

See documentation in the `/docs` directory of the DVD that comes with this book for information on how to configure and use Coyote Linux as a firewall.

Tiny Core Linux

Tiny Core Linux 3.1 is a very small Linux distribution in the tradition of Damn Small Linux (in fact it's developed by Robert Shingledecker, lead developer of DSL). Start with a core operating system that is only a few megabytes in size, and you can add only the components you need. Tiny Core is especially good on low-RAM, small disk-space devices and older, less-powerful hardware.

To boot Tiny Core Linux from the DVD that comes with this book, select `tinycore` from the boot prompt.

SLAX

The SLAX 6.1.2 CD image is included on the DVD that comes with this book. This live CD contains a well-stocked desktop Linux system. Chapter 24 describes SLAX.

To run SLAX live, insert the DVD into your PC's DVD drive, reboot, and select `slax`.

CentOS

The CentOS 5.5 live CD is included on the DVD that comes with this book. Because CentOS is built from source code used to create Red Hat Enterprise Linux, it is a good way to try out features of Red Hat Enterprise Linux before deciding to purchase subscriptions of Red Hat Enterprise Linux for your business or organization.

To run CentOS 5.5 live, insert the DVD into your PC's DVD drive, reboot, and select `centos`.

Creating Linux CDs or DVDs

Instead of using the Linux distributions that come with this book, you can download your own Linux distributions to use over the Internet. Once you have downloaded a Linux CD or DVD image, you can use several tools to create bootable CDs or DVDs for either installing or just running Linux live from those media. Before you begin, you must have the following:

- **DVD or CD ISO images** — Download the ISO images you want to burn to a physical DVD or CD.
- **Blank DVDs/CDs** — You need blank DVDs or CDs to burn the images to.
- **CD or DVD burner** — You need a drive that is capable of burning CDs or DVDs, depending on which you are burning.

Here's how to create bootable Linux CDs from a running Linux system (such as Fedora):

1. Download the ISO images you want to your computer's hard drive. (You'll need between 50MB and 700MB of hard disk space, depending on the size of the CD image you choose. Single-layer DVD images are usually under 4.7GB.)

2. Open a CD/DVD burning application. For this procedure, I recommend K3b CD/DVD Burning Facility (www.k3b.org). In Fedora, select the Applications menu and choose Sound & Video ➪ K3b (or type **k3b** from a Terminal window). The K3b CD Kreator window appears.

Note

If K3b is not installed on your Linux system, you can install it on most Linux distributions. For Fedora, install K3b by typing yum install k3b as root user from a Terminal window. ■

3. From the K3b window, select Tools ➪ Burn CD ISO Image to burn a CD image or Tools ➪ Burn DVD ISO Image to burn a DVD image. You are asked to choose an image file.

4. Browse to the image you just downloaded or copied to hard disk and select it. After you select the image you want, the Burn CD Image window appears, as does a checksum on the image. (Often, you can compare the checksum number that appears against the number in an md5 file from the download directory where you got the live CD to be sure that the CD image was not corrupted.) Figure A-1 shows the Burn CD Image window ready to burn an image of Damn Small Linux.

FIGURE A-1

Use K3b to burn your installation CDs.

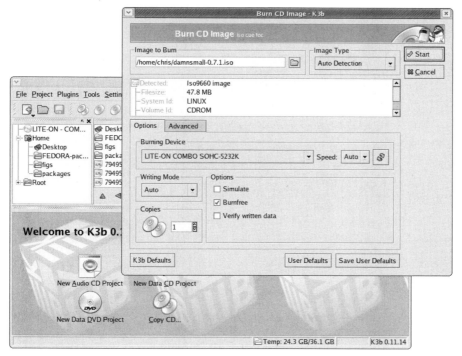

5. Insert a blank CD into the CD burner drive, which may be a combination CD/DVD drive. (If a CD/DVD Kreator window pops up, you can just close it.)

6. Check the settings in the Burn CD Image window (often the defaults are fine, but you may want to slow down the speed if you get some bad burns). You can also select the Simulate check box to test the burn before actually writing to the CD. Click Start to continue.

7. When the CD is done burning, eject it (or it may eject automatically) and mark it appropriately (information such as the distribution name, version number, and date).

Now you're ready to begin installing (or booting) the Linux distribution you just burned. Refer to Chapter 7 for general information on installing Linux. Then go to the chapter that covers your particular distribution to find its specific installation procedure.

If you don't have Linux installed or K3b available at the moment, you can burn CDs from any CD-burning application you have available. A nice overview of CD installation tools and how to use them to burn CDs is available at the Gentoo web site (`www.gentoo.org/doc/en/faq.xml#isoburning`). It describes disk-burning tools that are available on Windows, Mac OS X, and Linux systems.

If you have no GUI, or don't mind working from the shell, you can use the `cdrecord` command to burn the ISOs. With a blank CD inserted and the ISO image you want to burn in the current directory, here's a simple command line for burning a CD image to CD using `cdrecord`:

```
# cdrecord -v whatever.iso
```

See the `cdrecord` man page (`man cdrecord`) to see other options available with the `cdrecord` command.

Note
The `growisofs` command is another useful tool for burning CD and DVD ISO images. See the `growisofs` man page for further information. ■

Getting Source Code

To offer as many Linux distributions as possible on the limited media available with the book, I have included only binary versions of the software and no source code. However, every distribution included with the book offers the source code used to build it in a form that you can download from the Internet.

The following list contains URLs to where you can get the source code for all the Linux distributions included with the book. In some cases, you must choose a convenient mirror site from which to download the source code or use BitTorrent:

- **AntiX** — `http://antix.mepis.org/index.php?title=Main_Page#Downloads`
- **BackTrack** — `http://www.backtrack-linux.org/downloads`

- **CentOS** — http://centos.org/modules/tinycontent/index.php?id=15
- **Coyote** — http://sourceforge.net/projects/coyotelinux/files
- **Damn Small Linux** — www.damnsmalllinux.org/download.html
- **Debian** — www.debian.org/CD/netinst
- **Fedora** — http://fedoraproject.org/get-fedora
- **Gentoo** — www.gentoo.org/main/en/where.xml
- **INSERT** — http://sourceforge.net/projects/insert
- **KNOPPIX** — www.knopper.net/knoppix-mirrors/index-en.html
- **openSUSE** — http://download.opensuse.org/distribution
- **PCLinuxOS** — http://www.pclinuxos.com/?page_id=10
- **Puppy** — http://puppylinux.org/main/index.php?file=Download%20 Latest%20Release.htm
- **Slackware** — www.slackware.com/getslack
- **SLAX** — www.slax.org/get_slax.php
- **SystemRescueCd** — http://sourceforge.net/projects/systemrescuecd
- **Tiny Core** — www.tinycorelinux.com
- **Ubuntu** — www.ubuntu.com/desktop/getubuntu/download

Because links to Linux download sites change all the time, if the source code is not readily available from the links shown, try contacting the projects directly to find out where downloadable source code currently resides.

GNU General Public License

Version 2, June 1991

Copyright © 1989, 1991 Free Software Foundation, Inc.

59 Temple Place - Suite 330, Boston, MA 02111-1307, USA

Preamble

The licenses for most software are designed to take away your freedom to share and change it. By contrast, the GNU General Public License is intended to guarantee your freedom to share and change free software — to make sure the software is free for all its users. This General Public License applies to most of the Free Software Foundation's software and to any other program whose authors commit to using it. (Some other Free Software Foundation software is covered by the GNU Library General Public License instead.) You can apply it to your programs, too.

When we speak of free software, we are referring to freedom, not price. Our General Public Licenses are designed to make sure that you have the freedom to distribute copies of free software (and charge for this service if you wish), that you receive source code or can get it if you want it, that you can change the software or use pieces of it in new free programs; and that you know you can do these things.

To protect your rights, we need to make restrictions that forbid anyone to deny you these rights or to ask you to surrender the rights. These restrictions translate to certain responsibilities for you if you distribute copies of the software, or if you modify it.

For example, if you distribute copies of such a program, whether gratis or for a fee, you must give the recipients all the rights that you have. You must make sure that they, too, receive or can get the source code. And you must show them these terms so they know their rights.

We protect your rights with two steps: (1) copyright the software, and (2) offer you this license which gives you legal permission to copy, distribute and/or modify the software.

Also, for each author's protection and ours, we want to make certain that everyone understands that there is no warranty for this free software. If the software is modified by someone else and passed on, we want its recipients to know that what they have is not the original, so that any problems introduced by others will not reflect on the original authors' reputations.

Finally, any free program is threatened constantly by software patents. We wish to avoid the danger that redistributors of a free program will individually obtain patent licenses, in effect making the program proprietary. To prevent this, we have made it clear that any patent must be licensed for everyone's free use or not licensed at all.

The precise terms and conditions for copying, distribution and modification follow.

Terms and Conditions for Copying, Distribution and Modification

0. This License applies to any program or other work which contains a notice placed by the copyright holder saying it may be distributed under the terms of this General Public License. The "Program", below, refers to any such program or work, and a "work based on the Program" means either the Program or any derivative work under copyright law: that is to say, a work containing the Program or a portion of it, either verbatim or with modifications and/or translated into another language. (Hereinafter, translation is included without limitation in the term "modification".) Each licensee is addressed as "you".

Activities other than copying, distribution and modification are not covered by this License; they are outside its scope. The act of running the Program is not restricted, and the output from the Program is covered only if its contents constitute a work based on the Program (independent of having been made by running the Program). Whether that is true depends on what the Program does.

1. You may copy and distribute verbatim copies of the Program's source code as you receive it, in any medium, provided that you conspicuously and appropriately publish on each copy an appropriate copyright notice and disclaimer of warranty; keep intact all the notices that refer to this License and to the absence of any warranty; and give any other recipients of the Program a copy of this License along with the Program.

You may charge a fee for the physical act of transferring a copy, and you may at your option offer warranty protection in exchange for a fee.

2. You may modify your copy or copies of the Program or any portion of it, thus forming a work based on the Program, and copy and distribute such modifications or work under the terms of Section 1 above, provided that you also meet all of these conditions:

a) You must cause the modified files to carry prominent notices stating that you changed the files and the date of any change.

b) You must cause any work that you distribute or publish, that in whole or in part contains or is derived from the Program or any part thereof, to be licensed as a whole at no charge to all third parties under the terms of this License.

c) If the modified program normally reads commands interactively when run, you must cause it, when started running for such interactive use in the most ordinary way, to print or display an announcement including an appropriate copyright notice and a notice that there is no warranty (or else, saying that you provide a warranty) and that users may redistribute the program under these conditions, and telling the user how to view a copy of this License. (Exception: if the Program itself is interactive but does not normally print such an announcement, your work based on the Program is not required to print an announcement.)

These requirements apply to the modified work as a whole. If identifiable sections of that work are not derived from the Program, and can be reasonably considered independent and separate works in themselves, then this License, and its terms, do not apply to those sections when you distribute them as separate works. But when you distribute the same sections as part of a whole which is a work based on the Program, the distribution of the whole must be on the terms of this License, whose permissions for other licensees extend to the entire whole, and thus to each and every part regardless of who wrote it.

Thus, it is not the intent of this section to claim rights or contest your rights to work written entirely by you; rather, the intent is to exercise the right to control the distribution of derivative or collective works based on the Program.

In addition, mere aggregation of another work not based on the Program with the Program (or with a work based on the Program) on a volume of a storage or distribution medium does not bring the other work under the scope of this License.

3. You may copy and distribute the Program (or a work based on it, under Section 2) in object code or executable form under the terms of Sections 1 and 2 above provided that you also do one of the following:

a) Accompany it with the complete corresponding machine-readable source code, which must be distributed under the terms of Sections 1 and 2 above on a medium customarily used for software interchange; or,

b) Accompany it with a written offer, valid for at least three years, to give any third party, for a charge no more than your cost of physically performing source distribution, a complete machine-readable copy of the corresponding source code, to be distributed under the terms of Sections 1 and 2 above on a medium customarily used for software interchange; or,

c) Accompany it with the information you received as to the offer to distribute corresponding source code. (This alternative is allowed only for noncommercial distribution and only if you received the program in object code or executable form with such an offer, in accord with Subsection b above.)

The source code for a work means the preferred form of the work for making modifications to it. For an executable work, complete source code means all the source code for all modules it contains, plus any associated interface definition files, plus the scripts used to control compilation and installation of the executable. However, as a special exception, the source code distributed need not include anything that is normally distributed (in either source or binary form) with the major components (compiler, kernel, and so on) of the operating system on which the executable runs, unless that component itself accompanies the executable.

If distribution of executable or object code is made by offering access to copy from a designated place, then offering equivalent access to copy the source code from the same place counts as distribution of the source code, even though third parties are not compelled to copy the source along with the object code.

4. You may not copy, modify, sublicense, or distribute the Program except as expressly provided under this License. Any attempt otherwise to copy, modify, sublicense or distribute the Program is void, and will automatically terminate your rights under this License. However, parties who have received copies, or rights, from you under this License will not have their licenses terminated so long as such parties remain in full compliance.

5. You are not required to accept this License, since you have not signed it. However, nothing else grants you permission to modify or distribute the Program or its derivative works. These actions are prohibited by law if you do not accept this License. Therefore, by modifying or distributing the Program (or any work based on the Program), you indicate your acceptance of this License to do so, and all its terms and conditions for copying, distributing or modifying the Program or works based on it.

6. Each time you redistribute the Program (or any work based on the Program), the recipient automatically receives a license from the original licensor to copy, distribute or modify the Program subject to these terms and conditions. You may not impose any further restrictions on the recipients' exercise of the rights granted herein. You are not responsible for enforcing compliance by third parties to this License.

7. If, as a consequence of a court judgment or allegation of patent infringement or for any other reason (not limited to patent issues), conditions are imposed on you (whether by court order, agreement or otherwise) that contradict the conditions of this License, they do not excuse you from the conditions of this License. If you cannot distribute so as to satisfy simultaneously your obligations under this License and any other pertinent obligations, then as a consequence you may not distribute the Program at all. For example, if a patent license would not permit royalty-free redistribution of the Program by all those who receive copies directly or indirectly through you, then the only way you could satisfy both it and this License would be to refrain entirely from distribution of the Program.

If any portion of this section is held invalid or unenforceable under any particular circumstance, the balance of the section is intended to apply and the section as a whole is intended to apply in other circumstances.

It is not the purpose of this section to induce you to infringe any patents or other property right claims or to contest validity of any such claims; this section has the sole purpose of protecting the integrity of the free software distribution system, which is implemented by public license practices. Many people have made generous contributions to the wide range of software distributed through that system in reliance on consistent application of that system; it is up to the author/donor to decide if he or she is willing to distribute software through any other system and a licensee cannot impose that choice.

This section is intended to make thoroughly clear what is believed to be a consequence of the rest of this License.

8. If the distribution and/or use of the Program is restricted in certain countries either by patents or by copyrighted interfaces, the original copyright holder who places the Program under this License may add an explicit geographical distribution limitation excluding those countries, so that distribution is permitted only in or among countries not thus excluded. In such case, this License incorporates the limitation as if written in the body of this License.

9. The Free Software Foundation may publish revised and/or new versions of the General Public License from time to time. Such new versions will be similar in spirit to the present version, but may differ in detail to address new problems or concerns.

   Each version is given a distinguishing version number. If the Program specifies a version number of this License which applies to it and "any later version", you have the option of following the terms and conditions either of that version or of any later version published by the Free Software Foundation. If the Program does not specify a version number of this License, you may choose any version ever published by the Free Software Foundation.

10. If you wish to incorporate parts of the Program into other free programs whose distribution conditions are different, write to the author to ask for permission. For software which is copyrighted by the Free Software Foundation, write to the Free Software Foundation; we sometimes make exceptions for this. Our decision will be guided by the two goals of preserving the free status of all derivatives of our free software and of promoting the sharing and reuse of software generally.

NO WARRANTY

11. BECAUSE THE PROGRAM IS LICENSED FREE OF CHARGE, THERE IS NO WARRANTY FOR THE PROGRAM, TO THE EXTENT PERMITTED BY APPLICABLE LAW. EXCEPT WHEN OTHERWISE STATED IN WRITING THE COPYRIGHT HOLDERS AND/OR OTHER PARTIES PROVIDE THE PROGRAM "AS IS" WITHOUT WARRANTY OF ANY KIND, EITHER EXPRESSED OR IMPLIED, INCLUDING, BUT NOT LIMITED TO, THE IMPLIED WARRANTIES OF MERCHANTABILITY AND FITNESS FOR A PARTICULAR PURPOSE. THE ENTIRE RISK AS TO THE QUALITY AND PERFORMANCE OF THE PROGRAM IS WITH YOU. SHOULD THE PROGRAM PROVE DEFECTIVE, YOU ASSUME THE COST OF ALL NECESSARY SERVICING, REPAIR OR CORRECTION.

12. IN NO EVENT UNLESS REQUIRED BY APPLICABLE LAW OR AGREED TO IN WRITING WILL ANY COPYRIGHT HOLDER, OR ANY OTHER PARTY WHO MAY MODIFY AND/OR REDISTRIBUTE THE PROGRAM AS PERMITTED ABOVE, BE LIABLE TO YOU FOR DAMAGES, INCLUDING ANY GENERAL, SPECIAL, INCIDENTAL OR CONSEQUENTIAL DAMAGES ARISING OUT OF THE USE OR INABILITY TO USE THE PROGRAM (INCLUDING BUT NOT LIMITED TO LOSS

OF DATA OR DATA BEING RENDERED INACCURATE OR LOSSES SUSTAINED BY YOU OR THIRD PARTIES OR A FAILURE OF THE PROGRAM TO OPERATE WITH ANY OTHER PROGRAMS), EVEN IF SUCH HOLDER OR OTHER PARTY HAS BEEN ADVISED OF THE POSSIBILITY OF SUCH DAMAGES.

END OF TERMS AND CONDITIONS

Index

G

The books you read to succeed.

Get the most out of the latest software and leading-edge technologies
with a Wiley Bible—your one-stop reference.

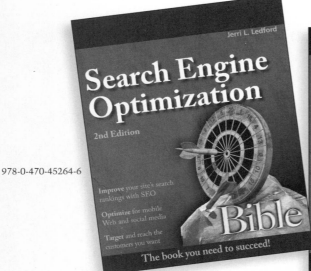

978-0-470-45264-6

Jerri L. Ledford

Search Engine Optimization
2nd Edition

Improve your site's search rankings with SEO

Optimize for mobile Web and social media

Target and reach the customers you want

Bible
The book you need to succeed!

Companion Web site

Jim Boyce

Windows 7

Explore the latest tools and features

Master inside tricks and best practices

Discover what you need, when you need it

Bible
The book you need to succeed!

978-0-470-50909-8

DVD Included!
• Trial versions of AutoCAD 2010 and AutoCAD LT 2010
• Drawings for the exercises, add-on programs, and more
• Videos on the big new features — Parametric Constraints and Mesh Solids

Ellen Finkelstein

AutoCAD 2010 & AutoCAD LT 2010
10th Anniversary Edition of the *AutoCAD Bible*

Start drawing today with the Quick Start tutorial

Create sophisticated 2D and 3D models

Learn how to customize and program AutoCAD

Bible
The book you need to succeed!

978-0-470-43640-0

DVD Included!
• Examples and content from the book
• Models and textures you can customize
• Searchable, full-color PDF of the book

Full-color Insert
• 16-page full-color insert with cutting-edge examples

Kelly L. Murdock

3ds Max 2010

Start creating today with a Quick Start tutorial

Master the basics through advanced techniques

Shine in the red-hot 3D gaming market

Bible
The book you need to succeed!

978-0-470-47191-3

Available wherever books are sold.

Wiley and the Wiley logo are registered trademarks of John Wiley & Sons, Inc.
All other trademarks are the property of their respective owners.

WILEY
Now you know.
wiley.com